Al-Maqrīzī's *al-Ḫabar ʿan al-bašar*
Volume IV, Section 2

Bibliotheca Maqriziana

OPERA MAIORA

Edited by

Frédéric Bauden (*Université de Liège*)

VOLUME 8

The titles published in this series are listed at *brill.com/bima*

Al-Maqrīzī's
al-Ḫabar ʿan al-bašar

Volume IV, Section 2:
The Idols of the Arabs

Critical Edition and Introduction by

Michael Lecker

Annotated Translation by

Yaara Perlman

BRILL

LEIDEN | BOSTON

Cover illustration: MS Fatih 4339 (Istanbul, Süleymaniye Kütüphanesi), fol. 30a.

Library of Congress Cataloging-in-Publication Data

Names: Maqrīzī, Aḥmad ibn ʿAlī, 1364-1442, author. | Maqrīzī, Aḥmad ibn ʿAlī, 1364-1442. Khabar ʿan al-bashar fī ansāb al-ʿArab wa-nasab Sayyid al-Bashar. Selections. | Lecker, Michael, editor. | Perlman, Yaara, translator.
Title: Al-Maqrīzī's al-Ḫabar 'an al-bašar. Volume IV, section 2: the idols of the Arabs / critical edition and introduction by Michael Lecker ; annotated translation by Yaara Perlman.
Other titles: Khabar ʿan al-bashar fī ansāb al-ʿArab wa-nasab Sayyid al-Bashar. Selections. English | Maqrīzī's al-Ḫabar 'an al-bašar. Volume IV, section 2: the idols of the Arabs
Description: Boston : Brill, 2022. | Series: Bibliotheca Maqriziana, 2211-6737 ; volume 8 | Includes bibliographical references and index.
Identifiers: LCCN 2021057536 (print) | LCCN 2021057537 (ebook) | ISBN 9789004499836 (hardback) | ISBN 9789004499867 (ebook)
Subjects: LCSH: Maqrīzī, Aḥmad ibn ʿAlī, 1364-1442. Khabar ʿan al-bashar fī ansāb al-ʿArab wa-nasab Sayyid al-Bashar. | Idolatry–Arabian Peninsula–History. | Idols and images–Worship.
Classification: LCC CS1549.5 .M36813 2022 (print) | LCC CS1549.5 (ebook) | DDC 202/.18–dc23/eng/20220104
LC record available at https://lccn.loc.gov/2021057536
LC ebook record available at https://lccn.loc.gov/2021057537

Typeface for the Latin, Greek, and Cyrillic scripts: “Brill”. See and download: brill.com/brill-typeface.

ISSN 2211-6737
ISBN 978-90-04-49983-6 (hardback)
ISBN 978-90-04-49986-7 (e-book)

This book is printed on acid-free paper and produced in a sustainable manner.

Contents

Preface IX
List of Plates and Map X
Abbreviations XI

Introduction 1

1 Idols in Conversion Reports 6
1.1 *Huḏayl: Sāʿidah al-Huḏalī and the Idol Suwāʿ of wadi Naʿmān* 6
1.2 *Sulaym: Rāšid b. ʿAbd Rabbihi, the Custodian of Suwāʿ of wadi Ruhāṭ (§ 66)* 7
1.3 *ʿUqayl: Abū Ḥarb b. Ḫuwaylid and the Divination Arrows* 9
1.4 *Saʿd b. Bakr: Ḍimām b. Ṯaʿlabah and the Idols* 10
1.5 *Kalb: ʿIṣām al-Kalbī, the Custodian of ʿAmrah* 10
1.6 *Ǧuhaynah: The Custodian ʿAmr b. Murrah* 12
1.7 *ʿUḏrah: Ziml b. ʿAmr and Ḥumām (§ 160)* 12
1.8 *Hamdān: al-ʿAwwām b. Ǧuhayl, the Custodian of Yaġūṯ* 13
1.9 *Saʿd al-ʿAshīrah: Ḍubāb and Farrā(ṣ/ḍ) (§ 157)* 13
1.10 *Ṭayyiʾ: Māzin b. al-Ġaḍūbah, the Custodian of Bāǧir* 15
1.11 *Baǧīlah: Ǧarīr b. ʿAbd Allāh and Ḏū l-Ḫalaṣah (§ 188–192)* 17
2 Mecca 20
2.1 *Household Idols* 20
2.2 *The Idol Buwānah near Yalamlam (cf. § 145)* 22
3 Medina (Yaṯrib) (§ 110–117) 23
3.1 *Household Idols* 24
3.2 *Idols of Noblemen* 29
3.3 *Idols of* baṭns 31
3.4 *The Ḥāriṯ b. al-Ḫazraǧ and Huzzam* 32
3.5 *The Ḫazraǧ and al-Ḫamīs (§ 141)* 32
3.6 *Al-Saʿīdah on Mount Uḥud (cf. § 206)* 32
3.7 *Manāt in or near Qudayd (§ 176, 182)* 33
4 Idols and Treasuries 35
4.1 *The Treasury of the Kaʿbah: A Community Fund* 36
4.2 *The Treasury of Allāt* 38
4.3 *The Treasury of Manāt* 40
4.4 *The Treasury of al-ʿUzzá* 41

Notes on the Edition and the Translation 42

Plates and Map 45

Abbreviations and Symbols 58

Critical Edition and Translation of al-Maqrīzī's al-Ḫabar ʿan al-bašar*, vol. IV, Section 2: The Idols of the Arabs*

Section on the Idols of the Arabs [Their *aṣnām* and *awṯān*] 60
Wadd 114
Suwāʿ 122
Yaġūṯ 126
Yaʿūq 128
Nasr 130
Hubal 134
Isāf and Nāʾilah 138
Saʿd 154
ʿĀʾim 156
Ḏū l-Šará 156
Ruḍā 158
Ḍamār 158
Al-Ḥarīš, Ṣaḫr, Šams, al-Bihām, al-Qayn, Šafr, al-Ḥibs, Ġayyān, Isāf, Samūl, Ḥusā, al-Ṭimm, al-Samḥ 162
Sāf, al-Dībāğ, al-Zabr 164
Huzzam 168
Manāf 168
Dawār 174
Al-Fals 174
Nuhm 180
Al-Suʿayr 184
Al-Uqayṣir 186
Al-ʿUrayf 190
Al-Ḥalāl 190
Aḥmas 192
ʿAmm Anas 192
Al-Šurayr, Ġanm, Ḏū l-Kaffayni 194
Al-Šāriq 198
Marsūġ 198

Al-Bayḍāʾ 198
Kulāl 200
Al-Ḫamīs 200
Al-Mukaymin 202
Yālīl 202
Barkulān 202
Qurs 202
Al-ʿAbd 202
Al-Ǧuṯā 204
Farrāḍ 210
Zaʿbal 212
Al-Ǧalsad 212
Ḥumām 214
ʿAwḍ 214
Saqb 218

Section on *al-ǧibt* and *al-ṭāġūt* 220
Al-ʿUzzá 224
Allāt 236
Manāt 246
Ḏū l-Kaʿabāt 248
Ḏū l-Ḫalaṣah 256
The Kaʿbah of Naǧrān 264
Riyām 268
Al-Qalīs/al-Qullays 268
Al-Huǧam 274
The account of Ḏāt Anwāṭ 276
Anṣāb 280
Ruḍā 282
Buss 284
Fire Temple 284
Al-Saʿīdah 284

Bibliography 287
List of Quoted Manuscripts 311
Index of Qurʾānic Verses 312
Index of Prophetic Traditions 314
Index of Verses of Poetry 315
Index of Names 318
Index of Quoted Titles in *al-Ḫabar ʿan al-bašar* 329

Index of Sources in *al-Ḫabar ʿan al-bašar* 330
Index of Glosses 331
Index of Technical Terms 332
Facsimile of MS Fatih 4339 (Istanbul, Süleymaniye Kütüphanesi),
Fols. 30a–48b 335

Preface

My acquaintance with al-Maqrīzī's *al-Ḫabar ʿan al-bašar* goes back a long time.[1] I am very grateful to my colleague Frédéric Bauden for inviting me to participate in the Maqriziana series. The chapters included in this volume are *Faṣl fī ḏikr aṣnām al-ʿarab wa-awṯānihā* (§ 1–162) and *Faṣl fī ḏikr al-ǧibt wa-l-ṭāġūt* (§ 163–206), corresponding to folios 30a–48b of MS Fatih 4339, preserved in the Süleymaniye Kütüphanesi in Istanbul.[2] Bauden generously put at my disposal all the necessary materials; it was my intention to edit a larger section of the book, but this was not possible.

Yaara Perlman's contribution to this volume is immense. She translated the text, often suggesting amendments to the edition, she added numerous parallel sources, edited the footnotes, adjusted the transliteration to the norms followed in the series, and prepared the indices. In fact, it is much more her project than mine.

In the process of editing an attempt was made to preserve al-Maqrīzī's own style; however, scribal errors were corrected between brackets {}, while the original Arabic text is recorded in the margin. In addition, here we have ensured that the *hamzah*, which al-Maqrīzī often omits, conforms to common usage. The holograph often has *alif* instead of *alif maqṣūrah* and the Qurʾān verses are only partially vocalized.

1 Cf. Lecker (1993).

2 For a detailed discussion of the author and the book see Bauden (2014) and Bauden (forthcoming).

Plates and Map

Plates

1 Istanbul/ Süleymaniye Kütüphanesi, MS Aya Sofya 3364, p. 411 47
2 Istanbul/ Süleymaniye Kütüphanesi, MS Aya Sofya 3364, p. 442 48
3 Istanbul/ Topkapı Sarayı Müzesi Kütüphanesi, MS 2926/4, fol. 22a 49
4 Istanbul/ Topkapı Sarayı Müzesi Kütüphanesi, MS 2926/4, fol. 40a 50
5 Istanbul/ Süleymaniye Kütüphanesi, MS Aya Sofya 3365, p. 42 51
6 Istanbul/ Süleymaniye Kütüphanesi, MS Aya Sofya 3365, p. 77 52
7 Cairo/Maktabat al-Azhar, MS Abāẓah 6733, fol. 123a 53
8 Cairo/Maktabat al-Azhar, MS Abāẓah 6733, fol. 128b 54
9 Strasbourg/Bibliothèque nationale et universitaire, MS 4244, fol. 128a 55
10 Strasbourg/Bibliothèque nationale et universitaire, MS 4244, fol. 133b 56

Map

1 Location map of several Arabian idols 57

Abbreviations

AO	*Archív Orientální*
BSOAS	*Bulletin of the School of Oriental Studies*
EAL	*Encyclopedia of Arabic Literature*
*EI*²	*The Encyclopaedia of Islam. New Edition*, ed. C.E. Bosworth et al. (Leiden: Brill, 1960–2007), 11 vols.
*EI*³	*The Encyclopaedia of Islam—Three*, ed. Kate Fleet et al. (Leiden: Brill, 2007 ff.).
EQ	*Encyclopaedia of the Qurʾān*, ed. J. Dammen McAuliffe (Leiden, Boston: Brill, 2001–2006), 6 vols.
GAS	F. Sezgin, *Geschichte des arabischen Schrifttums* (Leiden: Brill, 1967 ff.).
IOS	*Israel Oriental Studies*
JAOS	*Journal of the American Oriental Society*
JESHO	*Journal of the Social and Economic History of the Orient*
JNES	*Journal of Near Eastern Studies*
JRAS	*Journal of the Royal Asiatic Society*
JSAI	*Jerusalem Studies in Arabic and Islam*
JSS	*Journal of Semitic Studies*
SI	*Studia Islamica*
WO	*Die Welt des Orients*
ZDMG	*Zeitschrift der Deutschen Morgenländischen Gesellschaft*

Introduction

Many of the books quoted by al-Maqrīzī are no longer extant, hence the significance of his excerpts.[1,2] Al-Maqrīzī usually mentions the compilers of the books he quotes from (see index, under "Quoted sources"), but he rarely provides book titles (see index, under "Quoted titles"). By far, the authority quoted most often is ʿUmar b. Šabbah. Ibn Šabbah's lost monograph on the history of Mecca, *Kitāb Aḫbār Makkah*, the title of which appears twice, is the source of much of the new evidence, including the rare texts (§ 110 ff.) about idol worship in Medina at the time of the *hiǧrah*.[3]

Due to the lack of significant archaeological excavations in most of Arabia (in this introduction Arabia refers to the Arabian Peninsula), the primary sources, for all their weaknesses, remain indispensable. There are promising sites for future archaeological excavations, such as, for example, the site of the idol Manāt in or near Qudayd and that of the idol al-ʿUzzá in Buss, not far from Ḏāt ʿIrq (see map).[4] The *mīqāt* of Ḏāt ʿIrq is roughly 105 kilometers from the Kaʿbah (the *mīqāt* is the point at which the pilgrims enter a state of *iḥrām*).[5] We might expect to find the remains of temples, however modest, and bones of sacrificial animals in both sites, and indeed in many other sites in Arabia.

The role of idol worship is of crucial importance for the study of Arabia on the eve of Islam. The very existence of the Arabian idols has been questioned, but a thorough investigation of the primary sources suggests that their existence is beyond doubt. A large number of idols of various kinds must have been worshipped all over Arabia. While idolatry was, perhaps, in retreat elsewhere, in Arabia it showed no signs of decline. It may well be impossible to gauge the Arabs' devotion to their idols, but it stands to reason that idolatry formed a major obstacle for Muḥammad in both Mecca and Medina. There were many forms of idol worship. In al-Yamāmah, for example, a pilgrim would sit at the top of a hillock and then someone would grab his leg and pull him down to the bottom four times (§ 138).[6]

1 The introduction draws heavily on my earlier work, especially on a little known article: Lecker (2005a).

2 The significance of relatively late sources in the study of early Islam has recently been reinstated forcefully; see Munt (2012): 2–3.

3 Lecker (1993): 331.

4 On Buss, see Lecker (1989): 37–41. On al-ʿUzzá, see "al-ʿUzzā," in *EI*[2] (Macdonald & Nehmé).

5 *Iḥrām* is the state of temporary consecration of someone who is performing the *ḥaǧǧ* or *ʿumrah*; see "Iḥrām," in *EI*[2] (Wensinck & Jomier).

6 Lecker (forthcoming).

 | DOI:10.1163/9789004499867_002

The rejection of idol worship is a prominent element in the reports about the pre-Islamic *ḥanīf*s. Idols appear in legendary and stereotypic conversion reports of the Prophet's Companions (or alleged Companions) who lived in various parts of Arabia. The details regarding the idols are reliable, since they form the background information on which the legendary reports were based. More significantly, in Medina, where the spiritual influence of the dominant Jewish population was substantial, idol worship flourished on several levels of the tribal system. We can conclude that if it flourished in Medina, it flourished among the sedentary people everywhere in Arabia.

Nöldeke ascribed the ease with which the Arabs gave up idol worship to the spiritual progress that they had achieved before the rise of Islam.[7] Wellhausen argued that the Meccans clung to idol worship mainly for economic reasons; conversion to Islam was a political rather than a religious matter. Yet when a person converted, his pagan tribe stood by him when others fought against him.[8] Goldziher approvingly quoted Dozy's words that "religion, of whatever kind it may have been, generally had little place in the life of the Arabs, who were engrossed in worldly interests like fighting, wine, games and love."[9] Basing himself on Arabic poetry, Goldziher had in mind the tribes of central Arabia, whose religious belief he contrasted with the religious monuments of South Arabia. Nicholson argued:

7 "Die Araber hatten bis zum Anfang des 7. Jahrhunderts ausserordentliche geistige Fortschritte gemacht wie nicht leicht ein Volk in so ungünstigen Wohnsitzen. Sie waren ihrer alten Religion entwachsen und liessen diese daher fast ohne Widerstand fallen, als sich ihnen der Islâm mächtig imponierend darbot. Allderdings, im Vorbeigehn gesagt, vertauschten auch die meisten christlichen Araber ihr Christenthum ohne jedes Bedenken mit dem Islâm, der ihrem Wesen viel besser zusagte"; see Nöldeke's review of Wellhausen's *Reste arabischen Heidentums*: Nöldeke (1887): 720.

8 Wellhausen (1897): 220–221, and *passim*. Lammens agreed with Wellhausen regarding the weakness of the religious sentiment; Lammens (1928): 139, 181. In this context Buhl (1930): 93 mentioned the indifference of the business-minded Meccans. Paret did not think that the idols and their indifferent followers who only wanted to cling to their fathers' beliefs posed a serious challenge for Muḥammad. Paret (1957): 18 interpreted the passivity of the Arabs when their idols were destroyed at the time of Muḥammad as follows: "Die altarabischen Glaubensvorstellungen waren schon lange verblaßt, bevor sie endgültig durch den Islam abgelöst wurden." Paret was surprised that, of all places, Muḥammad should have appeared among the businessmen of Mecca; Paret (1957): 23. Stummer (1944): 393–394 argued: "Ja, schon Muḥammad traf auf ein Heidentum, dessen geistige Kraft bereits gebrochen und erlahmt war, denn offenbar waren die Einflüsse, die vom Judentum und Christentum auf das vorislamische Arabertum ausstrahlten, nicht unwirksam gewesen."

9 Goldziher (1966), 1:12.

> Religion had so little influence on the lives of the Pre-Islamic Arabs that we cannot expect to find much trace of it in their poetry … Of real piety the ordinary Bedouin knew nothing. He felt no call to pray to his gods, although he often found them convenient to swear by. He might invoke Allah in the hour of need, as a drowning man will clutch at a straw; but his faith in superstitious ceremonies was stronger. He did not take his religion too seriously ….[10]

By contrast, Levi Della Vida correctly observed that poetry and reports of battles from which we draw what we know of the life of pre-Islamic Arabs are not a true reflection of Bedouin life, and the verses that attribute religious indifference to the famous warriors should not be trusted.[11]

The incomplete and fragmentary nature of the literary evidence about the pre-Islamic idols is familiar from other aspects of pre- and early Islamic history. Medieval scholars specializing in *ḥadīṯ* and related topics were naturally interested in the idols mentioned in the Qur'ān, but not in those that only appear in the literary sources. However, philologists like Ibn al-Kalbī (d. ca. 204/818) recorded whatever they learned from their informants, whoever they were. The philologists' curiosity and their state of mind are demonstrated by Ibn al-Kalbī's comment regarding the seven divination arrows of the idol Hubal at the Kaʿbah: he admits that he could not find details about three of them.[12] Scholars of this

10 Nicholson (1966): 135.

11 Levi Della Vida (1938): 89–90. He is quoted by Henninger in connection with the common claim regarding the religious indifference of the Bedouins; namely, that pre-Islamic poetry is rigid, conventional, and limited with regard to its choice of subjects; Henninger (1981): 7–8. See also Krone (1992): 176 (she says that poetry fails to provide details on the religious life of the Bedouin, because religious themes were not among the motifs of the *qaṣīdah*). Still, while idols are rarely encountered in poetry, Allāh is mentioned very often, including by poets who had no link to Muḥammad, either because they lived before his time or because they were not influenced by him. This would demonstrate that religious elements can be found in pre-Islamic poetry, and that there was a decline in idol worship; Krone (1992): 183–186. However, Krone remarks, this "argument from silence" is not decisive: pre-Islamic poetry could easily be "Islamized" and manipulated. Krone realizes that the affair of the "Satanic verses" contradicts the assumption that idol worship at the time of Muḥammad was in decline ("stark im Niedergang"), and hence unconvincingly interprets it as a political rather than a religious affair; Krone (1992): 204–207. Andrae (1960): 16–17, however, found in Arabia "an undeveloped polytheism, in which a development had just barely begun which would have gradually produced a pantheon consisting of a hierarchy of gods, formed by associating together a number of independent individual divinities."

12 *Wa-ṯalāṯah lam tufassar* (!) *lī ʿalá mā kānat*; Yāqūt, *Muʿǧam al-buldān*, 5:391, s.v. Hubal; Ibn

kind were always on the lookout for evidence from every possible source. *Ḥadīṯ* scholars, by contrast, were selective in their choice of informants and faithfully transmitted to their disciples exact copies of what they had learned from their teachers.

A note about Ibn al-Kalbı's sources in *al-Aṣnām* may be in place here. He often quotes his father, who is referred to both in the first person (*ḥaddaṯa/nā l-Kalbī*, and *aḫbaranī abī*), or in the third person (*ʿan abīhi*).

Two sources merit special notice. Concerning al-Fals, the idol of Ṭayyi', Ibn al-Kalbī quotes Abū Bāsil al-Ṭā'ī, who in turn quotes his paternal uncle, ʿAntarah b. al-Aḫras whom one source describes as a Ǧāhilī poet,[13] while another source, which calls Abū Bāsil an expert on Ṭā'ī matters (*wa-kāna … ʿāliman bi-amr Ṭayyi'*), says that he was *muḫaḍram*, i.e. he also lived in early Islam.[14] These two members of the Ṭayyi' point to the tribal sources behind many of Ibn al-Kalbī's materials.

Far more significant is a source quoted by al-Kalbī's father, namely Abū Ṣāliḥ, who quotes Ibn ʿAbbās. This *isnād*, which appears in *al-Aṣnām* several times, is linked to the transmission of Ibn ʿAbbās's exegesis and is very common in Qur'ān exegesis and elsewhere. The Kufan Abū Ṣāliḥ al-Hāšimī (d. ca. 95/714 or ca. 115/733),[15] whose name was Bāḏām (or Bāḏān) was the *mawlá*, or manumitted slave, of Umm Hāni' bt. Abī Ṭālib (ʿAlī's sister, hence the *nisbah* al-Hāšimī).[16]

Certain idols are only known through their mention in poetry, because verse stood a better chance of being remembered and recorded than did prose. Often we learn about an idol from a (semi-)autobiographical report of its custodian or of the person who destroyed it. The custodians are supposed to have been the first to realize that after Muḥammad's mission, idol worship became futile. The fact that its creators were not interested in idol worship *per se* strengthens the weight of the source material; the idols were in the background, taken for granted. The personal viewpoint predominates. The same is true of the idol

---

al-Kalbī, *al-Aṣnām* 28. Cf. al-Azraqī, *Aḫbār Makkah*², 1:117–118, who quotes from Ibn Isḥāq a report about all seven arrows.

13 Al-ʿAwtabī, *al-Ansāb*, 1:313.

14 Ibn Ḥaǧar, *al-Iṣābah*², 5:163, calls him ʿAnbarah b. al-Aḫraš. He is also called after his grandmother on his mother's side ʿAntarah ibn ʿUkburah; al-Āmidī, *al-Mu'talif wa-l-muḫtalif* 225.

15 According to al-Buḫārī, he died in the last decade of the first Islamic century, while according to al-Ḏahabī he died in the second decade of the second Islamic century; al-Mizzī, *Tahḏīb al-kamāl*, 4:8, note. The earlier death date should perhaps be given priority, since some made the flimsy claim that he was a Companion of Muḥammad; Ibn al-Aṯīr, *Usd al-ġābah*, 6:167.

16 Rubin (2011a): 10.

destroyers who sought credit for their acts. The focus is not on the Ǧāhilī symbol but on the person. Typically, the person's offspring take part in preserving the story. In other words, the strong biographical bias of the Islamic literature is also evident in reports about idols. Differences and contradictions are an inevitable outcome.

There are numerous indications of a direct shift from idol worship to Islam. For example, when Yazīd b. al-Aswad al-Ǧarašī was asked how old he was, he answered that he had witnessed the cult of al-ʿUzzá in the town of his tribe.[17] ʿAmr b. Maymūn al-Awdī l-Maḏḥiǧī who lived in Muḥammad's time (although he was not a Companion) stated that he had worshipped Allāt in the Ǧāhiliyyah.[18] A member of the Ḫawlān tribe grew long hair (which reached his shoulders) in order to offer it to an unspecified idol (*li-ṣanam kānā lanā fī l-ǧāhiliyyah*). But God caused the sacrifice to be postponed, and the Ḫawlānī shaved his hair after he had converted to Islam.[19] It is not clear whether he was a Companion of Muḥammad,[20] but there can be no doubt that the interval was only a matter of several months or perhaps a year.[21]

The disputes regarding the identity of certain custodians indicate that even well into the Islamic period former custodians (or their descendants) gained prestige from their previous roles. The custodian's office, being a form of past prominence, was a source of pride. Some former custodians smoothly entered Muḥammad's nascent state. For example, Ḫuzāʿī b. ʿAbd Nuhm (§123), the former custodian of Muzaynah's idol Nuhm,[22] swore allegiance to Muḥammad on behalf of the Muzaynah tribe (*fa-bāyaʿahu ʿalá qawmihi Muzaynah*) and carried Muzaynah's banner (*liwāʾ*) during the conquest of Mecca.[23] Muḥammad put Rāšid al-Sulamī (§66), the last custodian of one of the two idols named Suwāʿ, in charge of his tribe (*wa-ʿaqada lahu ʿalá qawmihi*), which probably means that Muḥammad acknowledged his leadership. Rāšid participated in the

---

17 *Adraktu l-ʿUzzá tuʿbadu fī qaryat qawmī*; Ibn ʿAsākir, *Dimašq*, 65:107; al-Dāraquṭnī, *al-Muʾtalif wa-l-muḫtalif*, 2:945. Ibn ʿAbd al-Barr, *al-Istīʿāb*, 4:1570 has *al-aṣnām* instead of *al-ʿUzzá*.

18 Ibn ʿAsākir, *Dimašq*, 46:414. On ʿAmr see Cook (1999): 47–48.

19 *Asbaltu šaʿrī li-aǧuzzahu li-ṣanam kāna lanā fī l-ǧāhiliyyah fa-aḫḫara llāh ḏālika ḥattá ǧazaztuhu fī l-islām*; Ibn Saʿd, *al-Ṭabaqāt*², 9:439, no. 4622.

20 Ibn ʿAbd al-Barr, *al-Istīʿāb*, 4:1722–1724.

21 Compare the practice of the Aws and Ḫazraǧ at the end of the annual pilgrimage to Mecca: instead of shaving their hair there, together with the other pilgrims, they would shave it near Manāt; Lecker (2005a): 34.

22 Ibn al-Kalbī, *al-Aṣnām* 39–40.

23 Ibn Saʿd, *al-Ṭabaqāt*², 1:252–253; 5:143.

conquest of Mecca,[24] and Muḥammad appointed him to a certain administrative role in Naǧrān.[25]

1 Idols in Conversion Reports

Idols appear in many (semi-)autobiographical conversion reports. Although these reports are rather stereotypic and formulaic, they include valuable background information, which by definition is relatively reliable. Conversion reports often became family traditions. At a later stage some found their way into compilations of *dalāʾil al-nubuwwah* (the proofs of Muḥammad's prophethood), among other types of literature; however, their secondary usage does not detract from their significance for the study of Arabian society. Some of the reports about the *wufūd* (the tribal delegations that visited Muḥammad) refer to idols, while other reports do not. This does not mean that some tribes had idols, while others had none, rather some tribal informants concentrated on other themes, or their original reports were later curtailed. In any case, for the tribesmen, Muḥammad's mission was the antithesis of idol worship.[26]

1.1 *Huḏayl: Sāʿidah al-Huḏalī and the Idol Suwāʿ of wadi Naʿmān*

Ibn Saʿd quotes the following from al-Wāqidī < ʿAbd Allāh b. Yazīd (b. Qanṭas) al-Huḏalī[27] < ʿAbd Allāh b. Sāʿidah al-Huḏalī < his father. Sāʿidah heard a voice from within "their idol," Suwāʿ. Several Huḏalīs, including Sāʿidah, were leading two hundred scabby sheep to the idol in order to ask for its blessing, but a voice from within it announced that the deceit of the *ǧinn* was no longer effective: the *ǧinn* had been shot dead by falling stars because of a prophet called Aḥmad.[28]

---

24 Ibn Saʿd, *al-Ṭabaqāt*², 1:266; Lecker (1989): 54–55.

25 *Istaʿmala rasūlu llāh ṣ Abā Sufyān b. Ḥarb ʿalá Naǧrān fa-wallāhu l-ṣalāt wa-l-ḥarb wa-waǧǧaha Rāšid b. ʿAbd Rabbihi amīran ʿalá l-qaḍāʾ wa-l-maẓālim*; Ibn ʿAbd Rabbihi, *al-ʿIqd al-farīd*, 1:308; Lecker (1989): 59; Lecker (2005a): 16, n. 77.

26 The delegation of the Nahd declared: *bariʾnā ilayka yā rasūla llāh mina l-waṯan wa-l-ʿaṯan*; Ibn al-Aṯīr, *Usd al-ġābah*, 3:96 (printed: *wa-l-ʿanan*). *ʿAṯan* is interpreted as a small idol (*al-ṣanam*), while *waṯan* refers to a larger idol; Ibn Manẓūr, *Lisān al-ʿarab*, s.v. *ʿaṯan*. The Ḫawlān delegation promised Muḥammad that upon returning home, they would destroy their idol ʿUmyānis; Goldfeld (1973): 110–111.

27 Ibn ʿAdī, *al-Kāmil*, 4:1550.

28 *Qad ḏahaba kayd al-ǧinn wa-rumīnā bi-l-šuhub li-nabī smuhu Aḥmad*; Ibn Saʿd, *al-Ṭabaqāt*², 1:141. Cf. ibid., 1:140 (*lammā buʿiṯa Muḥammad ṣ duḥira l-ǧinn wa-rumū bi-l-kawākib, wa-kānū qabla ḏālika yastamiʿūna*). Ibn Ḥaǧar, who quotes this report from Abū Nuʿaym's *Dalāʾil al-nubuwwah*, declared the *isnād* "weak"; Ibn Ḥaǧar, *al-Iṣābah*², 3:7–8.

The idol, or rather the *ǧinnī* residing in it or associated with it, had a healing power.[29]

Al-Wāqidī quotes a similar report from the same ʿAbd Allāh b. Yazīd al-Huḏalī < Saʿīd b. ʿAmr al-Huḏalī < his father. ʿAmr had slaughtered the first slaughter animal which was a fat cow on their idol Suwāʿ, and then a voice was heard from within it announcing the appearance of a prophet in Mecca. When the Huḏalīs made inquiries in Mecca, only Abū Bakr could confirm the Prophet's appearance. The Huḏalīs refrained from embracing Islam then and there, which they later regretted.[30] The entry on ʿAmr b. Saʿīd al-Huḏalī in Ibn Ḥaǧar's biographical dictionary of Companions refers to three sources which adduce this report: Abū Nuʿaym's biographical dictionary of Companions, Abū Nuʿaym's *Dalāʾil al-nubuwwah* (which has a long version), and al-Ḫargūšī's *Šaraf al-muṣṭafá*.[31] So instead of Sāʿidah al-Huḏalī in this account we have ʿAmr (or ʿAmr b. Saʿīd) al-Huḏalī, and instead of sheep we find a cow. In any case, Huḏayl's association with Suwāʿ remains. Be it Sāʿidah or ʿAmr, it is a family tradition mainly interested in establishing a Companion status for the protagonist; the idol is in the background.

This Suwāʿ was in wadi Naʿmān; hence, it was not identical with the other Suwāʿ located in wadi Ruhāṭ (see map). The latter was worshipped by the Sulaym and the Huḏayl, and had a Sulamī custodian. The former was worshipped by the Kinānah, the Huḏayl, the Muzaynah, and the ʿAmr b. Qays ʿAylan. Its custodians were the Ṣāhilah from the Huḏayl.[32]

1.2 *Sulaym: Rāšid b. ʿAbd Rabbihi, the Custodian of Suwāʿ of wadi Ruhāṭ (§ 66)*

Ibn Saʿd, under *wafd* Sulaym (the Sulaym delegation), has three reports, the second of which deals with the former custodian of an idol belonging to the Sulaym, Rāšid b. ʿAbd Rabbihi. The Prophet replaced his pagan name, Ġāwī b.

29 A *šayṭān* named Misʿar that used to talk to the people through idols was killed by believing *ǧinnī*s, one of whom was Samḥaǧ; Abū Nuʿaym, *Dalāʾil al-nubuwwah* 109–110. The wording, *hāḏā šayṭān yukallimu l-nās fī l-awṯān*, may suggest that it was not associated with a specific idol.

30 Ibn Saʿd, *al-Ṭabaqāt*², 1:141.

31 Ibn Ḥaǧar, *al-Iṣābah*², 4:639.

32 Ibn Ḥabīb, *al-Muḥabbar* 316. Al-Yaʿqūbī, *Taʾrīḫ*, 1:255, only mentions the Kinānah as the owners of Suwāʿ, but perhaps the text is garbled. In Lecker (1989): 54, the statement associating Suwāʿ with wadi Naʿmān is presented as a variant version regarding its location. I now realize that there were two Suwāʿs, and this may have caused confusion. Cf. Hawting (1999): 119–121 (on p. 121, read Ṣāhilah instead of Ṣaḥālah). The most prominent member of the Ṣāhilah was the Prophet's Companion ʿAbd Allāh b. Masʿūd.

ʿAbd al-ʿUzzá, with an Islamic one. Rāšid became convinced of the fallacy of idolatry when he saw two foxes urinating on the idol. He smashed it and went to the Prophet, who granted him a place called Ruhāṭ that had a well (later called) ʿAyn al-Rasūl.[33] Ibn Saʿd does not specify his source, but the style is familiar from similar reports.

A family tradition going back to Rāšid (no doubt through his offspring) is preserved. It was paraphrased by Samhūdī, but even in its abridged form it includes illuminating evidence. Rāšid's report refers twice to *al-maʿlāt min Ruhāṭ*, or the upper part of wadi Ruhāṭ. This is where the idol Suwāʿ, which was worshipped by the Banū Ẓafar of Sulaym and the Huḏayl, was located, and it defined the Prophet's grant of land to Rāšid. That is, Rāšid received the site of the idol. The spring referred to as ʿAyn al-Rasūl was created miraculously by the Prophet's blessing (it is called Māʾ al-Rasūl). Rāšid heard a mysterious voice (*hātif*) from within Suwāʿ and from other idols announcing Muḥammad's prophethood. He also saw two foxes licking the ground around the idol, eating the gifts offered to it, and urinating on it.[34]

Rāšid's entry in Ibn Ḥağar's biographical dictionary of Companions has passages from earlier biographical dictionaries of Companions, including Abū Nuʿaym's. Abū Nuʿaym quotes Ibn Zabālah's lost book on the history of Medina, which was one of Samhūdī's main sources. Ibn Zabālah quotes from none other than Rāšid's grandson (or great-grandson), Ḥākim b. ʿAṭāʾ al-Sulamī. Ḥākim identified the idol as Suwāʿ and reported its location as al-Maʿlāt.[35] A slightly longer quotation from Abū Nuʿaym's dictionary states that Suwāʿ was *bi-l-maʿlāt min Ruhāṭ*.[36] Another passage in Ibn Ḥağar's entry is quoted from Ibn Ḥibbān al-Bustī's biographical dictionary of Companions. Rāšid's name (here it is Ġāwī b. Ẓālim) was replaced by the Prophet with the name Rāšid b. ʿAbd Allāh. One of the foxes, we are told, raised its leg and urinated on the idol. The differences are not relevant; these are versions of the story of Rāšid's conversion.[37]

Rāšid's offspring transmitted yet another report about their father. The *Manāsik* has the following *isnād*: Abū Muḥammad al-Warrāq, i.e. ʿAbd Allāh b.

33 Ibn Saʿd, *al-Ṭabaqāt*[2], 1:265–266.

34 Al-Samhūdī, *Wafāʾ al-wafā*, 4:1225; Lecker (1989): 52–59, with further discussion.

35 *Kāna l-ṣanamu llaḏī yuqālu lahu Suwāʿ* [printed: *Suwaʿ*] *bi-l-Maʿlāt, fa-ḏakara qiṣṣat islāmihi wa-kasrihi iyyāhu*; Ibn Ḥağar, al-*Iṣābah*[2], 2:434.

36 Al-Suyūṭī, *al-Ḫaṣāʾiṣ*, 2:193.

37 Ibn Ḥağar, *al-Iṣābah*[2], 2:434–435. Ibn Ḥibbān's book quoted here is probably *Asmāʾ al-ṣaḥābah*, on which see *GAS*, 1:191. Ibn ʿAbd al-Barr, *al-Istīʿāb*, 2:504, has a *kunyah*: Rāšid b. ʿAbd Allāh Abū Uṯaylah; his former name was Ẓālim or, according to some, Ġāwī b. Ẓālim, which the Prophet replaced with the name Rāšid b. ʿAbd Allāh. In Ibn Ḥibbān, *Taʾrīḫ al-ṣaḥābah* 100, he is called Rāšid b. Ḥafṣ al-Sulamī Abū Uṯaylah. He was from the people of the Ḥiğāz and the Prophet replaced his former name Ẓālim with the name Rāšid.

Abī Saʿd al-Warrāq[38] < Yaḥyá b. ʿAbd al-Malik b. Ismāʿīl al-Sulamī < Numayr b. Muḥammad b. ʿUqayl al-Ẓafarī (the Ẓafar were among the worshippers of Suwāʿ) < his grandfather (or great-grandfather), who informed him that their father Rāšid b. Rāšid, formerly known as Ẓālim b. Ġāwī, was with the Prophet in a wadi called Ruhāṭ. The latter granted him a spring which he had created miraculously, together with the declivity in which it ran. When the report was recorded, the place still belonged to Rāšid's offspring.[39] The above-mentioned ʿAyn al-Rasūl/Māʾ al-Rasūl is identical to ʿAyn al-Nabī mentioned elsewhere.[40] While there is no mention here of Rāšid's custodianhip, the mention of Ruhāṭ indicates that Rāšid b. Rāšid is in fact Rāšid the former custodian, and thus we have here other descendants who preserved a report about him. Note that there is a certain discrepancy between Rāšid's pedigree and that of his offspring: the informant who was Rāšid's descendant was from the above-mentioned Ẓafar, i.e. Ẓafar b. al-Ḥāriṯ b. Buhṯah b. Sulaym, while Rāšid's pedigree indicates that he was of the Kaʿb b. al-Ḥāriṯ b. Buhṯah b. Sulaym. However, elsewhere Rāšid is referred to as a member of the Ẓafar.[41] Perhaps the distinction between the brother clans Ẓafar and Kaʿb disappeared at a certain point in time, or a genealogical shift took place.[42]

1.3 *ʿUqayl: Abū Ḥarb b. Ḫuwaylid and the Divination Arrows*

The following is in fact a report of a near conversion. Among the ʿUqaylīs mentioned by Ibn Saʿd under the title *wafd* ʿUqayl b. Kaʿb one figure remained pagan, namely Abū Ḥarb b. Ḫuwaylid b. ʿĀmir b. ʿUqayl. He cast lots with arrows (*wa-ḍaraba bi-l-qidāḥ*) in order to decide between Islam and his own religion (*dīn*), and after the arrow of disbelief had emerged three times, he did not convert.[43] Ibn Saʿd quotes two reports on *wafd* ʿUqayl b. Kaʿb from Ibn al-Kalbī < a man of the ʿUqayl < their elders (*ašyāḫ qawmihi*).[44]

---

38 Anon., *al-Manāsik* 124–125.

39 Anon., *al-Manāsik* 350.

40 Anon., *al-Manāsik* 349. The unspecified Ẓafarī mentioned here must have been Rāšid. He asked the Prophet *an yasqiyahu bi-Ruhāṭ ʿaynan*, i.e. that he grant him a spring in Ruhāṭ. This is parallel to Rāšid's request that the Prophet grant him a *qaṭīʿah* in Ruhāṭ; al-Suyūṭī, *al-Ḫaṣāʾiṣ*, 2:194.

41 Anon., *al-Manāsik* 349.

42 Lecker (1989): 59.

43 Ibn Saʿd, *al-Ṭabaqāt*[2], 1:261. Contrast the famous report on Imruʾ al-Qays's breaking of the arrows of Ḏū l-Ḫalaṣah in Tabālah. His forceful action is thought to have put an end to the practice of divination (*istiqsām*) there; e.g. Ibn ʿAsākir, *Dimašq*, 9:239 (*fa-lam yustaqsam ʿinda Ḏī l-Ḫalaṣah ḥattá ǧāʾa llāh bi-l-islām*).

44 Ibn Ḥaǧar includes Abū Ḥarb in the first category of Companions, i.e. among those whose Companion status is mentioned in a *ḥadīṯ* of any level of reliability, or is proven otherwise;

1.4 *Sa'd b. Bakr: Ḍimām b. Ṯaʿlabah and the Idols*

Ibn Saʿd, under *wafd* Saʿd b. Bakr, quotes from al-Wāqidī the report on Ḍimām b. Ṯaʿlabah who arrived at Medina in Rağab 5/November–December 626. He returned to his people as a Muslim, having repudiated the idols.[45] According to al-Wāqidī, Ḍimām arrived in Rağab 5 in the first Arab delegation that came to Muḥammad.[46] Ibn Hišām, quoting Abū ʿUbaydah (Maʿmar b. al-Muthanná), dates Ḍimām's arrival to 9/630 or 631; Ibn Ḥağar, probably correctly, prefers the later date.[47]

Ḍimām began the report to his people about his visit to Muḥammad by cursing Allāt and al-ʿUzzá; his shocked audience warned him of the threat of leprosy, elephantiasis, and madness.[48]

Several versions of Ḍimām's report, which has legal implications, enjoy a high profile in the relevant Islamic literature. In the legal context the report is accompanied by respectable *isnād*s that avoid obscure tribal authorities.

1.5 *Kalb: ʿIṣām al-Kalbī, the Custodian of ʿAmrah*

ʿIṣām, a Kalbī of the ʿĀmir b. ʿAwf subdivision, was the custodian of a tribal idol called ʿAmrah (or ʿAmr?). No further details are given about him, perhaps because the report was not preserved by one of his descendants, but by members of another family. ʿAmr b. Ğabalah b. Wāʾilah al-Kalbī reports that they had an idol (*kāna lanā ṣanam*)—the wording and the existence of a custodian suggest that it was a tribal idol, not a household one. One day a voice from within the idol announced that idol worship had come to an end, following which ʿAmr and ʿIṣām went to Muḥammad and embraced Islam.[49] Ibn al-Kalbī and

---

Ibn Ḥağar, *al-Iṣābah*², 7:88; Ibn al-Kalbī, *Ğamharat al-nasab* 334. Abū Ḥarb demanded that his tribe be exempted from *ʿušr* and *ḥašr*; on these terms, see Lecker (2001): 32–38.

45 *Qad ḫalaʿa l-andād*; Ibn Saʿd, *al-Ṭabaqāt*², 1:259.

46 *Wa-kāna awwal man qadima min wafd al-ʿarab*: Ibn Baškuwāl, *Ġawāmiḍ al-asmāʾ*, 1:58. The *isnād* goes back to Muḥammad b. Muḥammad b. ʿUmar, i.e. al-Wāqidī's son < his father. For an *isnād* including Muḥammad b. Muḥammad b. ʿUmar al-Wāqidī < his father, see e.g. Abū Nuʿaym, *Ḏikr aḫbār Iṣbahān*, 2:44; al-Ḫaṭīb al-Baġdādī, *al-Asmāʾ al-mubhamah* 356. For an entry on al-Wāqidī's son, see al-Ḫaṭīb al-Baġdādī, *Taʾrīḫ Baġdād*, 3:196–197, s.v. Muḥammad b. al-Wāqidī (he transmitted from his father, among other books, the latter's *Kitāb al-taʾrīḫ*).

47 Ibn Ḥağar, *al-Iṣābah*², 3:487. In the report on Ḍimām in Ibn Hišām, *al-Sīrah al-nabawiyyah*, 4:219–221, note that there is no mention of Abū ʿUbaydah or the date of Ḍimām's arrival. Al-Wāqidī dates his arrival to the year of the Ḫandaq, after the departure of the *aḥzāb*, while another source dates his arrival to 7/628–629; al-Qurṭubī, *al-Ğāmiʿ*, 4:144.

48 Ibn Hišām, *al-Sīrah al-nabawiyyah*, 4:220; Ibn Šabbah, *Taʾrīḫ al-Madīnah*, 2:521–523; al-Ṭabarī, *Taʾrīḫ*, 1:1722–1724.

49 Ibn Ḥağar, *al-Iṣābah*², 4:501 (quoting al-Ḫargūšī's *Šaraf al-muṣṭafá*). The entry is entitled

Abū ʿUbayd al-Qāsim b. Sallām list ʿAmr b. Ǧabalah among those who paid a formal visit (*wafada*) to the Prophet.[50]

ʿAmr's grandson, namely Saʿīd b. al-Walīd b. ʿAmr al-Abraš al-Kalbī, was Hišām's *ḥāǧib* and one of the most influential figures in the Umayyad administration.[51] In another pedigree of al-Abraš, one which is perhaps more trustworthy, his grandfather's name is not ʿAmr but ʿAbd ʿAmr, which may suggest that the idol's name was ʿAmr rather than ʿAmrah.[52] In a variant of the above report the voice from within the idol addresses ʿAbd ʿAmr/Bakr. The report was recorded by Ibn al-Kalbī, whose informants were al-Ḥāriṯ b. ʿAmr and others. If indeed al-Ḥāriṯ b. ʿAmr was Ibn al-Kalbī's direct source, he could not have been the protagonist's son.[53]

By tracing al-Abraš's pedigree it is possible to identify the ʿĀmir b. ʿAwf subdivision of the Kalb tribe as ʿĀmir al-Akbar b. ʿAwf b. Bakr b. ʿAwf b. ʿUḏrah, more precisely ʿĀmir al-Ǧulāḥ b. ʿAwf b. Bakr b. ʿAwf b. ʿĀmir al-Akbar.[54] ʿAbd ʿAmr's brother, al-Nuʿmān, is said to have gone to the Prophet together with his brother.[55]

One assumes that the influential Abraš attempted to secure for his ancestor a place among the Prophet's Companions. In any case, the evidence concerning the idol's existence must be reliable.

"ʿIṣām b. ʿĀmir al-Kalbī," but I could not find support for his father's name. He was *min Banī Fāris* (?). ʿAmr's son, ʿAbd, appears to have played some role here, otherwise there would have been no entry on him in the *Iṣābah*. According to the entry, Wāʾilah's father was called al-Ǧulāḥ; Ibn Ḥaǧar, *al-Iṣābah*², 4:387 (printed: Wāʾil, instead of Wāʾilah).

50 Ibn Ḥaǧar, *al-Iṣābah*², 4:613 (Wāʾil instead of Wāʾilah; Wāʾil's father was Qays b. Bakr; see al-Abraš's pedigree below, where these two appear together with al-Ǧulāḥ). Perhaps Abū ʿUbayd compiled a monograph on the *wufūd*. For a possible quotation from this presumed monograph see Ibn Ḥaǧar, *al-Iṣābah*², 1:456, s.v. Ǧabalah b. Ṯawr al-Ḥanafī.

51 Ibn Ḥaǧar, *al-Iṣābah*², 4:613 (the "ibn" between "Saʿīd" and "al-Abraš" is superfluous).

52 Ibn al-Kalbī, *Nasab Maʿadd*, 2:608 (printed Saʿd instead of Saʿīd). A longer pedigree of al-Abraš makes him a great-great-grandson of ʿAbd ʿAmr, rather than a grandson: Saʿīd b. Bakr b. ʿAbd Qays b. al-Walīd b. ʿAbd ʿAmr b. Ǧabalah b. Wāʾil b. Qays b. Bakr b. al-Ǧulāḥ (referred to as Hišām's *wazīr*); Ibn Ḥazm, *Ǧamharat ansāb al-ʿarab* 458. The words "b. Bakr b. ʿAbd Qays" are superfluous, as he could not have had a grandfather called ʿAbd Qays who lived in the Islamic period. See al-Abraš's full pedigree in Ibn ʿAsākir, *Dimašq*, 7:295.

53 Here the idol is called ʿAyr, var. ʿAmr; Ibn Mandah, quoting Ibn al-Kalbī, in Ibn Ḥaǧar, *al-Iṣābah*², 1:322. See an entry on Bakr/ʿAbd ʿAmr in Ibn Saʿd, *al-Ṭabaqāt*², 6:310. Ibn Saʿd is quoted in Ibn ʿAsākir, *Dimašq*, 7:298. In Ibn al-Aṯīr, *Usd al-ġābah*, 1:410 (with reference to the biographical dictionaries of Ibn Mandah and Abū Nuʿaym), the idol's name is ʿ.t.r.

54 Ibn al-Kalbī, *Nasab Maʿadd*, 2:607–608; Caskel (1966), 1: table 289.

55 Ibn Ḥaǧar, *al-Iṣābah*², 6:441 (where the *nisbah* al-ʿUḏrī is misleading). Al-Nuʿmān is referred to as Ibn al-Ǧulāḥ in Ibn Durayd, *al-Ištiqāq* 541.

1.6 *Ǧuhaynah: The Custodian ʿAmr b. Murrah*

Ibn Saʿd, under *wafd* Ǧuhaynah, quotes two reports, both going back to Ibn al-Kalbī. One deals with two persons, while the other, dealing with one, refers to idol worship. Ibn al-Kalbī quotes Ḫālid b. Saʿīd < an unspecified man from the Ǧuhaynah, more precisely the Duhmān < his father, who was a Companion < ʿAmr b. Murrah: "We had an idol and we used to worship it (*nuʿaẓẓimuhu*). I was its custodian, and when I heard about the Prophet, I demolished it and set out for the Prophet in Medina."[56] The words "we had an idol" and the existence of a custodian indicate that the idol belonged to a tribal group.

1.7 *ʿUḏrah: Ziml b. ʿAmr and Ḥumām (§ 160)*

The idol of the ʿUḏrah, Ḥumām, is associated with the conversion of Ziml b. ʿAmr al-ʿUḏrī. Ibn Saʿd, under *wafd* ʿUḏrah, adduces two reports. One deals with the *wafd* as a whole, which included twelve members, four of whom are specified; the other, quoted from Ibn al-Kalbī < Šarqī b. al-Quṭāmī < Mudliǧ b. al-Miqdād b. Ziml b. ʿAmr, is about the informant's grandfather, Ziml b. ʿAmr. For part of the report Ibn al-Kalbī relied on another informant, namely Abū Zufar al-Kalbī (possibly quoting the same family *isnād*). Ziml's idol is not specified in this report. It states that Ziml went to the Prophet and informed him about what he had heard from within their idol. The Prophet replied: "This is a believer from among the *ǧinn*."[57] Elsewhere a report on this topic can be traced back to Abū l-Ḥāriṯ Muḥammad b. al-Ḥāriṯ, with a family *isnād* going back to Ziml b. ʿAmr. The idol belonged to the ʿUḏrah (not to Ziml alone) and its name was Ḥumām. More specifically, it was among (i.e. it belonged to) the Hind b. Ḥarām b. Ḍinnah b. ʿAbd b. Kabīr b. ʿUḏrah. Its custodian was called Ṭāriq and they used to sacrifice sheep (or goats, *yaʿtirūna*) at it.[58]

Ziml and some of his descendants were prominent in the Umayyad regime. Ziml, who received a house (*dār*) in Damascus from Muʿāwiyah, was in charge of Muʿāwiyah's *šurṭah* (internal security force). In the Battle of Ṣiffīn he reportedly carried the banner with which the Prophet had given him authority

---

56 Ibn Saʿd, *al-Ṭabaqāt*², 1:287–288; Ibn ʿAsākir, *Dimašq*, 46:343. ʿAmr abandoned the stone idols (*ālihat al-aḥǧār*), according to his verse that is attached to the report. In another report (Ibn ʿAsākir, *Dimašq*, 46:344), the custodian was ʿAmr's father.

57 Ibn Saʿd, *al-Ṭabaqāt*², 1:286. The same report is quoted from Ibn Saʿd in Ibn ʿAsākir, *Dimašq*, 19:77. Mudliǧ reports on the authority of his father, and Abū Zufar al-Kalbī is replaced by al-Ḥāriṯ b. ʿAmr b. Ǧuzayy (perhaps identical with Abū Zufar al-Kalbī) < his paternal uncle, ʿUmārah b. Ǧuzayy. In Ibn Ḥaǧar, *al-Iṣābah*², 2:567, no. 2818, where Ibn Saʿd is quoted, the text is garbled.

58 Ibn ʿAsākir, *Dimašq*, 11:489–490.

over his tribe. He was one of Muʿāwiyah's witnesses at the Ṣiffīn arbitration agreement (Ṣafar 37/August 657) and was killed in the Battle of Marǧ Rāhiṭ.[59]

For generations Ziml's report was preserved by his offspring, regardless of its incorporation in the general literary tradition. Tammām b. Muḥammad adduced it in his *Fawāʾid* on the authority of the above-mentioned Abū l-Ḥāriṯ Muḥammad b. al-Ḥāriṯ < his fathers.[60] In other words, the family tradition, which was probably written down at an early date, coexisted with the literature. Ziml's grandson, Mudliǧ b. al-Miqdād, transmitted his *ḥadīṯ* to his son, Hāniʾ, and to two non-family members, Šarqī b. al-Quṭāmī and Yazīd b. Saʿīd al-ʿAbsī.[61]

1.8 *Hamdān: al-ʿAwwām b. Ǧuhayl, the Custodian of Yaġūṯ*

Al-ʿAwwām b. Ǧuhayl al-Hamdānī was the custodian of Yaġūṯ, according to an autobiographical report from al-ʿAwwām himself (*kāna l-ʿAwwām yuḥaddiṯu baʿda islāmihi*).[62] He slept at the idol's sanctuary (*bayt al-ṣanam*), and after a stormy night he heard a mysterious voice (*hātif*) announcing the end of idolatry. Al-ʿAwwām set out for Medina and arrived in time to see the Hamdān delegation surrounding the Prophet.[63]

1.9 *Saʿd al-ʿAshīrah: Ḏubāb and Farrā(ṣ/ḍ) (§ 157)*

An idol called Farrāṣ[64] appears in the report on *wafd* Saʿd al-ʿAšīrah. Ibn al-Kalbī (< Abū Kubrān al-Murādī < Yaḥyá b. Hāniʾ b. ʿUrwah < ʿAbd al-Raḥmān b. Abī Sabrah al-Ǧuʿfī) quotes a report on the visit of Ḏubāb, a man of the Anas Allāh b. Saʿd al-ʿAšīrah, to the Prophet. When Ḏubāb and his fellow tribesmen heard about the appearance (*ḫurūǧ*) of the Prophet, Ḏubāb smashed the idol Farrāṣ

---

59 Ibn ʿAsākir, *Dimašq*, 19:76–77. Under Yazīd b. Muʿāwiyah he was in charge of the *ḫātam*; Ibn ʿAsākir, *Dimašq*, 21:95. Mudliǧ b. al-Miqdād b. Ziml who was a *šarīf* in Syria was married to Amīnah bt. ʿAbd Allāh al-Qasrī, Ḫālid al-Qasrī's sister; Ibn ʿAsākir, *Dimašq*, 57:189 (read al-Qasrī instead of al-Qušayrī); Ibn Ḥaǧar, *al-Iṣābah*², 2:568.

60 In Tammām's book the idol is called Ḫumām; Ibn ʿAsākir, *Dimašq*, 52:245; Ibn Ḥaǧar, *al-Iṣābah*², 2:568. On Tammām b. Muḥammad b. ʿAbd Allāh al-Rāzī (d. 414/1023) see GAS, 1:226–227; al-Kattānī, *al-Risālah al-mustaṭrafah* 71.

61 Ibn ʿAsākir, *Dimašq*, 57:189.

62 One assumes that the report was preserved by al-ʿAwwām's offspring.

63 Ibn Ḥaǧar, *al-Iṣābah*², 4:736–737, quoting Ibn al-Kalbī. Ibn Ḥaǧar quotes Ibn al-Kalbī's report from an unspecified treatise of Abū Aḥmad al-ʿAskarī, who in turn quotes Ibn Durayd's *al-Aḫbār al-manṯūrah*. In Ibn al-Aṯīr, *Usd al-ġābah*, 4:295, who similarly quotes Abū Aḥmad al-ʿAskarī, we find that Ibn Durayd quotes al-Sakan b. Saʿīd < Muḥammad b. ʿAbbād < Ibn al-Kalbī.

64 Wellhausen (1897): 67; Naṣr, *al-Amkinah*, 2:325.

and went to him.[65] Ibn al-Kalbī's immediate source was Abū Kubrān al-Ḥasan b. ʿUqbah al-Murādī.[66] Scholars of the Murādī tribe were naturally interested in the history of their fellow tribesmen, especially in connection with their tribe's first contact with the Prophet. Yaḥyá belonged to a subdivision of the Murād called Ġuṭayf (§ 20).[67] As to the Ǧuʿfī informant, note that Ǧuʿfī was a branch of the Saʿd al-ʿAšīrah. Moreover, the Anas Allāh b. Saʿd al-ʿAšīrah were incorporated into the Ǧuʿfī.[68]

A longer version of Ibn al-Kalbī's report is found in Ibn Šāhīn's biographical dictionary of Companions.[69] Saʿd al-ʿAšīrah's idol was called Qarrāṣ (the *fāʾ* and the *qāf* are only differentiated by a diacritical point) and the custodian's name was Ibn Waqšah. The custodian had a *ǧinnī* that was only visible to him (*raʾī mina l-ǧinn*) who informed him about the future. One day the *ǧinnī* informed Ibn Waqšah of something, then he turned to Ḏubāb and informed him of Muḥammad's appearance in Mecca. Ḏubāb smashed the idol and went to Muḥammad. The report is also found in Ibn Mandah's *Dalāʾil al-nubuwwah* (but not in his biographical dictionary of Companions), in al-Bayhaqī's *Dalāʾil al-nubuwwah*, and in al-Muʿāfá b. Zakariyyāʾ's *al-Ǧalīs al-ṣāliḥ*.[70] The literary merits of the report secured it a place in the last mentioned *adab* book.

The existence of Farrāṣ, the idol of the Saʿd al-ʿAšīrah, is arguably the only trustworthy detail in the report on Ḏubāb's conversion.

65 Ibn Saʿd, *al-Ṭabaqāt*², 1:295.

66 A report about Farwah b. Musayk al-Murādī's visit to the Prophet has the same *isnād* (Ibn al-Kalbī < Abū Kubrān al-Murādī < Yaḥyá b. Hāniʾ al-Murādī); Ibn Ḥaǧar, *al-Iṣābah*², 6:713. Abū Kubrān was also one of Sayf b. ʿUmar's sources; Ibn ʿAsākir, *Dimašq*, 63:246.

67 Ibn Ḥazm, *Ǧamharat ansāb al-ʿarab* 406. Farwah b. Musayk belonged to the same subdivision.

68 Ibn Ḥazm, *Ǧamharat ansāb al-ʿarab* 407 (*daḫalū fī aḫīhim Ǧuʿfī*). For an entry on ʿAbd al-Raḥmān see Ibn Ḥaǧar, *al-Iṣābah*², 4:308. For an entry on Abū Sabrah Yazīd b. Mālik al-Ǧuʿfī, see Ibn ʿAbd al-Barr, *al-Istīʿāb*, 4:1667.

69 Here Ibn al-Kalbī's informant is called al-Ḥasan b. Kaṯīr, probably due to a misprint.

70 Ibn Ḥaǧar, *al-Iṣābah*², 2:402–403; al-Bayhaqī, *Dalāʾil al-nubuwwah*, 2:259. In al-Muʿāfá, *al-Ǧalīs al-ṣāliḥ*, 1:557–558, the custodian is Ibn Waqšah/Ibn Daqšah. In Ibn al-Aṯīr, *Usd al-ġābah*, 2:208–209, the custodian is Ibn Ruqaybah/Waqšah. The entry is taken from the Companions dictionary of Abū Mūsá Muḥammad b. Abī Bakr b. Abī ʿĪsá l-Madīnī l-Iṣfahānī, *Ḏayl maʿrifat al-ṣaḥābah*, which includes corrections to Ibn Mandah's dictionary and additional materials. According to Ibn al-Aṯīr, *Usd al-ġābah*, 1:110, al-Madīnī's book was one-third shorter than Ibn Mandah's. See an entry on Abū Mūsá in al-Ḏahabī, *Siyar aʿlām al-nubalāʾ*, 21:152–159.

1.10 *Ṭayyiʾ: Māzin b. al-Ġaḍūbah, the Custodian of Bāǧir*

The Prophet's Companion Māzin b. al-Ġaḍūbah was of the Ṭayyiʾ, more precisely of the Ḫiṭāmah, hence his *nisbah* al-Ḫiṭāmī. Ḫiṭāmah was Māzin's great-great-grandfather.[71] The full version of Māzin's report was preserved in al-Ṭabarānī's *al-Muʿǧam al-kabīr*. Māzin was the custodian of an idol called Bāǧir[72] located in the ʿUmānī village Samāʾil (see map).[73] According to Māzin, he was in charge of his people (*fa-kuntu al-qayyim bi-umūrihim*). One day, when he and others were offering sheep (or goats, *fa-ʿatarnā ... ʿatīrah*) to the idol, he heard a voice from within it announcing the appearance of a prophet from Muḍar and calling upon him to abandon his stone idol. A rider from the Ḥiǧāz confirmed the appearance of Aḥmad, and Māzin broke the idol into pieces and traveled to the Prophet. The latter cured him of his excessive love for music, wine, and women of ill repute, and blessed the childless Māzin with a boy they named Ḥayyān. The *isnād* for this report goes back to ʿAlī b. Ḥarb al-Mawṣilī < Ibn al-Kalbī < his father < ʿAbd Allāh al-ʿUmānī < Māzin b. al-Ġaḍūbah.[74] ʿAlī b. Ḥarb b. Muḥammad b. ʿAlī[75] b. Ḥayyān b. Māzin b. al-Ġaḍūbah al-Ṭāʾī l-Mawṣilī (d. 265/878–879) was the great-great-grandson of Māzin's only child, Ḥayyān.[76] Al-Kalbī's source, ʿAbd Allāh al-ʿUmānī, was probably a member of Māzin's family who transmitted Māzin's report with all its embellishments and verse. ʿAlī b. Ḥarb transmitted *ḥadīṯ*, among others, from his father, Ḥarb b. Muḥammad, with whom he traveled to learn *ḥadīṯ*. ʿAlī was an expert on the history, genealogy, and wars of the Arabs (*aḫbār al-ʿArab wa-ansābihā wa-ayyāmihā*).[77] But to learn his own family history he turned to Ibn al-Kalbī. ʿAlī and other family members were referred to by the *nisbah* al-Māzinī after their famous ancestor, the former custodian Māzin.[78]

---

71 Ibn Ḥaǧar, *al-Iṣābah*², 5:704; Ibn ʿAbd al-Barr, *al-Istīʿāb*, 3:1344; Ibn al-Kalbī, *Nasab Maʿadd*, 1:261; al-Ḥāzimī, *ʿUǧālat al-mubtadī* 55, s.v. al-Ḫiṭāmī. An entry on Māzin can also be found in Ibn Qāniʿ, *Muʿǧam al-ṣaḥābah*, 3:121–122.

72 Or Bāḥir, or Nāǧir; see below.

73 Other variants are al-Simāl, Samāyā, and Sanābil. The last mentioned variant is from al-Ḥimyarī, *al-Rawḍ al-miʿṭār* 326, s.v. Sanābil. Regarding the idol's name, cf. Ibn al-Kalbī, *al-Aṣnām* 63, quoting Ibn Durayd: Bāǧ(a/i)r was worshipped by the Azd and their neighbors from the Ṭayyiʾ and Quḍāʿah; Ibn Durayd, *Ǧamharat al-luġah*, 1:267.

74 Al-Ṭabarānī, *al-Muʿǧam al-kabīr*, 20:337–339. See also al-Ṭabarānī, *al-Aḥādīṯ al-ṭiwāl* 154–156. The text in al-Hayṯamī, *Maǧmaʿ al-zawāʾid*, 8:247–248, is garbled.

75 Printed: Ḥarb (instead of ʿAlī).

76 Al-Mizzī, *Tahḏīb al-kamāl*, 20:361–365.

77 Al-Mizzī, *Tahḏīb al-kamāl*, 20:361, 20:363–364. ʿAlī's father was a merchant; al-Ḏahabī, *Siyar aʿlām al-nubalāʾ*, 12:251. His entry is followed by entries on three of his brothers; ibid., 12:253–256.

78 Al-Samʿānī, *al-Ansāb*, 5:165, who mentions a Māzinī called Salamah b. ʿAmr.

Al-Ṭabarānī (d. 360/971) received ʿAlī b. Ḥarb's report through Mūsá b. al-Ǧumhūr al-Tinnīsī l-Simsār. ʿAlī's great-grandson transmitted it in Baghdad in 338/949–950 to the *muḥaddiṯ* Muḥammad b. al-Ḥusayn al-Qaṭṭān. The latter transmitted it to Abū Bakr al-Bayhaqī (d. 458/1066), who included it in his *Dalāʾil al-nubuwwah*. ʿAlī's great-grandson included in the report, which he found in his great-grandfather's written source (*aṣl ǧaddī*), details which he had received from a friend in ʿUmān who referred to a local tradition (*ʿan salafihim*).[79]

Following his conversion, Māzin separated from his tribe[80] and established a mosque that had magical qualities. When someone who had been wronged prayed in it and cursed his oppressor, his prayer was accepted. In the margin of the manuscript (*aṣl al-samāʿ*) an anonymous hand added that a leper was almost cured there, and hence, to this day the mosque is called *mubriṣ* (curing from leprosy).[81] In this version of the report ʿAlī b. Ḥarb provides details about his meeting with Ibn al-Kalbī. When the latter found out that ʿAlī b. Ḥarb was a descendant of Ḫiṭāmah, he asked: "From the custodian's offspring?" Then Ibn al-Kalbī told him what he had heard from *šuyūḫ Ṭayyiʾ al-mutaqaddimīna* (the elders of the Ṭayyiʾ).

The family's attitude to Māzin's custodianship was far from being apologetic; it was its claim to fame.[82] It was very successful in securing for him Companion status, as is indicated by Māzin's entries in the biographical dictionaries of Companions[83] and by quotations in other types of literature. For example, it appears in al-Ṭabarānī's *al-Muʿǧam al-kabīr*, as quoted above. The *dalāʾil al-nubuwwah* literature merits special mention in this context.[84] Māzin's report was attractive for later compilers because of its legendary elements and verse,

79 Cf. Robinson (2000): 132.

80 The separation is mentioned in al-Ṭabarānī, *al-Muʿǧam al-kabīr*, 20:339, where it is reported that he "moved to the coast."

81 Al-Bayhaqī, *Dalāʾil al-nubuwwah*, 2:255–258.

82 In this version, Māzin was a custodian of several idols belonging to his family (*wa-kāna yasdunu l-aṣnām li-ahlihi*); he had an idol called Bāǧir, var. Nāǧir. ʿAlī b. Ḥarb also transmitted the report to the *muḥaddiṯ* ʿAbd al-Raḥmān b. Muḥammad al-Ḥanẓalī, whence it reached al-Ḥākim al-Naysābūrī (d. 405/1014–1015; it may appear in his *Taʾrīḫ Naysābūr*) via another transmitter; al-Bayhaqī, *Dalāʾil al-nubuwwah*, 2:258 (here the village is called al-Simāl).

83 Ibn Ḥibbān dissents from the consensus (quoted in Ibn Ḥaǧar, *al-Iṣābah*², 5:704: *yuqālu inna lahu ṣuḥbah*); see the same cautious remark in Ibn Ḥibbān, *al-Ṯiqāt*, 3:407.

84 Abū Nuʿaym, *Dalāʾil al-nubuwwah* 114–117 (the beginning of the report is garbled; the name of the village was Samāyā; the idol's name was Bāǧir); al-Bayhaqī, *Dalāʾil al-nubuwwah*, 2:255–258; al-Suyūṭī, *al-Ḫaṣāʾiṣ*, 1:256–257.

but historians looking for relatively solid evidence must depend on the background details, namely the existence of Māzin's idol in a certain village in ʿUmān.

Another family tradition is interwoven with the one discussed above. An Arab *mawlá* (manumitted slave) of Māzin, Abū Kaṯīr Ṣāliḥ (or Yasār/Našīṭ/Dīnār) b. al-Mutawakkil, is supposed to have been introduced by Māzin to the Prophet as his slave (*ġulām*). Prompted by the Prophet, Māzin manumitted him there and then. Ibn Mandah (d. 395/1005) received the report about the *mawlá* from none other than ʿAlī b. Ḥarb. ʿAlī in turn transmitted it from a descendant of the manumitted slave, al-Ḥasan b. Kaṯīr b. Yaḥyá b. Abī Kaṯīr < his father < his grandfather. Ibn Mandah reports that Ṣāliḥ and his master Māzin were killed in Barḏaʿah during ʿUṯmān's caliphate.[85]

Ṣāliḥ was useful to Māzin's offspring for transmitting a rather vague *ḥadīṯ* in favor of truthfulness, which Māzin reported on the Prophet's authority. It supported their claim that Māzin was a Companion of the Prophet.[86]

1.11 *Baǧīlah: Ǧarīr b. ʿAbd Allāh and Ḏū l-Ḫalaṣah* (*§ 188–192*)

Ibn Saʿd, under *wafd* Baǧīlah, quotes a report from al-Wāqidī, who in turn quotes a Medinan authority, ʿAbd al-Ḥamīd b. Ǧaʿfar < his father. The report includes details about the destruction of Ḏū l-Ḫalaṣah (which was located in Tabālah; see map), by Ǧarīr b. ʿAbd Allāh al-Baǧalī.[87] But a comparison with reports on the destruction found elsewhere indicates that Ǧarīr himself was the origin. A useful source is al-Ṭabarānī's *al-Muʿǧam al-kabīr* where all the reports go back to Ismāʿīl b. Abī Ḫālid < Qays b. Abī Ḥāzim, with two exceptions: Bayān b. Bišr al-Baǧalī < Qays b. Abī Ḥāzim, and Ṭāriq b. ʿAbd al-Raḥmān < Qays b. Abī Ḥāzim.[88]

The Kufan Ismāʿīl b. Abī Ḫālid al-Baǧalī l-Aḥmasī was a *mawlá* of the Aḥmas.[89] The Kufan jurist (*faqīh*) Qays b. Abī Ḥāzim was also of the Aḥmas,[90]

---

85 Quoted in Ibn Ḥaǧar, *al-Iṣābah*², 3:403. For an entry on Yaḥyá b. Abī Kaṯīr, see al-Mizzī, *Tahḏīb al-kamāl*, 31:504–511. He was tortured and flogged and his beard was shaved because he reviled the Umayyad rulers (*umtuḥina wa-ḍuriba wa-ḥuliqa li-kawnihi ntaqaṣa Banī Umayyah*); al-Ḏahabī, *Taḏkirat al-ḥuffāẓ*, 1:128.

86 Ibn Ḥaǧar, *al-Iṣābah*², 5:705, with reference to earlier biographical dictionaries of Companions and to Wakīʿ's *Nawādir al-aḫbār* (GAS, 1:376); al-Ṭabarānī, *al-Muʿǧam al-kabīr*, 20:337 (with some variants in the *isnād*).

87 Ibn Saʿd, *al-Ṭabaqāt*², 1:299–300.

88 Al-Ṭabarānī, *al-Muʿǧam al-kabīr*, 20:299–301, 310–312.

89 Al-Mizzī, *Tahḏīb al-kamāl*, 3:69–76.

90 Al-Mizzī, *Tahḏīb al-kamāl*, 24:10–16; Ibn Ḥazm, *Ǧamharat ansāb al-ʿarab* 389.

as was the Kufan Bayān b. Bišr[91] and the Kufan Ṭāriq b. ʿAbd al-Raḥmān.[92] The pattern is clear: only fellow Baǧalīs transmitted the report on Ǧarīr and Ḏū l-Ḫalaṣah. Although Ǧarīr did not belong to the Aḥmas but to another branch of the Baǧīlah, namely Qasr,[93] this is tribal history *par excellence*. The military power with which Ǧarīr set out to demolish Ḏū l-Ḫalaṣah was made of Aḥmasīs.

Ǧarīr came to Muḥammad in Ramaḍān 10/December 631,[94] in other words, news about Ḏū l-Ḫalaṣah's demolition reached Muḥammad shortly before his death. The demolition and the death of the Ḫaṯʿamīs who defended the sanctuary are in the background of the visit of *wafd* Ḫaṯʿam.[95] During the *riddah* wars Abū Bakr ordered Ǧarīr to fight the Ḫaṯʿamīs, who had rebelled because they were angry over Ḏū l-Ḫalaṣah and wanted to reinstate it.[96]

Ḏū l-Ḫalaṣah was not just another tribal idol; in fact, it was a cultic center. Ibn Saʿd, under *wafd* Baǧīlah, reports that when Ǧarīr came to the Prophet the first time and reported that the tribes had destroyed their idols, the Prophet specifically inquired about Ḏū l-Ḫalaṣah and found that it remained intact. Ǧarīr was sent to destroy it. He took what was on the idol (i.e. jewelry or weapons) and set fire to it.[97] The fact that Ḏū l-Ḫalaṣah lasted longer than the other idols, or at least most of them, is reflected in the Prophet's alleged statement that of the *ṭawāġīt* of the Ǧāhiliyyah only the *bayt*, or sanctuary, of Ḏū l-Ḫalaṣah remained.[98]

Ḏū l-Ḫalaṣah was al-Kaʿbah al-Yamāniyyah (the Yemeni Kaʿbah), while the Meccan Kaʿbah was al-Kaʿbah al-Šāmiyyah.[99] Ḏū l-Ḫalaṣah was probably the site of many idols.[100] Presumably, tribes associated with Ḏū l-Ḫalaṣah were not associated with the Kaʿbah. The Ḫaṯʿam, together with the Ṭayyiʾ and the Quḍāʿah, did not respect the sanctity of Mecca's *ḥaram* and that of the sacred

---

91 Al-Mizzī, *Tahḏīb al-kamāl*, 4:303–305.
92 Al-Mizzī, *Tahḏīb al-kamāl*, 13:345–348.
93 Ibn Ḥazm, *Ǧamharat ansāb al-ʿarab* 387.
94 Al-Balāḏurī, *Ansāb al-ašrāf*, 1:384.
95 Ibn Saʿd, *al-Ṭabaqāt*², 1:300.
96 ... *Wa-amarahu an yaʾtiya Ḫaṯʿam fa-yuqātila man ḫaraǧa ġaḍaban li-Ḏī l-Ḫalaṣah wa-man arāda iʿādatahu*; al-Ṭabarī, *Taʾrīḫ*, 1:1988.
97 Ibn Saʿd, *al-Ṭabaqāt*², 1:299.
98 Al-Ṭabarānī, *al-Muʿǧam al-kabīr*, 2:312.
99 Yāqūt, *Muʿǧam al-buldān*, 2:383, s.v. al-Ḫalaṣah.
100 Note the definition of al-Ḫalaṣah as *bayt aṣnām*; ibid. The word *al-zūn* is supposed to mean a place of this kind. It is interpreted as *mawḍiʿ tuǧmaʿu fīhi l-aṣnām wa-tunṣabu*; also: *al-zūn bayt al-aṣnām ayy mawḍiʿ kāna*; Yāqūt, *Muʿǧam al-buldān*, 3:159, s.v. Zūn. See also Ibn Manẓūr, *Lisān al-ʿarab*, the end of s.v. *zūn* (*wa-l-zūn mawḍiʿ tuǧmaʿu fīhi l-aṣnām wa-tunṣabu wa-tuzayyanu*).

months, while the other tribes made the pilgrimage to the Kaʿbah and respected it.[101] Ṭayyiʾ and Ḫaṯʿam did not make the pilgrimage to Mecca and were called *al-afǧarāni* (the two sinful tribes).[102]

The Azd al-Sarāt[103] were among the worshippers of Ḏū l-Ḫalaṣah.[104] The Ḫaṯʿam delegation only came to the Prophet after the demolition of their sanctuary, but some seventy or eighty men from (important?) families (*ahl bayt*) of the Daws (a subdivision of the Azd al-Sarāt), including Abū Hurayrah and ʿAbd Allāh b. Uzayhir, had come two years earlier, when the Prophet was in Ḫaybar.[105] The Daws are singled out among the former worshippers of Ḏū l-Ḫalaṣah as the ones most prone to return to their pagan ways. Abū Hurayrah transmitted the following on the authority of the Prophet: "Before the arrival of the Hour, the buttocks of the women of Daws will move from side to side around Ḏū l-Ḫalaṣah."[106] In other words, the Kaʿbah would remain intact in escatological times, and the southern tribes would yearn for idolatry and seek to revive the cultic center at Ḏū l-Ḫalaṣah.

There are probably more conversion reports involving idols. The less successful reports remained with the families and did not make it into the literature. The identification of the informants is often difficult because many of them did not transmit mainstream ("prestigious") *ḥadīṯ*, and hence were not included in the relevant biographical dictionaries. The main focus was entitlement to Companion status. At a later stage, through their inclusion in specialized types of literature, the conversion reports became part of the general Islamic heritage. The most relevant literature is the dictionaries of the Companions and compilations of *dalāʾil al-nubuwwah* (proofs of Muḥammad's prophethood), where the former idol worshippers—above all the custodians—bear

101 Kister (1965): 119. When Abū ʿUṯmān al-Nahdī (Quḍāʿah) refers to his pre-Islamic pilgrimages, he has in mind the idol Yaġūṯ, not the Kaʿbah; Ibn ʿAsākir, *Dimašq*, 35:472 (*aslamtu fī ḥayāt rasūli llāh ṣ wa-qad ḥaǧaǧtu bi-Yaġūṯ* [read probably *Yaġūṯa*] *wa-kāna ṣanaman min raṣāṣ li-Quḍāʿah timṯāla mraʾah wa-dawwartu l-adwirah*). The listing of the Ḫaṯʿam among the tribes of the *ḥums* is erroneous, while the reading Ǧušam is correct; Kister (1965): 132.

102 Kister (1965): 134, n. 5. Perhaps this is related to Ḫaṯʿam's participation in Abrahah's army which attacked Mecca; Kister (1972): 69–70, 72.

103 On the Sarāt mountains, see "al-Sarāt," in *EI*[2] (A. Grohmann-[E. van Donzel]).

104 Ibn al-Kalbī, *al-Aṣnām* 35; al-Balāḏurī, *Ansāb al-ašrāf*, 1:384.

105 Ibn Saʿd, *al-Ṭabaqāt*[2], 1:304; Ibn al-Ǧawzī, *al-Muntaẓam*, 3:304.

106 *Lā taqūmu l-sāʿah ḥattá taḍṭariba alyāt nisāʾ Daws ḥawla Ḏī l-Ḫalaṣah*; Muslim, *Ṣaḥīḥ*, 4:2230 (*Kitāb al-fitan wa-ašrāṭ al-sāʿah*). The following eschatological *ḥadīṯ* in this source speaks of a return to the worship of Allāt and al-ʿUzzá. For variants on the topic of Ḏū l-Ḫalaṣah, see Ibn Ḥammād, *al-Fitan* 302 (*iḏā ʿubidat Ḏū l-Ḫalaṣah ... kāna ẓuhūr al-Rūm ʿalá l-Šām*), 364 (Abū Hurayrah: ... *ka-annī bi-alyāt nisāʾ Daws qadi ṣṭafaqat yaʿbudūna Ḏā l-Ḫalaṣah*); Hawting (1999): 124.

witness to the collapse of idolatry. In any case, conversion reports involving idols go back to the very early days of Islam.[107]

2 Mecca

2.1 *Household Idols*

Conversion reports of Meccans, in the context of Muḥammad's conquest of his hometown, indicate the existence of a large number of household Meccan idols. Muḥammad is supposed to have purified Mecca of the idolatry, precisely as his ancestor Quṣayy b. Kilāb had done five generations earlier, when he drove out the corrupt Ḫuzāʿah.

Al-Wāqidī's reports about the destruction of household idols in Mecca aim at providing their protagonists with Islamic credentials. However, the background details are reliable. One report (< Saʿīd b. ʿAmr al-Huḏalī) starts with a general statement, followed by a specific example. After the conquest of Mecca, Muḥammad's announcer proclaimed that those who believe in Allāh and His messenger should break up every idol (*ṣanam*) in their houses. The Muslims started to break them up. Whenever ʿIkrimah b. Abī Ǧahl (of the Maḫzūm branch of Qurayš) heard of an idol in one of the houses of Qurayš, he went there to break it up. The report states that in the Ǧāhiliyyah, Abū Tiǧrāt used to make and sell them. At this point Saʿīd adds that his informant saw Abū Tiǧrāt manufacturing and selling them. Every Qurašī in Mecca had an idol in his house (*wa-lam yakun raǧul min Qurayš bi-Makkah illā wa-fī baytihi ṣanam*). According to the next report (< Ǧubayr b. Muṭʿim, d. 59/679), the announcer proclaimed that every idol had to be broken up or burnt, and that it was forbidden to sell them, i.e. to be used as firewood. Ǧubayr himself saw the idols being carried around Mecca (i.e. by peddlers). The Bedouin (*ahl al-badw*) would buy them and take them to their tents. Every Qurašī had an idol at home. He stroked it when he entered and when he left, so as to draw blessing from it.[108]

---

107 Cf. Krone (1992): 14: "Kunde über das arabische Heidentum geben uns zahlreiche Werke der Arabischen 'Gelehrten Literatur'. Zwar wurde in dem ersten Generationen nach dem Siegeszug des Islam noch bewußt auf eine Beschäftigung mit der Religion der Ǧāhiliyya verzichtet, um diese in Vergessenheit geraten zu lassen, doch schon im 2. Jh. der Hiǧra erwachte ein lebhaftes Interesse an der Erforschung des altarabischen Heidentums"; Krone assumes a gap of at least one hundred years between the end of idol worship and the beginning of scholarly interest in idols; ibid., 20.

108 See also al-Yaʿqūbī, *Taʾrīḫ*, 2:61 (*wa-nādá munādī rasūli llāh man kāna fī baytihi ṣanam fa-l-yaksirhu fa-kasarū l-aṣnām*). On the magical power of the *masḥ* see also Krone (1992): 395; Kohlberg (2003): 150–151.

Al-Wāqidī has another a report (< ʿAbd al-Maǧīd b. Suhayl) according to which when Hind bt. ʿUtbah embraced Islam, she started striking an idol in her house with an adze (*qadūm*), cutting oblong pieces from it (*fildah fildah*). She kept saying: "We have been deceived by you" (*kunnā minka fī ġurūr*).[109]

The reports about ʿIkrimah and Hind emphasize the zeal of the new converts. Hind was Abū Sufyān's wife and Muʿāwiyah's mother, hence the Umayyad court promoted her image. A (pseudo-)autobiographical report with a distinctly Umayyad chain of transmitters, including the caliphs ʿUmar II, Marwān I, and Muʿāwiyah—quoting his mother—elaborates on Hind's road from idolatry to Islam. The main component of this report is a dream that continued for three nights. On the first night, in pitch darkness, the Prophet appeared to her in a beam of light. On the second night she was on the road, with the idols Hubal and Isāf calling her on both sides and the Prophet in front of her, showing her the right path. On the third night she was on the brink of hell. Hubal called on her to enter, while the Prophet seized her by her clothes from behind. In the morning she went to an idol in her house. As she struck it she said: "You have misled me for a long time!" Then she converted to Islam at the Prophet's hands and pledged her allegiance to him.[110] All we need from this fictitious report is the background information, which clearly supports the testimony of other reports on the popularity of small wooden household idols in pre-Islamic Mecca.[111]

Some details are available about the Christian (*naṣrānī*) Meccan carpenter Abū Tiǧrāt[112] who carved wooden idols. His father's agnomen was Abū Fukayhah, after his daughter.[113] Abū Tiǧrāt was the son-in-law of a member of the Umayyad family, Muʿāwiyah b. al-Muġīrah b. Abī l-ʿĀṣ; this point was mentioned to the detriment of the Umayyad family in question.[114]

---

109 Al-Wāqidī, *al-Maġāzī*, 2:870–871. See Guillaume (1964). Abraham circumcised himself using the same tool; Kister (1994): 10–11 (where *qadūm* is rendered as a pick-axe).

110 Ibn ʿAsākir, *Dimašq*, 70:177 (*ṭāla mā kuntu minka illā fī ġurūr*). See also Ibn Saʿd, *al-Ṭabaqāt*², 10:225. Cf. the inferior reading in Ibn Ḥaǧar, *al-Iṣābah*², 8:156 (*kunnā maʿaka fī ġurūr*). Hind and ʿIkrimah's wife appear at the beginning of the list of Qurašī women who swore allegiance to Muḥammad after the conquest of Mecca; Ibn ʿAsākir, *Dimašq*, 70:179.

111 Fahd wrongly assumed that the idols in question were made of stone and that ʿIkrimah had manufactured them; Fahd (1968): 26–27, 29–30. Cf. Höfner (1970): 359: "Die Idole als solche waren Steine …"

112 Wellhausen (1882): 350, has Abū Baǧrāt, in error ("Abu Bajrāt machte und verkaufte sie; es wurde mit ihnen ein lebhafter Handel an die Beduinen getrieben").

113 Ibn Saʿd, *al-Ṭabaqāt*², 10:234. In another version the carpenter's father's name was Aflaḥ; Ibn Ḥaǧar, *al-Iṣābah*², 1:100.

114 *Wa-hum yuʿābūna bi-ḏālika*; al-Balāḏurī, *Ansāb al-ašrāf*, 4/i:479.

Al-Wāqidī's report about Abū Tiğrāt is based on an eyewitness account. Following ʿIkrimah's reported destruction of idols, al-Wāqidī says: *wa-kāna Abū Tiğrāt yaʿmaluhā fī l-ğāhiliyyah wa-yabīʿuhā, qāla Saʿd* [read: Saʿīd] *b. ʿAmr: aḫbaranī* [add: *abī*, see below] *annahu kāna yarāhu yaʿmaluhā wa-yabīʿuhā. Wa-lam yakun rağul min Qurayš bi-Makkah illā wa-fī baytihi ṣanam*. Al-Wāqidī's direct source is ʿAbd Allāh b. Yazīd [al-Huḏalī] < Saʿīd b. ʿAmr.[115] But the *isnād* is incomplete: Saʿīd b. ʿAmr's informant, namely his father, is missing. Elsewhere al-Wāqidī quotes from ʿAbd Allāh b. Yazīd < Saʿīd b. ʿAmr < his father, a report on the worship of Huḏayl's idol, Suwāʿ. As in the passage discussed here, the father's testimony is an eyewitness account: *ḥaḍartu maʿa riğāl min qawmī ṣanamanā Suwāʿ* ...[116] Saʿīd also received the report about Abū Tiğrāt from his father, ʿAmr.[117]

2.2 *The Idol Buwānah near Yalamlam (cf. § 145)*

The reports associating the Prophet Muḥammad with idol worship are of special interest. Two idols are relevant in this context, the famous al-ʿUzzá and the lesser-known Buwānah. According to Ibn al-Kalbī, Muḥammad said: "I offered al-ʿUzzá a white ewe, while I was still following the religious practices of my people" (*la-qad ahdaytu li-l-ʿUzzá šāt ʿafrāʾ wa-anā ʿalā dīn qawmī*).[118] As to the idol Buwānah (Buwānah is sometimes a place name), a report traced back to Ḥassān b. Ṯābit states that when he was tortured in Mecca before the *hiğrah*, Bilāl b. Rabāḥ repudiated Allāt, al-ʿUzzá, Hubal, (I)sāf, Nāʾilah, and Buwānah.[119] Buwānah was one of the idols "around Mecca," destroyed, after the conquest of Mecca, by Muslim expedition forces, the others being al-ʿUzzá, Manāt, Suwāʿ, and Ḏū l-Kaffayn.[120] The *ḥanīf* Zayd b. ʿAmr b. Nufayl was seen near Buwānah.[121] In one source a report mentioning Buwānah immediately follows a report concerning Zayd b. ʿAmr b. Nufayl, which seems to suggest that Buwānah is linked to Zayd's alleged spiritual influence on Muḥammad.[122] The

---

115 Al-Wāqidī, *al-Maġāzī*, 2:869–870.

116 Ibn Saʿd, *al-Ṭabaqāt*², 1:141.

117 In Abū Nuʿaym's biographical dictionary of Companions ʿAmr's father is called Saʿīd; Ibn Ḥağar, *al-Iṣābah*², 4:639.

118 Ibn al-Kalbī, *al-Aṣnām* 19; Kister (1970): 275.

119 Al-Balāḏurī, *Ansāb al-ašrāf*, 1:185.

120 Ibn Sayyid al-Nās, *ʿUyūn al-aṯar*, 2:243, quoting Ibn Saʿd; Ibn Saʿd, *al-Ṭabaqāt*², 2:128 (instead of *ḥawla l-Kaʿbah*, read: *ḥawla Makkah*). Ibn Saʿd is quoted in Hawting (1999): 121, n. 33.

121 Ibn Ḥağar, al-*Iṣābah*², 2:40, s.v. Ḥuğayr b. Abī Ihāb al-Tamīmī, quoting al-Fākihī, *Aḫbār Makkah*: *raʾaytu Zayd b. ʿAmr b. Nufayl wa-anā ʿinda ṣanam yuqālu lahu Buwānah.*

122 Cf. Kister (1970); Rubin (1990): 99–102.

Qurayš used to shave their hair at Buwānah, offer it to the idol, and worship the idol each year for one day until nightfall (*kāna bi-Buwānah* [read: *Buwānah*] *ṣanaman tuʿaẓẓimuhu Qurayš yaḥliqūna ruʾūsahum ʿindahu wa-tansuku lahu l-nasāʾik wa-yaʿkufūna ʿindahu yawman ilá l-layl wa-ḏālika yawm fī l-sanah*). When Muḥammad, who was reluctant to visit the idol, was finally convinced to do so (i.e. before the mission) he was prevented from approaching it by a mysterious tall man dressed in white.[123] A report about "the Buwānah idol" (*ṣanam Buwānah*) on the authority of Ǧubayr b. Muṭʿim states that a mysterious voice from within it announced the appearance of the Prophet. This took place one month before Muḥammad's first revelation.[124]

Beside Qurayš, two other tribes were associated with Buwānah. A member of the Ṯaqīf tribe, Kardam b. Sufyān al-Ṯaqafī, received Muḥammad's permission to slaughter ten camels "at Buwānah" (a place name) in fulfillment of a vow. Muḥammad made sure that when Kardam undertook the vow, there was no trace of the Ǧāhiliyyah in his heart.[125] In another source Muḥammad is more specific: he only granted his permission after making sure that there was no *waṯan* or *ṭāġiyah* in Buwānah.[126] Yet another version of the same report refers to a slaughter "on Buwānah."[127] The other tribe associated with Buwānah was Huḏayl. "An idol in Buwānah" appears in the report on ʿAmr al-Huḏalī (the father of Saʿīd b. ʿAmr) who regrets having missed an opportunity to convert to Islam early on. He heard a mysterious voice from within the idol.[128]

Buwānah was "below [i.e. south of] Mecca, near Yalamlam" (*asfal Makkah dūna Yalamlam*).[129] One assumes that the *mīqāt* of Yalamlam is meant here, not Yalamlam itself (see map). At this point the pilgrims coming from the south enter a state of *iḥrām*.

3 Medina (Yaṯrib) (§ 110–117)

There were diverse forms of idol worship in pre-Islamic Medina, a remarkable point considering the substantial influence of the Jewish tribes. There is no reason to assume that the situation was different among sedentary people else-

---

123 Al-Ḫargūšī, *Šaraf al-muṣṭafá*, 1:461–462. Muḥammad's words later in this report suggest that there was more than one idol at that place: *innī kullamā danawtu min ṣanam minhā* …

124 Ibn al-Aṯīr, *al-Kāmil fī l-taʾrīḫ*[1], 2:47: *kunnā ǧulūsan ʿinda ṣanam Buwānah* …

125 Ibn Saʿd, *al-Ṭabaqāt*[2], 8:75: *innī naḏartu an anḥara ʿašarat abʿirah lī bi-Buwānah.*

126 Ibn Ḥaǧar, *al-Iṣābah*[2], 8:133, s.v. Maymūnah bt. Kardam al-Ṯaqafiyyah.

127 Yāqūt, *Muʿǧam al-buldān*, 1:505: *innī naḏartu an aḏbaḥa ḫamsīna šāt ʿalá Buwānah.*

128 Al-Ḫargūšī, *Šaraf al-muṣṭafá*, 1:210–211. On ʿAmr see above, p. 7.

129 Al-Baġawī, *Šarḥ al-sunna*, 10:31.

where in Arabia, about whom we know next to nothing. The Islamic literature concentrates, for obvious reasons, on Mecca and Medina.

Wellhausen argued that the Medinans were even more indifferent to their idols than the Meccans. In his view, the Jews and Christians brought monotheism to the Anṣār and prepared them for Islam. Islam spread among the Anṣār very quickly, and even before the Prophet's *hiğrah* almost all the Anṣār were Muslims. Wellhausen suggests that their resistance to the Prophet was political and not religious: they mourned yesterday's freedom, not yesterday's idols.[130]

In fact, most Medinans did not convert to Islam before Muḥammad's *hiğrah*. Moreover, for several years after the *hiğrah* many Medinans remained pagan. Only the downfall of the Jewish Qurayẓah, on whom certain Medinans relied politically, economically, and militarily, turned them toward Islam.[131]

In the crucial negotiations which led to the *hiğrah* a significant role was played by Medinans who had acquired literacy in Arabic in the Jewish *Bayt al-Midrās*;[132] though most Medinans were immersed in private and public idol worship. Public idol worship can be associated with levels of the tribal system. It is impossible to measure the intensity of the religious sentiment among the Medinans,[133] and hence one should adhere to the evidence.

3.1 *Household Idols*

The existence of house or family idols has been known for many years, but has not been given its due weight.[134] Medinan household idols, like those in Mecca,

130 Wellhausen (1884–1899), 4:15–16. See also Watt (1953): 23 ("… it is generally agreed that the archaic pagan religion was comparatively uninfluential in Muḥammad's time"). On the inhabitants of Yaṯrib, Wensinck said: "Their receptiveness for monotheism can only be explained by their long contact with the Jews"; Wensinck (1975): 4.

131 Lecker (1995): 19–49.

132 Lecker (1997); Lecker (1993): 343.

133 Goldziher wrote: "At Yathrib the indigenous disposition of immigrant tribes from the south produced a mood more easily accessible to religious thought which was a great help to Muḥammed's success"; Goldziher (1966): 1:13 f. Goldziher had in mind the influence of Yemeni monotheism on the Arabs of Yaṯrib, who were supposed to have been more religious than other Arabs in central Arabia. Margoliouth (1905): 25 remarks cautiously, without specifically referring to Goldziher: "A great scholar, indeed, from whom it is unsafe to differ, finds a difference between the central and the southern Arabians, and supposes the latter to have been earnest worshippers, while the former were indifferent." According to Margoliouth, "the Arabs of Central Arabia were not wanting in piety."

134 Wellhausen mentions the *Hausgötze*. Lammens (1928): 139 correctly criticizes Wellhausen for conflating the "dieux domestiques" with the idols held by the leaders (on which see below). Lammens (1928): 140 erroneously assumed that the pre-Islamic Arabs knew only about a public cult, such as the one performed by the tribal group ("Inutile … de parler de culte privé, de dieux lares ou domestiques. L'Arabe de la préhégire n'a jamais entrevu

were made of wood. In Mecca they used to stroke the idols, and in Medina they did the same.[135]

A relatively large number of Medinan conversion reports involves idols, but only a handful of Meccan reports do. We can account for this by the different circumstances of conversion. When Muḥammad conquered Mecca in 8/630, its pagan inhabitants converted, or are supposed to have converted, within a short period. In Medina, by contrast, conversion was a long process accompanied by internal strife. The people of Mecca probably displayed more internal cohesion than the people of Medina, many of whom were prepared to defy the existing tribal system and leadership which were closely associated with the idols.

We know of a wooden idol that became an obstacle for Abū Ṭalḥah of the Naǧǧār (Ḫazraǧ) when he proposed to a Naǧǧārī woman, Umm Sulaym bt. Milḥān (Anas b. Mālik's mother). Abū Ṭalḥah wanted to marry her after the death of Anas's father, but she refused because he was a polytheist (*mušrik*). She reproached him for worshipping a stone and a piece of wood hewed for him by a carpenter (*ḫašabah ta'tī bihā l-naǧǧār fa-yanǧuruhā laka*). He agreed to embrace Islam and she accepted his conversion as dowry.[136]

Among the Naǧǧār subdivision called Ġanm b. Mālik b. al-Naǧǧār there was a man called ʿAmr b. Qays known as *ṣāḥib ālihatihim fī l-ǧāhiliyyah* (the person in charge of their idols in the Ǧāhiliyyah). He was once expelled from the Prophet's mosque, together with other *munāfiqūn* (hypocrites). While he was being expelled, he complained about his forcible removal from the *mirbad* (the drying floor for dates) of the Banū Ṯaʿlabah.[137] Since he was of the Ġanm b.

---

que la culte public, celui pratiqué par le clan, dont les rares manifestations suffissaient à épuiser sa courte dévotion").

135 This is shown by the report on Kaʿb b. ʿUǧrah: *Ista'ḫara islām Kaʿb b. ʿUǧrah wa-kāna lahu ṣanam yukrimuhu wa-yamsaḥuhu* ...; al-Ḏahabī, *Siyar aʿlām al-nubalā'*, 3:53 (quoting al-Wāqidī); Lecker (1993): 340–341.

136 The report is autobiographical; it is reported on the authority of Isḥāq b. ʿAbd Allāh b. Abī Ṭalḥah (d. 132/749–750 or 134/751–752), who quotes his grandmother, Umm Sulaym; Ibn Saʿd, *al-Ṭabaqāt*[2], 10:396. Abū Ṭalḥah was of the Maġālah, namely the ʿAdī b. ʿAmr b. Mālik b. al-Naǧǧār; Ibn Qudāmah, *al-Istibṣār* 49–50. Umm Sulaym belonged to the Ḥarām b. Ǧundab b. ʿĀmir b. Ġanm b. ʿAdī b. al-Naǧǧār; Ibn Qudāmah, *al-Istibṣār* 36–40. See an entry on Isḥāq in al-Mizzī, *Tahḏīb al-kamāl*, 2:444–446. Other reports (Ibn Saʿd, *al-Ṭabaqāt*[2], 10:397) refer to a wooden idol hewed by a slave who was a carpenter, and to an Ethiopian slave: *yanḥutuhā ʿabd āl fulān al-naǧǧār ... law ašʿaltum fīhā nāran la-ḥtaraqat ... šaǧarah tanbutu mina l-arḍ wa-innamā naǧarahā ḥabašī banī fulān*. In itself the verb *naḥata* is indifferent to the material used, but when it is linked to wood it is synonymous with *naǧara*; Lane (1863–1893), s.v. *naḥata*.

137 Ibn Hišām, *al-Sīrah al-nabawiyyah*, 2:175; Lecker (1993): 335. The identification put forward in Lecker (1993): 335 n. 25, is uncertain.

Mālik b. al-Naǧǧār, the Ṯaʿlabah in question are the Ṯaʿlabah b. Ġanm b. Mālik b. al-Naǧǧār.[138]

In connection with the Medinan idols we encounter the verb *laṭṭaḫa*, meaning to defile, or soil. The source of what follows is supposed to be ʿAlī b. Abī Ṭālib. During a funeral (of a Muslim, outside Medina), Muḥammad looked for a volunteer to break up every idol (*waṯan*) in Medina, level every tomb, and defile or besmear with slime every statue or figure (*ṣūrah*). An unidentified volunteer returned, but had not carried out the order, since he feared the people of Medina, so ʿAlī stepped in.[139] A variant of this report states that the Prophet ordered an Anṣārī to level every tomb and defile (*yulaṭṭiḫa*) every idol. The man refused to enter the houses of his people (*buyūt qawmī*), hence ʿAlī was sent for.[140] Regardless of its historical value, the report takes for granted a predominance of idol worship.

In the Ǧāhiliyyah Asʿad b. Zurārah (Naǧǧār) and Abū l-Hayṯam b. al-Tayyihān (a member of the Balī tribe who was a client of the ʿAbd al-Ašhal or the Zaʿūrāʾ) hated the idols and were disgusted by them; both men were monotheists.[141] The former was also involved in the actual destruction of idols (see below).

There are several reports about young Medinans who received Muḥammad enthusiastically and broke or smashed (*kasara/kassara*) the idols of their tribal groups. The idols were found among both the Aws and Ḫazraǧ, more specifically the ʿAbd al-Ašhal, Ḥāriṯah, ʿAmr b. ʿAwf, Ḫaṭmah, and Wāqif of the Aws, and the Salimah, Bayāḍah, Sāʿidah, Mālik b. al-Naǧǧār, and ʿAdī b. al-Naǧǧār of the Ḫazraǧ. The evidence regarding idol worship among the Salimah is relatively abundant; this was likely not because idolatry was more widespread among them, but because they were more numerous than the other subdivisions, or the Prophet had more supporters among them.

Idols are dominant in Medinan conversion reports. Let us begin with the Ḫazraǧ. Ziyād b. Labīd and Farwah b. ʿAmr of the Bayāḍah broke the idols of the Bayāḍah.[142] Saʿd b. ʿUbādah, al-Munḏir b. ʿAmr, and Abū Duǧānah of the Sāʿidah broke the idols of the Sāʿidah.[143] ʿUmārah b. Ḥazm, Asʿad b. Zurārah, and ʿAwf b. ʿAfrāʾ of the Mālik b. al-Naǧǧār broke the idols of the Mālik b. al-

138 Cf. Ibn Qudāmah, *al-Istibṣār* 56–64, especially 63–64 (on the two orphans who owned the *mirbad* on which the Prophet's mosque was built).

139 Ibn Ḥanbal, *al-Musnad*, 1:87; al-Hayṯamī, *Maǧmaʿ al-zawāʾid*, 5:172. Both texts are garbled. Ibn Manẓūr, *Lisān al-ʿarab*, s.v. *ṭalaḫa*, has instead of *laṭṭaḫa: ṭalaḫa*, or to besmear with slime.

140 Ibn Ḥanbal, *al-Musnad*, 1:139; al-Hayṯamī, *Maǧmaʿ al-zawāʾid*, 5:172–173.

141 Ibn Saʿd, *al-Ṭabaqāt*², 3:412; al-Ḏahabī, *Siyar aʿlām al-nubalāʾ*, 1:190; Lecker (1993): 336.

142 Ibn Saʿd, *al-Ṭabaqāt*², 3:553.

143 Ibn Saʿd, *al-Ṭabaqāt*², 3:567.

Naǧǧār.[144] Salīṭ b. Qays and Abū Ṣirmah of the ʿAdī b. al-Naǧǧār broke the idols of the ʿAdī b. al-Naǧǧār.[145] Perhaps there is confusion between Abū Ṣirmah and Abū Qays Ṣirmah b. Abī Anas, who embraced Islam at an advanced age after having rejected idol worship in the Ǧāhiliyyah.[146]

Among the Aws, Saʿd b. Muʿāḏ and Usayd b. al-Ḥuḍayr of the ʿAbd al-Ašhal broke the idols of the ʿAbd al-Ašhal.[147] Usayd belonged to ʿAbd al-Ašhal's leading family: his father, Ḥuḍayr, was the *raʾīs* (the battlefield commander) of the Aws in the Battle of Buʿāṯ. Ḥuḍayr was known, as was his son Usayd, as *al-kāmil* ("the highly accomplished one"), since they were both literate and excelled in swimming and archery.[148] Abū ʿAbs b. Ǧabr of the Ḥāriṯah and Abū Burdah b. Niyār, a client of the Ḥāriṯah from the Balī tribe, broke the idols of the Ḥāriṯah.[149] An alternative pedigree of Abū ʿAbs adds the name Maǧdaʿah before the eponym Ḥāriṯah.[150] This makes him a member of the Maǧdaʿah, whose most famous member was Muḥammad b. Maslamah. Abū ʿAbs's mother and two of the three women to whom he was married at different times were of the Maǧdaʿah: one of the women was Muḥammad b. Maslamah's sister, while the other was Muḥammad b. Maslamah's daughter.[151] Muḥammad b. Maslamah was a client (*ḥalīf*) of the ʿAbd al-Ašhal;[152] and one assumes that Abū ʿAbs was not a prominent figure in Medinan society before the advent of Islam. The same applies to Abū Burdah who was a client.

ʿAbd Allāh b. Ǧubayr and Sahl b. Ḥunayf used to break up idols and bring the pieces to the Muslims to use as firewood.[153] The two belonged to different

144 Ibn Saʿd, *al-Ṭabaqāt*², 3:451.

145 Ibn Saʿd, *al-Ṭabaqāt*², 3:474. According to some, Abū Ṣirmah was of the Māzin b. al-Naǧǧār, not of the ʿAdī; al-Mizzī, *Tahḏīb al-kamāl*, 33:426; Ibn ʿAbd al-Barr, *al-Istīʿāb*, 4:1691 (the Māzinī version regarding his origin was more widespread).

146 Ibn Ḥazm, *Ǧamharat ansāb al-ʿarab* 350 (*rafaḍa l-awṯān*); Ibn Hišām, *al-Sīrah al-nabawiyyah*, 2:156 (*wa-fāraqa l-awṯān*); al-Masʿūdī, *Murūǧ al-ḏahab*, 1:81 (*wa-haǧara l-awṯān*); Rubin (1990): 98. Note that the sources quoted by Rubin do not refer to him as a *ḥanīf*. The source of Ibn Isḥāq's report, which is missing in Ibn Hišām, is mentioned elsewhere: Muḥammad b. Ǧaʿfar b. al-Zubayr b. al-ʿAwwām; Ibn Ḥaǧar, *al-Iṣābah*², 3:422. Muḥammad's source may have been ʿAbd al-Raḥmān b. ʿUwaym b. Sāʿidah from whom Muḥammad quoted another report regarding Ṣirmah; Ibn Ḥaǧar, *al-Iṣābah*², 3:423. On Muḥammad see al-Mizzī, *Tahḏīb al-kamāl*, 24:579–580.

147 Ibn Saʿd, *al-Ṭabaqāt*², 3:389.

148 Ibn Saʿd, *al-Ṭabaqāt*², 3:558–559; Lecker (1997): 268, n. 64.

149 Ibn Saʿd, *al-Ṭabaqāt*², 3:415.

150 Ibn Ḥaǧar, al-*Iṣābah*², 7:266.

151 Ibn Saʿd, *al-Ṭabaqāt*², 3:415.

152 Ibn Qudāmah, *al-Istibṣār* 242.

153 Al-Balāḏurī, *Ansāb al-ašrāf*, 1:265; Lecker (1993): 333.

subdivisions of the ʿAmr b. ʿAwf, namely the Ṯaʿlabah and the Ḥanaš, respectively,[154] and the idols in question were those of the ʿAmr b. ʿAwf. Ḫuzaymah b. Ṯābit and ʿUmayr b. ʿAdī b. Ḫarašah of the Ḫaṭmah broke the idols of the Ḫaṭmah.[155] Hilāl b. Umayyah of the Wāqif broke the idols of the Wāqif.[156]

As we have seen, Abū Ṭalḥah's idol was made of wood; this is also clear with regard to the broken pieces used as firewood. In the case of another household idol wood is specifically mentioned. ʿAbd Allāh b. Rawāḥah rebuked its owner (who was perhaps Abū l-Dardāʾ, see below) for worshipping a piece of wood that he had crafted with his own hand. The owner replied that he had not attacked it because he feared for his young children.[157] In other words, the wooden household idol was perceived as tutelary.

Before ʿAbd Allāh b. Rawāḥah destroyed Abū l-Dardāʾs idol using an adze (*qadūm*), he brought it down (*fa-anzalahu*). This probably indicates that the idol was located in an elevated place, such as a shelf. It is also reported that Abū l-Dardāʾ hung a veil over his idol (*wa-qad waḍaʿa ʿalayhi mindīlan*).[158] In order to act against a household idol one had to enter the house.[159] These characteristics were perhaps shared by household idols elsewhere in Arabia.

Among the twenty-odd persons who reportedly destroyed idols, only three can be considered prominent members of society, namely Muʿāḏ b. ʿAmr b. al-Ǧamūḥ, who belonged to a leading family of the Salimah (Ḫazraǧ), Saʿd b. ʿUbādah of the Sāʿidah (Ḫazraǧ), and the "highly accomplished man" Usayd b. al-Ḥuḍayr of the ʿAbd al-Ašhal (Aws). There is a certain correlation between the idol breakers and those who were literate before Islam: at least five of the idol breakers, namely Saʿd b. ʿUbādah, al-Munḏir b. ʿAmr, Muʿāḏ b. Ǧabal, Usayd b. al-Ḥuḍayr, and Abū ʿAbs b. Ǧabr were literate; this means they were educated in *Bayt al-Midrās*.[160] However, typical idol breakers belonged to the rank-and-file of their tribal groups, and two of them were clients.

We do not have documentary or archival evidence on the idol breakers. But it is no accident that so many of them are found in Ibn Saʿd's third volume, which includes the biographies of those who fought in the Battle of Badr. More precisely, they are in the latter part of the volume, which is dedicated to the

---

154 Ibn Qudāmah, *al-Istibṣār* 320–323.

155 Ibn Saʿd, *al-Ṭabaqāt*², 5:297.

156 Al-Nawawī, *Tahḏīb al-asmāʾ*, 2:139; Ibn al-Aṯīr, *Usd al-ġābah*, 5:380–381.

157 Lecker (1993): 338.

158 Lecker (1993): 340.

159 Hence the above mentioned reluctance of the Anṣārī to enter the houses of his people (*buyūt qawmī*).

160 Lecker (1997): 267–271.

Badrīs among the Anṣār. All of those involved were unmistakably among the earliest and most enthusiastic supporters of Muḥammad in Medina.

3.2 *Idols of Noblemen*

Al-Maqrīzī quotes (§ 110–117) several rare reports on idol worship in Medina from Ibn Šabbah's *Aḫbār Makkah*. He says every nobleman (*rağul šarīf*) had an idol (§ 111). However, specific details are only given on three of them. ʿAmr b. al-Ğamūḥ had Manāf, al-Barāʾ b. Maʿrūr had al-Dībāğ, and al-Ğadd b. Qays had Zabr. All three belonged to the Salimah. Another characteristic of a nobleman was probably ownership of a tower house, since at least two of the above-mentioned noblemen owned a tower house.[161] There is no reason to assume that this type of idol was restricted to the Salimah. The fact that the three men belonged to leading families is also shown by Muḥammad's intervention on the issue of the leadership of the Salimah. According to one version, he replaced their *sayyid*, al-Ğadd b. Qays, with ʿAmr b. al-Ğamūḥ; according to another version, he replaced al-Ğadd with al-Barāʾ b. Maʿrūr's son, Bišr.[162] Al-Ğadd[163] and al-Barāʾ belonged to the ʿUbayd subdivision of the Salimah, while ʿAmr b. al-Ğamūḥ belonged to the Ḥarām subdivision.

The report on the shift of leadership from al-Ğadd to ʿAmr creates the false impression that it was associated with idols. Al-Ğadd was deposed and replaced by ʿAmr because of the former's stinginess, while ʿAmr "was in charge of their idols in the Ğāhiliyyah and used to hold a feast for the Messenger of God whenever he [the latter] got married" (*kāna ʿalá aṣnāmihim fī l-ğāhiliyyah wa-kāna yūlimu ʿalá rasūli llāh ṣ idhā tazawwağa*). The *isnād* goes back to Abū l-Zubayr < Ğābir b. ʿAbd Allāh.[164] Ğābir was ʿAmr's second cousin.[165] But idols are not related to stinginess, and the correct reading is *ʿalá aḍyāfihim* ("he was responsible for their guests in the Ğāhiliyyah").[166]

---

161 Lecker (1993): 336–338. In Abū Nuʿaym, *Dalāʾil al-nubuwwah* 310–312, read Manāf instead of Manāt (it was no doubt masculine); Ibn al-Ğawzī, *Ṣifat al-ṣafwah*, 1:643–644; al-Ḏahabī, *Siyar aʿlām al-nubalāʾ*, 1:253. Read Manāf instead of Manāt in Krone (1992): 537.

162 See e.g. Ḥassān, *Dīwān*, 1:460–461; Ibn ʿAsākir, *Dimašq*, 12:413. Ibn Isḥāq and Maʿmar, on the authority of al-Zuhrī, reported that al-Ğadd was replaced by Bišr. As we shall see, the version that mentions al-Ğadd's replacement by ʿAmr goes back to Ğābir b. ʿAbd Allāh.

163 Al-Wāqidī, *al-Maġāzī*, 1:169.

164 Ibn ʿAbd al-Barr, *al-Istīʿāb*, 3:1170–1171. See the entry on Abū l-Zubayr al-Makkī, Muḥammad b. Muslim (d. 126/743–744 or 128/745–746), in al-Mizzī, *Tahḏīb al-kamāl*, 26:402–411.

165 Ibn Qudāmah, *al-Istibṣār* 151–154.

166 Al-Bayhaqī, *Šuʿab al-īmān*, 7:431.

There are conflicting claims regarding ʿAmr b. al-Ǧamūḥ's conversion. According to ʿUrwah b. al-Zubayr, Muṣʿab b. ʿUmayr (from the Qurašī clan ʿAbd al-Dār) settled before the *hiǧrah* among the Ġanm b. Mālik b. al-Naǧǧār, with Asʿad b. Zurārah. Sometime after the conversion of the ʿAbd al-Ašhal, the Naǧǧār drove Muṣʿab out and harassed (*wa-štaddū ʿalá*) their fellow tribesman Asʿad. Muṣʿab moved to Saʿd b. Muʿāḏ of the ʿAbd al-Ašhal, where he continued his missionary work. Finally, in every court (*dār*) of the Anṣār there were Muslim men and women. Their noblemen, including ʿAmr b. al-Ǧamūḥ, embraced Islam. Their idols were broken and the Muslims became the strongest people in Medina.[167] Muṣʿab's expulsion from the court of the Naǧǧār and his shift to Saʿd b. Muʿāḏ—both seem to be historical facts—were left out of the *sīrah*, probably because they were embarrassing for the Naǧǧār. The conversion of the noblemen, particularly that of ʿAmr b. al-Ǧamūḥ who is the only one specified, and the breaking of the idols at this early stage (even before the second or major ʿAqabah meeting), are an invention. It is clear that ʿUrwah's report is favorable to ʿAmr.[168] According to Ibn Isḥāq, ʿAmr's conversion took place shortly after the major ʿAqabah meeting, following the repeated humiliation of his wooden idol, Manāf, at the hands of his son, Muʿāḏ b. ʿAmr b. al-Ǧamūḥ, who cooperated with Muʿāḏ b. Ǧabal and other young men of the Salimah.[169] The source of Ibn Isḥāq's report is missing in Ibn Hišām. ʿĀṣim b. ʿUmar b.

167 Al-Ṭabarānī, *al-Muʿǧam al-kabīr*, 20:362–364; al-Hayṯamī, *Maǧmaʿ al-zawāʾid*, 6:40–42; Abū Nuʿaym, *Ḥilyat al-awliyāʾ*, 1:106–107. Al-Wāqidī's combined report in Ibn Saʿd, *al-Ṭabaqāt*^{2}, 3:109–110, does not mention Muṣʿab's shift from the Naǧǧār to the ʿAbd al-Ašhal. It was probably omitted by al-Wāqidī while he was creating the combined report. However, in the entry on Saʿd b. Muʿāḏ in Ibn Saʿd, *al-Ṭabaqāt*^{2}, 3:389, it is reported that he moved Muṣʿab and Asʿad to his court—Saʿd and Asʿad were maternal cousins. The source of this report is Saʿd's grandson, Wāqid b. ʿAmr.

168 Also ʿIkrimah associated ʿAmr's conversion with Muṣʿab b. ʿUmayr; al-Ḏahabī, *Siyar aʿlām al-nubalāʾ*, 1:253 (quoting ʿIkrimah). Initially, ʿAmr apologized to Muṣʿab, arguing that he had to consult his fellow tribesmen whose *sayyid* he was: *inna lanā muʾāmarah fī qawminā, wa-kāna sayyid banī Salimah*. But soon afterwards the humiliation of his idol made him realize how weak and defenseless it was. Some themes of the humilation are known from Ibn Isḥāq's report on ʿAmr's conversion.

169 Ibn Hišām, *al-Sīrah al-nabawiyyah*, 2:95–96 (erroneously printed Manāt). ʿAmr was one of the *sayyid*s of the Salimah and one of their noblemen (*sayyidan min sādāt banī Salimah wa-šarīfan min ašrāfihim*). In his house he had a wooden idol, as was common among noblemen. They would take for themselves an idol, honor, and purify (i.e. consecrate) it (*kamā kānat al-ašrāf yaṣnaʿūna, tattaḫiḏuhu ilāhan tuʿaẓẓimuhu wa-tuṭahhiruhu*). The report on Muʿāḏ's idol in al-Maqdisī, *al-Badʾ wa-l-taʾrīḫ*, 5:117–118, is erroneous: Muʿāḏ should be replaced by Abū l-Dardāʾ; Lecker (1993): 339–340. On Muʿāḏ b. Ǧabal, see van Ess (2001).

Qatādah, who is often quoted by Ibn Isḥāq, stated that ʿAmr's conversion was delayed (*taʾaḫḫara*).[170] Moreover, according to Ibn al-Kalbī, ʿAmr was the last Anṣārī to embrace Islam.[171]

Muʿāḏ b. Ǧabal also figures in another report concerning idols. Muʿāḏ, Ṯaʿlabah b. ʿAnamah al-Salamī (of the Sawād subdivision of Salimah), and ʿAbd Allāh b. Unays al-Ǧuhanī, having converted to Islam, broke the idols of the Salimah.[172] Only Ṯaʿlabah was a full member of the Salimah. Muʿāḏ b. Ǧabal was a descendant of Udayy b. Saʿd, the brother of Salimah b. Saʿd. ʿAbd Allāh b. Unays al-Ǧuhanī was a client (*ḥalīf*) of the Salimah.

The idols of noblemen had names, and hence belonged to a category higher than that of household idols. Perhaps the noblemen's idols were larger or more richly decorated than the household ones.[173] They were probably anthropoid: the young attackers of ʿAmr b. al-Ǧamūḥ's idol threw it on its head, and at some stage ʿAmr hung a sword on it and demanded that it defend itself.[174] ʿAmr's idol was in a sanctuary (*bayt*) of its own;[175] this is probably true of the idols of noblemen in general. Regarding ʿAmr's idol, we are told that whenever people wanted to talk to it (i.e. consult it), an old woman would stand behind it and answer on its behalf.[176]

The Medinan idols discussed below were associated with the tribal system and belong to the public sphere, as opposed to the private realm discussed above.

3.3 *Idols of* baṭns

One level above the nobleman's idol we find the *baṭn*'s idol which had a name (§ 110). Among the *baṭns* mentioned as owners of idols were the subdivisions of the Nabīt branch (Aws), i.e. ʿAbd al-Ašhal, Ḥāriṯah, and Ẓafar; the Salimah; and

---

170 See the paraphrased fragment quoted in al-Ḏahabī, *Siyar aʿlām al-nubalāʾ*, 1:253–254. A report on ʿAmr's burial is quoted by Ibn Isḥāq from his father < *ašyāḫ* of the Salimah; Ibn Hišām, *al-Sīrah al-nabawiyyah*, 3:104.

171 Ibn Ḥağar, *al-Iṣābah*², 4:615.

172 Ibn Saʿd, *al-Ṭabaqāt*², 3:537, 540; Ibn Qudāmah, *al-Istibṣār* 136–137, 165, 166; Ibn Ḥağar, *al-Iṣābah*², 4:15–16 (ʿAbd Allāh b. Unays). The reports on these three breaking up the idols do not mention Muʿāḏ b. ʿAmr b. al-Ǧamūḥ.

173 In general, the decoration of idols seems to be suggested by the saying *aḥsan mina l-dumyah wa-mina l-zūn wa-humā l-ṣanam*; al-Maydānī, *Mağmaʿ al-amṯāl*, 1:227.

174 Ibn Hišām, *al-Sīrah al-nabawiyyah*, 2:95–96.

175 *Daḫalū bayt ṣanamihi*; al-Ḏahabī, *Siyar aʿlām al-nubalāʾ*, 1:254. This is also suggested by the expression *wa-daḫala ʿalá Manāf*; ibid., 1:253.

176 *Fa-aǧābat ʿanhu*; Abū Nuʿaym, *Dalāʾil al-nubuwwah* 311 (read Manāf instead of Manāt); Lecker (1993): 337.

three subdivisions of the Naǧǧār, namely ʿAdī b. al-Naǧǧār, Dīnār b. al-Naǧǧār, and Mālik b. al-Naǧǧār (Ḫazraǧ). Other *baṭns* in Medina are not listed as owners of idols, because the information is incomplete. The *baṭn*'s idol was placed in a sanctuary (*bayt*) and belonged to the whole *baṭn* (*li-ǧamāʿat al-baṭn*). Sacrifices were offered to it.[177] Under Islam sanctuaries may have been converted into mosques. An association between *baṭns* and worship was found in Kufa, where there were mosques belonging to *baṭns* of the Kindah.[178]

3.4 *The Ḥāriṯ b. al-Ḫazraǧ and Huzzam*

One level above the *baṭns* in the tribal system we find the branches or major subdivisions of the Aws and Ḫazraǧ. At present, we know of only one idol of this category, namely Huzzam, the idol of the Ḥāriṯ b. al-Ḫazraǧ. It was placed in their *maǧlis* (place of assembly), which carried the same name and was located in wadi Buṯḥān (§116). We can speculate that the other branches of the Aws and Ḫazraǧ had similar idols.[179] There is no mention of sacrifices, but since sacrifices were offered to the idols of the *baṭns*, we would expect to find them here as well.

3.5 *The Ḫazraǧ and al-Ḫamīs (§141)*

The Ḫazraǧ as a whole, together with the Sulaym tribe, worshipped an idol called al-Ḫamīs. Al-Ḫamīs appears in a verse attributed to the Prophet's grandfather, ʿAbd al-Muṭṭalib, who swore by it.[180]

3.6 *Al-Saʿīdah on Mount Uḥud (cf. §206)*

The idol al-Saʿīdah on Mount Uḥud was worshipped by the Azd—the Aws and Ḫazraǧ belonged to the Azd, and hence must have been among its worshippers—and by the whole of the Quḍāʿah (the Saʿd Huḏaym are mentioned specifically), with the exception of the Banū Wabarah. Al-Saʿīdah had custodi-

---

177 Regarding the association of *baṭns* to idols cf. Abbās (n.d.): 12: *wa-kānat awṯān al-ʿarab iḏ ḏāka musnadah ilá l-Kaʿbah ṯalāṯami'ah wa-sittīna waṯanan, li-kull ḥayy mina l-ʿarab waṯan, wa-kāna yakūnu fī l-ḥayy al-buṭūn al-kaṯīrah mina l-ʿarab, fa-kāna li-kull baṭn minhā waṯan.*

178 Lecker (1994): 344–345.

179 Cf. the expression *maǧālis al-anṣār*; Ibn ʿAsākir, *Dimašq*, 41:56.

180 *Abliġ banī l-Naǧǧāri in ǧi'tahum ... anniya minhum wa-bnuhum wa-l-Ḫamīs*; al-Ṭabarī, *Taʾrīḫ*, 1:1085; al-Balāḏurī, *Ansāb al-ašrāf*, 1:70; Ibn Ḥabīb, *al-Munammaq* 85. Cf. al-Ṭabarī, *History*, 6:12: "The meaning of *wa-l-khamīs* is somewhat obscure." Elsewhere the verse is attributed to al-Muṭṭalib b. ʿAbd Manāf; Ibn Saʿd, *al-Ṭabaqāt*[2], 1:63–64; Lecker (1989): 99 (a reference to the possibility that here "Ḫazraǧ" means both the Ḫazraǧ and the Aws; Ibn al-Kalbī, *al-Aṣnām* 14; al-Fākihī, *Aḫbār Makkah*, 4:236).

ans and a *talbiyah* of its own.[181] The custodians were the Banū l-ʿAǧlān,[182] who were the clients of the ʿAmr b. ʿAwf, more precisely the Banū Zayd b. Mālik b. ʿAwf b. ʿAmr b. ʿAwf.[183]

3.7 *Manāt in or near Qudayd (§176, 182)*

After al-Ḫamīs, worshipped by the Ḫazraǧ, and al-Saʿīdah, presumably worshipped by both the Aws and Ḫazraǧ, we arrive at the most significant idol of the two tribes, namely Manāt[184] which also had custodians and a *talbiyah* of its own. It was located in al-Mušallal near Qudayd (see map)[185] or, according to some, it was a rock in Qudayd belonging to the Huḏayl. Others argued that it belonged to the Huḏayl and the Ḫuzāʿah. Perhaps Huḏayl and Ḫuzāʿah had worshipped Manāt at an earlier stage, before the arrival of the Azd. In any case, in the immediate pre-Islamic period Manāt was worshipped, among other Azdīs, by the Aws and Ḫazraǧ. Its worshippers included the Azd Šanūʾah and other Azdīs, among them the groups of Ġassān.[186] Again, the Saʿd Huḏaym of the Quḍāʿah are mentioned specifically. At the end of the pilgrimage to Mecca the Aws and Ḫazraǧ would not shave their hair with the other pilgrims, but would stay near Manāt (*wa-aqāmū ʿindahu*) and shave their hair there. They believed that the pilgrimage was not complete without doing this. Reportedly, the Qurayš and all the other Arabs also worshipped Manāt. Its custodians were the Ġaṭārīf from the Azd.[187] The Ġaṭārīf were the family (*āl*) of al-Ḥāriṯ b.

---

181 Kister (1980a): 52 (read Saʿīda instead of Saʿīd). In the *talbiyah* the pilgrims declared that they did not come to the idol for (material) benefit nor for gain; cf. Tritton (1959): 194. The Quḍāʿah and some tribes of the Azd were among the *ḥillah* tribes that did not engage in trade during the pilgrimage; al-Yaʿqūbī, *Taʾrīḫ*, 1:257. When they were on pilgrimage, they only bought meat; Ibn Ḥabīb, *al-Muḥabbar* 181. According to Ibn Ḥabīb, *al-Muḥabbar* 179, the *ḥillah* included the Quḍāʿah (with the exception of ʿIlāf and Ǧanāb) and the Anṣār. Wellhausen (1897): 65, argued, following a verse in Yāqūt, *Muʿǧam al-buldān*, 4:116, s.v. al-ʿUzzá, that al-Saʿīdah was originally a nickname of al-ʿUzzá. See also Ibn al-Kalbī, *al-Aṣnām*, 19. Another idol with the same name was located near Sindād, or on the nearby bank of the Euphrates; Yāqūt, *Muʿǧam al-buldān*, 3:222, s.v. al-Saʿīdah.

182 Ibn Ḥabīb, *al-Muḥabbar* 316–317; Kister (1980a): 56.

183 Ibn al-Kalbī, *Nasab Maʿadd*, 2:711–712, lists six members of the ʿAǧlān who were Muḥammad's Companions; Ibn Ḥazm, *Ǧamharat ansāb al-ʿarab* 443; Lecker (1995): 135–137, and index. Serjeant (1989): 143, n. 49 identified ʿAǧlān with "ʿAjlān b. ʿAbdullāh of Rabīʿa" (he refers to Ibn Durayd, *al-Ištiqāq* 296; read: 297); but this is impossible. Besides, Ibn Durayd refers to the Qays ʿAylān, not to the Rabīʿah.

184 Krone (1992): 521–539.

185 King (2002): 94 locates Qudayd about 15 kilometers from Medina (!). He also locates Ruhāṭ near Yanbuʿ; ibid., 93, 95.

186 Lecker (2005a): 34.

187 Yāqūt, *Muʿǧam al-buldān*, 5:205, s.v. Manāt; Ibn al-Kalbī, *al-Aṣnām* 13–15; Ibn Ḥabīb, *al-*

ʿUbayd Allāh b. ʿĀmir al-Ġiṭrīf,[188] or Banū l-Ḥāriṯ b. ʿAbd Allāh b. Yaškur b. Mubaššir from the Azd. Their land was at the southernmost part of the Sarāt mountains, in an area called al-Ḥazz. The Ġaṭārīf conquered al-Ḥazz from the Amalekites, hence the name al-Ġaṭārīf, meaning "the noble ones."[189] The custodians may have been a family of the Ġaṭārīf that emigrated to northern Arabia.

A report on the authority of ʿAbd al-Malik b. ʿAbd al-ʿAzīz b. Saʿīd b. Saʿd b. ʿUbādah (a great-grandson of Saʿd b. ʿUbādah) praises his fathers. Saʿd's grandfather, Dulaym, used to donate ten camels to be sacrificed to Manāt every year. Saʿd's father, ʿUbādah, followed suit and Saʿd himself did the same before his conversion to Islam. Saʿd's son, Qays, used to donate the same number of camels to the Kaʿbah.[190] Idol worship is at the background of this report, which is about generosity and leadership. Obviously, the cult of Manāt continued to the very advent of Islam.

Manāt concludes the discussion of the idols worshipped by the people of Medina. The Aws or Ḫazraǧ had household idols; idols of noblemen were probably more impressive than household idols; the *baṭn* as a whole had an idol in a sanctuary. A branch of the Ḫazraǧ had an idol in its *maǧlis*; the Ḫazraǧ as a whole worshipped an idol; both the Aws and Ḫazraǧ worshipped al-Saʿīdah on Mount Uḥud; and finally, the Aws and Ḫazraǧ concluded their Meccan pilgrimage at their main idol, Manāt. None of this indicates that idol worship was in decline on the eve of Islam. Ibn Isḥāq's opinion about the influence of monotheism on the Arabs on the eve of Islam was that "it was merely superficial; the Arabs were illiterate, and what they heard from Jews and Christians had no effect on their lives." Guillaume, who adduced this statement, was surprised:

Muḥabbar 316. Wellhausen (1897): 28 argued that the two pilgrimages are incorrectly conflated here, one to Mecca and another to Manāt. Krone (1992): 537 said that the pilgrimage to Manāt could have been combined with the Meccan pilgrimage. On the sacrifice of hair cf. Krone (1992): 415–418. Al-Wāqidī, *al-Maġāzī*, 2:870, reports that Saʿd b. Zayd al-Ašhalī was sent by Muḥammad to demolish Manāt in Mušallal. The "Bakr" mentioned in the *talbiyah* of Manāt's worshippers and/or in that of the Qays ʿAylān were not the Bakr b. Wāʾil but the Bakr b. ʿAbd Manāt b. Kinānah, on whom see Ibn Ḥazm, *Ǧamharat ansāb al-ʿarab* 180–182; cf. Kister (1980a): 45. The Bakr b. ʿAbd Manāt b. Kinānah were among the *ḥillah* tribes; Ibn Ḥabīb, *al-Muḥabbar* 179. This would explain the threat they posed to pilgrims heading to Mecca. See also Ibn Ḥabīb, *al-Muḥabbar* 318; Kister (1980a): 57 (Hubal belonged to the Bakr, Mālik, and Milkān, and the rest of the Kinānah).

188 Ḥassān, *Dīwān*, 2:263 (on the affair of Abū Uzayhir).

189 Yāqūt, *Muʿǧam al-buldān*, 2:252, s.v. al-Ḥazz.

190 Ibn ʿAbd al-Barr, *al-Istīʿāb*, 2:595; Ibn ʿAsākir, *Dimašq*, 49:416–417.

> It must be remembered that he was talking about Western Arabia, and one would have thought that the influence of the synagogue or synagogues in Medina and its suburbs would have been considerable, especially when one bears in mind the close agreement between the Koran and the Talmud in teaching and terminology.[191]

Ibn Isḥāq's description of the situation in Medina on the eve of the *hiǧrah* is accurate.[192]

The power of idol worship in Arabia must not be underestimated. The evidence adduced above shows that idol worship flourished in Mecca, in Medina, and elsewhere. For ten frustrating years Muḥammad attempted to convert his fellow Meccans to Islam. Mecca's prosperity was based on the pilgrimage to Mecca and the fairs around. But the Meccans' rejection of Muḥammad was motivated by more than just concern about the economy. While we cannot gauge the intensity of their religious sentiment and their attachment to idols, clearly idols played a major role in their lives. The reports about the demolition of idols often provide medieval Muslim writers with an opportunity to ridicule the pagans and their cult, but the shock and fear attributed to the pagans reflect their belief in the power of their idols.

4 Idols and Treasuries

Finally, in what follows the treasuries of several idols are discussed in order to understand their social and economic role.

---

191 Guillaume (1960): 6–7. See also ibid., 21: "The Arabs were illiterate. They did not study writing. All that they knew of heaven and hell, the resurrection, the mission of prophets and so on was the little they had heard from Jews and Christians. This teaching had no effect on their lives." In Ibn Hišām, *al-Sīrah al-nabawiyyah*, 1:225 (< ʿĀṣim b. ʿUmar b. Qatādah), the Arabic text is as follows: *inna mimmā daʿānā ilá l-islām maʿa raḥmati llāh wa-hudāhu lanā la-mā kunnā nasmaʿu min riǧāl yahūd, wa-kunnā ahl širk aṣḥāb awṯān wa-kānū ahl kitāb, ʿindahum ʿilm laysa lanā* …

192 Serjeant, in his review of Guillaume's *New Light on the Life of Muhammad*, in BSOAS 26 (1963): 427–428, remarked with regard to Ibn Isḥāq's statement on the superficial influence of monotheism, that it "strikes the reviewer as very likely to be near the truth, and the existence of synagogues in ancient west Arabia is no more likely to have influenced the religious attitudes of tribesfolk than those in the Yemen (which were numerous enough until some twelve years ago) influenced the dominant Muslim population's outlook though relations were in other ways very close."

4.1 *The Treasury of the Kaʿbah: A Community Fund*

The Kaʿbah was a *bayt* (sanctuary), in fact, the Arabian sanctuary *par excellence*, according to the Islamic/Qurašī claim. *Bayt* is the common Arabic term describing a sanctuary of an idol; this could have been a humble construction or a lavish shrine, depending on the socio-economic level of the tribe(s) involved. Whenever there is reference to a sanctuary with a custodian, one can expect to find a treasury as well. The idol Suwāʿ in wadi Ruhāṭ, for example, had a treasury. Reportedly, ʿAmr b. al-ʿĀṣ ordered his men to destroy its treasury (*bayt ḫizānatihi*) and found nothing in it.[193]

The *ḫizānah* (treasury) of the Kaʿbah was in fact the treasury of the idol Hubal (*ḫizānah li-l-qurbān*, §80); its offerings were stored there. It is referred to as a *biʾr* (a pit); it was originally an uncovered area where jewels and other gifts were cast.[194] The pit was three cubits deep in the middle of the Kaʿbah, on the right side of one who entered it.[195] Elsewhere it is referred to as a *ǧubb* (which is synonymous with *biʾr*) dug by Abraham.[196] The treasury also included revenue from Hubal's divination arrows (*azlām*). The person in charge of the arrows (*ṣāḥib al-qidāḥ*) is said to have received 100 *dirhams* and a camel for sacrifice.[197] Swords are associated with this treasury and with other treasuries of idols. For example, Quṣayy b. Kilāb's maternal grandfather, Saʿd b. Sayal al-Azdī, gave Quṣayy's father two decorated swords that were deposited in the treasury of the Kaʿbah.[198] Perfume (*ḫalūq*) and aloes-wood (*muǧmar*) donated to the Kaʿbah before Islam were used to incense it both inside and outside.[199]

Beside the pit, the pre-Islamic *ḫizānat al-Kaʿbah* also included a dry storage place where precious textiles that were used to cover the Kaʿbah were stored.[200] During Ibn al-Zubayr's rebuilding of the Kaʿbah, its jewelry (*ḥilyah*) was stored in *ḫizānat al-Kaʿbah*, which was in the house of Šaybah b. ʿUṯmān of the ʿAbd al-Dār.[201]

193 Al-Wāqidī, *al-Maġāzī*, 2:870.
194 Al-Azraqī, *Aḫbār Makkah*², 1:87; Rubin (1986): 117.
195 Al-Azraqī, *Aḫbār Makkah*², 1:117.
196 Al-Suyūṭī, *al-Durr al-manṯūr*, 1:330.
197 Al-Azraqī, *Aḫbār Makkah*², 1:118.
198 Al-Kalāʿī, *al-Iktifāʾ*, 1:29.
199 Al-Azraqī, *Aḫbār Makkah*², 1:251. But cf. ibid., 1:253: Ibn al-Zubayr was the first to perfume (*ḫallaqa*) the inside (*ǧawf*) of the Kaʿbah. Al-Qalqašandī, *Maʾāṯir al-ināfah*, 1:123, states that Ibn al-Zubayr was the first to perfume the Kaʿbah both inside and outside. But elsewhere it is said that Muʿāwiyah was the first to use *ḫalūq* and *muǧmar* to incense the Kaʿbah; Yāqūt, *Muʿǧam al-buldān*, 4:467, s.v. al-Kaʿbah.
200 Al-Azraqī, *Aḫbār Makkah*², 1:251.
201 Al-Azraqī, *Aḫbār Makkah*², 1:207. See also ibid., 2:253 (Šaybah's house that included the

The Prophet is supposed to have found seventy thousand ounces of gold in the treasury of the Kaʿbah. ʿAlī advised him to use the funds for war expenses, but Muḥammad decided not to touch them, and Abū Bakr followed his example.[202] By contrast, the historian Yaʿqūbī supported the opposing view, that after the conquest of Mecca, Muḥammad distributed the contents of the treasury.[203] Reportedly, ʿUmar b. al-Ḫaṭṭāb did not touch it. Šaybah b. ʿUṯmān, the custodian of the Kaʿbah at the time of Muḥammad who lived to the end of Muʿāwiyah's caliphate, protected the treasury. A man who brought a gift from another man to the Kaʿbah told Šaybah that had it been his own property, he would not have donated it. Šaybah is supposed to have told him that ʿUmar had taken an oath to distribute the treasury's funds, but changed his mind after Šaybah convinced him not to. Šaybah told ʿUmar that the Prophet and Abū Bakr, who needed the funds more than he did, had not touched them.[204]

Among the precious items kept in the treasury was a golden gazelle which was stolen, among other items, by Muḥammad's parternal uncle, Abū Lahab.[205] In connection with this theft we find a crucial detail regarding the social and economic role of the treasury. Abū Musāfiʿ al-Ašʿarī, a client (*ḥalīf*) of the Maḫzūm, who was himself one of the culprits, referred to it in a verse as "the gazelle which you acquired together with its jewels for the calamities and the changing fortunes" (*inna l-ġazāla llaḏī kuntum wa-ḥilyatahū/taqnūnahū li-ḫuṭūbi l-dahri wa-l-ġiyarī*).[206] It follows that the gazelle—and no doubt the treasury as a whole—was a tribal community fund.[207]

treasury was located near *Dār al-Nadwah* and had a gate connecting it to the Kaʿbah). Cf. "Dār al-Nadwa," in *EI*³ (H. Munt).

202 Al-Azraqī, *Aḫbār Makkah*², 1:246–247.

203 Al-Yaʿqūbī, *Taʾrīḫ*, 2:61 (*wa-rawá baʿḍuhum anna rasūla llāh qasama mā kāna fī l-Kaʿbah mina l-māl bayna l-muslimīna wa-qāla āḫarūna aqarrahu*).

204 Ibn ʿAsākir, *Dimašq*, 23:259–260 (*qad raʾayā makānahu fa-lam yuḥarrikāhu wa-humā aḥwaǧu ilá l-māl minka*); cf. al-Azraqī, *Aḫbār Makkah*², 1:245–246. The Ǧurhum unjustly took the money donated to the Kaʿbah; al-Ṭabarī, *Taʾrīḫ*, 1:1131 (*wa-akalū māla l-Kaʿbah llaḏī yuhdá lahā*). When the caliph ʿUmar II turned one of his Meccan houses into a charitable endowment for the housing of pilgrims, he deposited the endowment document in the treasury of the Kaʿbah and instructed the custodians to look after the house; al-Azraqī, *Aḫbār Makkah*², 2:241.

205 Rubin (2007).

206 Al-ʿAskarī, *al-Awāʾil*, 1:65; Ibn Ḥabīb, *al-Munammaq* 62. Ibn al-Ǧawzī, *al-Muntaẓam*, 2:209, has a garbled text. Ibn Hišām, *al-Sīrah al-nabawiyyah*, 1:205, has a censored version of the report. It includes no names of Qurašīs, and the only name is that of Duyayk, a *mawlá* of the Ḫuzāʿah in whose house the unspecified "treasure belonging to the Kaʿbah" (*kanz li-l-Kaʿbah*) was found. Cf. Lecker (2014).

207 Possibly comparable to the community fund of the Jewish Banū l-Naḍīr; Lecker (2015).

4.2 *The Treasury of Allāt*

The prominence of the Ṯaqīf tribe in early Islamic politics and literature is reflected in the rich literary evidence about their idol, Allāt, and its treasury. Most of the evidence is legendary, but in the background there is a layer of relatively reliable detail. It is a matter of separating the wheat from the chaff.

The Ṯaqīf delegation that came to Medina in Ramaḍān 9/December 630–January 631 "asked to be exempted from having to demolish Allāt and al-ʿUzzá by themselves, to which he [Muḥammad] assented. Muġīrah b. Šuʿbah said: I was the one who demolished it."[208] Muġīrah was referring to Allāt. Muḥammad rejected their demand to keep Allāt for one year. His reply mentions *al-ṭāġiyah*, which is glossed as Allāt and al-ʿUzzá[209]—perhaps there was a statue of al-ʿUzzá in Ṭāʾif.[210]

The core report in the relatively long chapter on the Ṯaqīf delegation found in Ibn Šabbah's history of Medina goes back to Ibn ʿUqbah < Zuhrī. In the report, Ṯaqīf's idol is referred to as al-Rabbah. The Ṯaqīf feared that if the idol knew that they were rushing to destroy it, it would kill their families. This fear was voiced by the delegation head, ʿAbd Yālīl. Upon returning to Ṭāʾif the delegation members visited Allāt before proceeding to their homes.[211] The sanctuary of Allāt was in the middle of Ṭāʾif; it was veiled and received gifts of camels for sacrifice. They (i.e. the Ṯaqīf) made it similar to the Kaʿbah and worshipped it (*bayt kāna bayna ẓahrayi l-Ṭāʾif yustaru wa-yuhdá lahā* [sic] *l-hady, ḍāhaw bihi bayta llāh*

208 Ibn Saʿd, *al-Ṭabaqāt*², 1:271.

209 Kister (1979); al-Baġawī, *Tafsīr*, 4:140; al-Qurṭubī, *al-Ǧāmiʿ*, 10:299. It is noteworthy that the report refers to idols (plural) in general (*mattiʿnā bi-ālihatinā sanah ḥattá naʾḫuḏa mā yuhdá ilayhā fa-iḏā aḫaḏnāhu kasarnāhā wa-aslamnā*). The shrewd Ṯaqafīs knew what Muḥammad should tell the other Arabs, should they reprove him with regard to Ṯaqīf's prerogative (*in kāna bika malāmatu l-ʿarab fī kasr aṣnāmihim wa-tark aṣnāminā fa-qul lahum inna rabbī amaranī an uqirra Allāt bi-arḍihim sanah*); Muqātil, *Tafsīr*, 2:266–267; Kister (1979): 6–7. Muqātil does not mention his source, but he could have received it from his contemporary al-Kalbī. Ibn Šabbah, *Taʾrīḫ al-Madīnah*, 2:510–511, has an abridged version of the same report going back to al-Kalbī. Al-Kalbī's report as found in Ibn Šabbah was transmitted by Ḥammād b. Salamah; cf. an *isnād* in which Ḥammād quotes al-Kalbī in al-Ṭabarānī, *al-Muʿǧam al-kabīr*, 23:163. Since al-Kalbī's report specifically refers to Qurʾān 17:73, one assumes that it is from al-Kalbī's *Tafsīr*.

210 Cf. King (2002): 108. After the conclusion of their treaty with Muḥammad, the Ṯaqīf asked to keep Allāt for three years, and they continued haggling about it until they came down to a respite of one month after their return to Ṭāʾif. However, Muḥammad would not grant them a postponement for a definite period; Ibn Hišām, *al-Sīrah al-nabawiyyah*, 4:184–185; al-Wāqidī, *al-Maġāzī*, 3:968.

211 Having embraced Islam, ʿUrwah b. Masʿūd al-Ṯaqafī returned home without visiting al-Rabbah first, which the Ṯaqafīs found unusual; al-Wāqidī, *al-Maġāzī*, 3:960. They became suspicious when he did not approach Allāt and did not shave his head at it; ibid., 3:961.

wa-kānū ya'budūnahā). Muġīrah b. Šu'bah smashed the door and, together with others, leveled the sanctuary. Still, the *ṣāḥib al-mafātīḥ* (i.e. the custodian[212]) thought that the foundation would be provoked and the aggressors would be swallowed up (*la-yaġḍabanna l-asās wa-la-yuḥsafanna bihim*), so the foundation was dug up and the idol's jewels and covers (*ṯiyāb*) were removed.[213] These details regarding Allāt are from Zuhrī's report.

The Ṯaqīf were divided into two rival subdivisions, the Aḥlāf, or the allies, and the Mālik. In the Battle of Ḥunayn and during the siege of Ṭā'if, Qārib b. al-Aswad carried the banner of the Aḥlāf.[214] Muġīrah too belonged to the Aḥlāf, and the Aḥlāfī members of the Ṯaqīf delegation lodged with him.[215] When Muġīrah demolished Allāt, his clan, the Banū Mu'attib, gave him shelter.[216] The delegation head, 'Abd Yālīl, belonged to another branch of the Aḥlāf. The custodians of Allāt from the Aḥlaf were the Banū l-'Aǧlān b. 'Attāb b. Mālik b. Ka'b; 'Attāb may have been the first custodian.[217] Another source takes us one or two generations later: the custodians were the Banū Šubayl b. al-'Aǧlān. One of them is mentioned specifically, namely Munabbih b. Šubayl.[218] There is yet another claim regarding the custodians' identity, that they were the family (*āl*) of Abū l-'Āṣ of the Mālik.[219]

Allāt's treasury included funds (*māl*) in gold and onyx, in addition to jewels.[220] The *ġabġab*, or Allāt's treasury, was half a man's height deep and included

212 Al-Wāqidī, *al-Maġāzī*, 3:972, has *sādin*. A person referred to as *ṣāḥib al-mafātīḥ* held the keys to the treasury of the caliph 'Uṯmān; Miskawayh, *Taǧārib al-umam*, 1:455.

213 Ibn Šabbah, *Ta'rīḫ al-Madīnah*, 2:499–515; Zuhrī's report, 2:501–507. The passage on al-Rabbah, 2:503–504, is garbled (*law ta'lamu l-Rabbah annaka turīdu hadmahā qatalat ahlīnā*). A better reading is found in al-Wāqidī, *al-Maġāzī*, 3:967 (*law ta'lamu l-Rabbah annā awḍa'nā fī hadmihā qatalat ahlanā*).

214 Ibn Ḥaǧar, *al-Iṣābah*², 5:403.

215 Ibn Sa'd, *al-Ṭabaqāt*², 1:271.

216 Ibn Hišām, *al-Sīrah al-nabawiyyah*, 4:186; al-Wāqidī, *al-Maġāzī*, 3:971–972.

217 *Wa-ṣāḥibuhā minhum 'Attāb ... ṯumma banūhu ba'dahu*; al-Wāqidī, *al-Maġāzī*, 3:972. Wellhausen thought that Mu'attib and 'Attāb were the same, but this is not the case; Wellhausen (1897): 31; Caskel (1966), 1: table 118. See also Krone (1992): 427–429.

218 Ibn al-Kalbī, *Ǧamharat al-nasab* 388.

219 Ibn Ḥabīb, *al-Muḥabbar* 315. For Abū l-'Āṣ's pedigree see Ibn Ḥazm, *Ǧamharat ansāb al-'arab* 266. The family in question played a significant role in Islam. 'Uṯmān b. Abī l-'Āṣ, whose mother was Umayyad, was married to an Umayyad woman. He was Muḥammad's governor in Ṭā'if. Muḥammad instructed him to place the mosque of Ṭā'if at the former place of the idols (*ḥayṯu kānat ṭawāġītuhum*); al-Qurṭubī, *al-Ǧāmi'*, 8:255. The left minaret of the mosque was later built on the site of Allāt; al-Qurṭubī, *al-Ǧāmi'*, 17:99.

220 Ibn Hišām, *al-Sīrah al-nabawiyyah*, 4:186. See also "al-Mughīra b. Shu'ba," in *EI*² (Lammens): Muḥammad sent Muġīrah to Ṭā'if "to superintend the destruction of the national sanctuary and the liquidation of the treasure of al-Lāt."

its jewels and cover, in addition to perfume, gold, and silver (*balaġa niṣf qāmah wa-ntahá* [i.e. al-Muġīrah] *ilá l-ġabġab ḫizānatihā wa-ntazaʿū ḥilyatahā wa-kiswatahā wa-mā fīhā min ṭīb wa-min ḏahab aw* [read: *wa-*] *fiḍḍa*).[221] Muḥammad used the funds of Allāt's treasury (*māl al-ṭāġiyah* or *ḥuliyy al-Rabbah*) to repay a debt of two hundred gold *miṯqāl*s (*dīnār*s) left by the murdered ʿUrwah b. Masʿūd al-Ṯaqafī. He did this at the request of ʿUrwah's son, Abū Mulayḥ. He also repaid a debt of the same amount left by the former's brother, al-Aswad b. Masʿūd, at the request of the latter's son, Qārib.[222] There were also other unspecified beneficiaries, and some funds were spent on weapons for the *ǧihād*.[223]

The abolition of Allāt and appropriation of its treasury deprived the Ṯaqafīs of a central financial institution that may well have functioned as a bank, providing loans and guarantees. Through the Islamization of the Kaʿbah the Qurašīs in the rival town of Mecca preserved their own financial institution, namely the treasury of the Kaʿbah.

4.3 *The Treasury of Manāt*

Saʿd b. Zayd of the Anṣār, specifically of the ʿAbd al-Ašhal (Aws), is said to have destroyed Manāt. His expedition force found nothing in its treasury (*wa-lam yaǧidū fī ḫizānatihā šay'an*).[224] Abū Sufyān and ʿAlī b. Abī Ṭālib (separately) claimed credit for demolishing Manāt.[225] A somewhat vague reference to Manāt's treasury is linked to the latter, whom Muḥammad reportedly sent to Manāt, while he was going to conquer Mecca: "He took what belonged to her [i.e. Manāt] (*mā kāna lahā*) and brought it to the Messenger of God." Two swords are mentioned specifically.[226] Yet another who claimed credit is Ḫālid b. al-Walīd whom Muḥammad sent to destroy Manāt during the expedition of al-Muraysīʿ.[227] It is not at all clear who destroyed Manāt, but two reports about its destruction refer to its treasury.

---

221 Al-Wāqidī, *al-Maġāzī*, 3:972.

222 Ibn Hišām, al-*Sīrah al-nabawiyyah*, 4:187; al-Wāqidī, *al-Maġāzī*, 3:971; Ibn Saʿd, *al-Ṭabaqāt*², 8:66.

223 Al-Wāqidī, *al-Maġāzī*, 3:972 (*wa-aʿṭá … Abā Mulayḥ wa-Qāriban wa-nāsan wa-ǧaʿala fī sabīli llāh wa-fī l-silāḥ minhā*).

224 Ibn Sayyid al-Nās, *ʿUyūn al-aṯar*, 2:250.

225 Ibn Hišām, *al-Sīrah al-nabawiyyah*, 1:88.

226 Lecker (2005a): 34. Cf. Lecker (2012): 126–128. However, according to another version, ʿAlī found the swords when he destroyed al-F(a/i)ls (§ 121).

227 Ibn Kaṯīr, *Tafsīr*², 14:13.

4.4 *The Treasury of al-ʿUzzá*

Regarding the treasury at al-ʿUzzá, there is, for the time being, only circumstantial evidence. First, al-ʿUzzá had both a *bayt* (sanctuary), and custodians. (Differences regarding the sanctuary's shape and the identity of its custodians confirm the existence of both.) The combination of a sanctuary and custodians, as noted above, is indicative of a treasury. Second, there is evidence of votive gifts for which there must have been a treasury. Qurayš, for whom al-ʿUzzá was "the supreme idol," would visit it, bring it their tributes, and slaughter animals at it.[228]

---

228 *Wa-kānat aʿẓama l-aṣnām ʿinda Qurayš wa-kānū yazūrūnahā wa-yuhdūna ilayhā wa-yataqarrabūna ʿindahā bi-l-ḏabāʾiḥ*; Yāqūt, *Muʿǧam al-buldān*, 4:116, s.v. al-ʿUzzá. Ibn al-Kalbī has further detail regarding the special attachment of Qurayš to al-ʿUzzá, in which votive gifts played an essential part. See ibid., 4:118a: *wa-lam takun Qurayš bi-Makkah wa-man aqāma bihā mina l-ʿarab yuʿẓimūna šayʾan mina l-aṣnām iʿẓāmahumu l-ʿUzzá ṯumma Allāt ṯumma Manāt fa-ammā l-ʿUzzá fa-kānat Qurayš taḫuṣṣuhā dūna ġayrihā bi-l-hadiyyah wa-l-ziyārah wa-ḏālika fīmā aẓunnu li-qurbihā minhum.*

Notes on the Edition and the Translation

Edition

This edition was prepared from the holograph of al-Maqrīzī's *al-Ḫabar ʿan al-bašar*. The section on the idols is extant in volume 4 (fols. 30a–48b), preserved in the Süleymaniye Kütüphanesi in Istanbul, MS Fatih 4339. As for the previous volumes published in the *Bibliotheca Maqriziana*, the text was edited on the basis of the holograph, limiting editorial intrusion to the minimum. In the holograph, the section on the idols is clean and clear. As a consequence, we did not need to rely on the other copies of volume 4 identified below, in chronological order:

- Istanbul, Süleymaniye Kütüphanesi, MS Aya Sofya 3364, pp. 441–442
- Istanbul, Topkapı Sarayı Müzesi Kütüphanesi, MS Ahmet III 2926/4, fols. 22a–40a
- Istanbul, Süleymaniye Kütüphanesi, MS Aya Sofya 3365, pp. 42–77
- Cairo, Maktabat al-Azhar, MS Abāẓah 6733, fols. 123a–128b (with an important lacuna at the beginning of the section)
- Strasbourg, Bibliothèque nationale et universitaire, MS 4244, fols. 128a–133b (with the same lacuna at the beginning of the section as in the al-Azhar copy)
- Cairo, Dār al-Kutub al-Miṣriyyah, MS 5251 (a modern copy made from reproductions of volumes held in Istanbul)
- Cairo, Institut français d'archéologie orientale, MS 30/2 (a modern copy made on the basis of the al-Azhar manuscript)

The text was edited in line with the guidelines that have already been detailed in the previous volumes that appeared in this series.[1]

Translation

This translation attempts to provide a clear and faithful rendering of the original Arabic text. Where I felt it necessary, I used square brackets to insert explanatory comments, add words required for the sake of smoothness and clarity, and identify nouns to which pronouns in the Arabic text refer. Generally, I translated Arabic technical terms, but sometimes kept them transliterated

1 See particularly the latest volume edited and translated by Peter Webb on the Arab thieves.

 | DOI:10.1163/9789004499867_003

between parentheses. As far as possible, names of individuals are briefly identified in the footnotes, when first mentioned. I have also used the footnotes to indicate some instances in which parallel sources help elucidate difficult points in the text.

In preparing this translation I benefitted greatly from the assistance of Simon Hopkins, who offered valuable comments on some difficult passages in the text, and Michael Lecker, who read an earlier draft of the translation and saved me from numerous errors. I am also very grateful to Michael Brill, Noam Harris, Ahmad Al-Jallad, Ohad Kayam, Iyas Nasser, and Arik Sadan for their advice and suggestions. Needless to say, any inaccuracies and imprecisions that remain in the translation are my own responsibility.

Plates and Map

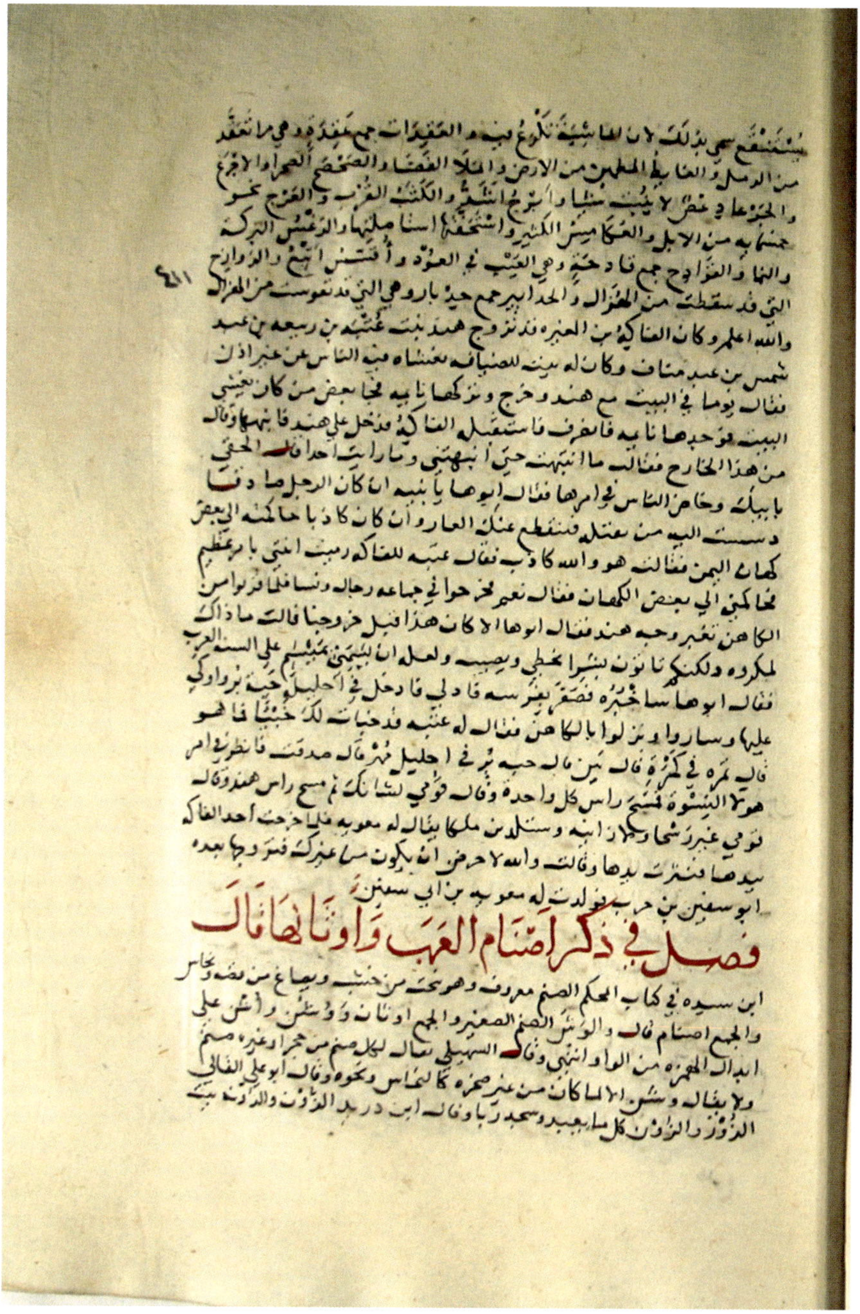

PLATE 1 Istanbul/ Süleymaniye Kütüphanesi, MS Aya Sofya 3364, p. 411

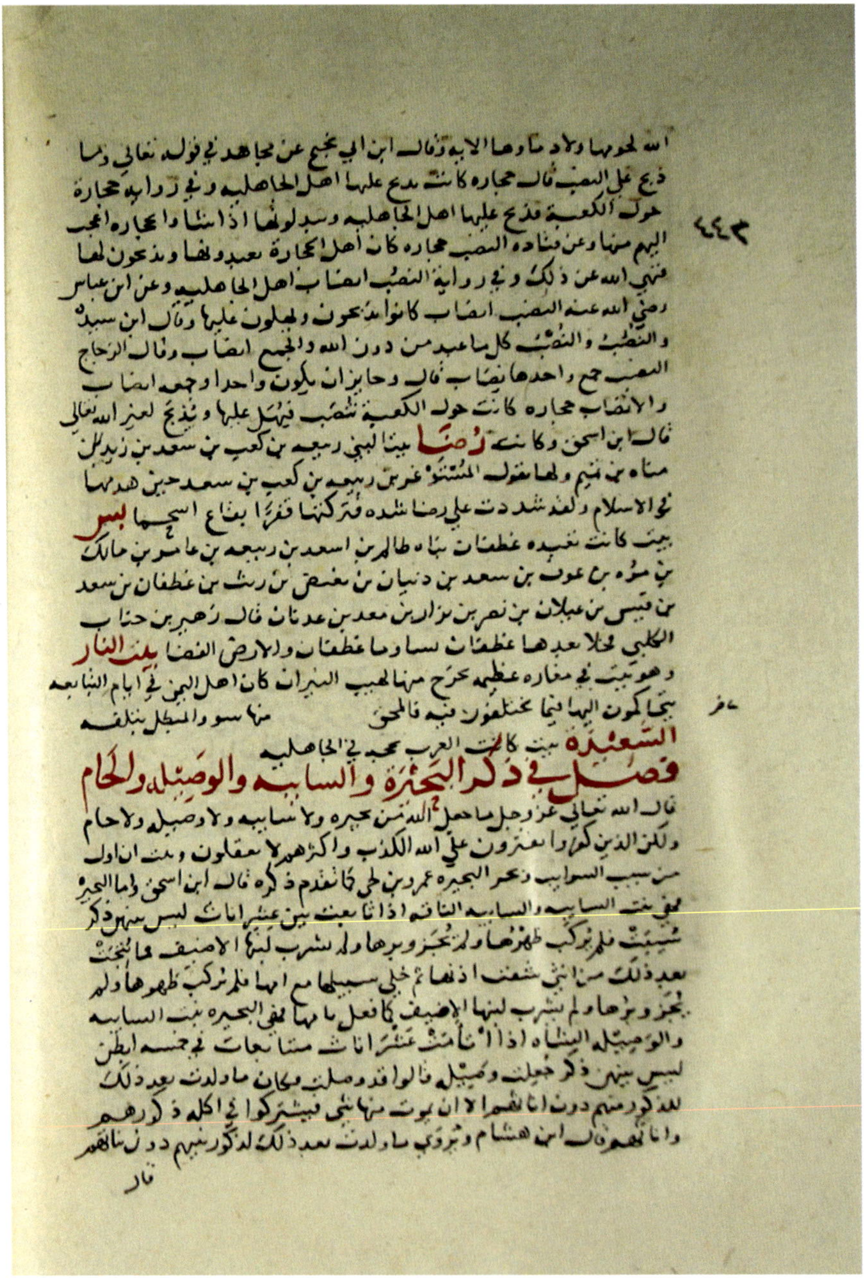

الله لحومها ولا دماؤها الاية وقال ابن ابي نجيح عن مجاهد في قوله تعالى وما
ذبح على النصب قال حجارة كانت يذبح عليها اهل الجاهلية وفي رواية حجارة
حول الكعبة تذبح عليها اهل الجاهلية ويبدلونها اذا شاؤوا بحجارة اعجب ٤٤٢
اليهم منها وعن قتادة النصب حجارة كان اهل الجاهلية يعبدونها ويذبحون لها
فنهى الله عن ذلك وفي رواية النصب انصاب اهل الجاهلية وعن ابن عباس
رضي الله عنه النصب انصاب كانوا يذبحون ويهلون عليها وقال ابن سيده
والنُّصْبُ والنُّصُبُ كل ما عبد من دون الله والجمع انصاب وقال الزجاج
النصب جمع واحدها نصاب قال وجائز ان يكون واحدا وجمعه انصاب
والانصاب حجارة كانت حول الكعبة تنصب فيهل عليها ويذبح لغير الله تعالى
قال ابن اسحق وكانت **رضا** بيتا لبني ربيعة بن كعب بن سعد بن زيد
مناة بن تميم ولها يقول المستوغر بن ربيعة بن كعب بن سعد حين هدمها
في الاسلام ولقد شددت على رضا شدة فتركتها قفرا بقاع اسحما **بس**
بيت كانت تعبده غطفان بناه ظالم بن اسعد بن ربيعة بن عامر بن مالك
بن مرة بن عوف بن سعد بن ذبيان بن بغيض بن ريث بن غطفان بن سعد
بن قيس بن عيلان بن نصر بن نزار بن معد بن عدنان قال زهير بن جناب
الكلبي فلا يعدها غطفان بسا وما غطفان والارض القضا **بيت النار**
وهو بيت في مغارة عظيمة يخرج منها لهيب النيران كان اهل اليمن في ايام التبابعة
يحتكمون اليها فيما يختلفون فيه فالمحق منهم يسلم والمبطل يتلفه
السعيدة بيت كانت العرب تحجه في الجاهلية

فصل في ذكر البحيرة والسائبة والوصيلة والحام

قال الله تعالى عز وجل ما جعل الله من بحيرة ولا سائبة ولا وصيلة ولا حام
ولكن الذين كفروا يفترون على الله الكذب واكثرهم لا يعقلون وقد ثبت ان اول
من سيب السوائب وبحر البحيرة عمرو بن لحي كما تقدم ذكره قال ابن اسحق واما البحيرة
فهي بنت السائبة والسائبة الناقة اذا تابعت بين عشر اناث ليس بينهن ذكر
سيبت فلم يركب ظهرها ولم يجز وبرها ولم يشرب لبنها الا ضيف فما نتجت
بعد ذلك من انثى شقت اذنها ثم خلي سبيلها مع امها فلم يركب ظهرها ولم
يجز وبرها ولم يشرب لبنها الا ضيف كما فعل بامها فهي البحيرة بنت السائبة
والوصيلة الشاة اذا اتأمت عشر اناث متتابعات في خمسة ابطن
ليس بينهن ذكر جعلت وصيلة قالوا قد وصلت فكان ما ولدت بعد ذلك
للذكور منهم دون اناثهم الا ان يموت منها شيء فيشتركوا في اكله ذكورهم
واناثهم قال ابن هشام ويروى ما ولدت بعد ذلك لذكور بنيهم دون بناتهم
قال

PLATE 2 Istanbul/ Süleymaniye Kütüphanesi, MS Aya Sofya 3364, p. 442

22

فينقطع عنك العار وان كان كاذبا حاكمته الى بعض كهان اليمن فقالت هو
والله كاذب فقال عتبة للفاكه رميت ابنتي بامر عظيم فحاكمني الى بعض
الكهان فقال نعم فخرجوا في جماعة رجال ونسا فلما قربوا من الكاهن تغير
وجه هند فقال ابوها الا كان هذا قبل خروجنا قالت ما ذاك لمكروه
ولكنكم تاتون بشرا يخطي ويصيب ولعله ان يسمني بميسم يبقى على السنة
العرب فقال ابوها سأخبره فصفر بفرسه فادلى فادخل في احليله حبة
بر واوكى عليها وساروا ونزلوا بالكاهن فقال له عتبة قد خبات لك
خبيا فما هو فقال ثمرة في كمرة قال بين قال حبة بر في احليل مهر
قال صدقت قال فانظر في امر هولا النسوة فمسح راس كل واحدة
وقال قومي لشانك ثم مسح راس هند وقال قومي غير رسحا ولا زانية
وستلدين ملكا يقال له معوية فلما خرجت اخذ الفاكه بيدها فنترت
يدها وقالت والله لاحرصن ان يكون من غيرك فتزوجها بعده ابو سفيان
ابن حرب فولدت معوية بن ابي سفيان

فصل في ذكر اصنام العرب واوثانها

قال ابن سيده في كتاب المحكم الصنم معروف وهو ينحت من خشب ويصاغ
من فضة ونحاس والجمع اصنام قال والوثن الصنم الصغير والجمع
اوثان ووثن واثن على ابدال الهمزة من الواو انتهى وقال السهيلي يقال
لكل صنم من حجر او غيره صنم ولا يقال وثن الا لما كان من غير صخرة كالنحاس
ونحوه وقال ابو علي القالي الزور والزون كل ما يعبد ويتخذ ربا
وقال ابن دريد الزون والزونة بيت الاصنام يتخذ ويزين والزونة
كالزينة يقال هذه زينة وزونة وقال المبرد قال ابن عباس في
قوله تعالى والذين لا يشهدون الزور قال هي اعياد المشركين وقد قيل
ان اصل وضع الاصنام في اول الدهر كان في عهد مهلاييل بن قينان بن انوش
ابن شيث بن ادم وقيل انما اخذ عن عاذيمون وهو عند الصابية شيث بن
ادم وعن هرمس الاول وهو عندهم ادريس بالواو وادريس اول من تكلم في
الجواهر العلوية والحركات النجومية وبنا الهياكل ومجد الله فيها قالوا ولما
علمنا ان للعالم صانعا مقدسا عن سمات الحدوث وجب علينا العجز عن ادراك

PLATE 3 Istanbul/ Topkapı Sarayı Müzesi Kütüphanesi, MS 2926/4, fol. 22a

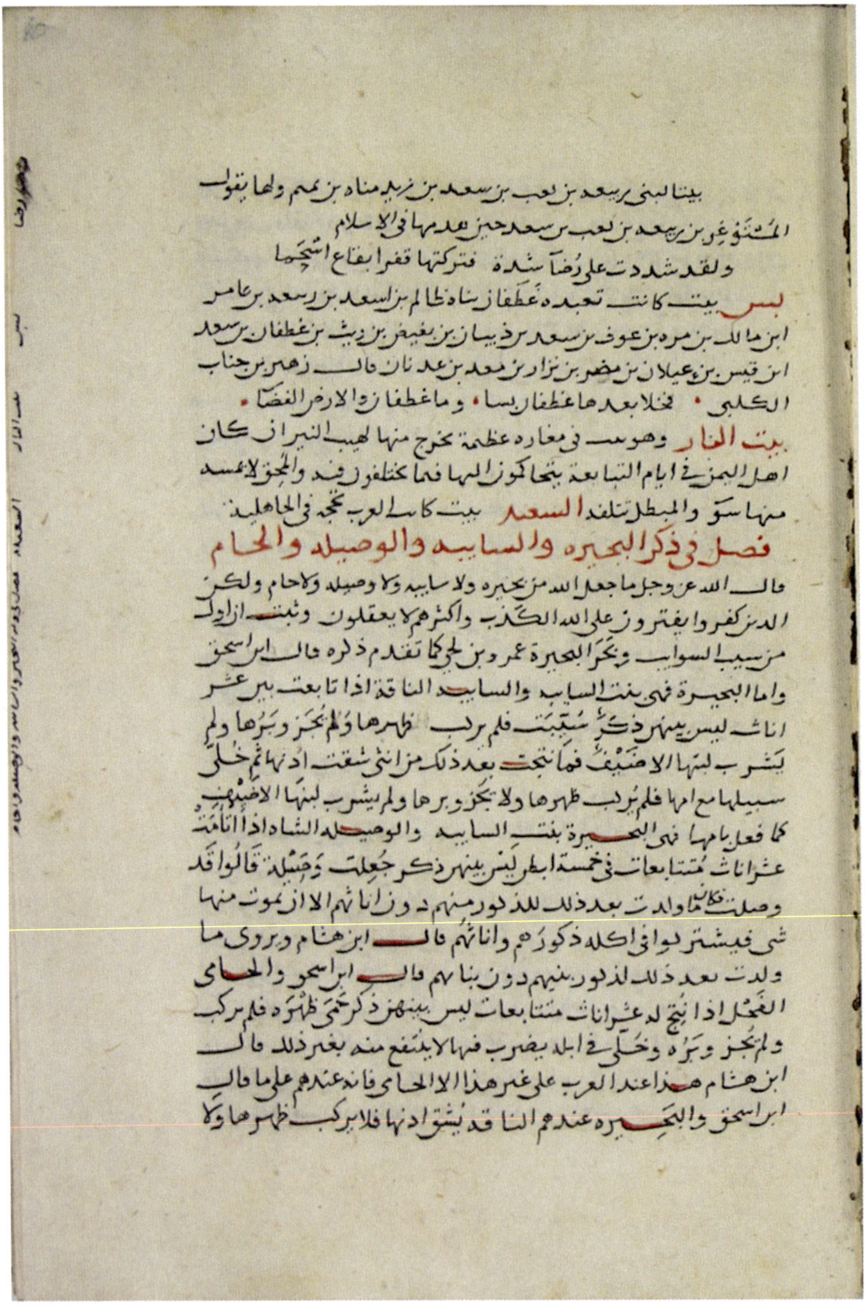

بيتا لبني ربيعة بن كعب بن سعد بن زيد مناة بن تميم ولها يقول
المستوغر بن ربيعة بن كعب بن سعد حين هدمها في الاسلام
ولقد شددت على رضا شدة فتركتها قفرا بقاع اسحما
بس بيت كانت تعبده غطفان بناه ظالم بن اسعد بن ربيعة بن عامر
ابن مالك بن مرة بن عوف بن سعد بن ذبيان بن بغيض بن ريث بن غطفان بن سعد
ابن قيس بن عيلان بن مضر بن نزار بن معد بن عدنان قال زهير بن جناب
الكلبي • فخلا بعدها غطفان بسا • وما غطفان والارض الفضاء •
بيت النار وهو بيت في مغارة عظيمة تخرج منها لهب النيران كان
اهل اليمن في ايام التبابعة يتحاكمون اليها فما يختلفون فيه والمحق لا تمسه
منها سوء والمبطل تتلفه السعير بيت كان للعرب تحجه في الجاهلية
فصل في ذكر البحيرة والسايبة والوصيلة والحام
قال الله عز وجل ما جعل الله من بحيرة ولا سايبة ولا وصيلة ولا حام ولكن
الذين كفروا يفترون على الله الكذب واكثرهم لا يعقلون وثبت ان اول
من سيب السوايب وبحر البحيرة عمرو بن لحي كما تقدم ذكره قال ابن اسحق
واما البحيرة فهي بنت السايبة والسايبة الناقة اذا تابعت بين عشر
اناث ليس بينهن ذكر سيبت فلم يركب ظهرها ولم يجز وبرها ولم
يشرب لبنها الا ضيف فما نتجت بعد ذلك من انثى شقت اذنها ثم خلي
سبيلها مع امها فلم يركب ظهرها ولا يجز وبرها ولم يشرب لبنها الا ضيف
كما فعل بامها فهي البحيرة بنت السايبة والوصيلة الشاة اذا اتامت
عشر اناث متتابعات في خمسة ابطن ليس بينهن ذكر جعلت وصيلة قالوا قد
وصلت فكان ما ولدت بعد ذلك للذكور منهم دون اناثهم الا ان يموت منها
شي فيشترك في اكله ذكورهم واناثهم قال ابن هشام ويروى ما
ولدت بعد ذلك لذكور بنيهم دون بناتهم قال ابن اسحق والحامي
الفحل اذا نتج له عشر اناث متتابعات ليس بينهن ذكر حمي ظهره فلم يركب
ولم يجز وبره وخلي في ابله يضرب فيها لا ينتفع منه بغير ذلك قال
ابن هشام هذا عند العرب على غير هذا الا الحامي فانه عندهم على ما قال
ابن اسحق والبحيرة عندهم الناقة تشق اذنها فلا يركب ظهرها ولا

PLATE 4 Istanbul/ Topkapı Sarayı Müzesi Kütüphanesi, MS 2926/4, fol. 40a

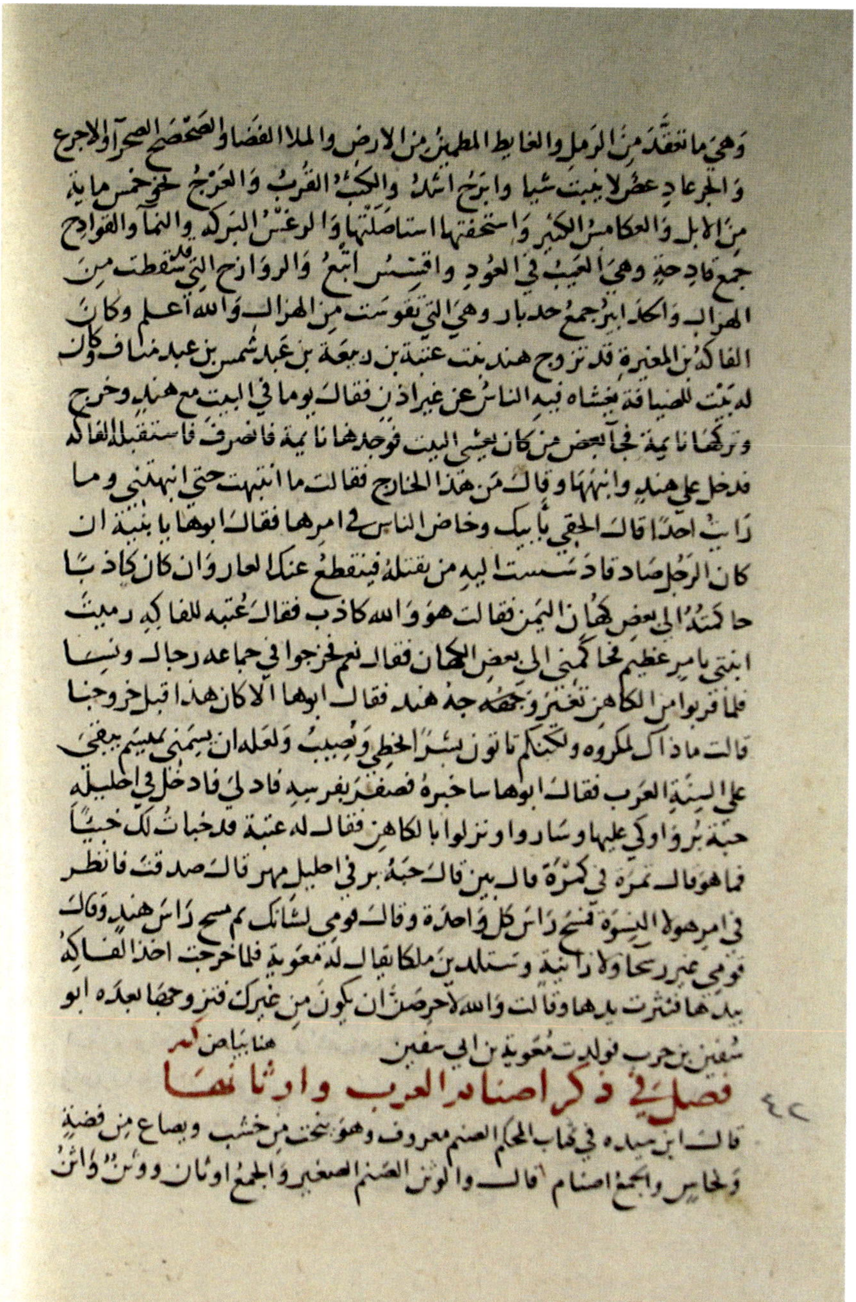

وهي ما تعقد من الرمل والغايط المطمئن من الارض والملا الفضاء والصحصح الصحرا والاجرع
والجرعا دعص لا ينبت شيا وابرح اشد والكثب القرب والعرج نحو خمس مائة
من الابل والعكامس الكثير واستحقتها استاصلتها والوغش البركة والنما والفوادح
جمع فادحة وهي العيب في العود واقتبس ابتع والروازح التي سقطت من
الهزال والكدابر جمع حدبار وهي التي نفوسنت من الهزال والله اعلم وكان
الفاكه بن المغيرة قد تزوج هند بنت عتبة بن ربيعة بن عبد شمس بن عبد مناف وكان
له بيت للضيافة يغشاه فيه الناس عن غير اذن فقال يوما في البيت مع هند وخرج
وتركها نايمة فجا بعض من كان يغشى البيت فوجدها نايمة فانصرف فاستقبله الفاكه
فدخل على هند وانبهها وقال من هذا الخارج فقالت ما انتبهت حتى انبهتني وما
رايت احدا قال الحقي بابيك وخاض الناس في امرها فقال ابوها يا بنية ان
كان الرجل صادقا فدسي اليه من يقتله فينقطع عنك العار وان كان كاذبا
حاكمته الى بعض كهان اليمن فقالت هو والله كاذب فقال عتبة للفاكه رميت
ابنتي بامر عظيم فحاكمني الى بعض الكهان فقال نعم فخرجوا في جماعة رجال ونسا
فلما قربوا من الكاهن تغير وجه هند فقال ابوها الا كان هذا قبل خروجنا
قالت ما ذاك لمكروه ولكنكم تاتون بشرا الخطي ويصيب ولعله ان يسمني بميسم يبقى
على السنة العرب فقال ابوها ساخبره فصفر بفرسه فادلى فادخل في احليله
حبة بر واوكى عليها وساروا ونزلوا بالكاهن فقال له عتبة قد خبات لك خبيا
فما هو قال ثمرة في كمرة قال ابين قال حبة بر في احليل مهر قال صدقت فانظر
في امر هولا النسوة فمسح راس كل واحدة وقال قومي لشانك ثم مسح راس هند وقال
قومي غير رسحا ولا زانية وستلدين ملكا يقال له معوية فلما خرجت اخذ الفاكه
بيدها فنترت يدها وقالت والله لاحرصن ان يكون من غيرك فتزوجها بعده ابو
سفين بن حرب فولدت معوية بن ابي سفين هنا بياض كبير

فصل في ذكر اصنام العرب واوثانها ٤٢

قال ابن سيده في كتاب المحكم الصنم معروف وهو ينحت من خشب ويصاغ من فضة
ونحاس والجمع اصنام قال والوثن الصنم الصغير والجمع اوثان ووثن واثن

PLATE 5 Istanbul/ Süleymaniye Kütüphanesi, MS Aya Sofya 3365, p. 42

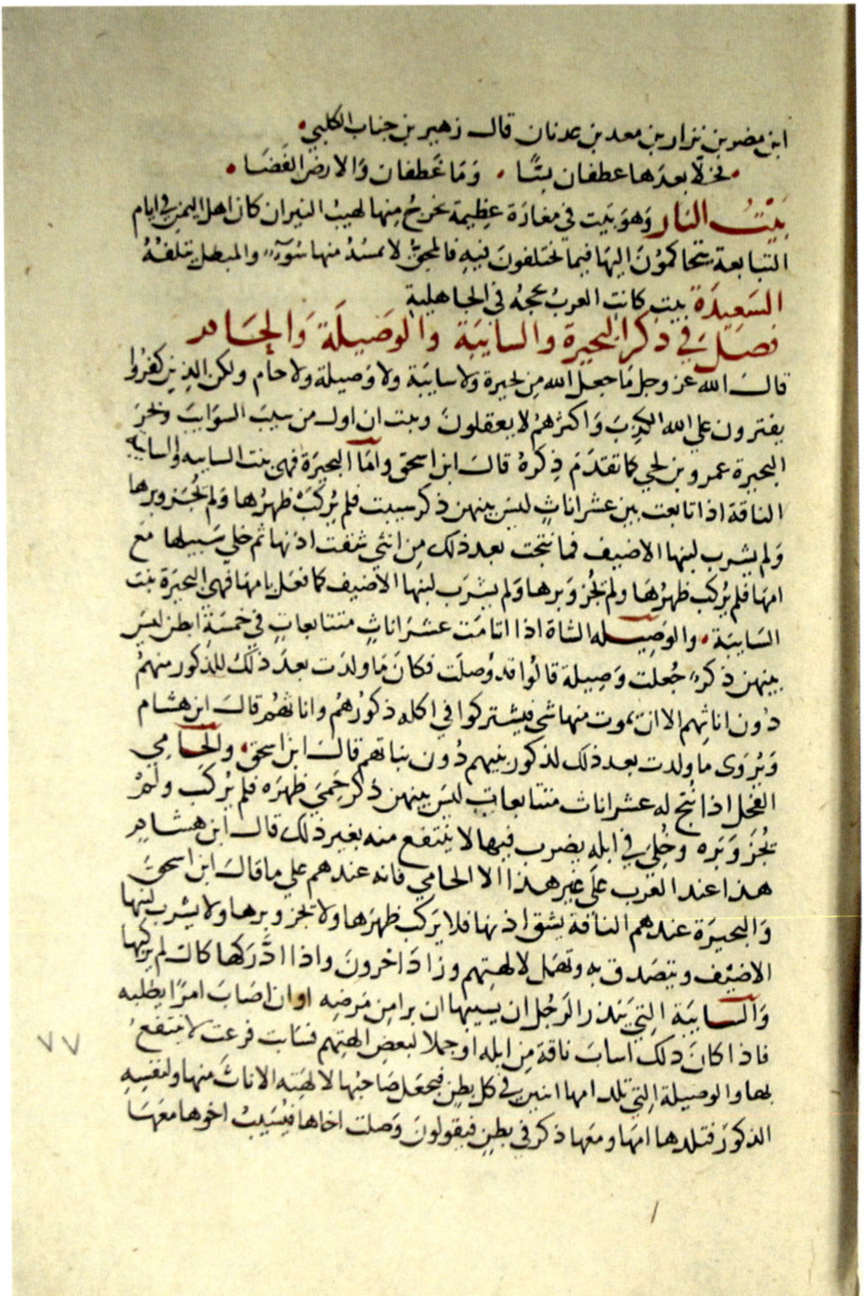

ابن مضر بن نزار بن معد بن عدنان قال زهير بن جناب الكلبي •
فخلا بعدها غطفان بتا • وما غطفان والارض الفضا •
بيت النار وهو بيت في مغارة عظيمة تخرج منها لهيب النيران كان اهل اليمن في ايام
التبابعة يتحاكمون اليها فيما يختلفون فيه فالمحق لا يمسه منها سوء والمبطل تلتقمه
السعيدة بيت كانت العرب تحجه في الجاهلية
فصل في ذكر البحيرة والسائبة والوصيلة والحام
قال الله عز وجل ما جعل الله من بحيرة ولا سائبة ولا وصيلة ولا حام ولكن الذين كفروا
يفترون على الله الكذب واكثرهم لا يعقلون وثبت ان اول من سيب السوائب وبحر
البحيرة عمرو بن لحي كما تقدم ذكره قال ابن اسحق واما البحيرة فهي بنت السائبة والسائبة
الناقة اذا تابعت بين عشر اناث ليس بينهن ذكر سيبت فلم يركب ظهرها ولم يجز وبرها
ولم يشرب لبنها الا ضيف فما نتجت بعد ذلك من انثى شقت اذنها ثم خلي سبيلها مع
امها فلم يركب ظهرها ولم يجز وبرها ولم يشرب لبنها الا ضيف كما فعل بامها فهي البحيرة بنت
السائبة • والوصيلة الشاة اذا اتامت عشر اناث متتابعات في خمسة ابطن ليس
بينهن ذكر جعلت وصيلة قالوا قد وصلت فكان ما ولدت بعد ذلك للذكور منهم
دون اناثهم الا ان يموت منها شي فيشتركوا في اكله ذكورهم واناثهم قال ابن هشام
ويروى ما ولدت بعد ذلك لذكور بنيهم دون بناتهم قال ابن اسحق • والحامي
الفحل اذا نتج له عشر اناث متتابعات ليس بينهن ذكر حمي ظهره فلم يركب ولم
يجز وبره وخلي في ابله يضرب فيها لا ينتفع منه بغير ذلك قال ابن هشام
هذا عند العرب على غير هذا الا الحامي فانه عندهم على ما قال ابن اسحق
والبحيرة عندهم الناقة يشق اذنها فلا يركب ظهرها ولا يجز وبرها ولا يشرب لبنها
الا ضيف ويتصدق به وتهمل لالهتهم وزاد اخرون واذا ادركها كان لم يركبها
والسائبة التي ينذر الرجل ان يسيبها ان برا من مرضه او ان اصاب امرا يطلبه
فاذا كان ذلك اساب ناقة من ابله او جملا لبعض الهتهم فسابت فرعت لا ينتفع ٧٧
بها والوصيلة التي تلد امها اثنين في كل بطن فيجعل صاحبها لالهته الاناث منها ولنفسه
الذكور فتلدها امها ومعها ذكر في بطن فيقولون وصلت اخاها فيسيب اخوها معها

PLATE 6 Istanbul/ Süleymaniye Kütüphanesi, MS Aya Sofya 3365, p. 77

PLATE 7 Cairo/Maktabat al-Azhar, MS Abāẓah 6733, fol. 123a

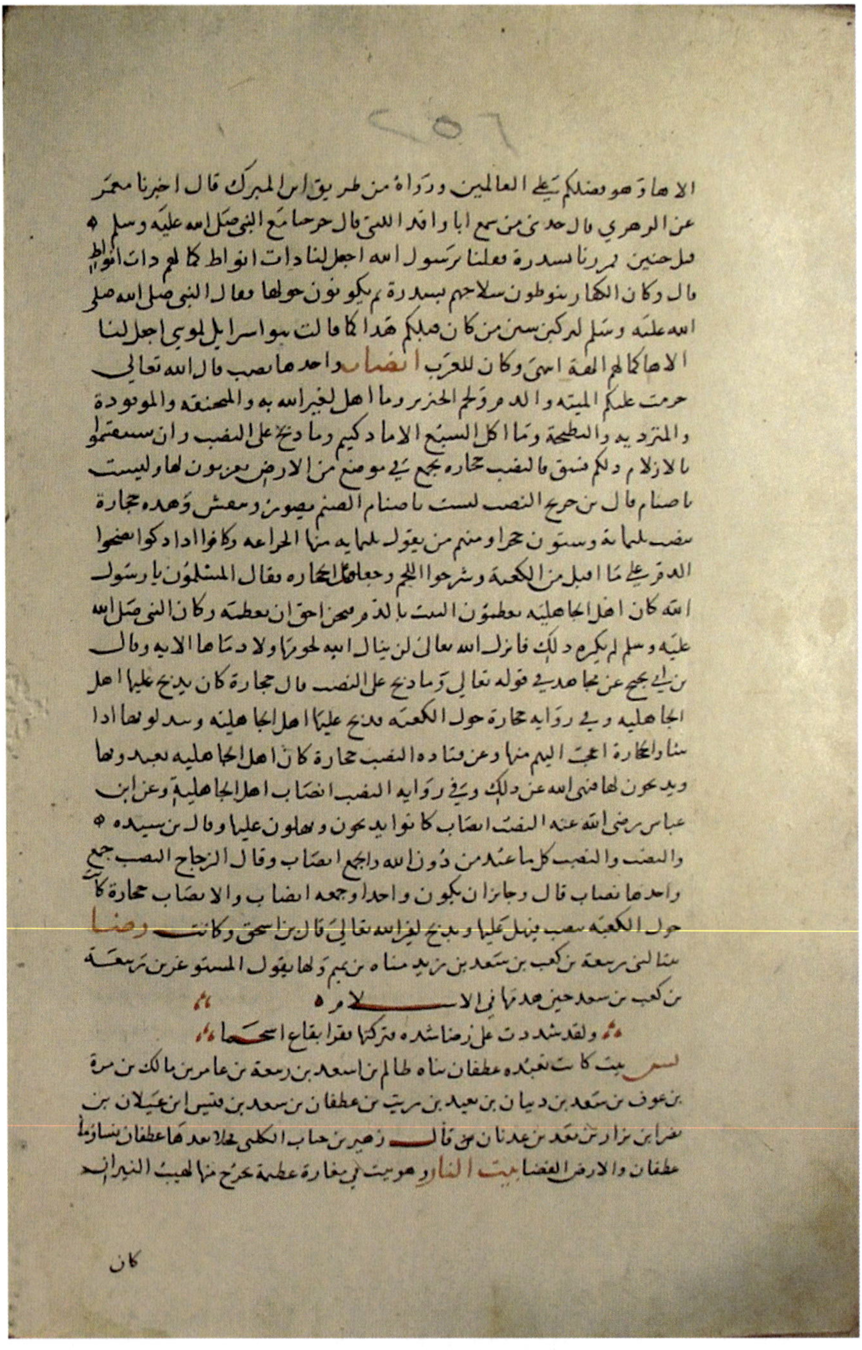

PLATE 8 Cairo/Maktabat al-Azhar, MS Abāẓah 6733, fol. 128b

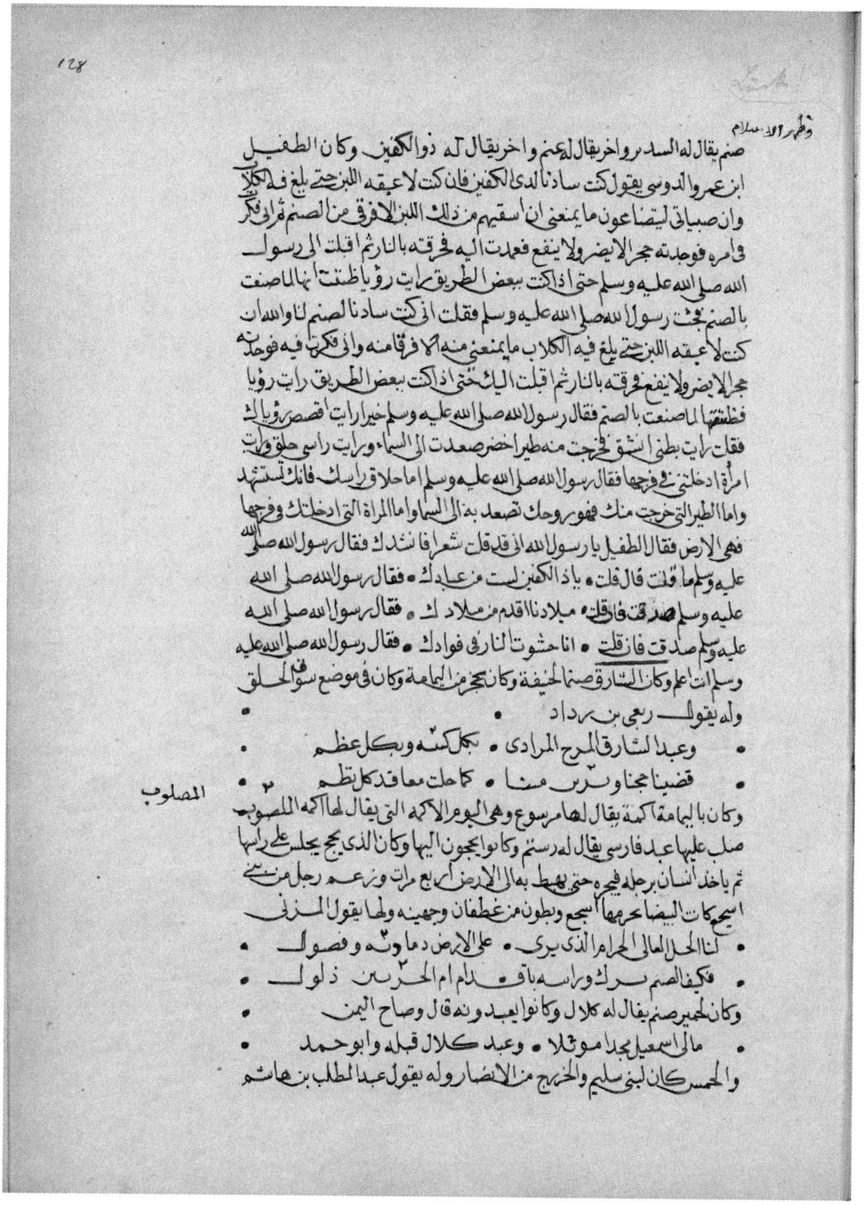
128

وظهر الاسلام

صنم يقال له السدر واخر يقال له عنم واخر يقال له ذو الكفين وكان الطفيل
ابن عمرو الدوسي يقول كنت سادنا لذي الكفين فان كنت لاعبقه اللبن حتى يبلغ فيه الكلاب
وان صبياني ليتضاعون ما يمنعني ان اسقيهم من ذلك اللبن الا فرقي من الصنم ثم اني فكرت
في امره فوجدته حجرا لا يضر ولا ينفع فعمدت اليه فحرقته بالنار ثم اقبلت الى رسول
الله صلى الله عليه وسلم حتى اذا كنت ببعض الطريق رايت رؤيا ظننت انها لما صنعت
بالصنم فجئت رسول الله صلى الله عليه وسلم فقلت اني كنت سادنا لصنم لنا والله ان
كنت لاعبقه اللبن حتى يبلغ فيه الكلاب ما يمنعني منه الا فرقا منه واني فكرت فيه فوجدته
حجرا لا يضر ولا ينفع فحرقته بالنار ثم اقبلت اليك حتى اذا كنت ببعض الطريق رايت رؤيا
فظننتها لما صنعت بالصنم فقال رسول الله صلى الله عليه وسلم خيرا رايت اقصص رؤياك
فقلت رايت بطني انشق فخرجت منه طيرا اخضر صعدت الى السماء ورايت راسي حلق ورايت
امراة ادخلتني في فرجها فقال رسول الله صلى الله عليه وسلم اما حلاق راسك فانك تستشهد
واما الطير التي خرجت منك فهو روحك تصعد به الى السما واما المراة التي ادخلتك في فرجها
فهي الارض فقال الطفيل يا رسول الله اني قد قلت شعرا فانشدك فقال رسول الله صلى الله
عليه وسلم ما قلت قال قلت • يا ذا الكفين لست من عبادك • فقال رسول الله صلى الله
عليه وسلم صدقت فان قلت • ميلادنا اقدم من ميلادك • فقال رسول الله صلى الله
عليه وسلم صدقت فان قلت • انا حشوت النار في فوادك • فقال رسول الله صلى الله عليه
وسلم انت اعلم وكان الشارق صنما لحنيفة وكان بحجر من اليمامة وكان في موضع سوق الحلق
وله يقول ربعي بن رداد • •
• وعبد الشارق المرج المرادي • بكل كسه وبكل عظم •
• قضينا نحبنا وسرين منا • كما حلت معاقد كل نظم •

المصلوب

وكان باليمامة اكمة يقال لها مرسوع وهي اليوم الاكمة التي يقال لها اكمة المصلوب
صلب عليها عبد فارسي يقال له رستم وكانوا يحجون اليها وكان الذي يحج يجلس على راسها
ثم ياخذ انسان برجله فيجره حتى يهبط به الى الارض اربع مرات وزعم رجل من بني
اسحم كانت البيضا بحرمها اسحم وبطون من غطفان وجهينه ولها يقول المزني
• لنا الحل العالي الحرام الذي يرى • على الارض دما دونه وفصول •
• فكيف الصنم سرك وراسه باقدام ام الحرسين ذلول •
وكان لحمير صنم يقال له كلال وكانوا يعبدونه قال وصاح اليمن •
• مالي اسعيل بحدا موثلا • وعبد كلال قبله وابو حمد •
والحمس كان لبني سليم والخزرج من الانصار وله يقول عبد المطلب بن هاشم

PLATE 9 Strasbourg/Bibliothèque nationale et universitaire, MS 4244, fol. 128a

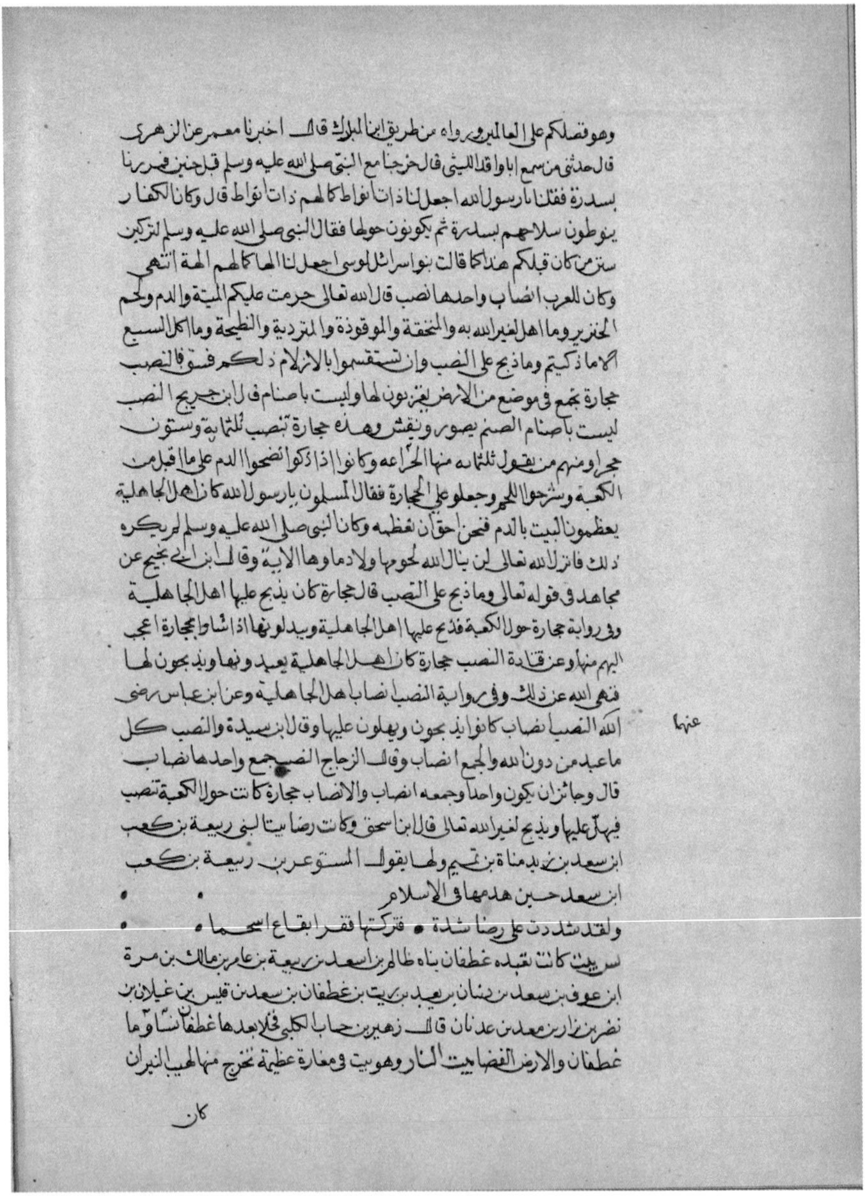

وهو فصلكم على العالمين ورواه من طريق ابن المبارك قال اخبرنا معمر عن الزهري
قال حدثني من سمع ابا واقد الليثي قال خرجنا مع النبي صلى الله عليه وسلم قبل حنين فمررنا
بسدرة فقلنا يا رسول الله اجعل لنا ذات انواط كما لهم ذات انواط قال وكان الكفار
ينوطون سلاحهم بسدرة ثم يكونون حولها فقال النبي صلى الله عليه وسلم لتركبن
سنن من كان قبلكم هذا كما قالت بنو اسرائيل لموسى اجعل لنا الها كما لهم الهة انتهى
وكان للعرب انصاب واحدها نصب قال الله تعالى حرمت عليكم الميتة والدم ولحم
الخنزير وما اهل لغير الله به والمنخنقة والموقوذة والمتردية والنطيحة وما اكل السبع
الا ما ذكيتم وما ذبح على النصب وان تستقسموا بالازلام ذلكم فسق فالنصب
حجارة تجمع في موضع من الارض يعتزبون لها وليست باصنام قال ابن جريج النصب
ليست باصنام الصنم يصور وينقش وهذه حجارة تنصب ثلثمائة وستون
حجرا ومنهم من يقول ثلثمائة منها الخزاعة وكانوا اذا ذكوا نضحوا الدم على ما اقبل من
الكعبة وشرحوا اللحم وجعلوه على الحجارة فقال المسلمون يا رسول الله كان اهل الجاهلية
يعظمون البيت بالدم فنحن احق ان نعظمه وكان النبي صلى الله عليه وسلم لم يكره
ذلك فانزل الله تعالى لن ينال الله لحومها ولا دماوها الاية وقال ابن ابي نجيح عن
مجاهد في قوله تعالى وما ذبح على النصب قال حجارة كان يذبح عليها اهل الجاهلية
وفي رواية حجارة حول الكعبة فذبح عليها اهل الجاهلية ويبدلونها اذا شاوا بحجارة اعجب
اليهم منها وعن قتادة النصب حجارة كان اهل الجاهلية يعبدونها ويذبحون لها
فنهى الله عن ذلك وفي رواية النصب انصاب اهل الجاهلية وعن ابن عباس رضي
الله عنهما النصب انصاب كانوا يذبحون ويهلون عليها وقال ابن سيدة والنصب كل
ما عبد من دون الله والجمع انصاب وقال الزجاج النصب جمع واحدها نصاب
قال وجائز ان يكون واحدا وجمعه انصاب والانصاب حجارة كانت حول الكعبة تنصب
فيهل عليها ويذبح لغير الله تعالى قال ابن اسحق وكانت رضا بيتا لبني ربيعة بن كعب
ابن سعد بن زيد مناة بن تميم ولها يقول المستوغر بن ربيعة بن كعب
ابن سعد حين هدمها في الاسلام
ولقد شددت على رضا شدة • فتركتها قفرا بقاع اسحما •
بس بيت كانت تعبده غطفان بناه ظالم بن اسعد بن ربيعة بن عامر بن مالك بن مرة
ابن عوف بن سعد بن ذبيان بن بغيض بن ريث بن غطفان بن سعد بن قيس بن عيلان بن
نضر بن نزار بن معد بن عدنان قال زهير بن جناب الكلبي فخلا بعدها غطفان نساء وما
غطفان والارض الفضا بيت للنار وهو بيت في مغارة عظيمة تخرج منها لهيب النيران
كان

PLATE 10 Strasbourg/Bibliothèque nationale et universitaire, MS 4244, fol. 133b

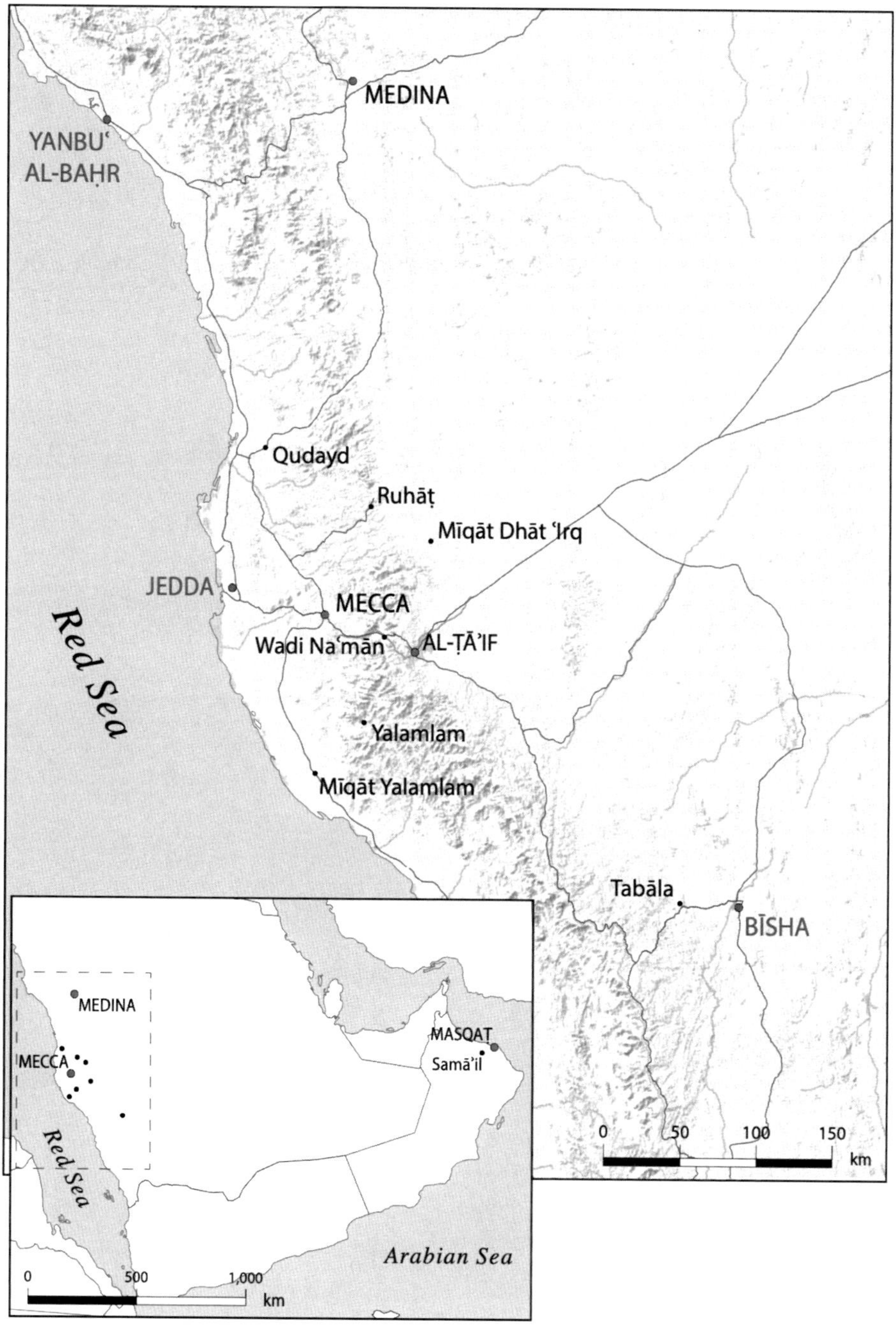

MAP 1 Location map of several Arabian idols

Abbreviations and Symbols

⟨…⟩	Interpolation (Arabic text)
{…}	Correction
[…]	Word(s) to be overlooked (Arabic text); interpolation (translation)
(…)	Blank in the MS
|	Used in the Arabic text to indicate the passage to the next folio (number indicated in the left margin)
الأصل	Istanbul, Süleymaniye Kütüphanesi, MS Fatih 4339

Text and Translation

of al-Maqrīzī's

al-Ḫabar ʿan al-bašar

كتاب الخبر عن البشر

The History of Mankind
Volume IV, Section 2
The Idols of the Arabs

∵

فصل في ذكر أصنام العرب وأوثانها

§1 قال ابن سيدة في **كتاب المحكم**: الصنم معروف وهو ينحت من خشب ويصاغ من فضة ونحاس والجمع أصنام. قال: والوَثَن الصنم الصغير والجمع أوثان وَوُثُن وأُثْن على إبدال الهمزة من الواو انتهى.[a] وقال السهيلي: يقال لكل صنم من حجر أو غيره صنم ولا يقال وثن إلا لما كان من غير صخرة كالنحاس ونحوه.

§2 وقال أبو علي القالي: الزُوْر والزُوْن كل ما يعبد ويتخذ ربا.[b]

قال ابن دريد: الزُوْن والزُوْنة بيت الأصنام يتخذ ويُزَين[c] والزُوْنة كالزينة. يقال: هذه زينة وزُوْنة.[d]

---

١ ذكر: الزيادة بخط المقريزي في الهامش الأيمن من الأعلى إلى الأسفل + صح، ويشير إليها رمز ⌐ بعد "في".
٢.62–٤ وقال ... المشركين: الزيادة بخط المقريزي في الهامش الأيمن من الأعلى إلى الأسفل ثم في الهامش الأسفل من الأسفل إلى الأعلى ويشير إليها رمز ⌐ بعد "انتهى".

---

a قارن ابن سيدة، المحكم، ١٠: ٢١٦ ("وَالْوَثَنُ: الصَّنَمُ ما كانَ. وقِيلَ: الصَّنَمُ الصَّغيرُ. والجَمعُ: أَوْثانٌ. ووُثُنٌ، ووُثْنٌ، وأُثُنٌ، على إِبْدالِ الهَمْزَةِ مِن الواو. وقد قُرِئَ: ﴿إِنْ يَدْعُونَ من دُونِهِ إِلَّا أُثُنًا﴾. حَكاهُ سِيبَوَيْهِ").

b راجع القالي، كتاب الأمالي، ٢: ٢٠٥.

c راجع ابن منظور، لسان العرب، "زون" ("والزُّون: الصنم، وكل ما عُبد من دون الله واتُّخذ إلهًا فهو زُونٌ وزُور"). وراجع أيضا ابن منظور، لسان العرب، "زين" ("والزُّونُ موضع تجمع فيه الأَصنام وتُنْصَبُ وتُزَيَّنُ. والزُّونُ: كل شيء يتخذ رَبًّا ويعبد من دون الله عزّ وجلّ لأَنه يُزَيَّنُ، والله أَعلم").

d راجع ابن دريد، جمهرة اللغة، ٢: ٨٣٠؛ وراجع أيضا ابن منظور، لسان العرب، "زون" ("والزُّونَةُ: كالزِّينة في بعض اللغات").

Section on the idols of the Arabs [their *aṣnām* and *awṯān*][1]

§1 Ibn Sīdah[2] said in *Kitāb al-Muḥkam*:[3] *Ṣanam* is a well-known thing. It is carved from wood, made of molten and cast silver and copper [or brass],[4] and its plural is *aṣnām*. *Waṯan* is a small *ṣanam*, and its plural forms are *awṯān*, *wuṯun*, and *uṯn* [or *uṯun*], where [i.e. in the plural form *uṯn* / *uṯun*] the *hamzah* is a substitute for a *wāw*. Unquote. Al-Suhaylī[5] said: Any idol made of stone (*ḥağar*) or other material is called a *ṣanam*. [The word] *waṯan* applies only to something which was made of [material] other than stone (*ṣaḫrah*), such as copper and the like.[6]

§2 Abū ʿAlī l-Qālī[7] said: *Zūr* and *zūn* are anything that is worshipped and taken as a lord.

Ibn Durayd[8] said: *Zūn* and *zūnah* are "a sanctuary of idols" (*bayt al-aṣnām*) which is taken and adorned.[9] *Zūnah* has the same meaning as *zīnah*. It is said: This is [both] a *zīnah* and a *zūnah* [i.e. the meaning of the two words is similar].

---

1 The distinction between the words *waṯan* and *ṣanam* is far from clear; see Guillaume (1964): 430.

2 For more on the Andalusian philologist and lexicographer Abū l-Ḥasan ʿAlī b. Ismāʿīl (d. 458/1066), known as Ibn Sīdah, see "Ibn Sīda," in *EI*² (M. Talbi).

3 *Al-Muḥkam wa-l-muḥīṭ al-aʿẓam* [The Greatest Masterful and Comprehensive (Dictionary)] is one of Ibn Sīdah's two important dictionaries. The other is *al-Muḫaṣṣaṣ*; "Ibn Sīda," in *EI*² (M. Talbi).

4 See also Lane (1863–1893): 1735: "a thing well known, that is carved of wood, and that is made of molten and cast silver and copper or brass."

5 Abū l-Qāsim ʿAbd al-Raḥmān b. ʿAbd Allāh al-Suhaylī (d. 581/1185), an Andalusian scholar whose famous work *al-Rawḍ al-unuf* is a commentary on Ibn Hišām's biography of the Prophet; see "al-Suhaylī," in *EI*² (W. Raven).

6 See also Guillaume (1964): 430.

7 For more Abū ʿAlī Ismāʿīl b. al-Qāsim al-Qālī (d. 356/967), whose best known work is *Kitāb al-Amālī*, see "al-Ḳālī," in *EI*² (R. Sellheim).

8 Abū Bakr Muḥammad b. al-Ḥasan of the Azd ʿUmān (d. 321/933) was a philologist and lexicographer whose works include *al-Ğamharah*, *al-Ištiqāq*, *al-Malāḥin*, and others; "Ibn Durayd," in *EI*² (J.W. *Fück*).

9 See the definitions of the word *zūn* in Ibn Manẓūr, *Lisān al-ʿarab*, s.v. *zūn* and Yāqūt, *Muʿğam al-buldān*, 3:159 (see also the introduction, note 100).

وقال المبرد: قال ابن عباس في قوله تعالى ﴿وَٱلَّذِينَ لَا يَشْهَدُونَ ٱلزُّورَ﴾، قال: هي أعياد المشركين.[a]

§3 وقد قيل إن أصل وضع الأصنام في أول الدهر كان في عهد {مهلائيل} بن قينان بن أنوش ابن شيث بن آدم وقيل إنما أخذ عن عاذيمون وهو عند الصابئة شيث بن آدم وعن هرمس الأول وهو عندهم إدريس.[b] قالوا: وإدريس أول من تكلم في الجواهر العلوية والحركات النجومية وبنى الهياكل ومجد الله تعالى فيها. قالوا: ولما علمنا أن للعالم صانعا مقدسا عن سِماتِ الحُدوث وجب

٣-٤ الدهر ... آدم : الزيادة بخط المقريزي في الهامش الأيسر في آخر السطر. ٣ مهلائيل : في الأصل: "مهلايل". ٤ وقيل إنما : كشط المقريزي عبارة أخرى قبل أن يصححها كما هي الآن. ٥ وبنى : في الأصل "وبنا".

a راجع المبرد، الكامل، ٣: ١٨١؛ وقارن ابن منظور، لسان العرب، "زور" ("وزَوَّرَ الشهادة: أبطلها، ومن ذلك قوله تعالى ﴿وَالَّذِينَ لَا يَشْهَدُونَ الزُّورَ﴾ قال ثعلب: الزُّورُ ههنا مجالس اللهو. قال ابن سيده: ولا أَدري كيف هذا إلا أَن يريد بمجالس اللهو هنا الشرك بالله، وقيل: أَعياد النصارى، كلاهما عن الزجاج، قال: والذي جاء في الرواية الشرك، وهو جامع لأَعياد النصارى وغيرها، قال: وقيل الزّورُ هنا مجالس الغِنَاء"). وراجع أيضا القرطبي، الجامع، ١٣: ٧٩ ("قوله تعالى: ﴿وَالَّذِينَ لَا يَشْهَدُونَ الزُّورَ﴾ أي لا يحضرون الكذب والباطل ولا يشاهدونه. والزور كل باطل زُوّر وزُخرِف، وأعظمه الشرك وتعظيم الأنداد. وبه فسر الضحاك وابن زيد وابن عباس. وفي رواية عن ابن عباس أنه أعياد المشركين").

b قارن الدمشقي، نخبة الدهر، ٤٤ ("وقيل إنّ الصابئة قسمان أحدهما القائلون بالهياكل وهم عبدة الكواكب والآخرون القائلون بالأشخاص وهم عبدة الأصنام فأما القائلون بالهياكل فإنهم يزعمون أنهم أخذوا ذلك عن عاديمون وهو شيث النبي عم وعاديمون أخذه عن أخنوخ وهو هرمس الهرامسة هذا زعمهم الباطل"). وقارن أيضا المقريزي، الخطط، ١: ٦١٧ ("ويُقالُ إنَّ الصَّابِئَةَ أَخَذَت هذه الهَياكِلَ عن عادٍ وثمُود (!) ويَزْعُمون أنَّه عن شيث بن آدم، وعن هِرْمس الأوّل—وهو إدريس").

Al-Mubarrad[10] said: Ibn ʿAbbās[11] said regarding His [Allāh's] saying, the Exalted, "And those who bear not false witness (*al-zūr*),"[12] [that the word *zūr*] means the festivals of the polytheists.

§ 3 It was said that the origin of the making of idols at the beginning of time was during the period of Mahlāʾīl b. Qaynān [Cainan] b. Anūš [Enosh] b. Šīṯ [Seth] b. Ādam. Others said that it [i.e. idolatry][13] was acquired from ʿĀḏīmūn [Agathadaimon], who is Seth b. Adam, according to the Sabians, and from Hermes the First, who is Idrīs[14] according to their view.[15] They said: Idrīs was the first to speak about celestial substances and the movements of the stars, and the first to build temples in which he praised Allāh, the Exalted. They said: When we learned that the world has a Creator who is sanctified beyond the characteristics of temporal origination, it was inev-

10 The Basran philologist al-Mubarrad (d. 286/900) was the compiler of *al-Kāmil fī l-adab*, *al-Fāḍil*, *al-Muqtaḍab*, and others; "al-Mubarrad," in EI² (R. Sellheim).

11 ʿAbd Allāh b. al-ʿAbbās (d. ca. 68/686–688) was a well-known scholar and Qurʾān commentator of the first generation of Islam; "ʿAbdallāh b. ʿAbbās," in EI³ (C. Gilliot).

12 Qurʾān (*al-Furqān*), 25:72; I have used Arberry's translation throughout, with some minor changes.

13 But cf. al-Dimašqī, *Nuḫbat al-dahr* 44. See also Green (1992): 117: "Dimashqi, for example, posited two different kinds of Sabians: those who acknowledge the cult of the celestial mansions (i.e., worship the stars), and those who believe in idols. The former asserted that they had acquired this doctrine from Agathadaimon or Seth the prophet, the son of Adam."

14 Idrīs, who is often identified with Enoch (Aḫnūḫ), is mentioned twice in the Qurʾān as a righteous man who was a prophet; "Idrīs," in EI² (G. Vajda).

15 Compare al-Dimašqī, *Nuḫbat al-dahr* 44: "They acquired this [doctrine] from ʿĀḏīmūn, who is Seth the prophet, and ʿĀḏīmūn acquired it from Aḫnūḫ, who is Hermes." See also Chwolson (1856), 2:398.

علينا العجز عن إدراك جلاله فتقربنا إليه بالمقَرَبينَ لديه وهم الروحانيون يعنون الملائكة ليكونوا لنا شُفَعاء ووسائط عنده.[a]

§4 قالوا: وهؤلاء الروحانيون هم الكواكب السبعة السيارة وهي زُحَل والمشْتَري والمرّيخ والشمس والزُهْرة وعطارد والقمر. قالوا: وأفلاك هذه الكواكب هي هياكلها فلكل روحاني هيكل ولكل هيكل فلك فنِسْبَة الروحاني إلى الهيكل نسبة الرُوْح إلى الجَسَد. قالوا: ولا بُد للمتوسِط من أن يُرَى فيتوجه إليه ويُسْتَفاد منه[b] فلذلك فزعنا إلى الهياكل التي هي السَيَّارَات السَبْع فعرفنا

---

٣ زُحَل: وضع المقريزي رمز "ح" تحت الكلمة إشارة إلى تلفظها بالحاء. ٤ روحاني: وضع المقريزي رمز "ح" تحت الكلمة إشارة إلى تلفظها بالحاء. ٥ الروحاني: وضع المقريزي رمز "ح" تحت الكلمة إشارة إلى تلفظها بالحاء.

---

a راجع الشهرستاني، الملل والنحل، ٢٠٣ ("ومذهب هؤلا: أن للعالم صانعًا فاطرًا حكيما، مقدّسًا عن سمات الحدثان والواجب علينا معرفة العجز عن الوصول إلى جلاله وإنما يتقرب إليه بالمتوسطات المقربين لديه وهم الروحانيون المطهرون المقدسون جوهراً وفعلًا وحالة"). وراجع أيضا ابن الأثير، الكامل في التاريخ²، ١: ٥٤-٥٥ ("فإن أصل مذهب الصابئين عبادة الروحانيين وهم الملائكة لتقربهم إلى الله تعالى زُلْفى، فإنهم اعترفوا بصانع العالم وأنه حكيم قادر مقدس إلا أنهم قالوا: الواجب علينا معرفة العجز عن الوصول إلى معرفة جلاله، وإنما نتقرب إليه بالوسائط المقربة لديه، وهم الروحانيون وحيث لم يعاينوا الروحانيين تقربوا إليهم بالهياكل وهي الكواكب السبعة السيارة لأنها مدبرة لهذا العالم عندهم ثم ذهبت طائفة منهم وهم أصحاب الأشخاص، حيث رأوا أن الهياكل تطلع وتغرب وترى ليلًا ولا ترى نهارًا إلى وضع الأصنام لتكون نصب أعينهم ليتوسلوا بها إلى الهياكل، والهياكل إلى الروحانيين، والروحانيون إلى صانع العالم. فهذا كان أصل وضع الأصنام أولا، وقد كان أخيرا في العرب من هو على هذا الاعتقاد").

b راجع المقريزي، الخطط، ١: ٦١٨ ("وزَعموا أنّه لا بدَّ من رُؤْية المُتَوَسِّط بين العِباد وبين بارِئِهم حتى يَتَوَجَّه إليه العَبْدُ بنَفْسه، ويستفيد منه").

itable that we would be rendered incapable of grasping His glory. We therefore sought His nearness by means of those who are drawn near to Him (*bi-l-muqarrabīna ladayhi*), namely, spiritual beings (*rūḥāniyyūna*)—i.e. angels (*malāʾikah*)[16]—so that they would be our intercessors and mediators before Him.

§ 4 They said: These spiritual beings are the seven planets,[17] namely, Saturn, Jupiter, Mars, the Sun, Venus, Mercury, and the Moon. They said: The spheres of these planets are their temples. Each spiritual being has a temple, and each temple has a sphere. The relation of the spiritual being with the temple is like that of the spirit with the body.[18] They said: The mediator must be seen and addressed, and one ought to benefit from it. Therefore, we sought protection at the temples, which are the seven planets. We became familiar

16 Note that the phrase *al-malāʾikah al-muqarrabūna* appears in Qurʾān (*al-Nisāʾ*), 4:172.

17 *Al-Kawākib al-sabʿah al-sayyārah* ("the seven wandering stars"); see "Zuḥal," in EI^2 (W. Hartner-[F.J. Ragep]).

18 See also Corbin (1986): 139.

بيوتها ومطالعها ومغاربها واتصالاتها الموافقة والمخالفة وما لها من الأيام وسَاعَاتها وما لها من الصُوَر والأشخاص والأقاليم. وسموا هذه السَبْعَة أرْبابا وآلهَةً.[a]

§5 وقالوا إن الله إلاه الآلهة ورب الأرباب وغلا بعضهم وهم جمهورهم فقالوا إنما رب الأرباب وإلاه الآلهة الشمس لأنها المُفِيْضَة أنوارها على الباقين وهي المُظْهرة آثارها فيهم. وعلى هذا كان القوم الذين بعث الله فيهم نوحا ثم إبرٰهيم عليهما السلام وعلى هذا القول منهم حاجهم | إبرٰهيم عليه 30b السلام وأثبت أن فوق الشمس قوة قاهرة للكل فكان من شأنه وشأنهم ما تقدم ذكره في أخبار إبرٰهيم عليه السلام.

§6 وكان القوم يتقربون إلى الهياكل تقربا إلى الروحانيين لتقربهم إلى البارئ تعالى لاعتقادهم أن الهياكل أبدان الروحانيين. قالوا: ومن تقرب إلى شخص فقد تقرب إلى روحه. فلما أصلوا هذا الاعتقاد بنوا اثني عشر هيكلا وهي هيكل العلة الأولى وهيكل العقل وهيكل السياسة[b] وهيكل الصُورَة[c] وهيكل النفس وكانت هذه الهياكل الخمسة كلها مُسْتَدِيْرة وهيكل زحل وهو مُسَدَّس وهيكل المشتري وهو مُثَلَّث وهيكل المريخ وهو مُرَبَّع وهيكل الشمس وهو مُربع أيضا وهيكل

١ وما ... من: الزيادة بخط المقريزي في الهامش الأيسر + صح، ويشير إليها رمز ⌐ بعد "وسَاعَاتها". ٥ منهم: الزيادة بخط المقريزي في الهامش الأيسر + صح، ويشير إليها رمز ⌐ بعد "القول". ‖ حاجهم: وضع المقريزي رمز "ح" تحت الكلمة إشارة إلى تلفظها بالحاء. ٦–٧ في ... السلام: الزيادة بخط المقريزي في الهامش الأيمن + صح، ويشير إليها رمز ⌐ بعد "ذكره". ١١ زحل: وضع المقريزي رمز "ح" تحت الكلمة إشارة إلى تلفظها بالحاء.

a قارن الشهرستاني، الملل والنحل، ٢٤٤ ("اعلم ان أصحاب الروحانيات لما عرفوا أن لا بد للانسان من متوسط ولا بد للمتوسط من أن يرى فيتوجه إليه ويتقرب به ويستفاد منه فزعوا إلى الهياكل التي هي السيارات السبع فتعرّفوا أوَّلا بيوتها ومنازلها وثانيًا مطالعها ومغاربها وثالثًا اتصالاتها على اشكال الموافقة والمخالفة مرتبة على طبائعها ورابعًا تقسيم الايام والليالي والساعات عليها وخامسًا تقدير الصور والاشخاص والاقاليم والامصار عليها").

b قارن الرازي، مفاتيح الغيب، ٢: ١٢٤ ("وهيكل السياسة المطلقة").

c قارن المسعودي، مروج الذهب، ٢: ٣٩١ ("ومن هياكل الصابية هيكل السياسة وهيكل الضرورة").

with their houses,[19] their rising and setting points,[20] their conjunctions and oppositions,[21] their days and their hours,[22] and their figures, representations,[23] and climes. They called these seven [planets] lords and gods.

§ 5 They said that Allāh is the God of gods and the Lord of lords. Some of them—who were in fact the majority—were extreme [in their belief], and said that the Lord of lords and the God of gods is the Sun, since it pours its light on those who remain [i.e. all living beings] and leaves its traces on them.[24] These were the beliefs of the people among whom Allāh sent Noah and then Abraham, may peace be upon them, and it was in relation to their saying that Abraham, may peace be upon him, argued with them, and asserted that there is a power above the sun which overcomes all. His story and theirs have already been mentioned in [the chapter titled] "The Traditions of Abraham, May Peace Be upon Him."[25]

§ 6 The people wanted to be close to the temples out of desire to be close to the spiritual beings, since they [the spiritual beings] were close to the Creator, the Exalted. [The people did this] because they believed that the temples are the bodies of the spiritual beings. They said: Whoever draws near a person draws near his spirit. Having firmly established this belief, they built twelve temples: The temple of the first cause, the temple of intelligence, the temple of world order, the temple of the form, the temple of the soul (all five of which were circular), Saturn's temple (hexagonal), Jupiter's temple (triangular), Mars's temple (a square), the Sun's temple (also a square), Venus's

19 Compare al-Šahrastānī, *al-Milal wa-l-niḥal* 244: *buyūtahā wa-manāzilahā* ("their houses and stations").

20 See "al-Maṭla'," in *EI*² (D.A. King).

21 Compare al-Šahrastānī, *al-Milal wa-l-niḥal* 244: *ittiṣālātihā 'alá aškāli l-muwāfaqah wa-l-muḫālafah*. See also Chwolson (1856): 2:407: "ihre Verbindungen nach den Formen der Conjunctionen und Oppositionen."

22 Compare al-Šahrastānī, *al-Milal wa-l-niḥal* 244: "the division of days, nights, and hours in them."

23 See "Ṣābi'a," in *EI*² (T. Fahd): "whence the necessity to have 'figures and representations' (*ṣuwar wa-ashkhāṣ*) by which the 'temples' may be reached and thereby the 'spiritual beings.'" And see Corbin (1986): 144: "The Sabians already descend from the order of pure spiritual beings (*rūḥānīyūn*) to the material Temples (*hayākil*) which are their personal Figurations (*ashkhāṣ*)."

24 Lit. "Makes its effects visible upon them."

25 Al-Maqrīzī deals with Abraham in the last volume (the sixth) of *al-Ḫabar 'an al-bašar*; this follows the section on idols. This may indicate that al-Maqrīzī changed his mind with regard to the internal organization of the work.

الزهرة وهو مثلث مستطيل في جوف مُربع وهيكل عطارد وهو مُثلث في جوف مربع مستطيل وهيكل القمر وهو مثمن.

§7 وكانت أصنامهم في هذه الهياكل ولها صَلَوات يُصَلونها لكل كوكب من السبعة يوم مخصوص يزعمون أنه رَب ذلك اليوم وتكون صلاتهم في ذلك اليوم ثلاث مرات عند طلوع الشمس وعند زوالها وعند غُروبها[a] فيصلون لزحل يوم السبت ويُصلون للمشتري يوم الأحد ويصلون للمريخ يوم الاثنين ويصلون للشمس يوم الثلاثاء ويصلون للزهرة يوم الأربعاء ويصلون لعطارد يوم الخميس ويصلون للقمر يوم الجمعة.

§8 وزعموا أن الكعبة البيت الحرام هيكل زحل وبهذا طال بقاؤه على مر الدهور وكر العصور لأن من شأن زحل الثبات.[b]

§9 وكان ببلخ نوبهار بناه منوشجهر أحد ملوك الطبقة الأولى من الفرس على اسم القمر[c] ليضاهي به الكعبة وجعل حوله الأصنام وألبسوه الحرير وعظموه وحجوا إليه من الآفاق كما تحج العرب

---

١١ الأصنام: زاد المقريزي هذه الكلمة فوق السطر. ١١–١.٧٠ وعظموه ... الكعبة: الزيادة بخط المقريزي في الهامش الأيمن + صح، ويشير إليها رمز ⌐ بعد "الحرير".

---

a قارن المقريزي، الخطط، ١: ٦١٨ ("وكانوا يُصَلُّون لكلِّ كَوْكَبٍ يومًا يَزْعمون أنَّه رَبّ ذلك اليوم، وكانت صَلاتُهم في ثلاثة أَوْقات: الأُولى عند طُلوع الشَّمْس، والثانية عند اسْتِوائها في الفَلَك، والثالثة عند غُروبِها").

b راجع المسعودي، مروج الذهب، ٢: ٣٨٠ ("وقد ذهب قوم منهم إلى أن البيت الحرام هو بيت زُحَل وإنَّما طال عندهم بقاء هذا البيت على مرور الدهور معظَّمًا في سائر الأعصار لأنَّه بيت زُحَل وأن زُحَل تولَّاه لأنَّ زحل من سأنه البقاء والثبوت، فما كان له فغيرُ زائل ولا داثر وعن التعظيم غير حائل").

c راجع المقريزي، الخطط، ١: ٦٢٠ ("ويُقالُ إنَّه كان للكواكِب السَّبْعَة السَّيَّارَة هياكِل، يَحُجُّ الناسُ إليها من سائرِ أَقْطار الدنيا، وَضَعَها القُدَماء، فجَعَلوا على اسْمِ كلِّ كَوْكَب هَيْكَلًا في ناحية من نواحي الأرض").

temple (an elongated triangle within a square),[26] Mercury's temple (a triangle within a rectangle), and the Moon's temple (an octagon).[27]

§ 7 The idols were in these temples, and [the people] recited prayers for them [for the idols]. Each of the seven planets was assigned one day, and they claimed that it [that planet] is the lord of that day.[28] During that day, they prayed three times: At sunrise, as the sun declined, and at sunset. They prayed to Saturn on Saturday, to Jupiter on Sunday, to Mars on Monday, to the Sun on Tuesday, to Venus on Wednesday, to Mercury on Thursday, and to the Moon on Friday.

§ 8 They claimed that the Kaʿbah, [which is] the Sacred House, is the temple of Saturn, and that this is the reason it survived the course of time and the periods, [i.e.] because Saturn is characterized by stability.

§ 9 The Nawbahār was in Balḫ.[29] Manūčihr,[30] one of the kings of the first dynasty of the Persians, built it as a dedication to the moon, [and sought] to rival the Kaʿbah with it [the Nawbahār]. He placed idols around it, and they put silk cloth on it, venerated it, and made pilgrimage[s] to it from

---

26 The "elongated triangle" (*muṯallaṯ mustaṭīl*) may refer to an isosceles triangle.

27 See also Chwolson (1856), 2:367; Corbin (1986): 140.

28 See also Corbin (1986): 140: "Each of these Temples was used, on the day especially consecrated to the star in question, for the performance of liturgy involving garnments whose colour corresponed to the planet, during which incense was burned in conformity with the importance which Sabians attached to the rite of perfumes."

29 The word derives from *nōva vihāra* ("new monastery") in Sanskrit; "al-Barāmika," in *EI*^{2} (W. Barthold [D. Sourdel]).

30 On Manūčihr, see Yarshater (2008), 3:433–434.

إلى الكعبة[a] إلى أن دانت الفرس بالمجوسية عملوه بيت نار. وقيل لسَادِنه ومتولي حجابته برمكا. وإنما سموه بهذا الاسم لأنهم شبهوا بيتهم بمكة فقالوا أَبْرَمكا وتفسيره والي مكة فصار من ولي ذلك يسمى بَرْمَكا.[b]

§10 وكانت ملوك الفرس من الأكاسرة وكابل شاه وملك السند وخراسان تدين بذاك الدين وتحج ذلك البيت فكانوا إذا حجوا إليه سجدوا له تعظيما له ثم قبلوا يد برمك وجعلوا لبرمك ما حول النوبهار من الأرضين وغير ذلك.[c] فلم يزل القائم بأمره وسدانته برمك بعد برمك ولهم أسماء بالعجمية سوى برمك حتى فتحت خراسان في خلافة عثمٰن رضي الله عنه صلحا وقد صارت البرمكة إلى برمك الأكبر أبي برمك الأصغر فوجه في الرهائن إلى عثمٰن وصارت البرمكة إلى بعض | ولده. 31a

---

١-٣ ومتولي ... بَرْمَكا: الزيادة بخط المقريزي في الهامش الأسفل+ صح. ١ برمكا: كذا في الأصل بدلا من "برمك". ٢ أَبْرمكا: وضع المقريزي الهمزة فوق الألف. ٤ وكانت ... شاه: كشط المقريزي جملة أخرى قبل أن يصححها كما هي الآن ونهاية الكلام في الهامش الأيسر. ٤-٩ وخراسان ... بعض: الزيادة بخط المقريزي في الهامش الأيسر من الأسفل إلى الأعلى، ثم في الهامش الأعلى من الأعلى إلى الأسفل + صح. ٩ ولده: كشط المقريزي كلمة أخرى (يظهر من التعقيبة في الصفحة المقبلة أن هذه الكلمة كانت "خالد") قبل أن يصححها كما هي الآن.

---

a راجع ياقوت، معجم البلدان، ٥: ٣٠٧ ("نُوبَهارُ ... ونوبَهار أيضًا: ببلْخ بناء للبرامكة، قال عمر بن الأزرق الكرماني: كانت البرامكة أهل شرف على وجه الدهر ببلخ قبل ملوك الطوائف وكان دينهم عبادة الأوثان فوُصفت لهم مكة وحالُ الكعبة بها وما كانت قريش ومن والاها من العرب يأتون إليها ويعظمونها فاتخذوا بيت النوبَهار مضاهاة لبيت الله الحرام ونصبوا حوله الأصنام وزينوه بالديباج والحرير وعلّقوا عليه الجواهر النفيسة").

b قارن المقريزي، الخطط، ١: ٦١٩ ("ويُقالُ إنَّه كان ببلْخ هَيْكَلٌ بَناه بنو حِمْيَر (!) على اسم القَمَر لتُعارِض به الكَعْبَة، فكانَت الفُرْس تَحُجّه وتَكْسُوه الحرير، وكان اسْمُه نُوبَهَار. فلما تَمَجَّسَت الفُرْس عَمِلَته بيْت نار، وقيل للمُوكَّل بسدانَتِه بَرْمَك—يعني والي مكّة").

c قارن ابن الفقيه، مختصر كتاب البلدان، ٣٢٣ ("وكانت ملوك الصين وكابل شاه تدين بذلك الدين فكانوا إذا حجوا سجدوا للصنم الأكبر فصيروا للبرمك ما حول النوبهار من الأرضين وسبع مائة سيب ماء ورُزْداقا بطخارسان يقال له زُونن ثمانية فراسخ في اربعة فراسخ").

distant lands, as the Arabs make pilgrimage[s] to the Kaʿbah. When the Persians adopted Zoroastrianism, they made it a fire temple.[31] Its custodian and guardian was called Barmak. They gave him this name only because they likened their sanctuary to Mecca. Thus, they said "*abar Makā*,"[32] which means "in charge of Mecca," and the person who was assigned that [office] came to be called Barmak.[33]

§10 The Kisrá kings of the Persians,[34] the Kābul Šāh, and the king of al-Sind and Ḫurāsān followed that religion and made pilgrimage[s] to that sanctuary. When they made pilgrimage[s] to it, they bowed down to it[35] as a sign of reverence, and then kissed Barmak's hand, and granted him the lands around the Nawbahār and other things. They remained responsible for its state and custodianship, one Barmak after another[36] (they had Iranian names besides Barmak), until Ḫurāsān was taken peacefully during the caliphate of ʿUṯmān,[37] may Allāh be pleased with him. The Barmak position had passed to Barmak al-Akbar ["Barmak the elder"],[38] who was the father of Barmak al-Aṣġar ["Barmak the younger"], but he was sent to ʿUṯmān among [other] hostages,[39] and the Barmak position passed to one of his sons.

---

31 Cf. "al-Barāmika," in *EI*² (W. Barthold [D. Sourdel]): "The later authors, who make this sanctuary a Zoroastrian Fire-Temple, were doubtless influenced by the tradition which envisaged the Barmakids as the descendants of the ministers of the Sāsānid Empire." See also Bosworth (1994): 271, n. 21.

32 The Middle Persian word *abar* means "on." In other sources, this phrase, which was meaningless to the copyists, was changed to *bāb Makkah* (the gate of Mecca) or *Ibn Makkah* (the son of Mecca); van Bladel (2010): 64, n. 92. And see also p. 68: "the title of the custodian, Barmak, is interpreted in the text by a tendentious folk etymology to prove that the Nawbahār was a pious and well-intended imitation of Mecca."

33 According to other explanations, Barmak originates from the Sanskrit word *pramukha*, which means "chief," or *paramaka*, which means "supreme"; "Barmakids," in *EI*³ (K. van Bladel).

34 Kisrá (pl. Akāsirah) is the title given in Islamic literature to the Sāsānid rulers (compare with Pharaoh and Negus); see "Kisrā," in *EI*² (M. Morony).

35 In other sources, it is said that they bowed down to "the greatest idol"; see Yāqūt, *Muʿǧam al-buldān*, 5:308; Ibn al-Faqīh, *Muḫtaṣar Kitāb al-Buldān* 323.

36 Lit. "Barmak after Barmak."

37 ʿUṯmān b. ʿAffān, the third of the rightly-guided caliphs (r. 23–35/644–655).

38 Barmak al-Akbar can be identified with the grandfather of Ḫālid b. Barmak; see van Bladel (2010): 63, n. 84, and 65, n. 97. For more on Ḫālid b. Barmak (d. 165/781–782), who participated in the ʿAbbāsid revolution, and received various appointments from al-Saffāḥ and al-Manṣūr, see "Barmakids," in *EI*³ (K. van Bladel).

39 This sentence and its variants are discussed in van Bladel (2010): 65, n. 98, n. 99.

§11 وأما برمك فإنه لما ورد المدينة أسلم رغبة في الإسلام وسمي عبد الله ثم رجع إلى بلاده والبرمكة لولده فقتله نيزك طرخان أحد ملوك خراسان وفر ابنه برمك بن برمك مع أمه وهو صغير إلى بلاد قشمير فنشأ بها على دين أهله وعاد إلى بلده فاجتمعوا إليه وأجلسوه موضع أبيه وسموه برمك فولي أمر النوبهار[a] إلى أن ولي أسد بن عبد الله البجلي خراسان ثم جنيد بن عبد الرحمن {المري}.

§12 ثم خرج يريد هشام بن عبد الملك حتى لقيه فداواه مما كان به حتى برأ فأكرمه ورغبه في الإسلام فأسلم على يد هشام بن عبد الملك بن مروان فسماه عبد العزيز وإليه تنسب البرامكة وعاد يريد خراسان فمات في جرجان وأقام بها ولده خالد بن برمك مع أمه.

---

١ وأما ... فإنه : كشط المقريزي عبارة أخرى قبل أن يصححها كما هي الآن. ١-٧ وأما ... الإسلام : الزيادة فوق كلمة "ولده" بخط المقريزي في الهامش الأعلى من الأسفل إلى الأعلى، ثم في الهامش الأيسر + صح. ٤ برمك : كذا. ٥ المري : في الأصل "الضبي". ٧ عبد العزيز : كشط المقريزي اسما آخر قبل أن يصححه كما هو الآن. ٧-٨ وعاد ... أمه : الزيادة بخط المقريزي في الهامش الأيمن من الأعلى إلى الأسفل + صح، ويشير إليها رمز ⌐ بعد "البرامكة".

---

a قارن ياقوت، معجم البلدان، ٥: ٣٠٨ ("فلم يزل يليه برمك بعد برمك إلى أن افتُتحت خراسان في أيام عثمان بن عفّان وانتهت السدانة إلى برمك أبي خالد بن برمك فسار إلى عثمان مع رهائن كانوا ضمنوا مالًا عن البلد، ثم إنه رغب في الإسلام فأسلم وسمي عبد الله ورجع إلى أهله وولده وبلده، فأنكروا إسلامه وجعلوا بعض ولده مكانه برمكًا، فكتب إليه نيزك طرخان أحد الملوك يعظم ما أتاه من الإسلام ويدعوه إلى الرجوع إلى دين آبائه، فأجابه برمك: إني إنما دخلت في هذا الدين اختيارًا له وعلمًا بفضله من غير رَهبة ولم أكن لأرجع إلى دينٍ بادي العوار مهتك الأستار، فغضب نيزك وزحف إلى برمك في جمع كثير، فكتب إليه برمك: قد عرفتَ حبي للسلامة وإني قد استنجدت الملوك فأنجدوني فاصرفْ عني أعِنّة خيلك وإلا حملتني على لقائك! فانصرفَ عنه ثم استغرّه وبيّته فقتله وعشرة بنين له فلم يبق له سوى طفل وهو برمك أبو خالد فإن أمه هربت به وكان صغيرًا إلى بلاد القشمير من بلاد الهند فنشأ هناك وتعلم علم الطبّ والنجوم وأنواعًا من الحكمة وهو على دين آبائه، ثم إن أهل بلده أصابهم طاعونٌ ووباء فتشاءَموا بمفارقة دينهم ودخولهم في الإسلام، فكتبوا إلى برمك حتى قدم عليهم فأجلسوه في مكان آبائه وتولى النوبَهار").

§11 As for Barmak [al-Akbar], when he arrived in Medina he willingly embraced Islam, and was given the name ʿAbd Allāh. Then he returned to his land, where his son held the position of Barmak, and Nīzak Ṭarẖān,[40] who was one of the kings of Ḫurāsān, killed him. His [Barmak al-Akbar's] son, Barmak b. Barmak,[41] who was at a young age, fled with his mother to the land of Kashmir,[42] and he was raised there according to the religion of his family.[43] Later he returned to his land, and they received him unanimously, seated him in his father's place, and named him Barmak. He was in charge of the Nawbahār until Asad b. ʿAbd Allāh al-Baǧalī[44] became governor of Ḫurāsān, succeeded by Ǧunayd b. ʿAbd al-Raḥmān al-Murrī.[45]

§12 Then he [Barmak b. Barmak] left, seeking Hišām b. ʿAbd al-Malik,[46] and when they met, he healed and cured him of his condition.[47] He [Hišām] honored him [Barmak b. Barmak], and made him [Barmak b. Barmak] want to become Muslim. He became a Muslim at the hands of Hišām b. ʿAbd al-Malik b. Marwān, who named him ʿAbd al-ʿAzīz. The Barmakids are traced back to him [Barmak b. Barmak, i.e. Ḫālid b. Barmak's father]. Then he set out to Ḫurāsān, but died in Ǧurǧān, and his son, Ḫālid b. Barmak, remained there with his mother.

---

40 Several rulers of Tokharistan were called Nīzak (or Nēzak) Ṭarẖān; see *EIr*, "Nēzak" (Frantz Grenet); van Bladel (2010): 65, n. 101.

41 Barmak b. Barmak can be identified with the father of Ḫālid b. Barmak; see van Bladel (2010), 66.

42 Regarding his education in Kashmir, see van Bladel (2010): 69–70.

43 The sequence of events is clearer in other sources. See van Bladel (2010): 66: "Then he [Nēzak Ṭarkhān] came to him by surprise with a night attack, and killed him and ten of his sons. He had no successor remaining except the Barmak, that is, the father of Khālid, for his mother fled with him, he being still a child, to the land of Qashmīr. He grew up there and studied astrology, medicine, and the branches of philosophy (*anwāʿan min al-ḥikma*), while remaining in the religion of his ancestors."

44 Asad b. ʿAbd Allāh al-Qasrī of the tribe of Baǧīlah (d. 120/737–738) was governor of Ḫurāsān on behalf of his brother Ḫālid b. ʿAbd Allāh for the years 106–109/724–727 and 117–120/735–738; "Asad b. ʿAbdallāh," in *EI*³ (E.L. Daniel); "Asad b. ʿAbd Allāh," in *EI*² (H.A.R. Gibb).

45 Ǧunayd b. ʿAbd al-Raḥmān al-Murrī (not al-Ḍabbī as erroneously given by al-Maqrīzī) was appointed by Hišām b. ʿAbd al-Malik as governor of Ḫurāsān in the year 111/729–730. He replaced Ašras b. ʿAbd Allāh al-Sulamī, who was governor of Ḫurāsān for the years 109–111/727–729; al-Ṭabarī, *History*, 25:2, 42, 65; Crone (1980): 98.

46 The tenth Umayyad caliph (r. 105–125/724–743).

47 Cf. van Bladel (2010): 73: "The Barmak's medical education was useful in Hishām's court. He is said to have treated Maslama [b. Hishām b. ʿAbd al-Malik] for his infertility (and this is, according to al-Kirmānī, on the authority of Maslama's own son, the product of the prescription)." See also Bosworth (1994): 271, 274.

§13 وخرب هذا الهيكل قيس بن الهيثم السلمي سنة إحدى وأربعين في أول خلافة معٰوية بن أبي سفيٰن.[a] وكان بناء عظيما حوله أروقة وثلاثمائة وستون مقصورة برسم سكنى سَدَنته وقومته.[b] ويقال بل خربه الفضل بن يحيى بن خالد بن برمك لما دخل بلخ وبنى فيه مسجدا.[c]

§14 ويقال إن غمدان بصنعاء بناه الضحاك المعروف بالازدهاق[d] على اسم الزهرة ثم سكنه الملوك من حمير إلى ⟨أن⟩ خربته الحَبَشُ ثم خرب ما بقي منه أمير المؤمنين عثمٰن بن عفان رضي الله عنه.[e]

§15 وكان في الجبل الفاصل بين جزيرة الأندلس وبين الأرض الكبيرة هيكل الزهرة يقال بنته كلاوبطره.[f]

---

٣ ويقال ... مسجدا: الزيادة بخط المقريزي في الهامش الأيسر ويشير إليها رمز ٦ بعد "وقومته". ‖ وبنى: في الأصل "وبنا". ٥ إلى ... خربته: في الأصل "الى خربته". ‖ الحَبَشُ: وضع المقريزي رمز "ح" تحت الكلمة إشارة إلى تلفظها بالحاء.

---

a راجع ياقوت، معجم البلدان، ٥: ٣٠٧ ("ولما فتح عبد الله بن عامر بن كُرَيز خراسان أنفذ قيس بن الهيثم حتى قدم مدينة بلخ وقدّم بين يديه عطاء بن السائب فدخل بلخ وخرّب النوبهار").

b راجع ياقوت، معجم البلدان، ٥: ٣٠٧ ("وكان حول البيت ثلثمائة وستون مقصورة يسكنها خُدّامه وقُوّامه وسدنته").

c راجع ابن خلكان، وفيات الاعيان، ٤: ٢٩ ("ومن مناقبه أنه لما تولى خراسان دخل إلى بلخ وهو وطنهم، وبها النوبهار وهو بيت النار التي كانت المجوس تعبدها، وكان جَدُّهم برمك خادم ذلك البيت—حسبما هو مشروح في ترجمة جعفر—فأراد الفضل هدم ذلك البيت، فلم يقدر عليه لإحكام بنائه، فهدم منه ناحية وبنى فيها مسجدا").

d راجع الطبري، تاريخ، ١: ٢٠١ ("ذكر بيوراسب، وهو الازدهاق، والعرب تُسمّيه الضحّاك فتجعل الحرف الذي بين السين والزاي في الفارسية ضادًا والهاء حاء والقاف كافا").

e راجع المقريزي، الخطط، ١: ٦١٩ ("وكان بصَنْعَاء قَصْرُ غَمْدان من بِنَاء الضَّحَّاك، وكان هَيْكَلَ الزُّهرَة، وهُدِمَ في خِلافَة عُثْمان بن عَفَّان"). وراجع أيضا الدمشقي، نخبة الدهر، ٣٢ ("ويقال إنّ الضحّاك المعروف بأزدهاك بناه على اسم الزهرة ثمّ كان مسكنا لسيف بن ذي يزن أحد ملوك حمير").

f راجع الدمشقي، نخبة الدهر، ٤٢ ("وبجبل طليطله بالأندلس هيكل للزهرة عظيم البناء بنته الملكة قلوبطرة").

§ 13 Qays b. al-Hayṯam al-Sulamī[48] destroyed this temple [Nawbahār] in the year 41 [/661–662], at the beginning of Muʿāwiyah b. Abī Sufyān's[49] caliphate. It [the temple] was a huge edifice surrounded by arcades and 360 compartments that were designated for the residence of its custodians and caretakers. According to others, al-Faḍl b. Yaḥyá b. Ḫālid b. Barmak[50] destroyed it [the temple] when he entered Balḫ, and built a mosque in it [i.e. in the place where the temple stood].

§ 14 It is said that Ġumdān in Ṣanʿāʾ was built by al-Ḍaḥḥāk, who is known as "al-Azdahāq,"[51] and that it [the temple] was dedicated to Venus. Then the kings of Ḥimyar lived there until the Ethiopians destroyed it, and afterward, the Commander of the Believers, ʿUṯmān b. ʿAffān, may Allāh be pleased with him, destroyed what was left of it.[52]

§ 15 The temple of Venus was on the chain of mountains that separates al-Andalus from the great land mass. It is said that Cleopatra built it.[53]

48 Muʿāwiyah's governor of Ḫurāsān: "Sulaym," in *EI*² (M. Lecker).

49 The first Umayyad caliph (r. 41–60/661–680).

50 Al-Faḍl b. Yaḥyá (d. 193/808) was appointed to several high offices during the ʿAbbāsid period. He was Hārūn al-Rašīd's foster-brother and a tutor of the future caliph al-Amīn; "Barmakids," in *EI*³ (K. van Bladel).

51 According to Persian legend, al-Ḍaḥḥāk was a demon tyrant on whose shoulders two snakes grew. The Avestan form Ažī dahāka was Arabicized into Azdahāq and then into al-Ḍaḥḥāk; see "Zuhāk," in *EI*² (E. Yarshater); al-Ṭabarī, *History*, 2:1.

52 On the castle of Ġumdān/Ġamdān, see Serjeant/Lewcock (1983): 44.

53 For the location of the temple of Venus, see also al-Andalusī (1991), 59.

§16 وكان بفرغانة بيت يقال له كاوسان بناه أحد ملوك الطبقة الأولى من الفرس على اسم الشمس خربه أمير المؤمنين أبو إسحٰق المعتصم.[a]

§17 وزعموا أن الكعبة بيت زحل وأن إدريس عليه السلام نص عليه ووصى أن يحج إليه. ويقال إن موضع جامع بني أمية بدمشق هو بيت المشتري بناه جيرون بن سعد بن عاد[b] وإن بيت المريخ بمدينة صُورْ من الساحل الشامي وإن عين شمس خارج القاهرة المعزية من أرض مصر كانت هيكل الشمس بناه أوشهنج أول ملوك الطبقة الأولى من الفرس على اسم الشمس وقيل بناه غيره وإن بيت الزهرة بمدينة منبج وبيت عطارد بمدينة صيدا من الساحل الشامي وبيت القمر هو قلعة مدينة حران يقال له المدور وما زال عامرا إلى أن خربه الططر في أعوام بضع وستين وسبع مائة عند تغلبهم على العراق والشام.[c]

---

٨ الططر: وضع المقريزي نقطة تحت كل من الطائين.

---

a قارن النويري، نهاية الأرب، ١: ٦٢ ("وبيت بفَرْغانة على اسم الشمس، يعرف بكاوسان، بناه كاوس أحد ملوك الفرس، وخربه المعتضد بالله"). وراجع الدمشقي، نخبة الدهر، ٤٣ ("ومن بيوت عطارد أيضا بيت بصيدا وبيت بفرغانه يسمّى كاوشان شاه بناه أحد ملوك الطبقة الأولى من الفرس على اسم عطارد أخربه المعتصم").

b قارن ياقوت، معجم البلدان، ٢: ١٩٩ ("وقال آخر من أهل السير: إن حصن جيرون بدمشق بناه رجل من الجبابرة يقال له جيرون في الزمن القديم ثم بنته الصابة بعد ذلك وبنت داخله بناءً لبعض الكواكب يقال إنه المشتري، ولباقي الكواكب أبنية عظام في أماكن مختلفة متفرقة بدمشق، ثم بنت النصارى الجامع").

c قارن النويري، نهاية الأرب، ١: ٦٢–٦٣ ("وحكى غير المسعودي أن البيت الأوّل الكعبة. ويذكرون أن إدريس (عليه السلام) أوصى به، وأوصى أن يكون الحج إليه وهو عندهم بيت زحل؛ والبيت الثاني وهو بيت المرّيخ، يزعمون انه كان بصور من الساحل الشاميّ؛ والبيت الثالث وهو بيت المشترِي، كان بدمشق بناه جيرون بن سعد بن عاد، وموضعه الآن الجامع الأمويّ؛ والبيت الرابع وهو بيت الشمس بمصر، ويسمى عين شمس، وآثاره باقية الى وقتنا هذا؛ والبيت الخامس وهو بيت الزهرة، كان بمَنْبج وخرب؛ والبيت السادس بيت عُطارد، وكان بصَيْدا من الساحل الشاميّ وخرِب؛ والبيت السابع وهو بيت القَمَر، كان بحرّان؛ وهو بيت الصابئة الأعظم").

§16 There was a sanctuary in Farġānah called Kāwusān,[54] which was built by one of the kings of the first dynasty of the Persians as a dedication to the Sun. The Commander of the Believers, Abū Isḥāq al-Muʿtaṣim,[55] destroyed it.

§17 They [the Sabians][56] claimed that the Kaʿbah is Saturn's sanctuary, and that Idrīs, may peace be upon him, determined this and exhorted [the people] to make pilgrimage[s] to it. It is said that the Banū Umayyah mosque in Damascus is located in [the place of] the sanctuary of Jupiter, which was built by Ǧayrūn b. Saʿd b. ʿĀd.[57] [It is also said] that the sanctuary of Mars is in the city of Ṣūr [Tyre] on the coast of al-Šām [greater Syria], and that ʿAyn Šams,[58] outside al-Qāhirah al-Muʿizziyyah[59] in the land of Egypt, was the Sun temple. Hūšang,[60] the first king of the first dynasty of the Persians, built it as a dedication to the Sun. Others said that someone else built it. [It is also said] that the sanctuary of Venus is in the city of Manbiǧ, the sanctuary of Mercury is in the city of Ṣaydā [Sidon] on the coast of al-Šām, and the sanctuary of the Moon is the citadel of the city of Ḥarrān.[61] It was called al-Mudawwar ["the circular"], and it remained in place until the Tatars destroyed it a few years after 760 [/1358], when they conquered Iraq and al-Šām.

---

54 Named after the mythical king Kay Kāʾūs who had allegedly built it; al-Nuwayrī, *Nihāyat al-arab*, 1:62. See also "Kay Kāʾūs," in *EI*² (Cl. Huart).

55 The ʿAbbāsid caliph who reigned from 218/833 to 227/842. According to other versions, al-Muʿtaḍid bi-llāh was the one who destroyed it; al-Nuwayrī, *Nihāyat al-arab*, 1:62.

56 See Dimašqī, *Nuḫbat al-dahr*, 40.

57 See Yāqūt, *Muʿǧam al-buldān*, 2:199, where one opinion has it that Ǧayrūn was the builder of Damascus. And see also the opinion in this source which suggests that it was the Sabians who built Jupiter's sanctuary.

58 See "ʿAyn S̲h̲ams," in *EI*² (C.H. Becker); Yāqūt, *Muʿǧam al-buldān*, 4:178–179.

59 Al-Qāhirah al-Muʿizziyyah ("The victorious [city] of al-Muʿizz") was the name given to Cairo by the Fāṭimid caliph al-Muʿizz li-Dīn Allāh, when he entered it in 362/973.

60 Hūšang was a mythical king who belonged to the Pīšdādiyān dynasty. See Firdawsī, *Epic of the Kings* 6–8; "Hūs̲h̲ang," in *EI*² (H. Massé).

61 That is, the citadel was originally the sanctuary of the moon; see Rice (1952), 43.

§18 وكان بمدينة منف التي يقال لها مدينة فرعون من أرض مصر البيت الأخضر وهو حجر مانع لا يعمل فيه الحديد إلا بجهد كان قطعة واحدة قد نقش فيه صور وكتابة وعلى وجه بابه صور حيات قد نشرت صدورها لو اجتمع آلاف من الناس لما قدروا أن يحركوه لعظمه وثقله. يقال إنه بيت القمر وإنه أحد بيوت سبعة | كانت بمنف على أسماء السبعة السيارة. ولم يزل هذا البيت 31b الأخضر بمنف حتى قطعه الامير شَيْخُو العُمَرِي في أعوام بضع وخمسين وسبع مائة ومنه أسكفة باب خانكاه شيخو بخط صَلِيبَة جامع ابن طولون ظاهر القاهرة المعزية.[a]

§19 وقد زعم قوم أن أول من عبد الأصنام قوم نوح عليه السلام وفيه نظر لأن الأصنام كانت قبل زمن نوح بدهر.

a راجع المقريزي، الخطط، ١: ٣٦٥-٣٦٦ ("وكان بمَنْف بَيْتٌ من الصَّوَّان الأخضر الماتِع الذي لا يَعْمَل فيه الحَديد قِطْعَة واحدة، وفيه صُوَر مَنْقوشَة وكِتابَةٌ، وعلى وَجه بابه صُوَر حَيَّات ناشِرة صُدُورها لو اجتمع أُلوفٌ من النَّاس على تَحْريكه ما قَدَرُوا لعِظَمِه وثِقَلِه. والصَّابِئَة تقول إنَّه بَيْتُ القَمَر. وكان هذا البيتُ من جُمْلَة سبعة بُيوت كانت بمَنف للكَواكِب السَّبْعَة. وهذا البَيْتُ الأَخْضر هَدَمَه الأميرُ سيفُ الدِّين شَيْخُو العُمَري، بعد سنة خمسين وسبع مائة، ومنه شيءٌ في خانقاهِه وجامِعِه الذي بخَطّ الصَّليبَة خارِج القاهِرَة"). وراجع أيضا القلقشندي، صبح الأعشى، ٣: ٣٢٠-٣٢١ ("وكان على القرب منهما بيت عظيم من حجر أخضر، قطعة واحدة: جوانبه الأربعة وأرضه وسقفه، ولم يزل على ذلك إلى الدولة الناصرية حسن بن الناصر محمد بن قلاوون، وأراد الأمير شيخو أتابك العساكر نقله إلى القاهرة صحيحا فعولج فانكسر فأمر بأن تنحت منه أعتاب فنحتت فجعل منها أعتاب خانقاه وجامعه بصليبة الجامع الطولوني"). وراجع أيضا القيسي، تحفة الألباب، ١٠٤ ("ورأيت في قصر فرعون [موسى] بيتا كبيرا من صخرة واحدة خضراء كالآس فيها صورة الأفلاك والنجوم ما لم أشاهد عجبا أحسن منه").

§ 18 The green house[62] was in the Egyptian city of Manf,[63] which was called the city of Pharaoh. It was [made of][64] strong stone on which iron did not have an effect, unless applied with great effort. It was [formed of] a single piece [of stone],[65] and images and writings were engraved[66] on it. There were images of snakes expanding their hoods on the front part of its gate. Even if thousands of men gathered together, they would not have been able to move it, due to its huge size and weight. Some say that it is the sanctuary of the Moon, and that it is one of seven sanctuaries which were [built] in Manf as a dedication to the seven planets. This green house remained in Manf until the amir Šayḫū l-ʿUmarī[67] broke it into pieces a few years after 750 [/1349]. The threshold of the Ḫānkāh of Šayḫū[68] in the Ṣalībah quarter of Ibn Ṭūlūn's mosque on the outskirts of al-Qāhirah al-Muʿizziyyah is made from it[s remains].

§ 19 Some people claimed that the first to worship idols were the people of Noah, may peace be upon him, but this is doubtful, since idols existed long before Noah's time.

62 This is a monolithic temple that is described in al-Maqrīzī's *Ḫiṭaṭ*, al-Qalqašandī's *Ṣubḥ al-aʿšá*, and ʿAbd al-Laṭīf's *al-Ifādah wa-l-iʿtibār*; see "Manf," in *EI*^{2} (U. Haarmann), and the references given there.

63 Regarding the city of Manf, see "Manf," in *EI*^{2} (U. Haarmann).

64 Compare al-Maqrīzī, *al-Ḫiṭaṭ*, 1:365. Al-Maqrīzī's text is translated in Reitemeyer (1903): 132; Wiet (1953): 93.

65 Compare al-Qalqašandī, *Ṣubḥ al-aʿšá*, 3:320, where it is said that its four sides, floor, and roof were formed of a single piece of stone.

66 Or painted (*nuqiša*).

67 The amir Sayf al-Dīn Šayḫū died in 758/1357; see Little (1974): 49.

68 On the Ḫānkāh (or Ḫānqāh) of Šayḫū, see Behrens-Abouseif (1989): 116–119.

§20 وخرج البخاري من حديث هشام عن ابن جريج وقال عطاء عن ابن عباس[a] رضي الله عنه: صارت الأوثان التي كانت في قوم نوح في العرب.[b] أما ود كانت لكلب بدومة الجندل[c] وأما سواع فكانت لهذيل وأما يغوث فكانت لمراد ثم لبني غُطَيف بالجوف عند سبأ[d] وأما يعوق فكانت لهمدان وأما نسر فكانت لحمير لآل ذي الكلاع[e] أسماء رجال صالحين من قوم نوح فلما هلكوا أوحى الشيطان إلى قومهم أن انْصِبُوا إلى مجالسهم التي كانوا يجلسُون أنْصَابًا وسموها بأسمائهم. ففعلوا فلم تُعبد فلما هلك أولئك ونُسِخَ العِلْم عُبِدَت.[f]

---

٢ كانت : كذا.

---

a راجع العيني، عمدة القاري، ١٤: ٢٨٧–٢٨٨ ("وهشام هو ابن يوسف الصنعاني أبو عبد الرحمن اليماني قاضيها وابن جريج هو عبد الملك بن عبد العزيز بن جريج قوله: وقال عطاء معطوف على شيء محذوف، كأنه كان في جملة أحاديث حدث بها ابن جريج عن عطاء، ثم قال: وقال عطاء عن ابن عباس").

b قارن البخاري، صحيح، ٤: ١٨٧٣ ("صَارَتِ الأَوْثَانُ الَّتِي كَانَتْ فِي قَوْمِ نُوحٍ فِي الْعَرَبِ بَعْدُ").

c قارن العيني، عمدة القاري، ١٣: ٤٣٨ ("أَمَّا وَدٌّ فَكَانَتْ لِكَلْبٍ بِدُومَةِ الْجَنْدَلِ").

d راجع ياقوت، معجم البلدان، ٢: ١٨٨ ("والجوف أيضًا: من أرض مُراد، له ذكر في تفسير قوله عز وجل: ﴿إِنَّا أَرْسَلْنَا نُوحًا إِلَى قَوْمِهِ﴾، رواه الحميدي الجرف ورواه النَّسَفي الحول، وهو فاسد، وهو في أرض سبأ").

e قارن أبو حيان، البحر المحيط، ١٠: ٢٨٥ ("فكان ودّ لكلب بدومة الجندل، وسواع لهذيل، وقيل: لهمدان، ويغوث لمراد، وقيل: لمذحج، ويعوق لهمدان، وقيل: لمراد، ونسر لحمير، وقيل: لذي الكلاع من حمير"). وراجع الثعلبي، الكشف والبيان، ١٠: ٤٦ ("وأما سواع فكان لآل ذي الكلاع يعبدونه").

f قارن القرطبي، الجامع، ١٨: ٣٠٨ ("وذكر الثعلبي عن ابن عباس قال: هذه الأصنام أسماء رجال صالحين من قوم نوح، فلما هلكوا أوحى الشيطان إلى قومهم أن انصِبوا في مجالسهم التي كانوا يجلسون فيها أنصابا وسمّوها بأسمائهم تذكروهم بها، ففعلوا، فلم تُعبد حتى إذا هلك أولئك ونسخ العلم عبدت من دون الله"). وراجع: العيني، عمدة القاري، ١٣: ٤٤٠ ("قوله: «وتنسخ» بلفظ الماضي من التفعيل أي تغير علمهم بصورة الحال وزالت معرفتهم بذلك، وفي رواية أبي ذر عن الكشميهني، ونسخ العلم فحينئذ عبدت على صيغة المجهول، وحاصل المعنى أنهم لما ماتوا وتغيرت صورة الحال وزالت معرفتهم جعلوها معابيد بعد ذلك").

§ 20 Al-Buḫārī[69] quoted Hišām's[70] *ḥadīṯ* on the authority of Ibn Ǧurayǧ,[71] [who said:] ʿAṭāʾ[72] said on the authority of Ibn ʿAbbās, may Allāh be pleased with him, that the idols of the people of Noah [later] became the property of the Arabs. Wadd belonged to Kalb in Dūmat al-Ǧandal,[73] Suwāʿ belonged to Huḏayl, Yaġūṯ belonged to the Banū Ġuṭayf of Murād in al-Ǧawf[74] near Sabaʾ, Yaʿūq belonged to Hamdān, and Nasr belonged to the Ḏū l-Kalāʿ branch of Ḥimyar. [These were the] names of pious men from the people of Noah. When they died, Satan inspired their people to set up statues (*anṣāb*) at the gathering places where they used to assemble, and to name them [the statues] after them [the pious men]. They did this, but they [the statues] were not worshipped. When those [people who set them up] had died and the knowledge [of the original purpose of the statues] was forgotten[75] they [i.e., the statues] began to be worshipped.

---

69 For more on Muḥammad b. Ismāʿīl al-Buḫārī (d. 256/870), the compiler of *Ṣaḥīḥ al-Buḫārī*, see "al-Bukhārī," in EI³ (Ch. Melchert).

70 Hišām b. Yūsuf al-Ṣanʿānī (d. 197/812–813); al-Ḏahabī, *Siyar aʿlām al-nubalāʾ*, 9:580–582.

71 Ibn Ǧurayǧ ʿAbd al-Malik b. ʿAbd al-ʿAzīz, a Meccan scholar who lived between the years 80/699 and 150/768; "Ibn Jurayj," in EI³ (H. Motzki).

72 Probably referring to ʿAṭāʾ b. Abī Rabāḥ (d. 114 or 115/732 or 733; "ʿAṭāʾ b. Abī Rabāḥ," in EI³ [H. Motzki]). Note that according to some, this was ʿAṭāʾ b. Abī Muslim al-Ḫurāsānī (d. 135/752). See al-Ḏahabī, *Siyar aʿlām al-nubalāʾ*, 6:140–143, especially 141; al-Qasṭallānī, *Iršād al-sārī*, 7:401.

73 An oasis located at the southeastern end of wadi Sirḥān; "Dūmat al-Dj̲andal," in EI² (L. Veccia Vaglieri).

74 A land of Murād; see Yāqūt, *Muʿǧam al-buldān*, 2:188.

75 The text has *nusiḫa l-ʿilm*. That is, the knowledge (of the original purpose of the statues) was forgotten and substituted for another.

§ 21 وحكى أبو جعفر محمد بن جَرير الطبري أن ودا وسواع ويغوث ويعوق ونسرا كانوا نفرا من بني آدم غير آلهة قوم نوح التي كانوا يعبدونها وأنهم كانوا قوما صالحين فيما بين آدم ونوح. وكان لهم أتباع يقتدون بهم فلما ماتوا قال أصحابهم الذين كانوا يقتدون بهم: "لو صورناهم كان أشوق لنا إلى العبادة إذا ذكرناهم." فصوروهم فلما ماتوا وجاء آخرون دَبّ إليهم إبليس فقال: "إنما كانوا يعبدونهم وبهم يُسْقون المطر." فعبدوهم[a] فابتدا عبادة الأوثان من ذلك الوقت.[b]

§ 22 وحكى أيضا أن هذه الخمسة هي أسماء أصنام قوم نوح وعزى القولين إلى جماعة.

§ 23 ورُوِيَ عن عُرْوة بن الزبير وغيره، قال: اشتكى آدم عليه السلام وعنده بنوه ود وسواع ويغوث ويعوق ونسر وكان ود أكبرهم وأبرهم به.

§ 24 وعن محمد بن كعب: كان لآدم {خمسة} بنين، ود وسواع ويغوث ويعوق ونسر، وكانوا عبادا. فمات رجل منهم فحزنوا عليه. فقال | الشيطان: "أنا أصور لكم مثله إذا نظرتم إليه ذكرتموه." 32a
قالوا: "افعل." فصوره في المسجد من صُفْر ورصاص[c] ثم مات آخر فصوره حتى ماتوا كلهم

١ كانوا: الزيادة بخط المقريزي في الهامش الأيسر من الأسفل إلى الأعلى + صح، ويشير إليها رمز ¬ بعد "نسرا". ٥ فابتدا: كذا. ٦ أيضا: الزيادة بخط المقريزي في الهامش الأيسر من الأسفل إلى الأعلى + صح، ويشير إليها رمز ¬ بعد "وحكى". ٩ خمسة: في الأصل "خمس".

a قارن الطبري، جامع البيان، ٢٣: ٣٠٣ ("فلما ماتوا وجاء آخرون، دبَّ إليهم إبليسُ فقال: إنما كانوا يَعْبُدُونهم وبهم يُسْقَون المطرَ. فعبَدُوهم").

b قارن القرطبي، الجامع، ١٨: ٣٠٨ ("وقال محمد بن كعب أيضا ومحمد بن قيس: بل كانوا قوما صالحين بين آدم ونوح، وكان لهم تَبَع يقتدون بهم، فلما ماتوا زيّن لهم إبليس أن يصوّروا صورهم ليتذكروا بها اجتهادهم، وليتسَلّوا بالنظر إليها، فصوّرهم. فلما ماتوا هُم وجاء آخرون قالوا: لَيْتَ شِعْرَنَا! هذه الصور ما كان آباؤنا يصنعون بها؟ فجاءهم الشيطان فقال: كان آباؤكم يعبدونها فترحمهم وتسقيهم المطر. فعبدوها فابتدئ عبادة الأوثان من ذلك الوقت").

c قارن الثعلبي، الكشف والبيان، ١٠: ٤٦ ("هل لكم أن أصور لكم في قبلتكم مثله إذا نظرتم إليه ذكرتموه، قالوا: نكره أن يجعل في قبلتنا شيئًا نصلي إليه، قال: فأجعله في مؤخّر المسجد. قالوا: نعم فصوره لهم من صفر ورصاص").

§ 21 Abū Ǧaʿfar Muḥammad b. Ǧarīr al-Ṭabarī[76] reported that Wadd, Suwāʿ, Yaġūṯ, Yaʿūq, and Nasr were the offspring of Adam, and not the gods that were worshipped by the people of Noah. These [people] were pious men who lived between the time of Adam and Noah, and they had followers who emulated them. When they died, their companions who emulated them said: "If we make images of them, it would increase our desire to engage in worship whenever we remember them." So they made images of them, and when they [the followers] died and others came, Satan crept into their minds and said: "They used to worship them and rain was sent down to them through them [the images]." Then they worshipped them, and this was the beginning of idol worship.

§ 22 He [al-Ṭabarī] also reported that these five [Wadd, Suwāʿ, Yaġūṯ, Yaʿūq, and Nasr] are the names of the idols of the people of Noah, and attributed these two opinions to several people.

§ 23 It was narrated on the authority of ʿUrwah b. al-Zubayr[77] and others that Adam, may peace be upon him, fell ill, and his sons Wadd, Suwāʿ, Yaġūṯ, Yaʿūq, and Nasr were present with him. Wadd was the eldest and most dutiful of them toward him [Adam].

§ 24 On the authority of Muḥammad b. Kaʿb:[78] Adam had five sons: Wadd, Suwāʿ, Yaġūṯ, Yaʿūq, and Nasr. They were all pious devotees. [When] one of them died, they mourned for him, and Satan said: "Shall I make for you an image of his likeness, [so that] whenever you look at it you will remember him?" They said: "Do it!" Thereupon he placed an image of him in their place of worship; [this image] was made of brass and lead. Then, [when] another one died, he [Satan] made an image of him and repeated this

76 Abū Ǧaʿfar Muḥammad b. Ǧarīr al-Ṭabarī (d. 310/923), the compiler of *Taʾrīḫ al-rusul wa-l-mulūk* and *Tafsīr al-Ṭabarī*; "al-Ṭabarī," in *EI*² (C.E. Bosworth).

77 On ʿUrwah b. al-Zubayr b. al-ʿAwwām of the tribe of Qurayš, who died in Medina in the year 93 or 94/711–712 or 712–713, see "ʿUrwa b. al-Zubayr," in *EI*² (G. Schoeler).

78 On Muḥammad b. Kaʿb al-Quraẓī (d. 117–120/735–738), see "Ḳurayẓa," in *EI*² (W.M. Watt).

{وصورهم}. {وَتَنقصَت} الأشياء كما {تنقص} اليوم إلى أن تركوا عبادة الله بعد حين.[a] فقال لهم الشيطان: "ما لكم لا تعبدون شيئا؟" قالوا: "وما نعبد؟" قال: "آلهتكم وآلهة آبائكم. ألا ترونها في مصلاكم؟" فعبدوها من دون الله حتى بعث الله تعالى نوحا عليه السلام فقالوا ﴿لَا تَذَرُنَّ آلِهَتَكُمْ وَلَا تَذَرُنَّ وَدًّا وَلَا سُوَاعًا﴾ الآية.

§25 ويقال إن سُواعا كان ابن شيث وإن يغوثَ كان ابن سواع وكذلك يعوق ونسر وهذه أسماء سريانية وقعت إلى الهند فسموا بها أصنامهم التي زعموا أنها صُور الدراري السبعة وربما كلمتهم الجن من جوفها ففتنتهم ثم أدخلها إلى العرب عمرو بن لحي أو غيره وعلمهم تلك الاسماء أو ألقاها الشيطان على ألسنتهم موافقة لما كان في عهد نوح.[b]

§26 ويروى عن ابن عباس رضي الله عنه أن نوحا كان يَحرُس جسدَ آدم على جبل بالهند فيمنع الكافرين من أن يطوفوا بقبره. فقال لهم الشيطان: "إن هؤلاء يفخرون عليكم ويزعمون أنهم بنو آدم دونكم وإنما هو جسد وأنا أصور لكم مثله تطوفون به." فصور لهم هذه الأصنام الخمسة وحملهم على عبادتها فلما كان أيام الطوفان دفنها الطين والتراب والماء فلم تزل مدفونة حتى أخرجها الشيطان لمشركي العَرب.

---

١ وصورهم: في الأصل "وصوروهم" (قارن القرطبي، الجامع). || وَتَنقصَت ... اليوم: في الأصل "وتنقضت الأشياء كما تنتقض اليوم" (قارن القرطبي، الجامع). ٣–٤ لَا ... سُوَاعًا: شكّل المقريزي الآية كما يلي: "لا تَذَرُنَّ الهتكم ولا نذرن وُدا ولا سُواعا". ٥–٨ ويقال ... نوح: الزيادة بخط المقريزي في الهامش الأيمن من الأعلى إلى الأسفل، ثم في الهامش الأسفل من الأسفل إلى الأعلى + صح، ويشير إليها رمز ⌐ بعد "الآية". ٩ يَحرُس: وضع المقريزي رمز "ح" تحت الكلمة إشارة إلى تلفظها بالحاء.

---

a قارن القرطبي، الجامع، ١٨: ٣٠٧–٣٠٨ ("فقال الشيطان: أنا أصوّر لكم مثله إذا نظرتم إليه ذكرتموه. قالوا: افعل. فصوّره في المسجد من صُفر ورصاص، ثم مات آخر، فصوّره حتى ماتوا كلهم فصوّرهم. وتنقّصت الأشياء كما تتنقّص اليوم إلى أن تركوا عبادة الله تعالى بعد حين"). وقارن العيني، عمدة القاري، ١٣: ٤٣٧ ("وتنغصت الأشياء").

b قارن السهيلي، الروض الأنف، ١: ٣٥٩ ("ثم أدخلها إلى العرب عَمْرو بن لُحَيٍّ كما ذكر أو غيره، وعلمهم تلك الأسماءَ، وألقاها الشيطانُ على ألسِنتهم موافقَةً لما كانوا فى عهد نوح").

[action, i.e., making images] until they [Wadd, Suwāʿ, Yaġūṯ, Yaʿūq, and Nasr] each died. Matters became increasingly worse[79] until, after a period of time, they abandoned the worship of Allāh. Satan then told them: "Why are you not worshipping anything?" They said: "What should we worship?" He said: "Your gods and the gods of your ancestors. Do you not see them in your place of prayer?" So they worshipped them apart from Allāh, until Allāh, the Exalted, sent Noah, may peace be upon him, and they said: "Do not leave your gods, and do not leave Wadd, nor Suwāʿ"[80] and so on with the verse.[81]

§ 25 It is said that Suwāʿ was the son of Seth, and that Yaġūṯ, Yaʿūq, and Nasr were the sons of Suwāʿ. These are Aramaic[82] names that spread to India; they gave these names to their idols, which, they claimed, had the shape of the seven shining stars. Sometimes, the *ǧinn* spoke to them [the people] from within them [the idols] and deceived them. Then ʿAmr b. Luḥayy[83] or someone else introduced them [the idols] to the Arabs and taught them those names. According to another version,[84] Satan cast them [the names] upon their tongues in accordance with what existed during the period of Noah.[85]

§ 26 It was narrated on the authority of Ibn ʿAbbās, may Allāh be pleased with him, that Noah used to guard Adam's body on a mountain in India to prevent the infidels from circumambulating his grave. Satan told them: "These [people] claim to be superior to you and allege that they alone are the sons of Adam. They are merely circumambulating a body. I shall make for you an image of his likeness, which you can circumambulate." Then he formed these five idols for them and induced them to worship them [the idols]. In the days of the flood, they [the idols] were buried under mud, dirt, and water, and they remained buried until Satan extracted them for the Arab polytheists.

---

79 Lit. "Matters gradually deteriorated, as they deteriorate today" (reading *tanaqqaṣat* and *tatanaqqaṣu* instead of *tanaqqaḍat* and *tantaqiḍu* as given by al-Maqrīzī).

80 Qurʾān (*Nūḥ*), 71:23.

81 A parallel version of this account is translated in Lecker (2012), 124.

82 *Suryānī* may mean Aramaic more generally here; see Tannous (forthcoming).

83 According to Muslim tradition, ʿAmr b. Luḥayy was the ancestor of the tribe of Ḫuzāʿah and the one who introduced idolatry to Arabia; "ʿAmr b. Luḥayy," in *EI*^{3} (U. Rubin).

84 The text has *aw* ("or"), but compare al-Suhaylī, *al-Rawḍ al-unuf*, 1:359, where it is said that ʿAmr b. Luḥayy or someone else introduced them to the Arabs and taught them those names, and then [*wa*] Satan cast them upon their tongues.

85 That is, Satan cast upon their tongues the names of the idols that had been worshipped during Noah's time.

§27 وقال ابن إسحٰق: وحدثني عبد الله بن أبي بكر بن محمد بن عمرو بن حَزْم عن أبيه، قال: حُدِّثْت أن رسول الله ﷺ قال: "رأيت عمرو بن لُحَي يَجُر قُصْبَه في النار فسألته عمن بيني وبينه من الناس فقال: 'هلكوا'."

§28 وخرجه عمر بن شبة في **كتاب أخبار مكة** فقال: ثنا عمرو بن قُسْط ثنا عبيد الله بن عمرو عن عبد الله بن محمد بن عقيل عن جابر والطفيل بن أُبي عن أبيه أن النبي ﷺ قال: "رأيت عمرو بن لحي يجر قصبه في النار وأشبه من رأيت به مَعْبَد بن أكثم الكعبي." قال معبد: "يٰرسول الله أيُخشى

٣.88–٤ وخرجه ... قال: الزيادة بخط المقريزي في الهامش الأيسر منقلبة + صح، ويشير إليها رمز ٦ بعد "هلكوا".

§ 27 Ibn Isḥāq[86] said: ʿAbd Allāh b. Abī Bakr b. Muḥammad b. ʿAmr b. Ḥazm[87] related to me [the following] on the authority of his father,[88] who said: It was related to me that the Messenger of Allāh, may Allāh bless and save him, said: "I saw ʿAmr b. Luḥayy dragging his intestines in hell. I asked him about the people [who have lived] between me and him [i.e. between my time and his], and he said: 'They perished'."

§ 28 ʿUmar b. Šabbah[89] quoted it [this *ḥadīṯ*] in *Kitāb Aḫbār Makkah* [The Book of the History of Mecca] and said: ʿAmr b. Qusṭ[90] related to us [that] ʿUbayd Allāh b. ʿAmr[91] related to him on the authority of ʿAbd Allāh b. Muḥammad b. ʿAqīl[92] < Ğābir[93] and al-Ṭufayl b. Ubayy[94] < his father,[95] that the Prophet, may Allāh bless and save him, said: "I saw ʿAmr b. Luḥayy dragging his intestines in hell, and Maʿbad b. Akṯam al-Kaʿbī[96] resembles him in appearance more than anyone I have ever seen." Maʿbad said: "O Messenger

86 On Muḥammad b. Isḥāq b. Yasār (d. ca. 150/767), the famous compiler of the biography of the Prophet, see "Ibn Isḥāḳ," in EI^{2} (J.M.B. Jones).

87 A Medinan traditionist who died in the year 130 or 135/747–748 or 752–753; Ibn Ḥağar, *Tahḏīb al-tahḏīb*, 5:146.

88 On Abū Bakr b. Muḥammad b. ʿAmr b. Ḥazm (d. ca. 120), who was appointed *qāḍī* and governor of Medina, see al-Ḏahabī, *Siyar aʿlām al-nubalāʾ*, 5:314–315; Ibn ʿAsākir, *Dimašq*, 66:41–48.

89 For more on Abū Zayd ʿUmar b. Šabbah (d. 262/878), who was a *mawlá* of the Banū Nuwayr, see "ʿUmar b. Shabba," in EI^{2} (S. Leder).

90 Or ʿAmr b. Qusayṭ, on whom see Ibn Abī Ḥātim, *al-Ğarḥ wa-l-taʿdīl*, 6:256.

91 On ʿUbayd Allāh b. ʿAmr b. Abī l-Walīd (d. 180/796), who was a *mawlá* of the tribe of Asad, see al-Ḏahabī, *Siyar aʿlām al-nubalāʾ*, 8:310–312.

92 Abū Muḥammad ʿAbd Allāh b. Muḥammad b. ʿAqīl (d. after 141/758) was the grandson of ʿAlī b. Abī Ṭālib's brother. His mother, Zaynab, was ʿAlī's daughter; al-Ḏahabī, *Siyar aʿlām al-nubalāʾ*, 6:204–205.

93 Ğābir b. ʿAbd Allāh (d. ca. 78/697) was one of the Prophet's Companions. He belonged to the Salimah branch of the tribe of Ḫazrağ; "Djābir b. ʿAbd Allāh," in EI^{2} (M.J. Kister).

94 Al-Ṭufayl b. Ubayy b. Kaʿb of the Banū l-Naǧǧār (Ḫazrağ); Ibn Saʿd, *al-Ṭabaqāt*^{1}, 7:79.

95 This tradition is narrated with two chains of transmission: the first one ends with ʿAbd Allāh b. Muḥammad b. ʿAqīl < Ğābir, and the second ends with ʿAbd Allāh b. Muḥammad b. ʿAqīl < al-Ṭufayl b. Ubayy < his father [Ubayy b. Kaʿb].

96 A member of the Kaʿb branch of the tribe of Ḫuzāʿah. Maʿbad and his father, Akṯam b. al-Ğawn/b. Abī l-Ğawn, are also mentioned in the accounts translated below. See also Abū Nuʿaym, *Maʿrifat al-ṣaḥābah*, 1:340. For Kaʿb as a branch of Ḫuzāʿah, see Caskel (1966): 1, tables 196 and 197. See also "ʿAmr b. Luḥayy," in EI^{3} (U. Rubin).

علي من شبهه؟ فإنه والد.» قال: "لا أنت مؤمن وهو كافر. هو أول من حمل العرب على عبادة الاصنام."

§29 قال ابن إسحٰق: وحدثني محمد بن إبرٰهيم بن الحٰرث التيمي أن أبا صالح السمان حدثه أنه سمع أبا هريرة رضي الله عنه يقول: سمعت رسول الله ﷺ يقول لأكثم بن الجوْن الخزاعي: "يا أكثم رأيتُ عمرو بن لحي بن قمعة بن خندف يجر قصبه في النار فما رأيت رجلا أشبه برجل منك به ولا بك منه." فقال أكْثَمَ: "عسى أن يضرني شبهه يا نبي الله." قال: "لا إنك مؤمن وهو كافر. إنه كان أول من غير دين إسمٰعيل فنصب الأوثان وبَحَرَ البَحِيْرَة وسَيَّبَ السائبة ووَصَل الوَصِيْلة وحَمى الحامي."

§30 أكثم بن أبي {الجون}: اسمه عبد العزى وقيل في أكثم إنه أبو معبد زوج أم معبد صاحبة

---

٣ ابن إسحٰق: كشط المقريزي عبارة أخرى قبل أن يصححها كما هي الآن. ٧ وبَحَرَ: وضع المقريزي رمز "ح" تحت الكلمة إشارة إلى تلفظها بالحاء. ‖ البَحِيْرَة: وضع المقريزي رمز "ح" تحت الكلمة إشارة إلى تلفظها بالحاء. ٩ أكثم ... الجون: الزيادة بخط المقريزي في الهامش الأيسر + حـ (يعني "حاشية"). ‖ الجون: في الأصل "الحرث".

of Allāh! Should I fear what might happen to me because of my resemblance to him? [After all] he is [my] ancestor."[97] He replied: "No, you are a believer whereas he was an infidel. He was the first who induced the Arabs to worship idols."

§ 29 Ibn Isḥāq said: Muḥammad b. Ibrāhīm b. al-Ḥāriṯ al-Taymī[98] related to me that Abū Ṣāliḥ al-Sammān[99] related to him that he had heard Abū Hurayrah,[100] may Allāh be pleased with him, say: I heard the Messenger of Allāh, may Allāh bless and save him, saying to Akṯam b. al-Ǧawn al-Ḫuzāʿī:[101] "O Akṯam! I saw ʿAmr b. Luḥayy b. Qamaʿah b. Ḫindif dragging his intestines in hell, and I have never seen two men so alike as you and he." Akṯam said: "Perhaps the resemblance to him will harm me, O Prophet of Allāh." He said: "No, you are a believer whereas he was an infidel. He was the first to change the religion of Ishmael, to set up idols, and institute the practices of *al-baḥīrah, al-sā'ibah, al-waṣīlah*, and *al-ḥāmī*."[102]

§ 30 Akṯam b. Abī l-Ǧawn's name[103] is ʿAbd al-ʿUzzá. According to Ibn al-Kalbī[104] and Ibn Ḥibbān,[105] Akṯam is [the same person as] Abū Maʿbad,[106] who was the husband of Umm Maʿbad from the story [of Umm Maʿbad al-

97 Note that ʿAmr b. Luḥayy is said to have been the ancestor of Ḫuzāʿah; see n. 83.

98 A *ḥadīṯ* transmitter (d. ca. 120/738) whose grandfather was reportedly one of the Prophet's Companions; al-Ḏahabī, *Siyar aʿlām al-nubalā'*, 5:294–296.

99 Abū Ṣāliḥ al-Sammān Ḏakwān b. ʿAbd Allāh (d. 101/719); al-Ḏahabī, *Siyar aʿlām al-nubalā'*, 5:36–37.

100 On Abū Hurayrah (d. 57, 58, or 59/678, 679, or 680), a Companion of the Prophet, and a well known *ḥadīṯ* transmitter, see "Abū Hurayra," in *EI*[3] (G.H.A. Juynboll).

101 The following account is also translated in Ibn Hišām, *The Life of Muhammad* 35.

102 These four words appear in Qur'ān (*al-Mā'idah*), 5:103, and according to the common interpretation of this verse, they refer to various animals that were dedicated to the idols. For more information, see Wellhausen (1897): 112–113.

103 Al-Maqrīzī wrote this, erroneously, as Akṯam b. Abī l-Ḥāriṯ.

104 Hišām b. Muḥammad b. al-Sā'ib al-Kalbī (d. 204 or 206/819 or 821), who is often called Ibn al-Kalbī, was the compiler of *Ǧamharat al-nasab, al-Aṣnām, Ansāb al-ḫayl*, and others; "al-Kalbī," in *EI*[2] (W. Atallah).

105 This is Abū Bakr Muḥammad b. Ḥibbān al-Tamīmī, a traditionist who was born in Bust, and who died in 354/965; "Ibn Ḥibbān," in *EI*[2] (J.W. Fück).

106 Akṯam's son Maʿbad was mentioned above; see § 28.

القصة. قاله ابن الكلبي وابن حبان. وعند العَسكري أكثم بن الجون بن أبي الجون.[a]

31 § حديث رأيت عمرو بن لحي يَجُر قُصْبه في النار خرجه البخاري ومسلم من طريق صالح بن كيسان عن ابن شهاب، قال: سمعت سعيد بن المسيب يقول: البحيرة التي يمْنَع دَرها للطواغيت فلا يحلبها أحد من الناس[b] والسائبة التي كانوا يُسَيّبونهَا لآلهتهم فلا يحمل عليها شيء.[c] 31**b

١ العَسكري : وضع المقريزي ثلاث نقط تحت الكلمة إشارة إلى تلفظها بالسين. ٢ حديث ... لحي : هذه ملاحظات للمقريزي كتبها على قصاصات ورقية صغيرة ووضعها بين الصفحات (٣١ و٣٢).

a قارن الزرقاني، شرح، ٢: ١٣١-١٣٢ ("فلما لبث أن جاء أبو معبد زوجها ... قال السهيلي: لا يعرف اسمه، وقال العسكري: اسمه أكثم بن أبي الجون، ويقال: ابن الجون"). وقارن أيضا ابن الأثير، أسد الغابة، ٦: ٢٨٦ ("أبو مَعْبَد الخُزَاعيّ، زوج أم معبد. مختلف في اسمه، فقال محمد بن إسماعيل: اسمه حُبَيش، وإنه سمع حديثه من أُم معبد في صفة النبيّ ﷺ").

b راجع ابن حجر، فتح الباري، ٩: ١٦٨ ("وأما قوله: "فلا يحلبها أحد من الناس" فهكذا أطلق نفي الحلب، وكلام أبي عبيدة يدل على أن المنفي إنما هو الشرب الخاص، قال أبو عبيدة: كانوا يحرمون وبرها ولحمها وظهرها ولبنها على النساء ويحلون ذلك للرجال، وما ولدت فهو بمنزلتها، وإن ماتت اشترك الرجال والنساء في أكل لحمها"). وراجع أيضا ابن منظور، لسان العرب، "صرب" ("وقد اصْطَرَب صَرْبة، وصَرَبَ بولَه يَصْرُبه ويَصْرِبه صربًا: حقنَه إذا طال حبسه، وخص بعضهم به الفحل من الإبل، ومنه قيل للبَحِيرة: صَرِبى على فَعْلى، لأَنهم لا يَحْلُبونها إلا للضيف، فيجتمع اللبن في ضرعها. وقال سعيد بن المسيب: البَحِيرة التي يمْنع دَرُّها للطواغيت، فلا يحلُبها أَحد من الناس").

c راجع البخاري، صحيح، ٤: ١٦٩٠؛ مسلم، صحيح، ٤: ٢١٩٢.

Ḫuzāʿiyyah].[107] According to al-ʿAskarī,[108] [his name is] Akṯam b. al-Ǧawn b. Abī l-Ǧawn.[109]

§ 31 The *ḥadīṯ*[110] [that reads] "I saw ʿAmr b. Luḥayy dragging his intestines in hell" was quoted by al-Buḫārī and Muslim[111] with a chain of transmission going back to[112] Ṣāliḥ b. Kaysān[113] on the authority of Ibn Šihāb,[114] who said: I heard Saʿīd b. al-Musayyab[115] say: *Al-baḥīrah* is [a female animal] whose milk is withheld for the *ṭawāġīt*,[116] and no man is allowed to milk her [for his own needs]. *Al-sāʾibah* is [a female animal] that they [i.e. the people of the Ǧāhiliyyah] used to set free (*kānū yusayyibūnahā*)[117] for their gods. Nothing was loaded on her.

---

107 "The story of Umm Maʿbad" refers to the traditions according to which the Prophet miraculously milked a sheep from Umm Maʿbad's herd, when he and Abū Bakr passed by her tent on their *hiǧrah* to Medina. Umm Maʿbad then described to her husband the details about the man who had visited them, and he responded that this was the Qurašī man of whom they had heard. Umm Maʿbad reportedly embraced Islam in Medina; Ibn Saʿd, *al-Ṭabaqāt*¹, 1:196–199. See also al-Ṭabarī, *Taʾrīḫ*, 3:2407–2414 (for a translation of this passage, see al-Ṭabarī, *History*, 39:138–144). Note that according to other accounts, Ibn Masʿūd was the one who milked a sheep for the Prophet and Abū Bakr; see Kister (1991): 275.

108 On Abū Hilāl al-Ḥasan b. ʿAbd Allāh b. Sahl al-ʿAskarī (d. ca. 400/1010), the compiler of *al-Awāʾil* and *Ǧamharat al-amṯāl*, see "al-ʿAskarī, Abū Hilāl," in *EI*³ (B. Gruendler).

109 Other sources say that according to al-ʿAskarī his name was Akṯam b. Abī l-Ǧawn; al-Zarqānī, *Šarḥ*, 2:132.

110 The following is from small pieces inserted between the pages of the MS.

111 Regarding Abū l-Ḥusayn Muslim b. al-Ḥaǧǧāǧ b. Muslim (d. 261/875), who is famous for his *al-Ǧāmiʿ al-ṣaḥīḥ* (usually called *al-Ṣaḥīḥ*), see "Muslim b. al-Ḥadjdjādj," in *EI*² (G.H.A. Juynboll).

112 Lit. "By way of" (*min ṭarīq*).

113 Ṣāliḥ b. Kaysān al-Madanī (d. after 140/757); al-Ḏahabī, *Siyar aʿlām al-nubalāʾ*, 5:454–456.

114 Ibn Šihāb al-Zuhrī (d. 124/742) was a prominent traditionist during the Umayyad period; "al-Zuhrī," in *EI*² (M. Lecker).

115 Saʿīd b. al-Musayyab al-Maḫzūmī of the tribe of Qurayš (d. ca. 94/713); al-Ḏahabī, *Siyar aʿlām al-nubalāʾ*, 4:217–246.

116 Pl. of *ṭāġūt*, see below §§ 163–164. See also Lane (1863–1893): 1674: "… whose milk was forbidden [by the pagan Arabs] for the sake of the idols … thus called [i.e. *ṣarbá*] because they used not to milk her save for the guest, so that her milk became collected [and retained] in her udder."

117 Note that *sāʾibah* and the verb *sayyaba* are derived from the same root. For the definitions of these words, see Lane (1863–1893): 1481–1482.

§32 قال ابن المسيب: وقال أبو هريرة: قال رسول الله ﷺ: "رأيت عمرو بن عامر الخزاعي يجر قُصْبَه في النار وكان أول من سيَّب السوائب."[a]

§33 زاد البخاري بعد هذا: والوَصِيْلَة الناقة البكر تُبَكِّر في أول نتاج الإبل ثم تُثني بعدُ بأنثى[b] وكانوا يُسَيِّبونها لطواغيتهم إن وصَلَت إحداهما بالأخرى ليس بينهما ذكر {والحامي} فحل الإبل يضرب الضِراب المعدود فإذا قضى ضرابه وَدَعُوه للطواغيت وأعْفَوه من الحمل فلم يحمل عليه شيء وسموه الحامي.[c]

---

٤ والحامي: في الأصل "والحام".

---

a راجع البخاري، صحيح، ٤: ١٦٩٠؛ مسلم، صحيح، ٤: ٢١٩٢.

b قارن الطبري، جامع البيان، ٩: ٣٨-٣٩ ("والوصيلةُ: الناقةُ البِكْرُ تُبَكِّرُ أولَ نتاجِ الإبلِ بأنثى، ثم تُثَنِّي بعدُ بأنثى"). وقارن أيضا الطبري، جامع البيان، ٩: ٣٦-٣٧ ("والوصيلةُ من الإبلِ: كانت الناقةُ تبتَكِرُ بأنثى ثم تُثَنِّي بأنثى"). وراجع ابن حجر، فتح الباري، ٩: ١٦٨ ("قوله: (والوصيلة الناقة البكر تبكر في أول نتاج الإبل بأنثى، ثم تثني بعد بأنثى) هكذا أورده متصلًا بالحديث المرفوع، وهو يوهم أنه من جملة المرفوع، وليس كذلك، بل هو بقية تفسير سعيد بن المسيب، والمرفوع من الحديث إنما هو ذكر عمرو بن عامر فقط، وتفسير البحيرة وسائر الأربعة المذكورة في الآية عن سعيد بن المسيب").

c راجع البخاري، صحيح، ٤: ١٦٩٠.

§ 32 Ibn al-Musayyab said [that] Abū Hurayrah said [that] the Messenger of Allāh, may Allāh bless and save him, said: "I saw ʿAmr b. ʿĀmir[118] al-Ḫuzāʿī dragging his intestines in hell. He was the first to institute the practice of the *sawāʾib* [pl. of *sāʾibah*]."

§ 33 After this, al-Buḫārī added:[119] *Al-waṣīlah* is a first-born she-camel that gives birth[120] [to a female][121] at her first delivery and then gives birth to [another] female at her second delivery. They used to set her free for their *ṭawāġīt* if she "joined" (*waṣalat*)[122] one of them to the other with no male in between them.[123] *Al-ḥāmī* is a male camel that was used for an assigned number of copulations. When he finished his [assigned number of] copulations, they left him for the *ṭawāġīt*, exempted him from carrying [loads], and did not load anything on him. They named him "*al-ḥāmī*."

118 In some accounts ʿĀmir appears as ʿĀmr's father, while Luḥayy appears as his grandfather; see "ʿAmr b. Luḥayy," in *EI*³ (U. Rubin).

119 I.e. after mentioning the previous *ḥadīṯ* which Abū Hurayrah had heard from the Prophet. The following explanation about the *waṣīlah* and *ḥāmī* is probably a part of the *ḥadīṯ* on the authority of Ṣāliḥ b. Kaysān < al-Zuhrī < Saʿīd b. al-Musayyab (§ 31). See also Ibn Ḥaǧar, *Fatḥ al-bārī*, 9:168.

120 The verb *tabtakiru* seems more appropriate in this context than *tubakkiru* given by al-Maqrīzī; see Lane (1863–1893): 240 (*ibtakarat bi-waladihā*); al-Ṭabarī, *Ǧāmiʿ al-bayān*, 9:36–37.

121 The word does not appear in al-Buḫārī's account, but can be found in other sources. See for instance al-Ṭabarī, *Ǧāmiʿ al-bayān*, 9:36–37.

122 Or perhaps, because she "joined" (reading *an waṣalat* instead of *in waṣalat*); al-ʿAynī, *ʿUmdat al-qārī*, 12:589. Note that *waṣalat* and *waṣīlah* are derived from the same root.

123 That is, they used to set free the she-camels that gave birth to two females successively with no male in between them.

§ 34 رواه ابن الهاد عن ابن شهاب عن سعيد عن أبي هريرة: سمعت النبي ﷺ. وقال لي أبو اليمان، انا شعيب عن الزهري، سمعت سعيدا قال: البحيرة بهذا، قال: وقال أبو هريرة: سمعت النبي ﷺ نحوه.[a]

§ 35 وخرج أبو زيد عمر بن شَبَّة في **كتاب أخبار مكة** من حديث عبيد الله بن عمرو عن | عبد الله 31**a ابن محمد بن عقيل عن جابر والطفيل بن أُبَي عن أبيه أن النبي ﷺ قال: "رأيت عمرو بن لُحَي يجر قصبه في النار وأشبه من رأيت به معبد بن أكثم الكعبي." قال معبد: "أيُخشى علي من شبهه؟ فإنه والد." قال: "لا أنت مؤمن وهو كافر. هو أول من حمل العرب على عبادة الأصنام."

---

٥ أُبَي : هذه إحدى الحالات النادرة التي تُكتب فيها الهمزة.   ٦ أيُخشى : في الأصل "ايُخْشا".

---

a قارن العيني، عمدة القاري، ١٢: ٥٩٠ ("وَقَالَ لِي أَبُو اليَمَانِ أخبَرَنا شُعَيْبٌ عَنِ الزُّهْرِيّ سَمِعْتُ سَعِيدًا قَالَ: يُخْبِرُهُ بِهٰذا قَالَ: قَالَ أَبُو هُرَيْرَةَ سَمِعْتُ النبيّ ﷺ نَحْوَهُ. قوله: «وقال لي أبو اليمان» رواية أبي ذر، وفي رواية غيره، قال أبو اليمان: بغير لفظة لي ... قوله: «يخبره» ... والضمير المرفوع فيه يرجع إلى سعيد بن المسيب، والمنصوب يرجع إلى الزهري، وفي رواية أبي ذر عن الحموي والمستملي: بحيرة ... وكأنه أشار به إلى تفسير البحيرة وغيرها كما في رواية إبراهيم بن سعد عن صالح بن كيسان عن الزهري. قوله: «قال وقال أبو هريرة» أي: قال سعيد بن المسيب. قال أبو هريرة: سمعت النبي ﷺ، قوله: «نحوه» أي: نحو ما رواه في الرواية الماضية"). وراجع ابن حجر، فتح الباري، ٩: ١٦٩ ("فإن المصنف أخرجه في مناقب قريش قال: حدثنا أبو اليمان أنبأنا شعيب عن الزهري سمعت سعيد بن المسيب قال: البحيرة التي يمنع درها إلخ، لكنه أورده باختصار قال: «وقال أبو هريرة عن النبي ﷺ رأيت عمرو بن عامر الخ»"). وراجع أيضا الطبري، جامع البيان، ٩: ٢٨ ("قال: ثني ابنُ الهادِ، عن ابنِ شهابٍ، عن سعيد بنِ المسيَّب، عن أبي هريرةَ، قال: سمِعتُ رسولَ الله صلى الله عليه وسلم يقولُ: «رأيتُ عمرَو بنَ عامرٍ الخزَاعيَّ يَجُرُّ قُصْبَه في النارِ، وكان أولَ مَن سيَّب السُّيَّبَ»").

§ 34 Ibn al-Hād[124] narrated it [this *ḥadīṯ*][125] on the authority of Ibn Šihāb < Saʿīd [b. al-Musayyab] < Abū Hurayrah [who said]: I heard the Prophet, may Allāh bless and save him [and so on with the *ḥadīṯ*]. Abū l-Yamān[126] told me, Šuʿayb[127] informed us on the authority of al-Zuhrī [who said]: I heard Saʿīd say: *Al-baḥīrah*, and so on with the *ḥadīṯ*.[128] [Saʿīd b. al-Musayyab] said [that] Abū Hurayrah said: I heard the Prophet, may Allāh bless and save him [and the rest of the *ḥadīṯ* was] similar to it [the *ḥadīṯ* that was ascribed to the Prophet (§ 32)].[129]

§ 35 Abū Zayd ʿUmar b. Šabbah quoted in *Kitāb Aḫbār Makkah* ʿUbayd Allāh b. ʿAmr's *ḥadīṯ* on the authority of ʿAbd Allāh b. Muḥammad b. ʿAqīl < Ǧābir and al-Ṭufayl b. Ubayy < his father,[130] that the Prophet, may Allāh bless and save him, said: "I saw ʿAmr b. Luḥayy dragging his intestines in hell, and Maʿbad b. Akṯam al-Kaʿbī resembled him in appearance more than anyone I have ever seen." Maʿbad asked: "Should I fear what might happen to me because of my resemblance to him? [After all,] he is [my] ancestor." He [the Prophet] replied: "No, you are a believer whereas he was an infidel. He was the first who induced the Arabs to worship idols."

---

124 Yazīd b. ʿAbd Allāh b. Usāmah b. al-Hād al-Layṯī was a narrator of *ḥadīṯ* who died in Medina in 139/756; Ibn Ḥaǧar, *Tahḏīb al-tahḏīb*, 11:295–296.

125 Referring to the *ḥadīṯ* that was ascribed to the Prophet (§ 32).

126 Abū l-Yamān al-Ḥakam b. Nāfiʿ, who was Šuʿayb's pupil (see below), died in Ḥimṣ in 221/836; al-Ḏahabī, *Siyar aʿlām al-nubalāʾ*, 10:319–326.

127 Šuʿayb b. Abī Ḥamzah was a *mawlá* from Ḥimṣ who died in 162 or 163/779 or 780; al-Ḏahabī, *Siyar aʿlām al-nubalāʾ*, 7:187–192.

128 Presumably, this means that Saʿīd's interpretation of the word *al-baḥīrah* (as well as the other words that refer to the various animals that were dedicated to the idols) in this chain of transmitters is similar to what was reported on the authority of Ṣāliḥ b. Kaysān < al-Zuhrī < Saʿīd b. al-Musayyab (see § 31). There are other versions in which the verb *yuḫbiruhu* (reporting to him [Saʿīd as the subject of the Arabic verb and al-Zuhrī as its direct object]) replaces *al-baḥīrah*. See al-ʿAynī, *ʿUmdat al-qārī*, 12:590.

129 See Ibn Ḥaǧar, *Fatḥ al-bārī*, 9:169.

130 See § 28.

§36 ومن طريق القعنبي عن مالك أن النبي ﷺ قال: "قد علمت أول من نصب النصب وسيب السوائب وغير دين إبرٰهيم عمرو بن لحي وقد رأيته يجر قصبه."

§37 ومن حديث ليث بن سعد عن يزيد بن الهاد عن ابن شهاب عن سعيد بن المسيب عن أبي هريرة عن النبي ﷺ أنه قال: "رأيت عمرو بن عامر يجر قصبه في النار كان سيب السائبة وَبحر البَحيرة."

§38 ومن حديث إبرٰهيم الهجري عن أبي الأحوص عن عبد الله عن النبي ﷺ، قال: "أول من سيب السوائب أبو خزاعة عمرو بن عامر وإني رأيته في النار يجر أمعاءه فيها."

§39 ومن حديث زهير بن حرب، ثنا جرير عن سهيل بن أبي صالح عن أبيه عن أبي هريرة عن النبي ﷺ، قال: "رأيت عمرو بن لحي بن قمعة بن خندف أبا بني كعب هؤلاء يجر قصبه في النار."

---

٢ قصبه : أضاف المقريزي "صح" تلو هذه الكلمة.

§ 36 [He also quoted the following *ḥadīṯ*] with a chain of transmission going back to[131] al-Qaʿnabī[132] on the authority of Mālik,[133] that the Prophet, may Allāh bless and save him, said: "I know the first [person] who set up stones (*nuṣub*),[134] instituted the practice of the *sawāʾib*, and changed the religion of Abraham. [It was] ʿAmr b. Luḥayy. I saw him dragging his intestines."

§ 37 [Ibn Šabbah also quoted] Layṯ b. Saʿd's[135] *ḥadīṯ* on the authority of Yazīd b. al-Hād < Ibn Šihāb < Saʿīd b. al-Musayyab < Abū Hurayrah < the Prophet, may Allāh bless and save him, who said: "I saw ʿAmr b. ʿĀmir dragging his intestines in hell. He instituted the practices of *al-sāʾibah* and *al-baḥīrah*."

§ 38 [He also quoted] Ibrāhīm al-Hağarī's[136] *ḥadīṯ* on the authority of Abū l-Aḥwaṣ[137] < ʿAbd Allāh [b. Masʿūd][138] < the Prophet, may Allāh bless and save him, who said: "The first to institute the practice of the *sawāʾib* was Abū Ḫuzāʿah[139] ʿAmr b. ʿĀmir. I saw him in hell dragging his intestines."

§ 39 [He also quoted] Zuhayr b. Ḥarb's *ḥadīṯ*[140] [with the following chain of transmission:] Ğarīr[141] related to us on the authority of Suhayl b. Abī Ṣāliḥ[142] < his father < Abū Hurayrah < the Prophet, may Allāh bless and save him, who said: "I saw ʿAmr b. Luḥayy b. Qamaʿah b. Ḫindif, the ancestor of the Banū Kaʿb, dragging his intestines in hell."

---

131 *Wa-min ṭarīq*; see note 112.

132 On ʿAbd Allāh b. Maslamah b. Qaʿnab (d. 221/836), who reportedly transmitted many *ḥadīṯ*s from Mālik's *al-Muwaṭṭaʾ*, see al-Ḏahabī, *Siyar aʿlām al-nubalāʾ*, 10:257–264.

133 Mālik b. Anas (d. 179/796) was the eponym of the Mālikī school of law. His greatest work is *al-Muwaṭṭaʾ*; "Mālik b. Anas," in *EI*² (J. Schacht).

134 See § 201–202.

135 Al-Layṯ b. Saʿd b. ʿAbd al-Raḥmān was a traditionist who died in Egypt in 175/791; "al-Layth b. Saʿd," in *EI*² (A. Merad).

136 Abū Isḥāq Ibrāhīm b. Muslim al-Hağarī; Ibn Ḥağar, *Tahḏīb al-tahḏīb*, 1:148–149.

137 Abū l-Aḥwaṣ ʿAwf b. Mālik b. Naḍlah al-Ğušamī from the Hawāzin; Ibn Saʿd, *al-Ṭabaqāt*¹, 8:302.

138 For more on ʿAbd Allāh b. Masʿūd (d. 32–33/652–654), who was one of the Prophet's Companions and a founder of one of the readings of the Qurʾān, see "Ibn Masʿūd, ʿAbdallāh," in *EI*³ (Sean Anthony).

139 See "ʿAmr b. Luḥayy," in *EI*³ (U. Rubin).

140 A traditionist who died in Baghdad in 234/849; "Zuhayr b. Ḥarb," in *EI*² (C.E. Bosworth).

141 Abū ʿAbd Allāh Ğarīr b. ʿAbd al-Ḥamīd al-Ḍabbī l-Kūfī (d. 188/804); al-Ḏahabī, *Siyar aʿlām al-nubalāʾ*, 9:9–18.

142 Suhayl b. Abī Ṣāliḥ was Ḏakwān al-Sammān's son.

§40 وخرج الزبير بن بكار في **كتاب نسب قريش** من حديث إبرٰهيم بن المنذر عن هشام بن سليمٰن المخزومي عن ابن جريج، قال: بلغني أن | رسول الله ﷺ قال: "رأيت عمرو بن لحي بن قمعة 31*b ابن خندف في النار يجر قُصْبه على رأسه فروة فقلت له: 'من معك في النار؟' فقال: 'من بيني وبينك من الأمم'." فقال المقداد بن الأسود: "ومَن عمرو بن لحي؟" قال: "أبو هؤلاء الحي من خزاعة وهو أول من غير الحنيفية دين إبرٰهيم وأول من نصب الأوثان حول الكعبة ومن جعل البحيرة والسائبة والوصيلة {والحامي}."

§41 حدثني عمر بن أبي بكر المؤمّلي عن عبد الحكيم بن أبي نَمِر وعثمٰن بن أبي سليمٰن وأبي عبيدة وابن مزروع أن رسول الله ﷺ قال: "أريت الجنة وأُرِيتُ النار فإذا فيها عمرو بن لحي يتأذى أهل

---

٤ الأسود: وضع المقريزي ثلاث نقط تحت هذه الكلمة إشارة إلى تلفظها بالسين. ٦ والحامي: في الأصل "والحام". ٨ يتأذى: في الأصل "يتاذا".

§ 40 Al-Zubayr b. Bakkār[143] quoted in *Kitāb Nasab Qurayš* [The Book of the Genealogy of Qurayš] Ibrāhīm b. al-Mundir's[144] *ḥadīt* on the authority of Hišām b. Sulaymān al-Maḫzūmī[145] < Ibn Ǧurayǧ, who said [that] it was reported to him that the Messenger of Allāh, may Allāh bless and save him, said: "I saw ʿAmr b. Luḥayy b. Qamaʿah b. Ḫindif in hell dragging his intestines and wearing a head scarf made of fur.[146] I said to him: 'Who are you with in hell?' He said: 'The peoples who are between me and you [i.e. the peoples who have lived between my time and yours]'." Al-Miqdād b. al-Aswad[147] asked: "Who is ʿAmr b. Luḥayy?" He said: "The ancestor of the tribe of Ḫuzāʿah. He is the first who changed the *ḥanīfiyyah*[148] [that is,] the religion of Abraham, and the first who set up idols around the Kaʿbah, and instituted the practices of *al-baḥīrah, al-sāʾibah, al-waṣīlah*, and *al-ḥāmī*."

§ 41 ʿUmar b. Abī Bakr al-Muʾammalī[149] narrated to me on the authority of ʿAbd al-Ḥakīm b. Abī Namir,[150] ʿUtmān b. Abī Sulaymān,[151] Abū ʿUbaydah,[152] and Ibn Mazrūʿ[153] that the Messenger of Allāh, may Allāh bless and save him, said: "I was shown paradise and I was shown hell, and there, suddenly, was

143 On the Qurašī scholar al-Zubayr b. Bakkār b. ʿAbd Allāh b. Muṣʿab (d. 256/870), see "al-Zubayr b. Bakkār," in *EI*² (S. Leder).

144 Abū Isḥāq Ibrāhīm b. al-Mundir al-Qurašī (d. 236/850); al-Dahabī, *Siyar aʿlām al-nubalāʾ*, 10:689–691.

145 Hišām b. Sulaymān b. ʿIkrimah b. Ḫālid b. al-ʿĀṣ al-Maḫzūmī of the tribe of Qurayš; al-Mizzī, *Tahdīb al-kamāl*, 30:211–212.

146 See Dozy (1881), 2:263.

147 Al-Miqdād b. al-Aswad of the Bahrāʾ (Quḍāʿah), who was one of the Companions of the Prophet. He was adopted by al-Aswad b. ʿAbd Yaġūt al-Zuhrī, but reportedly became known by the name al-Miqdād b. ʿAmr after the revelation of Qurʾān (*al-Aḥzāb*), 33:5, which declared adoption in Islam to be illegal; "al-Miḳdād b. ʿAmr," in *EI*² (G.H.A. Juynboll).

148 The *ḥanīfiyyah* was the religion of pure monotheism, which was known as *dīn Ibrāhīm* (the religion of Abraham). Those who are said to have followed the *ḥanīfiyyah* were called *ḥunafāʾ* (pl. of *ḥanīf*); see "Ḥanīf," in *EI*² (W.M. Watt); Rubin (1990).

149 ʿUmar b. Abī Bakr b. Muḥammad b. ʿAbd Allāh b. ʿAmr b. al-Muʾammal b. Ḥabīb; Ibn ʿAsākir, *Dimašq*, 43:547–551.

150 Perhaps this is ʿAbd al-Ḥakīm b. Sufyān b. Abī Namir, who is quoted elsewhere as one of al-Muʾammalī's sources; al-Fāsī, *Šifāʾ al-ġarām*, 2:115, 117.

151 ʿUtmān b. Abī Sulaymān al-Makkī l-Qurašī, a narrator of *ḥadīt* and *qāḍī* in Mecca; al-Mizzī, *Tahdīb al-kamāl*, 19:384–385.

152 Abū ʿUbaydah b. ʿAbd Allāh b. Abī ʿUbaydah b. Muḥammad b. ʿAmmār b. Yāsir. For another tradition narrated by al-Muʾammalī on the authority of Abū ʿUbaydah b. ʿAbd Allāh, see Ibn ʿAsākir, *Dimašq*, 9:241, and 50:79.

153 Perhaps this is Naṣr b. Mazrūʿ al-Kalbī. Ibn Mazrūʿ al-Kalbī is mentioned elsewhere as one of al-Muʾammalī's sources; see Ibn ʿAsākir, *Dimašq*, 46:348.

النار بريحه. فقلت: ’ما شأنه؟‘ فقالوا: ’هو أول من غير دين إبرٰهيم،‘ وأشبه من رأيت من ولده به أكثم بن أبي الجون الكعبي.“ فقال أكثم: ”أَتَخَشَّى يٰرسول الله أن يضرني شَبَهُه.“ قال: ”لا أنت مسلم وهو كافر.“

§ 42 حدثني عمر بن أبي بكر عن ابن أبي الزناد أن رسول الله ﷺ قال: ”أريت أبا بني [ابن] كعب هؤلاء عمرو بن لحي بن قمعة بن خندف يجر قصبه في النار قد آذى أهل النار بريحه. فقلت: ’ما شأنه؟‘ قالوا: ’إنه أول من غير دين إبرٰهيم وبحر البحيرة وسيب السائبة،‘ وأشبه من رأيت من ولده به أكثم بن أبي الجون.“ قال: فقام إليه أكثم | فقال: ”يٰرسول الله بأبي أنت وأمي أيضرني شبهه؟“ 31*a فقال: ”لا أنت مسلم وهو كافر.“

§ 43 قال وقال ابن أبي نمر: هو أول من غير دين إبرٰهيم وإسمٰعيل عليهما السلام وأحدث أشياء تابعه عليها بعض الناس وأباها عليه آخرون أحدث البحيرة والسائبة وكان أول من نصب وثنا بعد جرهم وهو الذي استخرج إساف ونائلة فنصبهما.

---

٢ شَبَهُه: كذا (التشكيل). ‖ مسلم: وضع المقريزي ثلاث نقط تحت هذه الكلمة إشارة إلى تلفظها بالسين.
٦ السائبة: وضع المقريزي ثلاث نقط تحت هذه الكلمة إشارة إلى تلفظها بالسين. ١١ فنصبهما: نهاية القصاصات الورقية.

ʿAmr b. Luḥayy. The people of hell were suffering from his smell. I asked: 'What is the matter with him?' They said: 'He is the first who changed the religion of Abraham.' Akṯam b. Abī l-Ǧawn al-Kaʿbī resembles him in appearance more than any of his descendants whom I have ever seen." Akṯam said: "O Messenger of Allāh! I fear that my resemblance to him would harm me." He replied: "No, you are a Muslim whereas he was an infidel."

§ 42 ʿUmar b. Abī Bakr related to me on the authority of Ibn Abī l-Zinād[154] that the Messenger of Allāh, may Allāh bless and save him, said: "The ancestor of the Banū Kaʿb, ʿAmr b. Luḥayy b. Qamaʿah b. Ḫindif, was shown to me dragging his intestines in hell. He hurt the people of hell with his smell. I asked: 'What is the matter with him?' They said: 'He is the first who changed the religion of Abraham, and instituted the practices of *al-baḥīrah* and *al-sāʾibah*.' Akṯam b. Abī l-Ǧawn resembles him in appearance more than any of his descendants whom I have ever seen." Akṯam then approached him and said: "O Messenger of Allāh! With my father may you be ransomed and with my mother! (*bi-abī anta wa-ummī*).[155] Would my resemblance to him be harmful to me?" He said: "No, you are a Muslim whereas he was an infidel."

§ 43 Ibn Abī Namir said: He [ʿAmr b. Luḥayy] was the first who changed the religion of Abraham and Ishmael, may peace be upon them, and introduced innovations that some people followed and others rejected. He introduced the practices of *al-baḥīrah* and *al-sāʾibah*, and he was the first to set up an idol after Ǧurhum.[156] He was the one who extracted Isāf and Nāʾilah[157] and set them up.[158]

---

154 Abū Muḥammad ʿAbd al-Raḥmān b. Abī l-Zinād (d. 174/790); al-Ḏahabī, *Siyar aʿlām al-nubalāʾ*, 8:167–170.

155 *Bi-abī anta wa-ummī* is used in this context to denote that the Prophet is as dear to Akṯam b. Abī l-Ǧawn as his parents. Regarding the meaning of this phrase, see Wright (1896–1898): vol. 2: § 56 (c., Rem. a).

156 For more on the tribe of Ǧurhum, see "D̲j̲urhum or D̲j̲urham," in *EI*^{2} (W. Montgomery Watt).

157 See § 84 ff.

158 This is the end of the small inserted paper in the MS.

32b § 44 قال ابن هشام: | حدثني بعض أهل العلم أن عمرو بن لحي خرج من مكة إلى الشام في بعض أموره فلما قدم {مآبَ} من أرض البلقاء وبها يومئذ العماليق وهم ولد عِمْلاق ويقال عِمْليق بن لاوَذ بن سام بن نوح رآهم يعبدون الأصنام فقال لهم: "ما هذه الأصنام التي أراكم تعبدون؟" قالوا له: "هذه أصنام نعبدها فنستمطرها فتُمطِرنا ونستنصرها فتنصرنا." فقال لهم: "أفلا تعطونني منها صنمًا فأسير به إلى أرض العرب فيعبدونه؟" فأعطوه صنمًا يقال له هُبَل فقدم به مكة فنصبه وأمر الناس بعبادته وتعظيمه انتهى.[a]

§ 45 وكان عمرو بن لحي—وهو ربيعة بن حارثة بن عمرو بن عامر بن ثعلبة بن امرئ القيس ابن مازن بن الأزد، أمه فُهَيرة بنت الحٰرث بن مُضاض الجرهمي وهو أبو خزاعة وكان يكنى أبا ثمامة وكان كاهنا {ومعه} رَئِي من الجن—حين غلبت خزاعة على البيت ونفت جرهم عن مكة قد جعلته العرب ربا لا يبتدع بدعة إلا اتخذوها شرعة لأنه كان يطعم الناس ويكسو في الموسم فربما نحر في الموسم عشرة آلاف بدنة وكسا عشرة آلاف حُلة وبلغ من أمره أنه فقأ عين عشرين بعيرا وكانوا {يفّقؤون} عين الفحل إذا بلغت الإبل ألفًا فإذا بلغت ألفين {فقؤوا} العين الأخرى

٢ مآبَ: في الأصل "مَاأَبَ". ٧–٩ وهو ... الجن: الزيادة بخط المقريزي في الهامش الأيمن منقلبة + صح، ويشير إليها رمز ⌐ بعد "لحي" ٨ يكنى: في الأصل "يكنا". ٩ ومعه: في الأصل "او معه". ‖ رَئِي: وضع المقريزي الهمزة فوق الياء. ١١ حُلة: وضع المقريزي رمز "ح" تحت الكلمة إشارة إلى تلفظها بالحاء. ‖ وبلغ من: كشط المقريزي عبارة أخرى قبل أن يصححها كما هي الآن. ١١–1.104 أمره ... ألفا: الزيادة بخط المقريزي في الهامش الأيسر من الأسفل إلى الأعلى ويشير إليها رمز ¬ بعد "من". ١٢ يفّقؤون: في الأصل "يفّقون". ‖ فقؤوا: في الأصل "فقوا".

a قارن المسعودي، مروج الذهب، ٢: ٣٨١ ("ثمّ نشأ عمرو بن لُحَيّ فساد قومه بمكّة واستولى على أمر البيت ثم سار إلى مدينة البلقاء من أعمال دمشق من أرض الشام فرأى قومًا يعبدُون الأصنام فسألهم عنها فقالوا: «هذه أرباب نتّخذها نستنصر بها فنُنصر ونستقي بها فنُسقى وكل ما نسألها نُعطى»، فطلب منهم صنمًا فدفعوا إليه هبل فسار به إلى مكة ونصبه على الكعبة ومعه إساف ونائلة، ودعا الناس إلى عبادتها وتعظيمها").

§ 44 Ibn Hišām[159] said: A learned man related to me that ʿAmr b. Luḥayy left Mecca for al-Šām on a certain matter. When he arrived at Maʾāb [Moab] in the land of Balqāʾ,[160] which was inhabited at that time by the Amalekites, who were the descendants of ʿImlāq or ʿImlīq b. Lāwaḏ [Lud] b. Sām [Shem] b. Nūḥ [Noah],[161] he saw them worshipping idols, and said to them: "What are these idols that I see you worshipping?" They told him: "These are idols that we worship. We ask them for rain and they give it to us, and we ask them for aid against our enemies and they grant it to us." He asked them: "Will you not give me one of these idols, so that I can take it to the land of the Arabs and they can worship it?" So they gave him an idol called Hubal, and he took it to Mecca, set it up, and ordered the people to worship and venerate it. Unquote.[162]

§ 45 As for ʿAmr b. Luḥayy—he [Luḥayy[163]] is Rabīʿah b. Ḥāriṯah b. ʿAmr b. ʿĀmir b. Ṯaʿlabah b. Imriʾ al-Qays b. Māzin b. al-Azd, and his [ʿAmr's] mother was Fuhayrah bt. al-Ḥāriṯ b. Muḍāḍ al-Ǧurhumī. He is Abū Ḫuzāʿah, and his *kunyah* was Abū Ṯumāmah. He was a soothsayer who had a *ǧinnī* that was visible to him (*raʾī*).[164] When Ḫuzāʿah conquered the House [i.e. the Kaʿbah] and banished Ǧurhum from Mecca, the Arabs made him [ʿAmr b. Luḥayy; their] master, and every undesirable innovation he made was accepted by them as religious law, because he used to feed the people and provide [them] with clothes during the season of the pilgrimage. He [ʿAmr b. Luḥayy] sometimes slaughtered ten thousand sacrificial animals[165] during the pilgrimage season and provided [the people] with ten thousand sets of clothes. He [ʿAmr b. Luḥayy] is reported to have gouged out one eye from [each of] twenty camels. They used to gouge out the eye of a male-camel when the total number of camels reached one thousand, and when it reached two thousand, they gouged out the other eye. He [ʿAmr b. Luḥayy; lived to]

---

159 ʿAbd al-Malik b. Hišām (d. 213 or 218/828 or 833) is known for his edition of Ibn Isḥāq's *Sīrah* (the biography of the Prophet); see "Ibn Hishām," in *EI*² (W.M. Watt).

160 For more on Hubal's place of origin, see "Hubal," in *EI*² (T. Fahd).

161 According to Muslim tradition, the Amalekites were ancient pre-Islamic people. The sources offer a variety of theories about their genealogy; see "ʿAmālīq," in *EI*³ (R. Tottoli); Lane (1863–1893): 2160.

162 This account is also translated in Ibn Hišām, *The Life of Muhammad* 701.

163 See al-Azraqī, *Aḫbār Makkah*¹, 1:164.

164 Compare Ibn al-Kalbī, *al-Aṣnām* 54, where it seems that Abū Ṯumāmah was the *ǧinnī*'s *kunyah*. But see also Ibn Ḥabīb, *al-Munammaq* 327.

165 *Badanah*; the word denotes a camel or a cow that is offered for sacrifice in Mecca; Lane (1863–1893): 169.

ورأى من ولده وولد ولده ألفا[a] وكان يَلُتّ السويق للحاج على صخرة معروفة تسمى صخرة اللّاتِّ. وكان الذي يلُت من ثقيف[b] فلما مات قال لهم عمرو بن لحي إنه لم يمت ولكن دخل في الصخرة ثم أمرهم بعبادتها وأن يبنوا عليها بيتًا يُسمَى اللَّاتَ. فدام أمره وأمر بنيه على هذا بمكة ثلاثمائة سنة فلما هلك عمرو سميت تلك الصخرة اللّاتَ مُخَفَّفة التاء واتخذت صنما.

§ 46 فهو أول من غير دين إبرٰهيم وإسمٰعيل وأول من بحر البحيرة وسيب السائبة وأول من نصب وثنا بعد جرهم ويقال إنه الذي استخرج إساف ونائلة ونصبهما.

§ 47 وقال ابن إسحٰق: ويزعمون أن أول ما كانت عبادة الحجارة في بني إسمٰعيل أنه كان لا يظعن من مكة ظاعن منهم حين ضاقت عليهم والتمسوا الفَسِيْح في البلاد إلا حمل معه حجرا من حجارة الحرم تعظيما للحرم فحيث ما نزلوا وضعوه فطافوا به كطوافهم بالكعبة حتى سَلَخ ذلك بهم إلى أن كانوا يعبدون ما استحسنوا من الحجارة وأعجبهم حتى خلفت الخلوف ونسوا ما كانوا عليه واستبدلوا بدين إبرٰهيم وإسمٰعيل غيره فعبدوا الأوثان وصاروا إلى ما كانت عليه الأمم قبلهم من الضلالات وفيهم على ذلك بقايا من عهد إبرٰهيم عليه السلام يتمسكون بها من | تعظيم البيت والطواف به والحج 33a

٥-٦ فهو ... ونصبهما: الزيادة بخط المقريزي في الهامش الأيمن ويشير إليها رمز ┌ بعد "صنما". ٥ بحر: وضع المقريزي رمز "ح" تحت الكلمة إشارة إلى تلفظها بالحاء.

a قارن الحلبي، السيرة الحلبية، ١: ١٨ ("وعاش عمرو بن لحي هذا ثلثمائة سنة وأربعين سنة، ورأى من ولده وولد ولده ألف مقاتل: أي ومكث هو وولده من بعده في ولاية البيت خمسمائة سنة").

b قارن السهيلي، الروض الأنف، ١: ٣٥٧ ("وكان عمرو بن لُحَيّ حين غلبت خزاعةُ على البيت، ونفت جُرْهم عن مكة، قد جعلته العرب رَبًّا لا يبتدع لهم بدعة إلا اتخذوها شرعة؛ لأنه كان يطعم الناس، ويكسو في الموسم، فربما نحر في الموسم عشرة آلاف بَدَنَة، وكسا عشرة آلاف حُلَّة حتى [قيل] إنه اللاتُّ الذى يَلُتُّ السّوبقَ للحَجِيج على صخرة معروفة تسمى: صخرة اللات، ويقال إن الذي يلُتُّ كان من ثقيف"). وقارن أيضا ابن الكلبي، الأصنام، ١٦ ("واللّاتُ بالطائف، وهي أحدث من مناةَ. وكانت صخرةً مُرَبَّعَةً. وكان يهوديٌّ يَلُتُّ عندها السَّوِيقَ").

see one thousand of his descendants and the sons of his descendants. He used to moisten (*yaluttu*) the *sawīq*[166] for the pilgrims on a well-known rock called the rock of al-Lātt.[167] [According to another opinion,][168] the one who moistened [the *sawīq*] was from Ṯaqīf. When he [the man from Ṯaqīf] died, ʿAmr b. Luḥayy told them that he [the man from Ṯaqīf] did not die, but entered the rock. Then he [ʿAmr b. Luḥayy] ordered them to worship it [the rock] and to build a sanctuary on it and call it al-Lātt. It continued thus during his [ʿAmr b. Luḥayy's] own lifetime and that of his [ʿAmr b. Luḥayy's] descendants in Mecca for three hundred years,[169] and when ʿAmr died, that rock was named Allāt—without a *šaddah* over the *tāʾ*—and it became an idol.[170]

§ 46 He [ʿAmr b. Luḥayy] was the first to change the religion of Abraham and Ishmael, the first to institute the practices of *al-baḥīrah* and *al-sāʾibah*, and the first to set up an idol after Ǧurhum. It is said that he was the one who extracted Isāf and Nāʾilah and set them up.

§ 47 Ibn Isḥāq said: They claim that stone worship began among the sons of Ishmael because they would not leave Mecca unless they carried with them one of the stones of its sacred territory (*al-ḥaram*) as a sign of reverence to it. This was at a time when Mecca had become too small for them and they wanted more room in the land. Wherever they settled, they would place [the stone] and then circumambulate it, as they circumambulated the Kaʿbah, and this led them[171] to worship the stones that they deemed good and which pleased them. Eventually, as generations passed away, they forgot their former beliefs, exchanged the religion of Abraham and Ishmael for another, worshipped idols, and repeated the errors of the peoples before them. Still, they adhered to remnants from the time of Abraham, may peace be upon him—such as venerating the House [i.e. the Kaʿbah], circumambulating it, making the *ḥaǧǧ* and the *ʿumrah*,[172] performing the *wuqūf* on

166 A kind of porridge made of wheat or barley and moistened with water or clarified butter.

167 See also § 175.

168 See al-Suhaylī, *al-Rawḍ al-unuf*, 1:356.

169 See also Lane (1863–1893): 2649.

170 For explanations concerning the etymology of the name Allāt, see Krone (1992): 43–49.

171 The meaning of the verb *salaḫa* in this sentence can be inferred from the context. See also Stummer (1944): 378.

172 The greater and lesser pilgrimages, respectively.

والعمرة والوقوف على عرفة والمزدلفة وهدي البدن والإهلال بالحج[a] والعمرة مع إدخالهم فيه ما ليس منه.

§48 فكانت كنانة وقريش إذا أهلوا قالوا: "لبيك اللهم لبيك لبيك لا شريك لك إلا شريك هو لك تملكه وما ملك." فيوَحدونه بالتلبية ثم يُدخِلون معه أصنامهم ويجعلون مِلكَها بيده. يقول الله تبارك وتعالى لمحمد ﷺ ﴿وَمَا يُؤْمِنُ أَكْثَرُهُمْ بِٱللَّهِ إِلَّا وَهُمْ مُشْرِكُونَ﴾ أي ما يوحدونني بمعرفة حقي إلا جعلوا معي شريكا من خلقي.[b]

§49 وذكر ابن شبة أن إسمٰعيل عليه السلام لما سكن مكة وولد له بها أولاد وكثروا بها حتى {ملؤوها} وما حولها ونفوا من كان بها من العماليق ضاقت عليهم مكة فاضطربوا في البلاد فكان سَبَب عبادتهم الأوثان والحجارة أنه كان لا يظعن من مكة ظاعن إلا احتمل معه حجرا من حجارة الحرم معظما له وصبابة بمكة[c] فحيث ما حلوا وضعوه وطافوا به كطوافهم بالكعبة ثم خرجوا من ذلك إلى أن عبدوا ما استحسنوا واستبدلوا بدين إبرٰهيم وإسمٰعيل غيره فنصبوا الأوثان ثم ذكر نحو ما تقدم.

---

٥ وَمَا ... مُشْرِكُونَ : شكل المقريزي الآية كما يلي: "وما يُؤْمِنُ اكثَرهم بالله الا وهو مشركون".
٧–١٠ وذكر... له : كشط المقريزي نصا آخر قبل أن يكتب النص الحالي وتابعه في الهامش الأيسر.
٨ ملؤوها : في الأصل "ملوها". ٩ احتمل : وضع المقريزي رمز "ح" تحت الكلمة إشارة إلى تلفظها بالحاء.
١٠–١٢ وصبابة ... تقدم : الزيادة بخط المقريزي في الهامش الأيسر منقلبة في آخر السطر.

---

a راجع ابن منظور، لسان العرب، "هلل" ("والإِهْلالُ بالحج: رفعُ الصوت بالتَّلْبية").

b قارن السهيلي، الروض الأنف، ١: ٣٥١ ("أي ما يوحِّدونني لمعرفة حقِّي إلا جعلوا معي شريكا من خَلقي").

c قارن ابن الكلبي، الأصنام، ٦ ("حدَّثنا أبي وغيرُه—وقد أثبتُّ حديثَهم جميعًا—أنّ إسماعيل بن إبراهيم (صلّى الله عليهما) لمّا سكن مكّة ووُلِدَ له بها أولادٌ كثيرٌ حتّى ملأوا مكّة ونفَوْا مَن كان بها من العماليق، ضاقت عليهم مكّةُ ووقعتْ بينهم الحروبُ والعداواتُ وأخرج بعضُهم بعضًا فتفسَّحوا في البلاد والتماس المعاش. وكان الذي سَلَخَ بهم إلى عبادة الأوْثان والحجارة أنه كان لا يَظْعَنُ من مكّة ظاعنٌ إلّا احتمَل معه حَجَراً من حجارة الحَرَم، تعظيمًا للحَرَم وصَبابةً بمكّة").

ʿArafah and al-Muzdalifah,[173] offering the *budn*[174] as sacrifices, and raising their voices when uttering the *talbiyah*[175] during the *ḥaǧǧ* and the *ʿumrah*[176]—while also introducing practices that were not part of it [the religion of Abraham].[177]

§ 48 When Kinānah and Qurayš raised their voices while uttering the *talbiyah*, they said: "At your service (*labbayka*), O Allāh, at your service, at your service! You have no partner except the partner that You have. You own him and whatever he owns." They would declare His oneness in the *talbiyah*, and then include their idols with Him, and place what they own in His hand. Allāh, the Blessed and Exalted, said to Muḥammad, may Allāh bless and save him: "And the most of them believe not in Allāh, but they associate other gods [with Him],"[178] i.e. they do not declare My oneness, while knowing My right [to be worshipped alone], without ascribing to Me a partner of My own creation.

§ 49 Ibn Šabbah reported that when Ishmael, may peace be upon him, lived in Mecca and begot children, they multiplied there until they filled Mecca and its surroundings and banished the Amalekites who inhabited it, and because Mecca became too small for them, they began roaming the land. They worshipped idols and stones because no one left Mecca without carrying with him one of the stones of its sacred territory, out of reverence for it [the sacred territory] and deep affection for Mecca. Wherever they settled, they would place [the stone] and then circumambulate it as they circumambulated the Kaʿbah. Then they forsook this [practice], and worshipped what they deemed good, exchanged the religion of Abraham and Ishmael with another, and set up idols. Afterwards, he reported something similar to what has already been mentioned.

173 Regarding *al-wuqūf*, or "the standing" of the pilgrims, see "al-Wuḳūf," in *EI*² (P. Lory); "Ḥadjdj," in *EI*² (A.J. Wensinck-[J. Jomier]); "ʿArafāt," in *EI*³ (Uri Rubin).

174 Plural of *badanah*, see above, n. 165.

175 A formula repeated by pilgrims entering the state of *iḥrām* (ritual purity). Different tribes had different *talbiyas* dedicated to their idols; see "Talbiya," in *EI*² (T. Fahd); Kister (1980a).

176 *Al-ihlāl bi-l-ḥaǧǧ wa-l-ʿumrah*. For the meaning of the word *ihlāl* in this context, see Klinke-Rosenberger (1941): 75, n. 34 (and the references given there).

177 This account is also translated in Ibn Hišām, *The Life of Muhammad* 33–34.

178 Qurʾān (*Yūsuf*), 12:106.

§50 ويقال إن آدم عليه السلام لما مات افترق أولاده فرقتين فرقة تمسكت بالدين والصلاح وفرقة مالت إلى المعاصي والفساد واعتزل أهل الصلاح وصعدوا الجبل الذي أهبط عليه آدم بالهند ويقال له نُوْد[a] فجعلوا تابُوتَه في مغارة هناك[b] وأقام أهل الفساد في الأرض فكانوا يسْتَغْوُون من نزل إليهم من أهل الجبل هذا وقد {استولوا} على تابوت آدم فصور لهم الشيطان صورة آدم ليتخذوها بدلا من تابوته فعظموها دهرا طويلا حتى جاء بعدهم من غلا في تعظيمها حتى رأى عبادتها دينا فعبدها وصارت صنما وعمل مثلها عدة أصنام.[c]

§51 ويقال إن آدم مات بالهند على الجبل الذي أهبط عليه فكانوا يطوفون بقبره تبركا به ثم افترقوا في الديانة فأوحى الله تعالى إلى {متوشلخ} بن {أخنوخ} بن يرد بن {مهلائيل} بن قينان بن أنوش ابن شيث بن آدم أن لا يطوف بقبر آدم كافر وأن يحول بينهم وبينه فلا يَصِلون إليه وأن يخلي بين المؤمنين وبين قبره. فكان المؤمنون من ولد آدم يطوفون بقبره كلما أرادوا ومنعوا أهل الكفر أن يدنوا منه فاشتد ذلك عليهم وحزنوا لمفارقته فلما رأى إبليس ذلك منهم قال لهم: | "إن هؤلاء 33b

٢-٣ الذي ... في: الزيادة بخط المقريزي في الهامش الأيمن من الأعلى إلى الأسفل + صح، ويشير إليها رمز ⌐ بعد "الجبل". ٣ مغارة هناك: كشط المقريزي عبارة أخرى قبل أن يصححها كما هي الآن مع الزيادة في الهامش الأيمن. ٤ استولوا: في الأصل "اسفوا" (راجع الماوردي، الحاوي الكبير). ٨ متوشلخ: في الأصل "متوشلخ". ‖ أخنوخ: في الأصل "حنوح" ‖ مهلائيل: في الأصل "مهلايل".

a قارن ياقوت، معجم البلدان، ٥: ٣١٠ ("نَوْذ: بالفتح ثم السكون وذال معجمة: جبل بسرنديب عنده مهبط آدم، عليه السّلام، وهو أخصب جبل في الأرض، ويقال: أمرَع من نَوْذ وأجدبُ من برَهُوت، وبرهوت: واد بحضرموت، ذكر في موضعه"). وقارن الطبري، تاريخ، ١: ١٢٠-١٢١ ("قال وأُهبط آدم على جبل بالهند يقال له بوذ ... وقال آخرون بل اهبط آدم بسَرَنْديب على جبل يُدعَى بوذ").

b قارن ابن الكلبي، كتاب الأصنام، ٥٠ ("أوّلُ ما عُبِدَتِ الأصنام أنّ آدم عليه السلام لمّا مات، جعله بنو شيث بن آدَمَ في مغارة في الجبل الذي أُهْبِطَ عليه آدمُ بأرض الهند").

c قارن الماوردي، الحاوي الكبير، ٩: ٥٦٤ ("حكي أن آدم لما مات افترق أولاده فريقين فريق تمسكوا بالدين والصلاح وفريق مالوا إلى المعاصي والفساد ثم اعتزل أهل الصلاح فصعدوا جبلا وأخذوا معهم تابوت آدم ومكث أهل المعاصي والفساد في الأرض فكانوا يستغوون من نزل إليهم من أهل الجبل، واستولوا على تابوت آدم فصور لهم إبليس صورة آدم ليتخذوا بدلًا من التابوت فعظموها ثم حدث بعدهم من رأى تعظيمها فعبدها فصارت أصنامًا معبودة").

§ 50 It is said that when Adam, may peace be upon him, died, his descendants became divided into two groups: One group adhered to religion and righteousness, while the other inclined to disobedience and corruption. The righteous people separated themselves and climbed the mountain on which Adam was cast down in India. It was called Nūd.[179] They placed his [Adam's] coffin in a cave there. The corrupt people remained in the plains, and used to lead astray the people of the mountain who came down to them. They took possession of[180] Adam's coffin, and Satan made an image of Adam for them, so that they could adopt it instead of his coffin. They venerated it [his image] for a long period of time, and eventually those who lived after them exaggerated their veneration of it [so much] that they considered its worship to be a religion, and therefore worshipped it. It [Adam's image] became an idol, and he [Satan?] made several idols similar to it.[181]

§ 51 It is said that Adam died in India on the mountain upon which he was cast down, and that they used to circumambulate his grave to draw its blessing. Then they became divided with regard to their religion, and Allāh, the Blessed and Exalted, inspired Matūšalaḫ [Methuselah] b. Aḫnūḫ [Enoch] b. Yard [Jared] b. Mahlāʾīl b. Qaynān b. Anūš b. Šīṯ b. Ādam to prevent the infidels from circumambulating Adam's grave, separate them from it so that they could not reach it, and let the believers access his grave freely. The believers who descended from Adam used to circumambulate his grave whenever they pleased, and they prevented the infidels from approaching it. This was difficult for them [the infidels], and it saddened them to be separated from it. When Satan saw this [i.e. the grief of the infidels], he said to

179 There are diverse explanations of the name of this mountain. See al-Ṭabarī, *Taʾrīḫ*, 1:119–125; idem, *History*, 1:290–295.

180 The translation follows the text found in al-Māwardī, *al-Ḥāwī l-kabīr*, 9:564 (*wa-stawlaw*) instead of the version given by al-Maqrīzī (*wa-asifū*).

181 Or perhaps, several idols similar to it were made.

يفخرون عليكم ويزعمون أنهم بنو آدم دونكم. فهل يسركم أن أجعل لكم شبه آدم فتأتونه كل وقت فتطوفون به؟" فقالوا: "وددنا ذلك." فنحت لهم خمسة أصنام وهي ود وسواع ويغوث ويعوق ونسر فعبدوها وما زالوا على عبادتها حتى بعث الله تعالى نوحا فنهاهم عن عبادتها فأبوا عليه تركها فلما كان الطوفان جعل الموج يدفعها بشدة جرية الماء حتى قذفها إلى بحر جُدة فلما نضب ماء الطوفان اندفنت.

§ 52 ويقال إن ودا وسواع ويغوث ويعوق ونسرا كانوا قوما صالحين فماتوا جميعا في نحو شهر فجزع عليهم {ذوو} قراباتهم. فأتاهم رجل من بني قابيل بن آدم يقال له الرحال فقال لهم عندما اشتد حزنهم: "يا قوم قد علمتم أني أتقن الناس كَفّيْن. فهل لكم أن أعمل مثل صورهم؟ لا تنكرون منهم قليلا ولا كثيرا غير أني لا أقدر أن أنفخ فيهم[a] الروح." قالوا: "نعم." فنحت لهم الأصنام الخمسة على صُوَرهم وذلك على عهد يَرْد بن {مهلائيل} بن قينان بن أنوش بن شيث بن آدم.

§ 53 فكان الرجل منهم يجيء فإذا نظر إلى الأصنام ذكر عمه وابن عمه كأنهم هم فيستغفر لصاحبه ويترحم عليه حتى هلك ذلك القرن[b] ثم جاء قرن بعدهم فعظموا تلك الأصنام أشد تعظيما من القرن الأول ثم جاء القرن الثالث فقالوا: "ما عظم أولنا هؤلاء إلا وهم يرجون شفاعتهم عند الله." فعَبَدُوهم وبالغوا في تعظيمهم وصار الأمر يزداد عظما حتى اعتقدوا أنها تنفع وتضر.

---

٦ ونسرا : وضع المقريزي ثلاث نقط تحت الكلمة إشارة إلى تلفظها بالسين. ٧ ذوو : في الأصل "ذووا". || الرحال : وضع المقريزي رمز "ح" تحت الكلمة إشارة إلى تلفظها بالحاء. ٩ فنحت : وضع المقريزي رمز "ح" تحت الكلمة إشارة إلى تلفظها بالحاء. ١٠ مهلائيل : في الأصل "مهلايل".

---

a قارن ابن الجوزي، المنتظم، ١: ٢٣٢ ("غَيْر أني لا أقدر أن أجعل فيها أرواحًا").

b قارن ابن الجوزي، المنتظم، ١: ٢٣٢ ("وكان الرجل يأتي أخاه وعمه وابن عمه ليعظمه ويسعى حوله حتى ذهب ذلك القرن الأول").

them: "These [people] claim superiority over you and allege that they alone are the sons of Adam. Would you like me to make for you [an image] similar to Adam, so that you can visit it any time and circumambulate it?" They [the infidels] said: "We would like that." Thereupon he sculpted five idols for them—Wadd, Suwāʿ, Yaġūṯ, Yaʿūq, and Nasr, and they [the infidels] worshipped them. They kept worshipping them until Allāh, the Exalted, sent Noah. He [Noah] forbade them [the infidels] from worshipping them [the idols], but they refused his order to leave them. When the flood came, the waves pushed them with the force of the water until they were cast into the sea of Jedda,[182] and when the water of the flood receded, they were buried.

§ 52 It is said that Wadd, Suwāʿ, Yaġūṯ, Yaʿūq, and Nasr were righteous people. They all died in the space of about a month, and their kin were grief-stricken over them. Then a man of the Banū Qābīl [Cain] b. Ādam, who was called al-Raḥḥāl, came to them when their grief was intense, and he told them: "O people! You know that I have the most skillful hands. Would you like me to make [statues] that will resemble their images? The only fault you will find with them is that I am not able to breathe spirit into them." They [the people of Wadd, Suwāʿ, Yaġūṯ, Yaʿūq, and Nasr] said: "Yes." So he sculpted for them the five idols in their image. This was during the time of Yard b. Mahlāʾīl b. Qaynān b. Anūš b. Šīṯ b. Ādam.

§ 53 One of them would come, and when he looked at the idols, he remembered his uncle and cousin as if they were them. He would beg forgiveness for his relative and express compassion for him. [They did this] until that generation passed away, and after them came another generation who venerated these idols even more than the first one. Then came the third generation, and they said: "Our ancestors venerated these [people;[183] i.e. Wadd, Suwāʿ, Yaġūṯ, Yaʿūq, and Nasr] only because they sought their intercession with Allāh." So they worshipped them, exaggerated their veneration of them, and the gravity of the situation gradually increased until they believed that they [the idols] could benefit and harm [them].

182 Regarding Jedda, the port of Mecca on the Red Sea, see "Jidda," in *EI*³ (U. Freitag); Hawting (1984).

183 The masculine plural pronouns in this paragraph may refer to the idols. See also Ibn al-Kalbī, *al-Aṣnām* 52, n. 6, n. 7.

§ 54 فلما بعث الله إليهم {أخنوخ} وهو إدريس بن يرد بن {مهلائيل} نبيا دعاهم إلى عبادة الله ورفض الأصنام فأبوا ذلك فرفعه الله إليه ولم يزْدد الأمر إلا عظما حتى أدرك نوح وبينه وبين آدم عشرة أجيال فبعثه الله إليهم رسولا وهو ابن أربع مائة وثمانين سنة فدعاهم في نبوته مائة وعشرين سنة ثم أمره الله أن يصنع الفلك ويحمل فيها ما أمره فركب معه ثمانون نفسا[a] وأرسل الله الطوفان | فاحتمل الماء الأصنام حتى ألقاها إلى جدة فنضب الماء عنها واندفنت فلم تزل مندفنة 34a حتى استخرجها إبليس لمشركي العرب فدعاهم إليها فأجابوه.

§ 55 فأخذت قضاعة ودا فعبدوه في دومة الجندل ثم توارثوه حتى صار إلى كلب فعبدوه حتى جاء الإسلام وأخذت أَعْلَى وأنعم ابنا عمرو بن طيئ يغوث وكان لكهلان يعوق ثم توارثه {بنوه} حتى صار إلى همدان وكان لبني معد بن عدنان سواع حتى صار لهذيل وكان لحمير نَسْر.[b]

§ 56 وذكر أبو زيد عمر بن شبة أن عمرو بن لحي قال له رَئِيُه يوما: "أَجِبْ أبا ثمامة." فقال له: "لبيك مِنْ تِهَامَة." فقال له: "ارْحَل بلا مَلامة." قال: "خير ولا إقامة." قال: "ائْتِ ضَفّ جُدّة تَجِد فيها

١ أخنوخ : في الأصل "حنوح". ‖ مهلائيل : في الأصل "مهلايل". ٨ بنوه : في الأصل "بنوهما". ١٠ وذكر : كشط المقريزي كلمة أخرى قبل أن يصححها كما هي الآن. ‖ رَئِيُه : وضع المقريزي الهمزة فوق الياء. ١١ ارْحَل : وضع المقريزي رمز "ح" تحت الكلمة إشارة إلى تلفظها بالحاء.

a قارن ابن كثير، البداية والنهاية، ١: ١٢٨ ("وقد اختلف العلماء في عدة من كان معه في السفينة، فعن ابن عباس: كانوا ثمانين نفسًا معهم نساؤهم، وعن كعب الأحبار: كانوا اثنين وسبعين نفسًا. وقيل: كانوا عشرة").

b قارن الثعلبي، الكشف والبيان، ١٠: ٤٦ ("فاتخذت قضاعة ودًّا فعبدوها بدومة الجندل، ثمّ توارثه بنوه الأكابر فالأكابر حتّى صارت إلى كلب فجاء الإسلام وهو عندهم، وأخذ أعلى وأنعم وهما من طي يغوث فذهبوا به إلى مراد فعبدوه زمانًا، ثمّ إن بني ناجية أرادوا أن ينزعوه من أعلى وأنعم، ففروا به إلى الحصين أخي بني الحرث بن كعب، وأما يعوق فكان لكهلان، ثمّ توارثه بنوه الأكبر فالأكبر، حتّى صار إلى همدان، وأما نسر فكان لخثعم يعبدونه، وأما سواع فكان لآل ذي الكلاع يعبدونه").

§ 54 When Allāh sent them Aḫnūḫ [Enoch], who is Idrīs b. Yard b. Mahlā'īl,[184] as a prophet, he [Aḫnūḫ] called them to worship Allāh and abandon the idols, but they refused to do this. Then Allāh raised him [Aḫnūḫ] to Himself, and the gravity of the situation increased until the time of Noah. Ten generations separate him from Adam. Allāh sent him [Noah] to them as a messenger when he was at the age of 480, and for 120 years he called them [to worship Allāh], according to his prophecy. Then Allāh ordered him to build the ark and load it with what He [Allāh] had ordered him [to load it with]. Eighty persons traveled with him. Afterwards, Allāh sent the flood, the water carried the idols until it cast them upon Jedda, and when the water receded, they were buried. They remained buried until Satan extracted them for the Arab polytheists. He [Satan] called them to [worship] them [the idols] and they complied with his call.

§ 55 Quḍāʿah took Wadd and worshipped it in Dūmat al-Ǧandal. Then they inherited it from one another[185] until it became the property of Kalb, who worshipped it until the advent of Islam. Aʿlá and Anʿam, who were sons of ʿAmr b. Ṭayyi',[186] took Yaġūṯ. Yaʿūq belonged to Kahlān, and afterwards, his descendants inherited it from each other[187] until it became the property of Hamdān. Suwāʿ belonged to the Banū Maʿadd b. ʿAdnān, until it became the property of Huḏayl, and Nasr belonged to Ḥimyar.

§ 56 Abū Zayd ʿUmar b. Šabbah related that one day ʿAmr b. Luḥayy's *ǧinnī*[188] said to him: "Answer [my call], O Abū Ṯumāmah!" He said to him: "I am at your service from Tihāmah!"[189] He [the *ǧinnī*] told him [ʿAmr b. Luḥayy]: "Leave without delay."[190] He [ʿAmr b. Luḥayy] said: "Very well, there shall be no tarrying." He [the *ǧinnī*] said: "Go to the shores of Jedda, where

184 For the identification of Enoch with Idrīs, see note 14.

185 Compare al-Ṯaʿlabī, *al-Kašf wa-l-bayān*, 10:46: *ṯumma tawāraṯahu banūhu l-akābir fa-l-akābir* ("Then his descendants inherited it, one great and noble [descendant] from another great and noble [descendant]"). For this use of the verb *tawāraṯa*, see also Lane (1863–1893): 2934: "توارثوه كابرا عن كابر [They inherited it by degrees, one great in dignity and nobility from another great in dignity and nobility]."

186 Later in the text (§ 67), Anʿam is given the *nisbah* al-Murādī, though he originally belonged to the tribe of Ṭayyi'. See Crone (2016): 442–443, n. 125.

187 See note 185 above.

188 *Ra'ī*; see also § 45.

189 The coastal plain between the Red Sea and the southern Arabian Peninsula; "Tihāma," in *EI*² (G.R. Smith).

190 Perhaps this is the meaning of *malāmah* in this account. The verb *talawwama* from the same root means to tarry, linger, take one's time. The alternative is to translate *malāmah* as reproach, rebuke, or blame.

أصناما مُعَدَّة فأَورِدْها أرضَ تهامة ولا تهَب ثم ادْعُ العربَ إلى عبادتها تُجَبْ.» فأتى ساحل جدة فاستثارها.[a]

§ 57 ثم حملها حتى ورد بها تهامة وحضر الحج فرفعها ودعا العرب إلى عبادتها. فأجابه عوف بن كنانة بن عوف بن عُذْرَة بن زيد فدفع إليه وُدًا فحمله فكان بدومة الجندل وسمى ابنَه عبْدَ وُدٍّ فهو أول عربي سُمي عبد ود ثم سميت العرب ‹به› بعده[b] وجعل عوف ابنه {عامرا} الذي يقال له عامر الجادر[c] سادنا له فلم تزل بنوه يَسْدُنُونَه حتى جاء الله بالإسلام.[d]

---

١ فأتى: في الأصل "فاتا". ٤ وُدًا: كذا في الأصل بدلا من "وَدًّا". ‖ وسمى: في الأصل "وسما". ‖ وُدٍّ: كذا في الأصل بدلا من "وَدٍّ". ٥ عامرا: في الأصل "عامر".

---

a قارن ابن حبيب، المنمق، ٣٢٧ ("قال: وكان عمرو بن ربيعة وهو خزاعة كاهنًا له رئي من الجن وكان عمرو يكنى أبا ثمامة فأتاه رئيه فقال: أجب أبا ثمامة، فقال: لبيك من تهامة، فقال له: ارحل بلا ملالة، قال له: جير ولا إقامة، قال: ائت صف جدة، فيها أصناما معدة، فأورد بها تهامة، ولا تهب ثم ادع العرب إلى عبادتها تجب. فأتى عمرو ساحل جدة فوجد بها ودا وسواعا ويغوث ويعوق ونسرا وهي الأصنام التي عبدت على عهد إدريس ونوح عليهما السلام، ثم إن الطوفان طرحها هناك فسفى عليها الرمل فواراها، واستثارها عمرو وحملها إلى تهامة وحضر الموسم فدعا العرب إلى عبادتها فأجابوه"). وقارن أيضا ابن الكلبي، الأصنام، ٥٤ ("عَجِّلْ بالمسير والظَّعْن من تِهَامَه بالسعد والسلامَة! قال: جَيْر ولا إقامَه").

b قارن ياقوت، معجم البلدان، ٥: ٣٦٨ ("وسمى ابنه عبد وَد، فهذا أول من سمى عبد ود ثم سمت العرب به بعده").

c قارن ابن منظور، لسان العرب "جدر" ("وعامِرُ الأَجْدَارِ: أَبو قبيلة من كَلْبٍ، سمّي بذلك لِسِلَعٍ كانت في بدنه").

d قارن ابن الكلبي، الأصنام، ٥٤-٥٥ ("ثم حملها حتَّى ورد تِهامَةَ. وحضر الحجُّ، فدعا العربَ إلى عبادتها قاطبةً. فأجابه عوْفُ بن عُذْرَةَ بن زيد اللاتِ بن رُفَيْدَةَ بن ثور بن كلب بن وَبَرَةَ بن تَغْلِبَ بن حُلوانَ بن عِمْرانَ بن إلحافِ بن قُضاعةَ فدفع إليه وَدًّا فحمله [إلى وادي القُرى فأقرّه] بدُومَة الجندل. وسَمّى ابنَه عبدَ وَدٍّ. فهو أوّل من سُمِّيَ به، وهو أوّل من سَمَّى عبدَ وَدّ. ثم سمَّت العربُ به بعدُ.
وجَعَلَ عوفٌ ابنَه عامرًا الذي يقال له عامر الأَجْدَار سادنًا له. فلم تزل بنوه يَسْدُنونه حتَّى جاء الله بالإسلام"). وقارن ابن حبيب، المحبر، ٣١٦ ("وكان وَد لبني وبرة. وكان موضعه بدومة الجندل. وكان سدنته بني الفرافصة بن الأحوص، من كلب").

you will find idols that are ready [for taking]. Bring them to the land of Tihāmah, and fear not. Then summon the Arabs to worship them, and your summons shall be heeded."[191] He [ʿAmr b. Luḥayy] thereupon went to the coast of Jedda and dug them up.

§ 57 Then he [ʿAmr b. Luḥayy] carried them and arrived with them at Tihāmah, and during the time of the pilgrimage he [ʿAmr b. Luḥayy] raised them and summoned the Arabs to worship them. ʿAwf b. Kinānah b. ʿAwf b. ʿUḏrah b. Zayd[192] complied with his [ʿAmr b. Luḥayy's] call, so he [ʿAmr b. Luḥayy] gave him Wadd. He [ʿAwf b. Kinānah] carried it [with him], and it was [placed] in Dūmat al-Ǧandal. He [ʿAwf b. Kinānah] named his [ʿAwf b. Kinānah's] son ʿAbd Wadd, and he became the first Arab to be given the name ʿAbd Wadd. Afterwards, the Arabs were given this name. ʿAwf made his son ʿĀmir, who was called ʿĀmir al-Ǧādir,[193] custodian of it, and his descendants remained its custodians until the advent of Islam.

191 The translation of this paragraph does not convey the rhythmic effect of the original Arabic text. For a more poetic translation of the parallel text in Ibn al-Kalbī's *al-Aṣnām*, see Faris (1952): 47.

192 He was from the tribe of Kalb. See Caskel (1966), 1: table 290.

193 Or read ʿĀmir al-Aǧdār instead of ʿĀmir al-Ǧādir. See for instance Ibn al-Kalbī, *al-Aṣnām* 55; Ibn Durayd, *al-Ištiqāq* 541–542. ʿĀmir al-Aǧdār is a branch of Kalb; see Caskel (1966): 1, table 292; "Wadd," in *EI*² (Ch. Robin). However, ʿĀmir al-Ǧādir seems to be associated in the sources with the builder of the *ǧidār* ("barrier") of the Kaʿbah, who belonged to the Azd; see Ibn Saʿd, *al-Ṭabaqāt*¹, 1:53. Regarding the *ǧidār* of the Kaʿbah, see Rubin (1986): 99.

§58 فكان مالك بن حارثة الجدري يذكر أنه رآه وقال: كان أبي يبعثني إليه باللبن فيقول: "اسقه إلٰهك" فأشربه.[a] قال: ثم رأيت خالد بن الوليد بعد كسَره أجذاذا[b] وكان النبي ﷺ وجهه لهدمه من غزوة تبوك فحالت بينه وبين هدمه بنو عبد ود وبنو عامر الجادر فقاتلهم فهزمهم فكسره. فقتل يومئذ رجل من بني عبد ود يقال له قطن بن شريح فأقبلت أمه وهو مقتول فقالت: [الوافر]

ألا تلك المسرة لا تدوم ... ولا يبقى على الدهر النعيمُ
ولا يبقى على الحدثان غُفْر ... بشاهقة له أم رَؤُوْمُ[c] | 34b

ثم قالت: [البسيط]

يا جَامِعًا جامعُ الأحشاء والكبد ... يا ليت أمك لم تولد ولم تلد[d]

ثم أكبت عليه فشهقت شهقة فماتت. وقتل أيضا يومئذ حسان بن مصاد ابن عم الأكيدر.

---

١ حارثة : قد تكون القراءة الأصح "جارية". ٥ يبقى : في الأصل "يبقا". ٦ يبقى : في الأصل "يبقا". ‖ رَؤُوْمُ : وضع المقريزي الهمزة فوق الواو.

---

a راجع ابن الكلبي، الأصنام، ٥٥ ("قال وكان أبي يبعثني باللبن إليه، فيقول: اِسْقِه إلٰهَكَ. قال: فأشربُهُ").

b قارن ابن الكلبي، الأصنام، ٥٥ ("ثم رأيتُ خالد بن الوليد بعدُ كَسَرَهُ فجعله جُذَاذًا").

c قارن ابن الكلبي، الأصنام، ٥٦ ("ولا يَبْقَى على الحَدَثَانِ غُفْرٌ ... له أمٌّ بشاهقةٍ رَءُومُ").

d قارن ابن عبد ربه، العقد الفريد، ٣: ٢١٦ ("وقالت أعرابية ترثي ولدها:

يا قرحةَ القلب والأحشاءِ والكبِدِ ... يا ليت أُمَّك لم تَحْبَلْ ولم تَلِدِ").

وقارن أيضا ابن دريد، تعليق، ١٢٧ ("وعن الكلبي، قال: وجّه النَّبيّ صلى الله عليه وسلَّم خالدَ بنَ الوليد إلى وَدّ—صنمٍ لكلب—فكَسَّرَه جُذاذا وقاتَلَ دونَه ناسٌ من كلبٍ، فقُتِل منهم رجال، وقُتِلَ منهم غلامٌ يقالُ له جامِع، فجاءَت أُمّه تَتَصفَّح القَتْلَى، فلما وَجَدَتْه قالت:

أَلا تِلْكَ المَسَرّةُ لا تَدُومُ ... ولا يَبْقَى على الدَّهْر النعيمُ
ولا يَبْقى على الحَدَثان غُفْرٌ ... بشاهِقَةٍ لهُ أمٌّ رَؤوم

ثم أَسندته إلى صَدْرِها وقالت:

يا جامِعًا جامِعَ الأَحْشاءِ والكَبدِ ... يا لَيْتَ أمَّك لم تُولَد ولم تَلِدِ

ثم شَهِقَتْ شَهْقَة اتبعتْها نَفْسها").

§ 58 Mālik b. Ḥāriṯah al-Ǧadarī[194] related that he had seen it [Wadd]. He said: My father used to send me to it with milk and say "Give it to your god to drink," but I would drink it myself. Afterwards I saw Ḫālid b. al-Walīd.[195] He smashed it [Wadd] into pieces. The Prophet, may Allāh bless and save him, had sent him [Ḫālid b. al-Walīd] from the expedition of Tabūk to destroy it. The Banū ʿAbd Wadd and the Banū ʿĀmir al-Ǧādir prevented him from destroying it, so he fought them, defeated them, and then smashed it [the idol, Wadd]. A man of the Banū ʿAbd Wadd named Qaṭan b. Šurayḥ was killed on that day, and his mother came across his body and said: [*al-wāfir*]

Surely, that joy shall not last
nor will pleasure withstand time,
nor will the young of a mountain goat that has a loving mother
withstand the adversities of fate on a steep cliff.[196]

Then she said: [*al-basīṭ*]

O you who hold together! You who hold the intestines and liver together!
I wish your mother was never born nor ever gave birth.[197]

Then she fell over him, uttered a single cry, and died. Ḥassān b. Maṣād, who was Ukaydir's[198] cousin, also died on that day.

194 Or read Mālik b. Ǧāriyah al-Aǧdārī (Ḥāriṯah and Ǧāriyah are only differentiated by diacritic marks); Lecker (2012): 127.

195 Ḫālid b. al-Walīd b. al-Muġīrah al-Maḫzūmī (d. 21/646) was a famous general at the time of the early conquests. He was also sent by the Prophet to destroy al-ʿUzzá (see below); "Khālid b. al-Walīd," in *EI*[2] (P. Crone).

196 The version of this verse in *al-Aṣnām* gives the impression that the mother was on the steep cliff. For its translation, see Grunebaum (1953): 46; Atallah (1969): 46.

197 This verse is also translated in Klinke-Rosenberger (1941): 60. For a less literal translation of the first hemistich, see Faris (1952): 48: "O thou the centre of my love / The source of all my oy and mirth!"

198 Ukaydir b. ʿAbd al-Malik al-Kindī was the Christian king of Dūmat al-Ǧandal at the time of Muḥammad; "Ukaydir b. ʿAbd al-Malik," in *EI*[2] (M. Lecker).

§59 فكان مالك بن حارثة يصف ودا يقول: كان على صورة رجل كأعظم ما يكون من الرجال مؤتزرا بحلة مُرتَديا بأخرى عليه سيف متقلده وقد تنكب قوسا وبين يديه حربة فيها لواء وكِنانة فيها سهام.[a]

§60 وفي ود يقول الحُطَيئَة العبْسي: [الطويل]

فحياك {ود} ما هداك لفتية   وركبٍ بأعلى ذي غَوانَةَ هُجَّدِ[b]

١ حارثة: وضع المقريزي رمز "ح" تحت الكلمة إشارة إلى تلفظها بالحاء. ٤ الحُطَيئَة: وضع المقريزي الهمزة فوق الياء. ٥ ود: في الأصل "ودًا". ‖ بأعلى: في الأصل "باعلا".

a قارن ياقوت، معجم البلدان، ٥: ٣٦٨ ("قال ابن الكلبي: فقلت لمالك بن حارثة: صفْ لي ودًّا حتى كأني أنظر إليه، قال: تمثال رجل كأعظم ما يكون من الرجال قد دُثّر عليه، أي نُقِش عليه، حُلّتان متّزر بحُلّة ومرتد بأخرى عليه سيفٌ قد تنكّب قوسًا وبين يديه حَرْبة فيها لواء ووفضة أي جعبة فيها نبلٌ، فهذا حديث ودّ"). وقارن ابن الكلبي، الأصنام، ٥٦ ("قد ذُبِرَ عليه حُلَّتان").

b قارن أبو علي الفارسي، الحجة، ٦: ٣٢٨ ("فحَيَّاكِ وَدٌّ مَنْ هَدَاكِ لِفِتْيَةٍ وخُوْصٍ بأعلى ذي نُضَالَةَ هُجَّدِ. وقال أبو الحسن: ضمّ أهل المدينة الواو وعسى أن يكون لغة في اسم الصنم، قال: وسمعت هذا البيت:

حيّاك وُدٌّ فإنّا لا يَحِلُّ لنا   فضلُ النساءِ وإنّ الدّين قَدْ عَزَمَا

الواو مضمومة. قال: وسمعت مَن يقول: إن الواو مفتوحة"). وقارن أيضا ياقوت، معجم البلدان، ٤: ٤٥ ("طُوَالَةُ بالضم: موضع ببُرْقان فيه بئر، قاله ثعلب في قول الحطيئة:

وفي كل مُمسَى ليلة ومعرَّس   خيالٌ يوافي الركبَ من أمّ مَعْبَدِ

فحيّاك وُدٌّ ما هداك لفتية   وخُوصٍ بأعلى ذي طوالة هُجّدِ").

وقارن أيضا: ابن سيدة، المخصص، ١٣: ٢٦٢ ("والهاجِدُ—المُصَلِّي بالليل والنّائمُ وأنشد

فَحَيَّاكِ وُدٌّ مَا هَدَاكِ لِفِتْيةٍ   وخُوصٍ بأَعْلَى ذِي طُوالَةَ هُجَّدِ").

وقارن أيضا: ابن سيدة، المخصص، ٥: ١٠٤ ("فَحَيَّاكَ وُدٌّ مَنْ هَداكَ لِفِتْيةٍ   وخُوصٍ بأعْلَى ذي عَوانة هُجَّدِ"). وراجع: لسان العرب، "هجد" ("والهاجِد: والهَجود: المُصَلي بالليل، والجمع هُجودٌ وهُجّد؛ قال مرة بن شيبان:

أَلا هَلَكَ امْرُؤٌ قامَتْ عليه   بِجَنْبِ عُنَيْزَةَ البَقَرُ الهُجُودُ

وقال الحطيئة:

فَحَيَّاكِ وُدٌّ ما هداكِ لِفِتْيَةٍ   وخُوص بأَعلى ذِي طُوالةَ هُجَّدِ").

§ 59 Mālik b. Ḥāriṯah used to describe Wadd, saying: It was a figure of a man of the largest stature, clothed with one garment around the waist and another covering the upper part of its body.[199] It carried a sword, had a bow on its shoulder, and in front of it there was a spear to which a banner was attached and a quiver with arrows.

§ 60 Al-Ḥuṭay'ah al-ʿAbsī[200] said about Wadd: [*al-ṭawīl*]

May Wadd[201] grant you [fem. sg.] longevity! What has led you to young men
and to camel riders[202] who sleep[203] at the upper part of Ḏū Ġawānah?[204]

---

199 Compare with other versions of this account, in which it seems that the garments were engraved or painted on Wadd; Ibn al-Kalbī, *al-Aṣnām* 56; Yāqūt, *Muʿǧam al-buldān*, 5:368. See also Wellhausen (1897): 17; Klinke-Rosenberger (1941): 60, 136.

200 Ḥuṭay'ah ("the midget") was the nickname of the *muḫaḍram* poet Ǧarwal b. Aws; "al-Ḥuṭay'a," in *EI*[3] (N. Papoutsakis).

201 The following two verses were also recited with the vocalization Wudd; see Abū ʿAlī l-Fārisī, *al-Ḥuǧǧah*, 6:328. According to some Qur'ān reciters, Wudd was the name of the idol mentioned in Qur'ān (*Nūḥ*), 71:23. Note that there was reportedly another idol named Wudd, which was worshipped by the tribe of Qurayš. See Lecker (2012): 124.

202 Other variants of this verse have *ḫūṣ* (pl. of *aḫwaṣ*; a camel whose eyes are sunk) or *ṣuhb* (pl. of *aṣhab*; according to one definition, the word denotes a camel with red fur on his upper body and white fur on his underside); al-Ḥuṭay'ah, *Dīwān* 73; idem, *Der Dīwān* 86–88; Lane (1863–1893): 822, 1737. In light of this, it is worth mentioning that the word *rukb* is also the plural of *arkab*, i.e. a camel with one knee larger than the other (Lane [1863–1893]: 1145). Note also that the word *al-rakb* (in the sense of "owners of camels"/"riders of camels") appears in the previous line of this poem: al-Ḥuṭay'ah, *Dīwān* 73.

203 In this verse, *huǧǧad* may also be rendered as "to young men and to camel riders who pray in the night at the upper part of Ḏū Ġawānah." The verb *haǧada* is one of the *aḍdād*, i.e. a word that has two contrary meanings. It means both "to remain awake in the night"/"pray in the night," and "to sleep"; see Ibn Sīdah, *al-Muḫaṣṣaṣ*, 13:262; Lane (1863–1893): 2879.

204 Other sources that quote this verse mention the places Ṭuwālah, ʿUwādah, and ʿAwānah; al-Ḥuṭay'ah, *Dīwān* 73.

§61 وله يقول النابغة الذبياني: [البسيط]

حياك {وُد} فإنا لا يحل لنا   لهو النساء وإن الدِينْ قد عَزَما

§62 قال ابن شبة: حدثنا محمد بن حاتم ثنا يونس بن محمد ثنا يعقوب القمي ثنا أبو المطهر عن أبي جعفر محمد بن علي أنهم ذكروا عنده وهو قائم يصلي يزيد بن المهلب فلما انفتل من صلاته قال: "ذكرتم يزيد بن المهلب. أما إنه قتِل في أول أرض عُبد فيها غير الله." ثم ذكر ودا فقال: "كان ود رجلا مسلما كان مُحببا في قومه فلما مات عسكروا حول قبره وجزعوا عليه.[a] فلما رأى إبليس جزعهم عليه تشبه في صورة إنسان فقال: 'أرى جزعكم على هذا. فهل لكم أن أصور لكم مثله فيكون في بلدكم فتذكرونه به؟' قالوا: 'نعم'." قال: "فصور لهم مثله فوضعوه في ناديهم وجعلوا يذكرونه. فلما رأى ما بهم من ذكره قال لهم: 'فهل لكم أن أجعل في منزل كل رجل منكم {تمثالا} مثله فيكون في بيته فتذكرونه؟'[b]

٢ وُد: في الأصل "وُدٍ". ٣ ابن شبة: الزيادة بخط المقريزي في الهامش الأيسر من الأسفل إلى الأعلى في آخر السطر. ٩ تمثالا: في الأصل "مثالا".

a قارن الصالحي، سبل الهدى، ٢: ٢٤٠ ("عسكروا حول قبره في أرض بابل").

b قارن ابن كثير، البداية والنهاية، ١: ١٢٢ ("فلما رأى ما بهم من ذكره قال: هل لكم أن أجعل في منزل كل واحد منكم تمثالا مثله ليكون له في بيته فتذكرونه؟").

§ 61 Al-Nābiġah al-Ḏubyānī[205] said, referring to it: [*al-basīṭ*]

May Wadd grant you [fem. sg.] longevity! It is unlawful for us
to dally with women since the religion has become strict.[206]

§ 62 Ibn Šabbah said: Muḥammad b. Ḥātim[207] related to us, Yūnus b. Muḥammad[208] related to us, Yaʿqūb al-Qummī[209] related to us, Abū l-Muṭahhar related to us on the authority of Abū Ǧaʿfar Muḥammad b. ʿAlī [al-Bāqir][210] that they mentioned Yazīd b. al-Muhallab[211] in his [al-Bāqir's] presence while he was standing in prayer. When he turned away from his prayer, he said: "You have mentioned Yazīd b. al-Muhallab. Indeed, he was killed in the land in which [deities] other than Allāh were first worshipped."[212] Then he mentioned Wadd and said: "Wadd was a Muslim man who was beloved among his people. When he died, they gathered around his grave and were grief-stricken over him. When Satan saw their grief over him, he assumed the form of a human and said: 'I see your grief over this [man]. Would you like me to make an image for you that will resemble him? It will be in your land and you can remember him through it.' They said: 'Yes.' So he [Satan] made an image of his [Wadd's] likeness for them, and they placed it in their place of assembly and remembered him. When he saw their interest in remembering him, he [Satan] told them: 'Would you like me to put in the house of each one of you a statue that will resemble him? It would be in your house and

205 A pre-Islamic poet who belonged to the Banū Murrah of Ġaṭafān; "al-Nābigha al-Dhubyānī," in EI^2 (A. Arazi).

206 See also Wellhausen (1897): 17.

207 Muḥammad b. Ḥātim b. Sulaymān al-Zammī (d. 246/860); al-Ḏahabī, *Siyar aʿlām al-nubalāʾ*, 11:452–453.

208 Yūnus b. Muḥammad al-Baġdādī (d. 207 or 208/822 or 823); al-Ḏahabī, *Siyar aʿlām al-nubalāʾ*, 9:473–476.

209 Abū l-Ḥasan Yaʿqūb b. ʿAbd Allāh al-Qummī (d. 174/790); al-Ḏahabī, *Siyar aʿlām al-nubalāʾ*, 8:299–300.

210 The fifth Imām of the Twelver Šīʿah. He became Imām in 94/712–713 or 95/713–714; "Muḥammad b. ʿAlī Zayn al-ʿĀbidīn, Abū Djaʿfar, called al-Bāḳir," in EI^2 (E. Kohlberg).

211 Yazīd b. al-Muhallab b. Abī Ṣufrah al-Azdī was governor under the Umayyads. His career is discussed in detail in "al-Muhallabids," in EI^2 (P. Crone).

212 Regarding the place in which Yazīd is said to have died, see "al-Muhallabids," in EI^2 (P. Crone): "Yazīd was defeated by Maslama b. ʿAbd al-Malik at ʿAḳr in Ṣafar 102/August 720; he himself was killed, and his supporters fled to Sind (where Ḥabīb b. al-Muhallab had recently been governor), only to be caught and killed or sent to Syria for execution."

قالوا: ’نعم‘.“ قال: ”فمثل لكل أهل بيت تمثالا مثله فجعلوا يذكرونه وأدرك أبناؤهم فجعلوا يرون ما يصنعون وتناسلوا ودرس أمر ذكرهم إياه حتى اتخذوه إلاها من دون الله أولاد أولادهم. فكان أول ما عبد غير الله في الأرض ود.“[a]

§63 قال أبو زيد عمر بن شبة: وأجابت عمرو بن لحي هذيلُ بن مدركة فدفع إلى رجل منهم يقال له الحٰرث بن تميم بن سعد بن هذيل سُوَاعًا وكانت هذيل وكنانة وسُلَيم وسعد بن بكر وسافلة قيس يعبدونه | وكان برُهَاط من أرض الحجاز.[b] 35a

---

٤ عمر … شبة : الزيادة بخط المقريزي في الهامش الأيسر من الأسفل إلى الأعلى + صح، ويشير إليها رمز ٦ بعد "أبو زيد".

---

٦ برُهَاط : أضاف المقريزي الحاشية التالية في الهامش الأعلى: ”رُهَاط بضم أوله قرية جامعة على ثلاثة أميال من مكة وهي بطرف جبل يقال له شمنصير بفتح أوله وثانيه بعده نون وصاد مهملة مكسورة وياء وراء مهملة وهو جبل ململم لم يعله قط أحد ولا درى ما على ذروته وبأعلاه القرود والمياه حواليه ينابيع وبغربيه قرية يقال لها الحُديبية ومن الحديبية إلى مكة مرحلة قاله البكري.“ راجع: العيني، عمدة القاري، ٥: ٥٣ (”قلت لعطاء: ما القرية الجامعة؟ قال: ذات الجماعة والأمير والقاضي والدور المجتمعة الآخذ بعضها ببعض، مثل جدة“). وقارن البكري، معجم ما استعجم، ٣: ٨١٠ (”[شَمَنْصِير] بفتح أوّله وثانيه، بعده نون ساكنة، وصاد مهملة مكسورة، وياء وراء مهملة: جَبَل … قال ابن دُرَيْد: ويقال شَمَاصِيرُ، بألف مكان النون، وهو جَبَلٌ مُلَمْلَمٌ من جبال تِهَامَة، يتّصل بجبال ذروة، ولم يَعْلُهُ قطّ أحد، ولا أدري ما على ذَرْوَتِهِ. وبأَعْلاه القُرُود، والمِيَاهُ حواليه ينابيعُ تنساب، عليها النَّخْلُ وغيرها. وبطرف شمنصير قرية يقال لها رُهاط، وهي بوَادٍ يُسَمَّى غُرَابا … وبغَرْبِي شَمَنْصِير قرية يقال لها الحُدَيْبِيَة، لَيْسَت بِالْكَبِيرة، وبحذائِها جبل صغير يقال له ضُعَاضِع، وعنده حبس كبير يجتمع فيه الماءُ“).

---

a قارن الصالحي، سبل الهدى، ٢: ٢٤١ (”هل لكم أن أجعل في منزل كل رجل منكم تمثالا فيكون في بيته فيذكر به؟ قالوا: نعم. فمثَّل لكل أهل بيت تمثالا مثله فجعلوا يذكرونه به وأدرك أبناؤهم فجعلوا يرون ما يصنعون به وتناسَلوا ودرَس أَمرُ ذِكْرهم إياه حتى اتخذوه إلهًا يعبدونه من دون الله تعالى فكان أولَ من عُبد من دون الله وَدٌّ“).

b قارن ابن الكلبي، الأصنام، ٥٧ (”قال: وأجابت عمْرَو بن لُحَيٍّ مُضَرُ بن نِزَار، فدفع إلى رجُل من هُذَيْلٍ، يقال له الحارث بن تميم بن سعد بن هُذَيْل بن مُدْرِكَة بن اليأس بن مُضَرَ سُواعًا. فكان بأرضٍ يقال لها رُهَاطُ من بطن نخلة، يعبُدُهُ من يليه من مُضَرَ“). وقارن أيضا ابن الكلبي، الأصنام، ٩–١٠ (”وكان أوّلَ

you can remember him.' They said: 'Yes.' So he made each family[213] a statue of his [Wadd's] likeness, and they remembered him [Wadd]. Their sons grew to maturity and started to see what they were doing. They begot offspring, their memory of him [Wadd] vanished, and finally the children of their children adopted it [the statue] as a god apart from Allāh. The first [deity] other than Allāh that was worshipped on earth was Wadd."

§ 63 Abū Zayd ʿUmar b. Šabbah said: Huḏayl b. Mudrikah complied with ʿAmr b. Luḥayy's call, so he [ʿAmr b. Luḥayy] gave Suwāʿ to one of their men whose name was al-Ḥāriṯ b. Tamīm b. Saʿd b. Huḏayl.[214] Huḏayl, Kinānah, Sulaym, Saʿd b. Bakr, and lower Qays [ʿAylān] worshipped it, and it was [placed] in Ruhāṭ in the land of al-Ḥiǧāz.[215]

من اتخذ تلك الأصنام، (من ولد إسماعيل وغيرِهم من الناس [و]سَمَّوْها بأسمائها على ما بَقِيَ فيهم من ذكرها حينَ فارقوا دِين إسماعيل) هُذَيْلُ بن مُدْرِكَةَ. اِتَّخذوا سُوَاعا. فكان لهم بِرُهَاطٍ من أرض يَنْبُع (!). ويَنْبُع عِرْضٌ من أعراض المدينة. وكانت سَدَنَتَه بنو لحيان. ولم أسمع لِهُذَيْلٍ في أشعارها له ذكرًا، إلا شعر رجل من اليمن.").

---

11 in Ruhāṭ : Ruhāṭ has a *ḍammah* over the first letter. It is a great town with a large population (*qaryah ǧāmiʿah*; the term appears to refer to a town that was an administrative center) at a distance of three miles (*amyāl*) from Mecca (but see the map), on the side of a mountain called Šamanṣīr—with a *fatḥah* over the first and second letters, then a *nūn*, a *ṣād* vocalized with a *kasrah*, and then a *yāʾ*, and a *rāʾ*. Šamanṣīr is a round-shaped mountain that no one has ever climbed, and no one knows what lies on its summit. There are apes at its top, springs around it, and west of it there is a town called al-Ḥudaybiyyah, which is one day's journey from Mecca. This was said by al-Bakrī (marginal gloss in al-Maqrīzī's hand). For more on the geographer Abū ʿUbayd ʿAbd Allāh b. ʿAbd al-ʿAzīz al-Bakrī (d. 487/1094), see *EI*², "Abū ʿUbayd al-Bakrī" (É. Lévi-Provençal).

---

213 Or, important family (*ahl bayt*).

214 See Caskel (1966): 1, table 58.

215 For more information on the location of Suwāʿ, see Lecker (2005a): 9, who argues that there were in fact two idols known by this name.

§64 فقال رجل من العرب يذكره: [الوافر]

تراهم حول {قيلهم} عكوفا   كما عكفت هذيل على سُوَاع
تظل جَنابَه صَرْعى لديه   عَتَائر من ذخائر كل راع[a]

§65 وقال أبو خراش الهذلي يذكر سواعا: [الوافر]

ألم يَرْهَبك من عز وخوف   جُنوح الآثمين على سُواع

§66 وله يقول راشد بن عبد ربه السُلَمي ونظر إلى ثعلبين وهما يبولان عليه: [الطويل]

أرب يبول الثعلَبان برأسه   لقد ذل من بالت عليه الثعالب

---

٢ قيلهم: في الأصل "قبلتهم" (راجع ابن الكلبي، كتاب الأصنام، ٥٧).

a قارن الزبيدي، تاج العروس، "سوع" ("يَظَلُّ جَنابَهُ برُهاط صَرْعَى   عَتائِرُ من ذَخائِرِ كُلِّ رَاعِ").

§ 64 One of the Arabs said, mentioning it: [*al-wāfir*]

You see them crowding around their prince[216]
as the Huḏayl crowded around Suwāʿ.
Sacrificial animals from the most valuable possessions of every herdsman
remained alongside it, lying prostrate before it.[217]

§ 65 Abū Ḫirāš al-Huḏalī[218] said, mentioning Suwāʿ: [*al-wāfir*][219]

Does not the leaning of the sinful ones on Suwāʿ
frighten you[220] with power and fear? [?][221]

§ 66 Rāšid b. ʿAbd Rabbihi al-Sulamī[222] said [the following verse] about it as he was looking at two foxes urinating on it: [*al-ṭawīl*]

Is this a lord on whose head two foxes[223] urinate?
He upon whom the foxes urinate is humiliated.[224]

---

216 This follows the reading found in Ibn al-Kalbī, *al-Aṣnām* 57 (*qaylihim*) instead of the word given by al-Maqrīzī (*qiblatihim*).

217 See also Wellhausen (1897): 18 (who translated the variant of this verse in *Tāǧ al-ʿarūs*); Klinke-Rosenberger (1941): 60.

218 Abū Ḫirāš Ḫuwaylid b. Murrah al-Huḏalī was a *muḫaḍram* poet who died during the caliphate of ʿUmar b. al-Ḫaṭṭāb; "Abū Khirāsh," in *EI*² (Ch. Pellat).

219 Cf. Ibn al-Kalbī, *al-Aṣnām* 10, where Ibn al-Kalbī is reported to have said that there is no mention of Suwāʿ in the poetry of Huḏayl. See also Lecker (1989): 53, n. 16.

220 Reading *yurhibka* instead of *yarhabka* as given by al-Maqrīzī.

221 The phrase *mina l-ġār wa-l-ḫawf* ("from jealousy and fear"), which only differs slightly from *min ʿizz wa-ḫawf*, appears in a different verse attributed to Abū Ḫirāš; Ibn Manẓūr, *Lisān al-ʿarab*, s.v. *wabīl*.

222 On whom see Lecker (1989): 54–59.

223 There are some disagreements as to whether there are two foxes (*ṯaʿlabāni*) mentioned in this verse or only one (*ṯuʿlubān*); Lane, *Arabic English Lexicon* 338.

224 These verses are also translated in Hawting (1999): 108; Lecker (1989): 55; Lane, *Arabic English Lexicon* 338.

§67 قال وأجابت مذحجُ عمرَو بن لحي فدفع إلى أَنْعَم بن عَمْرو المرادي يغوث فكان بأكمةٍ باليمن يقال لها مذحج تعبده مذحج ومن والاها. وقال غيره إن عمرو بن لحي دفع يغوث إلى أظلم وهو أنعم بن عَمْرٍو وإلى أعلى بن عمرو فكانت مذحج ومن والاها تعبده فأرادت ناجية من مراد أخذه فهربوا به إلى الحصين بن يزيد الحارثي[a] فرحب بهم وأكرمهم وزوج صاحبه ابنته بغير مهر وساقها إليه وهو رجل من أعلى وفيه قيل: [الوافر]

وسار بنا يغوث إلى مراد   فناجزناهم قبل الصباح

§68 وقال ابن إسحٰق: وأنعم من طيئ وأهل جرش من مذحج اتخذوا يغوث بجرش.

٣ أعلى: في الأصل "اعلا". ٥ أعلى: في الأصل "اعلا".

١ أَنْعَم: أضاف المقريزي الحاشية التالية في الهامش الأيسر: "حـ أنعم قال ابن هشام: وطيئ بن أدد بن مالك ومالك مذحج بن أدد ويقال طيئ بن أدد بن زيد بن كهلان بن سبأ وذكر الكلبي وأبو عبيد والبلاذري أنعم بن زاهر بن عمرو بن عوبثان بن زاهر بن مراد." راجع: مغلطاي، إكمال تهذيب الكمال، ٥: ١٩٣ ("وفي «الجمهرة» للكلبي: أنعم بن عمرو بن الغوث بن ظبي بن أدد بن زيد يشجب بن عريب بن زيد بن كهلان بن سبأ، انتقل إلى مراد فقيل انعم بن زاهر عن عامر بن عوثبان بن زاهر ابن مراد").

a قارن ياقوت، معجم البلدان، ٥: ٤٣٩ ("ولم يزل في هذا البطن من مراد أَنْعُم وأعلى إلى أن اجتمعت أشراف مراد وقالوا: ما بال إلهنا لا يكون عند أعزّائنا وأشرافنا وذوي العدد منا! وأرادوا أن ينتزعوه من أعلى وأنعم ويضعوه في أشرافهم، فبلغ ذلك من أمرهم إلى أعلى وأنعم فحملوا يغوث وهربوا به حتى وضعوه في بني الحارث"). وقارن أيضا القرطبي، الجامع، ١٨: ٣٠٩ ("وأخذت أعلى وأنعم—وهما من طيئ—وأهل جُرَش من مَذْحِج يَغُوث فذهبوا به إلى مُرَاد فعبدوه زمانا. ثم إن بني ناجية أرادوا نزعه من [أعلى] وأنعم، ففرّوا به إلى الحُصَين أخي بن الحارث بن كعب من خُزاعة").

§ 67 He [Ibn Šabbah] said: Maḏḥiǧ complied with ʿAmr b. Luḥayy's call, so he [ʿAmr b. Luḥayy] gave Yaġūṯ to Anʿam b. ʿAmr al-Murādī. It [the idol Yaġūṯ] was on a hill in Yemen called Maḏḥiǧ, where it was worshipped by Maḏḥiǧ and by those in their vicinity. Others said that ʿAmr b. Luḥayy gave Yaġūṯ to Aẓlam, who is Anʿam b. ʿAmr, and to Aʿlá b. ʿAmr, and that Maḏḥiǧ and those in their vicinity worshipped it. The [Banū] Nāǧiyah of Murād wanted to take it, so they fled with it to al-Ḥuṣayn b. Yazīd al-Ḥāriṯī.[225] He welcomed and honored them, gave his daughter in marriage without dowry to the person who was entrusted with it [i.e. the person who brought the idol], and sent her to him. He was a man from Aʿlá. [The following verse] was said about it [Yaġūṯ]: [*al-wāfir*]

Yaġūṯ led us to Murād,
and we fought them before the morning.[226]

§ 68 Ibn Isḥāq said: Anʿum[227] of Ṭayyiʾ and the people of Ǧuraš of Maḏḥiǧ adopted Yaġūṯ in Ǧuraš.[228]

---

2 Anʿam : Anʿam['s tribal affiliation]: Ibn Hišām said: [the pedigree of Ṭayyiʾ (to which Anʿam is said to have belonged) is] Ṭayyiʾ b. Udad b. Mālik, and Mālik is Maḏḥiǧ b. Udad. Some say [Ṭayyiʾ is] Ṭayyiʾ b. Udad b. Zayd b. Kahlān b. Sabaʾ. Al-Kalbī, Abū ʿUbayd [al-Qāsim b. Sallām], and al-Balāḏurī reported [that Anʿam is] Anʿam b. Zāhir b. ʿAmr b. ʿAwbaṯān b. Zāhir b. Murād (marginal gloss in al-Maqrīzī's hand). On Anʿam's affiliation with Murād, see note 186.

---

225 On Muḥammad's Companion Ḥuṣayn b. Yazīd b. Šaddād al-Ḥāriṯī, whose epithet was Ḏū l-Ġuṣṣah ("one who has a thing lying across the throat"), see Ibn Ḥaǧar, *al-Iṣābah*[1], 2:81–82; Ibn ʿAbd al-Barr, *al-Istīʿāb*, 2:470–471.

226 This line is also translated in Klinke-Rosenberger (1941): 35; Faris (1952): 9; Atallah (1969): 7. For more details on the quarrel over the control of the idol Yaġūṯ, see Yāqūt, *Muʿǧam al-buldān*, 5:439; Wellhausen (1897): 19–22.

227 According to Ibn Isḥāq, his name was Anʿum; al-Suhaylī, *al-Rawḍ al-unuf*, 1:352.

228 For more details on Ǧuraš, see Yāqūt, *Muʿǧam al-buldān*, 2:126–127; Graf (2010).

§69 قال أبو زيد: وأجابت همدان فدفع عمرو بن لحي إلى مالك بن مرثد بن جشم بن حاشد بن جشم بن خيوان بن نوف بن همْدان يعوق فكان بقرية يقال لها خيوان تعبده همدان ومن والاها من أهل اليمن.[a] وقال غيره: خيوان من صنعاء على ليلتين مما يلي مكة.[b]

§70 وفي يعوق يقول مطعم الأرحبي[c] لنهم في شأن قتيل كان منهم: [الرجز]

قُولا لِنهْم اقصدي   يا نهْم حاربك؟ الطريق
يا قومنا لا تعتدوا   بيني وبينكم يَعُوْق

§71 وقال مالك بن نَمَط الهمْداني: [الوافر] | 35b

يَريش الله في الدنيا ويَبْري   ولا يبري يعوق ولا يَريش

---

٥ حاربك: وضع المقريزي رمز "ح" تحت الكلمة إشارة إلى تلفظها بالحاء.

---

a قارن ابن حزم، جمهرة أنساب العرب، ٣٩٤ ("ومن بطون همدان أيضا بطن يقال لهم بنو قابض بن يزيد بن مالك بن جُشَم بن حاشد بن جُشَم. وكان عمرو بن لحيّ دفع الى قابض المذكور صَنَمًا اسمُهُ يَعُوق فجعله في قرية باليمن يقال لها خَيْوان"). وقارن الهمداني، الإكليل، ١٠: ٧٢ ("وأولد زيد بن مالك بن جشم بن حاشد مالكًا وهو خيوان بطن وقابضًا بطن وإلى خيوان بن زيد دفع عمرو بن لحي يعوق الصنم وكان في قرية خيوان"). وقارن السهيلي، الروض الأنف، ١: ٣٥٢ ("قال ابن إسحاق: وخَيْوانُ بَطْنٌ من هَمْدان، اتخذوا يَعُوقَ بأرض هَمْدان من أرض اليمن").

b قارن ياقوت، معجم البلدان، ٢: ٤١٥ ("خَيْوَانُ: بفتح أوله وتسكين ثانيه وآخره نون: مخلاف باليمن ومدينة بها؛ قال أبو علي الفارسي: خَيْوان فَيْعال منسوب إلى قبيلة من اليمن، وقال ابن الكلبي: كان يعوقُ الصنمُ بقرية يقال لها خَيْوان من صنعاءَ على لَيْلَتين مما يلي مكة").

c راجع الهمداني، الإكليل، ١٠: ١٥٤ ("فأولد طفيل جلهما ومطعما ومالكا فأولد جلهم مالكا وعترا وحوثرة وأولد مطعم مكرمان وأولد مكرمان المعمر فأولد المعمر مطعما فأولد مطعم أبا رهم الشاعر هاجر وهو ابن خمسين ومئة سنة").

§ 69 Abū Zayd[229] said: Hamdān complied [with ʿAmr b. Luḥayy's call], so he gave Yaʿūq to Mālik b. Marṯad b. Ǧušam b. Ḥāšid b. Ǧušam b. Ḫaywān[230] b. Nawf b. Hamdān.[231] It [Yaʿūq] was [placed] in a village called Ḫaywān, where it was worshipped by the Hamdān and the people of Yemen who were in their vicinity. Others said: Ḫaywān is at a distance of two nights' journey from Ṣanʿāʾ in the direction of Mecca.[232]

§ 70 Muṭʿim al-Arḥabī[233] said [the following verses] about Yaʿūq, [addressing them] to the Nihm,[234] concerning a murdered man who belonged to them [the Nihm]: [*al-rağaz*]

Tell [dual] Nihm: Act in a moderate manner,
O Nihm! […?]
O our people! Do not act aggressively!
Yaʿūq is between me and you [pl.; i.e. as an arbiter]!

§ 71 Mālik b. Namaṭ al-Hamdānī[235] said: [*al-wāfir*]

Allāh feathers arrows in this world and pares them,
but Yaʿūq neither pares nor feathers arrows.[236]

229 I.e. ʿUmar b. Šabbah.

230 Elsewhere this appears as Ḫayrān. See Caskel (1966), 1: table 227. Note that Mālik is not attested in this chart as one of Marṯad's sons.

231 Compare Ibn Ḥazm, *Ǧamharat ansāb al-ʿarab*, 394, where it is said that ʿAmr b. Luḥayy gave Yaʿūq to Qābiḍ b. Yazīd (read Zayd) of Hamdān. And see also al-Hamdānī, *al-Iklīl*, 10:72, where ʿAmr b. Luḥayy is said to have given this idol to Ḫaywān (= Mālik), who was Qābiḍ's brother. For Qābiḍ and Ḫaywān, see Caskel (1966), 1: table 228.

232 On the location of Ḫaywān, see also: "Yaʿūḳ," in *EI*² (Ch. Robin): "K̲h̲aywān is situated well to the north of Sanʿāʾ in the direction of Mecca, at a distance of 105 km, midway between Ṣanʿaʾ and Ṣaʿda."

233 More details concerning the pedigree of Muṭʿim al-Arḥabī (of Hamdān) are found in al-Hamdānī, *al-Iklīl*, 10:154. His son, Abū Ruhm b. Muṭʿim al-Arḥabī, who was reportedly also a poet, is said to have made the *hiğrah* at the age of 150; Ibn al-Aṯīr, *Usd al-ġābah*, 6:113.

234 Perhaps this is the Nihm branch of Hamdān. See Caskel (1966), 1: table 230.

235 Mālik b. Namaṭ (or his father Namaṭ according to another opinion) was reportedly part of the delegation of Hamdān that came from Yemen to see the Prophet. According to Ibn al-Kalbī, he descended from Sufyān b. Arḥab of Hamdān; Ibn al-Aṯīr, *Usd al-ġābah*, 5:46–47. See also Caskel (1966), 1: table 231.

236 I.e. Yaʿūq brings neither harm nor benefit. See also Lane (1863–1893): 1200; Ibn Hišām, *The Life of Muhammad* 701.

§72 قال عمر بن شبة: وأجابت حمير عمرو بن لحي فدفع إلى رجل من ذي رُعَين يقال له مَعْدي كرب نَسْرًا فكان بموضع من أرض سبأ يقال له بَلْخَعُ تعبده حمير ومن والاها.

فلم يزالوا يعبدونه {حتى هودهم ذو} نُواس.[a]

§73 ولم تزل هذه الأصنام تعبد حتى بعث الله تبارك وتعالى محمدا ﷺ وأمر بهدمها وبعث جرير ابن عبد الله البجلي إلى نسر فهدمه.

§74 وفي هذه الخمسة الأصنام أنزل الله تعالى ﴿وَقَالُوا لَا تَذَرُنَّ آلِهَتَكُمْ وَلَا تَذَرُنَّ وَدًّا وَلَا سُوَاعًا وَلَا يَغُوثَ وَيَعُوقَ وَنَسْرًا وَقَدْ أَضَلُّوا كَثِيرًا وَلَا تَزِدِ الظَّالِمِينَ إِلَّا ضَلَالًا﴾.

§75 وقال غيره لم تزل حمير تعبد نسرا إلى أن انتقلت أيام تبع عن عبادة الأصنام إلى اليهودية.

§76 وفي نسر يقول رجل من آل ذي رعين في قتيل قتله رجل من بني أود بن صعب بن سعد العشيرة: [المنسرح]

---

٣ حتى ... ذو: في الأصل "هم وذو" (راجع ابن الكلبي، كتاب الأصنام، ٥٨).

---

a قارن ياقوت، معجم البلدان، ٥: ٢٨٤ ("وَنَسْرٌ: أحد الأصنام الخمسة التي كان يعبدها قوم نوح، عليه السلام، وصارت إلى عمرو بن لُحَيّ، كما ذكرنا في ودّ، ودَعا القوم إلى عبادتها فكان فيمن أجابه حِمير فأعطاهم نسرًا ودفعه إلى رجل من ذي رُعين يقال له معدي كرب فكان بموضع من أرض سبأ يقال له بلخع فعبدته حمير ومن والاها فلم تزل تعبده حتى هَوَّدَهم ذو نُوَاس").

§ 72 ʿUmar b. Šabbah said: Ḥimyar complied with ʿAmr b. Luḥayy's call, so he gave Nasr to a man from Ḏū Ruʿayn whose name was Maʿdī Karib.[237] It [Nasr] was in a place in the land of Saba' called Balḫaʿ,[238] where it was worshipped by Ḥimyar and by those in their vicinity.[239]

They kept worshipping it until Ḏū Nuwās[240] turned them to Judaism.[241]

§ 73 These idols continued to be worshipped until Allāh, the Blessed and Exalted, sent Muḥammad, may Allāh bless and save him, and he ordered them to be destroyed. He sent Ǧarīr b. ʿAbd Allāh al-Baǧalī[242] to Nasr to destroy it.

§ 74 Allāh, the Exalted, revealed [the following verses] regarding these five idols: "and they[243] have said, 'Do not leave your gods, and do not leave Wadd, nor Suwāʿ, Yaġūṯ, Yaʿūq, neither Nasr.' And they have led many astray. And [my Lord] do not increase the evildoers except in error!"[244]

§ 75 Others said: Ḥimyar continued to worship Nasr until they abandoned idol worship for Judaism during the days of Tubbaʿ.[245]

§ 76 A man of the people of Ḏū Ruʿayn said [the following verse] about Nasr, concerning a man who was killed by a member of the Banū Awd b. Ṣaʿb b. Saʿd al-ʿAšīrah:[246] [*al-munsariḥ*]

---

237 He was reportedly one of the *muʿammarūn*, i.e. those who are said to have lived to an exceptionally advanced age; Ibn Ḥamdūn, *al-Taḏkirah al-Ḥamdūniyyah*, 6:38.

238 See "Yaʿūḳ," in *EI*[2] (Ch. Robin): "a Sabaean town known only through traditions relating to idols." See also Hawting (1999): 116.

239 For more on Nasr, see Müller (1994).

240 Yūsuf As'ar Yaṯ'ar, whose epithet in Muslim sources is Ḏū Nuwās, was the Ḥimyarī king who persecuted the Christians of Naǧrān in the year 523. See "D̲h̲ū Nuwās," in *EI*[2] (M.R. Al-Assouad); "People of the Ditch," in *EQ* (R. Tottoli).

241 This follows the reading in Ibn al-Kalbī, *al-Aṣnām* 58: *ḥattā hawwadahum Ḏū Nuwās* (They kept worshipping it until Ḏū Nuwās turned them to Judaism), instead of the reading provided by al-Maqrīzī: *hum wa-Ḏū Nuwās* ("they and Ḏū Nuwās").

242 Ǧarīr b. ʿAbd Allāh of the tribe of Baǧīlah was also the one sent to destroy Ḏū l-Ḫalaṣah (see below, § 189 and § 191). See also Ibn Saʿd, *al-Ṭabaqāt*[1], 8:145; "Bad̲j̲īla," in *EI*[2] (W.M. Watt).

243 See § 78.

244 Qur'ān (*Nūḥ*), 71:23–24.

245 Tubbaʿ is the term used in Muslim sources for the rulers of Ḥimyar between the late third and early sixth centuries; "Tubbaʿ," in *EI*[2] (A.F.L. Beeston). Perhaps Tubbaʿ in this tradition refers to Asʿad Abū Karib (see the tradition on the idol Ri'ām below, § 194).

246 Caskel (1966), 1: table 270.

حلفت بالنَسْر لا أصالحكم   ما اهتز في رأس أثلة ورق

§77 وذكر ابن شبة عن قتادة في قوله تعالى ﴿{لَا} تَذَرُنَّ آلِهَتَكُمْ وَلَا تَذَرُنَّ وَدًّا وَلَا سُوَاعًا﴾ الآية، قال: كان ود لهذا الحي من كلب بدومة الجندل[a] وكان سُواع لهذيل برهاط وكان يغوث لبني غطيف من مراد بالجوف من سبأ وكان يعوق لهمْدان ببلخع وكان نسْر لذي الكلاع من حمير وكانت هذه الآلهة التي يعبدها هؤلاء هي التي عبدها قوم نوح والله ما عدا ما تسمعون عُوْدا أو طينة أو حجرا عبدها العرب بعد ذلك.[b]

§78 وعن عروة بن الزبير وذكر رد قوم نوح عليه وقول بعضهم لبعض ﴿لَا تَذَرُنَّ آلِهَتَكُمْ وَلَا تَذَرُنَّ وَدًّا وَلَا سُوَاعًا وَلَا يَغُوثَ وَيَعُوقَ وَنَسْرًا﴾، قال: كانت هذه في قوم نوح ثم صارت في العرب. وقال مجاهد: كانت هذه الأسماء أسماء قوم صالحين فماتوا فعبدهم قوم نوح واتخذوهم آلهة فدعاهم إلى تركها فقالوا ﴿لَا تَذَرُنَّ آلِهَتَكُمْ﴾ هذه الأسماء.

§79 وعن الحسن في قوله تعالى ﴿إِنْ يَدْعُونَ مِنْ | دُونِهِ إِلَّا إِنَاثًا﴾ قال: كان لكل حي من العرب 36a
صنم يعبدونها يسمونها أنثى بني فلان. فأنزل الله تعالى ﴿إِنْ يَدْعُونَ مِنْ دُونِهِ إِلَّا إِنَاثًا وَإِنْ يَدْعُونَ إِلَّا شَيْطَانًا مَرِيدًا﴾.

٢ لَا : في الأصل "ولا".   ٥ ما تسمعون : كذا.   ١١ وعن ... مِنْ : كشط المقريزي عبارة أخرى قبل أن يصححها كما هي الآن.

a قارن الطبري، جامع البيان، ٢٣: ٣٠٤ ("فكان وَدٌّ لكَلْبٍ بدُومةِ الجَنْدَلِ").

b قارن الطبري، جامع البيان، ٢٣: ٣٠٤ ("وكانت هذه الآلهةُ يَعْبُدُها قومُ نوحٍ، ثم اتخذَها العربُ بعد ذلك، واللهِ ما عدا خشبةً أو طينةً أو حجراً").

I swore by Nasr that I shall not reconcile with you
as long as leaves quiver at the top of [the] tamarisk [tree].

§ 77 Ibn Šabbah reported [the following tradition] on the authority of Qatādah,[247] regarding His saying, the Exalted, "Do not leave your gods, and do not leave Wadd, nor Suwāʿ"[248] and so on with the verse: Wadd belonged to the tribe of Kalb in Dūmat al-Ǧandal, Suwāʿ belonged to Huḏayl in Ruhāṭ, Yaġūṯ belonged to the Banū Ġuṭayf of Murād in al-Ǧawf of Sabaʾ, Yaʿūq belonged to Hamdān in Balḫaʿ, and Nasr belonged to Ḏū l-Kalāʿ of Ḥimyar. These gods that were worshipped by these [people] are those that the people of Noah had worshipped. By Allāh, [these idols,] as you hear, [are?] nothing but wood, clay, or stone which the Arabs worshipped thereafter.

§ 78 On the authority of ʿUrwah b. al-Zubayr regarding the response of the people of Noah to his call, and their saying to one another, "Do not leave your gods, and do not leave Wadd, nor Suwāʿ, Yaġūṯ, Yaʿūq, neither Nasr":[249] These [idols] were among the people of Noah, and then they became the property of the Arabs. Muǧāhid[250] said: These names [i.e. Wadd, Suwāʿ, Yaġūṯ, Yaʿūq, and Nasr] were the names of righteous people. They died, and then the people of Noah worshipped them, and adopted them as gods. He [Noah] called on them [the people] to abandon them [the idols], but they said [to each other]: "Do not leave your gods,"[251] [i.e. those called by] these names.

§ 79 On the authority of al-Ḥasan[252] regarding His saying, the Exalted, "Instead of Him, they pray not except to female beings":[253] Every Arab tribe had a [female] idol that they worshipped and which they called the female being of such and such tribe. Allāh, the Exalted, revealed: "Instead of Him, they pray not except to female beings; they pray not except to a rebel Satan."[254]

247 For more on the Qurʾānic commentator Qatādah b. Diʿāmah al-Sadūsī (d. ca. 117/735), see "Ḳatāda b. Diʿāma," in *EI*² (Ch. Pellat).

248 Qurʾān (*Nūḥ*), 71:23.

249 Qurʾān (*Nūḥ*), 71:23.

250 Abū l-Ḥaǧǧāǧ Muǧāhid b. Ǧabr al-Makkī (d. between 100/718 and 104/722); "Mudjāhid b. Djabr al-Makkī," in *EI*² (A. Rippin).

251 Qurʾān (*Nūḥ*), 71:23.

252 Abū Saʿīd al-Ḥasan b. Abī l-Ḥasan Yasār al-Baṣrī (d. 110/728); "Ḥasan al-Baṣrī," in *EI*² (H. Ritter).

253 Qurʾān (*al-Nisāʾ*), 4:117.

254 Qurʾān (*al-Nisāʾ*), 4:117.

§80 قال عمر بن شبة: وهبل كان موضعه في الكعبة على الجب الذي كان فيها[a] وكان من خرز العقيق على صورة الإنسان وكانت يده اليمنى مكسورة أدركته قريش كذلك فجعلت له يدا من ذهب وكان أول من نصبه خزيمة بن مدركة بن إلياس بن مضر وجعلت له خزانة للقربان[b] وجعلت له سبعة أقداح يضرب بها على الميت والعذرة والنكاح وكان أكثر قربانه مائة وجُعِل له جناحان وكان يقال له هبل خزيمة وكانوا إذا {جاؤوا} هبل بالقربان ضربوا بالقداح وهم يقولون: [الرجز]

إنا اختلفنا فهب {السراحا} ثلاثة يا هبل فصاحا
الميت والعُذْرة والنكاحا ومبرئ المرضى والصحاحا
إن لم {تقله} {فمر} القداحا[c]

١ وهبل : كشط المقريزي كلمة أخرى قبل أن يصححها كما هي الآن. ٥ جاؤوا : في الأصل "جاوا". ٦ السراحا : في الأصل "السواحا". ٨ تقله : في الأصل "يقله". || فمر : في الأصل "فمن" (راجع الأزرقي، أخبار مكة).

a قارن الواقدي، كتاب المغازي، ٢: ٨٣٢ ("وحول الكعبة ثلاثمائة صَنَمٍ وستّون صَنَمًا مُرَصَّصةٌ بالرَّصاص وكان هُبَل أعظمها وهو وُجاهَ الكعبة على بابها").

b راجع الأزرقي، أخبار مكة١، ١: ١١٥ ("قال: وحفر إبراهيم عليه السلام جُبًّا في بطن البيت على يمين من دخله يكون خزانة للبيت، يلقى فيه ما يُهدى للكعبة، وهو الجُبّ الذي نصب عليه عمرو بن لحي هُبَل، الصَّنَمَ الذي كانت قريش تعبده وتستقسم عنده بالأزلام حين جاء به من هيت من أرض الجزيرة").

c قارن الأزرقي، أخبار مكة١، ١: ١٨٩ ("وقال محمد بن إسحاق: كان هُبَل من خَرَزِ العقيق على صورة إنسان، وكانت يده اليمنى مكسورة، فأدركته قريش فجعلت له يدًا من ذهب، وكان له خزانة للقُرْبان، وكانت له سبعة قداح يُضرب بها على الميت والعُذْرة والنكاح، وكان قربانه مائة بعير، وكان له حاجب، وكانوا إذا جاءوا هُبَل بالقربان ضربوا بالقداح، وقالوا:

إنا اختلفنا فهب السراحا ثلاثة يا هُبَل فصاحا
الميت والعذرة والنكاحا والبرء في المرضى [وفي] الصحاحا
إن لم تقله فَمُرِ القِداحا").

وقارن أيضا الأزرقي، أخبار مكة١، ١: ١٨٨ ("وكانوا إذا أرادوا أن يختنوا غلامًا أو ينكحوا منكحا أو يدفنوا ميتًا أو [شكُّوا] في نسب أحد منهم: ذهبوا به إلى هُبَل ومائة درهم وجزُور فأعطوها صاحب القداح الذي يضرب بها، ثم قرّبوا صاحبهم الذي يريدون به ما يريدون"). وقارن أيضا ابن الكلبي، أصنام، ٢٧–

§ 80 ʿUmar b. Šabbah said: Hubal's location was inside the Kaʿbah, above the pit[255] which was there. It was made of cornelian, shaped like a man, and its right hand was broken off. Qurayš received it in this form, so they made a hand of gold for it. The first one to set it up was Ḫuzaymah b. Mudrikah b. Ilyās [or al-Yās] b. Muḍar.[256] A treasury for offerings was made for it, and seven arrows, which used to be cast [to answer questions] pertaining to a dead person, virginity, or marriage, were made for it [as well]. The most common offering made to it was one hundred [sacrificial animals/camels/dirhams].[257] Two wings were made for it, and it was called "Hubal of Ḫuzaymah." When they brought an offering to Hubal, they cast the arrows saying: [*al-rağaz*]

We have a disagreement, so give [us] relief.
    Three pure ones [?], O Hubal:
A dead person, virginity, and marriage.
    You who restores the sick and healthy!
If you will not say it, then command the arrows! [?]

---

٢٨ ("كانت لقريش أصنامٌ في جوف الكعبة وحولها. وكان أعظمها عندهم هُبَل. وكان فيما بلغني من عقيق أحمَر على صورة الإنسان، مكسورَ اليدِ اليُمْنى. أدركتْه قريشٌ كذلك، فجعلوا له يدًا من ذهبٍ. وكان أوّلَ من نَصَبَهُ خُزَيْمَةُ بن مُدْرِكة بن اليأس بن مُضَر. وكان يقال له هُبَلُ خُزَيْمَةَ. وكان في جوف الكعبة، قُدّامَه سبعةُ أَقْدُحٍ. مكتوبٌ في أوّلها: "صريحٌ" والآخر: "مُلْصَقٌ" فإذا شكُّوا في مولود، أهدَوْا له هَدِيّةً، ثم ضربوا بالقِدَاح. فإن خرج: "صريحٌ" ألحقوه، وإن [خرج: "ملصقٌ"] دفعوه. وقِدْحٌ على الميّت، وقِدْحٌ على النكاح، وثلاثةٌ لم تُفَسَّرْ لي على ما كانت. فإذا اختصموا في أمرٍ أو أرادوا سفرا أو عملا أَتَوْهُ فاستقسموا بالقِدَاح عنده. فما خَرَجَ، عَمِلوا به وانتَهَوْا إليه").

---

255 Or perhaps, beside the pit (but see § 83). See also al-Ṭabarī, *History*, 6:3. Regarding this pit, see Hawting (1980): 51; Rubin (1986): 117–118.

256 He was an ancestor of the Qurayš; "Khuzāʿa," in *EI*² (M.J. Kister).

257 Or, the maximum quantity offered to it was one hundred [camels and others]. Compare al-Azraqī, *Aḫbār Makkah*¹, 1:189: "Hubal's offering consisted of one hundred camels."

§ 81 وله يقول أبو سفيٰن بن حرب يوم أحد: "اعْل هُبل."[a] فقال رسول الله ﷺ: "الله أعلى وأجل."
وله يقول ابن الزبعرى:

جمع صخر يوم قال اعل هُبل

صخر أبو سفيٰن بن حرب

§ 82 وقال غيره: كان هبل أعظم أصنام قريش وجاء به عمرو بن لحي من هِيْتَ بأرض الجزيرة حتى وضعه في الكعبة.

§ 83 وقال الزبير بن بكار: كانت في الكعبة بئر ذراعٍ وشبر يقال لها بئر أُدَد على رأسها صنم من جزعة حمراء يقال له هبل يطرح {فيها} ما يُهدى للكعبة[b] ويقال هي الحطيم[c] وكان هبل من أعظم أصنامهم عندهم.

---

٥ عمرو بن: كشط المقريزي عبارة أخرى قبل أن يصححها كما هي الآن. ٧–1.138 وقال ... إسمٰعيل: الزيادة بخط المقريزي في الهامش الأيمن من الأسفل إلى الأعلى، ثم في الهامش الأعلى من الأسفل إلى الأعلى ويشير إليها رمز ⌐ بعد "الكعبة". ٨ فيها: في الأصل "فيه". || يُهدى: في الأصل "يُهدا".

---

a قارن ابن الكلبي، الأصنام، ٢٨ ("وهو الذي يقول له أبو سُفْيَانَ بْنُ حَرْبٍ حين ظَفِرَ يوم أُحُدٍ: أُعْلُ هُبَلُ! أي علا دينُك. فقال رسول الله (ﷺ): اللهُ أعلى وأَجَلّ!"). وقارن أيضا ياقوت، معجم البلدان، ٥: ٣٩١ ("أعلِ هُبل، أي أعل دينك").

b قارن الطبري، جامع البيان، ٨: ٧٦ ("كانت هُبَلُ أعظمَ أصنامِ قُرَيْشٍ بمكةَ، وكانت على بئرٍ في جوفِ الكعبةِ، وكانت تلك البئرُ هي التي يُجْمَعُ فيها ما يُهْدَى للكعبةِ"). وقارن أيضا الأزرقي، أخبار مكة١، ١: ١٨٧ ("أخبرني محمد بن إسحاق، قال: إن البئر التي كانت في جوف الكعبة كانت على يمين من دخلها، وكان عمقها ثلاثة أذرع، يقال: إن إبراهيم وإسماعيل حفراها ليكون فيها ما يُهدى للكعبة"). وقارن أيضا السنجاري، منائح الكرم، ١: ٣٦٩ ("قال الزبير وقال محمد بن حسن عن محمد بن طلحة عن عثمان بن عبد الرحمن قال: كانت في الكعبة بئر ذراع [وربع] وشبر يقال لها بئر أدد على رأسها صنم من جَزْعَة حمراء يقال له هبل يُطرح فيها ما يُهدى للكعبة").

c راجع ابن حجر، فتح الباري، ٧: ٥٤٧ ("وقال غيره: الحطيم هو بئر الكعبة التي كان يلقى فيها ما يهدى لها").

§ 81 During the Battle of Uḥud, Abū Sufyān b. Ḥarb[258] said, referring to it: "Be exalted, Hubal!" The Messenger of Allāh, may Allāh bless and save him, said: "Allāh is more exalted and more sublime." Ibn al-Ziba'rá[259] said, referring to it:

Ṣaḫr mustered [his army] on the day he said: Be exalted, Hubal![260]

Ṣaḫr is Abū Sufyān b. Ḥarb['s name].

§ 82 Others said that Hubal was the greatest idol of Qurayš. 'Amr b. Luḥayy brought it from Hīt in the land of al-Ǧazīrah, and placed it inside the Ka'bah.

§ 83 Al-Zubayr b. Bakkār said: There was a well inside the Ka'bah which measured a cubit and *šibr*[261] and which was called the well of Udad. On top of it was an idol made of red onyx called Hubal, and into it gifts to the Ka'bah were cast. Some say that it is *al-ḥaṭīm*.[262] Hubal was one of their greatest idols.

258 The father of the first Umayyad caliph, Mu'āwiyah b. Abī Sufyān. He is reported to have died between 32/653 and 34/655; "Abū Sufyān," in *EI*³ (Kh.M.G. Keshk).

259 'Abd Allāh b. al-Ziba'rá l-Sahmī was a Qurašī poet who was one of the Prophet's adversaries; "Ibn al-Ziba'rā," in *EI*² (J.W. Fück).

260 Or, Ṣaḫr['s army] was mustered on the day he said: Be exalted, Hubal!
Or, The mustering of Ṣaḫr['s army took place] on the day he said: Be exalted, Hubal!
Or, The mustering of Ṣaḫr['s army] on the day he said: Be exalted, Hubal!

261 *Šibr* is the distance between the little finger and the thumb when they are extended; see Lane (1863–1893): 1496.

262 Nowadays, the *ḥaṭīm* is the semi-circular wall opposite the northwest wall of the Ka'bah, but originally it was probably the area opposite the front wall of the Ka'bah. See Rubin (1986): 113–118.

وعن مجاهد: كان الحطيم زَرْبا لـ〈غنم〉 إسمٰعيل.[a]

35*a §84 وذكر أبو عبد الله محمد بن عبد الرحيم القيسي في كتاب **تحفة الألباب** أنه وجد في جبال مكة أزج تحت الأرض فيه صورة رجل وامرأة من صخر من أجمل الصور وعندهما لوح من رخام مكتوب فيه هذه الأبيات: [الخفيف]

أنا مأوى الفخار ساف بن عمْرو 〈و〉ربيع الأنام في كل عصر
كنت في جرهم أُعَد رئيسا وإذا ما أمرت فالأمر أمري
كان حكمي عليهم وعلى من حج ذا البيت في البرية يجْري
فهويت التى ترون أمامي فتبطنتها على غير مهر
من رآني فلا يُلِمَّ بأنثى ذات بعل ولا يهم بعَهْر[b]

36a §85 قال عمر بن شبة: وكان إساف ونائلة رجل وامرأة من جرهم يقال لهما إساف بن يعلى ونائلة بنت زيد. فوقع إساف على نائلة في الكعبة فمسخهما الله تعالى حجرين فأخرجا من 〈جوف

٢–٩ وذكر ... بعَهْر: كتب هذا المقطع على ورقة صغيرة وضعها المقريزي بين الصفحات. ٥ وربيع: الواو ناقصة في الأصل. ١٠ وكان: وردت الكلمة بين الأسطر بحجم صغير وهي زيادة متأخرة. ‖ رجل: كذا في الأصل بدلا من "رجلا". ١١–1.140 جوف ... وعليهما: قارن الأزرقي، أخبار مكة¹، ١: ١٩٠.

---

١٠ إساف: أضاف المقريزي الحاشية التالية في الهامش الأيمن من الأعلى إلى الأسفل: "إساف من أسَاف الرجلُ ذهب ماله." راجع: ابن منظور، لسان العرب، سوف ("والسَّوافُ والسُّوافُ: الموتُ في الناسِ والمال، سافَ سَوْفًا وأسافَه الله، وأَسافَ الرجلُ: وقَع في ماله السَّوافُ أي الموت"). وراجع أيضا: ابن منظور، لسان العرب، أسف ("وأَسافٌ وإِسافٌ: اسم صنم لقريش").

---

a راجع السيوطي، در، ١: ٣٣٠ ("وجعل ابراهيم عليه السلام الحجر الى جنب البيت عريشا من أراك تقتحمه العنز، فكان زربًا لغنم اسماعيل، وحفر ابراهيم جبا في بطن البيت على يمين من دخله يكون خزانة للبيت يلقي فيه ما يهدى للكعبة").

b قارن القيسي، تحفة الألباب، ١٢
("من رآني فلا يلمّ بانثى ذات بعل ولا يهمّ بِقَهْرٍ").

On the authority of Muǧāhid: The *ḥaṭīm* was a pen for Ishmael's sheep.[263]

§ 84 Abū ʿAbd Allāh Muḥammad b. ʿAbd al-Raḥīm al-Qaysī reported in *Kitāb Tuḥfat al-albāb* [The Book of the Gift of the Hearts] that in the mountains of Mecca an underground chamber was found that contained an image of a man and a woman made of stone. It was one of the most beautiful images. There was a marble tablet next to them [these images], on which these verses were written: [*al-ḫafīf*]

I am the shelter of glory, [I]sāf[264] b. ʿAmr,
and the one who provides plentiful subsistence to mankind in every period of time.
I was considered a leader among Ǧurhum.
When I gave an order, it was carried out.
My authority over them and over whoever
performed the pilgrimage to this shrine was valid throughout mankind.
I desired she whom you [masc. pl.] see in front of me,
and had sexual intercourse with her without [giving any] dowry.
Whoever sees me [punished in stone], let him not have sexual contact with a woman
who has a husband, and let him not consider [committing] fornication.

§ 85 ʿUmar b. Šabbah said: Isāf and Nāʾilah were a man and woman from Ǧurhum whose names were Isāf b. Yaʿlá and Nāʾilah bt. Zayd. Isāf had sexual intercourse with Nāʾilah inside the Kaʿbah, and Allāh, the Exalted, transformed them into two stones. Then they were removed from the interior of

22 Isāf : Isāf [or Asāf]: [Derived] from *asāfa l-raǧulu*, [which means:] his [the man's] cattle died (marginal gloss in al-Maqrīzī's hand). This idol's name is given as both Asāf and Isāf in Ibn Manẓūr, *Lisān al-ʿarab*, s.v. Asāf and Isāf.

263 According to other accounts, the *ḥiǧr* was a pen for Ishmael's sheep. See al-Azraqī, *Aḫbār Makkah*[1] 1:115; al-Suyūṭī, *al-Durr al-manṯūr* 330. See also Rubin (1986): 106–107.

264 See Wright (1896–1898), 2:§ 234 (a).

الكعبة وعليهما› ثيابهما فجعل أحدهما بلصق الكعبة والآخر عند زمزم فجعل يطرح بينهما مما يُهْدى للكعبة وكان يُسمى حطيم الكعبة. وإنما نصبا ليعتبر بهما فلم يزل أمرهما يدرس حتى جعلا وثنين يُعْبدان وجعلوا كلما بليت ثيابهما أخلفوا لهما ثيابا أخرى ثم أخذ الذي بلصق الكعبة فجعل مع الذي عند زمزم فكان الناس يذبحون عندهما.[a]

§86 ولهما يقول السجاعة: | 36b

إن إسافا وإن نائله قد بنيا للسابله كل الذي نطق فيه القائله

§87 ولإساف يقول بشْر بن أبي خازم الأسدي: [الوافر]

عليه الطير ما يَدنُون منه مقامات العوارك من إساف[b]

٢ يُهْدى: في الأصل "يُهدا". ‖ يُسمى: في الأصل "يُسما".

a قارن ياقوت، معجم البلدان، ١: ١٧٠ ("إساف ونائلة صنمان كانا بمكة. قال ابن إسحاق: هما مَسْخان وهما إساف بن بُغَاءَ ونائلة بنت ذئب؛ وقيل: إساف بن عمرو ونائلة بنت سُهَيْل وإنهما زنيا في الكعبة فُمسخا حَجَرَيْن فنُصبا عند الكعبة؛ وقيل: نُصب أَحدهما على الصَّفا والآخر على المَرْوَة ليُعْتَبَرَ بهما، فقَدُم الأمرُ فأمر عمرو بن لُحَيّ الخُزاعي بعبادتهما، ثم حَوَّلهما قصيٌّ فجعل أحدهما بِلصْق البيت وجعل الآخر بزمزم وكان ينحر عندهما وكانت الجاهلية تمسّح بهما"). وقارن أيضا الأزرقي، أخبار مكة[١]، ١: ١٩٠ ("ويقال: جعلهما جميعًا في موضع زمزم، فكان ينحر عندهما، فكان أهل الجاهلية يمرّون بإساف ونائلة ويتمسّحون بهما"). وقارن أيضا مسلم، صحيح، ٢: ٩٢٨ ("إِنَّمَا كَانَ ذَاكَ أَنَّ الْأَنْصَارَ كَانُوا يُهِلُّونَ فِي الْجَاهِلِيَّةِ لِصَنَمَيْنِ عَلَى شَطِّ الْبَحْرِ. يُقَالُ لَهُمَا إِسَافٌ وَنَائِلَةُ. ثُمَّ يَجِيئُونَ فَيَطُوفُونَ بَيْنَ الصَّفَا وَالْمَرْوَةِ").

b راجع ياقوت، معجم البلدان، ٥: ٢٠٣ ("كان من أصنام العرب صنم يقال له مناف وبه كانت قريش تسمّي عبد مناف، ولا أدري أين كان ولا من كان نصبه، ولم تكن الحُيّض من النساء يدنون من أصنامهم ولا يتمسحن بها وإنما كانت تقف الواحدة ناحية منها؛ وفي ذلك يقول بلعاء بن قيس بن عبد الله بن يعمر، ويعمر هو الشُّدّاخ الليثي: ... وقَرْن قد تركت الطير منه كمُعْتَرَك العوارك من مناف").

the Kaʿbah with their clothes on. One of them was placed close to the Kaʿbah and the other near Zamzam,[265] and some of the gifts to the Kaʿbah were cast between them. It [the area between them] was named the *ḥaṭīm* of the Kaʿbah. They were only set up so [people] would take warning from them, but in time their origin was forgotten, and they became two idols that were worshipped.[266] Whenever their clothes became worn out, they [the people] would replace them with other clothes. Afterwards, the one that was close to the Kaʿbah was taken and placed with that which was near Zamzam, and people slaughtered [sacrifices] beside them.

§ 86 A person who composed many verses of rhymed prose (*saǧʿ*) said, referring to them:

> Isāf and Nāʾilah have built for the travelers
> all that the speakers are talking about [?].

§ 87 Bišr b. Abī Ḫāzim al-Asadī[267] said about Isāf: [*al-wāfir*]

> Birds sit upon him. They do not approach him [Isāf].
> The positions of the menstruating women before Isāf.[268]

---

265 The famous well located near the corner of the Kaʿbah.

266 See also Hawting (1999): 102.

267 A pre-Islamic poet who belonged to the Banū Asad b. Ḫuzaymah; "Bis͟hr b. Abī K͟hāzim," in *EI*² (J.W. Fück).

268 Compare Klinke-Rosenberger (1941): 45: "Er bleibt unbeweglich, als ob Vögel auf ihm säßen; man nähert sich ihm nicht." Es ist die Haltung der Menstruierenden vor *Isâf*. And compare also to Faris (1952): 35: "Full of awe, they draw not nigh unto it, / But stand afar off like the menstruating women before Isāf." Parallel sources quote a similar verse with regard to another idol called Manāf (for a translation of this verse, see Grunebaum [1953]: 45), and explain that the menstruating women did not come near their idols and did not stroke them, but stood apart from them; Yāqūt, *Muʿǧam al-buldān*, 5:203; Ibn al-Kalbī, *al-Aṣnām* 32. See also Klinke-Rosenberger (1941): 107, n. 201.

§88 ولهما يقول عبد المطلب بن هاشم: [الطويل]

وملقى رحال الأشعرين ركابهم بمفضى السيول بين ساف ونائل[a]

§89 وهما اليوم حجران بمكة قد بني بهما في دار عباس بن عبد المطلب التي في المسْعَى.[b]

§90 حدثنا عبد الوهاب بن عبد المجيد ثنا محمد بن عمرو عن أبي سلمة ويحيى بن عبد الرحمٰن بن حاطب عن أسامة بن زيد بن حارثة عن أبيه، قال: خرج النبي ﷺ وهو مردفي إلى نصب من

٢ رحال: وضع المقريزي رمز "ح" تحت الكلمة إشارة إلى تلفظها بالحاء. ٣ المسْعَى: في الأصل "المسْعَا". ووضع المقريزي في آخر الكلمة رمز ⌐ إشارة إلى حاشية أو زيادة في الهامش الأيمن ولكن لا توجد أي زيادة أو حاشية هناك.

a قارن ابن الكلبي، الأصنام، ٢٩ ("فلهما يقول أبو طالب (وهو يحلف بهما، حينَ تحالفت قريشٌ على بني هاشم في أمر النبيّ عليه السلام):

أَحْضَرْتُ عند البيت رَهْطي ومَعْشَرِي وأمسَكْتُ من أثوابه بالوصائلِ
وحيثُ يُنيخُ الأشعَرُون رِكابَهم بِمُفْضَى السيولِ من إسافٍ ونائلِ")

b راجع المقريزي، إمتاع الأسماع، ٤: ٣٦١ ("وكان إذا انصرف خرج على دار ابن أبي حُسين، وكان طريقه حتى يَجزع المسعى، ثم يسلك بين دار عباس بن عبد المطلب وبين دار ابن أزهر بن عبد عَوْف الزهري، ثم على دار الأخنس بن شَريق، حتى يدخل بيته").

§ 88 ʿAbd al-Muṭṭalib b. Hāšim[269] said about them: [*al-ṭawīl*]

And where the saddles of the camels of the Ašʿarūn[270] are put down,
at the place to which the streams flow, between [I]sāf and Nāʾilah.[271]

§ 89 Today they are two stones in Mecca, which were used in the construction of ʿAbbās b. ʿAbd al-Muṭṭalib's[272] court in *al-masʿá*.[273]

§ 90 ʿAbd al-Wahhāb b. ʿAbd al-Maǧīd[274] related to us, Muḥammad b. ʿAmr[275] related to us on the authority of Abū Salamah[276] and Yaḥyá b. ʿAbd al-Raḥmān b. Ḥāṭib[277] < Usāmah b. Zayd b. Ḥāriṯah[278] < his father,[279] who said: The Prophet, may Allāh bless and save him, set out to one of the

---

269 Other sources ascribe this verse to Abū Ṭālib (see below). ʿAbd al-Muṭṭalib was the Prophet's grandfather. He was the son of Hāšim b. ʿAbd Manāf of Qurayš and Salmá bt. ʿAmr of the tribe of Ḫazraǧ; "ʿAbd al-Muṭṭalib b. Hāshim," in *EI*³ (U. Rubin).

270 I.e. members of the Yemeni tribe of Ašʿar.

271 The full poem, of which this verse is a part, can be found in Abū Ṭālib, *Dīwān*, 63–74 (see verse no. 9).

272 ʿAbbās b. ʿAbd al-Muṭṭalib (d. ca. 32/653) was the Prophet's uncle and the eponym of the ʿAbbāsids; "al-ʿAbbās b. ʿAbd al-Muṭṭalib," in *EI*³ (A. Görke).

273 I.e. the course taken by the pilgrims.

274 On ʿAbd al-Wahhāb b. ʿAbd al-Maǧīd al-Ṯaqafī, who died in Baṣra in 194/810, see Ibn Saʿd, *al-Ṭabaqāt*¹, 9:290–291.

275 Abū l-Ḥasan Muḥammad b. ʿAmr b. ʿAlqamah al-Layṯī (d. 144 or 145/761 or 762); al-Ḏahabī, *Siyar aʿlām al-nubalāʾ*, 6:136–137.

276 Abū Salamah b. ʿAbd al-Raḥmān b. ʿAwf al-Zuhrī (Qurayš) was a *ḥadīṯ* transmitter who died in Medina in 94/713; al-Ḏahabī, *Siyar aʿlām al-nubalāʾ*, 4:287–292.

277 For more on Yaḥyá b. ʿAbd al-Raḥmān b. Ḥāṭib b. Abī Baltaʿah (d. 104/722), who was a client of the Banū Asad, see Ibn ʿAsākir, *Dimašq*, 64:305–311.

278 Usāmah b. Zayd b. Ḥāriṯah was born in Mecca and died in al-Ǧurf around 54/674; "Usāma b. Zayd," in *EI*² (V. Vacca).

279 On Zayd b. Ḥāriṯah (d. 8/629), who was Muḥammad's adopted son, see "Zayd b. Ḥāritha," in *EI*² (M. Lecker).

الأنصاب فذبحنا له شاة[a] وجعلناها في الإرة[b] فلقينا زيد بن عمرو بن نفيل فأبى أن يأكل منها.

وكان صنمان من نحاس يقال لهما إساف ونائلة مستقبل الكعبة يتمسح بهما الناس إذا طافوا. فقال النبي ﷺ: "لا تمسهما ولا تمسح بهما." فقلت في نفسي: "لأمسنهما حتى أنظر ما يقول." فمسستهما فقال: "ألم تُنْه عن هذا؟" فلا والذي أكرمه ما مسستهما حتى أنزل عليه الكتاب.[c]

---

١ فذبحنا: وضع المقريزي رمز "ح" تحت الكلمة إشارة إلى تلفظها بالحاء. ‖ فأبى: في الأصل "فابا".

---

a راجع ابن منظور، لسان العرب، "نصب" ("قال ابن الأثير، قال الحربيُّ: قوله ذَبحنا له شاةً له وجهان: أَحدهما أَن يكون زيد فعله من غير أَمر النبي، ﷺ، ولا رِضاه، إِلاَّ أَنه كان معه، فنُسِب إِليه، ولأَنَّ زيداً لم يكن معه من العِصْمة ما كان مع سيدنا رسول الله، ﷺ. والثاني أَن يكون ذبحها لزاده في خروجه، فاتفق ذلك عند صنم كانوا يذبحون عنده، لا أَنه ذبحها للصنم، هذا إِذا جُعِلَ النُّصُب الصَّنم، فأَما إِذا جُعِلَ الحجر الذي يذبح عنده، فلا كلام فيه، فظن زيد بن عمرو أَن ذلك اللحم مما كانت قريش تذبحه لأَنصابها، فامتنع لذلك، وكان زيد يخالف قريشًا في كثير من أُمورها، ولم يكن الأَمْرُ كما ظَنَّ زيد").

b راجع الحربي، غريب الحديث، ٢: ٧٥٢ ("«صَنَعْنَاهَا فِي الإِرَه» أَخْبَرَنَا عَمْرُو عَنْ أَبِيهِ: الْإِرَةُ: حُفْرَةٌ يُوقَدُ فِيهَا. وَذَكَرَ عَنِ الْوَالِبِيِّ: الْإِرَةُ: النَّارُ: يَقُولُ: عِنْدَكُمْ إِرَةٌ: أَيْ نَارٌ. أَخْبَرَنِي أَبُو نَصْرٍ، عَنِ الْأَصْمَعِيِّ: الْإِرَةُ: الْحُفْرَةُ الَّتِي حَوْلَهَا الْأَثَافِيُّ، تَقُولُ: وَرَتْ إِرَةٌ")، وراجع أيضا ابن منظور، لسان العرب، "أري" ("وفي الحديث: ذُبِحَت لرسول الله صلى الله عليه وسلم شاةٌ ثم صُنِعَتْ في الإِرَة؛ الإِرَةُ: حفرة توقد فيها النار، وقيل: هي الحفرة التي حولها الأَثافيُّ. يقال: وَأَرْتُ إِرَةً، وقيل: الإِرَةُ النارُ نَفْسُها، وأَصل الإِرَة إِرْيٌ، بوزن عِلْم، والهاء عوض من الياء. وفي حديث زيد بن حارثة: ذبحنا شاة وصنعناها في الإِرَة حتى إذا نَضِجَت جعلناها في سُفْرَتنا").

c قارن البيهقي، دلائل النبوة، ٢: ٣٤ ("عن زيد بن حارثة، قال: كان صنم من نحاس يقال له: إِسَافٌ، أو نَائِلَة، يتَمَسَّح به المشركون إذا طافوا. فطاف رسول الله، ﷺ، فطفت معه، فلما مررت مسحت به، فقال رسول الله، ﷺ: لا تمسه! فقال زيد: فطفت فقلت في نفسي لَأَمَسَّنَّهُ حتى أنظر ما يكون، فمسحته، فقال رسول الله، ﷺ، ألم تنه؟").

anṣāb,[280] and took me [with him,] behind him on the same riding animal. We slaughtered a sheep for it [the *nuṣub*][281] and put it in a pit.[282] Then Zayd b. ʿAmr b. Nufayl[283] met us, and he refused to eat from it [what we had slaughtered].

There were two idols made of copper that were called Isāf and Nāʾilah; they faced the Kaʿbah, and the people would stroke them as they performed the circumambulation. The Prophet, may Allāh bless and save him, said: "Do not touch them, and do not stroke them!" I said to myself: "I shall touch them to see what he [the Prophet] says." So I touched them, and he said: "Were you not forbidden to do this?" And no, I swear by He who honored him, I did not touch them until the Book was revealed to him.

280 In this tradition the word *nuṣub* (singular of *anṣāb*) is explained as denoting either an idol or a stone; Kister (1970): 272.

281 Some commentators who interpreted this *ḥadīṯ* attempted to show that the Prophet did not slaughter a sheep for the *nuṣub*. For more information, see Kister (1970): 272–273.

282 *Ǧaʿalnāhā fī l-irah*. According to *Ġarīb al-ḥadīṯ* of al-Ḥarbī, the word *irah* denotes either a pit (*ḥufrah*) in which fire is kindled, fire, or a pit surrounded by stones on which a cooking pot is placed (*al-aṯāfī*); al-Ḥarbī, *Ġarīb al-ḥadīṯ*, 2:752.

283 Zayd b. ʿAmr b. Nufayl was reportedly one of the *ḥanīf*s who rejected the idol worship of the Qurayš; "Zayd b. ʿAmr b. Nufayl," in *EI*[2] (M. Lecker).

§91 قال: وثنا محمد بن المنكدر قال: قام النبي ﷺ والكعبة محفوفة بالأوثان. قال: وثنا أبو عاصم عن موسى بن عبيدة [موسى] وثنا يعقوب بن زيد قال: ومع النبي ﷺ قضيب يشير به إليها حتى أتى على يساف ونائلة فأمر بهما فعُفرا وطرحا. ثم قال: "قولوا." قالوا: "يٰرسول الله ما نقول؟" قال: "قولوا: صدق الله وعده ونصر عبده وهزم الأحزاب وحده."[a]

§92 ثنا محمد بن حاتم ثنا يونس بن محمد ثنا شيبان عن قتادة ﴿وَٱلرُّجْزَ فَٱهْجُرْ﴾، قال: هما صنمان كانا عند إساف ونائلة يمسح وجوههما من أتى عليهما من المشركين فأمر الله تعالى نبيه ﷺ أن يهجرهما ويجانبهما.[b]

---

١ قال[١] ... قال[٣]: الزيادة بخط المقريزي في الهامش الأيسر من الأسفل إلى الأعلى + صح، ويشير إليها رمز ¬ بعد "الكتاب". ٣ أتى: في الأصل "اتا". ‖ يساف: كذا في الأصل بدلا من "إساف". ٦ أتى: في الأصل "اتا".

---

a قارن الفاكهي، أخبار مكة، ٢: ٢٤٢ ("حدّثنا محمد بن علي المَرْوَزي، قال: ثنا [عبيد الله] بن موسى، قال: ثنا موسى بن عُبيدة، عن يعقوب بن زيد، ومحمد بن المنكدر، قالا: فكان بها يومئذ—يعني يوم فتح مكة—ستة وثلاثون [وثنًا]، على الصفا صنم، وعلى المروة صنم، وما بينهما محفوف بالأوثان"). وقارن أيضا المتقي، كنز العمال، ١٠: ٥٣٠–٥٣١ ("حدثنا عبد الله بن موسى أنبأنا موسى بن عبيد (!) عن يعقوب بن زيد بن طلحة التيمي ومحمد بن المنكدر قالا: كان بمكة يوم الفتح ستون وثلثمائة وثنٍ (!) على الصفا وعلى المروةِ صنمٌ وما بينهما محفوفٌ بالأوثانِ والكعبةُ قد أُحيطت بالأوثانِ، قال محمد بن المنكدر: فقام رسول الله صلى الله عليه وسلم ومعه قضيبٌ يشيرُ به إلى الأوثانِ فما هو إلا أن يُشيرَ إلى شيءٍ منها فيتساقط حتى أتى إساف ونائلةَ وهما قدام المقامِ مستقبلَ باب الكعبةِ فقال: عَفِّروهما فألقاهُما المسلمون"). وقارن أيضا الواقدي، المغازي، ٢: ٨٣٢ ("فجعل رسول الله صلَّى الله عليه وسلَّم كلّما مرَّ بصنَمٍ منها يُشير بقضيبٍ في يده [ويقول]: ﴿جَاءَ ٱلْحَقُّ وَزَهَقَ ٱلْبَاطِلُ إِنَّ ٱلْبَاطِلَ كَانَ زَهُوقًا﴾. فيقع الصنم لوجهه. قال: حدّثني ابن أبي سَبْرَةَ، عن حُسَيْن بن عبد الله، عن عِكْرِمَة، عن ابن عبّاس رضي الله عنه، قال: ما يزيد رسول الله صلَّى الله عليه وسلَّم أن يُشير بالقضيب إلى الصَّنم فيقع لوجهه").

b قارن السيوطي، الدر المنثور، ٨: ٣٢٥ ("﴿وَٱلرُّجْزَ فَٱهْجُرْ﴾ قَالَ: هما صنمان كانا عند البيت أساف ونائلة يمسح وجوههما من أتى عليهما من المشركين، فأمر الله نبيه محمدًا أن يهجرهما ويجانبهما").

§ 91 He said: Muḥammad b. al-Munkadir[284] related to us that when the Kaʿbah was surrounded by idols, the Prophet, may Allāh bless and save him, stood up [...]. He said: Abū ʿĀṣim[285] related to us on the authority of Mūsá b. ʿUbaydah,[286] and Yaʿqūb b. Zayd[287] related to us that the Prophet, may Allāh bless and save him, held a rod which he pointed at them.[288] Then he reached Isāf and Nāʾilah, gave an order, and they were rolled in the dust and thrown away. Afterwards, he said: "Speak!" They said: "O Messenger of Allāh! What shall we say?" He said: "Say: 'Allāh fulfilled His promise, granted victory to His servant, and He alone defeated the parties'."[289]

§ 92 Muḥammad b. Ḥātim related to us, Yūnus b. Muḥammad related to us, Šaybān[290] related to us on the authority of Qatādah, who said [referring to the word *ruǧz*[291] in the verse] "and defilement (*wa-ruǧz*) flee! (*fa-hǧur*)":[292] They are two idols that were beside [the House.[293] They were called] Isāf and Nāʾilah. The polytheists who approached them used to stroke their faces. Allāh, the Exalted, ordered his Prophet, may Allāh bless and save him, to avoid (*an yahǧurahumā*) and shun them.

---

284 On Muḥammad b. al-Munkadir b. ʿAbd Allāh of the Taym b. Murrah (Qurayš), who died in Medina in 130/748 or 131/749, see Ibn Saʿd, *al-Ṭabaqāt*¹, 7:440–444.

285 Abū ʿĀṣim al-Ḍaḥḥāk b. Maḫlad al-Šaybānī; al-Ḏahabī, *Siyar aʿlām al-nubalāʾ*, 9:480–485.

286 On Mūsá b. ʿUbaydah b. Našīṭ al-Rabaḏī, who died in Medina in 153/770, see Ibn Saʿd, *al-Ṭabaqāt*¹, 7:555.

287 Yaʿqūb b. Zayd b. Ṭalḥah al-Taymī (Qurayš) was a *ḥādiṯ* transmitter and a *qāṣṣ* (storyteller) who died at the beginning of Abū Ǧaʿfar's caliphate; Ibn Saʿd, *al-Ṭabaqāt*¹, 7:469–470.

288 Parallel sources add the following sentence here: "And no sooner had he pointed at one of them, than it fell down." See al-Muttaqī, *Kanz al-ʿummāl*, 10:530–531.

289 The text has *al-aḥzāb*, that is, the parties that opposed Muḥammad.

290 Šaybān b. ʿAbd al-Raḥmān was a *mawlá* of Tamīm who died in Baghdad in 164/781; Ibn Saʿd, *al-Ṭabaqāt*¹, 8:498.

291 Or *riǧz*, according to some Qurʾān reciters; Abū ʿAlī l-Fārisī, *al-Ḥuǧǧah*, 6:338.

292 Qurʾān (*al-Muddaṯṯir*), 74:5.

293 The words *ʿinda l-bayt* ("beside the House") are missing from the text but can be found in other sources. See al-Suyūṭī, *al-Durr al-manṯūr*, 8:325.

§93 وذكر بسنده عن سعيد بن جبير: كان إساف ونائلة رجلا وامرأة فجرا في الكعبة فمسخا حجرين فاتخذا صنمين يعبدان من دون الله فلما افتتح النبي ﷺ مكة أمر بهما فكسرا.

§94 وعن مطر قال: عُبد إساف ونائلة أربعين سنة.

§95 ثنا أبو حاتم ارنا هشيم ارنا داود بن أبي هند عن الشعبي قال: كان على | الصفا وثن يقال له 37a إساف وعلى المروة وثن يقال له نائلة فكان المشركون يطوفون بينهما فلما كان الإسلام قال ناس لرسول الله ﷺ إن أهل الجاهلية كانوا يطوفون بين الصفا والمروة للوثنين اللذين كانا عليهما وليسا من شعائر الله فنزلت هذه الآية ﴿إِنَّ ٱلصَّفَا وَٱلْمَرْوَةَ مِنْ شَعَآئِرِ ٱللَّهِ فَمَنْ حَجَّ ٱلْبَيْتَ أَوِ ٱعْتَمَرَ فَلَا جُنَاحَ عَلَيْهِ أَنْ يَطَّوَّفَ بِهِمَا﴾.

§96 وفي رواية عن إسمٰعيل بن إبرٰهيم عن داود عن عامر قال: كان على الصفا وثن يقال له إساف وعلى المروة وثن يقال له نائلة فكان أهل الجاهلية إذا طافوا بينهما مسحوهما فلما جاء الإسلام قال

---

١ وذكر: الزيادة بخط المقريزي في الهامش الأيسر من الأسفل إلى الأعلى + صح، ويشير إليها رمز ٦ بعد "ويجانبهما". || بسنده: وضع المقريزي ثلاث نقط تحت هذه الكلمة إشارة إلى تلفظها بالسين. ٩ إسمٰعيل ... عن٢: الزيادة بخط المقريزي في الهامش الأيمن من الأعلى إلى الأسفل + صح، ويشير إليها رمز ٢ بعد "عن".

§ 93 He reported, with a chain of transmitters going back to Saʿīd b. Ǧubayr,[294] that Isāf and Nāʾilah were a man and a woman who fornicated inside the Kaʿbah. Then they were transformed into two stones, and adopted as idols that were worshipped apart from Allāh. When the Prophet, may Allāh bless and save him, conquered Mecca, he ordered that they be destroyed, and they were destroyed.

§ 94 It was reported on the authority of Maṭar[295] that Isāf and Nāʾilah were worshipped for forty years.

§ 95 Abū Ḥātim related to us, Hušaym[296] informed us, Dāwūd b. Abī Hind[297] informed us on the authority of al-Šaʿbī,[298] that he said: There was an idol on al-Ṣafā called Isāf, and an idol on al-Marwah called Nāʾilah. The polytheists used to circumambulate between them. When Islam came, some people told the Messenger of Allāh, may Allāh bless and save him: "The people of the Ǧāhiliyyah used to circumambulate between al-Ṣafā and al-Marwah because of the two idols which were on top of them [al-Ṣafā and al-Marwah], and they are not among the religious rites that were decreed by Allāh (*laysā min šaʿāʾiri llāh*)." Thereupon, this verse was revealed: "Safa and Marwa are among the waymarks of Allāh (*min šaʿāʾiri llāh*); so whosoever makes the Pilgrimage to the House, or the Visitation, it is no fault in him to circumambulate them."[299]

§ 96 According to Ismāʿīl b. Ibrāhīm,[300] who narrated [the following *ḥadīṯ*] on the authority of Dāwūd < ʿĀmir [i.e. al-Šaʿbī], there was an idol on al-Ṣafā called Isāf and an idol on al-Marwah called Nāʾilah. When the people of the Ǧāhiliyyah circumambulated between them, they stroked them, and when

294 Saʿīd b. Ǧubayr b. Hišām was a Kufan scholar who was a *mawlá* of the Banū Wālibah b. al-Ḥāriṯ, a branch of the Banū Asad b. Ḫuzaymah; "Saʿīd b. Djubayr," *in EI*² (H. Motzki).

295 Abū Raǧāʾ b. Ṭahmān Maṭar al-Warrāq al-Ḫurāsānī (d. 129/747); al-Ḏahabī, *Siyar aʿlām al-nubalāʾ*, 5:452–453.

296 Hušaym b. Bašīr was a *mawlá* of the Banū Sulaym (d. 183/799); Ibn Saʿd, *al-Ṭabaqāt*¹, 9:315.

297 Dāwūd b. Abī Hind (d. 139 or 140/756 or 757); al-Ḏahabī, *Siyar aʿlām al-nubalāʾ*, 6:376–379.

298 On ʿĀmir b. Šarāḥīl b. ʿAbd al-Kūfī (d. between 103/721 and 110/728), who is often cited as al-Šaʿbī or as ʿĀmir, see "al-Shaʿbī," in *EI*² (G.H.A. Juynboll).

299 Qurʾān (*al-Baqarah*), 2:158.

300 Ibn ʿUlayyah Ismāʿīl b. Ibrāhīm b. Miqsam was a *ḥadīṯ* transmitter and a *mawlá* of the tribe of Asad. ʿUlayyah was the name of his mother; al-Ḏahabī, *Siyar aʿlām al-nubalāʾ*, 9:107–120.

المسلمون إن أهل الجاهلية إنما كانوا يسعون بينهما من أجل هذين الصنمين. قال: فنزلت ﴿إِنَّ ٱلصَّفَا وَٱلْمَرْوَةَ مِن شَعَآئِرِ ٱللَّهِ فَمَنْ حَجَّ ٱلْبَيْتَ أَوِ ٱعْتَمَرَ فَلَا جُنَاحَ عَلَيْهِ أَن يَطَّوَّفَ بِهِمَا وَمَن تَطَوَّعَ خَيْرًا فَإِنَّ ٱللَّهَ شَاكِرٌ عَلِيمٌ﴾، قال: فجعله تطوع خير.

97 § ثنا زهير ثنا جرير عن أشعث عن جعفر عن سعيد قال: لما كان يوم فتح مكة جاءت عجوز شمطاء حبشية تخمشت وجهها ودعت بالويل. قال: فذكر ذلك للنبي ﷺ فقال: "تلك نائلة. قد يئست أن تعبد في بلدكم هذا أبدا."

98 § ثنا أحمد بن يونس ثنا يعقوب عن جعفر عن سعيد بن عبد الرحمن بن أبزى قال: لما كسرت نائلة جاءت عجوز حبشية شمطاء تخمش وجهها وتدعو بالويل. فقيل للنبي ﷺ فقال: "تلك نائلة. أيست أن تعبد ببلادكم هذه أبدا."

---

٢ يَطَّوَّفَ : شكل المقريزي الكلمة كما يلي "يَطّوَّف". ٦ يئست : لقد وضع المقريزي النقطتين تحت الياء الثانية فقط. ٧ سعيد ... الرحمن : الزيادة بخط المقريزي في الهامش الأيمن من الأعلى إلى الأسفل + صح، ويشير إليها رمز ⌐ بعد "عن".

Islam came, the Muslims said: “The people of the Ǧāhiliyyah performed the *saʿy*[301] between them only because of these two idols.” Thereupon, [this verse] was revealed: “Safa and Marwa are among the waymarks of Allāh; so whosoever makes the Pilgrimage to the House, or the Visitation, it is no fault in him to circumambulate them; and whoso volunteers good (*taṭawwaʿa ḫayran*), Allāh is All-grateful, All-knowing.”[302] He [Allāh] decreed that it [the circumambulation between al-Ṣafā and al-Marwah] is an act of doing good that is not obligatory (*ǧaʿalahu taṭawwuʿ ḫayr*).[303]

§ 97 Zuhayr[304] related to us, Ǧarīr[305] related to us on the authority of Ašʿaṯ[306] < Ǧaʿfar[307] < Saʿīd,[308] who said: On the day of the conquest of Mecca, an old, gray haired Ethiopian woman came scratching her face and crying out in affliction. This was reported to the Prophet, may Allāh bless and save him, and he said: “That was Nāʾilah. She has lost hope of ever being worshipped again in this land of yours.”

§ 98 Aḥmad b. Yūnus[309] related to us, Yaʿqūb[310] related to us on the authority of Ǧaʿfar[311] < Saʿīd b. ʿAbd al-Raḥmān b. Abzá, who said: When Nāʾilah was destroyed, an old, gray haired Ethiopian woman came scratching her face and crying out in affliction. It was reported to the Prophet, may Allāh bless and save him, and he said: “That was Nāʾilah. She has lost hope of ever being worshipped again in this land of yours.”

301 The stage of the pilgrimage when the pilgrims walk briskly/jog between the hills of al-Ṣafā and al-Marwah; see “Saʿy,” in *EI*^{2} (T. Fahd).

302 Qurʾān (*al-Baqarah*), 2:158.

303 See also Lane (1863–1893): 1871.

304 Zuhayr b. Ḥarb: see note 140.

305 Ǧarīr b. ʿAbd al-Ḥamīd: see note 141.

306 Ašʿaṯ b. Isḥāq b. Saʿd b. ʿĀmir b. Mālik al-Ašʿarī; Abū Nuʿaym, *Taʾrīḫ Iṣfahān*, 1:272.

307 For more on the traditionist Ǧaʿfar b. Abī l-Muġīrah al-Qummī, see Abū Nuʿaym, *Taʾrīḫ Iṣfahān*, 1:291–292.

308 This may refer to Saʿīd b. ʿAbd al-Raḥmān b. Abzá, on whom see al-Mizzī, *Tahḏīb al-kamāl*, 10:524–525. See also § 98.

309 Aḥmad b. ʿAbd Allāh b. Yūnus b. ʿAbd Allāh b. Qays of the Banū l-Yarbūʿ (Tamīm) died in 227/842; al-Mizzī, *Tahḏīb al-kamāl*, 1:375–378.

310 Yaʿqūb al-Qummī (see note 209).

311 See above, note 307.

§ 99 وقال بعضهم إن إسافا ونائلة لم يفجرا في البيت ولكن قبلها[a] فمسخا حجرين فنصبا ليعتبر بهما الناس ثم دعا عمرو بن لحي إلى عبادتهما فعبدا ثم حولهما قصي بن كلاب تجاه الكعبة يُذبَح عندهما في موضع زمزم.[b]

§ 100 وقال ابن قُتَيبة: إساف ونائلة من بني عبد الدار.[c]

§ 101 وقال الزبير بن بكار: ويقال لما وقع إساف على نائلة مسخهما الله تعالى حجرين فأخرجا من جوف الكعبة وعليهما ثيابهما فجعل أحدهما بلصق الكعبة والآخر عند زمزم وكان يطرح بينهما ما كان يهدى للكعبة وكان ذلك المكان يسمى الحطيم. وإنما نصبا هنالك ليعتبر بهما الناس فلم يزل أمرهما يدرس حتى جعلا صنمين يعبدان.

§ 102 وفيهما يقول أبو طالب: [الطويل]

وحيث يُنيخُ الأشعرون ركابهم بمُفضى السيول بين {ساف} ونائل

١–5.154 وقال ... قصي: الزيادة بخط المقريزي في الهامش الأيسر منقلبة، ثم في الهامش الأعلى من الأعلى إلى الأسفل، ثم في الهامش الأيمن من الأعلى إلى الأسفل، ثم في الهامش الأسفل من الأسفل إلى الأعلى ويشير إليها رمز ٦ بعد "أبدا". ٧ يهدى: في الأصل "يهدا". ‖ يسمى: في الأصل "يسما". ١٠ بمُفضى: في الأصل "بمُفضا".

---

a قارن الإصبهاني، الأغاني، ١٥: ١٣ ("وقيل إنّه لم يَفْجُر بها في البيت، ولكنه قبَّلَها في البيت"). وقارن أيضا ابن كثير، السيرة النبوية، ١: ٧٠ ("وقد قيل إن الله لم يُمهلهما حتى فجَرا فيها، بل مَسخهما قبل ذلك، فعند ذلك نصبا عند الصفا والمروة").

b قارن الأزرقي، أخبار مكة١، ١: ١٥٠ ("ثم حَوَّلهما قُصَيّ بن كلاب بعد ذلك فوضعهما يذبح عندهما وجاه الكعبة عند موضع زمزم"). وقارن أيضا الإصبهاني، الأغاني، ١٥: ١٣ ("فأُخرِجا من الكعبة، ونُصِبا ليعتبر بهما من رآهما، ويزدجر النّاسُ عن مِثْلِ ما ارتكبا، فلما غَلَبَتْ خُزاعةُ على مكة ونُسِيَ حديثُهما، حوَّلهما عَمْرُو بن لحيّ بن كلابٍ (!) بعد ذلك فجعلهما تُجاهَ الكعبةِ يُذبحُ عندَهما عندَ موضع زمزم").

c قارن ابن قتيبة، غريب الحديث، ٢: ٧ ("وأمّا اساف ونائِل، ويقال: نائلة فهما صَنَمان. وروى أنَّهما كانا إنْسانَيْن من بني عبد الدار، طافا بالكعبة فصادَفا منها خَلوة، فأراد أحدهما صاحبه فنكسهما الله نحاسًا").

§ 99 Some said[312] that Isāf and Nāʾilah did not fornicate in the House [i.e. the Kaʿbah], but rather that he kissed her, and then they were transformed into two stones and set up so that people would take warning from them. ʿAmr b. Luḥayy then called [people] to worship them, and they were worshipped. Afterwards, Quṣayy b. Kilāb[313] moved them in front of the Kaʿbah, so that [sacrificial animals] would be slaughtered beside them in the site of Zamzam.[314]

§ 100 Ibn Qutaybah[315] said: Isāf and Nāʾilah belonged to the Banū ʿAbd al-Dār.

§ 101 Al-Zubayr b. Bakkār said: It is said that when Isāf had sexual intercourse with Nāʾilah, Allāh, the Exalted, transformed them into two stones, and they were removed from the interior of the Kaʿbah with their clothes on. One of them was placed close to the Kaʿbah and the other near Zamzam, and gifts to the Kaʿbah were cast between them in a place called the *ḥaṭīm*. They were merely set up there so that people would take warning from them, but in time their origin was forgotten, and they became two idols that were worshipped.

§ 102 Abū Ṭālib[316] said about them: [*al-ṭawīl*]

And where the Ašʿarūn make their camels kneel,
at the place to which the streams flow between [I]sāf and Nāʾilah.

---

312 This may have been just one person's statement (*wa-qāla baʿḍuhum*).

313 Quṣayy b. Kilāb b. Murrah b. Kaʿb b. Luʾayy b. Fihr (or Qurayš b. Ġālib) was one of Muḥammad's ancestors. According to legendary accounts, he united the scattered clans of the Qurayš and organized the worship of the Kaʿbah. He is also reported to have been the custodian of the Kaʿbah; "Ḳuṣayy," in *EI*² (G. Levi Della Vida); Nicholson (1966): 64–65.

314 That is, in the site where the well of Zamzam was reportedly later dug by the Prophet's grandfather, ʿAbd al-Muṭṭalib. See Rubin (1986): 116.

315 Abū Muḥammad ʿAbd Allāh b. Muslim al-Dīnawarī, the compiler of *Adab al-kātib, al-Anwāʾ, Maʿānī l-šiʿr, al-Maʿārif, al-Šiʿr wa-l-šuʿarāʾ*, and *Ġarīb al-ḥadīṯ*; "Ibn Ḳutayba," in *EI*² (G. Lecomte).

316 On whom see "Abū Ṭālib," in *EI*³ (U. Rubin).

§103 ويقال: اتخذت قريش إسافا ونائلة على موضع زمزم ينحرون عندهما.[a]

§104 وقال ابن إسحٰق عن صالح بن حيان: قلت لابن بريدة: "ما إساف ونائلة؟" فقال: "كانا شابين من قريش فكانا يطوفان بالكعبة فأصابا {منها} خلوة فأراد أحدهما صاحبه فنكسهما الله نحاسا فجاء بهما قريش فقالوا: 'لولا أن الله رضي أن يُعبد {هذان الإنسانان} لما نكسهما نحاسا'." قال ابن بريدة: "أما إساف فرجل وأما نائلة فامرأة من بني عبد الدار بن قصي."

§105 قال ابن شبة: وكان سَعْد صنما لبني ملكان ومالك ابني كنانة بن خزيمة بساحل جدة وكان صخرة طويلة. ويقال: كان لبني لهب. فأقبل رجل منهم بإبل له يطيفها بسعد يرجو بركته فلما رأت الإبل ما عليه من الدماء والذبائح نفرت وتفرقت فلم تكد تُجمع. فرماه الكناني بحجر وقال: [الطويل]

أتينا إلى سعد ليجمع شملنا فشتتنا سعد فلا نحن من سعد
وهل سعد إلا صخرة بتنوفة من الأرض لا تدعو لغي ولا رشد[b]

---

٣ منها: في الأصل "منه". ٤ هذان الإنسانان: في الأصل "هذين الانسانين". ‖ الإنسانان: وضع المقريزي ثلاث نقط تحت الكلمة إشارة إلى تلفظها بالسين.

---

a قارن السهيلي، الروض الأنف، ١: ٣٥٤ ("قال ابن إسحاق: واتخذوا إسافا ونائلة على موضع زمزم ينحرون عندهما").

b قارن السهيلي، الروض الأنف، ١: ٣٥٣–٣٥٤ ("قال ابن إسحاق: وكان لِبَني مِلْكان بن كِنانة بن خُزيمة بن مُدْرِكة بن الياس بن مُضَر صنم، يقال له: سَعْد: صَخْرة بفلاة من أرضهم طويلة، فأقبل رجل من بني مِلْكان بإبلٍ له مُؤَبَّلة؛ ليقفها عليه، التماسَ بركته—فيما يزعم—فلما رأته الإبل وكانت مَرْعِيَّة لا تُركَب، وكان يُهْراق عليه الدماء نفرتْ منه، فذهبتْ في كل وجه، وغَضِب ربها المِلْكاني فأخذ حجرا فرماه به، ثم قال: لا بارك الله فيك، نفَّرت عليّ إبلي، ثم خرج في طلبها حتى جمعها، فلما اجتمعت له قال:
أتَيْنا إلى سَعْدٍ ليجمَعَ شَملنا فَشَتَّتَنا سعدٌ فلا نَحْنُ من سَعْدِ
وهل سَعدُ إلَّا صخرةٌ بتَنُوفَةٍ من الأرْضِ لا تدْعو لِغَيٍّ ولا رُشْدِ")

§ 103 It is said that Qurayš adopted Isāf and Nāʾilah by the site of Zamzam and slaughtered [sacrificial animals] beside them.[317]

§ 104 Ibn Isḥāq said on the authority of Ṣāliḥ b. Ḥayyān:[318] I asked Ibn Buraydah,[319] "What are Isāf and Nāʾilah?" He said: "They were two youths from Qurayš, who used to circumambulate the Kaʿbah. [One day,] they found it empty and desired one another, and thereupon, Allāh turned them into copper. Qurayš then brought them and said: 'Had Allāh not been pleased with the worship of these two persons, he would not have turned them into copper'." Ibn Buraydah said: "As for Isāf, he was a man. As for Nāʾilah, she was a woman from the Banū ʿAbd al-Dār b. Quṣayy."

§ 105 Ibn Šabbah said: Saʿd was an idol of the Banū Milkān and [Banū] Mālik, who [Milkān and Mālik] were sons of Kinānah b. Ḫuzaymah. It [the idol] was a long rock on the coast of Jedda. Some say that it belonged to the Banū Lihb. One of them [the Banū Milkān][320] came with his camels, and walked them around Saʿd hoping to draw its blessing, but when the camels saw the blood and sacrifices on it, they shied away and dispersed, and could barely be gathered together again. The Kinānī[321] then pelted [the idol] with a stone and said: [*al-ṭawīl*]

We came to Saʿd so that he would bring us together
but Saʿd dispersed us, so we have nothing to do with Saʿd.
Is Saʿd not merely a rock in a desert tract
of land, summoning neither to error nor to a right path?[322]

---

317 See also Ibn Hišām, *The Life of Muhammad* 37.
318 Ṣāliḥ b. Ḥayyān al-Qurašī l-Kūfī; al-Ḏahabī, *Siyar aʿlām al-nubalāʾ*, 7:373–374.
319 ʿAbd Allāh b. Buraydah b. al-Ḥuṣayb al-Aslamī; Ibn Saʿd, *al-Ṭabaqāt*[1], 9:220.
320 See al-Suhaylī, *al-Rawḍ al-unuf*, 1:303–304.
321 The Milkān belonged to the Kinānah tribal federation.
322 For a translation of these verses, see also Lane (1863–1893): 1361; Klinke-Rosenberger (1941): 50, 117, n. 273; Ibn Hišām, *The Life of Muhammad* 37.

§106 وكان للأزد بالسراة صنم يقال له عائم وله يقول زيد الخيل: [الطويل] | 37b

تخبر من لاقيت أن قد هزمتهم {ولم} تدر ما سيماهم لا وعائم[a]

§107 وكان بالسراة صنم يقال له ذو {الشرى}. كان لبني الحٰرث من يَشْكر ولدوس. وله يقول رجل من الغطارف: [الطويل]

إذًا لحللنا دون ما حول ذي {الشرى} وشج العِدَى منا خميس عرمرم[b]

٢ ولم: في الأصل "ولو". ٣ الشرى: في الأصل "الشوا". ٥ الشرى: في الأصل "الشوا".

a قارن ابن الكلبي، الأصنام، ٤٠ ("وكان لأزْد السَّرَاةِ صنمٌ يقال له عائمٌ. وله يقول زيد الخيّرِ، وهو زيد الخيّل الطائيُّ:
تُخَبِّرُ مَنْ لَاقَيْتَ أَنْ قد هَزَمْتَهُمْ ولم تَدْرِ ما سِيمَاهُمُ، لا، وعائمِ!").
وقارن أيضا ياقوت، معجم البلدان، ٤: ٧٣ ("تخبّر من لاقيتَ أني هزمتُهم ولم ندرِ ما سِيماهمُ لا وعائم"). وقارن أيضا الإصبهاني، الأغاني، ١٧: ٢٧٠ ("تُخبِّر مَنْ لاقيتُ أن قد هزمتهم ولم تَدر ما سيماهُمُ والعمائم (!)").

b راجع ياقوت، معجم البلدان، ٣: ٣٣٠-٣٣١ ("وذو الشرى: صنم كان لدوس وكانوا قد حموا له حمى، وفي حديث الطفيل بن عمرو لما أسلم ورجع إلى أهله بالنور في رأس سوطه دنَت منه زوجته فقال لها: إليك عني فلستُ منكِ ولستِ مني! قالت: لِمَ بأبي أنت وأمّي؟ فقال: فرّق بيني وبينك دينُ الإسلام، فقالت: ديني دينك! فقال لها: اذهبي إلى حنا ذي الشرى، بالنون، ويقال حمى ذي الشرى، فتطهري منه؛ قال: وكان ذو الشرى صنمًا لدوس وكان الحنا حمًى حَمَوْه له به وشَلٌ من ماء يهبط من جبل، قال: قالت بأبي أنت وأمّي أخشى على الصبية من ذي الشرى شيئًا، فقال: أنا ضامنٌ لك، فذهبتْ واغتسلتْ ثمّ جاءت فعرض عليها الإسلام فأسلمت؛ وقال الكلبي: وكان لبني الحارث بن يشكُر بن مبشّر من الأزد صنم يقال له ذو الشرى وله يقول أحد الغطاريف:
إذًا لَحَلَلنا حول ما دون ذي الشّرَى وشَجّ العِدَى منّا خَميسٌ عرَمرَمُ").

§106 The Azd had an idol in al-Sarāt[323] called ʿĀʾim.[324] Zayd al-Ḫayl[325] said, referring to it: [*al-ṭawīl*]

You [masc. sg.] tell those you meet that you have defeated them,
but you do not even know their distinguishing mark. No, [I swear] by ʿĀʾim![326]

§107 There was an idol in al-Sarāt called Ḏū l-Šará.[327] It belonged to the Banū l-Ḥāriṯ of Yaškur[328] and to Daws.[329] A man of the Ġaṭārif[330] said, referring to it: [*al-ṭawīl*]

Then, we alighted before the area surrounding Ḏū l-Šará,
and a huge army of our [people] crushed the heads of the enemies.[331]

323 Al-Sarāt is the name of the mountain chain that runs along the western part of the Arabian Peninsula; "al-Sarāt," in *EI*² (A. Grohmann [E. van Donzel]).

324 Cf. Ibn al-Kalbī, *al-Aṣnām* 40: "the Azd al-Sarāt had an idol called ʿĀʾim." See also Wellhausen (1897): 66; Klinke-Rosenberger (1941): 51.

325 Zayd al-Ḫayl ("Zayd of the horses") was a poet and a tribal chief who belonged to the tribe of Ṭayyiʾ; Ibn Ḥağar, *al-Iṣābah*¹, 2:513–515; "Zayd al-Khayl," in *EAL* (J.E. Montgomery).

326 This line is also translated in Faris (1952): 36; Atallah (1969): 33. The version of this line in al-Iṣfahānī, *al-Aġānī*, 17:270 has *wa-l-ʿamāʾim* ("and the turbans") instead of *wa-ʿĀʾim* ("[I swear] by ʿĀʾim"). Zayd al-Ḫayl reportedly addressed this verse to Qays b. ʿĀṣim of the tribe of Tamīm, whom he accused of falsely taking credit for defeating the Banū ʿIğl.

327 Al-Maqrīzī erroneously read the name Ḏū l-Šawā.

328 Of the Azd.

329 Cf. "Dhu 'l-Sharā," in *EI*² (G. Ryckmans): "Ibn Hishām records that Dhu 'l-Sharā 'was an image belonging to Daus and the *ḥimā* was the temenos which they had made sacred to him; in it there was a trickle of water from a rivulet from the mountain' … This tradition is resumed in the *Ḳamūs*: *dhu 'l-Sharā ṣanam daws*. The tradition arose from confusion among the Arabs between Duserani, 'the worshippers of Dusares,' a naming for the Nabataeans, and the tribe of Daws."

330 Of the Azd. They are usually called "al-Ġaṭārīf"; Ibn Ḥabīb, *al-Muḥabbar* 316. See also the introduction, pp. 33–34.

331 See also Wellhausen (1897): 49; Klinke-Rosenberger (1941): 50.

§108 ورُضا كان لربيعة وطيئ وله يقول طفيل الخيل: [الطويل]

وقالوا وألقوا ما حَبَوا في رحالهم   هُم ورُضًا مَن قَد تخافون فاذهبوا[a]

§109 وكان ضَمَار صنما لبني سُلَيم. كان منهم لمرداس بن أبي عامر أبي عباس بن مرداس وكان قد جعل عليه سيفين من ذهب وجعله في بيت فكان يتعاهده في الأيام فيسأله عن الشيء فيكلمه الشيطان من جوفه. فلما هلك مرداس أوصى به ابنه عباسا فكان عباس يتعاهد منه ما كان أبوه يتعاهد منه. فسمع عباس ليلة من البيت الذي فيه الصنم صوتا فخرج يسحب ثوبه حتى أتاه فسمع صوتا من جوف الصنم يقول:[b] [الكامل]

أَوْدَى ضَمار وكان يُعبَد مرة   قبل الكتاب إلى النبي محمد
قل للقبائل من سُلَيم كلها   هلك الأنيس وعاش أهل المسجد
إن الذي ورث النبوة والهدى   بعد ابن مريم من قريش مهتد

---

٢ حَبَوا: وضع المقريزي رمز "ح" تحت الكلمة إشارة إلى تلفظها بالحاء. ‖ رحالهم: وضع المقريزي رمز "ح" تحت الكلمة إشارة إلى تلفظها بالحاء. ٨ أَوْدَى: في الأصل "أَوْدَا" ووضع المقريزي الهمزة فوق الألف.

---

٣ ضَمَار: أضاف المقريزي الحاشية التالية في الهامش الأيسر من الأسفل إلى الأعلى: "ضَمار بفتح الضاد المعجمة والميم وبراء مهملة في آخره".

---

a قارن طفيل الغنوي، ديوان، ٢٢ ("فقال بصيرٌ يَسْتَبِينُ رِعالَها: هُمُ والإلهِ مَنْ تَخَافِين فاذْهَبِي
ويُرْوَى ولَعَلَّهَا رِوَايَةُ أَبِي عُبَيْدَةَ:
وقال بَصيرٌ قد أَبَانَ رِعالَها   فهِيَّ: ورُضَى مَنْ تَخافِينَ، فاذْهَبِي
ورُضَى، إِسْمُ صَنَمٍ كَانَ لِطَيِّئٍ").

b راجع الإصبهاني، الأغاني، ١٤: ٢٩٥ ("عن العَبَّاس بن مِرداس بن أبي عامر أنه قال: كان لأبي صنم اسمه ضمار، فلمَّا حضره الموتُ أوصاني به وبعبادته والقيام عليه، فعمَدتُ إلى ذلك الصنم فجعلته في بيت، وجعلت آتيه في كل يوم وليلة مرَّة، فلما ظهر أمرُ رسول الله صلى الله عليه وسلم سمعتُ صوتًا في جوف الليل راعني، فوثبتُ إلى ضمار، فإذا الصَّوت في جوفه يقول").

§ 108 Ruḍā[332] belonged to Rabīʿah and Ṭayyiʾ. Ṭufayl al-Ḫayl[333] said, referring to it: [*al-ṭawīl*]

And they said, having cast what they gave [?] in their saddles:[334]
[I swear] by Ruḍā, they are those you certainly fear, so leave![335]

§ 109 Ḍamār was an idol of the Banū Sulaym. It belonged to Mirdās b. Abī ʿĀmir of the Banū Sulaym, who was ʿAbbās b. Mirdās's father.[336] He [Mirdās] placed two gold swords upon it [Ḍamār, the idol], and put it in a sanctuary. He used to visit it frequently during the day and ask it about something, and a devil would speak to him from within it. When Mirdās died, he entrusted it to his son, ʿAbbās, who used to visit it frequently, as his father had. One night, ʿAbbās heard a voice from the sanctuary in which the idol was placed. He went out, dragging along his garment, and when he reached it, he heard a voice from within the idol saying: [*al-kāmil*]

Ḍamār has perished. It was once worshipped
before [the revelation of] the Book to the Prophet Muḥammad.
Tell the tribal groups of Sulaym, all of them,
that the close friend [i.e. Ḍamār] has passed away, and the people of the mosque are alive.
The member of Qurayš who inherited the prophecy and the right path,
following the son of Maryam, is rightly guided.[337]

---

5 Ḍamār : Ḍamār has a *fatḥah* over the *ḍād* and *mīm*, and a *rāʾ* at the end (marginal gloss in al-Maqrīzī's hand).

---

332 Or perhaps Ruḍá.

333 For more on the poet and warrior Ṭufayl b. ʿAwf al-Ġanawī, who was also known as Ṭufayl al-Ḫayl and al-Muḥabbir, see "Ṭufayl b. ʿAwf al-Ghanawī," in EAL (J.E. Montgomery).

334 Or, in their dwellings.

335 Compare Ṭufayl al-Ġanawī, *Dīwān* 22 (Arabic text; Abū ʿUbaydah's version): "And a wise man (*baṣīr*) examining their troops of horses (*riʿālahā*) said: They, [I swear] by Ruḍá, are those you fear, so leave!" This variant of the verse is also translated in Ṭufayl al-Ġanawī, *Dīwān* 5 (English text).

336 For more on al-ʿAbbās b. Mirdās, who died between 18/639 and 35/656, see "al-ʿAbbās b. Mirdās," in EI3 (G.E. von Grunebaum and G. Tamer).

337 This line may also be translated as follows: "He who inherited the prophecy and the right path after the son of Maryam is a rightly guided [man] from Qurayš." For a translation of these verses see also Wellhausen (1897): 66.

فكتم ذلك عباس ولم يذكره لأحد وخرج إلى إبل له بعقيق نَمِرَة فبينما هو {مستلق} في روضة من رياض العقيق إذ سمع صوتا وهو يقول:

بشر الجن وإبلاسها   أن قد وضعت المطي أحلاسَها
ومنعت السماء أحراسها[a]

فرفع رأسه فإذا هو بطير فطلبه فدخل في بعض تلك الجبال فلم يقدر عليه فرجع إلى مكانه فبينما هو هنالك إذ سمع صوتا يقول:

إن النور الذي وقع من السماء   يوم الاثنين وليلة الثلاثاء
في دار بني العنقاء

فرفع رأسه فإذا هو بحيال على نَشَز فطلبه فاضمحل حتى لم يره. فرجع إلى أهله فقال: "هل أتاكم
خبر من قبل مكة؟" قالوا: "نعم. بلغنا أن نبيا خرج بمكة." فوقع في قلبه الإسلام فخرج متوجها إلى
مكة وقال لأهله: "إني منطلق إلى مكة. فإن كان محمد محقا لم أُسْبَق إليه وإن كان | مبطلا لم أغلب 38a
عليه."[b] فخرج حتى أتى مكة فوجد النبي ﷺ قد هاجر إلى المدينة فطلبه حتى جاء المدينة فأسلم.

١ مستلق: في الأصل "مستلقي". ٣ أحلاسَها: وضع المقريزي رمز "ح" تحت الكلمة إشارة إلى تلفظها بالحاء. ٤ أحراسها: وضع المقريزي رمز "ح" تحت الكلمة إشارة إلى تلفظها بالحاء. ٩ بحيال: كذا. وضع المقريزي رمز "ح" تحت الكلمة إشارة إلى تلفظها بالحاء.

a قارن الإصبهاني، الأغاني، ١٤: ٢٩٥ ("بَشِّر الجِنّ وأجناسَها أن وضعت المَطِيّ أحلاسها وكفت السماء أحراسَها وأن يُغصِّ السَّوْقُ أنفاسَها"). وراجع ابن كثير، تفسير، ٧: ٢٧٤ ("ألم ترَ الجنّ وإبلاسها ويأسها من بعد إنكاسِها").

b راجع الإصفهاني، الأغاني، ١٤: ٢٩٦ ("فإن كان خيرًا لم أُسبَق إليه، وإن كان شرًّا نصرتُهُ نخؤولته، على أني قد رأيت الفضلَ البيّنِ وكرامةَ الدنيا والآخرة في طاعته ومؤازرته، واتّباعه ومبايعته، وإيثار أمره على جميع الأمور").

ʿAbbās kept this to himself and did not mention it to anyone. He went to some of his camels in the valley of Namirah, and as he was lying down in one of the meadows of the valley, he heard a voice saying:

Bring the *ǧinn* and their despair the good tidings
that the riding animals put on their saddle cloths
and that heaven protected its guards.

He raised his head, and suddenly there was a bird. He tried to catch it, but it flew into one of the mountains, so he could not reach it. Then he returned to the previous place, and while he was there, he heard a voice saying:

The light that descended from the sky
on Monday and the night before Tuesday morning
is in the territory of the Banū l-ʿAnqāʾ.[338]

He raised his head, and suddenly, it [the bird] was on the opposite side in a high place [?]. He tried to catch it, but it retreated until he could no longer see it. He returned to his family and said: "Did you receive any news from Mecca?" They said: "Yes. We heard that a prophet appeared in Mecca." [Upon hearing this,] his heart inclined to Islam, and so he left, heading toward Mecca, and told his family: "I am setting out to Mecca. If Muḥammad is truthful, no one will reach him before me, and if he is a liar, no one will overcome me in reaching him."[339] Then he left, but when he arrived in Mecca, he discovered that the Prophet, may Allāh bless and save him, had already made the *hiǧrah* to Medina, so he went after him until he reached Medina and embraced Islam.

338 Al-ʿAnqāʾ in this verse probably refers to Ṯaʿlabah al-ʿAnqāʾ, who was an ancestor of the Aws and Ḫazraǧ.

339 Compare al-Iṣfahānī, *al-Aġānī*, 14:296: "If he is good, no one will reach him before me, and if he is bad, I will help him due to our maternal relations [*naṣartuhu li-ḫuʾūlatihi*]." The word *ḫuʾūlah* denotes "[t]he relationship of a maternal uncle [and of a maternal aunt]"; see Lane (1863–1893): 825. This sentence should probably be linked to the traditions that ascribe to the Prophet the statement that he is "the son of the ʿAwātik [pl. of ʿĀtikah] from Sulaym." For more details on this tradition, see Lecker (1989): 114–116.

§110 قال: كان لكل بطن من الأوس والخزرج وهم الأنصار صنم في بيت لجماعة البطن يكرمونه ويعظمونه ويذبحون له. وكان في بني عبد الأشهل صنم يدعى الحريش وإليه نسب عبد حريش بن مرة بن عمرو بن حنظلة بن يربوع جد عبد قيس بن خفاف بن عبد حريش الشاعر[a] وصنم في بني حارثة يقال له صَخْر وصنم في بني ظَفَر يقال له شمس وصنم في بني معْوية يقال له البِهَام وصنم في بني عمرو بن عوف يقال له القين وصنم في بني {خَطْمَة} يقال له شفر وصنم للقواقلة يقال له الحِبْس وصنم في بني أمية يقال له غيان وصنم في بني سَلِمة يقال له إساف وصنم في بني عدي بن النجار يقال له سَمول وصنم في بني دينار بن النجار يقال له حُسَا وصنم في بني مالك بن النجار يقال له الطِم وصنم في بني زُريق يقال له السمْح.

---

٢ يدعى : في الأصل "يدعا". ‖ الحريش : وضع المقريزي رمز "ح" تحت الكلمة إشارة إلى تلفظها بالحاء. ٢-٣ وإليه ... الشاعر : الزيادة بخط المقريزي في الهامش الأيسر وتبتدئ في آخر السطر أمام "الحريش". ٤ حارثة : وضع المقريزي رمز "ح" تحت الكلمة إشارة إلى تلفظها بالحاء. ‖ البِهَام : كذا (التشكيل). ٥ خَطْمَة : في الأصل "حَطْمَة". ووضع المقريزي رمز "ح" تحت الكلمة إشارة إلى تلفظها بالحاء. ٦ الحِبْس : كذا (التشكيل). ووضع المقريزي رمز "ح" تحت الكلمة إشارة إلى تلفظها بالحاء ٧ حُسَا : وضع المقريزي رمز "ح" تحت الكلمة إشارة إلى تلفظها بالحاء. ٨ الطِم : كذا (التشكيل). ‖ السمْح : وضع المقريزي رمز "ح" تحت الكلمة إشارة إلى تلفظها بالحاء.

---

a قارن الدارقطني، المؤتلف والمختلف، ٢: ٦١١-٦١٢ ("وأمّا جَرِيش، فهو صَنَمٌ كان في الجاهلية، نُسب إليه رَجل، فقيل: عَبْد جَرِيش، وهو جَدّ عبد قَيْس بن خُفَاف بْنِ عَبْدِ جَرِيش بن مُرَّة بن عَمرو الشَّاعِر، وهو من بني عَمرو بن حَنظلة بن مالك بن زيد مَناة").

§110 He [Ibn Šabbah][340] said: Every clan of the Aws and Ḫazraǧ, who are the Anṣār,[341] had an idol in a sanctuary that belonged to the entire clan; they honored and venerated it, and they made sacrifices to it. There was an idol in [the territory of] the Banū ʿAbd al-Ašhal[342] called al-Ḥarīš.[343] ʿAbd Ḥarīš b. Murrah b. ʿAmr b. Ḥanẓalah b. Yarbūʿ, the grandfather of the poet ʿAbd Qays b. Ḫufāf b. ʿAbd Ḥarīš, was named in reference to it [the idol al-Ḥarīš].[344] There was also an idol in [the territory of] the Banū Ḥāriṯah[345] called Ṣaḫr, an idol in [the territory of] the Banū Ẓafar[346] called Šams, an idol in [the territory of] the Banū Muʿāwiyah[347] called al-Bihām, an idol in [the territory of] the Banū ʿAmr b. ʿAwf[348] called al-Qayn, an idol in [the territory of] the Banū Ḫaṭmah[349] called Šafr, an idol of the Qawāqilah[350] called al-Ḥibs, an idol in [the territory of] the Banū Umayyah[351] called Ġayyān,[352] an idol in [the territory of] the Banū Salimah[353] called Isāf, an idol in [the territory of] the Banū ʿAdī b. al-Naǧǧār[354] called Samūl, an idol in [the territory of] the Banū Dīnār b. al-Naǧǧār[355] called Ḥusā,[356] an idol in [the territory of] the Banū Mālik b. al-Naǧǧār[357] called al-Ṭimm, and an idol in [the territory of] the Banū Zurayq[358] called al-Samḥ.

---

340 See Lecker (1993), 331, and see also the introduction.
341 The Medinan "helpers" of the Prophet Muḥammad.
342 Of the Aws.
343 Al-Ḥarīš was also the eponym of the Banū l-Ḥarīš, a brother clan of the ʿAbd al-Ašhal. At some point, the Ḥarīš clan was incorporated into the ʿAbd al-Ašhal; Lecker (1993): 333–334.
344 Compare al-Dāraquṭnī, *al-Muʾtalif wa-l-muḫtalif*, 2:611, where the idol's name is said to have been Ǧarīš, and the poet's pedigree is given as ʿAbd Qays b. Ḫufāf b. ʿAbd Ǧarīš b. Murrah b. ʿAmr of the Banū ʿAmr b. Ḥanẓalah b. Mālik b. Zayd Manāt.
345 Of the Aws.
346 Of the Aws.
347 Of the Aws.
348 Of the Aws.
349 Of the Aws. Al-Maqrīzī erroneously reads the name Ḥaṭmah.
350 Of the Ḫazraǧ.
351 Of the Aws.
352 The Banū Umayyah were a subgroup of Ḫaṭmah. Note that Ġayyān was also the name of a subgroup of Ḫaṭmah, which suggests that al-Maqrīzī's statement about the Umayyah worshipping Ġayyān involves two different subgroups of this clan. See Lecker (1993): 333–334.
353 Of the Ḫazraǧ.
354 Of the Ḫazraǧ.
355 Of the Ḫazraǧ.
356 Or Ḥusāʾ.
357 Of the Ḫazraǧ.
358 Of the Ḫazraǧ.

§111 ولكل رجل شريف صنم من هذه الأصنام وكان في بيت عَمرو بن الجُموح صنم يقال له سَاف كسره معاذ بن جبل رضي الله عنه ومعاذ بن عمرو بن الجموح وللبراء بن معرور صنم يقال له الديباج وصنم للجد بن قيس يقال له الزبّر.

§112 فلما قدم السبعون الذين شهدوا العقبة جعلوا يكسرون الأصنام. فدخل عبد الله بن رواحة رضي الله عنه على شيخ منهم قديم فربَط مع صنمه ميتة ثم وضعه على بابه فأصبح الشيخ فرآه فقال: "من صنع هذا بإلاهنا؟" فقيل له: "هذا عمل ابن رواحة." فأتاه ابن رواحة فقال له: "أما تستحيي وأنت من كبرائنا تعبد خشبة أنت عملتها بيدك؟" فقال الشيخ: "إني غير متعرض له. أخاف على صبيتي." فضحك بَشير بن سعد وقال: "وهَل عنده ضر أو نفْع؟" فكسره عبد الله بن رواحة وأسلم الشيخ.

§ 111 Every nobleman had one of these idols. There was an idol in the house of ʿAmr b. al-Ǧamūḥ[359] called Sāf[360] which was destroyed by Muʿāḏ b. Ǧabal,[361] may Allāh be pleased with him, and by Muʿāḏ b. ʿAmr b. al-Ǧamūḥ. Al-Barāʾ b. Maʿrūr[362] had an idol called al-Dībāǧ, and there was also an idol called al-Zabr which belonged to al-Ǧadd b. Qays.[363]

§ 112 When the seventy who participated in the ʿAqabah meeting[364] arrived, they started to destroy the idols. ʿAbd Allāh b. Rawāḥah,[365] may Allāh be pleased with him, entered [the house of] an old man who belonged to them,[366] tied a carcass to his idol, and laid it by his door. The old man woke up and saw it, and he said: "Who did this to our god?" He was then told: "This is the doing of Ibn Rawāḥah." Ibn Rawāḥah approached him and said to him: "Are you not ashamed, as one of our elders, of worshipping a piece of wood which you made with your own hands?" The old man said: "I do not assail it. I fear for my boys." Bašīr b. Saʿd[367] laughed and said: "Does it have [the power to] harm or benefit?" Thereupon, ʿAbd Allāh b. Rawāḥah destroyed it, and the old man embraced Islam.

---

359 One of the tribal leaders of the Banū Salimah (Ḫazraǧ); Ibn al-Aṯīr, *Usd al-ġābah*, 4:195.

360 Note that the idol Isāf was mentioned earlier in the text as the idol of the Banū Salimah. This idol is probably identical to Manāf (see below, § 117); Lecker (1993): 337.

361 According to the sources, Muʿāḏ b. Ǧabal was one of the men who destroyed the idols of the Banū Salimah. He is also said to have participated in the ʿAqabah meeting; Ibn Saʿd, *al-Ṭabaqāt*[1], 3:539–546.

362 Al-Barāʾ b. Maʿrūr belonged to the ʿUbayd subdivision of the Salimah. He is reported to have been a *naqīb* following the ʿAqabah meeting, and to have participated in the Battle of Badr; Ibn Saʿd, *al-Ṭabaqāt*[1], 3:571–572; "Al-Barāʾ b. Maʿrūr," in *EI*[3] (Andreas Görke).

363 Al-Ǧadd b. Qays also belonged to the ʿUbayd subdivision of the Banū Salimah; Lecker (1993): 338.

364 The Anṣār are said to have first met the Prophet in a series of meetings in al-ʿAqabah, a mountain road between Mecca and Miná. These meetings reportedly laid the foundations for the Prophet's arrival in Medina. For more details, see Melamede (1934): 17–58; Yazigi (2008): 292–298.

365 ʿAbd Allāh b. Rawāḥah (d. 8/629) was the *naqīb* of the Banū l-Ḥāriṯ branch of the Ḫazraǧ. He was literate before Islam, and was reportedly a zealous opponent of idol worship among the Banū l-Ḥāriṯ in Medina; "ʿAbdallāh b. Rawāḥa," in *EI*[3] (Sarah Mirza); Lecker (1993): 339.

366 The old man probably belonged to ʿAbd Allāh b. Rawāḥah's branch, the Banū l-Ḥāriṯ b. al-Ḫazraǧ; Lecker (1993): 338.

367 Bašīr b. Saʿd was also a member of the Banū l-Ḥāriṯ b. al-Ḫazraǧ. Like ʿAbd Allāh b. Rawāḥah, he was literate before Islam; "Bashīr b. Saʿd," in *EI*[3] (M. Lecker).

§113 وكان أبو الدرداء آخر دَارِه إسلاما[a] فكان عبد الله بن رواحة يدعوه إلى الإسلام فيأبى وكان له صديقا فتحينه فلما خرج أبو الدرداء دخل عبد الله منزله فكسر صنمه وهو يقول: [الطويل]

38b تبرأ من اسماء الشياطين كلها ألا كل ما يُدعى مع الله باطل |

فقالت امرأته: "أهلكتني يٰابن رواحة." وخرج وجاء أبو الدرداء وامرأته تبكي فقال: "ما لك؟" قالت: "أخوك ابن رَواحة دخل فصنع ما ترى." فغضب ثم فكر فقال: "لو كان عند هذا خير لدفع عن نفسه." فأتى النبي ﷺ فأسلم.[b]

§114 وكان كعب بن عُجْرَة تأخر إسلامه وله صنم في بيته وكان عُبادة بن الصامت له صديقا فدخل منزله يوما وكعب غائب عن منزله فكسر صنمه فلما جاء كعب فرأى ما صنع به قال: "ما

١ فيأبى: في الأصل "فيابا". ٢ فتحينه: وضع المقريزي رمز "ح" تحت الكلمة إشارة إلى تلفظها بالحاء.
٣ يُدعى: في الأصل "يُدعا".

a قارن ابن سعد، الطبقات٢، ٤: ٣٥١ ("وكان أبو الدرداء آخِرَ أهل داره إسلَامًا").

b قارن ابن عساكر، تاريخ مدينة دمشق، ٤٧: ١٠٦ ("قالوا: وكان أَبُو الدَّرْدَاء أهل آخر داره (!) إسلاما، متعلقًا بصنم له قد وضع عليه منديلًا، فكان عَبْد الله بن رواحة يدعوه إلى الإسلام فيأبى ممسكًا بذلك الصنم، فتحيّنه عَبْد الله بن رَوَاحة وكان له أخًا في الجاهلية والإسلام، فلما رآه قد خرج من بيته خالف فدخل بيته، وأعجل امرأته وأنها لتمشط رأسها، فقال: أين أَبُو الدَّرْدَاء؟ قالت: خرج أخوك آنفًا، فدخل إلى بيته الذي كان فيه ذلك الصنم ومعه القدّوم قال: فانتزله وجعل يقلد قلدًا قلدًا وهو يرتجز ويقول:

تَبَرَّأت (!) من اسماء الشياطين كلها ألا كلما يدعى مع الله باطل

قال ثم خرج وسمعت المرأة ضرب القدوم وهو يضرب ذلك الصنم، فقالت: أهلكتني يا ابن رَوَاحة، قال: فخرج على ذلك، فلم يكن شئ حتى أقبل أَبُو الدَّرْدَاء إلى منزله، فدخل فوجد المرأة قاعدة تبكي شفقًا منه، فقال: ما شأنك؟ فقالت: أخوك عبد الله بن رَوَاحة دخل إليّ فصنع ما ترى، فغضب غضباً شديدًا ثم فكّر في نفسه فقال: لو كان عنده خيرٌ لدفع عن نفسه، فانطلق حتى أتى رَسُول الله (صلى الله عليه وسلم) ومعه ابن رَوَاحة، فأسلم").

§ 113 Abū l-Dardāʾ[368] was the last of his clan[369] to embrace Islam. ʿAbd Allāh b. Rawāḥah used to urge him to embrace Islam, but he [Abū l-Dardāʾ] refused. He [ʿAbd Allāh b. Rawāḥah] was his [Abū l-Dardāʾ's] friend, and he [ʿAbd Allāh b. Rawāḥah] waited for the right time to act. When Abū l-Dardāʾ left, ʿAbd Allāh entered his [Abū l-Dardāʾ's] house and destroyed his idol, saying: [*al-ṭawīl*]

Free yourself [masc. sg.] from the names of the devils, all of them!
Surely, anything that is prayed to along with Allāh is false.

His [Abū l-Dardāʾ's] wife said: "You have ruined me, Ibn Rawāḥah." Then he left, and Abū l-Dardāʾ came, while his wife was still crying. He asked: "What is the matter with you?" She said: "Your brother,[370] Ibn Rawāḥah, entered and did what you see." He was angry, but then he thought [about it] and said: "Had there been any good in this [idol], it would have defended itself." Then he went to the Prophet, may Allāh bless and save him, and embraced Islam.

§ 114 Kaʿb b. ʿUǧrah's[371] conversion to Islam was belated. He had an idol in his house. ʿUbādah b. al-Ṣāmit[372] was his friend; one day he entered Kaʿb's house when Kaʿb was absent and destroyed his idol. When Kaʿb came and saw what he had done to it, he said: "This [idol] is useless." Then he [Kaʿb]

368 Abū l-Dardāʾ also belonged to the Banū l-Ḥāriṯ b. al-Ḫazraǧ; Ibn Saʿd, *al-Ṭabaqāt*[1], 4:351–358; "Abū l-Dardāʾ," in *EI*[3] (Christopher Melchert).

369 *Āḫir dārihi Islāman*: he was the last person in the territory (or court) of his tribal group (or family) to embrace Islam. See also Lecker (1993): 339.

370 Note that some accounts say that Abū l-Dardāʾ and ʿAbd Allāh b. Rawāḥah were maternal brothers, but the more prevalent opinion in the sources states that they were maternal cousins. See Ibn ʿAsākir, *Dimašq*, 28:35; Ibn Saʿd, *al-Ṭabaqāt*[1], 4:351. See also Lecker (2002): 113, n. 18.

371 According to some, Kaʿb b. ʿUǧrah was a full-fledged member of the Anṣār, and according to others, he was their client. The version in which he was their client is preferable. See Lecker (1993): 341.

372 ʿUbādah b. al-Ṣāmit was reportedly the *naqīb* of the Qawāqilah. He played a prominent role in the expulsion of the Jewish Banū Qaynuqāʿ tribe from Medina; Ibn Saʿd, *al-Ṭabaqāt*[1], 3:506; Ibn Ḥaǧar, *al-Iṣābah*[1], 3:505–507.

عند هذا طائل.» وأتى منزل عبادة فظن عبادة أنه يريد أن يقع به فقال: "قد رأيت أنه لو كان عنده طائل ما تركك تفعل به ما رأيت."[a]

§ 115 قال: وكانت حواء بنت يزيد امرأة قيس بن الخطيم فقالت: كان قيس لا يُرام فعَدوت يوما على صنمه فكسرته فلما دخل نظر إليه وقال: "ما هذا؟ أأنت فعلت هذا؟" قالت: "لا ولكن الشاة نطحته." فقام إلى الشاة فذبحها.

§ 116 قال: واتخذت بلْحرث بن الخزرج صنما يقال له هُزَم وكان موضعه في مجلسهم الذي يقال له هُزّم ببطحان.

§ 117 وكان لبني سَلِمة صنم يقال له مناف. فعدا عليه رجل منهم يقال له الجموح فَرَبَطه بكلب ثم طرحه في بئر فوجد فيها. فقال الجموح: [الرجز]

٧ هُزّم: كذا (التشكيل).

a قارن ابن عساكر، تاريخ مدينة دمشق، ٥٠: ١٤٥-١٤٦ ("وكان كَعْب بن عُجْرَة قد استأخر إسلامه وكان له صنم في بيته يكرمه ويمسحه من الغبار، ويضع عليه ثوبًا، وكان يكلّم في الإسلام فيأباه، وكان عُبَادة بن الصَّامت له خليلًا، فقعد له يومًا يرصده، فلمّا خرج من بيته دخل عُبَادة ومعه قدوم وزوجته عند أهلها فجعل يفلّذه فلذة فلذة وهو يقول:

أَلَا كلّ ما يُدعى مع الله باطلُ

ثم خرج وأغلق الباب، فرجع كعب إلى بيته، فنظر إلى الصنم قد كسر فقال: هذا عمل عُبادة، فخرج مغضباً وهو يريد أن يشاتم عُبَادة إلى أن فكر في نفسه فقال: ما عند هذا الصنم من طائل، لو كان عنده طائل حيث جعله جُذاذًا لامتنع، ومضى حتى دق على عُبادة فأشفق عُبادة أن يقع به، فدخل عليه فقال: قد رأيت أن لو كان عنده طائل ما تركك تصنع به ما رأيت، وإنّي أشهد أن لا إله إلّا الله، وأنّ مُحَمَّدًا رَسُول الله").

went to ʿUbādah's house, and ʿUbādah suspected that he wanted to hurt him. But he said: "I realize that if it had been of any use, it would not have let you do to it what I have seen."

§ 115 He [Ibn Šabbah] said: Ḥawwāʾ bt. Yazīd[373] was Qays b. al-Ḫaṭīm's[374] wife. She said: Qays was a man whom no one dared to challenge. One day, I assaulted his idol and destroyed it. When he entered, he looked at it and said: "What is this? Did you do this?" She said: "No, the sheep butted it." So he went to the sheep and slaughtered it.

§ 116 He [Ibn Šabbah] said: The Banū l-Ḥāriṯ b. al-Ḫazraǧ adopted an idol called Huzzam. It was located in their place of assembly which was [also] called Huzzam in [wadi] Buṭḥān.[375]

§ 117 The Banū Salimah had an idol called Manāf.[376] One of them [the Banū Salimah], whose name was [Muʿāḏ b. ʿAmr b.][377] al-Ǧamūḥ, assaulted it, tied it to [a carcass of] a dog, and then threw it into a well in which it was [later] found. [ʿAmr b.] al-Ǧamūḥ said: [*al-raǧaz*]

---

373 Ḥawwāʾ bt. Yazīd belonged to the Zaʿūrāʾ, a Jewish clan that was incorporated into the ʿAbd al-Ašhal (Aws); Lecker (1993): 333.

374 He was a poet who belonged to the Ẓafar clan of the Aws; "Ḳays b. al-Khaṭīm," in *EI*^{2} (T. Kowalski).

375 Note that some of the Banū l-Ḥāriṯ lived east of wadi Buṭḥān; Lecker (1993): 340, n. 46.

376 According to other sources, the idol's name was Manāt, but the reading Manāf is preferable; Lecker (1993): 337.

377 See Lecker (1993): 336.

الحمد لله الجليل ذي المنن   قبح بالفعل منافا ذا {الدرن}
أقسم لو كنت إلاها لم تكن   أنت وكلب وسط بئر في قَرَن[a]

§118 قال: وكان الدَوَار أن العرب تأخذ من الحَرَم سبعة أحجار كقدر عرض الكعبة وطولها إلا أنه مُدَور ثم يدورون حوله فيدور الرجال أربعة أطواف والنساء ثلاثة. وكانت دَوَار في سبع قبائل من العرب ليس في غيرهم في ضَبَّة ونُمَيْر ومُرة وجُهينة وبلي وعُذْرة وسُلَيم.

وفي ذلك يقول عامر بن الطفيل ورأي قينات لغَني بن أعْصُر يطفن وفيهن جَمال: [الوافر]

ألا ⟨يا⟩ ليت إخواني غنيا   عليهم كلما أمْسَوا دَوَارُ[b]

١ الدرن: في الأصل "الـ رن". ولا يظهر أن المقريزي كشط حرفا بل ترك بياضا بين أداة التعريف والحرفين الأخيرين.   ٦ أعْصُر: في الأصل "اعصَر".

a قارن ابن الأثير، أسد الغابة، ٤: ١٩٥ ("وكان عمرو بن الجموح سيدًا من سادة بني سَلِمة، وشريفًا من أشرافهم، وكان قد اتخذ في داره صنمًا من خَشَب يقال له «مناة» يعظمه ويطهّره، فلما أَسلم فتيان بني سلمة: ابنه معاذ بن عمرو، ومعاذ بن جبل في فتيان منهم، كانوا ممن شهد العقبة، فكانوا يدخلون بالليل على صنم عمرو فيحملونه فيطرحونه في بعض حُفَر بني سلمة، وفيها عِذَر الناس مُنكسًا عَلَى رأسه، فإذا أَصبح عمرو، قال: ويلكم! من عدا على آلهتنا هذه الليلة؟ ثم يغدو فيلتمسه، فإذا وجده غسله وطَيَّبه، ثم يقول: والله لو أَعلم من يَصْنَعُ بك هذا لأُخْزِينَّه، فإذا أَمسى ونام عَمْرو عَدَوا عليه ففعلوا به ذلك، فيغدو فيجده، فيغسله ويطيبه. فلما أَلحوا عليه استخرجه فغسله وطيّبه، ثم جاءَ بسيفه فعلقه عليه، ثم قال: إني والله لا أَعلم من يصنع بك ذلك، فإن كان فيك خير فامتنع، هذا السيف معك! فلما أمسى عَدَوا عليه، وأَخذوا السيف من عُنُقه، ثم أَخذوا كَلْبًا ميتًا فقرنوه بحبل، ثم أَلقوه في بئر من آبار بني سَلِمة فيها عِذَرُ الناس. وغدا عمرو فلم يجده، فخرج يبتغيه حتى وجده مقرونًا بكلب، فلما رآه أَبصر رشده وكلمه من أَسلم من قومه، فأَسلم وحسن إسلامه").

b قارن ابن الكلبي، الأصنام، ٤٢ ("كانت للعرب حجارةٌ غُبْرٌ منصوبةٌ، يطوفون بها ويَعْتِرُون عندها. يُسَمُّونَها الأنصابَ، ويُسَمُّونَ الطَّوافَ بها الدَّوَارَ. وفي ذلك يقول عامر بن الطُّفَيْل (وأتى غَنِيَّ بن أعْصُرَ يومًا وهم يطوفون بنُصُبٍ لهم، فرأى في فَتَيَاتِهِم جَمالا وهُنَّ يَطُفْنَ به) فقال:
أَلَا يَا لَيْتَ أخوالِي غَنِيًّا   عليهم كُلَّما أَمْسَوْا دَوَارُ!").

Praise be to Allāh, the Great, the Benevolent.
Indeed, He has revealed the ugliness of Manāf, the filthy one.
I swear that had you been a god,
you and a dog would not have been tied together in the middle of a well.

§118 He[378] said: The [practice called] *dawār* [was the following:] The Arabs would take seven stones from the sacred territory of Mecca [and arrange them] according to the width and length of the Kaʿbah but in a circular shape. Then they would circle it [the demarcated area]. The men would circle it four times, and the women [would circle it] three times. The *dawār* was only practiced by seven Arab tribes: The Ḍabbah, Numayr, Murrah, Ğuhaynah, Balī, ʿUḏrah, and Sulaym.

ʿĀmir b. al-Ṭufayl[379] recited [the following verse] about it, after seeing beautiful female slaves[380] of the Ġanī b. Aʿṣur[381] perform the circumambulation: [*al-wāfir*]

O would that my brothers, the Ġanī,
perform the *dawār* whenever they enter upon the evening.[382]

---

378 Possibly referring to Ibn Šabbah.

379 ʿĀmir b. al-Ṭufayl was an Arab poet and warrior who belonged to ʿĀmir b. Ṣaʿṣaʿah. He was one of the Prophet's adversaries, and reportedly attacked the Muslims in Biʾr Maʿūnah; "ʿĀmir b. al-Ṭufayl," in *EI*^{2} (W. Caskel).

380 *Qaynāt*; Ibn al-Kalbī, *al-Aṣnām*, 42, has *fatayāt* (young women).

381 An Arab tribe of Qays ʿAylān; "Ghanī b. Aʿṣur," in *EI*^{2} (J.W. Fück).

382 For a translation of the version of this verse in *al-Aṣnām*, where the word *aḫwālī* ("my maternal uncles") replaces *iḫwānī* ("my brothers"), see Lyall (1913): 122; Klinke-Rosenberger (1941): 52.

وقال المبرد: دَوَار نُسُك كانوا ينسكون عنده في الجاهلية.[a]

ويقال إن عامرا كان عاهرا عاقرا.[b]

وكانت هذه الحجارة التي كانوا يدورون حولها وتسمى الدَوَار يقال لها أيضا النُصُبُ وكانت {غير} | منصوبة وكانوا يذبحون عندها عتائرهم. 39a

§119 وعن مجاهد في قوله ﴿وَمَا ذُبِحَ عَلَى ٱلنُّصُبِ﴾ قال: كان حول الكعبة حجر يذبح عليه أهل الجاهلية ويبدلونه إذا {شاؤوا} {بحجر} أحب إليهم منه.[c]

---

١ وقال ... الجاهلية : الزيادة بخط المقريزي في الهامش الأيسر من الأسفل إلى الأعلى + صح. ‖ دَوَار: في الأصل "دَوَارٍ". ٤ غير : في الأصل "عنر". ٥ ٱلنُّصُبِ : شكل المقريزي الكلمة كما يلي: "النصُب". ٦ شاؤوا : في الأصل "شاوا". ‖ بحجر : في الأصل "بالحجر".

---

a راجع المبرد، الكامل، ١: ١٣٠؛ قارن ابن قتيبة، المعاني، ١: ١٠٥ ("الدوار نسك للجاهلية يدورون فيه لصنم أو غيره"). وقارن أيضا التبريزي، شرح، ١١٤–١١٥

("فَعَنَّ لَنَا سِرْبٌ كَأَنَّ نِعَاجَهُ عَذَارَى دَوَارٍ في مُلَاءٍ مُذَيَّلِ

ومعنى البيت أنه يصف أن هذا القطيعَ من البقر يَلُوذُ بعضُه ببعض، وتَدُور كما تَدُور العذارى حول دَوَار، وهو نُسُك كانوا في الجاهلية يدورون حوله").

b راجع ابن منظور، لسان العرب، عقر ("ورجل عاقِرٌ وعَقِيرٌ: لا يولد له، بيِّن العُقْر، بالضم، ولم نسمع في المرأة عقيرا. وقال ابن الأعرابي: هو الذي يأتي النساء فيُحَاضِنُهنّ ويلامِسُهنّ ولا يولد له").

c قارن مقاتل، تفسير، ١: ٢٧٩ ("﴿وَمَا ذُبِحَ عَلَى ٱلنُّصُبِ﴾ يعني وحرم ما ذبح على النصب، وهي الحجارة التي كانوا ينصبونها في الجاهلية ويعبدونها، فهو حرام البتة، وكان خزان الكعبة يذبحون لها، وإن شاءوا بدلوا تلك الحجارة بحجارة أخرى، وألقوا الأولى"). وقارن مجاهد، تفسير، ٣٠٠ ("قال: حجارة كانت حول الكعبة، كان يذبح لها أهل الجاهلية، ويبدلونها إذا شاءوا، وإذا رأوا ما هو أعجب إليهم منها"). وقارن أيضا الطبري، جامع البيان، ٨: ٧١ ("عن مجاهدٍ قوله: ﴿وَمَا ذُبِحَ عَلَى ٱلنُّصُبِ﴾. قال: كان حولَ الكعبةِ حجارةٌ كان يَذْبَحُ عليها أهلُ الجاهليةِ ويُبدلونها إذا شاءوا بحجرٍ هو أحبُّ إليهم منها").

Al-Mubarrad said: The *dawār* was a [place of] ritual, beside which they used to perform their religious rites in the Ǧāhiliyyah.[383]

It is said that ʿĀmir was an adulterer and that he had no offspring.

These stones, which they used to circle and which were called *dawār*,[384] were also called *nuṣub*. They were not standing stones.[385] They used to slaughter their sacrificial animals beside them.

§ 119 On the authority of Muǧāhid regarding His saying "as also things sacrificed to idols (*al-nuṣub*)":[386] There were stones around the Kaʿbah on which the people of the Ǧāhiliyyah used to make sacrifices, and which they would replace, if they wished, with [other] stones that were more to their liking.

---

383 According to the dictionaries, *dawār* was the name of an idol the Arabs set up. They made a space around the idol, and walked around it. The word *dawār* applies both to the idol and the space around it; Lane (1863–1893): 931.

384 According to *al-Aṣnām*, the practice of walking around the stones was called *dawār*; Ibn al-Kalbī, *al-Aṣnām* 42.

385 *Wa-kānat ġayr manṣūbah* (read perhaps *ġayr* instead of عنر). Ibn al-Kalbī has: *wa-kānat li-l-ʿArab ḥiǧāratun ġubrun* (غبر) *manṣūbatun* (the Arabs had set up dust-colored stones); Ibn al-Kalbī, *al-Aṣnām* 42. See also Klinke-Rosenberger (1941), 51: "Die Araber besaßen staubfarbige Steine, die sie aufgestellt hatten." Faris (1952): 42 has: "The Arabs also had relic stones [that they obtained from ancient ruins] and erected."

386 Qurʾān (*al-Māʾidah*), 5:3.

§120 وقال دريد بن الصِمّة: [المتقارب]

ويوم {بخربَةَ} لا ينقضي   كأن أناسًا به دَوّروا[a]

ويوم {خربة} كان لبني جُشَم رهط دُريد على محارب.

ومعنى دوروا كأنهم عكوف حول صنم الدَوَار. وكان الطواف في الجاهلية حول الأصنام.

§121 قال ابن شبة: وكان لطيئ صنم يقال له {الفلس} وكان أحمر طويلا في وسط جبلهم الذي يقال له أجَأ[b] أسود[c] كأنه تمثال إنسان فكانوا يعبدونه ويهدون له ويذبحون عنده ولا يأتيه خائف

١–٤ وقال ... الأصنام: الزيادة بخط المقريزي في الهامش الأيمن من الأعلى إلى الأسفل، ويشير إليها رمز ⌐ بعد "منه". ٢ بخربَةَ: في الأصل "نخْرِبَةَ". ٣ خربة: في الأصل "نجربة". ٥ الفلس: في الأصل "القُلْس". وأضاف المقريزي نقطة بجانب القاف فيما بعد وتوجد أيضا ثلاث ضمات فوق القاف.

a قارن البكري، معجم ما استعجم، ٢: ٤٩٠ ("[الخَرْبَة] بفتح أوله وإسكان ثانيه وبالباءِ المعجمة بواحدة وهاء التأنيث أرض في ديار غَسَّان، وفي وادٍ من أوديتها نَحَرَ الحارث بن ظالم لِقْحَةَ الملك يزيد بن عمرو الغَسَّاني، وكان ذلك سَبَبَ قَتْلِهِ واخْفارِ الذِّمّة فيه. وقال دُرَيْد بن الصِّمَّة:

ويوم بخَرْبَةَ لا يَنْقَضِي   كأَنَّ أُنَاسًا به دَوَّرُوا

وهذا اليوم كان لبني جُشَمَ رهطِ دُرَيْد على مُحَارب").

b راجع: ياقوت، معجم البلدان، ١: ٩٤ ("وقال أبو عبيد السكوني: أَجَأُ أحد جَبَلَيْ طيِّئٍ وهو غربي فيد، وبينهما مسير ليلتين وفيه قُرًى كثيرة").

c قارن ياقوت، معجم البلدان، ٤: ٢٧٣ ("وقيل: الفلس أنفُ أحمَرُ في وسط أجإٍ وأجأُ أسودُ").

§ 120 Durayd b. al-Ṣimmah[387] said: [*al-mutaqārib*]

> And a "day" [i.e. battle; *wa-yawmun*] in Ḫarbah does not come to an end![388]
> As if people are going round in circles with it (*bihi dawwarū*).

The Battle of Ḫarbah was a battle in which the Banū Ǧušam, Durayd's clan, defeated [the Banū] Muḥārib.

The meaning of [the verb] *dawwarū* is: As if they are going around the idol al-Dawār.[389] During the Ǧāhiliyyah, circumambulation was performed around the idols.

§ 121 Ibn Šabbah said: Ṭayyi' had an idol called al-Fals.[390] It was red and long, [and it was located] in the center of their mountain called Aǧa',[391] [which was] black. It was as if it [al-Fals] had the shape of a man. They used to worship it, bring gifts to it, and make sacrifices beside it. Every man who was in

---

387 For more on the poet Durayd b. al-Ṣimmah, a tribal leader of the Banū Ǧušam b. Mu'āwiyah, see "Durayd b. al-Ṣimma," in *EI*² (K. Petráček).

388 Or perhaps, many a "day" [*wa-yawmin*] in Ḫarbah comes to no end!

389 *Ṣanam al-dawār*. Dawār/Duwār was also the name of a certain idol; see "Circumambulation," in *EI*³ (U. Rubin): "The form Duwār (also Duwwār, Dawwār, Dawār) occurs as the name of an idol that the pre-Islamic Arabs reportedly used to circumambulate; it is mentioned on line 63 of the *mu'allāqa* of Imru' al-Qays (d. c. 550 C.E.), who compares the wild cows to 'the young virgins (*adhārā*) of Duwār/Dawār, moving in long trailing robes.'" The phrase *ṣanam al-dawār* may also refer to "the *dawār* idol," i.e. the idol that they circled.

390 For more information on this idol, see Wellhausen (1897): 51–53. Al-Maqrīzī systematically renders the name of this idol al-Quls.

391 See "Adja' and Salmā," in *EI*² (W. Caskel).

إلا أمن عنده ولا يطرد أحد طريدة لأحد فيلجئها إليه إلا {تركت} فلم يُخْفَر.[a] فكان آخر من سدنه بنو بولان وبولان هو الذي بدأ بعبادته فكان آخر من سَدَنه منهم رجل يقال له صيفي.[b]

فانطلق صيفي يوما فاطرد ناقة خلية لامرأة من كلب من بني عُلَيم كانت جارة لمالك بن كلثوم ابن ربيعة بن عمرو بن تيم بن {نسوة} بن قيس بن مُصْلح بن شَمَجى بن ثعلبة بن عمرو بن الغوث ابن طيئ الشَمَجي وكان شريفا فارسا فانطلق بها حتى وقفها بفناء {الفلس} وخرجت جارة مالك تلك فأخبرته بذهابه بناقتها فركب فرسه عريانا[c] وأخذ رمحه ثم خرج في أثره فأدركه وهو عند {الفلس} والناقة موقوفة عند {الفلس} فقال له: "خل عن ناقة جارتي." فقال: "إنها لربك." قال: "خل سبيلها." فقال: "أتخْفِر إلاهك؟" فبوأ له الرمح فحل عقالها فانصرف بها مالك. وأقبل السادن على {الفلس} ونظر إلى مالك ثم رفع يده فقال:[d] [الرجز]

---

١ تركت : في الأصل "تُرك". ٤–٥ بن١ ... طيئ : الزيادة بخط المقريزي في الهامش الأيسر في آخر السطر بجانب "كلثوم". ٤ نسوة : في الأصل "نسو". ٥ الفلس : في الأصل "القلس". ٧ الفلس : في الأصل "القلس". || الفلس : في الأصل "القلس". ٩ الفلس : في الأصل "القلس".

---

a قارن ابن الكلبي، الأصنام، ٥٩ ("وكانوا يعبدُونه ويُهدُون إليه ويَعترون عنده عتائرهم، ولا يأتيه خائفٌ إلا أَمِنَ عنده، ولا يَطْرُد أحدٌ طريدةً فيلجأ بها إليه إلا تُرِكَتْ له ولم تُخْفَرْ حَوِيّتُه"). وقارن أيضا ابن دريد، الاشتقاق، ٣٩٤ ("ومنهم: مالك بن كُلْثوم بن ربيعة، وهو الذي يقال له «مُخْفِر الفِلْس» والفِلْس: صنَم كان لطِيِّء، وكان لا تُخْفَر ذمّتُه، فأَخْفره مالك، وله حدث").

b قارن ابن دريد، الاشتقاق، ٣٩٧ ("منهم: بنو بَوْلان. وبَوْلان: فَعْلان من قولهم: رجلٌ بُوَلَةٌ: كثير البَول والبُوَال: داءٌ يصيب الغنمَ فتبولُ حتّى تموت. فمن بني بولان: مِعْتَرٌ، أحد فُرسانهم، قَتَل ملكا من ملوك بنو جَفْنة كان غَزَاهم. ومنهم: بنو صَيْفِيّ، وهو سادن الفِلْس").

c قارن ابن الكلبي، الأصنام، ٦٠ ("فركِبَ فَرَسًا عُرْيًا، وأخذ رُمحَه، وخرج في أَثَرِه"). راجع ابن حجر، فتح الباري، ٦: ١٦١ ("باب ركوب الفرس العري) بضم المهملة وسكون الراء، أي ليس عليه سرج ولا أداة، ولا يقال في الآدمين إنما يقال عريان قاله ابن فارس، قال: وهي من النوادر انتهى").

d قارن ياقوت، معجم البلدان، ٤: ٢٧٣ ("فنَوَّلَه الرمح وحلَّ عقالَها وانصرف بها مالكٌ وأقبل السادن إلى الفلس ونظر إلى مالك ورفع يده وهو يشير بيده إليه ويقول").

fear and came to it was safe beside it, and when one caught an animal[392] belonging to someone and drove it to it [al-Fals], it [the animal] remained [by the idol, as its property], and the idol's sanctity was not violated.[393] Its last custodians were the Banū Bawlān.[394] Bawlān was the first to worship it. Its last custodian from among them [the Banū Bawlān] was a man named Ṣayfī.

One day Ṣayfī drove away[395] a milch-camel,[396] which belonged to a woman of the Banū ʿUlaym of Kalb.[397] She was under the patronage of Mālik b. Kulṯūm[398] al-Šamaǧī who was a nobleman and horseman. He [Ṣayfī] took her [the she-camel], and brought her to the space in front of al-Fals, and then the woman who was under Mālik's patronage came out and told him [Mālik] that he [Ṣayfī] had taken her she-camel. Thereupon, he rode his horse without a saddle, took his lance, and went out after him [Ṣayfī]. He overtook him [Ṣayfī] by al-Fals, while the she-camel was held beside al-Fals, and told him: "Release my protégée's she-camel!" He said: "She [the she-camel] belongs to your lord." He said: "Release her!" He replied: "Are you violating the sanctity of your god?" Then, he pointed his lance toward him [Ṣayfī], he [Ṣayfī] untied the rope with which she was bound, and Mālik left with her [the she-camel]. The custodian then approached al-Fals, looked at Mālik, and raised his hand saying: [*al-raǧaz*]

392 The text has *ṭarīdah*, which denotes a wild animal that is caught; Lane (1863–1893): 1839.

393 Compare Ibn al-Kalbī, *al-Aṣnām* 59: *wa-lam tuḫfar ḥawiyyatuhu* (read *ḥurmatuhu*?). In this context the term may apply to the sacred space of the idol. Compare also Ibn Durayd, *al-Ištiqāq* 394: *wa-kāna lā tuḫfaru ḏimmatuhu*, that is, the protection given by the idol was not violated. See also Klinke-Rosenberger (1941): 138–139.

394 A subdivision of the tribe of Ṭayyiʾ; Caskel (1966), 1: table 252.

395 *Iṭṭarada*. See also Brünnow and Fischer (2008): 67: "*iṭṭarada*: to drive away as booty (cattle and the like)."

396 *Nāqah ḫaliyyah*; the dictionaries provide several meanings for this phrase. According to one explanation, it denotes a she-camel that gives birth when she has an abundance of milk. Her offspring is then taken from beneath her and put under another she-camel, and afterwards, she is left alone (*tuḫallá*) to be milked; see Ibn al-Kalbī, *al-Aṣnām* 60, n. 1.

397 See Caskel (1966), 1: table 280.

398 Al-Maqrīzī provides Mālik b. Kulṯūm's full pedigree: [Kulṯūm was the] son of Rabīʿah b. ʿAmr b. Taym b. Niswah (elsewhere Našwah) b. Qays b. Muṣliḥ b. Šamaǧá b. Ṯaʿlabah b. ʿAmr b. al-Ġawṯ b. Ṭayyiʾ (Marginal gloss in al-Maqrīzī's hand). See also Caskel (1966), 1: table 252.

رب أريك مالك بن كلثوم[a] أخفرك اليوم بناب علكوم
وكنت قبل اليوم غير مَغْشُوم

يحرضه عليه.

وألفى ذلك اليوم عدي بن حاتم قد ذبح عنده وجلس هو ومن معه يتحدثون بما صنع مالك وفزع لذلك عدي بن حاتم وقال: "انظروا ما يصيبه في يومه أو غده."[b] فلما مضت له أيام ولم يصبه شيء رفض عدي عبادته وعبادة الأصنام وتنصر فلم يزل نصرانيا حتى جاء الله بالإسلام.[c]

فكان مالك أول من أخفره وكان بعد ذلك إذا طرد السادن طريدة أخذت منه. فلم يزل {الفلس} يُعبد حتى ظهر النبي ﷺ فبعث إليه علي بن أبي طالب | رضي الله عنه فهدمه وأخذ 39b
سيفين كان الحٰرث بن أبي شمر ملك غسان قلدهما إياه أحدهما يقال له مُخَذِّم والآخر رسوب.[d]

ولهما يقول علقمة بن عبدة التميمي: [الطويل]

٤ وألفى : في الأصل "والفا". ٨ الفلس : في الأصل "الفلس". ٩ مُخَذِّم : كذا في الأصل بدلا من "مِخْذَم" (راجع ابن منظور، لسان العرب، "خذم").

a قارن ياقوت، معجم البلدان، ٤: ٢٧٣ ("يا ربِّ إن يكُ مالكُ بن كُلثوم").وقارن أيضا ابن الكلبي، الأصنام، ٦١ ("يارِبِّ إن مالكَ بنَ كُلْثُوم").

b قارن ابن الكلبي، الأصنام، ٦١ ("وعَدِيُّ بن حاتم يومئذ [قد] عَتَرَ عنده وجلس هو ونَفَرٌ معه يتحدثون بما صنع [مالكٌ]. وفَزِعَ لذلك عَدِيُّ بن حاتم وقال: اُنظروا ما يُصيبه في يومه هذا").

c قارن ابن الكلبي، الأصنام، ٦١ ("فلم يزل متنصِّرا حتّى جاء الله بالإسلام، فأسلم").

d قارن المقريزي، إمتاع الأسماع، ٧: ١٤٢ ("وبعث رسول الله صلى الله عليه وسلم عليّ بن أبى طالب رضى الله عنه إلى الفُلْس صنم طيِّئ، فوجده مقلداً سيفين يقال لهما: مجذم ورسوب، وهما سيفان كانا للحارث بن أبى شمر الغسّاني، يتقلدهما عن يمينه وشماله، فنذر لئن ظفر ببعض أعاديه، ليهديهما إلى الفُلْس، فظفر به فأهداهما إليه"). وقارن أيضا الزبيدي، تاج العروس، "رسب" ("وقال البلاذُرِيّ في سرِيَّة عليّ رضي الله عنه لمّا تَوَجَّهَ إلى هَدْمِ الفَلْس صَنَمِ لِطَيِّءٍ، كانَ الصَّنَمُ مُقَلَّداً بسَيْفَيْنِ أَهْدَاهُمَا إِلَيْهِ الحارِثُ بنُ أَبِي شمِرٍ، وهما مِخْذَمٌ ورسُوبٌ، كانَ نَذَرَ لَئِنْ ظَفِرَ بِبَعْضِ أَعْدَائِه لَيُهْدِيَنَّهُمَا إلى الفَلْس فَظَفِرَ فَأَهْدَاهُمَا لَهُ").

My lord, I show you Mālik b. Kulṯūm.
He has violated your sanctity today with an old and sturdy she-camel.
Before this day you were not wronged.

He [Ṣayfī] was inciting it [the idol] against him [Mālik].

He found[399] ʿAdī b. Ḥātim[400] on that day making a sacrifice beside it [al-Fals], and sitting with those who were with him, discussing what Mālik had done. ʿAdī b. Ḥātim was terrified because of it, and he said: "Watch what will befall him [Mālik] today or tomorrow." When several days had passed and nothing befell him, ʿAdī abandoned its [al-Fals's] worship as well as the worship of [the other] idols, and adopted Christianity.[401] He remained a Christian until the advent of Islam.

Mālik was the first who violated its sanctity. Afterwards, whenever the custodian caught an animal, it was taken away from him [the custodian]. Al-Fals continued to be worshipped until the arrival of the Prophet, may Allāh bless and save him. The Prophet sent ʿAlī b. Abī Ṭālib,[402] may Allāh be pleased with him, to it [al-Fals,] whereupon he destroyed it and took the two swords with which al-Ḥāriṯ b. Abī Šamir, the King of Ġassān,[403] had girded it.[404]One of them [the swords] was called Miḫḏam[405] and the other [sword was called] Rasūb. ʿAlqamah b. ʿAbadah al-Tamīmī[406] said, referring to them: [*al-ṭawīl*]

399 The use of the Arabic verb *wa-alfá* ("he found") is perhaps an attempt to connect this sentence to what has previously been said.

400 ʿAdī b. Ḥātim (d. ca. 66/686) was the son of the famous Ḥātim al-Ṭāʾī. See "ʿAdī b. Ḥātim," in *EI*³ (E. Kohlberg).

401 See "ʿAdī b. Ḥātim," in *EI*³ (E. Kohlberg): "Following an incident involving the idol al-Fuls/al-Fals, ʿAdī forsook idol worship and adopted Christianity (or *al-rakūsiyya*, said to be a mixture of Christianity and the Sabaean religion)."

402 The fourth of the rightly-guided caliphs.

403 For more information on al-Ḥāriṯ b. Abī Šamir, see King (2004): 223.

404 According to other accounts, al-Ḥāriṯ b. Abī Šamir granted these swords to Manāt; Ibn al-Kalbī, *al-Aṣnām* 15.

405 Al-Maqrīzī erroneously reads this word Muḫaḏḏim and, below, Muḫdim.

406 For more on ʿAlqamah b. ʿAbadah b. Nāširah b. Qays b. ʿUbayd al-Tamīmī, who is also known by the epithet al-Faḥl, see "ʿAlqama," in *EI*³ (A. Arazi).

يُظاهِر سِربالَيْ حديد عليهما عَقِيلا سُيوف مُخْذِم ورَسُوْبُ[a]

فقدم بهما علي رضي الله عنه على النبي ﷺ. فقال قائل: وهبهما لعلي السيفين جميعا. وقال قائل: وهب له أحدهما.

§122 وقال ابن الكلبي: وكانت سَدنته زيد بن صيفي بن صَعْتَرَة بن عمرو بن مِعْتَر بن بَوْلان بن عمرو بن الغوث بن طيئ[b] وكان مالك بن كلثوم بن ربيعة بن عمرو بن تيم بن نسوة بن قيس بن مصلح بن شمجى بن جرم هو مُخْفِر {الفلس}.

§123 قال ابن شبة: وكان لمُزَينة صنم يقال له نهم وبه كان يسمى عبد نُهْم كان لمزينة وكان بثنية ذات جبلين وكان سادنه خزاعي—ابن عبد نهم بن عَفيف بن سُحيم بن ربيعة بن عدي بن ثعلبة ابن ذؤيب بن سعد بن عَداء بن عثمٰن بن مزينة وهو عمرو بن أد ⟨بن⟩ طابخة بن اليأس بن مضر ابن نزار بن معد بن عدنان—المُزَني[c] فلما سمع بالنبي ﷺ عمد إلى الصنم فكسره وقال: [الطويل]

---

١ حديد: وضع المقريزي رمز "ح" تحت الكلمة إشارة إلى تلفظها بالحاء. ‖ مُخْذِم: كذا في الأصل بدلا من "مِخْذَم". ٤ وكانت ... صيفي: كذا في الأصل. ٥ مالك ... كلثوم: كشط المقريزي عبارة أخرى قبل أن يصححها كما هي الآن. ‖ نسوة: وضع المقريزي ثلاث نقط تحت الكلمة إشارة إلى تلفظها بالسين. ٦ شمجى: في الأصل "شمجا". ‖ الفلس: في الأصل "القلس". ٧–٨ كان ... جبلين: الزيادة بخط المقريزي في الهامش الأيسر من الأسفل إلى الأعلى ويشير إليها رمز ⌐ بعد "نهم". ٨–١٠ ابن ... عدنان: الزيادة بخط المقريزي في الهامش الأيمن منقلبة ويشير إليها رمز ⌐ بعد "خزاعي". ١٠ المُزَني: كشط المقريزي عبارة أخرى قبل أن يصححها كما هي الآن.

---

a قارن ابن الكلبي، الأصنام، ١٥ ("مُظاهرُ سِرْبَالَيْ حديدٍ عليهما عقيلا سيوفٍ: مِخْذَم ورَسوبُ"). وراجع الأخفش الأصغر، كتاب الاختيارين، ٦٥٤ ("«عَقيلةُ» كلِّ شيء: خِيارُهُ. «مظاهر سربالي حديد» يقول: عليه دِرعانِ، واحدةٌ فوقَ واحدة").

b قارن ابن الكلبي، نسب معد، ٢٦٤–٢٦٥ ("وهؤُلاءِ بنو بَوْلان بن عَمْرو ... فوَلَدَ صَيْفِيُّ بن صَعْتَرَةَ: زَيْداً، وهم سَدَنَةُ الفِلْس").

c راجع ابن الأثير، أسد الغابة، ٢: ٦٢٦ ("شُرَيْح بن ضَمْرة المُزَنِيّ، وهو من ولد لُحَيّ بن جُرَش بن لاطِم بن عثمان بن مُزَيْنَة، وهي أمه، وأَبوه عمرو بن أد بن طابِخَة بن إِلياس بن مضر، نسب ولده إِليها، فيقال لولد عثمان وأَوس ابني عمرو: مزينة نسبة إِلى أمهما مزينة بنت كلب بن وَبرة"). وراجع أيضا ابن حزم، جمهرة

> Wearing two coats of iron mail one over another,[407] on which hang
> two precious swords: Miḫḏam and Rasūb.[408]

ʿAlī, may Allāh be pleased with him, brought them to the Prophet, may Allāh bless and save him. Some say that he [the Prophet] gave both swords to ʿAlī, while others say that he gave him one of them.

§ 122 Ibn al-Kalbī said: Its custodians were [the Banū] Zayd b. Ṣayfī b. Ṣaʿtarah b. ʿAmr b. Miʿtar b. Bawlān b. ʿAmr b. al-Ġawṯ b. Ṭayyiʾ. Mālik b. Kulṯūm b. Rabīʿah b. ʿAmr b. Taym b. Niswah b. Qays b. Muṣliḥ b. Šamağá b. Ğarm was the one who violated the sanctity of al-Fals.

§ 123 Ibn Šabbah said: Muzaynah had an idol called Nuhm. The name ʿAbd Nuhm is traced back to it [this idol]. It belonged to Muzaynah, and was [located] in the narrow pass of Ḏāt Ğabalayni. Its custodian was Ḫuzāʿī l-Muzanī, who was the son of ʿAbd Nuhm b. ʿAfīf b. Suḥaym b. Rabīʿah b. ʿAdī b. Ṯaʿlabah b. Ḏuʾayb b. Saʿd b. ʿAddāʾ b. ʿUṯmān b. Muzaynah. [ʿUṯmān] was [the son of][409] ʿAmr b. Udd b. Ṭābiḫah b. al-Yaʾs b. Muḍar b. Nizār b. Maʿadd b. ʿAdnān.[410] When he [Ḫuzāʿī] heard about the Prophet, may Allāh bless and save him, he approached the idol, destroyed it, and said: [*al-ṭawīl*]

أنساب العرب، ٤٨٠ ("مُزَيْنة، وهم بنو عُثمان وأَوس ابني عمرو بن أدّ بن طابخة بن الياس بن مُضَر ابن نزار بن مَعَد بن عَدْنان").

407 The text has *yuẓāhiru*, but perhaps the variant *muẓāhiru* is better. See al-Aʿlam al-Šantamarī, *Šarḥ dīwān ʿAlqamah*, 29; see also the translation of this line in Lyall (1918): 330.

408 See Klinke-Rosenberger (1941): 37; Grunebaum (1953): 44.

409 ʿUṯmān was ʿAmr b. Udd's son. The pedigree of ʿUṯmān's descendants is traced back to Muzaynah, who was his mother; Ibn al-Aṯīr, *Usd al-ġābah*, 1:336.

410 On Ḫuzāʿī b. ʿAbd Nuhm, see Ibn al-Aṯīr, *Usd al-ġābah*, 2:169.

ذَهَبْتُ إلى نُهْـم لأذبـح عـنـده   عتيرة نسك كالذي كنت أفعل
فقلت لنفسي حين راجعت عقلها   أهذا إلاه إنه لـيس يعـقــل[a]

ثم لحق بالنبي ﷺ فأسلم وضمن له إسلام قومه مُزينة وكان على قبض المغانم.[b]

§124 وله يقول أمية بن الأسكر الليثي: [الرجز]

إذا لقيت راعيين في غنم   أَسَيدين يحلفان بنُهَم
{من بطن عمق} ذي الجليل والسَلم[c]   فامض ولا {يأخُذك} للحم القرَم
وإن نجوتَ سالما فلا تُذم[d]

٣ وكان ... المغانم : الزيادة بخط المقريزي في الهامش الأيمن منقلبة ويشير إليها رمز ⌐ بعد "مُزينة".
٥ يحلفان : وضع المقريزي رمز "ح" تحت الكلمة إشارة إلى تلفظها بالحاء. ٦ من ... عمق : في الأصل "ينظر عتق" (قارن حسان، ديوان). || يأخُذك : في الأصل "تاخُذك".

a قارن ابن الأثير، أسد الغابة، ٢: ١٦٩ ("فَقُلْتُ لِنَفْسِي حِينَ رَاجَعْتُ حَزْمَهَا   أَهٰذَا إِلٰهٌ أَبْكَمُ لَيْسَ يَعْقِلُ؟"). وقارن أيضا ابن الكلبي، الأصنام، ٤٠ ("أهذا إلهٌ أبكم ليس يعقِلُ؟").

b راجع ابن حجر، الإصابة١، ٢: ٢٣٧ ("وفد خُزَاعي بن أسود فأسلم، ووعد أن يأتي بقومه، فأبطأ"). وراجع أيضا ابن الأثير، أسد الغابة، ٢: ١٦٩ ("فبايع النبي ﷺ وبايعه على مزينة، وقدم من قومه معه عشرة رهط [منهم]: بلال بن الحارث، وعبد الله بن دُرَّةَ، وأبو أسماء، والنعمان بن مقرّن، وبشر بن المحتفر، وأسلمت مزينة، ودفع رسول الله ﷺ إليه لواءهم يوم الفتح، وكانوا ألف رجل، وكان على قَبَض مغانم النبي ﷺ").

c راجع حسان، ديوان، ١: ٣٩٢ ("من بَطْنِ عَمْقٍ ذي الْجَلِيلِ وَالسَّلَمْ").

d قارن ابن الكلبي، الأصنام، ٤٠
("إذا لَقِيتَ راعِيَيْنِ في غَنَمْ   أُسَيِّدَيْنِ يَحْلِفَانِ بنُهُمْ
بينهما أَشْلاءُ لَحْمٍ مُقْتَسَمْ   فامْضِ ولا يأْخُذْكَ بالَّحْمِ القَرَمْ").

I went to Nuhm to sacrifice a sacrificial animal[411]
beside it as I used to do,
but I said to myself when I consulted my reason:
Is this a god? It has no brains![412]

Then he joined the Prophet, may Allāh bless and save him, embraced Islam, and ensured him [the Prophet] that his [Ḫuzāʿī's] tribe, Muzaynah, would [also] embrace Islam. He [Ḫuzāʿī] was put in charge over the spoils that were taken.[413]

§ 124 Umayyah b. al-Askar al-Layṯī[414] said referring to it [Nuhm]: [*al-rağaz*]

When you meet two blackish sheep
herdsmen who swear by Nuhm,[415]
from the valley of ʿAmq,[416] Ḏū l-Ğalīl, and [Ḏū] l-Salam,[417]
Leave! Let not your greed for meat overcome you!
If you escape unhurt, you shall not be blamed.

411 *ʿAtīrat nusk*; *ʿatīrah* denotes a sheep or goat offered for sacrifice; see Lane (1863–1893): 1946.

412 Other versions have the word *abkam* (dumb; mute) instead of *innahū*. The verse, in this case, should be translated as follows: Is this a god? A mute that has no brains! See also Klinke-Rosenberger (1941): 51, 119–120.

413 I.e. he was responsible for guarding and dividing them; see Lane (1863–1893): 2483.

414 On Umayyah b. al-Askar al-Layṯī, see Ibn Ḥağar, *al-Iṣābah*[1], 1:264–267.

415 Vocalized "Nuham" for reasons of meter. In other sources, the following line is added here: "with [the] remains of meat divided between them." See Ibn al-Kalbī, *al-Aṣnām* 40. For a translation of this version of the verses, see Wellhausen (1897): 58.

416 According to al-Bakrī, *Muʿğam mā staʿğam*, 3:967, ʿAmq was a water source located in the land of Muzaynah.

417 *Ğalīl* and *salam* are species of trees; see Lane (1863–1893): 438, 1414. The phrase Ḏū l-Ğalīl and [Ḏū] l-Salam in this verse may refer to the place where these trees grew. Note that the name Ḏū Salam (without the definite article) appears in another verse that is attributed to a man of Muzaynah; Yāqūt, *Muʿğam al-buldān*, 4:190; al-Samhūdī, *Wafāʾ al-wafā*, 4:325.

§125 وكان لعنزة صنم يقال له السُّعَيْر.[a] فخرج جعفر بن أبي خَلَّاس بن مالك بن امرئ القيس ابن عِمّيْت بن كعب بن عبد الله بن كنانة بن بكر بن عوف بن عذرة بن زيد اللات بن رُفيدة بن ثور بن كلب بن وبَرة بن {تغلب} بن حلوان بن عمران بن الحاف بن قضاعة الكلبي على ناقته فمر به وقد عُتِرَتْ عنده عَتِيرة فنفرت ناقته منه فأنشأ يقول:[b] [الكامل]

نفَرَت قلوصي من عتائر صُرِّعَتْ حول السُّعَيْر تَزُورُه ابنا يَقْدُم
وجميع يذكر مُطِعين جَنابَه ما إن يُحِيْرُ إليهم بتكَلُّم[c]

§126 وقال ابن الكلبي: مر به جعفر بن امرئ القيس بن عمّيت بن كعب بن عبد الله بن كنانة ابن بكر بن عوف بن عذرة فنفرت قلوصه منه ومن الدماء التي تُعْتَر | للصنم فأراد هدمه فقيل له 40a إنه إلاه فتركه وقال فذكر البيتين.

١–٣ بن٢ ... قضاعة: الزيادة بخط المقريزي في الهامش الأيسر من الأسفل إلى الأعلى ويشير إليها رمز ٦ بعد "خَلَّاس". ٣ تغلب: في الأصل "ثعلبة".

---

١ خَلَّاس: أضاف المقريزي الحاشية التالية في الهامش الأيمن منقلبة: "حـ قيده الدارقطني والأمير بفتح الخاء المعجمة وتشديد اللام." ٥–٦ يَقْدُم ... يذكر: أضاف المقريزي الحاشية التالية في الهامش الأيسر من الأعلى إلى الأسفل: "يقدم ويذكر ابنا عنزة".

---

a قارن ابن منظور، لسان العرب، "عوض"
("حَلَفْتُ بمائراتٍ حَوْلَ عَوْضٍ وأنْصابٍ تُرِكْنَ لدَى السعير
قال: والسعير اسم صنم لعنزة خاصّةً").

b قارن ابن الكلبي، الأصنام، ٤١ ("فخرج جعفر بن أبي خلاسٍ الكلبيّ على ناقته. فمرّت به، وقد عَتَرَتْ عَنَزَةُ عنده، فنَفَرَتْ ناقتُهُ منه. فأنشأ يقول").

c قارن ياقوت، معجم البلدان، ٣: ٢٢٢ ("وجموعُ يَذْكُرَ مُطعين جنابة ما أن يجيز إليهمُ بتكلّم. يقدُم ويذكر: ابنا عَنَزَةَ، فرأى بني هؤلاء يطوفون حول السعير").

§ 125 ʿAnazah had an idol called al-Suʿayr.[418] Ǧaʿfar b. Abī Ḫallās al-Kalbī, who was the grandson of Mālik b. Imriʾ al-Qays b. ʿImmīt b. Kaʿb b. ʿAbd Allāh b. Kinānah b. Bakr b. ʿAwf b. ʿUḏrah b. Zayd Allāt b. Rufaydah b. Ṯawr b. Kalb b. Wabarah b. Taġlib[419] b. Ḥulwān b. ʿImrān b. al-Ḥāf b. Quḍāʿah, went out on his she-camel and passed by it [al-Suʿayr], after an animal had just been sacrificed beside it. Upon seeing this, his she-camel shied, and he recited [the following verses], saying: [*al-kāmil*]

My young she-camel shied away from sacrificial animals that were lying prostrate
around al-Suʿayr. The two sons of Yaqdum visit it,
as do all [the offspring] of Yaḏkur; they stand alongside it with their eyes fixed on it,
but it does not speak back to them.[420]

§ 126 Ibn al-Kalbī said: Ǧaʿfar b. Imriʾ al-Qays b. ʿImmīt b. Kaʿb b. ʿAbd Allāh b. Kinānah b. Bakr b. ʿAwf b. ʿUḏrah passed by it, and his young she-camel shied away from it and from the blood that was offered as a sacrifice for the idol. He wanted to destroy it, but was told that it is a god, so he left it and recited the two verses.

---

1 Ḫallās : Al-Dāraquṭnī and al-Amīr [Ibn Mākūlā] dotted and vocalized it with a *fatḥah* over the *ḫāʾ* and a *šaddah* over the *lām* (marginal gloss in al-Maqrīzī's hand). 10–11 Yaqdum ... Yaḏkur : Yaqdum and Yaḏkur are the two sons of ʿAnazah (marginal gloss in al-Maqrīzī's hand).

---

418 There are different opinions concerning the vocalization of this idol's name; see below note 506.

419 Al-Maqrīzī erroneously read the name as Ṯaʿlabah.

420 These lines are also translated in Wellhausen (1897): 61; Klinke-Rosenberger (1941): 51; Grunebaum (1953): 45–46.

§127 قال ابن شبة: وكان لقضاعة ولخم وجذام وأهل الشام ومن والاهم من غطفان صنم يقال له الأقيصر[a] وكانوا يحجونه فيحلقون {رؤوسهم} عنده. فكان كلما حلق رجل منهم رأسه ألقى مع شعره قبضة من دقيق. فكانت هوازن تنتابهم في ذلك الوقت فإن أدركه قبل أن يلقي الدقيق مع ذلك {الشعر} قال بعضهم: "أعطنيه فإني من هَوازنَ ضَارِعٌ." وإن فاته أخذ ذلك {الشعر} بما فيه مع {القمل} والدقيق نخبزه وأكله.[b]

§128 فاختصمت جرم وبنو جعدة إلى النبي ﷺ في ماء يقال له العقيق[c] فقضى به ﷺ لجرم.[d] فقال معٰوية بن عبد العزى بن زرّاع الجَرْمي: [الطويل]

٢ فيحلقون: وضع المقريزي رمز "ح" تحت الكلمة إشارة إلى تلفظها بالحاء. || رؤوسهم: في الأصل "روسهم". ٤ الشعر١: في الأصل "الشعير". || الشعر٢: في الأصل "الشعير". ٥ القمل: في الأصل "القضل".

a قارن ابن الكلبي، الأصنام، ٣٨ ("وكان لقُضاعَةَ ولَخْمٍ وجُذَام وعامِلَةَ وغَطَفانَ صنمٌ في مَشَارف الشام يقال له: الأُقَيْصِرُ").

b راجع الجاحظ، الحيوان، ٥: ٣٧٧-٣٧٨ ("وقال ابنُ الكلبيّ: عُيِّرَتْ هَوَازنُ وأسدٌ بأكل القُرَّة. وهما بنو القملة. وذلك أن أهل اليمن كانوا إذا حلقوا رؤوسهم [بمِنًى وضع كل رجل منه على رأسِهِ قُبْضَةً من دقيق. فإذا حلقوا رؤوسهم] سقط ذلك الشعرُ مع ذلك الدقيق، ويجعلون الدقيق صدقةً. فكان ناسٌ من الضُّرَكاء وفيهم ناسٌ من قيس وأسد يأخذون ذلك الشعر بدقيقه فيرمُون بالشعرِ وينتفعون بالدقيق"). وراجع أيضا ابن منظور، لسان العرب، "قرر" ("قال ابن الكلبي: عُيِّرَتْ هَوازِنُ وبنو أَسد بأَكل القُرَّة، وذلك أَن أَهل اليمن كانوا إِذا حلقوا رؤوسهم بمنًى وَضَع كلُّ رجل على رأْسه قُبْضَةَ دقيق فإِذا حلقوا رؤوسهم سقط الشعر مع ذلك الدقيق ويجعلون ذلك الدقيق صدقة فكان ناس من أَسد وقيس يأْخذون ذلك الشعر بدقيقه فيرمون الشعر وينتفعون بالدقيق").

c راجع ياقوت، معجم البلدان، ٤: ١٣٩-١٤٠ ("ومنها العقيق: ماء لبني جعدة وجَرْم تخاصموا فيه إلى النبيّ، ﷺ، فقضى به لبني جَرْم، فقال معاوية بن عبد العزّى بن ذراع الجرمي أبياتًا ذكرناها في الأُقَيْصر").

d قارن ابن عبد البر، الاستيعاب، ١: ٨٧ ("أسماء بن رَبَّان الجَرْمي من بني جَرْم بن ربّان، وهو الذي خاصم بني عقيل في العقيق وقضى به رسولُ الله ﷺ للجَرْمي، وهو ماءٌ في أرض بني عامر بن صعصعة، وهو القائل:

وإني أخو جَرْم كما قد علمتمُ إذا اجتمعت عند النبيِّ المَجَامِعِ
فإن أنتم لم تقنعوا بقضائه فإني بما قَالَ النبيّ لقانعُ").

§ 127 Ibn Šabbah said: The Quḍāʿah, Laḫm, Ǧuḏām, the people of al-Šām, and [the branches of] Ġaṭafān that were in their vicinity had an idol called al-Uqayṣir, to which they used to make pilgrimage[s], and beside which they used to shave their heads. Whenever one of them shaved his head, he threw a handful of grain with his hair [as a gift for the idol].[421] The Hawāzin used to come to them repeatedly at that time. If one of them [Hawāzin] caught up with him [the pilgrim] before he threw the grain with that hair,[422] he would say: "Give it to me, I am a frail man from Hawāzin!" If he was too late in arriving, he would take the hair[423] mixed with the lice and grain, bake it and eat it.

§ 128 The Ǧarm and the Banū Ǧaʿdah claimed their right to a watering-place called al-ʿAqīq,[424] and came to the Prophet, may Allāh bless and save him, for his decision. [The Prophet], may Allāh bless and save him, decided in favor of the Ǧarm, and thereupon Muʿāwiyah b. ʿAbd al-ʿUzzá b. Zarrāʿ al-Ǧarmī[425] said: [*al-ṭawīl*]

421 They used to throw their offerings for the idol into the *ḥafr* (trench/well); see below, and see also "al-Uḳayṣir," in *EI*² (F. Fahd).

422 Al-Maqrīzī erroneously read the word *šaʿīr* instead of *šaʿr*.

423 Al-Maqrīzī erroneously read the word *šaʿīr* instead of *šaʿr*.

424 According to some sources, the water source was in the land of the Banū ʿĀmir b. Ṣaʿṣaʿah. See Ibn ʿAbd al-Barr, *al-Istīʿāb*, 1:87.

425 Other sources refer to him as Muʿāwiyah b. Abī Rabīʿah al-Ǧarmī (Ibn Ḥaǧar, *al-Iṣābah*¹, 6:119), or Muʿāwiyah b. ʿAbd al-ʿUzzá b. Ḏirāʿ al-Ǧarmī (Ibn al-Kalbī, *al-Aṣnām* 48).

وإني أخو جرم كما قد علمتم   إذا اجتمعت عند النبي المجامع
فإن أنتم لم تقنعوا بقضائه   فإني بما قال النبي لقانع
ألم تر جرما أنجدت وأبوكم   مع القمل في حفر الأقيصر شارع[a]
إذا قِرّة[b] جاءت يقول أصِبْ بها   سِوَى القمل إني من هوازن ضارع
فما أنتم من هؤلا الناس كلهم   بلى ذنب ما أنتم وأكارع
{وإنكم} كالخنصرين أُخِسَّتا   وفاتهما من طولهن الأصابع

§129 وقال سراقة بن مالك بن جعشم المدلجي من بني كنانة: [الطويل]

ألم ينهكم عن شتمنا لا أبا لكم   جذام ونخم أعرضت في المواسم[c]
وكل قضاعي كأن جفانَه   حياض بِرَضْوَى والأنوف رواغم
بما انتهكوا من قبضة الذُل منكم[d]   فلا {المرء} يسْتَحْيِي ولا {المرء} طاعم

٣ حفر: وضع المقريزي رمز "ح" تحت الكلمة إشارة إلى تلفظها بالحاء.   ٤ قِرّة: كذا في الأصل بدلا من "قُرّة". وأضاف المقريزي فوقها رمز "ك" (يعني "كذا") بالحبر الأحمر إشارة إلى شكه في القراءة الصحيحة.
٦ وإنكم: في الأصل "وانكما".   ١٠ المرء١: في الأصل "المرو". ‖ المرء٢: في الأصل "المرو".

a قارن ابن منظور، لسان العرب، "قرر" ("ألم تَرَ جَرْمًا أَنْجَدَتْ وأَبوكُمُ   مَعَ الشَّعْرِ، في قَصِّ المُلَبَّدِ، سارِعُ").

b راجع الزبيدي، تاج العروس، "قرر" ("والقُرَّةُ، بالضَّمّ: الضِّفْدَعُ وَقَالَ ابنُ الكَلْبِيّ: عُيِّرَتْ هَوَازِنُ وبَنُو أَسَد بأَكْلِ القُرَّة"). وراجع أيضا الجاحظ، البخلاء، ٢: ١٨٤–١٨٥ ("وقال معاوية بن أبي رَبيعةَ الجَرْميُّ في القرّة، وهو يُعيِّر بني أسد وناسا من هَوازِنَ، هما بنو القَمليّة:

ألم تر جرما أمجدت وأبوكم   مع الشَّعر في قصّ الملبَّد شارعُ
إذا قرة جاءت يقول: أصب بها   سوى القمل، إنّي من هَوازنَ ضارعُ

... والقُرَّة: الدقيقُ المختلطُ بالشَّعرِ. كان الرجل منهم لا يحلق رأسه إلّا وعلى رأسه قُبضةٌ من دقيق للأكل. فهو معيب").

c قارن ابن الكلبي، الأصنام، ٥٠
("أَلَمْ يَنْهَكُمْ عن شَتْمِنا لا أَبَا لَكُمْ   جُذَامٌ وَنَخْمٌ أَعْرَضتْ والمواسِمُ").

d قارن ابن الكلبي، الأصنام، ٥٠ ("بما انتهكوا من قَبْضَة الذُّلِّ فيكُمُ").

I belong to the Ǧarm, as you well know,
when the crowds assemble by the Prophet.
If you are not satisfied with his decision,
I am satisfied with what the Prophet said.
Have you not seen that the Ǧarm have prevailed,[426] while your father
went into the trench of al-Uqayṣir with the lice?
When a handful of grain was offered, mixed with hair,[427] he would
say: Throw it
without the lice. I am a frail man of the Hawāzin.
What are you among these people, all of them?
Certainly! The tail is what you are and the shanks.
You are like the two weak little fingers,
which were exceeded in length by [the rest of] the fingers.[428]

§129 Surāqah b. Mālik b. Ǧuʿšum al-Mudliǧī[429] of the Banū Kinānah said: [*al-ṭawīl*]

Has he not forbidden you [masc. pl.]—may you have no father[430]—
from vilifying us?
Ǧuḏām and Laḫm show themselves at the fairs,
as does every Quḍāʿī whose bowls are as if they are
tanks in Raḍwá[431] as they stand humiliated[432]
because of the handful of shame which they took pains to receive
from you.
The man does not feel shame, and the man does not eat.[433]

---

426 *Anǧadat*; variant: *amǧadat*: "gained glory, became glorious"; al-Ǧāḥiẓ, *al-Buḫalāʾ*, 2:184. According to Ibn Qutaybah, in this verse *anǧadat* means: "lived in Naǧd." See Ibn Qutaybah, *al-Maʿānī*, 1:426.

427 *Qurrah*; according to *al-Aṣnām*, the meaning of this word is "a handful" (*qubḍah*); Ibn al-Kalbī, *al-Aṣnām* 48. In *al-Buḫalāʾ* the word is interpreted as "grain mixed with hair" (*al-daqīq al-muḫtaliṭ bi-l-šaʿr*); al-Ǧāḥiẓ, *al-Buḫalāʾ*, 2:185. Regarding this word see also Wellhausen (1897): 63.

428 For a translation of these lines, see also Klinke-Rosenberger (1941): 56.

429 On Surāqah b. Mālik b. Ǧuʿšum al-Mudliǧī, who is said to have embraced Islam during the conquest of Mecca, see Ibn Ḥaǧar, *al-Iṣābah*[1], 3:35–36.

430 The phrase *lā abā laka* ("may you have no father") was commonly used by poets to fill gaps in verses; Lyall (1918): 163.

431 Regarding the mountain named Raḍwá, see Yāqūt, *Muʿǧam al-buldān*, 3:51.

432 Lit. "while the noses cleave to the dust."

433 A slightly different version of this poem is translated in Klinke-Rosenberger (1941): 56.

§130 وللأقيصر يقول زهير بن أبي سُلْمى المزني: [الطويل]

حلفت يمينا بالأقيصر جاهدا وما {سُحقت} فيه المقاديم والقَملُ[a]

§131 وكان صنم يقال له **العُرَيف** لبني نهد أيضا وله يقول جابر بن الصقعب النهدي: [المنسرح]

إني وما مار بالعُرَيْفِ وما قرقر بالجلهتين من شَرْب[b]

§132 وإلاه ربيعة كان بالنجفة وكان لطيئ وربيعة وله يقول سنان بن أبي حارثة {المري}: [الكامل]

فالقريتين إلى إلاه ربيعةٍ آثارها كملاعب المُتَيَقِن | 40b

§133 **والحَلال** كان صنما لبني مُرة وقيل لبني فزارة وكان على ماء يقال له الصلب وله يقول الشاعر: [الوافر]

---

٢ سُحقت: في الأصل "سُفحت". ٤ شَرْب: كذا (التشكيل). ٥ حارثة: وضع المقريزي رمز "ح" تحت الكلمة إشارة إلى تلفظها بالحاء. || المري: في الأصل "المزني". ٨ وقيل ... فزارة: الزيادة بخط المقريزي في الهامش الأعلى من الأسفل إلى الأعلى فوق كلمة "مُرة".

---

a قارن ابن الكلبي، الأصنام، ٣٨ ("وله يقول زُهَيْر بن أبي سُلْمى:
حَلَفْتُ بأنصاب الأُقَيْصِر جاهِدًا وما سُحِقَتْ فيه المقاديمُ والقَمْلُ")
وقارن أيضا ابن منظور، لسان العرب، "سحف" ("سَحَفَ رأسَه سَحْفًا وجَلَطَه وسَلَتَه وسَحَته: حَلَقَه فاستأْصل شَعْرَه، وأَنشد ابن بري:
فأَقْسَمْتُ جَهْدًا بالمَنازِلِ من مِنًى وما سُحِفَتْ فِيهِ المَقادِيمُ والقَمْلُ
أَي حُلِقَتْ").

b قارن الجاحظ، الحيوان، ٥: ٣٧٦ ("وقال عبد الله بن العَجْلان النهديُّ:
إني وما مارَ بالفُريقِ وما قَرْقَرَ بالجَلْهَتَيْنِ من سُرُبِ
[جماعة من القطا وغيره، واحدتها سُرْبَة وعبر بها ها هنا عن الحُجّاج]").

§ 130 Zuhayr b. Abī Sulmá l-Muzanī[434] said about al-Uqayṣir: [*al-ṭawīl*]

I solemnly swore an oath by al-Uqayṣir,
and by the place where the foreparts of the heads and the [hair with] lice are shaved.[435]

§ 131 There was an idol called al-ʿUrayf which also belonged to Banū Nahd.[436] Ǧābir b. al-Ṣaqʿab al-Nahdī[437] said about it: [*al-munsariḥ*]

I swear by what flows in [the wadi beside the idol] al-ʿUrayf, and by the water[438] that gurgles between the two sides of the valley.

§ 132 The god of Rabīʿah [or: Ilāh of Rabīʿah?] was in al-Naǧafah.[439] It belonged to Ṭayyiʾ and Rabīʿah. Sinān b. Abī Ḥāriṯah al-Murrī[440] said about it: [*al-kāmil*]

And al-Qaryatayni [?][441] to/towards/belong to [?] the god of Rabīʿah/Ilāh of Rabīʿah.
Their [?] remains are like the playgrounds of al-Mutayaqqin [?].[442]

§ 133 Al-Ḥalāl was an idol that belonged to the Banū Murrah. Some say that it belonged to the Banū Fazārah.[443] It was [located] by a watering-place called al-Ṣ.l.b. A poet said about it: [*al-wāfir*]

---

434 For more details on the pre-Islamic poet Zuhayr b. Abī Sulmá, see "Zuhayr b. Abī Sulmā," in *EI*[2] (Lidia Bettini).

435 Reading *suḥiqat* instead of what al-Maqrīzī gives: *sufiḥat*. This verse is also translated in Wellhausen (1897): 62; Klinke-Rosenberger (1941): 50, 118–119; "al-Uḳayṣir," in *EI*[2] (T. Fahd).

436 No other idol of the Nahd was mentioned earlier in the text.

437 In *al-Ḥayawān*, this verse is attributed to ʿAbd Allāh b. al-ʿAǧlān al-Nahdī; al-Ǧāḥiẓ, *al-Ḥayawān*, 5:376.

438 Reading *širb* instead of *šarb*, as given by al-Maqrīzī.

439 A place between Baṣra and Baḥrayn; Yāqūt, *Muʿǧam al-buldān*, 5:272.

440 Not al-Muzanī as given by al-Maqrīzī. Sinān b. Abī Ḥāriṯah was one of the tribal leaders of Ġaṭafān; al-Iṣfahānī, *al-Aġānī*, 11:109.

441 Perhaps this is the oblique case of "al-Qaryatāni" (although in the present verse one expects the nominative). Al-Qaryatāni may refer to a place that was close to al-Nibāǧ, on the way to Mecca from Baṣra; Yāqūt, *Muʿǧam al-buldān*, 4:336.

442 Or, the playgrounds of the one convinced [?].

443 Likely referring to the Murrah subgroup of Ġaṭafān, as Fazārah, which is likewise mentioned in this account, was also a subgroup of this tribe.

مَنَحْناهُن مُرة يوم أضحى غداة حجيج أحمس والحَلال

§134 **وأحمس** كان صنما لبني فزارة وله يقول الأعشى: [الطويل]

رضِيْعَي لبانِ ثُدِيّ أُمٍ تقاسما بأحمس عَوْض الدهر لا نتفرق[a]

§135 **وعَمُ أنس** كان لخولان بأرضها وكان يُقسَم له مع قَسم الله تعالى.[b] قال ابن إسحٰق: وهم بطن من خولان يقال ⟨لهم الأديم⟩.[c] قال مجاهد: كانت خولان إذا ذكت ذبيحة يسمون عليها باسم الله واسم صنمهم ويقسمون له من زرعهم فإذا هبت الريح فأمالت ما جعلوا لصنمهم إلى ما جعلوا لله لم يجعلوا لله فيه شيئا وإذا هبت الريح فأمالت ما جعلوا لله إلى ما جعلوه لصنمهم جعلوه للصنم. فأنزل الله عز وجل في ذلك ﴿وَجَعَلُوا لِلَّهِ مِمَّا ذَرَأَ مِنَ ٱلْحَرْثِ وَٱلْأَنْعَامِ نَصِيباً فَقَالُوا هٰذَا لِلَّهِ بِزَعْمِهِمْ وَهٰذَا لِشُرَكَائِنَا فَمَا كَانَ لِشُرَكَائِهِمْ فَلَا يَصِلُ إِلَى ٱللَّهِ وَمَا كَانَ لِلَّهِ فَهُوَ يَصِلُ إِلَى شُرَكَائِهِمْ سَاءَ مَا يَحْكُمُونَ﴾.

١ مَنَحْناهُن: وضع المقريزي رمز "ح" تحت الكلمة إشارة إلى تلفظها بالحاء. ‖ والحَلال: وضع المقريزي رمز "ح" تحت الكلمة إشارة إلى تلفظها بالحاء. ٣ لبانِ ثُدِيّ: كذا في الأصل بدلا من "لِبَانٍ ثَدْيَ". ٤–٥ قال ... الأديم: الزيادة بخط المقريزي في الهامش الأيسر من الأسفل إلى الأعلى في آخر السطر بجانب كلمة "تعالى". ٥ لهم الأديم: الكلمتان غير ظاهرتين في الأصل بسبب قطع الورق في الهامش.

a قارن الأعشى، ديوان شعر الأعشى، ١٥٠
("رَضِيعَيْ لِبَانٍ ثَدْيَ أُمٍّ تَحَالَفَا بِأَسْحَمَ دَاجٍ عَوْضَ لا نَتَفَرَّقُ
وَيُرْوَى تَقَاسَمَا. رَوَى أَبُو عُبَيْدَةَ بِأَسْحَمَ عَوْضَ الدَّهْرِ لا نَتَفَرَّقُ وَعَوْضُ عَنْهُ بِالرَّفْعِ يُرِيدُ أَبَدَ الدَّهْرِ").

b قارن ابن الكلبي، الأصنام، ٤٣ ("وكان لخَوْلَانَ صنمٌ يقال له عُمْيَانِسُ بأرض خَوْلان. يقسِمون له من أنعامهم وحروثهم قِسْمًا بينه وبين الله (عزَّ وجلَّ) بزعمهم").

c قارن ابن الكلبي، الأصنام، ٤٤ ("وهم بطنٌ من خَوْلَانَ يقال لهم الأَدُومُ وهم الأُسُومُ"). وقارن أيضا ياقوت، معجم البلدان، ٤: ١٥٩ ("وهم بطن من خولان يقال لهم الاذوم وهم الاسوم").

We gave them [fem.] to Murrah on the day he acted in the morning,
in the daybreak of the pilgrims of Aḥmas and al-Ḥalāl [?].

§ 134 Aḥmas was an idol that belonged to the Banū Fazārah. Al-Aʿšá[444] said about it: [*al-ṭawīl*]

[Like] two foster brothers suckling milk from the breast of one mother, swearing
by Aḥmas never to become separated.[445]

§ 135 ʿAmm Anas[446] belonged to Ḫawlān [and was placed] in their land. They used to assign to it a portion of their share along with the portion that was assigned to Allāh, the Exalted. Ibn Isḥāq said: They are a clan of Ḫawlān called al-Adīm.[447] Muǧāhid said: When Ḫawlān slaughtered a sacrificial animal, they used to invoke the name of Allāh and the name of their idol over it,[448] and assign to it [the idol] some of their crops. When the wind blew and moved what they placed for their idol over to what they placed for Allāh, they would not apportion any of it to Allāh. But when the wind blew and moved what they placed for Allāh over to what they placed for their idol, they would apportion it to the idol. Allāh, the Great and Mighty, revealed [the following verse] regarding this: "They appoint to Allāh, of the tillage and cattle that He multiplied, a portion, saying, 'This is for Allāh'—so they assert—'and this is for our associates.' So what is for their associates reaches not Allāh; and what is for Allāh reaches their associates. Evil is their judgment!"[449]

---

444 Abū Baṣīr Maymūn b. Qays b. Ǧandal al-Aʿšá ("the night blind"), who belonged to the Qays b. Ṯaʿlabah tribe (Bakr b. Wāʾil). See "al-Aʿshā," in *EI*³ (B. Jockers).

445 Others do not associate the verse with this idol, and read *asḥam* for *aḥmas*. See for instance Lane (1863–1893): 1321. See also al-Aʿšá, *Dīwān šiʿr al-Aʿšá*, 150.

446 For a translation of parallel versions of this account, see Ibn Hišām, *The Life of Muhammad* 36–37; Faris (1952): 37–38; Goldfeld (1977); Robin (2009): 539. Note that the sources provide various readings for this idol's name. For more on its form and vocalization, see Robin (2009): 541–543 (who opts for ʿAmmīʾanas).

447 For a hypothesis about this group's origin, see Robin (2009). The scanned page was truncated and MS Dār al-Kutub was consulted. Regarding the truncated part, see Bauden (forthcoming).

448 They did this by saying *bi-smi llāh* (in the name of Allāh) and, presumably, a similar formula that included their idol's name.

449 Qurʾān (*al-Anʿām*), 6:136.

§136 واتخذت دَوْس أصناما منها صنم يقال له الشُرَيْر وآخر يقال له غنم وآخر يقال له ذو الكفين.[a] فكان الطفيل بن عمرو الدوسي يقول: كنت سادنا لذي الكفين. فإن كنت لأغْبقه اللبن حتى تلغ فيه الكلاب وإن صبياني ليتضاغون ما يمنعني أن أسقيهم من ذلك اللبن إلا فَرَقي من الصنم ثم إني فكرت في أمره فوجدته حجرا لا يضر ولا ينفع فعمدت إليه فحرقته بالنار[b] ثم أقبلت إلى رسول الله ﷺ حتى إذا كنت ببعض الطريق رأيت رؤيا ظننت أنها لما صنعت بالصنم. فجئت رسول الله ﷺ فقلت: "إني كنت سادنا لصنم لنا. والله إن كنت لأغبقه اللبن حتى {تلغ} فيه الكلاب ما يمنعني منه إلا فرقا منه وإني فكرت فيه فوجدته حجرا لا يضر ولا ينفع فحرقته بالنار ثم أقبلت إليك حتى إذا كنت ببعض الطريق رأيت رؤيا فظننتها لما صنعت بالصنم."

---

٦ تلغ: في الأصل "يلغ".

---

a قارن ابن الكلبي، الأصنام، ٣٧ ("وكان لدَوْس ثم لبني مُنْهِب بن دَوْس صنمٌ يقال له ذو الكَفَّيْن").

b قارن السهيلي، الروض الأنف، ٣: ٣٦٧ ("ثم لم أزَل مع رسول الله ﷺ حتى إذا فتح اللهُ عليه مكةَ، قال: قلت: يا رسول الله، ابعثني إلى ذي الكفَّين، صنمِ عمرو بن حُمَمَة حتى أُحْرقه. قال ابن إسحاق: فخرج إليه").

§136 Daws adopted several idols, including an idol called al-Šurayr, another one called Ġanm, and yet another called Ḏū l-Kaffayni [lit., "he who has two palms"]. Al-Ṭufayl b. ʿAmr al-Dawsī[450] used to say: I was custodian of Ḏū l-Kaffayni, and in fact used to give it a draft of milk in the evening [so much] that the dogs would lap it up, while my children were actually screaming [with hunger]. Nothing prevented me from giving them some of that milk except my fear of the idol. Then I gave it some thought and found it to be a stone that brings no harm or benefit, so I approached it, and set it on fire. Afterwards, I went to the Messenger of Allāh, may Allāh bless and save him, and when I was on the way, I had a dream that I thought was caused by what I had done to the idol. I went to the Messenger of Allāh, may Allāh bless and save him, and said: "I was custodian of an idol of ours. By Allāh, I used to give it a draft of milk in the evening [so much] that the dogs would lap it up. Nothing prevented me from using it [the milk; for my own family needs] except that [I acted as I did] out of fear of it [the idol]. Then I gave it some thought, found it to be a stone that brings no harm or benefit, and set it on fire. Afterwards, I came to you, and when I was on the way, I had a dream, and I thought that it was caused by what I had done to the idol."

450 A tribal leader and a poet from the Daws tribe; Abū Nuʿaym, *Maʿrifat al-ṣaḥābah*, 3:1561–1565.

فقال رسول الله ﷺ: "خيرا رأيت. اقصص رؤياك." فقلت: "رأيت بطني انشق فخرجت منه طير خضر صعدت إلى السماء ورأيت رأسي حلق ورأيت امرأة أدخلتني في فرجها." فقال رسول | 41a الله ﷺ: "أما حِلَاقُ رأسك فإنك تستشهد وأما الطير التي خرجت منك فهو رُوْحك يُصْعَد به إلى السماء وأما المرأة التي أدخلتك في بطنها فهي الأرض."[a] فقال الطفيل: "يٰرسول الله إني قد قلت شعرا فأنشدك." فقال رسول الله ﷺ: "أنشد ما قلت." قال: قلت: [الرجز]

يا ذا الكفين[b] لست من عبادك

فقال رسول الله ﷺ: "صدقتَ." قال: قلت:

ميلادنا أقدم من ميلادك[c]

---

٣ رُوْحك : وضع المقريزي رمز "ح" تحت الكلمة إشارة إلى تلفظها بالحاء.

---

a قارن السهيلي، الروض الأنف، ٣: ٣٦٨ ("قال: ثم رجع إلى رسول الله ﷺ فكان معه بالمدينة حتى قَبض اللهُ رسولَه—صلى الله عليه وسلم—فلما ارتدّت العرب، خرج مع المسلمين فسار معهم حتى فرَغُوا من طُليحة ومن أرض نَجْد كلِّها. ثم سار مع المسلمين إلى اليمامة—ومعه ابنُهُ عَمْرو بن الطُّفيل—فرأى رؤيا وهو متوجِّه إلى اليمامة فقال لأصحابه: إني قد رأيت رؤيا، فاعبرُوها لي، رأيتُ أن رأسي حُلِق وأنه خرج من فمي طائرٌ وأنه لقِيَتْني امرأةٌ فأدخلتني في فَرْجها وأرى ابني يَطلبني طَلَبا حَثيثا ثم رأيتُه حُبس عني، قالوا: خيرا، قال: أمّا أنا والله فقد أوَّلتُها، قالوا: ماذا؟ قال: أمّا حلْق رأسي فَوضْعه وأما الطائر الذي خرج من فِي فَرُوحي وأما المرأة التي أدخلتني فرجها فالأرض تُحْفَرُ لي فأُغيَّب فيها وأما طَلب ابني إياي ثم حَبْسه عني فإني أراه سَيجْهد أنْ يصيبه ما أصابني، فُقتل رحمه الله شهيدا باليمامة وجُرح ابنه جراحة شديدة ثم استبَلّ منها ثم قُتل عام اليَرموك في زمن عمر رضي الله عنه شهيدا").

b راجع السهيلي، الروض الأنف، ٣: ٣٧٦-٣٧٧ ("وقوله: يا ذا الْكَفَيْنِ لست من عبادك. أراد: الكّفين بالتشديد، فخفف للضرورة غير أن في نسخة الشيخ أن الصنم كان يسمى: ذا الكَفَيْنِ، وخفف الفاء بخطِّه بعد أن كانت مشددة، فدل أنه عنده مخفف في غير الشعر"). وقارن الزبيدي، تاج العروس، "كفف" ("وذُو الكُفَيْنِ، كزُبيّر: صَنَمٌ لدوس، عَن نَصر؛ وِمنه قوله: يَا ذَا الكُفَيْن لسْت من عبادِكَا").

c قارن ابن حبيب، المحبر، ٣١٨-٣١٩ ("وكان ذو الكفين لخزاعة ودَوس. فلما كسره عمرو بن حممة الدوسي قال: «يا ذا الكفين لستُ من تلادك. ميلادنا أكبر من ميلادك").

The Messenger of Allāh, may Allāh bless and save him, said: "You have dreamt a good dream, tell me about it." I said: "I saw my stomach split open, and green birds that rose toward the sky emerged from it. I also saw that my head had been shaved, and that a woman inserted me into her private parts." The Messenger of Allāh, may Allāh bless and save him, said: "The shaving of your head means that you will die as a martyr, the birds that emerged from you are your spirit, which will be raised to heaven, and the woman who inserted you into her womb (*baṭn*) is the earth."[451] Al-Ṭufayl said: "O Messenger of Allāh! I composed some poetry. Shall I recite [it] to you?" The Messenger of Allāh, may Allāh bless and save him, said: "Recite what you have composed." I said: [*al-rağaz*]

O Ḏū l-Kaffayni![452] I am not one of your worshippers.

And the Messenger of Allāh, may Allāh bless and save him, said: "You have said the truth!" I said:

Our birth is more ancient than your birth.

---

451 Other sources narrate a different story regarding al-Ṭufayl b. ʿAmr's dream. See Guillaume's translation of a parallel version of this account in the *Sīrah*: "He [al-Ṭufayl b. ʿAmr] returned to Medina to the apostle and remained with him until God took him. When the Arabs revolted he sided with the Muslims and fought with them until they disposed of Ṭulayḥa and the whole of Najd. Then he went with the Muslims to the Yamāma with his son ʿAmr, and while on the way he saw a vision of which he told his companions asking for an interpretation. 'I saw my head had been shaved and a bird was coming out of my mouth and a woman met me and took me into her womb, and I saw my son seeking me anxiously; then I saw him withheld from me.' They said that they hoped it would prove a good omen, but he went on to say that he himself would provide the interpretation of it. The shaving of his head meant that he would lay it down; the bird which flew from his mouth was his spirit; and the woman who received him into her womb was the earth which would be opened for him and he would be hidden therein; his son's vain search for him meant that he would try to attain what he had attained. He was slain as a martyr in al-Yamāma while his son was severely wounded and recovered later. He was actually killed in the year of the Yarmūk in the time of ʿUmar, dying as a martyr." Ibn Hišām, *The Life of Muhammad* 177.

452 In this verse it is vocalized "Kafayni," for reasons of meter. These lines are also translated in Klinke-Rosenberger (1941): 50; Ibn Hišām, *The Life of Muhammad* 177.

فقال رسول الله ﷺ: "صدقت." قال: قلت:

أنا حشوت النار في فؤادك[a]

فقال رسول الله ﷺ: "أنت أعلم."

§ 137 وكان الشارق صنما لحنيفة وكان بحَجْر من اليمامة وكان في موضع سوق الخلق وله يقول ربعي بن رداد: [الوافر]

وعند الشارق المَرح المُرَادي   بكل كتيبة وبكل عُظْم
قضينا حجنا وبَرِئن منا   كما حُلّت معاقد كل نَظْم

وبشارق هذا سُمي عبد الشارق بن (...).

§ 138 وكان باليمامة أكمة يقال لها مَرْسُوغ وهي اليوم الأكمة التي يقال لها أكَمَةُ المصلوب صلب عليها عبد فارسي يقال له رستم. وكانوا يحجون إليها وكان الذي يحج يجلس على رأسها ثم يأخذ إنسان برجله فيجره حتى يهبط به إلى الأرض أربع مرات.

§ 139 وزعم رجل من أشجع قال: كانت البيضاء تحرمها أشجع وبطون من غطفان وجهينة.[b] ولها يقول المزني: [الطويل]

---

٨ وبشارق ... بن: الزيادة بخط المقريزي في الهامش الأيمن من الأسفل إلى الأعلى ويشير إليها رمز ٮ بعد "نَظْم" ويبدو أنه لم يتم الكلام.

---

a قارن الواقدي، المغازي، ٢: ٨٧٠ ("أنا حَشَشتُ النارَ في فُؤادِكا").

b راجع ياقوت، معجم البلدان، ١: ٥٣٠-٥٣١ ("والبيضاء موضع بقرب حِمَى الربذة").

And the Messenger of Allāh, may Allāh bless and save him, said: "You have said the truth!" I said:

I have stuffed your heart with fire.

And the Messenger of Allāh, may Allāh bless and save him, said: "You know best."

§ 137 Al-Šāriq was an idol that belonged to [the tribe of] Ḥanīfah. It was [located] in Ḥağr of al-Yamāmah, at the site of the [later] second-hand clothes market. Ribʿī b. Raddād said about it: [*al-wāfir*]

At the cheerful al-Šāriq that destroys [?]
every troop and every large group.
We completed our pilgrimage and they [fem.] withdrew from us
like the knots of every string of pearls are undone.[453]

ʿAbd al-Šāriq b. […] was named after this Šāriq.[454]

§ 138 There was a hillock in Yamāmah called Marsūġ.[455] Today,[456] it is the hillock called Akamat al-Maṣlūb [lit., "the hillock of the crucified man"]. A Persian slave named Rustam was crucified on it. They used to make pilgrimage[s] to it [the hillock]. The pilgrim would sit at its top, and then someone would grab his leg and pull him down to the ground. [This was practiced] four times.[457]

§ 139 A man of Ašğaʿ claimed that al-Bayḍāʾ was declared sacred by Ašğaʿ and by branches of the Ġaṭafān and Ğuhaynah. Al-Muzanī [i.e. a man of Muzaynah] said about it: [*al-ṭawīl*]

---

453 See Lecker (forthcoming).

454 Al-Maqrīzī added this line in the margin and left what follows the name blank, as if he had intended to add a fuller name.

455 *Marsūġ* means "tethered by the forelegs"; Lane (1863–1893): 1080.

456 I.e. at the time of al-Maqrīzī's source.

457 For more information on the idol al-Šāriq, see Lecker (forthcoming).

لنا الجبل العالي الحرام الذي ترى   على الأرض ذا مَاذِيّة وفضول
فكيف نَعاف الضيمَ تِرك؟ ورأسه   بأقدام أم الحَرَتين ذلول

§140 وكان لحمير صنم يقال له كُلَال وكانوا يعبدونه. قال وضاح اليمن:[a] [الطويل]

بنى لي إسْمعيل مجدا مؤثلا   وعبد كلال قبله وأبو جَمْدْ[b]

§141 والخميس كان لبني سُليم والخزرج من الأنصار وله يقول عبد المطلب بن هاشم: [السريع]

أبلغ بني النجار إن جئتهم   أني منهم وابنهم والخميس

٢ تِرك: وضع المقريزي نقطة بالحبر الأحمر فوق الكاف ربما يريد الإشارة إلى شكه في القراءة الصحيحة.
٤ بنى: في الأصل "بنا". || جَمْد: كذا في الأصل بدلا من "جمَدْ" (راجع الإصفهاني، الأغاني ٦: ٢٤٩–٢٥٠).

a راجع الإصبهاني، الأغاني، ٦: ٢٢٢ ("وَضّاح لقب غلب عليه لجماله وبهائه، واسمه عبد الرحمن بن إسماعيل بن عبد كُلال بن داذ بن أبي جَمَد").

b قارن الإصبهاني، الأغاني، ٦: ٢٢٣ ("وقال أيضًا يفتخر بجَدّه أبي جَمَد:
بَنَى لِيَ إسماعيلُ مجدًا مُؤَثّلًا   وعبدُ كُلال بعده وأبو جَمَدْ").

We have the high and sacred mountain that you see
  on the land like [a warrior clad in] Median chain mail, and [we also have] benefits.
How can a t.r.k [?] loathe injustice, when his head
  is humbled by the feet of Umm al-Ḥarratayn? [?]

§ 140 Ḥimyar had an idol called Kulāl, which they worshipped. Waḍḍāḥ al-Yaman[458] said: [*al-ṭawīl*]

Ismāʿīl built[459] for me a [legacy of] deeply rooted nobility,
  as did ʿAbd Kulāl and Abū Ǧamad prior to him.[460]

§ 141 Al-Ḫamīs[461] belonged to the Banū Sulaym and to the Ḫazraǧ[462] of the Anṣār. ʿAbd al-Muṭṭalib b. Hāšim[463] said, referring to it: [*al-sarīʿ*]

If you come to the Banū l-Naǧǧār, tell them
  that I am one of them, and [that I am] their son, [I swear] by al-Ḫamīs.

---

458 Waḍḍāḥ al-Yaman ('the bright from Yemen') was an Umayyad poet whose name was ʿAbd al-Raḥmān b. Ismāʿīl (d. ca. 90/707). There are contradictory traditions on his Yemeni origin; see "Waḍḍāḥ al-Yaman," in *EI*² (A. Arazi); "Waḍḍāḥ al-Yaman," in *EAL* (T. Seidensticker).

459 See Lane (1863–1893): 260: "بِنَايَة is sometimes used in relation to nobility."

460 Waḍḍāḥ al-Yaman takes pride in his ancestry in this line. According to *al-Aġānī*, his pedigree is ʿAbd al-Raḥmān b. Ismāʿīl b. ʿAbd Kulāl b. Dāḏ b. Abī Ǧamad; al-Iṣfahānī, *al-Aġānī*, 6:222.

461 Regarding this idol, see Lecker (1989): 99; Lecker (2005a): 33.

462 It is possible that this idol was also worshipped by the Aws tribe, since some sources remark that the name Ḫazraǧ refers to both the Ḫazraǧ and the Aws; see Ibn al-Kalbī, *al-Aṣnām* 14; Lecker (1989): 99, n. 4.

463 The Prophet's grandfather; on whom see above, note 269. In *Kitāb al-Ṭabaqāt* the line is attributed to al-Muṭṭalib b. ʿAbd Manāf; Ibn Saʿd, *al-Ṭabaqāt*¹, 1:63–64; Lecker (2005a): 33.

§142 وكان {بجماء العاقر} بالعقيق من المدينة صنم يقال له المُكَيْمن لا أدري | من كان يعبده.[a] 41b

§143 وياليل كان صنما لجهينة بالحوراء من أرض الحجاز على ساحل البحر.[b]

§144 وكان للمعافر صنم يقال له بَرْكُلَان.[c]

§145 وكان لبني عامر بن ربيعة صنم يقال له قُرس وكان بثنية بوانة.[d] وله يقول البلوي: [الوافر]

وما قُرس وإن أعظمتموه بذي دَفْع يُعد ولا قبال

§146 والعَبْد كان لطيئ وكان بمُوهق.

١ بجماء العاقر: في الأصل "بالجماء المعاقر". ووضع المقريزي نقطة بالحبر الأحمر فوق الكلمة الثانية إشارة إلى شكه في القراءة الصحيحة؟ ٤ البلوي: أضاف المقريزي هذا الاسم في الهامش الأيسر في آخر السطر بجانب كلمة "يقول".

a راجع السمهودي، وفاء الوفاء، ٤: ٤٨٠–٤٨١ ("مُكَيْمِن: تصغير مكمن، ويقال: مكيمن الجمَّاء، وهو الجبل المتصل بجمَّاء تضارع ببطن العقيق. وفي أخبار مكة لابن شَبَّة: أنه كان بجمَّاء العاقر بعقيق المدينة صنمٌ يقال له: «المكيمن»، فلعله سبب التسمية لقرب جمَّاء العاقر منه").

b راجع ابن الكلبي، الأصنام، ٤٥ ("وكان رجلٌ من جُهَيْنَةَ، يقال له عبد الدار بن حُدَيْبٍ، قال لقومه: هَلُمَّ نبني بيتا (بأرض من بلادهم يقال لها الحوراء) نُضاهي به الكعبة ونُعَظِّمُهُ حتَّى نستميل به كثيرا من العرب. فأعظموا ذلك وأبَوْا عليه").

c راجع ياقوت، معجم البلدان، ٥: ١٠٩ ("مَرْكَلان: بالفتح ثم السكون، وآخره نون، والرَّكْل الضربُ بالرِّجل، والرَّكْل الكُرّاثُ: وهو موضع، عن ابن دريد").

d راجع ابن عساكر، تاريخ مدينة دمشق، ١٩: ٥٠٣–٥٠٤ ("رأيت زيد بن عمرو وأنا عند صنم بُوَانَة بعدما رجع من الشام وهو يراقب الشمس").

§ 142 There was an idol in Ǧammāʾ al-ʿĀqir[464] in the ʿAqīq of Medina[465] called al-Mukaymin.[466] I do not know who used to worship it.

§ 143 Yālīl was an idol of Ǧuhaynah in al-Ḥawrāʾ[467] in the land of al-Ḥiǧāz, on the sea coast.

§ 144 The Maʿāfir had an idol called Barkulān.

§ 145 The Banū ʿĀmir b. Rabīʿah[468] had an idol called Qurs, which was in the narrow pass of Buwānah.[469] Al-Balawī [i.e. a man of Balī] said about it: [*al-wāfir*]

Qurs, even though you treat it with reverence,
is not considered to have [the power to] repel or fight.

§ 146 Al-ʿAbd belonged to Ṭayyiʾ and was [located] in Mūhiq.

---

464 The word Ǧammāwāt (pl. of Ǧammāʾ) refers to three mountains in the area of Medina: Ǧammāʾ Tuḍāriʿ (or Tuḍāruʿ), Ǧammāʾ Umm Ḫālid, and Ǧammāʾ al-ʿĀqir. On these Ǧammāwāt, see al-Samhūdī, *Wafāʾ al-wafā*, 4:42–48; Yāqūt, *Muʿǧam al-buldān*, 2:32, 158–159.

465 See "al-ʿAḳīḳ," in *EI*² (G. Rentz): "The best known of the ʿAḳīḳs is the valley passing just west of Medina, from which it is separated by Ḥarrat al-Wabra. It continues northwards to join Wādī al-Ḥamḍ, the classical Iḍam, which empties into the Red Sea south of al-Wadjh. The mountain ʿAyr south of Medina rises above the right bank of al-ʿAḳīḳ, which draws much of its water from the neighbouring lava beds."

466 Al-Maqrīzī's source for the account of Mukaymin is Ibn Šabbah's *Aḫbār Makkah*. See al-Samhūdī, *Wafāʾ al-wafā*, 4:480–481.

467 Al-Ḥawrāʾ was in the territory of Ǧuhaynah; "Ḳuḍāʿa," in *EI*² (M.J. Kister).

468 The Banū ʿĀmir b. Rabīʿah should probably be identified with the offspring of ʿĀmir b. Rabīʿah b. ʿĀmir b. Ṣaʿṣaʿah. Ibn Ḥazm, *Ǧamharat ansāb al-ʿarab* 280–281.

469 Buwānah is mentioned in the sources as the name of an idol or as the name of a place associated with idols: Hawting (1999): 121–122. See also the introduction, pp. 22–23.

§147 والجثا كان صنما لبني نهد[a] وله يقول {ابن} عجلان النهدي: [الطويل]

فقلنا إذا لا ينكل القوم عنكم   لعَمْرو الجُثَا اللاتي الدماء تَمُورها[b]

§148 وعن سعيد بن جبير عن ابن عباس رضي الله عنه في قوله تعالى ﴿أَفَرَأَيْتَ مَنِ ٱتَّخَذَ إِلَٰهَهُ هَوَاهُ﴾ قال: كان أحدهم يعبد الحجر فإذا رأى ما هو أحسن منه رمى به وعبَد الآخر.

§149 وقال حماد بن سلمة عن حميد عن أبي عثمٰن قال: كنّا في الجاهلية إذا حملنا حجرا على بعير نعبده فرأينا حجرا أحسن منه ألقيناه وأخذنا الذي هو أحسن. وكنّا إذا سقط الحجر عن البعير قلنا: "قد سقط إلاهكم، فالتمسوا حجرا آخر."

§150 وعن قتادة قال: حدثت عن أبي عثمٰن قال: كان أهل الجاهلية إذا حجوا عمدوا إلى حجرهم الذي كانوا يعبدونه فشدوه على بعير من إبلهم فإذا سار ذلك البعير نادى مناديهم: "إن ربكم قد سار فسيروا." فإن سار يومه أجمع ساروا معه وإن هو برك من ساعته نادى مناديهم: "إن ربكم قد نزل فانزلوا." وإن وجدوا حجرا أحسن من حجرهم الأول أخذوه ورموا بالآخر. فإذا كان يوم دوارهم

١ ابن : في الأصل "ان".

a راجع الزبيدي، تاج العروس، "جثو" ("وقِيلَ: الجُثَا صَنَمٌ كانَ يُذْبَحُ لَهُ").

b قارن الإصبهاني، الأغاني، ٢٢: ٢٤٢ ("فقلنا:

إذا لا نَنْكُل الدهرَ عنكُم   بصُمِّ القنا اللائي الدماء تُميرها").

§ 147 Al-Ǧuṯā[470] was an idol that belonged to the Banū Nahd. Ibn ʿAǧlān al-Nahdī[471] said about it: [*al-ṭawīl*]

> We said: Hence, the people will not shrink from you [pl.],
> [I swear] by the life of[472] al-Ǧuṯā over which blood pours.[473]

§ 148 On the authority of Saʿīd b. Ǧubayr < Ibn ʿAbbās, may Allāh be pleased with him, who said [the following] regarding His saying, the Exalted, "Have you seen him who has taken his caprice to be his god":[474] Someone worshipped a stone, and when he saw something [i.e. a stone] that was better than it, he discarded it and worshipped the other one.

§ 149 Ḥammād b. Salamah[475] said on the authority of Ḥumayd[476] < Abū ʿUṯmān,[477] who said: In the Ǧāhiliyyah, when we carried a stone on a camel in order to worship it and then saw a stone that was better than it [the first one], we discarded it and took the better one. When the stone fell from the camel, we said: "Your god fell down, look for another stone."

§ 150 On the authority of Qatādah, who said: It was related to me on the authority of Abū ʿUṯmān, that when the people of the Ǧāhiliyyah made pilgrimage[s], they approached the stone that they used to worship, and bound it to one of their camels. When the camel departed, their crier called out: "Your lord has departed. Depart!" If it [the camel] walked all day long, they walked with it, and if it quickly kneeled down, their crier called out: "Your lord has stopped for a rest. Stop!" If they found a stone that was better than the first stone, they took it and discarded the other [first] one. During the

470 See also Lane (1863–1893): 380: "الجثا is also said to have been a certain idol, to which sacrifices were performed."

471 For more on the pre-Islamic poet ʿAbd Allāh b. al-ʿAǧlān al-Nahdī (Quḍāʿah), see al-Iṣfahānī, *al-Aġānī*, 22:238–246.

472 The letter *wāw* in the word *la-ʿamr* seems superfluous.

473 A variant of this line appears in *al-Aġānī* (al-Iṣfahānī, *al-Aġānī*, 22:242), but there is no mention of al-Ǧuṯā.

474 Qurʾān (*al-Ǧāṯiyah*), 45:23.

475 Ḥammād b. Salamah b. Dīnār (d. 167/783); al-Ḏahabī, *Siyar aʿlām al-nubalāʾ*, 7:444–456.

476 On Ḥumayd b. Abī Ḥumayd al-Ṭawīl (d. ca. 142/759), who was Ḥammād b. Salamah's maternal uncle, see al-Mizzī, *Tahḏīb al-kamāl*, 7:355–366.

477 Abū ʿUṯmān al-Nahdī, ʿAbd al-Raḥmān b. Mull, or Malī, according to another opinion; al-Ḏahabī, *Siyar aʿlām al-nubalāʾ*, 4:175–178.

صبوا عليه ألبانهم وأطعمتهم وذبحوا له فيظل أولادهم جياعا وتظل كلابهم شباعا يتضحك بهم الشيطان ويتلعب بهم.[a]

§151 وعن أبي رجاء قال: كنا نصلي للحجر الأبيض ونرى أحسن منه الحجر الأسود فنصلي ونجمع الرمل فنحلب فيه ونصلي له.[b]

§152 وعن مجاهد في قوله ﴿مَنْ كَانَ يُرِيدُ ٱلْعِزَّةَ﴾ قال: بعبادة الأوثان.[c]

§153 وعن سعيد بن جبير في قوله تعالى ﴿إِنَّ ٱلَّذِينَ تَدْعُونَ مِنْ دُونِ ٱللَّهِ عِبَادٌ أَمْثَالُكُمْ﴾ يقول: ما الذين تدعون من | دون الله يعني الأوثان يقول ما هم إلا مثلكم.[d] 42a

---

a قارن ابن سعد، الطبقات٢، ٩: ٩٧ ("سمعتُ أبا عثمان النّهديّ يقول: كنّا في الجاهليّة نعبد حجرًا فسمعنا مناديًا ينادي يا أهل الرِّحال إنّ ربّكم قد هَلَكَ فالتَمِسُوه، قال: فخرجنا على كلّ صعب وذَلُول، فبينا نحن كذلك نطلب إذا منادٍ ينادي إنّا قد وجدنا ربكم أو شبهه، قال: فجئنا فإذا حجرٌ، قال: فنحرنا عليه الجُزُر").

b قارن ابن قيم الجوزية، إغاثة اللهفان، ٢: ٢٦٢ ("سمعت أبا رجاء العُطارِدِيَّ يقول: لما بُعث النبي صلى الله عليه وسلم فسمعنا به لحقنا بمسَيلِمة الكذاب فلحقنا بالنار، قال: وكنا نعبدُ الحجرَ في الجاهلية، فإذا وجدنا حجرًا هو أحسن منه نُلْقِي ذلك ونأخذه، فإذا لم نجدْ حجرًا جمعنا حَثْيَةً من تُراب، ثم جئنا بغَنَم فحلبناها عليه، ثم طُفنا به. وقال أبو رَجاء أيضًا: كنا نعمدُ إلى الرَّملِ فنجمعه ونَحلِبُ عليه فنعبده، وكنا نعمِدُ إلى الحجر الأبيض فنعبدهُ زمانًا، ثم نلقيه"). وراجع أيضا أبو نعيم، حلية الأولياء، ٢: ٣٠٦ ("سمعت أبا رجاء يقول: كنا نجمع التراب في الجاهلية فنجعل وسطه حفرة فنحلب فيها ثم نسعى حولها، ونقول لبيك لا شريك لك إلا شريكا هو لك تملكه وما ملك").

c راجع أبو حيان، البحر المحيط، ٩: ١٧ ("﴿مَنْ كَانَ يُرِيدُ ٱلْعِزَّةَ﴾: أي المغالبة، ﴿فَلِلَّهِ ٱلْعِزَّةُ﴾: أي ليست لغيره، ولا تتم إلا به، والمغالب مغلوب. ونحا إليه مجاهد وقال: ﴿مَنْ كَانَ يُرِيدُ ٱلْعِزَّةَ﴾: بعبادة الأوثان، وهذا تمثيل لقوله: ﴿وَٱتَّخَذُوا مِنْ دُونِ ٱللَّهِ آلِهَةً لِيَكُونُوا لَهُم عِزًّا﴾").

d قارن القرطبي، الجامع، ٧: ٣٤٢ ("وقرأ سعيد بن جُبير: ﴿إنِ الذين تدعون من دون الله عبادًا أمثالَكُمْ﴾ بتخفيف "إن" وكسرها لالتقاء الساكنين، ونصب "عبادًا" بالتنوين، "أمثالكم" بالنصب. والمعنى: ما الذين تدعون من دون الله عبادًا أمثالكم، أي هي حجارة وخشب؛ فأنتم تعبدون ما أنتم أشرف منه").

day of their *dawār*,[478] they poured their milk and food[479] on it, and made sacrifices for it. Their children remained hungry, while their dogs were sated. Satan mocked them and made fun of them.

§ 151 [The following tradition] was reported on the authority of Abū Raǧāʾ,[480] who said: We used to pray to a white stone, but then we thought the black stone was better than it, so we prayed [to the black stone]. We would also pile up sand, milk [our animals] on it, and pray to it.

§ 152 It was reported on the authority of Muǧāhid that His saying "Whosoever desires superior power (*ʿizzah*)" [refers to those who seek to gain such power] by worshipping idols.[481]

§ 153 It was reported on the authority of Saʿīd b. Ǧubayr that His saying, the Exalted, "Those on whom you call apart from Allāh, are servants like you,"[482] [should be interpreted as follows:] Those on whom you call apart from Allāh—i.e. the idols—are like you.[483]

---

478 I.e. During the day in which they performed the *dawār*; see above, § 118.

479 *Aṭʿimah* (pl. of *ṭaʿām*). The common meaning of the word is wheat, but it may also denote barley or dates; Lane (1863–1893): 1854.

480 On Abū Raǧāʾ al-ʿUṭāridī, ʿImrān b. Milḥām al-Tamīmī (d. ca. 107/725), who is reported to have embraced Islam after the conquest of Mecca, see al-Ḏahabī, *Siyar aʿlām al-nubalāʾ*, 4:253–257.

481 Qurʾān (*Fāṭir*), 35:10.

482 Qurʾān (*al-Aʿrāf*), 7:194.

483 This sentence is incongruous with parallel sources that say that Saʿīd read this verse with *in al-nāfiyah*, and that the meaning of the verse is: "Those on whom you call apart from Allāh are not servants like you": al-Qurṭubī, *al-Ǧāmiʿ*, 7:342.

§154 وقال أبو بكر بن أبي شيبة: ثنا شبابة ثنا نعيم بن حكيم عن أبي مريم عن علي رضي الله عنه قال: انطلق بي رسول الله ﷺ حتى أتى الكعبة. فقال: "اجلس." فجلست إلى جنب الكعبة وصعد على منكبي. ثم قال: "انهض". فنهضت به. فلما رأى ضعفي تحته قال: "اجلس". فجلست فنزل عني وجلس لي وقال لي: "يا علي اصعد على منكبي." فصعدت على منكبه فلما نهض بي خيل إلي أني لو شئت نلت أفق السماء. فصعدت على الكعبة وتنحى رسول الله فقال لي: "ألق صنمهم الأكبر صنم قريش." وكان من نحاس وكان موتدا بأوتاد من حديد إلى الأرض.[a] فقال لي رسول الله: "عالجه." فجعلت أعالجه والنبي ﷺ يقول: "إيه إيه." فلم أزل أعالجه حتى استمكنت منه فقال لي: "ألقه." فقذفته ونزوت أو نزلت.[b]

§155 وقال الكلبي عن أبي صالح عن ابن عباس قال: كانت العرب تعبد النجوم وكانت حمير تعبد الشمس وذلك قول الله تعالى ﴿وَجَدتُّهَا وَقَوْمَهَا يَسْجُدُونَ لِلشَّمْسِ مِن دُونِ ٱللَّهِ﴾. وكانت كنانة تعبد القمر وكانت تميم تعبد الدبران وكانت لخم وجذام تعبد المشتري وكانت طيئ تعبد الثريا

٥ وتنحى: في الأصل "وتنحا".

a قارن الحلبي، السيرة الحلبية، ٣: ٢٩ ("وفي رواية: لما ألقى الأصنام لم يبق إلا صنم خزاعة موتدا بأوتاد من الحديد").

b قارن الحلبي، السيرة الحلبية، ٣: ٣٠ ("وفي الكشاف: ألقاها جميعها وبقي صنم خزاعة فوق الكعبة وكان من قوارير صفر، فقال ﷺ: يا علي ارم به، فحمله رسول الله ﷺ حتى صعد فرمى به فكسره، فجعل أهل مكة يتعجبون ويقولون: ما رأينا أسحر من محمد. وفي خصائص العشرة لصاحب الكشاف زيادة، وهي: ونزلت من فوق الكعبة وانطلقت أنا والنبي ﷺ نسعى، وخشينا أن يرانا أحد من قريش هذا كلامه، وهذا يدل على أن ذلك لم يكن يوم فتح مكة فليتأمل"). وقارن أيضا الزيلعي، تخريج الأحاديث، ٢: ٢٨٨ ("فصعدت على الكعبة وعليها تمثال من صفر أو نحاس، فجعلت أعالجه يميناً وشمالاً وقدام ومن بين يديه ومن خلفه؛ حتى إذا استمكنت منه قال لي رسول الله صلى الله عليه وسلم «اقذفه» فقذفت به فكسرته كما تكسر القوارير، ثم نزلت، فانطلقت أنا ورسول الله صلى الله عليه وسلم يستبق حتى توارينا بالبيوت خشية أن يلقانا أحد من الناس").

§ 154 Abū Bakr b. Abī Šaybah[484] said, Šabābah[485] related to us, Nuʿaym b. Ḥakīm[486] related to us on the authority of Abū Maryam[487] that ʿAlī, may Allāh be pleased with him, said: The Messenger of Allāh, may Allāh bless and save him, went away with me until he [the Prophet] reached the Kaʿbah. He [the Prophet] said: "Sit!" So I sat beside the Kaʿbah, and he [the Prophet] climbed on my shoulders. Then he [the Prophet] said: "Get up!" So I rose with him [on my shoulders], but when he [the Prophet] saw my weakness beneath him, he [the Prophet] said: "Sit!" So I sat, and he [the Prophet] got down from atop me, sat for me [so that I could climb on his shoulders], and told me: "O ʿAlī! Climb on my shoulders." So I climbed on his shoulders, and when he rose with me [on his shoulders], it seemed to me that if I wished, I could have reached the horizon of the sky. Then I climbed on top of the Kaʿbah, and the Messenger of Allāh stepped aside and said to me: "Cast down their largest idol, the idol of Qurayš." It was made of copper and was fixed to the surface [of the Kaʿbah] by iron pegs. The Messenger of Allāh told me: "Struggle with it [i.e. release the idol]." So I struggled with it, as the Prophet was saying: "Go on! Go on!" I kept struggling with it until I had control over it, and then he told me: "Throw it." So I cast it down and leaped (*nazawtu*) [i.e. from the top of the Kaʿbah], or [according to another version], came down (*nazaltu*).[488]

§ 155 Al-Kalbī[489] said on the authority of Abū Ṣāliḥ[490] that Ibn ʿAbbās said: The Arabs used to worship the stars. Ḥimyar worshipped the Sun, and this is [the implication of] Allāh's saying, the Exalted: "I found her and her people prostrating to the sun, apart from Allāh."[491] Kinānah worshipped the Moon, Tamīm worshipped Aldebaran, Laḫm and Ǧuḏām worshipped Jupiter, Ṭayyiʾ worshipped Pleiades, Qays worshipped Sirius, the Banū Asad

484 For more on the Kufan traditionist Ibn Abī Šaybah (d. 235/849), see "Ibn Abī Shayba," in *EI*^{2} (Ch. Pellat).

485 Abū ʿAmr Šabābah b. Sawwār al-Fazārī was a *ḥadīṯ* transmitter who died in Mecca in the year 206/821; al-Ḏahabī, *Siyar aʿlām al-nubalāʾ*, 9:513–516.

486 On Nuʿaym b. Ḥakīm (d. 148/765), see al-Ḏahabī, *Mīzān al-iʿtidāl*, 4:267.

487 Abū Maryam al-Ṯaqafī l-Madāʾinī; al-Ḏahabī, *Mīzān al-iʿtidāl*, 4:573.

488 Note the orthographic similarity between *nazawtu* (نزوت) and *nazaltu* (نزلت).

489 Muḥammad b. al-Sāʾib al-Kalbī (d. 146/763) was Ibn al-Kalbī's father; "al-Kalbī," in *EI*^{2} (W. Atallah).

490 Abū Ṣāliḥ Bāḏām, or Bāḏān, a *mawlá* of Umm Hāniʾ bt. Abī Ṭālib; Ibn Saʿd, *al-Ṭabaqāt*^{1}, 8:413.

491 Qurʾān (*al-Naml*), 27:24.

وكانت قيس تعبد الشعرى وكانت بنو أسد تعبد عطارد وكانت ربيعة تعبد المرزم وذلك قول الله تعالى ﴿أَلَمْ تَرَ أَنَّ ٱللَّهَ يَسْجُدُ لَهُۥ مَن فِي ٱلسَّمَٰوَٰتِ وَمَن فِي ٱلْأَرْضِ وَٱلشَّمْسُ وَٱلْقَمَرُ وَٱلنُّجُومُ﴾ أي إن هذا كله مسخر له.

§156 وعن مجاهد في قوله تعالى ﴿وَأَنَّهُۥ هُوَ رَبُّ ٱلشِّعْرَىٰ﴾ قال: كوكب خلف الجوزاء[a] كان يعبد.[b]

§157 وكان لسعد العشيرة صنم يقال له فَرَّاض وكانوا يعظمونه. وكان يقال لسادنه ابن وقَشَةَ وهو من بني أنس الله بن سَعْد العشيرة وكان له رَئي من الجن يخبره بما يكون فأتاه يوما وعنده رجل من بني أنس الله يقال له ذُبَابُ فأخبره بشيء فنظر إلى ذباب فقال:[c]

---

٤ ٱلشِّعْرَىٰ: شكل المقريزي هذه الكلمة كما يلي: "الشِعْرى". ٦ وكانوا يعظمونه: الزيادة بخط المقريزي في الهامش الأيمن من الأعلى إلى الأسفل + صح، ويشير إليها رمز ٢ بعد "فَرَّاض". ٨ إلى: كتب المقريزي هذه الكلمة مرتين، أولا في آخر السطر وثانيا في بداية السطر التالي وشطب الأولى فيما بعد.

---

a راجع ابن منظور، لسان العرب، "شعر" ("الشِّعْرَى: كوكب نيِّرٌ يقال له المِرْزَمُ يطلعُ بعد الجَوْزاءِ، وطلوعه في شدة الحرّ").

b راجع مقاتل، تفسير، ٣: ٢٩٤ ("قال مقاتل: الشعرى اليمانية النيرة الجنوبية كوكب مضيء، وهي التي تتبع الجوزاء، ويقال: لها المزن والعبور، كان أناس من الأعراب من خزاعة وغسان وغطفان يعبدونها، وهي الكوكب الذي يطلع بعد الجوزاء"). وراجع أيضا البيهقي، دلائل النبوة، ١: ١٨٢ ("وبلغني أن أبا كَبْشَةَ أول مَنْ عَبَدَ الشِّعْرَى وخالف دينَ قومه، فلما خالفَ النبيُّ، ﷺ، دين قريشٍ وجاءَ بالحنيفية—شَبَّهُوهُ بأَبي كَبْشَةَ ونسبوه إليه، فقالوا: ابن أَبي كَبْشَةَ").

c راجع ابن الأثير، أسد الغابة، ٢: ٢٠٨ ("روى يحيى بن هانئ بن عروة المرادي، عن أبي خيثمة عبد الرحمن بن أبي سبرة الجعفي قال: كان لسعد العشيرة صنم يقال له: فرّاص، يعظمونه، وكان سادنه رجلًا من أنس الله بن سعد العشيرة، يقال له: ابن رقبية، وقيل: وقشة. قال عبد الرحمن بن أبي سبرة: فحدثني ذباب بن الحارث، رجل من أنس الله، قال [كان] لابن رقبية، أو وقشة—على اختلاف الروايتين—رَئِيٌّ من الجن يخبره بما يكون، فأتاه ذات يوم فأخبره بشيء، فنظر إليّ فقال:").

worshipped Mercury, and Rabīʿah worshipped Bellatrix. This is [the implication of] Allāh's saying, the Exalted: "Have you not seen how to Allāh bow all who are in the heavens and all who are on the earth, the sun and the moon, the stars [and the mountains, the trees and the beasts, and many of mankind],"[492] i.e. this in its entirety is subjected to Him.

§ 156 It was reported on the authority of Muǧāhid [that the word Sirius] in His saying, the Exalted, "and that it is He who is the Lord of Sirius"[493] [refers to] a star behind al-Ǧawzāʾ[494] that was worshipped.[495]

§ 157 Saʿd al-ʿAšīrah had an idol called Farrāḍ,[496] which they venerated. Its custodian, a man named Ibn Waqšah, belonged to the Banū Anas Allāh b. Saʿd al-ʿAšīrah. He had a *ǧinnī* that was visible to him, who told him what would happen [in the future]. One day, it [the *ǧinnī*] came to him when a man of the Banū Anas Allāh named Ḏubāb[497] was present with him, and told him something. Then he [Ibn Waqšah] looked at Ḏubāb and said:

---

492 Qurʾān (*al-Ḥaǧǧ*), 22:18.

493 Qurʾān (*al-Naǧm*), 53:49.

494 On al-Ǧawzāʾ see "Minṭaḳat al-Burūdj," in *EI*² (W. Hartner-[P. Kunitzsch]).

495 Some say that Abū Kabšah of Ḫuzāʿah was the first to worship this planet; "al-Shiʿrā," in *EI*² (P. Kunitzsch).

496 Parallel sources mention the names Farrāṣ (فراص) and Qarrāḍ (قراض); Lecker (2005a): 17–18.

497 On Ḏubāb b. al-Ḥāriṯ, see Ibn al-Aṯīr, *Usd al-ġābah*, 2:208–209. See also the introduction, pp. 13–14.

يا ذباب يا ذُباب   اسمَعْ لِلعَجب العجاب
بعث الله أحمد بالكتاب   يدعو بمكة فلا يُجاب

فقال له ذباب: "ما تقول؟" فقال: "ما أدري هكذا | قال لي." قال: فلم يكن إلا قليل حتى سمعنا 42b
بظهور النبي ﷺ. فثُرْت إلى الصنم فحطمته ثم أتيت النبي ﷺ فقلت: [الطويل]

تبعت رسولَ الله إذ جاء بالهدى   وخلفت فرَّاضًا بدار هوان
شددت عليه شدة فتركته   كأن لم يكن والدهر ذو حَدَثان
فلما رأيتُ اللهَ أظهر دينَه   أجبتُ رسولَ الله حين دعاني
فأصبحتُ للإسلام ما عشتُ ناصرًا   وألقيت فيه كلكلي وجِراني
فمن مبلغ سعدَ العشيرة أنني   شرَيْت الذي يبقى بآخَر فاني[a]

§158 زعبل صنم لبني حنيفة.

§159 الجَلْسَد صنم.[b] قال: [السريع]

١ يا ذُباب ٢: الزيادة بخط المقريزي في الهامش الأيسر + صح، ويشير إليها رمز ¬ بعد "ذباب". ٤ فثُرْت ... ﷺ: الزيادة بخط المقريزي في الهامش الأيسر من الأعلى إلى الأسفل + صح، ويشير إليها رمز ¬ بعد "وسلم". ٩ يبقى: في الأصل "يبقا".

a قارن النويري، نهاية الأرب، ١٨: ١٨

("تَبِعتُ رسولَ الله إذْ جاء بالهُدى   وخَلَّفْت فَرّاضًا بِدارِ هَوانِ
شَدَدْتُ عَلَيه شَدَّةً فتركْتُه   كَأَنْ لم يكُنْ والدّهْرُ ذو حَدَثانِ
فلمّا رأيْتُ اللهَ أَظْهَرَ دينَه   أَجَبْتُ رسولَ الله حِينَ دَعَانِي
فأصبَحْتُ لِلْإِسْلامِ ما عِشْتُ ناصِرا   وأَلْقَيْتُ فيها (!) كَلْكَلِي وجِرانِي
فَمَنْ مُبلِـغٌ سَعْدَ الْعَشِيرةِ أَنَّني   شَرَيْتُ الَّذي يَبْقى بآخَرَ فانِي").

b راجع ياقوت، معجم البلدان، ٢: ١٥١ ("الجَلْسَدُ: اسم صنم كان بحضرموت ولم أجد ذكره في كتاب الأصنام لأبي المنذر هشام بن محمد الكلبي، ولكني قرأت في كتاب أبي أحمد الحسن بن عبد الله العسكري: أخبرنا ابن دُرَيْد قال أخبرني عمي الحسين بن دريد قال أَخْبرني حاتم بن قبيصة المهلّبي عن هشام بن الكلبي عن أَبي مسكين قال: كان بحضرموت صنم يسمى الجَلْسَد تعبده كندة وحضرموت").

O Ḏubāb! O Ḏubāb!
Listen to the wonder of wonders.
Allāh sent Aḥmad with the Book.
He calls in Mecca [to embrace Islam], but no one complies [with his call].

Ḏubāb then said to him: "What are you saying?" And he replied: "I do not know. This is what it [the *ǧinnī*] said to me." Not long after this we heard of the arrival of the Prophet, may Allāh bless and save him. Thereupon, I assaulted the idol, broke it, and then went to the Prophet, may Allāh bless and save him, and said: [*al-ṭawīl*]

I followed the Messenger of Allāh when he brought the right path,
and left Farrāḍ behind in an abode of disgrace.
I attacked it and abandoned it
as if it did not exist. Indeed, time begets vicissitudes.
When I saw that Allāh revealed His religion,
I complied with the Messenger of Allāh['s call] when he called me.
I became a supporter of Islam for as long as I live,
and invested my entire being in it.[498]
Who shall inform Saʿd al-ʿAšīrah that I
obtained that which is enduring in exchange for something else ephemeral?

§ 158 Zaʿbal was an idol of the Banū Ḥanīfah.[499]

§ 159 Al-Ǧalsad was an idol. [A poet][500] said:[501] [*al-sarīʿ*]

498 Lit. "I threw upon it the weight of my chest and front (or inner) part of my neck."

499 For more information on this idol, see Lecker (forthcoming).

500 Some say that the poet's name was al-Muṯaqqib al-ʿAbdī, while others say that it was ʿAdī b. Wadāʿ (or b. al-Riqāʿ); Ibn Manẓūr, *Lisān al-ʿarab*, s.v. *bayqara*, Ǧalsad.

501 The full line is recorded in Ibn Manẓūr, *Lisān al-ʿarab*, s.v. *bayqara*.

(...) كما   يبْقَر من يمشي إلى الجلْسَدِ[a]

يعني بقوله يبْقَر أي مشى منكسا رأسه.

§160 حُمَام صنم كان لبني عُذرة وكانوا يعظمونه وكان في بني هند بن حرام بن ضنة بن عبد بن كبير بن عذرة وكانوا يعْتِرون عنده.[b]

§161 عَوْض صَنَم لبكر بن وائل كلها. قال رجل من عَنَزَةَ قديم: [الوافر]

---

٣ حُمَام: وضع المقريزي رمز "ح" تحت الكلمة إشارة إلى تلفظها بالحاء.   ٥ بن وائل: الزيادة بخط المقريزي في الهامش الأيسر من الأسفل إلى الأعلى + صح، ويشير إليها رمز ˥ بعد "لبكر".

---

a راجع ابن منظور، لسان العرب، "بقر" ("والبيْقَرَةُ: إسراع يطأطئ الرجل فيه رأسه، قال المثَقِّبُ العَبْدِيّ، ويروى لِعَدِيّ بن وَدَاع:
فَبَاتَ يَجْتابُ شُقَارَى، كما   بيْقَرَ مَنْ يَمْشِي إلى الجلْسَدِ
وشُقَارَى، مخفف من شُقَّارَى: نبت، خففه للضرورة، ورواه أبو حنيفة في كتابه النبات: من يمشي إلى الخلَصَة، قال: والخلَصَةُ الوَثَنُ، وقد تقدم في فصل جسد"). وقارن ابن منظور، لسان العرب، "جلسد" ("والجلْسَد: صنم كان يُعبد في الجاهلية؛ قال:
.... كما   كَبَّرَ مَنْ يَمْشِي إلى الجلْسَد").

b راجع ابن عساكر، تاريخ مدينة دمشق، ١١: ٤٨٩-٤٩٠ ("حَدثني أبي عَن أبيه عَن جده عن زمل بن عَمْرو العُذري، قال: كان لبني عذرة صنمٌ يقال له حمام وكانوا يعظمونه، وكان في بني هند بن حَرَام بن ضِنَّة بن عَبْد بن كبير بن عُذرة، كان سادنه رَجُلًا يقال له طَارق، وكان يَعْتِرُون عنده").

[…] as those who
approach al-Ǧalsad walk while stooping their heads (*bayqara*).

The verb *bayqara* means: He walked while stooping his head.[502]

§ 160 Ḥumām was an idol which belonged to the Banū ʿUḏrah, and which they used to venerate. It was in [the territory of] the Banū Hind b. Ḥarām b. Ḍinnah b. ʿAbd b. Kabīr b. ʿUḏrah, and they used to sacrifice [their sheep or goats] beside it.[503]

§ 161 ʿAwḍ was an idol that belonged to the Bakr b. Wāʾil in their entirety.[504] A man of ʿAnazah who lived in ancient times said:[505] [*al-wāfir*]

502 For more information on al-Ǧalsad, see Lecker (forthcoming); Wellhausen (1897): 53–56.

503 Regarding this idol, see Lecker (2005a): 7–8.

504 I.e. it belonged to all the sub-tribes of the Bakr b. Wāʾil.

505 Or, an old man of ʿAnazah (*raǧul min ʿAnazah qadīm*). Note that the following verse is attributed elsewhere to Rušayd b. Rumayḍ al-ʿAnzī (i.e. of ʿAnz b. Wāʾil) or al-ʿAnazī (i.e. of ʿAnazah).

حَلَفتُ بمائرَاتٍ حول عَوْضٍ وأنْصَابٍ تُرِكْنَ لدى السُعَيْر
أَجُوبُ الدهرَ أَرضًا شطرَ عُمري ولَا يَلقَى مِسَاحَتَها بعيري[a]

وقال الأعشى: [البسيط]

لا أعْرِفَنَّكَ إن جدَّت عداوتُنا والتُمِسَ النَصْر منكم عَوْضُ واحْتَمِلوا[b]

٥ عَوْضُ بالضَّم قسَم واحْتُمِلَ الرجل غضب.

---

١ حَلَفتُ : وضع المقريزي رمز "ح" تحت الكلمة إشارة إلى تلفظها بالحاء. ‖ بمائرَاتٍ : وضع المقريزي رمز "ك" (يعني "كذا") إشارة إلى شكه في القراءة الصحيحة. ‖ لدى : في الأصل "لدا". ٤ واحْتَمِلوا : كتب المقريزي هذه الكلمة في الهامش الأيسر في نهاية السطر بجانب كلمة "عَوْضُ".

---

٣ وقال : وضع المقريزي رمز "ح" (يعني "حاشية") فوق هذه الكلمة ولكن لا توجد أي حاشية في الهامش. ٤ لا : وضع المقريزي رمز "ح" (يعني "حاشية") فوق هذه الكلمة وكتب الحاشية على السطر التالي. ٥ عَوْضُ ... غضب : وضع المقريزي رمز "ح" (يعني "حاشية") فوق هذه الكلمة ووضع كلمة "الى" (يعني "الى هناك") إشارة إلى أول الحاشية وآخرها.

---

a قارن البكري، معجم ما استعجم، ١: ٨٤
("أُجوبُ الدَّهْرَ أرضا شَطْرَ عمرٍو ولا يُلْفَى بسَاحَتِها بَعِيري").
وقارن أيضا: البغدادي، خزانة الأدب، ٧: ١٤١
("أَجوبُ الأَرْضَ دهرًا إِثرِ عمرٍو ولا يُلقَى بساحتِه بَعِيري").

b قارن التبريزي، شرح، ٥٠٣
("لَا أَعْرِفَنَّكَ إنْ جَدَّتْ عَدَاوتُنَا وَالتُمِس النَّصْرُ مِنْكُمْ عَوْضُ تُحْتَمَلُ
... عوضُ: اسمٌ للدهر، ويروى عَوْضَ—بفتح الضاد—مثل حيثُ وحيثَ، يقول: لا أعرفَنّكَ إن التُمِسَ النَّصرُ منك دهرك، واحتمل القوم: احتملتهم الحَمِيَّةُ والحربُ، أي أُغْضِبوا، ويروى «واحْتَملوا» أي ذهبوا من الحمية أو الغيظ، وتَحتَمل: أي تذهب وتخلّي قومك"). وقارن أيضا الأعشى، ديوان شعر الأعشى، ٤٦
("لأعرِفنَّكَ (!) إنْ جدّتْ عداوَتُنَا وَالتُمِس النّصرُ منكُمْ عوضُ تُحْتَمَلُ
وَرَوَى أَبو عُبَيْدَةَ عَوْضُ تَحْتَمِلُ وَعَوْضَ تَحْتَمِلُوا. أَبُو عَمْرٍو: [احْتُمِلَ] الرَّجُلُ أُغْضِبَ. وَمَنْ رَوَى تَحْتَمِلُ أَرادَ تَذْهَبُ وَتُخَلِّي قَوْمَكَ").

I swore by streams of blood flowing around ʿAwḍ,
and by stones (*anṣāb*) that were left beside al-Suʿayr[506]
that I shall never cross a land during any part of my life,[507]
and that my camel will never set foot in [lit. encounter, or meet] its area [i.e. of this land].[508]

Al-Aʿšá said: [*al-basīṭ*]

I swear I shall never (*ʿawḍu*) acknowledge you [masc. sg.] if our animosity is serious
and aid is requested from you [masc. pl.] and they become angry (*wa-ḥtumilū*).[509]

[The word] *ʿawḍu* with [the vowel] *ḍammah* [on the final letter] is used in oaths.[510] *Uḥtumila l-rağul* means: He [the man (*al-rağul*)] became angry.

506 This line is also translated in Lane (1863–1893): 2744; Wellhausen (1897): 66. The idol's name is vocalized "al-Suʿayr" in the text, but the word *baʿīr* (camel) at the end of the second line may suggest that the reading "al-Saʿīr" is preferable. For the different vocalizations of this idol's name, see Wellhausen (1897): 61; "al-Suʿayr," in *EI*[2] (T. Fahd).

507 *Šaṭra ʿamrī*. The word *šaṭr* means "half," "part," or "direction." *Muʿğam mā staʿğama* has *šaṭra ʿamrin* (ʿAmr as a proper name; al-Bakrī, *Muʿğam mā staʿğama*, 1:84) which should perhaps be understood as "in the direction of ʿAmr."

508 Compare al-Bakrī, *Muʿğam mā staʿğama*, 1:84: "and that my camel will not be found in its area" (*wa-lā yulfá bi-sāḥatihā baʿīrī*).

509 For the variants of this verse, see Geyer (1928): 49. A variant of this line is also quoted in Ullmann (1970–2004), 2/3:1372.

510 The word *ʿawḍu* in this verse does not seem to relate directly to the idol named ʿAwḍ. Perhaps the supposition is that the oath *ʿawḍu* is derived from the proper name ʿAwḍ. See also Robertson Smith (1907): 61: "And this seems to be correct, i.e., the particle عوض is simply a shortened form of the oath by the deity, ʿAuḍ, which must therefore have been widely spread"; Robertson Smith (1972): 43. See also Fahd (1968): 48. On *ʿawḍu* as an oath, see Lane (1863–1893): 2197.

§162 السَقْبُ من ولد الناقة الذكَر ولا يقال للأنثى سَقْبَة. وكان لبني بكر بن وائل بن قاسط بن أفْصَى بن دعمي سَقْب يعبدونه فأغار عليهم عمرو بن حبيب بن عمرو بن شيبان بن محارب بن فهر ابن مالك بن النَضْر بن كنانة فأخذ السقب الذي يعبدونه فأكله فقيل له آكِلُ السَّقْبِ لذلك.[a]

٢ بن دعمي: الزيادة بخط المقريزي في الهامش الأيسر من الأسفل إلى الأعلى ويشير إليها رمز ٦ بعد "أفْصَى".

a راجع ابن عساكر، مختصر تاريخ دمشق، ١١: ١٥٦ ("ضرار بن الخطاب بن مرداس بن كبير بن عمرو بن حبيب بن عمرو بن شيبان بن محارب بن فهر بن مالك بن النضر بن كنانة، الفهري له صحبة. أسلم يوم فتح مكة، وشهد مع أبي عبيدة فتوح الشام. وكان ضرار يوم الفجار على بني محارب بن فهر، وكان أبوه خطاب بن مرداس يأخذ المرباع. وهو الذي غزا بني سليم، وهو رئيس بن فهر. وجده عمرو بن حبيب هو آكل السَّقْب. وذلك أنه أغار على بني بكر، ولهم سَقْب يعبدونه، فأخذ السَّقب فأكله").

§162 *Saqb* is the male offspring of a she-camel. The female is not called *saqbah*. The Banū Bakr b. Wā'il b. Qāsiṭ b. Afṣá b. Du'mī had a *saqb* that they worshipped. [One day,] 'Amr b. Ḥabīb b. 'Amr b. Šaybān b. Muḥārib b. Fihr b. Mālik b. al-Naḍr b. Kinānah[511] raided them, took the *saqb* that they worshipped, and ate it; therefore he ['Amr] was nicknamed "the *saqb* eater."

511 'Amr b. Ḥabīb b. 'Amr was the great-great grandfather of the poet Ḍirār b. al-Ḫaṭṭāb b. Mirdās b. Kaṯīr/Kabīr b. 'Amr, who was one of the Prophet's Companions; Ibn 'Asākir, *Muḫtaṣar Ta'rīḫ Dimašq*, 11:156. See also Caskel (1966), 1: table 34.

§163 قال الله تبٰرك وتعالى ﴿أَلَمْ تَرَ إِلَى ٱلَّذِينَ أُوتُوا نَصِيبًا مِنَ ٱلْكِتَابِ يُؤْمِنُونَ بِٱلْجِبْتِ وَٱلطَّاغُوتِ وَيَقُولُونَ لِلَّذِينَ كَفَرُوا هٰؤُلَاءِ أَهْدَى مِنَ ٱلَّذِينَ آمَنُوا سَبِيلًا﴾. يعني تعالى بذلك اليهود. ونزلت هذه الآية في كعب بن الأشرف وحُيَيّ بن أخطب لما لقيا قريشا فقال لهما المشركون:[a] "أنحن أهدى أم محمد وأصحابه؟ فإنا أهل السِّدَانَة والسِقَاية وأهل الحرَم." فقالا: "بل أنتم أهدى من محمد"، وهما يعلمان أنهما كاذبان وإنما حملهما على ذلك الحسد. فأنزل الله تعالى هذه الآية. فعن ابن عباس رضي الله عنه أنه قال: الجبت الأصنام والطاغوت تراجمة الأصنام.[b]

§164 وعن مجاهد وابن زيد: الجبت السِحْر والطاغوت الشيطان.

وعن سعيد بن جبير: الجبت الساحر والطاغوت الكاهن.

وعن الضحاك: الجبت حُيَي بن أخطب والطاغوت كعب بن الأشرف.

وقال الزجاج: كل ما عُبد من دون الله فهو جبت وطاغوت.

---

٢ بِٱلْجِبْتِ: شكل المقريزي الكلمة كما يلي: "بالجِبْتِ". ٣ أَهْدَى: شكل المقريزي الكلمة كما يلي: "اهْدَى". ٤ وحُيَيّ: وضع المقريزي رمز "ح" تحت الكلمة إشارة إلى تلفظها بالحاء. ٨ السِحْر: وضع المقريزي رمز "ح" تحت الكلمة إشارة إلى تلفظها بالحاء.

---

a قارن الطبري، جامع البيان، ٧: ١٤٦-١٤٧ ("ذُكِر لنا أن هذه الآيةَ أُنْزِلَتْ في كعبِ بنِ الأشرفِ وحُيَيِّ بنِ أخطبَ ورجُلَيْن مِن اليهودِ من بني النضيرِ، لَقِيا قريشًا بمَوسمٍ، فقال لهم المشركون").

b راجع الثعلبي، الكشف والبيان، ٣: ٣٢٦-٣٢٧ ("عطية عن ابن عباس: الجبت: الأصنام، والطاغوت: تراجمة الأصنام الذين يكونون بين أيديهم يفترون عنها الكذب ليضلوا النّاس"). وراجع ابن عطية، المحرر الوجيز، ٤: ٩٩ ("وقال ابن عباس: الجبت: الأَصنام، والطاغوت: القوم المترجمون عن الأصنام الذين يضلون الناس بتعليمهم إياهم عبادة الأَصنام").

 | DOI:10.1163/9789004499867_007

Section on *al-ǧibt* and *al-ṭāġūt*

§ 163 Allāh, the Blessed and Exalted, said: "Have you not regarded those who were given a share of the Book believing in demons and idols (*bi-l-ǧibt wa-l-ṭāġūt*), and saying to the unbelievers, 'These are more rightly guided on the way than the believers.'"[512] By that [i.e. those referred to in the verse, Allāh], the Exalted, meant the Jews. This verse was revealed regarding Kaʿb b. al-Ašraf[513] and Ḥuyayy b. Aḫṭab.[514] They met the Qurayš, and the polytheists asked them: "Are we more rightly guided or are Muḥammad and his Companions [more rightly guided]? We are the custodians of the Kaʿbah, those who provide the pilgrims with water, and we are the people of the sacred territory of Mecca." They [Kaʿb and Ḥuyayy] said: "You are more rightly guided than Muḥammad," even though they knew that they were lying. It was just envy that made them say this. Thereupon, Allāh, the Exalted, revealed this verse. It was reported on the authority of Ibn ʿAbbās, may Allāh be pleased with him, that *al-ǧibt* means idols (*al-aṣnām*) and *al-ṭāġūt* means the 'interpreters' of the idols (*tarāǧimat al-aṣnām*).[515]

§ 164 On the authority of Muǧāhid and Ibn Zayd:[516] *Al-ǧibt* refers to sorcery and *al-ṭāġūt* applies to Satan.

On the authority of Saʿīd b. Ǧubayr: *Al-ǧibt* is a sorcerer and *al-ṭāġūt* is a soothsayer.

On the authority of al-Ḍaḥḥāk:[517] *Al-ǧibt* is Ḥuyayy b. Aḫṭab and *al-ṭāġūt* is Kaʿb b. al-Ašraf.

Al-Zaǧǧāǧ[518] said: Anything that was worshipped apart from Allāh is *ǧibt* and *ṭāġūt*.

---

512 Qurʾān (*al-Nisāʾ*), 4:51.

513 Kaʿb b. al-Ašraf was a poet who recited verses against the Prophet and incited the tribe of Qurayš against the Muslims. He was assassinated in Medina by members of the Aws. Kaʿb's mother belonged to the Jewish tribe of al-Naḍīr, and his father was a member of Nabhān (Ṭayyiʾ); "Kaʿb b. al-As̲h̲raf," in *EI*² (W.M. Watt).

514 Ḥuyayy b. Aḫṭab of the Banū l-Naḍīr was one of the Prophet's adversaries in Medina. He was executed with the men of the tribe of Qurayẓah, and following the fall of Ḫaybar, his daughter, Ṣafiyyah, became one of the Prophet's wives.

515 That is, oracles who speak on behalf of the idol and lead people astray.

516 ʿAbd al-Raḥmān b. Zayd b. Aslam (d. 182/798); Ibn Ḥaǧar, *Tahḏīb al-tahḏīb*, 6:162–163.

517 For more on the Qurʾānic commentator al-Ḍaḥḥāk b. Muzāḥim al-Hilālī (d. ca. 105/723), see al-Ḏahabī, *Siyar aʿlām al-nubalāʾ*, 4:598–600.

518 The grammarian Abū Isḥāq Ibrāhīm b. al-Sarī l-Zaǧǧāǧ (d. 311/923); see "al-Zad̲j̲d̲j̲ād̲j̲," in *EI*² (C.H.M. Versteegh).

وقال قطرب: الجبت الجِبْش وهو الذي لا خير عنده قلبت الشين تاء.[a]

وقال الراغب: الجبت والطاغوت في الأصل اسمان لصنمين ثم صارا يستعملان في كل باطل ولذلك قيل ما عُبد من دون الله فهو طاغوت ولذلك فسر مرة بالصنم ومرة بالشيطان ومرة بالسِحْر ومرة بكل ما {يُعْبد} من دون الله.[b]

وقال الرازي: وهما كلمتان وضعتا لمن كان في غاية في الشر والفساد.[c]

وقال الماتريدي: والطاغوت مشتق من الطغيان. سمي بذلك كل من انتهى في الطغيان غايته حتى استجاز أن يعبد دون الله.[d]

وقال ابن سِيْدَةَ: والطاغوت ما عبد من دون الله عز وجل. يقع على الواحد والجميع والمذكر

---

٣ بالسِحْر: وضع المقريزي رمز "ح" تحت الكلمة إشارة إلى تلفظها بالحاء. ٤ يُعْبد: في الأصل "يُعْيد".

---

a قارن ابن عطية، المحرر الوجيز، ٤: ١٠٠ ("وذكر بعض الناس أن الجبت هو من لغة الحبشة، وقال قطرب: الجبت: أصله الجبس، وهو الثقيل الذي لا خير عنده"). وقارن أيضا ابن منظور، لسان العرب، "جبس" ("الجِبْس: الجَبانُ الفَدْمُ، وقيل: الضعيف اللئيم، وقيل: الثقيل الذي لا يجيب إلى خير، والجمع أَجْباسٌ وجُبُوسٌ").

b قارن الراغب الإصفهاني، تفسير، ٤: ١٢٧٢–١٢٧٣ ("الجبت والطاغوت: في الأصل اسمان لصنمين، ثم صارا يستعملان في كُل باطل، ولذلك قيل: ما عُبِدَ من دون الله فهو طاغوت، ولذلك فُسِّر مرة بالصنم، ومرّة بالشيطان، ومرّة بالسحر، ومرّة بكل معظّم من دون الله").

c قارن الرازي، مفاتيح الغيب، ١٠: ١٣٣ ("وبالجملة فالأقاويل كثيرة، وهما كلمتان وضعتا علمين على من كان غاية في الشر والفساد").

d راجع الماتريدي، التأويلات، ١: ٤٣٤ ("الطّاغُوتُ: هو اسْمٌ مُشْتَقٌّ مِنَ الطُّغْيانِ كالرَّحَمُوتِ والرَّهَبوتِ مِنَ الرَّحْمَةِ والرَّهْبَةِ ونحو ذلكَ سُمِّيَ بِهِ كلُّ مَنِ انْتَهى مِن الطُّغيانِ غايَتَهُ حتى اسْتَحَلَّ أَنْ يُعْبَدَ هو دُونَ اللهِ، فهو طاغوتٌ"). وراجع أيضا الرازي، مفاتيح الغيب، ١٠: ١٣٢ ("وأما طاغوت فإنه مأخوذ من الطغيان، وهو الاسراف في المعصية، فكل من دعا إلى المعاصي الكبار لزمه هذا الاسم، ثم توسعوا في هذا الاسم حتى أوقعوه على الجماد").

Quṭrub[519] said: *Al-ǧibt* is *al-ǧibš* [read: *al-ǧibs*], which means he who [or that which] has no good in him [or it].[520] The letter *šīn* [read: *sīn*] was changed into *tāʾ*.

Al-Rāġib[521] said: *Al-ǧibt* and *al-ṭāġūt* are originally the names of two idols, but then they came to denote every false object [of worship]. For this reason, it was said that what was worshipped apart from Allāh is a *ṭāġūt*, and for this reason it was interpreted sometimes as an idol, sometimes as Satan, sometimes as sorcery, and sometimes as anything that is worshipped apart from Allāh.

Al-Rāzī[522] said: They are two words that were used to denote those who were extremely evil and corrupt.

Al-Māturīdī[523] said: [The word] *al-ṭāġūt* derives from *al-ṭuġyān*;[524] it applies to anyone whose *ṭuġyān* has reached such a level that he thought it was permissible to be worshipped apart from Allāh.[525]

Ibn Sīdah said: *Al-ṭāġūt* signifies what was worshipped apart from Allāh, the Great and Mighty. It refers to the singular, plural, masculine, and femin-

---

519 Quṭrub is the cognomen of the grammarian and lexicographer Muḥammad b. al-Mustanīr, who died in Baghdad in 206/821; see "Ḳuṭrub," in *EI*² (G. Troupeau).

520 See also Lane (1863–1893): 373: "الجِبْتُ ... said to be originally الجِبْسُ, i.e., (Bḍ,) he, or that, wherein is no good." And see Jeffery (1938): 99: "It was generally agreed that it was an Arabic word, Baiḍ., e.g., claiming that it was a dialectal form of جبس, a theory that was taken up by Rāghib, *Mufradāt*, and others."

521 On Abū l-Qāsim al-Ḥusayn b. Muḥammad, al-Rāġib al-Iṣfahānī, who died in the early 5th/11th century, see "al-Rāghib al-Iṣfahānī," in *EI*² (E.K. Rowson).

522 Abū ʿAbd Allāh Muḥammad b. ʿUmar, known as Faḫr al-Dīn al-Rāzī (d. 606/1209); "Fakhr al-Dīn al-Rāzī," in *EI*² (G.C. Anawati).

523 Abū Manṣūr al-Samarqandī l-Māturīdī (d. ca. 333/944); "al-Māturīdī," in *EI*² (W. Madelung).

524 The root *ṭġw/y* has the general meaning of "exceeding the limit," particularly with regard to disobedience, infidelity, and wrongdoing; see Lane (1863–1893): 1856–1857; "Ṭāghūt," in *EI*² (T. Fahd).

525 Cf. al-Māturīdī, *Taʾwīlāt*, 1:434: *ḥattá staḥalla an yuʿbada huwa dūna llāhi.*

والمؤنث. وزنه فَعَلُوت. إنما هو طَيَغُوْت[a] قُدِمَت الياء قبل الغين وهي مفتوحة وقبلها فتحة فقلبت أَلِفًا.[b]

§165 وقال ابن إسحق: وكانت العرب قد اتخذت مع الكعبة طواغيت وهي بيوت تعظمها كتعظيم الكعبة | لها سدنة وحجاب وتُهْدي لها كما تهدي إلى الكعبة وتطوف بها كطوافها بها 43b وتنحر عندها وهي تعرف فضل الكعبة عليها لأنها قد عرفت أنها بيت إبرٰهيم ومسجده.

§166 فكانت لقريش وبني كنانة العُزَّى في نخلة على {خمسة} فراسخ من مكة وكانت ثلاث سمرات. وأول من دعا إلى عبادتها عمرو بن لحي والحٰرث بن كعب. فقال له عمرو: "إن ربكم كان يتصيف {باللات} بالطائف لبردها ويشتو بالعزى التي بتهامة." وكان في كل واحدة منها شيطان.[c] وكان سدنتها وحجابها بني شيبان من سُلَيم حلفاء بني هاشم. قال ابن هشام: حُلفاء أبي طالب خاصة.[d]

---

٢ أَلِفًا: هذه إحدى الحالات النادرة التي تُكتب فيها الهمزة. ٦–٨ على ... شيطان: الزيادة بخط المقريزي في الهامش الأيمن ويشير إليها رمز ⌐ بعد "بنخلة". ٦ خمسة: في الأصل "خمس". ٨ باللات: كتب المقريزي هذه الكلمة في المكان غير الصحيح بعد "إن ربكم". ‖ ويشتو: في الأصل "ويشتوا". ‖ بالعُزى: في الأصل "بالعُزا".

---

a راجع ابن سيدة، المحكم، ٦:٤٣؛ قارن ابن منظور، لسان العرب، "طغي" ("والطاغوتُ، يقعُ على الواحد والجمع والمذكر والمؤنث: وزْنُه فَعَلُوتٌ إنما هو طَغَيُوتٌ، قُدِّمتِ الياءُ قبل الغَيْن، وهي مفتوحة وقبلها فَتْحَةٌ فَقُلِبَتْ أَلِفًا").

b وقارن الخازن، تفسير، ١: ٣٨٩ ("وقيل هما صنمان كانا لقريش وهما اللذان سجد اليهود لهما لمرضاة قريش").

c قارن الأزرقي، أخبار مكة[١]، ١: ١٩٨ ("وكان أول من دعا إلى عبادتهما عمرو بن ربيعة والحارث بن كعب. وقال لهم عمرو: إن ربكم يتصيّف [باللات] لبرد الطائف، ويشتو بالعُزّى لحرّ تهامة، وكان في كل واحدة شيطان يعبد"). وقارن أيضا الأزرقي، أخبار مكة[١]، ١: ١٩٩ ("قال الكلبي: وكانت اللات والعُزّى ومَنَاة في كل واحدة منهنّ شيطانة تكلّمهم").

d قارن ابن حبيب، المحبر، ٣١٥ ("وكانت العزى شجرة بنخلة عندها وثن تعبدها غطفان. سدنتها من بني صِرمة بن مرة").

ine.[526] Its pattern is *faʿalūt*. The form is *ṭayaġūt*,[527] in which the *yāʾ* precedes the *ġayn* [after changing the original form *ṭaġayūt* to *ṭayaġūt*], and since it [the letter *yāʾ*] was vocalized with a *fatḥah* and preceded by a *fatḥah*, it was changed into an *alif* [*ṭayaġūt* to *ṭāġūt*].[528]

§165 Ibn Isḥāq said: Along with the Kaʿbah, the Arabs adopted *ṭawāġīt*, which were sanctuaries that they venerated in the same manner they venerated the Kaʿbah. They had custodians and guardians, and they [i.e. the Arabs] also brought gifts to them [to the *ṭawāġīt*] as they brought gifts to the Kaʿbah, circumambulated them [the *ṭawāġīt*] as they circumambulated it, and slaughtered [sacrificial animals] beside them. Yet they acknowledged the superiority of the Kaʿbah over them, since they knew that it was Abraham's sanctuary and mosque.

§166 Al-ʿUzzá belonged to the Qurayš and the Banū Kinānah, [and it was located] in Naḫlah,[529] at a distance of five *farsaḫs* [ca. 30 kilometers] from Mecca. It was three *samurah* [acacia] trees. The first who summoned to worship it were ʿAmr b. Luḥayy and al-Ḥāriṯ b. Kaʿb. ʿAmr told him: "Your lord spent the summer at Allāt in al-Ṭāʾif for its cool weather, and during the winter he stayed at al-ʿUzzá which is in Tihāmah."[530] There was a devil inside each one of them. Its custodians and guardians were the Banū Šaybān of Sulaym,[531] who were allies of the Banū Hāšim. Ibn Hišām said: In particular [they were] allies of Abū Ṭālib.

526 See for instance Qurʾān (*al-Baqarah*), 2:257, where *ṭāġūt* is masculine plural, and Qurʾān (*al-Zumar*), 39:17, where the feminine singular pronoun in the verb *yaʿbudūhā* refers to this word; Hawting (1999): 55–56.

527 Ibn Manẓūr, *Lisān al-ʿarab*, s.v. *ṭāġūt* has *ṭaġayūt* (of the pattern *faʿalūt*).

528 For the various explanations concerning the origin of the word *ṭāġūt*, see Lane (1863–1893): 1857; Jeffery (1938): 202–203.

529 Naḫlah is the name of two valleys on the road between Mecca and al-Ṭāʾif; "Nakhla," in *EI*² (W.M. Watt); Lecker (1989): 39–41.

530 Compare al-Azraqī, *Aḫbār Makkah*¹, 1:198: "and during the winter he stayed at al-ʿUzzá because of the warmth of Tihāmah." See also Wellhausen (1897): 45.

531 Regarding the custodians of al-ʿUzzá, see Lecker (1989): 38, 42.

§167 قال ابن إسحٰق: وقال شاعر من العرب: [الطويل]

لقد أُنكحَت أسماءُ رأسَ بُقَيْرةٍ من الأُدْم أهداها امرؤ من بني غَنْم
رأى قَدَعًا في عَينها إذ يَسوقها إلى غبْغَب العُزى فوسعَ في القَسْم[a]

وكذلك كانوا يصنعون إذا نحروا هديا قسموه فيمن حضرهم. والغبغب المنحر مُهْراق الدماء. قال ابن هشام: هاذان البيتان لأبي خراش الهذلي واسمه خويلد بن مرة في أبيات له. والسَدَنة الذين يقومون بأمر الكعبة.

§168 وقال عمر بن شبة: كانت العُزّى بنخلة بواد منها يقال له حراض تعظمها كل العرب وكانت سدانتها وهي حجابتها إلى بني {شيبان} من حلفاء بني هاشم. ولها يقول زيد بن عمرو بن نفيل: [الوافر]

---

٧ حراض: وضع المقريزي رمز "ح" تحت الكلمة إشارة إلى تلفظها بالحاء. ٨ شيبان: في الأصل "شبيل".

٨ شيبان: أضاف المقريزي الحاشية التالية في الهامش الأيمن من الأعلى إلى الأسفل: "شبيل بن عجلان بن عتاب بن مالك بن كعب بن عمرو بن سعد بن عوف بن قسي وهو ثقيف."

---

a قارن ابن الكلبي، الأصنام، ٢٠ ("فله يقول الهُذَليُّ وهو يهجو رجُلا تزوّج امرأةً جميلةً يقال لها أسماءُ:

لقد أُنْكِحَتْ أسماءُ لَحْيَ بُقَيْرَةٍ من الأُدْمِ أهداها امْرُؤٌ من بني غَنْم!
رأى قَذَعًا في عينها إذ يَسُوقُها إلى غَبْغَبِ العُزَّى فوضَّعَ في القَسْمِ.

فكانوا يقسِمون لُحومَ هداياهم فيمن حضرها وكان عندها"). وقارن أيضا الزمخشري، الفائق، ٣: ٧٤ ("قَالَ الْهُذَلِيّ:

رأى قَدَعًا فِي عَيْنِها حين قُرِّبَتْ إلى غَبْغَبِ العُزَّى فنصَّفَ فِي القَسْم

وهو من قَدَعته؛ أي كففته وردعه فَقَدِع؛ لِأَن المرتدع مُنْخَزِلٌ ضَعِيف"). وراجع السهيلي، الروض الأنف، ١: ٣٦٥–٣٦٨ ("رأى قَدَعًا في عَيْنِها. والْقَدَع: ضَعف البصر من إدمان النظر. وقوله في الْغَبْغَب: وهو الْمَنْحر ومراق الدم، كأنه سُمِّي بحكاية صوتِ الدم عند انبعاثِه، ويجوز أن يكون مقلوبًا من قولهم: بئر بُغْبُغٌ وبُغَيْبِـغٌ إذا كانت كثيرة الماء. قال الراجز: بُغَيْبِـغٌ قصيرةُ الرِشاءِ. ومنه قيل لعين أبي نَيْزَر: البُغَيْبِغَةُ. ومعنى هذا البيت: الذَّمُّ وتشبيهُ هذا الْمَهْجُوِّ برأسِ بقرةٍ قد قربت أن يذهب بصرُها، فلا تصلح إلا للذبح والقسم").

§167 Ibn Isḥāq said that an Arab poet said: [*al-ṭawīl*]

Asmāʾ was given in marriage to a head of a small reddish cow
that a man of the Banū Ġanm had offered as sacrifice.
He saw the weakening of the sight in her [the cow's] eye as he led her [the cow]
to the Ġabġab of al-ʿUzzá, and was generous in the distribution [of her meat].[532]

When slaughtering [animals] as sacrificial offerings, it was their practice to divide [the meat] among those present. [The word] *ġabġab* denotes a place where sacrificial animals are slaughtered. It is a place where blood pours out.[533]

Ibn Hišām said: These two verses were composed by Abū Ḫirāš al-Huḏalī,[534] whose name is Ḫuwaylid b. Murrah. [They appear] among [other] verses that he composed.[535] The custodians are those who take care of the Kaʿbah.

§168 ʿUmar b. Šabbah said: Al-ʿUzzá was in one of the valleys of Naḫlah, which was called Ḥurāḍ. It was venerated by all of the Arabs. Its custodianship (*sidānatuhā*), i.e. its guardianship (*ḥiǧābatuhā*), belonged to the Banū Šaybān, who were allies of the Banū Hāšim. Zayd b. ʿAmr b. Nufayl said, referring to it: [*al-wāfir*]

19 Šaybān : Šubayl b. ʿAǧlān b. ʿAttāb b. Mālik b. Kaʿb b. ʿAmr b. Saʿd b. ʿAwf b. Qasī, who [= Qasī] is Ṯaqīf (marginal gloss in al-Maqrīzī's hand in reference to the word Šubayl in the manuscript, which was corrected to Šaybān). The custodians of al-ʿUzzá belonged to the tribe of Sulaym. As for the Banū Šubayl b. ʿAǧlān, some say that they were custodians of Allāt. See Crone (2016): 441, n. 118.

532 For a translation of parallel versions of these lines, see Klinke-Rosenberger (1941): 40, 99, n. 154; Grunebaum (1953): 44; Ibn Hišām, *The Life of Muhammad* 38; Atallah (1969): 15.

533 See Lane (1863–1893): 2222: "غبغب ... A place where victims are sacrificed."

534 On whom see above, note 218.

535 I.e., they are a part of a longer poem. See Ibn Hišām, *The Life of Muhammad* 702. The verses are found in the *mulḥaqāt* (appendices) of the *dīwān* of Abū Ḫirāš; Hell (1933), 2:78 (Arabic text, poem no. 39, verses 7–8).

تركت اللات والعُزى جميعا   كذلك يفعل الجلد الصبور
فلا العزى أَدِيْنُ ولا ابنتيها   ولا أُطمي بني طسم أدور
ولا غنما أزور وكان ربا   لنا في الدهر إذ حلمي صغير[a]

§169 قال أبو غسان: وأخبرت أن سعيد بن العاص أبا أحيحة مرض فأتاه أبو لهب عائدا له فوجده يبكي فقال له: "ما يبكيك؟ أمن الموت؟" قال: "لا ولكن أخاف أن لا تُعبَد العزى بعدي." قال أبو لهب: "والله ما عبدت لحياتك ولا تترك لموتك." فقال سعيد: "الآن علمت أن لها من يمنعها بعدي." قال: وأعجبه قول أبي لهب.[b] وبعث إليها رسول الله ﷺ خالد بن الوليد بن المغيرة المخزومي يهدمها فلما جاءها هدم منها ثم انصرف. فقال له رسول الله ﷺ: "ما فعلت؟" قال: "هدمتها." قال:

---

١ تركت ... الصبور: الزيادة بخط المقريزي في الهامش الأيسر من الأسفل إلى الأعلى في آخر السطر وبجانب كلمة "نفيل". ٣ ولا ... صغير: الزيادة بخط المقريزي في آخر السطر وفي الهامش الأيسر من الأعلى إلى الأسفل. ٤ أحيحة: وضع المقريزي رمز "ح" تحت الكلمة إشارة إلى تلفظها بالحاء.

---

٢ فلا ... أدور: أضاف المقريزي الحاشية التالية في الهامش الأيمن أمام البيت الثاني ووضع فوق الكلمة الأولى رمز "خ" (يعني "نسخة أخرى"): "فلا العزى أدين ولا ابنتيها ولا صنمي بني طسم أزور."

---

a قارن الزبير بن بكار، جمهرة نسب قريش، ١: ٢٥٤
("عَزَلْتُ الجِنَّ والجنَّان عَني   كذلك يفعَلُ الجَلْدُ الصَّبُورُ
فلا العُزَّى أَدِينُ ولَا ابنتيها   ولا أُطُمَيْ بَنِي طَسْمٍ أُدِيرُ
ولا غَنْمَا أَدِينُ وكان رَبًّا   لنا في الدَّهرِ إذْ حِلْمِي صغيرُ")
وقارن ابن الكلبي، الأصنام، ٢٢
("فلا العُزَّى أَدِينُ ولا ابنتَيْهَا   ولا صَنَمَيْ بني غَنْمٍ أَزُورُ
ولا هُبَلا أَزورُ وكانَ رَبًّا   لنا في الدهرِ إذْ حِلْمِي صَغيرُ")

b قارن ابن الكلبي، الأصنام، ٢٣ ("قال أبو لهب: "واللهِ ما عُبِدَتْ حياتَكَ [لأجلك]، ولا تُتْرَكُ عبادتُها بعدَكَ لموتك!" فقال أبو أُحَيْحَةَ الآن علمت أن لي خليفة وأعجبه شدة نصبه في عبادتها"). وقارن أيضا الواقدي، المغازي، ٣: ٨٧٤ ("وكان سادِنها أفلح بن نَضْر الشَّيبانيّ من بني سُلَيم، فلمّا حضرته الوفاة دُخل عليه وهو حزين، فقال له أبو لَهَب: ما لي أراك حزينًا؟ قال: أخاف أن تضيع العُزَّى من بعدي. قال له أبو لَهَب: فلا تَحْزَنْ، فأنا أَقوم عليها بعدك").

I have abandoned Allāt and al-ʿUzzá, both of them,
as befits [any] intrepid [and] tenacious [man].[536]
I serve neither al-ʿUzzá nor her two daughters,
nor do I circle the two tower houses of the Banū Ṭasm,
nor do I visit Ġanm, who was one of our lords,
at the time when my *ḥilm* was small [i.e. during the Ǧāhiliyyah].[537]

§169 Abū Ġassān[538] said: I was informed that Saʿīd b. al-ʿĀṣ Abū Uḥayḥah[539] fell ill, and Abū Lahab[540] came to visit him, found him crying, and asked him: "Why are you crying? Is it because [you fear] death?" He said: "No, but I fear that al-ʿUzzá will not be worshipped after me." Abū Lahab said: "By Allāh, it was not worshipped because you were alive,[541] and it shall not be abandoned because of your death." Saʿīd said: "Now I know that it [al-ʿUzzá] has someone who will protect it after me." Abū Lahab's words impressed him. The Messenger of Allāh, may Allāh bless and save him, sent Ḫālid b. al-Walīd b. al-Muġīrah al-Maḫzūmī to destroy it [al-ʿUzzá], and when he reached it, he destroyed a part of it, and then left. The Messenger of Allāh, may Allāh

---

3–4 I ... Ṭasm : Al-Maqrīzī adds on the margin another variant of this verse: I serve neither al-ʿUzzá nor her two daughters, nor do I visit the two idols of the Banū Ṭasm.

---

536 *Al-Ǧald al-ṣabūr*. In certain contexts, *ṣabr* may denote endurance, fortitude, or tenacity; "Ṣabr," in *EI*² (A.J. Wensinck). It is also noteworthy that in the Qurʾān *ṣabr* sometimes connotes "the vice of 'stubborn persistence' in the worship of ancestral deities"; see "Trust and patience," in *EQ* (S.C. Alexander). The adjective *ǧald* applies to someone who has both *quwwah* (strength) and *ṣabr*. It denotes both physical and mental strength (*al-ǧaladu: al-quwwah wa-l-ṣabr ... kāna aḫwafa ǧaldan ay qawiyyan fī nafsihi wa-ǧasadihi*; Ibn Manẓūr, *Lisān al-ʿarab*, s.v. *ǧalad*). See also Bravmann (1972): 40, who says with regard to this verse that "the war-like atmosphere is also underscored by the expression *al-ǧald al-ṣabūr*."

537 The term *ḥilm* includes a number of qualities, such as forbearance, self-control, and moderation. It is often contrasted with *ǧahl*; see "Ḥilm," in *EI*² (Ch. Pellat). The last verse is also translated in Goldziher (1966): 1:208.

538 This is probably Abū Ġassān al-Madanī, Muḥammad b. Yaḥyá l-Kinānī: al-Mizzī, *Tahḏīb al-kamāl*, 26:636–639.

539 Saʿīd b. al-ʿĀṣ b. Umayyah b. ʿAbd Šams b. ʿAbd Manāf; see Ibn al-Kalbī, *al-Aṣnām* 23.

540 Abū Lahab ("father of flame") was Muḥammad's half uncle, and one of his inveterate enemies in Mecca. His and his wife's hostile behavior toward Muḥammad was reportedly the occasion for the revelation of *Sūrat al-Masad* (111); "Abū Lahab," in *EI*² (W.M. Watt). According to *al-Maġāzī*, the dying man who was worried about the worship of al-ʿUzzá was Aflaḥ of the Banū Sulaym, who was al-ʿUzzá's custodian; see al-Wāqidī, *al-Maġāzī*, 3:874; Hawting (1999): 27.

541 Compare Ibn al-Kalbī, *al-Aṣnām*, 23: *wa-llāhi mā ʿubidat ḥayātaka li-ağlika* ("By Allāh, it was not worshipped for your sake during your lifetime").

"فما رأيت؟" قال: "ما رأيت شيئا." قال: "ما فعلت شيئا. فارجع." فرجع فهدمها فخرجت منها امرأة سوداء عريانة ثائرة الرأس تسعى وتولول. فقال سادنها: [الطويل]

فيا عُز شُدِّي شَدّة لا شَوى لها   على خالد ألقي القناعَ وشمِري[a] | 44a
ويا عُز إن لم تقتلي {المرء} خالدا   فبوئي بإثم عاجل أو تَنَصَّري

فأقبل إليها خالد بالسيف وهو يقول: [الرجز]

يا عُز كفرانك لا سبحانك   إني رأيت الله قد أهانك

فضربها خالد بالسيف ثم انصرف إلى النبي ﷺ فأخبره الخبر. فقال: "تلك العزى ولن تُعبَد العُزى بعد اليوم أبدا."[b]

§ 170 قال: وبلغني أنهم حموا لها واديا يقال له سقام وهو من ناحية حراض يشبهونه بحرم الكعبة[c] وأنه لم يحم لسُواع. وبلغني أنهم كانوا يدْعُون اللاتَ والعزى ومناةَ الثالثة الأخرى بنات الله ويقولون إذا طافوا بالكعبة: "اللات والعزى ومناة الثالثة الأخرى فإنهن الغرانيق العلى وإن

---

٣ شَوى: في الأصل "شَوا". ٤ المرء: في الأصل "المرو".

---

a قارن ابن الكلبي، الأصنام، ٢٦
("أعُزَّاءُ، شُدِّي شَدَّةً لا تُكَذِّبِي   على خالدٍ! أَلْقِي الخِمَارَ وشَمِّرِي!")
وقارن أيضا البغدادي، خزانة الأدب، ٧: ٢١٦ ("عزَّايَ شُدِّي شدّةً لا تكذِّبي").

b قارن ابن الكلبي، أصنام، ٢٦ ("فقال خالدٌ:
[يا عُزُّ] كُفرانكِ لا سبحانكِ   إنِّي رأيتُ الله قد أهانَكِ!
ثم ضربها ففَلَق رأْسها، فإذا هي حُمَمَةٌ. ثم عضَدَ الشجرة، وقَتَلَ دُبيَّةَ السادِنَ. ثم أتى النبيّ (ﷺ) فأخبره. فقال: "تلك العُزَّى، ولا عُزَّى بعدها للعرب! أَمَا إنَّها لن تُعْبَدَ بعدَ اليوم!"").

c قارن ابن الكلبي، أصنام، ١٩ ("وكانت قريش قد حَمَتْ لها شِعْباً من وادي حُرَاضٍ يُقال له سُقَامٌ. يضاهون به حَرَم الكعبة").

bless and save him, asked him: "What did you do?" He replied: "I destroyed it." He asked: "And what did you see?" He replied: "I did not see anything." He said: "You did not do a thing. Go back!" So he went back and destroyed it, and then a black, naked woman, with disheveled hair, emerged from it [the idol], running and wailing. Its custodian said: [*al-ṭawīl*]

O al-ʿUzzá![542] Make a mortal attack
upon Ḫālid. Throw aside your veil and tuck up your garment.
O al-ʿUzzá![543] If you do not kill this man Ḫālid,
then bear a swift punishment or help yourself![544]

Ḫālid then approached it [al-ʿUzzá] with a sword, saying: [*al-rağaz*]

O al-ʿUzzá,[545] may you be denied, not praised.
Verily, I see that Allāh has humiliated you.

Ḫālid struck it with the sword, and then returned to the Prophet, may Allāh bless and save him, and told him what had happened. He [the Prophet] said: "That was al-ʿUzzá, and al-ʿUzzá will never be worshipped after this day."

§170 He said: I was informed that they [the Qurayš][546] declared a valley called Suqām in the area of Ḥurāḍ as its [i.e. al-ʿUzzá's] *ḥimá* [protected space],[547] likening it to the sacred territory around the Kaʿbah, and that this valley was not declared as Suwāʿs *ḥimá*. I was also informed that they used to call Allāt, al-ʿUzzá, and Manāt the third, the other,[548] the daughters of Allāh, and that when they circumambulated the Kaʿbah they used to say: "[By][549] Allāt and al-ʿUzzá, and Manāt the third, the other. They are the exalted

542 Vocalized "ʿUzzu" (or "ʿUzza") for reasons of meter.

543 See note 542.

544 See Grunebaum (1953): 45. And see also Ibn Hišām, *The Life of Muhammad* 565; al-Ṭabarī, *History*, 8:188, where *tanaṣṣarī* is translated as "become a Christian."

545 See note 542.

546 See the parallel text in Ibn al-Kalbī, *al-Aṣnām* 19.

547 *Ḥimá* (a protected or forbidden place) was a protected pastureland. It was a place that people were prohibited from approaching, where they were not allowed to pasture their animals; see "Ḥimā," in *EI*² (J. Chelhod); Munt (2014): 28–31; Crone (2016): 436–438.

548 Manāt is referred to in the Qurʾān (al-Nağm, 53:19) as "the third, the other" (*al-ṯāliṯah al-uḫrá*). Regarding this phrase, see Seidensticker (2010), 304.

549 The letter *wāw* which is used in oaths is missing from the text, but compare Ibn al-Kalbī, *al-Aṣnām* 19; Yāqūt, *Muʿğam al-buldān*, 4:116.

شفاعتهن لترتجى."[a] قال الله تعالى ﴿أَفَرَأَيْتُمُ ٱللَّاتَ وَٱلْعُزَّى وَمَنَاةَ ٱلثَّالِثَةَ ٱلْأُخْرَى أَلَكُمُ ٱلذَّكَرُ وَلَهُ ٱلْأُنْثَى تِلْكَ إِذًا قِسْمَةٌ ضِيزَى إِنْ هِيَ إِلَّا أَسْمَاءٌ سَمَّيْتُمُوهَا أَنْتُمْ وَآبَاؤُكُمْ مَا أَنْزَلَ ٱللَّهُ بِهَا مِنْ سُلْطَانٍ﴾.

§171 وقال يونس بن محمد عن شيبان عن قتادة قال: بعث النبي ﷺ خالد بن الوليد رضي الله عنه إلى شعب سقام ليكسر العزى فقال سادنها: "يا خالد بن الوليد أحذركها إن لها شدة لا يقوم لها شيء." فمشى إليها خالد بن الوليد بالفأس فهشم أنفها.[b]

§172 وقال الوليد بن جميع عن أبي الطفيل قال: لما افتتح النبي ﷺ مكة بعث خالد بن الوليد إلى العزى فأتاها وهي على ثلاث سمرات فهدم البيت وقطع السمرات ثم أتى النبي ﷺ فأخبره فقال: "ارجع. فإنك {لم} تصنع شيئا." فرجع فلما رأته السدنة وهم حجابها امتنعوا وأمعنوا في الجبل وقالوا:[c]

٢ إذًا ... ضِيزَى: شكل المقريزي هذه الكلمات كما يلي: "اذًا قِسْمة ضِيْزَى." ٨ لم: في الأصل "لن".

a قارن ابن الكلبي، الأصنام، ١٩ ("وكانت قريشٌ تطوف بالكعبة وتقول: واللاتِ والعُزّى وَمَنَاةَ الثالثةِ الأُخرى! فإنهنّ الغرانيقُ العُلى وإن شفاعتهنّ لَتُرْتجى!").

b راجع الجاحظ، الحيوان، ٦: ٢٠١ ("وفي بعض الرِّواية أنهم كانوا يسمعون في الجاهلية من أجواف الأوثان هَمهمةً، وأن خالد بن الوليد حين هَدَمَ العُزّى رمَته بالشّرَر حتى احترقَ عامّةُ فخذه، حتى عادهُ النبي صلى الله عليه وسلم").

c قارن ابن كثير، تفسير، ٧: ٤٢٣-٤٢٤ ("لما فتح رسول الله صلى الله عليه وسلم مكة بعث خالد بن الوليد إلى نخلة، وكانت بها العزى فأتاها خالد وكانت على ثلاث سمرات، فقطع السمرات وهدم البيت الذي كان عليها، ثم أتى النبي صلى الله عليه وسلم فأخبره فقال: «ارجع فإنك لم تصنع شيئا» فرجع خالد، فلما أبصرته السدنة وهم حجبتها أمعنوا في الحيل وهم يقولون"). وقارن أيضا ابن كثير، السيرة النبوية، ٥: ٥٩٨ ("أمْعَنوا هربًا في الجبل").

cranes (*al-ġarānīq al-ʿulá*),[550] and their intercession is hoped for."[551] Allāh, the Exalted, said: "Have you considered Allāt and al-ʿUzzá and Manāt the third, the other? What, have you males, and He females? That were indeed an unjust division. They are naught but names yourselves have named, and your fathers; Allāh has sent down no authority touching them."[552]

§ 171 Yūnus b. Muḥammad said on the authority of Šaybān < Qatādah, who said that the Prophet, may Allāh bless and save him, sent Ḫālid b. al-Walīd, may Allāh be pleased with him, to the ravine of Suqām to destroy al-ʿUzzá, and its custodian said: "O Ḫālid b. al-Walīd! Beware of it! It [al-ʿUzzá] is strong. Nothing can stand against it." Ḫālid b. al-Walīd then went toward it with a pickaxe and crushed its [al-ʿUzzá's] nose.

§ 172 Al-Walīd b. Ǧumayʿ[553] said on the authority of Abū l-Ṭufayl,[554] who said that when the Prophet, may Allāh bless and save him, conquered Mecca, he sent Ḫālid b. al-Walīd to [destroy] al-ʿUzzá, which was on top of three *samurah* trees. He [Ḫālid] approached it, destroyed the sanctuary, and cut down the *samurah* trees. Then he went to the Prophet, may Allāh bless and save him, and told him [what had happened]. He [the Prophet] said: "Go back! You did not do a thing." So he went back, and when the custodians (*al-sadanah*)—i.e. its guardians (*ḥuǧǧābuhā*)—saw him, they held back,[555] fled to the mountain,[556] and said: "O al-ʿUzzá! Drive him out of his senses! O al-

---

550 For more on the meaning and significance of the *ġarānīq*, see Lichtenstaedter (1975), 54–61.

551 According to the Muslim sources, Satan cast these words, which appear in this account as a formula uttered by the Qurayš when they circumambulated the Kaʿbah, upon the Prophet's tongue, and the latter mistook them as Qurʾānic verses. These verses, which according to Muslim tradition were later abrogated, are referred to as "satanic verses" by modern scholars; see "Satanic Verses," in *EQ* (Sh. Ahmed); Rubin (1995): 156–166.

552 Qurʾān (*al-Naǧm*), 53:19–23.

553 Al-Walīd b. ʿAbd Allāh b. Ǧumayʿ al-Zuhrī l-Kūfī; al-Mizzī, *Tahḏīb al-kamāl*, 31:35.

554 On Abū l-Ṭufayl ʿĀmir b. Wāṯilah (d. ca. 100/718), see Ibn ʿAbd al-Barr, *al-Istīʿāb*, 2:798–799.

555 Perhaps *imtanaʿū* should be translated as "they resisted." This translation would fit the reading *amʿanū fī l-ḥiyal*, which appears in other sources (see below, note 556).

556 *Amʿanū fī l-ǧabal.* Compare with other versions that have *amʿanū fī l-ḥiyal* (the words *ǧabal* and *ḥiyal* are differentiated only by the diacritical marks), which should be rendered as something like: "they were intent on using stratagems"; see Ibn Kaṯīr, *Tafsīr*[1], 7:423–424.

"يا عزى خبليه. يا عزى أعوريه." فأتاها فإذا امرأة عريانة ناشرة شعرها تحثو التراب على رأسها فعممها بالسيف[a] حتى قتلها ثم أتى النبي ﷺ فأخبره فقال: "تلك العزى."

§173 وعن عمر بن عبد العزيز وسعيد بن جبير أنهما قالا: كان المشركون يعبدون العزى وهو حجر أبيض الحين من الدهر ثم يجدون ما هو أحسن منه من | الحجارة فيعبدون الآخر ويطرحون 44b
الأول.[b] فأنزل الله تعالى ﴿أَفَرَأَيْتَ مَنِ ٱتَّخَذَ إِلَٰهَهُۥ هَوَىٰهُ﴾ ثلاث آيات.

§174 وقال حماد بن سَلَمَة عن داود بن أبي هند عن محمد بن عباد المخزومي إن قريشا قالت: "قيضوا لأصحاب محمد. قيضوا لكل رجل منهم وليه يأخذه."[c] فقيضوا لأبي بكر الصديق رضي الله عنه طلحة ابن عبيد الله فأتاه فقال: يٰأبا بكر قم إلي." قال: "إلى ما تدعوني؟" قال: إلى اللات والعزى." قال: "وما اللات؟" قال: "{وثن}." قال: "وما العزى؟" قال: "بناته."[d] قال: "فمن أمهن إذا؟" قال: فسكت وأقبل على القوم فقال: "أجيبوه عني." فسكتوا. فقال: "يٰأبا بكر قم إلي. أشهد أن لا إله الا الله وأن

---

١ تحثو: في الأصل "تحثوا". ٣ وسعيد ... قالا: الزيادة بخط المقريزي في الهامش الأيمن من الأعلى إلى الأسفل + صح، ويشير إليها رمز ٮ بعد "العزيز". ٩ وثن: في الأصل "وثنا".

---

a قارن ابن كثير، تفسير، ٧: ٤٢٤ ("فغمسها بالسيف حتى قتلها").

b قارن الطبري، جامع البيان، ٢١: ٩٣ ("كانت قريشٌ تَعْبُدُ العُزَّى—وهو حجرٌ أبيضُ—حيناً من الدهرِ، فإذا وجَدوا ما هو أحسنُ منه، طرَحوا الأوَّلَ وعبَدوا الآخرَ").

c قارن البلاذري، أنساب الأشراف، ٥: ١٨٥ ("أنّ قريشًا قالت: قِيِّضوا لكلِّ رجل من أصحابِ محمدٍ وليَّه ليأخذه").

d قارن البلاذري، أنساب الأشراف، ٥: ١٨٥ ("فقال أبو بكر: وما اللاتُ والعزّى؟ قال: بنات الله، قال: فمن أمّهما؟ فسكَت طلحة فلم يُجِبْهُ").

ʿUzzá! Make him blind in one eye!" He approached it, and suddenly there was a naked woman with disheveled hair,[557] throwing dust upon her head. He struck her in the head with a sword and killed her, and then he went to the Prophet, may Allāh bless and save him, and told him [what had happened]. He [the Prophet] said: "That was al-ʿUzzá!"

§ 173 It was reported on the authority of ʿUmar b. ʿAbd al-ʿAzīz[558] and Saʿīd b. Ǧubayr that for a period of time the polytheists used to worship al-ʿUzzá, which was a white stone, and then they would find a stone which was better than it, worship the other one, and discard the first. Allāh, the Exalted, revealed three verses, [the first being:] "Have you seen him who has taken his caprice to be his god."[559]

§ 174 Ḥammād b. Salamah said on the authority of Dāwūd b. Abī Hind < Muḥammad b. ʿAbbād al-Maḫzūmī[560] that Qurayš said: "Assign [guardians] for Muḥammad's Companions, assign for each one of them a guardian, so that he would take him [with him]." For Abū Bakr al-Ṣiddīq,[561] may Allāh be pleased with him, they assigned Ṭalḥah b. ʿUbayd Allāh;[562] and he [Ṭalḥah] approached him [Abū Bakr] and said: "O Abū Bakr! Come here!" He [Abū Bakr] asked: "What do you summon me for?" He [Ṭalḥah] answered: "[The worship of] Allāt and al-ʿUzzá." He [Abū Bakr] asked: "What is Allāt?" He [Ṭalḥah] answered: "An idol." He [Abū Bakr] asked: "And what is al-ʿUzzá?" He [Ṭalḥah] answered: "Its daughters."[563] He [Abū Bakr] asked: "In that case, who is their mother?" He [Ṭalḥah] became silent, approached the people, and said: "Answer him on my behalf." But they became silent [too]. Then he said: "O Abū Bakr! Come here! I bear witness that there is no god but

557 Lit. "Spreading out her hair."

558 The eighth Umayyad caliph (r. 99–101/717–720).

559 Qurʾān (*al-Ǧāṯiyah*), 45:23.

560 Muḥammad b. ʿAbbād b. Ǧaʿfar al-Maḫzūmī l-Makkī; al-Ḏahabī, *Siyar aʿlām al-nubalāʾ*, 5:106.

561 The first of the rightly-guided caliphs (d. 22/634).

562 Ṭalḥah b. ʿUbayd Allāh (d. 36/656) was one of Muḥammad's Companions. Ṭalḥah and Abū Bakr both belonged to the clan of Taym b. Murrah of Qurayš. See "Ṭalḥa," in EI^2 (W. Madelung).

563 The attached pronoun in the word *banātuhu* ("its daughters") seems to refer to the word *waṯan* ("idol"). The version of this account in *Ansāb al-ashrāf* states that after Abū Bakr asked: "What are Allāt and al-ʿUzzá," the reply was that they are the daughters of Allāh; al-Balāḏurī, *Ansāb al-ašrāf*, 5:185.

محمدا عبده ورسوله.» قال: وأنزل الله تعالى ﴿وَمَنْ يَعْشُ عَنْ ذِكْرِ ٱلرَّحْمَٰنِ نُقَيِّضْ لَهُ شَيْطَانًا فَهُوَ لَهُ قَرِينٌ﴾.

175§ قال ابن شبة: واللات كانت لثقيف بالطائف وموضعها الذي كانت به تحت منارة مسجد الطائف اليسرى.[a] وكانت اللات صخرة مربعة. يقال إن رجلا فيما مضى كان يقعد على صخرة لثقيف يبيع السمن للحاج إذا مروا به ويلت سويقهم وكان ذا غنم وسمن فسميت الصخرة اللات وقد قرأ عبد الله بن عامر قارئ أهل الشام ﴿أَفَرَأَيْتُمُ ٱللَّاتَّ وَٱلْعُزَّىٰ﴾ بالتشديد وهذا يدل على ما تقدم من الحديث. وكانت سدانتها من ثقيف إلى بني عتاب بن مالك الثقفيين. وكان سفينٰ بن عيينة يقول: هي شجرة. ولها يقول صخر بن الجعد الخُضري: [الطويل]

وإني وتركي وصل كاس لكالذي تبرأ {من لات} وكان يدينها[b]

176§ وقال أبو الجوزاء عن ابن عباس رضي الله عنه في قوله تعالى ﴿ٱللَّاتَ وَٱلْعُزَّىٰ﴾ قال:

---

١ يَعْشُ : شكل المقريزي هذه الكلمة كما يلي: "يَعْشُ". ٣ واللات : كشط المقريزي كلمة أخرى قبل أن يصححها كما هي الآن. ٤–٧ يقال ... الحديث : الزيادة بخط المقريزي في الهامش الأيسر من الأسفل إلى الأعلى، ثم في الهامش الأعلى من الأعلى إلى الأسفل، ويشير إليها رمز ˥ بعد "مربعة". ٦ ٱللَّاتَّ وَٱلْعُزَّىٰ : شكل المقريزي هاتين الكلمتين كما يلي: "اللاتَّ والعُزّى". ٩ من لات : في الأصل "من اللاتي".

---

a قارن الطبري، جامع البيان، ٢٢: ٤٦–٤٧ ("واختلَفَت القرأةُ في قراءةِ قولِه: ﴿ٱللَّٰتَ﴾ فقرأَته عامةُ قرأةِ الأمصارِ بتخفيفِ التاءِ على المعنى الذي وصَفْتُ. وذُكِر أن اللاتَ بيتٌ كان بنَخْلَةَ تَعْبُدُه قريشٌ. وقال بعضُهم: كان بالطائفِ").

b قارن ابن الكلبي، الأصنام، ١٦ ("ولها يقول عمرو بن الجُعَيْد:

فإِنِّي وتَرْكِي وَصْلَ كأْسٍ لَكَالَّذي تبرَّأَ منْ لاتٍ، وكان يَدِينُها!").

Allāh, and that Muḥammad is His servant and messenger." Allāh, the Exalted, revealed: "Whoso blinds himself to the remembrance of the All-merciful, to him We assign a Satan as a comrade."[564]

§ 175 Ibn Šabbah said: Allāt belonged to Ṯaqīf in al-Ṭāʾif. It was located under the left side minaret of [what was later the] mosque of al-Ṭāʾif. Allāt was a cube-shaped rock. It is said that in the past, a man used to sit on a rock that belonged to Ṯaqīf, selling clarified butter to the pilgrims when they passed by him, and moistening (*yaluttu*) their *sawīq*. He had sheep and clarified butter. The rock was called al-Lātt. ʿAbd Allāh b. ʿĀmir, the Qurʾān reciter of the people of al-Šām,[565] recited, "Have you considered al-Lātt and al-ʿUzzá" [and so on with the verse][566] with a *šaddah* [over the letter *tāʾ* in the word al-Lātt]; this [reading] points to what has already been mentioned in this *ḥadīṯ*. Its custodianship belonged to the Banū ʿAttāb b. Mālik of Ṯaqīf. Sufyān b. ʿUyaynah[567] said: It was a tree. Ṣaḫr b. al-Ǧaʿd al-Ḫuḍrī[568] said about it: [*al-ṭawīl*]

By my abstinence from contact with a cup of wine I am like he who
has renounced Allāt[569] after having been one of her followers.[570]

§ 176 Abū l-Ǧawzāʾ[571] said on the authority of Ibn ʿAbbās, may Allāh be pleased with him, who said about His [Allāh's] saying, the Exalted, "Allāt

564 Qurʾān (*al-Zuḫruf*), 43:36.

565 For more on Abū ʿUmar ʿAbd Allāh b. ʿĀmir al-Yaḥṣubī (d. 118/736), see "Ibn ʿĀmir," in *EI*² (ed.).

566 Qurʾān (*al-Naǧm*), 53:19.

567 Sufyān b. ʿUyaynah b. Maymūn al-Hilālī (d. 196/811); "Sufyān b. ʿUyayna," in *EI*² (Susan A. Spectorsky).

568 On the poet Ṣaḫr b. al-Ǧaʿd al-Ḫuḍrī, see Ibn ʿAsākir, *Dimašq*, 23:414–418. In *al-Aṣnām* this verse is attributed to ʿAmr b. al-Ǧuʿayd; see Ibn al-Kalbī, *al-Aṣnām* 16.

569 Vocalized *Lāt* for reasons of meter.

570 See also Wellhausen (1897): 30; Faris (1952): 14; Atallah (1969): 11.

571 Abū l-Ǧawzāʾ Aws b. ʿAbd Allāh al-Rabaʿī l-Baṣrī (d. 83/702); al-Ḏahabī, *Siyar aʿlām al-nubalāʾ*, 4:371–372.

كان رجل يلت السويق.[a] وعن قتادة في قوله ﴿أَفَرَأَيْتُمُ ٱللَّاتَ وَٱلْعُزَّىٰ﴾ قال: أما اللات فكانت بالطائف وأما العُزى فكانت بسقام شعب بطن نخلة وأما مناة فكانت بقديد آلهة يعبدونها.[b]

§177 وقال جعفر عن سعيد: كانت قريش يعبدون اللات وهو حجر أبيض حينا من الدهر فإذا وجدوا ما هو أحسن منه طرحوا الأول وعبدوا الآخر. فأنزل الله تعالى فيهم ﴿أَفَرَأَيْتَ مَنِ ٱتَّخَذَ إِلَٰهَهُۥ هَوَاهُ﴾ الآية.

§178 قال عمر بن شبة: حدثني أبو غسان حدثني عبد العزيز بن عمران الزهري قال: إن النبي ﷺ بعث إلى اللات المغيرة بن شعبة يهدمها[c] فلما قدم قال: "والله لألعبن بثقيف." فلما صعد عليها تخانق ثم صرع. فقالت | ثقيف: "كلا. زعم المغيرة أنه يهدم الربَّة. هي والله أمنع من ذاك."[d] فوقف عليه 45a
الأسود بن عمرو فقال: "يا مغيرة أتهدم الربة؟ كلا ورب الكعبة. لهي أمنع من ذاك." فوثب المغيرة وهو يقول: "أف لكم لا تتركون ضلالتكم ولا كفركم. والله ما كنت إلا أعبث بكم فوجدتكم إلى الكفر أسرع منكم إلى الإيمان. والله لأهدمنها حتى لا أبقي منها حجرا." فهدمها وهدم البيت الذي كان يلقى فيه ما يُهْدى إليها واسمه الغبغب. وله يقول ابن الحدادية الخزاعي: [الطويل]

---

٢ آلهة: في الأصل "آلهةً". ١٢ يلقى: في الأصل "يلقا". || يُهْدى: في الأصل "يُهْدا".

---

a قارن البخاري، صحيح، ٤: ١٨٤١ ("حدّثنا مُسْلِمُ بْنُ إِبْرَاهِيمَ: حَدَّثَنَا أَبُو الْأَشْهَبِ: حَدَّثَنَا أَبُو الجَوْزَاءِ، عَنِ ابْنِ عَبَّاسٍ رَضِيَ اللَّهُ عَنْهُمَا، فِي قَوْلِهِ: ﴿اللَّاتَ وَالْعُزَّى﴾ كان اللَّاتُ رَجُلًا يَلُتُّ سَوِيقَ الحَاجِّ"). وقارن أيضا الطبري، جامع البيان، ٢٢: ٤٨ ("حدّثني أحمدُ بنُ يوسُفَ، قال: ثنا أبو عبيد، قال: ثنا عبدُ الرحمنِ، عن أبي الأشْهَبِ، عن أبي الجَوْزاءِ، عن ابن عباسٍ، قال: كان يَلُتُّ السويقَ للحاجِّ").

b قارن الطبري، جامع البيان، ٢٢: ٥٠ ("أما مَناةُ فكانت بقُدَيْدٍ، آلهةٌ كانوا يَعْبُدونها. يعني اللاتَ والعُزَّى ومَناةَ").

c قارن ابن حبيب، المحبر، ٣١٥ ("وكان اللات بالطائف لثقيف على صخرة. وكانوا يسترون ذلك البيت ويضاهون به الكعبة. وكان له حجبة وكسوة. وكانوا يحرمون واديه. فبعث رسول الله صلى الله عليه أبا سفيان بن حرب والمغيرة بن شعبة فهدماه").

d قارن الواقدي، المغازي، ٣: ٩٧٢ ("فلمّا ضرب المُغيرة ضربةً بالمِعْوَل سقط مَغْشيًّا عليه يرتكض، فصاح أَهل الطائف صيحةً واحدة: كلَّا! زعمتم أَنَّ الرَّبَّة لا تمتنع، بلى واللهِ لتمتنعن!").

and al-ʿUzzá":[572] There was a man [called al-Lātt, lit. "the moistener"] who moistened (*yaluttu*) the *sawīq*.[573] On the authority of Qatādah, who said [the following] with regard to His saying, "Have you considered Allāt and al-ʿUzzá":[574] Allāt was in al-Ṭāʾif; al-ʿUzzá was in Suqām, a ravine of Baṭn Naḫlah; and Manāt was in Qudayd.[575] [These were the] gods that they [i.e. the Arabs] worshipped.

§ 177 Ǧaʿfar [b. Abī l-Muġīrah] said on the authority of Saʿīd [b. Ǧubayr]: For a period of time the Qurayš used to worship Allāt, which was a white stone, and when they found something [i.e. a stone] which was better than it, they would discard the former [stone], and worship the other one. Allāh, the Exalted, revealed [the following verse] with regard to them: "Have you seen him who has taken his caprice to be his god" and so on with the verse.[576]

§ 178 ʿUmar b. Šabbah said: Abū Ġassān related to me, ʿAbd al-ʿAzīz b. ʿImrān al-Zuhrī[577] related to me that the Prophet, may Allāh bless and save him, sent al-Muġīrah b. Šuʿbah[578] to destroy Allāt, and when he [al-Muġīrah] arrived, he said: "By Allāh, I shall dupe the Ṯaqīf." So when he [al-Muġīrah] climbed upon it [Allāt], he pretended to be choking, and then fell on the ground. Ṯaqīf said: "Not at all! Al-Muġīrah claimed that he would destroy al-Rabbah [i.e. the idol of Ṯaqīf], but, by Allāh, its power of resistance is greater than this." Al-Aswad b. ʿAmr stood by him [al-Muġīrah] and said: "O al-Muġīrah! Are you [trying to] destroy al-Rabbah? Not at all! By the lord of the Kaʿbah, its power of resistance is greater than this!" Thereupon, al-Muġīrah leaped up and said [to members of the tribe of Ṯaqīf]: "Ugh! You have not abandoned your error and infidelity. By Allāh, I was merely joking with you, but I have found that you are quicker to follow infidelity than you are to follow belief. By Allāh, I shall destroy it until I shall not leave a stone of it untouched." Then he [al-Muġīrah] destroyed it, and he also destroyed the sanctuary into which its gifts were cast. It was called al-Ġabġab. Ibn al-Ḥudādiyyah al-Ḫuzāʿī[579] said, referring to it: [*al-ṭawīl*]

---

572 Qurʾān (*al-Naǧm*), 53:19.

573 I.e. the deity was named after him.

574 Qurʾān (*al-Naǧm*), 53:19.

575 Located between Mecca and Medina (see the map).

576 Qurʾān (*al-Ǧāṯiyah*), 45:23.

577 On whom see Ibn Saʿd, *al-Ṭabaqāt*[1], 7:614.

578 Al-Muġīrah b. Šuʿbah al-Ṯaqafī belonged to the Banū Muʿattib, who were the custodians of Allāt: "al-Mughīra b. Shuʿba," in *EI*[2] (H. Lammens).

579 This is Qays b. al-Ḥudādiyyah, who was born to a woman from the Banū Ḥudād of Kinānah; his father's name was Munqiḏ; see Ibn al-Kalbī, *al-Aṣnām* 21.

يميني ببيت الله أول حَلْفَةٍ وإلا فأنصابٍ نُجِرْن بغبغب[a]

وله يقول النابغة: [الكامل]

يا عام لو قدرت عليك رماحنا والراقصات إلى منى فالغبغب[b]

١ حَلْفَةٍ: في الأصل "حِلْفَةٍ". ‖ نُجِرْن: في الأصل: "نحرن". ٣ منى: في الأصل "منا". ‖ فالغبغب: كتبت الكلمة في الهامش الأيسر مائلة إلى أعلى.

a قارن ابن الكلبي، الأصنام، ٢١ ("وله يقول قيس بن مُنْقِذ بن عُبَيْد بن ضاطر بن حبشيَّة بن سَلُول [الخزاعيّ] (ولدته امرأةٌ من بني حُدَاد من كِنانة وناسٌ يجعلونها من حُدَادِ مُحارِبٍ) وهو قَيْس بن الحُدَادِيّة الخُزاعيّ:

تَلَّيْنا بيت الله أَوَّلَ حَلْفَةٍ وإلا فأنصابٍ يَسُرْنَ بغبغبِ")

وراجع أيضا الأخفش الأصغر، كتاب الاختيارين، ٢٢٠

("يَمِينًا، بِرَبِّ الرّاقِصاتِ، عَشِيَّةً وإلّا فأَنْصابٍ، يُمِرْن، بِغَبْغَبِ").

b قارن ابن الكلبي، الأصنام، ٢١ ("فلغبغبٍ يقول نُهَيْكَةُ الفَزارِيُّ لعامرِ بن الطُّفَيْل:

يا عامِ! لو قَدَرَتْ عليك رِماحُنا والراقصاتِ إلى مِنًى فالغَبْغَبِ!

[لَتَقِيتَ بالوَجْعاء طعنة فاتكٍ مُرَّانَ أَوْ لثَوَيْتَ غير مُحَسَّبِ]")

وراجع أيضا ابن منظور، لسان العرب، "حسب" ("قال نَهِيك الفَزارِيُّ، يخاطب عامر بن الطفيل:

لتَقِيتَ، بالوَجْعاءِ، طَعْنَةَ مُرْهَفٍ مُرَّانَ، أَو لثَوِيتَ غَيْرَ مُحَسَّبِ

الوَجْعاءُ: الاسْتُ. يقول: لو طَعَنْتُكَ لَوَلَّيْتَنِي دُبُرَكَ، واتَّقَيْتَ طَعْنَتِي بوَجعائِكَ، ولثَوَيْتَ هالِكًا، غير مُكَرَّم لا مُوَسَّدٍ ولا مُكَفَّنٍ؛ أو معناه: أنه لم يَرْفَعْكَ حَسَبُكَ فيُنْجِيَكَ من الموت، ولم يُعَظَّم حَسَبُكَ"). وقارن أيضا الآلوسي، روح المعاني، ١٠: ١١٢ ("وقرئ (ولأرقصوا) من رقصت الناقة إذا أسرعت وأرقصتها ومنه قوله:

يا عام لو قدرت عليك رماحنا والراقصات إلى منى فالغبغب").

My oath by the House of Allāh is the first oath;
otherwise, [the oath is] by stones (*anṣāb*) that were carved (*nuǧirna*)[580] in Ġabġab.

Al-Nābiġah[581] said, referring to it: [*al-kāmil*]

O ʿĀmir![582] If our spears could reach you,
[I swear] by the [camels] that go quickly[583] toward Miná and al-Ġabġab.[584]

580 The use of the verb *naǧara* in the verse is unusual, since it is typically used in relation to wood. Parallel sources have *yasurna* ("to rise"; Ibn al-Kalbī, *al-Aṣnām* 21) or *yamurna* (a verb that probably relates to the blood that was poured over the stones; al-Aḫfaš al-Aṣġar, *Kitāb al-Iḫtiyārayn* 220). For a translation of the version of this verse in *al-Aṣnām*, see Faris (1952): 19; Klinke-Rosenberger (1941): 40; Atallah (1969): 16.

581 *Al-Aṣnām* states that the poet was Nuhaykah al-Fazārī; Ibn al-Kalbī, *al-Aṣnām* 21. See also Ibn Manẓūr, *Lisān al-ʿarab*, s.v. *ḥassaba*, where he is called Nahīk al-Fazārī.

582 Vocalized *yā ʿĀmi* (or *yā ʿĀmu*); see Wright (1896–1898), 2:§ 38 (Rem. c.). According to *al-Aṣnām*, this verse was addressed to ʿĀmir b. al-Ṭufayl (on whom see note 379); Ibn al-Kalbī, *al-Aṣnām* 21.

583 For the translation of *wa-l-rāqiṣāti* see Grunebaum (1953): 44; Wright (1896–1898), 2:§ 168 (the last example).

584 Parallel sources add the following line here: "you would have avoided, by turning your hind part, the thrust of a whetted [weapon made of] dogwood tree (*ṭaʿnat murhaf murrān*), or you would have taken your resting place without honor (*ġayr muḥassab*)." The translation of this line follows the text in Ibn Manẓūr, *Lisān al-ʿarab*, s.v. *ḥassaba*. See also Lane (1863–1893): 565, who provides various possible meanings of *ġayr muḥassab*. This line was also added to Ibn al-Kalbī, *al-Aṣnām* 21 (with *fātik* ["bold warrior"] instead of *murhaf*). For its translation, see Klinke-Rosenberger (1941): 40, who prefers the variant *ḥarrān* over *murrān*: "thirsty"; Faris (1952): 19; Grunebaum (1953): 44.

§179 وعن مجاهد أنه كان يقول: اللات رجل كان على طريق الطائف على صخرة له غنم وكان يخلط السمن والأقط والزبيب فيطعمه من يضيفه[a] فسمي اللات فلما مات عُبد. وفي رواية: كان رجل يقال له اللات كان يلت السويق فلما مات عكفوا على قبره. وعن ابن عباس: كان رجلا يلت السويق يسقيه الحاج. وفي رواية: إنما سمي اللات لأنه كان يلت عليه السويق.[b] وفي رواية أن اللات هو لات السويق والعُزى العزى.[c]

§180 وعن عاصم بن بهدلة: اللات لات السويق. وعن مجاهد: اللات الذي كان يلت السويق بالطائف فعكفوا على قبره والعزى سمرات ومناة الثالثة الأخرى حجارة.

§181 قال أبو زيد عمر بن شبة: ثنا أحمد بن معٰوية قال: سمعت أبا الخطاب الكاني من أهل بيت المقدس قال ثنا عطاء الخراساني قال: قال عمر بن الخطاب رضي الله عنه: كانت للخطاب بُهَيمات كنت أرعاها وكان رجلا فظا غليظا ضروبا شتوما. وكان سمرتان كنت أخبطهما للبهَم وكانت

٤–٨ وفي ... شبة: الزيادة بخط المقريزي في الهامش الأيمن من الأعلى إلى الأسفل، ثم في الهامش الأسفل من الأسفل إلى الأعلى + صح، ويشير إليها رمز ⌐ بعد "عُبد".

---

a قارن ابن حجر، فتح الباري، ٩: ٥٩٤ ("فروى الفاكهي من طريق مجاهد قال: كان رجل في الجاهلية على صخرة بالطائف وعليها له غنم، فكان يسلو من رسلها ويأخذ من زبيب الطائف والأقط فيجعل منه حيسًا ويطعم من يمر به من الناس، فلما مات عبدوه").

b قارن الماوردي، النكت والعيون، ٥: ٣٩٧ ("فمن خففها فلهم فيها قولان: أحدهما: أنه كان صنماً بالطائف زعموا أن صاحبه كان يلت عليه السويق لأصحابه، قاله السدي").

c راجع ابن منظور، لسان العرب "عزز" ("قال ابن سيده: أراه تأنيث الأَعَزّ، والأَعَزُّ بمعنى العَزيزِ، والعُزَّى بمعنى العَزِيزَة؛ قال بعضهم: وقد يجوز في العُزَّى أَن تكون تأنيث الأَعَزِّ بمنزلة الفُضْلى من الأَفْضَل والكُبْرَى من الأَكْبَرِ، فإِذا كان ذلك فاللام في العُزَّى ليست زائدة بل هي على حد اللام في الحَارِثِ والعَبَّاسِ، قال: والوجه أَن تكون زائدة لأَنا لم نسمع في الصفات العُزَّى كما سمعنا فيها الصُّغْرى والكُبْرَى").

§ 179 It was reported on the authority of Muǧāhid that al-Lātt was a man on a rock on the road to al-Ṭā'if; he had sheep. He used to mix clarified butter, dried curd, and raisins, and feed it to his guests. He was called al-Lātt, and when he died, he was worshipped. According to another version,[585] there was a man named al-Lātt who used to moisten (*yaluttu*) the *sawīq*. When he died, they [the people] clung to his grave [to worship it]. On the authority of Ibn ʿAbbās: He [al-Lātt] was a man who moistened the *sawīq* and gave it to the pilgrims to drink. According to another version, he was named al-Lātt because he used to moisten (*yaluttu*) the *sawīq* on it.[586] According to another version, al-Lātt is "the moistener of the *sawīq*" [based on the logic that *lātt* is the active participle of the verb *latta*, which means "to moisten"], and al-ʿUzzá is "the mighty one" [based on the logic that *ʿuzzá* is the feminine form of *aʿazz*].[587]

§ 180 On the authority of ʿĀṣim b. Bahdalah:[588] Al-Lātt is the moistener of the *sawīq*. On the authority of Muǧāhid: Al-Lātt was the one who moistened the *sawīq* in al-Ṭā'if. They clung to his grave [to worship it]. Al-ʿUzzá was *samurah* trees, and Manāt the third, the other,[589] was stones.[590]

§ 181 Abū Zayd ʿUmar b. Šabbah said that Aḥmad b. Muʿāwiyah[591] related to him, and said: I heard Abū l-Ḫaṭṭāb al-Kinānī of the people of Bayt al-Maqdis [i.e. Jerusalem], say, ʿAṭā' al-Ḫurāsānī[592] related to us and said that ʿUmar b. al-Ḫaṭṭāb,[593] may Allāh be pleased with him, said: Al-Ḫaṭṭāb [his father] had little lambs that I used to take to pasture. He [al-Ḫaṭṭāb] was a churlish, rude, and insolent man who was wont to beat [others] viciously. There were two *samurah* trees that I used to beat with a staff for the lambs [to feed them the

585 The scanned page was truncated and MS Dār al-Kutub was consulted.

586 *Summiya l-lātt li-annahu kāna yaluttu ʿalayhi l-sawīq*. Perhaps the masculine singular pronoun attached to the preposition *ʿalá* refers to the word *ṣanam*, which is missing from this account. Compare al-Māwardī, *al-Nukat wa-l-ʿuyūn*, 5:397.

587 See Lane (1863–1893): 2032. Al-ʿUzzá might also mean "the all-powerful"; see "al-ʿUzzā," in *EI*² (M.C.A. Macdonald & L. Nehmé).

588 ʿĀṣim b. Bahdalah, who is also known by the name ʿĀṣim b. Abī l-Naǧūd, was a *mawlá* of the tribe of Asad; al-Mizzī, *Tahḏīb al-kamāl*, 13:473–480.

589 See § 170.

590 Or perhaps Manāt the third, the other, was made of stone? (read *min ḥiǧārah* instead of *ḥiǧārah*).
The scanned page was truncated and MS Dār al-Kutub was consulted.

591 This is probably Aḥmad b. Muʿāwiyah b. Bakr al-Bāhilī; Ibn Quṭlūbuġā, *al-Ṯiqāt*, 1:249–250.

592 On whom see note 72.

593 The second of the rightly-guided caliphs (r. 13–23/634–644).

إحداهما حلوة والأخرى مرة وكنت إذا خبطتهما بدأت بالمرة فخبطتها لهن فأَصَبْنَ منها ثم أدِيرهن إلى الحلوة فيُصِبْنَ منها فأنصرف بهن وهن بِطَانٌ وكن إذا سبَقْنَني بدأن بالحلوة فأَصَبْنَ منها ثم أديرهن إلى المرة ولا يُصِبْنَ منها كثيرا فأنصرف بهن خِماصا فيُؤذِيْني. فغدوت يوما بهن وكنت أمر بالمسجد الحرام وباللات والعزى وفيه نحو من سبعين صنما فلما كدت أن أخرج من باب المسجد سمعت صوتا يصيح وهو يقول: "يا ذريح يا ذريح أمر نجيح رجل يصيح لا إله إلا الله."[a]

فالتفت فلم أر أحدا في المسجد ورجعت إلى اللات والعزى فلم أر أحدا فانصرفت حتى إذا كنت عند باب المسجد سمعت صوتا وهو يصيح يقول: "يا ذريح يا ذريح | أمر نجيح رجل يصيح 45b يقول لا إله إلا الله."

قال: قلت: "أجعل الآلهة إلها واحدا؟" فعجبت مما سمعت ثم خرجت فسمعت أن محمدا قد بعث.

---

a قارن البيهقي، دلائل النبوة، ٢: ٢٥٢-٢٥٣ ("ثم أنشأ عمر يقول: كنا يومًا في حيٍّ من قريش يقال له آل ذريح، وقد ذبحوا عجلا والجزَّار يعالجه إذ سمعنا صوتًا من جوف العجل وما نرى شيئًا، وهو يقول: يا آل ذريح أمرٌ نجيحٌ. صائح يصيح بلسان فصيح يشهد أن لا إله إلا الله"). وقارن أيضا ابن الجوزي، كشف المشكل، ١: ١٠١ ("وقوله: يا جليح: اسم شخص. أَمر نجيح: أَي سريع، من النّجاح: وَهو الظَّفَر بالمراد. وهذا من الهواتف المنذرة ببعثة النبي صلى الله عليه وسلم ... حدَّثنا شيخٌ أدرك الجاهلية يقال له ابن عبس قال: كنتُ أسوقُ بقرةً لآلٍ لنا، فسمعْتُ من جوفها: يالَ ذريح، قولٌ فصيح، رجلٌ يصيح: أَن لا إِله إِلَّا الله. قال: فقَدِمْنا مكَّة، فوجدنا النبي صلى الله عليه وسلم قد خرج بمكة")؛ والدينوري، المجالسة، ٥: ٣٨٧ ("أن بني غفار قربوا عجلا ليذبحوه، فناذى العجل: يا آل ذريح! لأمرٍ نجيح، لصائحٍ يصيح، بلسان فصيح، بمكة يدعو لا إلٰه إلا الله")؛ والسهيلي، الروض الأنف، ٢: ٣١٩ ("والصوت الذي سمعه عمر من العجل يا جَلِيح سمعت بعض أشياخنا يقول: هو اسم شيطان، والجليح فى اللغة: ما تطاير من رؤس النبات وخف نحو القطن وشبهه، والواحدة: جليحة، والذي وقع في السيرة: يا ذريح، وكأنه نِداء للعِجل المذبوح لقولهم: أحمر ذَرِيحِيٌّ، أي: شديد الحمرة، فصار وصفا للعجل الذبيح من أجل الدم: ومن رواه: يا جليح، فمآله إلى هذا المعنى؛ لأن العجل قد جُلح أي: كشف عنه الجلد، فالله أعلم")؛ وراجع ابن حجر، فتح الباري، ٧: ٥٧٥ ("قوله: (يا جليح) بالجيم والمهملة بوزن عظيم ومعناه الوقح المكافح بالعداوة، قال ابن التين: يحتمل أن يكون نادى رجلًا بعينه، ويحتمل أن يكون أراد من كان بتلك الصفة قلت: ووقع في معظم الروايات التي أشرت إليها «يا آل ذريح» بالذال المعجمة والراء وآخره مهملة، وهم بطن مشهور في العرب").

leaves]. One of them [the trees] was sweet and the other bitter. Whenever I beat them, I began with the bitter one, beat it for them, and they ate from it. Then I would direct them to the sweet one, they would eat from it, and I would walk away with them when their bellies were full. When they were ahead of me, they began with the sweet [tree] and ate from it. Then I would direct them to the bitter [tree], but they would not eat much from it, so I would walk away with them when they had empty bellies, and it would cause me pain. One day, I walked with them early in the morning, and passed by the Holy Mosque of Mecca, Allāt, and al-ʿUzzá. There were approximately seventy idols there. When I was about to leave from the door of the mosque, I heard a voice crying out and saying: "O Ḏarīḥ![594] O Ḏarīḥ! A matter accomplished with success! A man cries out: There is no god but Allāh."

I turned around, but did not see anyone in the mosque. I returned to Allāt and al-ʿUzzá, but did not see anyone either. So I went away, and when I was near the door of the mosque, I heard a voice crying out, saying: "O Ḏarīḥ! O Ḏarīḥ! A matter accomplished with success! A man cries out saying: There is no god but Allāh."

I said: "Has he made the gods one God?"[595] I was amazed by what I had heard, and then I left, and heard that Muḥammad had been sent.

594 The meaning of the word Ḏarīḥ is uncertain. Some say that *āl Ḏarīḥ* ("the people of Ḏarīḥ") were a subgroup (*ḥayy*) of Qurayš (al-Bayhaqī, *Dalāʾil al-nubuwwah*, 2:252–253; compare Ibn al-Ǧawzī, *Kašf al-muškil*, 1:101. The name Ḏarīḥ is also recorded in *Lisān al-ʿarab* as a name of an Arab tribe; Ibn Manẓūr, *Lisān al-ʿarab*, s.v. Banū Ḏarīḥ). Some sources say that the voice came from within a calf or a cow (al-Bayhaqī, *Dalāʾil al-nubuwwah*, 2:252–253; Ibn al-Ǧawzī, *Kašf al-muškil*, 1:101), so the word *ḏarīḥ* may also be associated with the animal's blood (*aḥmar ḏarīḥī* means "intensely red"; Lane [1863–1893]: 960. See also Ibn Hišām, *The Life of Muhammad* 93, where the phrase is translated: "O blood red one"). Some sources cite this verse with the word *ǧalīḥ* instead of *ḏarīḥ*. *Ǧalīḥ* is interpreted in the sources as a name (Ibn al-Ǧawzī, *Kašf al-muškil*, 1:101), an epithet of an impudent person (Ibn Ḥağar, *Fatḥ al-bārī*, 7:575: *al-waqiḥ al-mukāfiḥ bi-l-ʿadāwah*), a name of a devil, or in reference to a sacrificial animal (compare with *ḏarīḥ*); al-Suhaylī, *al-Rawḍ al-unuf*, 2:319.

595 Cf. Qurʾān (*Ṣād*), 38:5: "What, has he made the gods One God? This is indeed a marvelous thing."

§182 وقال ابن إسحٰق: وكانت اللات لثقيف بالطائف وكان سدنتها وحجابها بني مُعَتِّب من ثقيف. وكانت مَنَاةُ للأوس والخزرج ومن دان بدينهم من أهل يثرب على ساحل البحر من ناحية المُشَلَّل بقديد.

قال ابن هشام: وقال الكميت بن زيد: [الوافر]

وقد آلَتْ قَبائل لا تُولي   مناةَ ظهورها متحرفينا

فبعث رسول الله ﷺ إليها أبا سفيٰن بن حرب فهدمها. ويقال علي بن أبي طالب رضي الله عنه.[a]

§183 وقال عمر بن شبة: وكانت مناة للأوس والخزرج وكانت خزاعة أيضا تعبدها وكانت بالمُشَلَّل بين مكة والمدينة. ولها يقول عبد العزيز بن وديعة المزني: [الكامل]

إني حلفت يمين صدق مُؤْلِيًا   بمناة عند محل آل الخزرج[b]

§184 وفي مناة واللات والعزى أنزل الله تعالى ﴿أَفَرَأَيْتُمُ ٱللَّاتَ وَٱلْعُزَّىٰ وَمَنَاةَ ٱلثَّالِثَةَ ٱلْأُخْرَىٰ﴾.

١٠ وَٱلْعُزَّى: شكل المقريزي هذه الكلمة كما يلي: "العُزى".

a قارن ابن سعد، الطبقات٢، ٢: ١٣٦ ("ثمّ سريّة سعد بن زيد الأشهلي إلى مَناة في شهر رمضان سنة ثمان من مُهاجَر رسول الله، ﷺ. قالوا: بعث رسول الله ﷺ حين فتح مكّة سعد بن زيد الأشهلي إلى مَناة").

b قارن ابن الكلبي، الأصنام، ١٤ ("فلإعظام الأوْس والخزرج يقول عبد العُزَّى بن وَدِيعة المُزَنيُّ، أو غيْرُه من العرب:

إنّي حَلَفْتُ يمينَ صدقٍ برَّةً   بِمَناةَ عند محلِّ آل الخَزْرَجِ!

وكانت العرب جميعا في الجاهلية يُسَمُّونَ الأَوْسَ والخزرجَ جميعا: الخزرجَ. فلذلك يقول: 'عند محلِّ آلِ الخزرجِ'.").

§ 182 Ibn Isḥāq said: Allāt belonged to the Ṯaqīf in al-Ṭā'if. Its custodians and guardians were the Banū Mu'attib of Ṯaqīf. Manāt belonged to the Aws and Ḫazraǧ and to the people of Yaṯrib who followed their religion. It was on the seashore, close to the area of al-Mušallal[596] in Qudayd.

Ibn Hišām said that al-Kumayt b. Zayd[597] said: [*al-wāfir*]

Tribes swore not to turn their backs
on Manāt, or face away [from it].[598]

The Messenger of Allāh, may Allāh bless and save him, sent Abū Sufyān b. Ḥarb to destroy it [Manāt]. Others say [that he sent] 'Alī b. Abī Ṭālib, may Allāh be pleased with him.[599]

§ 183 'Umar b. Šabbah said: Manāt belonged to the Aws and Ḫazraǧ, and the Ḫuzā'ah also worshipped it. It was in al-Mušallal, between Mecca and Medina. 'Abd al-'Azīz b. Wadī'ah al-Muzanī[600] said about it: [*al-kāmil*]

I took a truthful oath, swearing
by Manāt,[601] near the place where the people of the Ḫazraǧ make their sacrifices.[602]

§ 184 Allāh, the Exalted, revealed [the following verses] regarding Manāt, Allāt, and al-'Uzzá: "Have you considered Allāt and al-'Uzzá and Manāt the

596 A mountain (or mountain path; *ṯaniyyah*) overlooking Qudayd; Yāqūt, *Mu'ǧam al-buldān*, 5:136; al-Bakrī, *Mu'ǧam mā sta'ǧam*, 3:723. According to Yāqūt, it is seven miles (*amyāl*) from Medina; Yāqūt, *Mu'ǧam al-buldān*, 5:204.

597 Al-Kumayt b. Zayd al-Asadī was an Arab poet who lived between 60/680 and 126/743; "al-Kumayt b. Zayd al-Asadī," in *EI*² (J. Horovitz and Ch. Pellat).

598 This verse is also translated in Wellhausen (1897): 26; Ibn Hišām, *The Life of Muhammad* 702. See also Kumayt b. Zayd, *Dīwān* 452.

599 According to other accounts, Sa'd b. Zayd al-Ašhalī was sent to destroy it; Ibn Sa'd, *al-Ṭabaqāt*¹, 3:405.

600 Elsewhere he is named 'Abd al-'Uzzá; Ibn al-Kalbī, *al-Aṣnām* 14.

601 Parallel sources have the word *barratan* instead of *mu'liyan*; see Ibn al-Kalbī, *al-Aṣnām* 14. For a translation of this version of the line, see Kowalski (1934): 69; Klinke-Rosenberger (1941): 36.

602 See the definition of *maḥill* in Lane (1863–1893): 622. According to *al-Aṣnām*, the word al-Ḫazraǧ in this verse refers to both the Aws and Ḫazraǧ tribes (see note 462).

فكانت قريش والعرب كلها تعظم مناة {وتسمى} بها عَبدُ مناة. وبعث النبي ﷺ إليها عليا رضي الله عنه عام الفتح فهدمها.

§185 قال: واتخذت بكر بن وائل وتغلب وإياد بيتا يقال له ذو الكعبات وكان بمكان يقال له سنداد وتحجه خثعم.[a] وله يقول الأسود بن يَعْفُر التميمي وهو الأعشى: [الكامل]

أهل الخورنق والسدير وبارق والبيت ذي الكعبات من سِنْداد

قال كاتبه وجامعه: الأسود بن يعفر هذا كنيته أبو نهشل من بني نهشل بن دارم شاعر فصيح جاهلي ليس بالمكثر كان يفد على النعمن بن المنذر. وأول هذا الشعر: [الكامل]

---

١ وتسمى: في الأصل "وتَسم". ٤ وتحجه خثعم: الزيادة بخط المقريزي في الهامش الأيسر من الأسفل إلى الأعلى ويشير إليها رمز ⌐ بعد "سنداد".

---

٤ يَعْفُر: أضاف المقريزي الحاشية التالية في الهامش الأيمن منقلبة: "ح بفتح الياء في أوله وبضمها أيضا." ٥ والبيت: أضاف المقريزي الحاشية التالية في الهامش الأيسر من الأعلى إلى الأسفل: "هذا البيت هو الخورنق." وكتب المقريزي فوق هذه الكلمة كلمة "والقصر" وأضاف رمز "خ" (يعني "نسخة: أخرى"). ‖ سِنْداد: أضاف المقريزي الحاشية التالية في الهامش الأيسر في آخر السطر بجانب الكلمة: "سنداد بكسر أوله ويقال بفتحه أيضا."

---

a قارن الإصبهاني، الأغاني، ٢٢: ٣٥٧ ("حدثني الكَلبيّ عن الشَّرقي بن القُطامي قال: كان سببُ غزو كسرى إيادًا أن بلادهم أجدبتْ، فارتحلوا حتى نزلوا بِسنداد ونواحيها، فأقاموا بها دهرًا حتى أَخصبوا وكثُروا، وكانوا يَعبدون صنمًا يقال له: ذو الكَعبين، وعبدته بكرُ بنُ وائل من بعدهم").

third, the other?"[603] The Qurayš and all the Arabs venerated Manāt. The name ʿAbd Manāt is traced back to it [the idol]. The Prophet, may Allāh bless and save him, sent ʿAlī, may Allāh be pleased with him, to it [Manāt] during the year of the conquest of Mecca, and he destroyed it.

§185 He [Ibn Šabbah?] said: Bakr b. Wāʾil, Taġlib, and Iyād adopted a sanctuary called Ḏū l-Kaʿabāt. It was in a place called Sindād, and Ḫaṯʿam made pilgrimage[s] to it. Al-Aswad b. Yaʿfur al-Tamīmī, who is [known as] al-Aʿšá,[604] said about it: [*al-kāmil*]

The people of al-Ḫawarnaq,[605] al-Sadīr, Bāriq,
and the sanctuary of Ḏū l-Kaʿabāt at Sindād.

Its [the book's] author and compiler [i.e. al-Maqrīzī] said: Al-Aswad b. Yaʿfur's *kunyah* is Abū Nahšal. He belonged to the Banū Nahšal b. Dārim. He was an eloquent Ǧāhilī poet, who did not compose many poems, and who used to pay formal visits to al-Nuʿmān b. al-Munḏir.[606] The poem begins as follows: [*al-kāmil*]

7 Yaʿfur : [Yaʿfur] may have a *fatḥah* over the *yāʾ* at the beginning, or a *ḍammah* (marginal gloss in al-Maqrīzī's hand). 10 sanctuary : This sanctuary (*al-bayt*) is al-Ḫawarnaq (marginal gloss in al-Maqrīzī's hand). Al-Maqrīzī also wrote the word *wa-l-qaṣr* ("and the castle") above this word, offering an alternative reading of this line. ‖ Sindād : Sindād is vocalized with a *kasrah* over the first letter; others say it may also be vocalized with a *fatḥah* (marginal gloss in al-Maqrīzī's hand).

603 Qurʾān (*al-Naǧm*), 53:19–20.

604 On the pre-Islamic poet al-Aswad b. Yaʿfur (or Yuʿfur), who was also known as Aʿšá Nahšal (the night-blind man of the Nahšal), see "al-Aswad b. Yaʿfur," in *EI*³ (Gert J.A. Borg).

605 Al-Ḫawarnaq is a castle in the vicinity of al-Ḥīrah which was built in the time of the Laḫmid ruler al-Nuʿmān (d. after 418 CE). This castle is associated with Sinnimār, the architect who built it and who, according to legend, was cast down from its heights by al-Nuʿmān; see "al-Khawarnaḳ," in *EI*² (L. Massignon); Nicholson (1966): 40–41.

606 The last Laḫmid ruler of al-Ḥīrah (r. ca. 580–602 CE); see "al-Nuʿman (iii) b. al-Mundhir," in *EI*² (I. Shahîd); Nicholson (1966): 45.

نام الخلي وما أُحِس رقادي   والهَم مُحْتَضِر لدَيَّ وِسَادي
ولقد علمت لو ان علمي نافعي[a]   أن السبيل سبيل ذي الأعواد
إن المنيةَ والحُتُوفَ كلاهما   يُوفِي المخارِم يرقبان سَوادي[b]
ماذا أؤمل بعد آل مُحَرق   تركوا منازلهم وبعْدَ إياد | 46a
أهل الخورنق والسدير وبارق   والقصر ذي الشرفات من سنْداد
أرض تخيرها لطيب مقيلها   كعب بن مامة وابن أم دؤاد[c]

---

٤ مُحَرق : وضع المقريزي رمز "ح" تحت الكلمة إشارة إلى تلفظها بالحاء.   ٦ أرض ... دؤاد : الزيادة بخط المقريزي في الهامش الأعلى، في الركن الأيسر، من الأسفل إلى الأعلى.

---

٢ ذي الأعواد : أضاف المقريزي الحاشية التالية في الهامش الأيمن منقلبة: "حـ ذي الأعوادِ رجل من العرب قد تقدم ذكره."   ٤ آل مُحَرق : أضاف المقريزي الحاشية التالية في الهامش الأسفل من الأعلى إلى الأسفل تحت كلمة "مُحَرق": "هما ملكا الحـ‹ـيرة› عمرو بن هنـ‹ـد و›الـ‹ـحرث› بن عمرو ‹بن عدي› ابن أخت جـ‹ـذيمة› الأبرش". قطعت بعض الكلمات عند التجليد.   ٥ والسدير : أضاف المقريزي الحاشية التالية في الهامش الأعلى من الأسفل إلى الأعلى: "موضع بالحيرة بناه المنذر الأكبر." ‖ وبارق : أضاف المقريزي الحاشية التالية في الهامش الأعلى من الأسفل إلى الأعلى: "حـ بارق موضع به سميت القبيلة." ‖ والقصر : أضاف المقريزي الحاشية التالية في الهامش الأعلى من الأسفل إلى الأعلى: "ح والبيت ذي الكعبات." وفي الهامش الأيسر: "ح والقصر ذي الكعبات." ‖ سنْداد : أضاف المقريزي الحاشية التالية في الهامش الأعلى من الأسفل إلى الأعلى: "حـ بفتح السين وكسرها."

---

a قارن المفضل الضبي، المفضليات، ٢١٦ ("ولقد علِمتُ سِوَى الذي نبَّأْتني"). وقارن أيضا ابن كثير، السيرة النبوية، ١: ٧٢
("ولقد علمتُ وإن تطاول بِي المَدَى   أنَّ السبيل سبيل ذي الأعوادِ").

b راجع الأخفش الأصغر، كتاب الاختيارين، ٥٦٠ ("«المَخارمُ»: جمعُ مَخرِم. وهو مُنقَطَعُ أنفِ الجبلِ، وأَنفِ الغلَظِ. وقوله «يوفي»: يَعْلُو. يقال: أَوفَيتُ على الجبَلِ، إذا عَلَوتَ عليه. قال: ومعنى «يَرْقُبانِ»: ينتظرانِ. و«سَوادُهُ»: شَخصُهُ").

c قارن المفضل الضبي، المفضليات، ٢١٧ ("أَرضًا تَخَيَّرَها لِدَارِ أَبيهم")؛ والأخفش الأصغر، كتاب الاختيارين، ٥٦١ ("أَرضٌ تَخَيَّرَها لِبَرْدِ مَقِيلِها").

The carefree one sleeps, but I feel no sleep.
  Care is present at my pillow with me.[607]
I know, if my knowledge is of any benefit to me,
  that the road [I have taken] is the road of Ḏū l-Aʿwād.
Verily, fate and death both
  ascend upon the mountaintops, and watch for my dark figure.[608]
What can I hope for, after the family of Muḥarriq
  has left its dwellings, and after the Iyād [have done the same]?[609]
The people of al-Ḫawarnaq,[610] al-Sadīr, Bāriq,
  and the castle with pinnacles (*šurufāt*) at Sindād.
A land that Kaʿb b. Māmah[611] and Ibn Umm Duʾād[612]
  chose for the pleasantness of its resting place.

---

4 Ḏū l-Aʿwād : Ḏū l-Aʿwād refers to an Arab man who was mentioned earlier (marginal gloss in al-Maqrīzī's hand). In this verse, the meaning of Ḏū l-Aʿwād is obscure. According to one opinion, it was the nickname of a particular man, while according to another, it is the plural of *ʿūd* (bier). 7 the … Muḥarriq : [The family of Muḥarriq] refers to the two kings of al-Ḥīrah, ʿAmr b. Hind and al-Ḥāriṯ b. ʿAmr b. ʿAdī, who was the nephew of Ǧaḏīmah al-Abraš (Marginal gloss in al-Maqrīzī's hand). The scanned page was truncated and MS Dār al-Kutub was consulted. The comment is in disorder: Ǧaḏīmah's nephew was in fact ʿAmr b. ʿAdī l-Laḫmī. 9 al-Sadīr : [Al-Sadīr] refers to a place in al-Ḥirah built by al-Munḏir al-Akbar (marginal gloss in al-Maqrīzī's hand). ‖ Bāriq : Bāriq refers to a place after which the tribal group [i.e. Banū Bāriq] was named (marginal gloss in al-Maqrīzī's hand). See also al-Bakrī, *Muʿǧam mā staʿǧam*, 1:221, where it is said that Bāriq was the name of a mountain. Saʿd b. ʿAdī b. Ḥāriṯah b. Imriʾ al-Qays who lived there was given the name Bāriq after this mountain, and his offspring were called Banū Bāriq. Compare Yāqūt, *Muʿǧam al-buldān*, 1:319, where it is said that Bāriq was the name of a watering-place. But see also Lyall (1918): 164, who argues that Bāriq in this poem likely refers to a name of a building. 10 the … pinnacles : Al-Maqrīzī adds on the margin two variants of the phrase "and the castle with pinnacles" (*wa-l-qaṣr ḏī l-šurufāt*): the first is "and the sanctuary of Ḏū l-Kaʿabāt" (*wa-l-bayt ḏī l-Kaʿabāt*), and the second is "and the castle of Ḏū l-Kaʿabāt" (*wa-l-qaṣr ḏī l-Kaʿabāt*). ‖ Sindād : [Sindād is vocalized] with either a *fatḥah* or a *kasrah* over the *sīn* (marginal gloss in al-Maqrīzī's hand).

---

607 The following lines are also translated in Lyall (1918): 161–162; Jones (2011): 426–432. The translation of the first line closely follows Jones's translation.

608 See also Lyall (1918): 163. On the loose grammatical structure and meaning of this line, see Jones (2011): 428.

609 The grammatical structure of this line is discussed in Bravmann (1977): 303; Beeston (1981): 21.

610 Parallel sources have *arḍ* ("land") instead of *ahl* ("people"), a reading that might be preferable in this context, as it may suggest that this line and the following one both refer to the dwellings (*manāzil*) mentioned in the previous line. See Jones (2011): 411.

611 Kaʿb b. Māmah of the Iyād tribe was famous for his generosity.

612 The identity of Ibn Umm Duʾād is not clear; see Jones (2011): 430.

جرت الرياح على محل ديارهم فكأنهم كانوا على ميعاد
ولقد غنوا فيها بأكرم عيشة في ظل ملك ثابت الأوتاد
فإذا النعيم وكل ما يُلْهَى به يوما يصير إلى بلى ونفاد

§186 ذكر الكلبي في **كتاب البلدان** أن السَّدِيْر سمي سديرا لأن أبصار العرب سدرت لسواد نخله. 45*a فقالوا عند ذلك: ما هذا إلا سَدِيْر. وقال الجواليقي: أي له ثلاث قباب متداخلة. وقال ابن دريد: هو موضع بالحيرة بناه المنذر الأكبر لبعض ملوك العجم. وقال أبو حاتم: قال أبو عبيدة: هو السدلى فعرب فقيل سدير.[a]

٣ وكل ما: كشط المقريزي ما يلي اللام، ثم غير شكل اللام وكتب فيما بعد "ما". ٣.256–٤ ذكر... شرُفة: كتب هذا المقطع على جزازة وضعها المقريزي بين الصفحات (٤٥ و٤٦). ٦ بالحيرة: وضع المقريزي رمز "ح" تحت الكلمة إشارة إلى تلفظها بالحاء.

٢ غنوا: أضاف المقريزي الحاشية التالية في الهامش الأيمن من الأعلى إلى الأسفل: "حـ غنوا أي أقاموا في سرور والمغنى (في الأصل "المغنا") المنزل ولا يكون إلا الإقامة في خفض وسرور ولا يكون للشقاء." || ثابت الأوتاد: أضاف المقريزي الحاشية التالية في الهامش الأيسر في آخر السطر: "أي متمكن."

a قارن الزبيدي، تاج العروس، "سدر" ("وهو بالفارسيّة «سهْ دِلَّى» أَي ثلاث شُعَبٍ أو ثلاث مُداخَلَات. وفي الصّحاح: وأَصْله بالفارسيّة «سِهْ دِلَّى» أي فيه قِبَابٌ مُدَاخَلَة مِثْلُ الحارِيّ بكُمَّيْنِ. وقال الأَصمعِيّ: السَّدِير فارِسيَّة كأَن أَصله «سهْ دِل» أَي قُبَّة فِي ثَلاَث قِبَاب مُدَاخَلَة، وهي التي تُسَمِّيه اليومَ الناسُ سِدِلَّى. فأَعْربته العرب فقالوا: سَدِيرً. قلْت: وما ذَكَره من أَن السدِلَّى بمعنَى القِبَاب المُتداخِلة فهو كَذٰلك فِي العُرْف الآن، وهٰكذا يُكْتَب فِي الصُّكُوك المستعمَلة. وأَمَّا كَون أَنّ السَّدِير مُعرّب عنه فمَحَلُّ تأَمُّلٍ، لأَن الذي يَقتضيه اللسانُ أَن يكون مُعَرَّبًا عَن «سِهْ دره» أَي ذا ثلاثةِ أَبواب، وهذا أَقرب من «سِهْ دلَّى» كما لا يَخْفَى"). وراجع ابن خلكان، وفيات الأعيان، ١: ١٧٨ ("والسِّدِلِّي—بكسر السين المهملة والدال المهملة وبعدها لام مشددة مكسورة أيضا—قبة في القصر مبنية على ثلاث دعائم، وهو لفظ عجمي معناه ثلاث دعائم").

The winds blew over the place of their residences,
as if they had a fixed time.[613]
They dwelt there in contentment, without need of anything, in the most honorable way of life,
in the shadow of a kingdom that is solid and stable (*ṯābit al-awtād*).
And then, pleasure and everything that brings distracting delight[614]
will one day turn to decay and come to an end.

§186 Al-Kalbī reported in *Kitāb al-Buldān* [The Book of the Lands] that al-Sadīr was given this name because the Arabs were dazzled (*li-anna abṣāra l-ʿarab sadarat*) by the dark color of its palm trees.[615] Upon seeing this, they said: This is a *sadīr*! Al-Ǧawālīqī[616] said: [It is named al-Sadīr] because it has three intersecting domes.[617] Ibn Durayd said: It is a place in al-Ḥīrah, which was built by al-Munḏir al-Akbar[618] for one of the kings of the Persians. Abū Ḥātim[619] said that Abū ʿUbaydah[620] said: It [comes from the word] *sidillī* which was Arabicized to *sadīr*.[621]

---

3 in … anything : [The verb] *ġanū* means they lived in contentment. [The word] *maġnan* denotes a place where people dwell with ease and contentment, where there is no distress (marginal gloss in al-Maqrīzī's hand). 5 solid … stable : That is, [with reference to the meaning of *ṯābit al-awtād*], firmly established (marginal gloss in al-Maqrīzī's hand). Lit. "In the shadow of a kingdom whose tent pegs are planted in the ground." See also Lyall (1918): 164; Jones (2011): 431.

---

613 See also Jones (2011): 431: "It is as though they had [only] a fixed time [to live there]"; Lyall (1918): 161 has "as though their lords had been set a time and no more to be."

614 See Jones (2011): 432.

615 I.e. the palm trees seemed "black" to them from a distance. See Lane (1863–1893): 1462; "Sawād," in *EI*[2] (H.H. Schaeder).

616 On al-Ǧawālīqī ("maker of sacks"), or Ibn al-Ǧawālīqī, Abū Manṣūr Mawhūb b. Aḥmad (d. 539/1144), see "al-Djawālīḳī," in *EI*[2] (H. Fleisch).

617 See note 621 below.

618 Al-Munḏir III (d. 554).

619 For more on the Arab philologist Abū Ḥātim al-Siǧistānī (d. 255/869), see "Abū Ḥātim al-Sijistānī," in *EI*[3] (R. Weipert).

620 On Abū ʿUbaydah Maʿmar b. al-Muṯanná (d. ca. 210/825), a *mawlá* of the Banū Taym b. Murrah, see "Abū ʿUbayda," in *EI*[3] (R. Weipert).

621 See Lane (1863–1893): 1333–1334: "سدلي … an arabicized word, originally, in Pers., سِهْ دِلَّهْ ['three-hearter'], as though it were three chambers in one chamber …"; see also al-Ṭabarī, *History*, 5:81, n. 218: "Some of the Arabic philologists sought a forced etymology for its name in *si dihlī*(*z*) 'having three compartments, portices.'"

وذكر أبو العباس المبرد في **كتاب الاشتقاق**: سمي بذلك لاتصال بنيته ومن هذا سمي السِدْر لأن ورقه باق ولا ينتثر حيث يَعدم الشجر ورقه. وقال الحازمي: هو من أبنية آل المنذر عند الحيرة. وقال ابن حبيب: سدير النخل سواده وشخوصه.[a] يقال سدير إبل وسدير نخل.[b]

§187 وسنداد قال الكلبي عن الشرقي: هو بناء على الفرات {يرفأ} فيه لأن سفن الهند كانت ترسى

---

٤ يرفأ: في الأصل "ترفا".

---

a راجع ابن منظور، لسان العرب، دهم ("وأنشد ابن الأعرابي في صفة نخل:

دُهْمًا كأَنَّ الليل في زُهَائِها   لا تَرْهَبُ الذِّئب على أطلائها

يعني أنها خُضْر إلى السواد من الرِّيّ، وأن اجتماعها يُرِي شُخُوصَها سودًا، وزهاؤها شخوصها"). وراجع ابن منظور، لسان العرب، سدر ("وسديرُ النخل: سوادُه ومُجتَمَعُه").

b قارن ياقوت، معجم البلدان، ٣: ٢٠١ ("وقال ابن السكيت: قال الأصمعي السدير فارسية أصله سه دل، أي قبة فيها ثلاث قباب متداخلة، وهو الذي تسميه الناس اليوم سِدِلّى فعربته العرب فقالوا سدير، وفي نوادر الأصمعي التي رواها عنه أبو يعلى قال: قال أبو عمرو بن العلاء السدير العُشب، انقضى كلام أبي منصور؛ وقال العمراني: السدير موضع معروف بالحيرة، وقال: السدير نهر، وقيل: قصر قريب من الخورنق كان النعمان الأكبر اتخذه لبعض ملوك العجم، قال أبو حاتم: سمعت أبا عبيدة يقول هو السِّدِلّى أي له ثلاثة أبواب، وهو فارسيّ معرّب، وقيل: سمي السدير لكثرة سواده وشجره، ويقال: إني لأرى سدير نخل أي سواده وكثرته، وقال الكلبي: إنّما سمي السدير لأن العرب حيث أقبلوا ونظروا إلى سواد النخل سدرت فيه أعينهم بسواد النخل فقالوا: ما هذا إلّا سدير؛ قال: والسدير أيضًا أرض باليمن تنسب إليها البرود؛ قال الأعشى:

وبيداء قفر كبُرد السدير   مشاربها دائرات أُجُن

وقد ذكر بعض أهل الأثر أنّه إنّما سمّي السدير سديرًا لأن العرب لما أشرفت على السواد ونظروا إلى سواد النخل سدرت أعينهم فقالوا: ما هذا إلّا سدير، وهذا ليس بشيء لأنّه سمّي سديرًا قبل الإسلام بزمن، وقد ذكره عدي بن زيد، وكان هلاكه قبل الإسلام بمدة، والأسود بن يعفر، وهو جاهليّ قديم، بقوله:

أهل الخوَرنق والسّدير وبارقٍ   والقصر ذي الشرفات من سِنداد").

Abū l-ʿAbbās al-Mubarrad reported in *Kitāb al-Ištiqāq* [The Book of Derivation]: It was given this name because its structure remained intact.[622] The *sidr* tree[623] was given its name for the same reason, since its leaves remain and do not fall off when the trees lose their leaves. Al-Ḥāzimī[624] said: It is one of the edifices of the family of al-Mundir near al-Ḥīrah. Ibn Ḥabīb[625] said: The word *sadīr*, when used in relation to palm trees (*sadīr al-naḫl*), refers to their dark color [i.e. when seen from a distance]. It is used in relation to camels (*sadīr ibil*) and palm trees [i.e. in reference to their dark color when seen from a distance].

§ 187 As for Sindād, al-Kalbī said on the authority of al-Šarqī:[626] It is an edifice on the Euphrates to which ships were brought; the ships of India

622 Lit. "Due to the connectedness of its structure."

623 For more on the species of tree called *sidr*, see "Sidr," in *EI*² (R. Kruk). This tree is also mentioned in the accounts concerning Ḏāt Anwāṭ (see below, § 199 and § 200).

624 Abū Bakr Muḥammad b. Mūsá l-Ḥāzimī (d. 584/1188), the compiler of *al-Nāsiḫ wa-l-mansūḫ*, *al-Muʾtalif wa-l-muḫtalif fī asmāʾ al-buldān*, and others; al-Ḏahabī, *Siyar aʿlām al-nubalāʾ*, 21:167–172.

625 Abū Ǧaʿfar Muḥammad b. Ḥabīb, the compiler of *al-Muḥabbar* and *al-Munammaq*; "Muḥammad b. Ḥabīb," in *EI*² (I. Lichtenstädter).

626 Al-Šarqī b. al-Quṭāmī (d. ca. 150/767 or ca. 155/772); "al-Sharḳī b. al-Ḳuṭāmī," *in EI*² (W.P. Heinrichs).

إليه.[a] وفي **كتاب الأمصار** للجاحظ: هو قصر بظهر الكوفة. وفي **مأدبة الأدباء**: | هو الذي كانت 45*b تحجه الأعراب في الجاهلية الجهلاء. وفي **ديوان الأدب** للفارابي: سنداد اسم نهر[b] والشرفات الشماريخ واحدها شُرفة.

46a §188 ذو الخَلَصَة. قال البكري: بفتح أوله وثانيه وفتح الصاد المهملة. بيت بالعبلاء كانت خثعم تحجه انتهى.[c] والعبلاء على ثلاث مراحل من مكة قريب من الطائف ومن تُربة. وإنما سمي ذا الخلَصَة بخرزة كانت على رأسه.

قال أبو زيد عمر بن شبة: واتخذت خثعم ودوس بيتا يقال له ذو الخَلَصَة عليه {كهيئة} التاج. وقال مرة: كان مروة بيضاء منقوشة عليها {كهيئة} التاج. وكان بتبَالَة بين مكة واليمن على مسيرة {ثماني} ليال من مكة.[d] وكان سدنتها بنو أُبامة من باهلة بن أعصر[e] وكان خثعم وبجيلة وأزد السراة

٤–٦ قال ... رأسه: الزيادة بخط المقريزي في الهامش الأيسر ويشير إليها رمز ٦ بعد "الخلَصَة". ٧ كهيئة: في الأصل "كهية". ٨ كهيئة: في الأصل "كهية". ٩ ثماني: في الأصل "ثمان".

---

a راجع المسعودي، مروج الذهب، ١: ١١٧–١١٨ ("وقد كان الفرات الأكثر من مائه ينتهي إلى بلاد الحِيرة ونهرها بيّن الى هذا الوقت، وهو يُعرف بالعَتِيق، وعليه كانت وقعة المسلمين مع رُسْتَم وهي وقعة القادِسيَّة، فيصبّ في البحر الحبَشي، وكان البحر يومئذٍ في الموضع المعروف بالنَّجَف في هذا الوقت، وكان يقدم هنالك سفُن الصين والهِند ترِد إلى ملوك الحيرة").

b راجع الفارابي، ديوان الأدب، ٢: ٧٣ ("سِنْداد: اسْمُ نهر").

c راجع البكري، معجم ما استعجم، ٢: ٥٠٨.

d قارن ابن حبيب، المحبر، ٣١٧ ("وكان ذو الخلصة له بيت تعبده بجيلة وخثعم والحارث بن كعب وجرم وزبيد والغوث بن مر بن اد وبنو هلال بن عامر، وكانوا سدنته. وكان بين مكة واليمن، كان بالعبلاء على أربع مراحل من مكة. وهو اليوم بيت قصّار، فيما اخبرت"). وقارن أيضا: الأزرقي، أخبار مكة[1]، ١: ١٩٦ ("نصب عمرو بن لُحَيّ الخلَصة بأسفل مكة، فكانوا يكسونها القلائد ويهدون إليها الشعير والحنطة ويصبّون عليها اللبن ويذبحون لها ويعلّقون عليها بَيْض النّعام، ونصب على الصفا صنمًا يقال له: نهيك مُجاودُ الريح، ونصب على المروة صنمًا يقال له: مُطعِم الطير").

e قارن ابن الكلبي، الأصنام، ٣٥ ("وكان سَدَنَتَها بنو أُمَامَةَ من باهِلَةَ بنِ أَعْصُرَ").

anchored there. In *Kitāb al-Amṣār* [The Book of Capital Cities][627] of al-Ǧāḥiẓ[628] [it is said that] it is a castle on the outskirts of Kufa. In *Maʾdubat al-udabāʾ* [Instructing the *udabāʾ* in *adab*],[629] [it is said that] it is [the place] to which the Bedouins made pilgrimage[s] in the Ǧāhiliyyah.[630] In *Dīwān al-adab*[631] of al-Fārābī[632] [it is said that] Sindād is the name of a river, and *šurufāt*, whose singular is *šurufah*, are the highest portions (*šamārīḫ*).[633]

§188 Ḏū l-Ḫalaṣah: Al-Bakrī said that it has a *fatḥah* over its first and second letters, and a *fatḥah* over the *ṣād*. [It was] a sanctuary in al-ʿAblāʾ to which Ḫaṯʿam made pilgrimage[s]. Unquote. Al-ʿAblāʾ is at a distance of three days' journey from Mecca, near al-Ṭāʾif and Turabah.[634] It was called Ḏū l-Ḫalaṣah because of a precious stone that was on its [the idol's] head.

Abū Zayd ʿUmar b. Šabbah said: Ḫaṯʿam and Daws adopted a sanctuary called Ḏū l-Ḫalaṣah, upon which there was [something] in the shape of a crown. On another occasion, he said: It was a sculpted white flint rock, upon which there was [something] in the shape of a crown.[635] It was in Tabālah,[636] between Mecca and Yemen, at a distance of eight nights' journey from Mecca. Its custodians were the Banū Ubāmah[637] of Bāhilah b. Aʿṣur. The

627 For more detail on *al-Amṣār wa-ʿaǧāʾib al-buldān* [The Book of Capital Cities and the Wonders of Countries], see Pellat (1969): 22.

628 Abū ʿUṯmān ʿAmr b. Baḥr (d. 255/868), who is known by the name al-Ǧāḥiẓ, was a well-known compiler of several *adab* works; "al-Djāḥiẓ," in *EI*² (Ch. Pellat).

629 The author of this work is al-Ḥasan b. al-Muẓaffar al-Nīsābūrī, who, according to *al-Wāfī bi-l-wafayāt* died in 442/1050 or 1051. See al-Ṣafadī, *al-Wāfī bi-l-wafayāt*, 12:169.

630 *Fī l-ǧāhiliyyah al-ǧahlāʾ*. According to one explanation, the adjective *ǧahlāʾ* in this phrase is used to emphasize the intensity of the Ǧāhiliyyah; Lane (1863–1893): 478.

631 The full title of this work is *Dīwān al-adab fī bayān luġat al-ʿarab* [Collected *Adab* Traditions Explaining the Language of the Arabs].

632 Abū Ibrāhīm Isḥāq b. Ibrāhīm al-Fārābī (d. 350/961); "al-Fārābī," in *EI*² (H. Fleisch).

633 The word *šamārīḫ* denotes the uppermost parts of clouds, mountains, and trees; Lane (1863–1893): 1596. In this context, it probably refers to the highest portions of edifices or castles.

634 For Turabah, see Yāqūt, *Muʿǧam al-buldān*, 2:21.

635 *Kāna marwah bayḍāʾ manqūšah ʿalayhā ka-hayʾati l-tāǧ*. This sentence may also be translated as follows, "it was a white flint rock upon which [something] in the shape of a crown was sculpted." See also: Stummer (1944): 378; Hawting (1999): 129, n. 57.

636 See "Tabāla," in *EI*² (G.R. Smith).

637 Elsewhere, this appears as Umāmah; see "Dhu 'l Khalaṣa," in *EI*² (T. Fahd).

ومن قاربهم من بطون العرب من هوازن تعظمها وتهدي لها. وفيها يقول {خداش} بن زهير لعثعث ابن {وحشي} الخثعمي في عقد كان بينهم فغدر به: [الطويل]

وذكّرته بالله بيني وبينه   وما بيننا من مُدة لو تذكرا
وبالمروة البيضاء يوم تبالة   ومحبَسة النعمٰن حيث تنصرا[a]

§189 وذكر أبو الفرج في **كتاب الأغاني** أن امرأ القيس بن حُجْر الكندي لحق بقيل من الأقيال فأمده وتبعه شُذاذ من العرب وسار إلى بني أسد[b] ومر بتبالة وبها ذو الخلصة فاستقسم عنده

١ خداش : في الأصل "خراش". ٢ وحشي : في الأصل "وحنس" (راجع ابن الكلبي، كتاب الأصنام، ٣٥)، ووضع المقريزي رمز "ح" تحت الكلمة إشارة إلى تلفظها بالحاء. ٦ شُذاذ : الذالان مهملتان في الأصل.

a قارن البغدادي، خزانة الأدب، ١: ١٩٠ ("وما بيننا من هذه (!) لو تذكّرا"). وقارن أيضا: ياقوت، معجم البلدان، ٢: ٣٨٣

("وبالمروة البيضاء ثم تبالة   ومجلسة النعمان حيث تنصّرا")

وراجع زهير بن خداش، شعر زهير بن خداش، ٧٤

("فأبّي وأيُّ ابنِ الحُصَينِ وعَثْعَثٍ   إذا ما التَقَيْنَا كان بالحِلْفِ أغْدَرَا

ولعل البيت مع البيتين السابقين من قصيدة في هجاء عثعث الخثعمي"). وراجع أيضا سيبويه، كتاب سيبويه، ٢: ٤٠٣

("فأبّي وأيُّ ابنِ الحُصَينِ وعَثْعَثٍ   غداةَ التَقَيْنا كان عندك أعْذَرا")

b قارن الإصبهاني، الأغاني، ٩: ١١٠–١١١ ("وقال ابن الكلبيّ والهَيْثم بن عَدِيّ وعمر بن شَبَّة وابن قُتَيْبة: فلمّا امتنعتْ بكرُ بن وائل وتَغْلِب من اتّباع بني أسد خرج من فَوْره ذلك إلى اليمن فاستنصر أَزْد شَنُوءَةَ، فأبَوْا أن ينصروه وقالوا: إخواننا وجيراننا. فنزل بقَيْلٍ يُدْعَى مَرْثَد الخير بن ذي جَدَن الحِمْيَريّ، وكانت بينهما قَرابة، فاستنصره واستمدّه على بني أسد، فأمدّه بخمسمائة رجل من حِمْيَرَ، ومات مرثد قبل رحيل امرئ القيس بهم، وقام بالمملكة بعده رجلٌ من حمير يقال له قَرْمَل بن الحميم وكانت أمُّه سوداء، فتردَّد امرأ القيس وطوّل عليه حتى همّ بالانصراف وقال:

وإذ نحن ندعو مَرْثَد الخيرِ ربَّنا   وإذ نحن لا نُدْعَى عَبيدًا لقَرْمَلِ

فأنفذ له ذلك الجيشَ، وتبعه شُذَّاذٌ من العرب، واستأجر من قبائل العرب رجالًا، فسار بهم إلى بني أسد").

Ḫaṯʿam, Bağīlah, Azd al-Sarāt, and the Bedouin clans of Hawāzin that were in their proximity venerated it, and offered gifts to it. Ḫidāš b. Zuhayr[638] said [the following verses] about it, [and addressed them] to ʿAṯʿaṯ b. Waḥšī[639] l-Ḫaṯʿamī, regarding a treaty that existed between them, but was broken by him [ʿAṯʿaṯ]: [*al-ṭawīl*]

And I reminded him of Allāh between me and him,[640]
and of the truce (*muddah*)[641] between us—if he had only remembered—
and of the white flint rock on the day of Tabālah,[642]
and the prison of al-Nuʿmān, where he became a Christian.[643]

§189 Abū l-Farağ[644] reported in *Kitāb al-Aġānī* [The Book of Songs] that Imruʾ al-Qays b. Ḥuğr al-Kindī[645] reached one of the [Ḥimyarī] princes,[646] and he [the prince] supplied him [with warriors]. Bedouins who were not living among their tribes also followed him, and he went [to fight] the Banū Asad. He passed by Tabālah, where Ḏū l-Ḫalaṣah was located; he sought

638 For more on the *muḫaḍram* poet Ḫidāš (not Ḫirāš as read by al-Maqrīzī) b. Zuhayr al-ʿĀmirī of the Banū ʿĀmir b. Ṣaʿṣaʿah, see "Khidāsh b. Zuhayr al-Aṣghar," in EI² (Ch. Pellat).

639 Not وحنس as read by al-Maqrīzī.

640 I.e. That Allāh is our witness. Regarding the formula *Allāh baynī wa-baynaka* ("Allāh is between me and you"), see Klinke-Rosenberger (1941): 115, n. 260.

641 For the meaning of *muddah*, see Dozy (1881), 2:581.

642 Or perhaps this refers to the battle of Tabālah (?). See also Ḫidāš b. Zuhayr, *Šiʿr*, 73.

643 See also Klinke-Rosenberger (1941): 48–49, 116; Grunebaum (1953): 45.

644 Abū l-Farağ al-Iṣfahānī (or al-Iṣbahānī; d. after 360/971); "Abū l-Faraj al-Iṣfahānī," in EI³ (S. Günther).

645 Imruʾ al-Qays was a sixth-century pre-Islamic poet. According to the sources, he was the youngest son of Ḥuğr, who was the last king of Kindah, but the king expelled him from court twice because of his poetry, and he lived the life of a vagabond. When news reached him that his father was assassinated by the Banū Asad, he devoted his life to avenging his death; see "Imruʾ al-Ḳays b. Ḥudjr," in EI² (S. Boustany).

646 *Bi-qayl mina l-aqyāl*. Regarding the word *qayl* see al-Ṭabarī, *History*, 5:184, n. 473; "Ḳayl," in EI² (A.F.L. Beeston).

بقداحه الآمِر والناهي والمتربص فخرج الناهي فكسرها وضرب بها وجهه وقال: "مَصَصْتَ[a] بَظْرَ أمك. لو قتِل أبوك ما عوقتني." ثم خرج فظفر ببني أسد وقال: [الرجز]

لو كنت يا ذا الخَلَصَةِ الموتورا   دُوْني وكان شيخك المقبورا[b]
لم تنه عن قتل العُدَاة زُوْرا

فلم يُسْتَقْسَم عند ذي الخلصة بقِدح حتى جاء الإسلام وهدمه جرير بن عبد الله.

§190 قال أبو علي: ذو الخلصَة بفتح الخاء واللام. وقال غيره: أسكن امرؤ القيس هذا للضرورة. وذكر المبرد عن أبي عبيدة أن موضع ذي الخلصة مسجد جامع لبلدة يقال لها العبلات من أرض خثعم.[c]

---

٤ زُوْرا: أضاف المقريزي الحاشية التالية في الهامش الأيسر: "حـ نصب زورا على الحال من المصدر الذي هو النهي. أراد نهيا زورا."

---

a راجع ابن منظور، لسان العرب، "مصص" ("قال الأزهري: ومن العرب من يقول مَصَصْتُ الرّمانَ أَمُصُّ، والفصيح الجيدَ مَصِصْت، بالكسر، أَمَصُّ").

b قارن ابن الكلبي، الأصنام، ٣٥ ("قال رجل منهم:
لو كُنْتَ ياذا الخلَص المَوْتُورَا   مِثْلِي وكان شَيْخُكَ المقبورَا")

c راجع المبرد، الكامل، ٤: ٥٥؛ قارن ابن حجر، فتح الباري، ٨: ٣٩٩ ("وحكى المبرد أن موضع ذي الخلصة صار مسجدًا جامعًا لبلدة يقال لها العبلات من أرض خثعم، ووهم من قال إنه كان في بلاد فارس"). وقارن أيضا أبو عبيدة، الديباج، ٣٦ ("كانت بنو الحارث تسمى المنتشر مجدّعًا فطلبُوه فلم يقدروا عليه حتّى حجّ ذا الخلصة وهو بيت بالعَبْلاء كانت خَثْعمُ ومن وَلِيَهم من قيّسٍ وغيرهم يَحُجُّونه قال: وهو اليوم مسجد العَبْلاء")؛ وياقوت، معجم البلدان، ٤: ٨٠ ("والعبلاء، وقيل العَبَلات: بلدة كانت لخثعم بها كان ذو الخلَصة بيتُ صنمٍ، وهي من أرض تبَالة").

divine guidance there by consulting its arrows: The commanding [arrow], the forbidding [arrow], and the awaiting [arrow]. The forbidding one came out, so he broke them, struck them against its [the idol's] face, and said: Go suck your mother's clitoris! If your father had been killed you would not have hindered me. Then he left, defeated the Banū Asad, and said:[647] [*al-rağaz*]

If you, O Ḏū l-Ḫalaṣah,[648] were the one in my place,[649] seeking blood revenge for the murder
of a relative, and if your father (*šayḫ*) was the one who was buried,
you would not have falsely (*zūrā*) forbidden the slaying of the enemies.

[From then on] arrows were not consulted for divine guidance near Ḏū l-Ḫalaṣah until the advent of Islam. It was destroyed by Ğarīr b. ʿAbd Allāh.

§ 190 Abū ʿAlī said: Ḏū l-Ḫalaṣah has a *fatḥah* over the *ḫāʾ* and *lām*. Others said: Imruʾ al-Qays pronounced it [the letter *lām* in the verse] without a vowel out of poetic necessity.

Al-Mubarrad reported on the authority of Abū ʿUbaydah[650] that Ḏū l-Ḫalaṣah was located in the [place of what was later the] congregational mosque of a town called al-ʿAbalāt[651] in the land of Ḫaṯʿam.

---

9 falsely : He [the poet] put the word *zūr* in the accusative because it is a circumstantial phrase (*ḥāl*) of the verbal noun (*maṣdar*), which is "forbiddance" (*al-nahy*; the *maṣdar* was omitted from the literal utterance). He had in mind the phrase "false forbiddance" (*nahyan zūran*) (marginal gloss in al-Maqrīzī's hand). The grammatical function of the word *zūr* in this line is discussed in more detail in al-Suhaylī, *al-Rawḍ al-unuf*, 1:374.

---

647 According to *al-Aṣnām*, the attribution of these verses to Imruʾ al-Qays is incorrect; Ibn al-Kalbī, *al-Aṣnām* 35.

648 See below (§ 190) for more information on the vocalization of this word in the verse.

649 *Dūnī*; other sources have *miṯlī* (like me); see Ibn al-Kalbī, *al-Aṣnām* 35; Klinke-Rosenberger (1941): 48.

650 On whom see n. 620.

651 Compare Abū ʿUbaydah, *al-Dībāğ*, 36, which has al-ʿAblāʾ.

§191 وخرج| البخاري ومسلم من حديث قيس عن جرير قال: كان بيت في الجاهلية يقال له 46b
ذو الخلصة والكعبة اليمانية والكعبة الشامية.[a] فقال لي النبي ﷺ: "ألا تُرِيحُني من ذي الخلَصَة؟" فنفرت في مائة وخمسين راكبا من أَحْمَس فكسرناه وقتلنا من وجدنا عنده فأتيت النبي ﷺ فأخبرته فدعا لنا ولأَحْمس.

وقال فيه مسلم: وكان يقال له الكعبة اليمانية والكعبة الشامية. وقال فيه: "هل أنت مريحي من ذي الخلصة والكعبة اليمانية والشامية؟" ولم يقل فيه البخاري "من أحمس".[b] وذكره البخاري في المناقب وكرره هو ومسلم بزيادة.[c]

§192 وقال ابن شَبَّة: وذو الخلصة اليوم عتبة باب مسجد تبالة. وبلغنا أن رسول الله ﷺ قال: "لا تذهب الدنيا حتى تصطك أليات نساء دَوْس على ذي الخلصة[d] يعبدونها كما كانت تعبد."

---

٢ الشامية : في الأصل "الشأمية". ٥ مسلم : وضع المقريزي ثلاث نقط تحت الكلمة إشارة إلى تلفظها بالسين.

---

a راجع ابن حجر، فتح الباري، ٨: ٣٩٩–٤٠٠ ("والكعبة اليمانية والكعبة الشامية) كذا فيه. قيل: وهو غلط والصواب اليمانية فقط، سموها بذلك مضاهاة للكعبة، والكعبة البيت الحرام بالنسبة لمن يكون في جهة اليمن شامية فسموا التي بمكة شامية والتي عندهم يمانية تفريقًا بينهم. والذي يظهر لي أن الذي في الرواية صواب وأنها كان يقال لها اليمانية باعتبار كونها باليمن والشامية باعتبار أنهم جعلوا بابها مقابل الشام"). وقارن أيضا ابن كثير، السيرة النبوية، ١: ٧١ ("وكان ذو الخلَصة لدَوْس وخَثْعم وبجِيلة ومن كان ببلادهم من العرب بتَبالَة، وكان يقال له الكعبة اليمانية، ولبيت مكة الكعبة الشامية").

b راجع ابن حجر، فتح الباري، ٨: ٣٩٨ ("فَنَفَرْتُ فِي مِائَةٍ وَخَمْسِينَ رَاكِبًا فَكَسَرْنَاهُ").

c راجع مسلم، صحيح، ٤: ١٩٢٥–١٩٢٦؛ البخاري، صحيح، ٣: ١٣٩٠. راجع أيضا البخاري، صحيح، ٤: ١٥٨٢–١٥٨٣.

d قارن ابن حجر، فتح الباري، ٨: ٣٩٩ ("لا تقوم الساعة حتى تضطرب أليات نساء دوس حول ذي الخلصة").

§ 191 Al-Buḫārī and Muslim quoted Qays's[652] *ḥadīṯ* on the authority of Ǧarīr [b. ʿAbd Allāh], who said: There was a sanctuary in the Ǧāhiliyyah known by the names Ḏū l-Ḫalaṣah, al-Kaʿbah al-Yamāniyyah, and al-Kaʿbah al-Šāmiyyah.[653] The Prophet, may Allāh bless and save him, said to me: "Will you not relieve me of Ḏū l-Ḫalaṣah?" Thereupon, I left with one hundred fifty riders from Aḥmas,[654] and we destroyed it and killed whomever we found near it. Then I went to the Prophet, may Allāh bless and save him, informed him [of what had happened], and he invoked a blessing upon us and upon Aḥmas.

Muslim said in it [i.e. in his *ḥadīṯ* about Ḏū l-Ḫalaṣah]: It was called [both] al-Kaʿbah al-Yamāniyyah and al-Kaʿbah al-Šāmiyyah. He also said in it [his *ḥadīṯ*]: "Will you relieve me of Ḏū l-Ḫalaṣah, and al-Kaʿbah al-Yamāniyyah and al-Šāmiyyah?" Al-Buḫārī did not mention in it [i.e. in his *ḥadīṯ*; the words] "from Aḥmas." Al-Buḫārī reported it [the *ḥadīṯ*] in [the chapter titled] "The virtues" (*al-Manāqib*), and both he and Muslim repeated it several times with additional wording.

§ 192 Ibn Šabbah said: Today, Ḏū l-Ḫalaṣah is the threshold of the mosque of Tabālah. We were informed that the Messenger of Allāh, may Allāh bless and save him, said: "This world shall not perish until the buttocks of the women of Daws shake beside Ḏū l-Ḫalaṣah, while they [i.e. the Daws] worship it in the manner that it was worshipped [before Islam]."[655]

---

652 Qays b. Abī Ḥāzim al-Baǧalī; al-Ḏahabī, *Siyar aʿlām al-nubalāʾ*, 4:198–202.

653 According to this account, the names al-Kaʿbah al-Šāmiyyah and al-Kaʿbah al-Yamāniyyah both refer to Ḏū l-Ḫalaṣah. Indeed, some explain that Ḏū l-Ḫalaṣah was called al-Kaʿbah al-Šāmiyyah because its door faced al-Šām. However, others claim that Ḏū l-Ḫalaṣah was called al-Kaʿbah al-Yamāniyyah whereas the Kaʿbah in Mecca was called al-Kaʿbah al-Šāmiyyah, and therefore, the identification of Ḏū l-Ḫalaṣah with al-Kaʿbah al-Šāmiyyah is incorrect; Ibn Ḥaǧar, *Fatḥ al-bārī*, 8:399–400; Lane (1863–1893): 786. See also "Dhu l Khalaṣa," in *EI*² (T. Fahd).

654 Note that Ǧarīr was not a member of Aḥmas. He belonged to the Qasr, another branch of the Baǧīlah. See the introduction.

655 Regarding this *ḥadīṯ* and its variants, see Hawting (1999): 124; Lecker (2005a): 23. And see also Klinke-Rosenberger (1941): 49.

ومن خرافات العرب أن امرأة فاجرة ساحرة دعت غلاما من أهل اليمن إلى نفسها فأبى عليها فسحرته فصار نعامة وكانت له أم صالحة فدعت عليها الله تعالى فمسخت حجرا فهي الطاغوت الذي كان يسمى ذا الخلصة معبود دوس وخثعم وبجيلة ومن كان ببلادهم من العرب.

§193 وكانت كعبة نجران لبني الحٰرث بن كعب من نجران بناها بنو عبد المدان على بناء الكعبة.[a] وقيل هي قبة من أدم إذا نزل بها مستجير ⟨أجير⟩[b] أو طالب حاجة قضيت. ولها يقول أعشى بني بكر بن وائل يمدح بني عبد المدان: [المتقارب]

١-٣ ومن ... العرب: الزيادة بخط المقريزي في الهامش الأيمن منقلبة، ويشير إليها رمز ⌐ بعد "تعبد". ٤-٥ بناها ... قضيت: الزيادة بخط المقريزي في الهامش الأيسر في آخر السطر بجانب كلمة "نجران"، من الأسفل إلى الأعلى، ثم من الأعلى إلى الأسفل. ٥ أجير: قارن الإصبهاني، كتاب الأغاني.

a قارن البكري، معجم ما استعجم، ٢: ٦٠٣ ("[دير نجرْان] وهو المسمى كَعْبة نَجران، كان لآل عبد المَدَان بن الدّيّان، سادة بني الحارث بن كعب. وكان بَنَوْه (!) مُرَبَّعًا مُستوي الأضلاع والأقطار، مرتفعا من الأرض، يُصعَد إليه بدرجة، على مثال بناء الكَعْبة، فكانوا يَحُجُّونه هم وطوائف من العرب، ممن يُحِلّ الأشهر الحُرُم، ولا يَحُجُّون الكعبة، وتَحُجُّه خثعم قاطبة"). وقارن ياقوت، معجم البلدان، ٥: ٢٦٨-٢٦٩ ("وكعبة نجران هذه يقال بيعة بناها بنو عبد المدان بن الدّيّان الحارثي على بناء الكعبة وعظموها مضاهاة للكعبة وسموها كعبة نجران وكان فيها أساقفة مُعتَمّون وهم الذين جاؤوا إلى النبي، ﷺ، ودعاهم إلى المباهلة، وذكر هشام بن الكلبي أنها كانت قبّة من أدم من ثلثمائة جلد، كان إذا جاءها الخائفُ أمن أو طالبُ حاجة قُضيت أو مسترفد أُرفد، وكان لعظمها عندهم يسمّونها كعبة نجران، وكانت على نهر بنجران، وكانت لعبد المسيح بن دارس بن عدي بن معقل، وكان يستغلّ من ذلك النهر عشرة آلاف دينار وكانت القبّة تستغرقها").

b قارن الإصبهاني، الأغاني، ١١: ٣٨٢ ("وكان إذا نزل بها مستجيرٌ أُجِير، أو خائف أَمِن، أو طالبُ حاجة قُضيت، أو مسترفد أُعْطي ما يُريده").

One of the fantastical stories of the Arabs has it that a wicked sorceress invited a young man of the people of Yemen to take her [i.e., she attempted to seduce him], but he refused, so she bewitched him, and he became an ostrich. He had a pious mother, who invoked Allāh, the Exalted, against her, and she [the sorceress] was transformed into stone. She [the sorceress] is the *ṭāġūt* which was called Ḏū l-Ḫalaṣah, the idol (*maʿbūd*) of the Daws, Ḫaṯʿam, Baǧīlah, and the Bedouins who were in their lands.

§193 The Kaʿbah of Naǧrān belonged to the Banū l-Ḥāriṯ b. Kaʿb of Naǧrān.[656] The Banū ʿAbd al-Madān built it according to the structure of the Kaʿbah. It was said: It was a dome-shaped structure made of pieces of leather. When someone who sought protection stayed there he was protected, and when someone was in need help was provided. Aʿšá of the Banū Bakr b. Wāʾil[657] said [the following verses] about it, extolling the Banū ʿAbd al-Madān: [*al-mutaqārib*]

656 On the Kaʿbah of Naǧrān, see Shahid (1979): 70–74.

657 On whom see note 444.

〈و〉كعبة نجران حتم عليـ	ـك حتى تُنـاخي بأبوابها
تزور {يزيد وعبد المسيح}	وقيسًا هُـم خير أربابها[a]
وشاهدنا الجُلُّ والياسميـ	ـنُ والمُسْمِعات {بقُصابها}
وبَرْبَطُها دائم مُعْمَلٌ	فأيُ الثلاثة أزْرَى بها[b]

الجُل الورد. وأزرى 〈بها〉 أي بالمُسْمِعات وقيل بناقته.[c]

---

١ وكـعبة : كشط المقريزي الواو ولكن هي لازمة للعروض. ‖ حـتم : وضع المقريزي رمز "ح" تحت الكلمة إشارة إلى تلفظها بالحاء. ٢-٥ تزور ... بناقته : الزيادة بخط المقريزي في وسط السطر بعد كلمة "بأبوابها"، ثم في الهامش الأيسر من الأعلى إلى الأسفل. ٢ يزيد ... المسيـح : في الأصل "يزيد بن عبد المسيـح" (راجع الأعشى، ديوان، ١٢٢). ٣ بقُصابها : في الأصل "بقُضْبانها" (راجع ابن منظور، لسان العرب، "قصب": وقال الأصمعي: أراد الأعشى بالقُصَّاب الأَوْتارَ التي سُوِّيَتْ مِنَ الأَمْعاءِ؛ وقال أَبو عمرو: هي المزامير). ٤ أزْرَى : في الأصل "ازرا".

---

a قارن الأعشى، ديوان شعر الأعشى، ١٢٢ ("[نَزُو]رُيَزِيدَ وَعَبْدَ ٱلْمَسِيحِ وَقَيْسًا هُمُ خَيْرُ أَرْبَابِهَا").

b قارن الأعشى، ديوان شعر الأعشى، ١٢٢ ("وَمِزْمَرُنَا مُعْمَلُ دَائِمٌ فَأَيُّ الثّلاثَةِ أُزْرَى بِهَا").

c قارن ابن قتيبة، المعاني، ١: ٤٦٨-٤٦٩ ("أزرى بها يقال بالمسمعات وقيل بالباقة").

And the Kaʿbah of Nağrān is imposed upon
you [fem. sing.] until you are knelt down by its doors.
You [masc. sg.] visit Yazīd, ʿAbd al-Masīḥ[658]
and Qays, they are its best lords.
The roses (*al-ğull*) and jasmine flower are present with us,
while the songstresses [perform] on their lute strings.[659]
Their [or its] lute[660] is employed continuously.
Which of the three disgraced them [or it; *azrá bihā*]?[661]

[The word] *al-ğull* means "the roses," and [the attached pronoun *hā* in] *azrá bihā* refers to the songstresses or to his she-camel,[662] according to another opinion [?].

658 Not Yazīd b. ʿAbd al-Masīḥ as read by al-Maqrīzī.

659 Read *bi-quṣṣābihā* not *bi-quḍbānihā* as al-Maqrīzī did. Compare Howell (1880–1911): part 1, vol. 3a: 892: "And our witness is the rose and the jasmine and the songstresses with their flutes." And see also Lane (1863–1893): 2529, where the word *aqṣābihā* replaces *quṣṣābihā*: "The rose being present with us, and the jasmine, and the songstresses with their chords of gut … or, as some relate it, he said بِقُصَّابِهَا, meaning with their musical reeds, or pipes."

660 Other versions of this line have "our lute"; al-Iṣfahānī, *al-Aġānī*, 11:381.

661 Or perhaps, "Which of the three disgraces it most?"

662 Other accounts have *bāqah* instead of *nāqatihi*, which is perhaps better in this context (Ibn Qutaybah, *al-Maʿānī*, 1:468–469). *Bāqah* means "a bundle" or "a bouquet," and it is possible that this refers to the roses and jasmine. Perhaps the "three" who are mentioned in the poem were Yazīd, ʿAbd al-Masīḥ, and Qays. Note that the lines above appear in a different order in al-Aʿšá, *Dīwān šiʿr al-Aʿšá* 121–122.

194§ وكان لحمير بصنعاء بيت يقال له رِيَام كانوا يتحاكمون إليه ويكلمهم منه شيطان: فلما تهود تبع قالت الأحبار: "إنما هذا الذي يكلمهم من البيت شيطان فنحن نخرجه لكم." فدخلوا بالتورية فدرسوها حتى خرج من البيت كلب أسود فهدموه. وأشار عليه بهدمه الحبران اللذان كانا {ينهيانه} عن هدم الكعبة حين كان سار إلى الحجاز والتهمه.[a]

195§ قال: ولما غزا يوسف الذي قتل أصحاب الأخدود بنجْران وعبرت الحبش إلى صنعاء بنى أبرهة الأشرم الحبشي القليس بصنعاء وجعل فيه بيتا.[b] وكتب إلى النجاشي:[c] "إني قد بنيت لك بيتا لم تبن العرب مثله ولا العجم {ولن} أنتهي حتى أصرف حج العرب إليه." وكانت فيه خشبة طولها ستون ذراعا من ساج يقال لها كُعَيْب وكانت معها خشبة أخرى مثلها يقال لها امرأة كُعَيب

---

٢ الأحبار: وضع المقريزي رمز "ح" تحت الكلمة إشارة إلى تلفظها بالحاء. ٣ ينهيانه: في الأصل "ينهياه". ٥ بنى: في الأصل "بنا". ٧ ولن: في الأصل "ولم".

---

a راجع ابن الكلبي، الأصنام، ١٢ ("فلما انصرف تُبَّعٌ من مَسيرِهِ الذي سار فيه إلى العِراق قَدِمَ معه الحَبْرانِ اللذان صَحِباه من المدينة، فأمراه بهدم رِئام. قال: شَأْنُكُما به. فهدماه وتهود تُبَّعٌ وأهلُ اليَمَن").وراجع أيضا ياقوت، معجم البلدان، ٣: ١١٠ ("وكان تُبّع تبان لما قدم المدينة صحبه حبران من اليهود وهما اللّذان هَوّداه وردّا النار الّتي كانت تخرج من أرض باليمن في قصة فيها طول، فقال الحبران لتبّع: إنّما يكلمهم من هذا الصنم شيطان يفتنهم فخلّ بيننا وبينه، قال: فشأنكما، فدخلا إليه فاستخرجا منه فيما زعم أهل اليمن كلباً أسود فذبحاه ثمّ هدما ذلك البيت، فبقاياه إلى اليوم، كما ذكر ابن إسحاق عمّن أخبره، بها آثار الدماء الّتي كانت تُهراق عليه؛ وفي رواية يونس عن ابن إسحاق: أن رئامًا كان فيه شيطان وكانوا يملؤون له حياضًا من دماء القربان فيخرج فيصيب منها ويكلّمهم، وكانوا يعبدونه، فلمّا جاء الحبران مع تبّع نشرا التوراة عنده وجعلا يقرآنها فطار ذلك الشيطان حتى وقع في البحر").

b قارن ابن الكلبي، الأصنام، ٤٦ ("وقد كان أَبْرَهَةُ الأَشْرَمُ قد بنى بيتا بصنعاءَ، كنيسةً سمَّاها القَلِيسَ، بالرُّخام وجيِّد الخشب المُذْهَبِ").

c راجع الأزرقي، أخبار مكة١، ١: ٢١٣ ("حدثني من أثق به من مشيخة أهل اليمن بصنعاء أن يوسف ذا نواس—وهو صاحب الأخدود الذي حرق أهل الكتاب بنجران—لما غرقه الله، جاءت الحبشة إلى أرض اليمن، فعبروا من دَهْلَك حتى دخلوا صنعاء وحرقوا غمدان، وكان أعظم [قصر] يعلم في الأرض، وغلبوا على اليمن، وبنى أبرهة الحبشي للنجاشي القُلَّيس، وكتب إليه").

§194 Ḥimyar had a sanctuary in Ṣanʿāʾ called Riyām.[663] They used to seek its judgment, and a devil would speak to them from within it. When Tubbaʿ embraced Judaism,[664] the rabbis said: "That which speaks to them from the sanctuary is merely a devil. We shall draw it out for you." So they entered [the sanctuary] with the Torah, read it until a black dog emerged from the sanctuary, and then they destroyed it [the sanctuary]. The two rabbis,[665] who forbade him [Tubbaʿ] to destroy the Kaʿbah when he set out to al-Ḥiǧāz and "devoured" it [?], advised him to destroy it.[666]

§195 He said: When Yūsuf,[667] who killed "the people of the ditch (*aṣḥāb al-uḫdūd*)"[668] at Naǧrān, carried out the raid, and the Ethiopians crossed over [the sea to reach] Ṣanʿāʾ, Abrahah al-Ašram the Ethiopian[669] built al-Qalīs [or al-Qullays][670] in Ṣanʿāʾ,[671] assigned a [place for a] sanctuary in it, and wrote to the Negus: "I have built a sanctuary for you, the like of which no Arab or non-Arab has ever built, and I shall not cease until I divert the Arabs' pilgrimage to it." There was a piece of teak wood inside it that was sixty cubits tall, and was called Kuʿayb, and with it there was another similar piece of

---

663 Or Riʾām. See also Klinke-Rosenberger (1941): 35, 86, n. 87; al-Ṭabarī, *History*, 5:171, n. 438.

664 This most likely refers to Tubbaʿ Asʿad Abū Karib.

665 They should perhaps be identified with Suḫayt/Suḫayt and Munabbih of the Banū Hadl, who were clients of the Jewish tribe of Qurayẓah; Lecker (1995a): 134–135.

666 For more information on the traditions of Tubbaʿ and the Jewish *aḥbār*, see Lecker (1995a). See also al-Ṭabarī, *History*, 5:165 ff.

667 On whom see note 240.

668 *Aṣḥāb al-uḫdūd* is a term mentioned in the Qurʾān (*al-Inšiqāq*), 84:4; many commentators associate them with the Christians of Naǧrān who were persecuted by Ḏū Nuwās in the year 523: "[Al-]Ukhdūd," in *EQ* (Ch.J. Robin).

669 Abrahah al-Ašram (lit., "split-nosed") was the Christian king of South Arabia during the middle of the sixth century; see "Abraha," in *EI*³ (U. Rubin).

670 For more on this church, see Shahid (1979): 81–83; Serjeant/Lewcock (1983): 44–48; al-Ṭabarī, *History*, 5:217–218, n. 539; Robin (2015).

671 There are several opinions concerning the location of this church; Kister (1972): 63.

فكانوا يتبركون بهما[a] ويعظمونهما ويزعمون أن كعيبا يكلمهم ويخبرهم ببعض ما يحبون ويكرهون. فبلغ ما كتب به أبرهة إلى النجاشي أهل مكة | فدعا رجل من النسأة[b] من بني مالك بن كنانة فتيين 47a منهم فأمرهما أن يذهبا إلى البيت الذي فيه القليس فيُحدثا فيه. ففعلا ذلك[c] فدخل أبرهة البيت فرأى آثارهما فقال: "من فعل هذا؟" فقيل له: "رجلان من العرب." فغضب وقال: "لا أنتهي حتى أهدم البيت الذي بمكة." فسار وكان من أمر الفيل ما كان.

فلم يزل كعيب والخشبة التي معه في القليس حتى هدمه العباس بن الربيع الحارثي في خلافة أبي جعفر وهو عامل على اليمن وأخرج كعيبا من القليس فابتاعه رجل من أهل العراق فقطعه وبنى به دارا لجذم فقال رعاع من الناس: "هذا {لشرائه} كعيبا."

§196 وقال السهيلي: وسميت هذه الكنيسة القَلِيْسَ لارتفاع بنائها وعلوها.[d] قال: وكان أبرهة قد استذل أهل اليمن في بنيان هذه الكنيسة وجشمهم فيها أنواعا من السُخَر.[e] وكان ينقل إليها العُدد

---

٨ وبنى : في الأصل "وبنا". ‖ لشرائه : في الأصل "لشراه".

---

a قارن الأزرقي، أخبار مكة[١]، ١: ٢١٦ ("وكان في القبة أو في البيت خشبة ساج منقوشة، طولها ستون ذراعًا [يقال] لها: كعيب، وخشبة من ساج نحوها في الطول يقال لها: امرأة كعيب، كانوا يتبركون [بهما] في الجاهلية، وكان يقال لكعيب الأحوزي، والأحوزي بلسانهم: الحر").

b راجع السهيلي، الروض الأنف، ١: ٢٤٣ ("والنَّسأَة: الذين كانوا يَنسَئون الشهور على العرب في الجاهلية، فيحلّون الشهر من الأشهر الحرم، ويحرّمون مكانه الشهر من أشهر الحلّ، ويؤخِّرون ذلك الشَّهر").

c قارن الطبري، تاريخ، ٢: ٩٣٤ ("فلما تحدّثت العرب بكتاب ابرهة ذلك إلى النجاشيّ غضب رجل من النساة احد بني فقيم ثم احد بني مالك، فخرج حتى أتى القليس فقعد فيها ثم خرج فلحق بأرضه").

d راجع السهيلي، الروض الأنف، ١: ٢٤٤-٢٤٥ ("وسميت هذه الكنيسة: الْقُلَّيْس لارتفاع بنائها وعلوها، ومنه القلانس لأنها في أعلى الرؤوس، ويقال: تَقَلْنَسَ الرجل وتقلَّس إذا لبس الْقَلَنْسُوة، وقَلَسَ طعاما أي: ارتفع من معدته إلى فيه"). وراجع أيضا ابن كثير، ٨: ٤٥٩ ("سمتها العرب القليس لارتفاعها لأن الناظر إليها تكاد تسقط قلنسوته عن رأسه من ارتفاع بنائها").

e قارن ابن كثير، السيرة النبوية، ١: ٣٠ ("فذكر السهيلي أن أبرهة استذل أهل اليمن في بناء هذه الكنيسة الخسيسة، وسخرهم فيها أنواعا من السخر، وكان من تأخر عن العمل حتى تطلع الشمس يقطع يده لا محالة").

wood called "Ku'ayb's wife." They used to draw blessings from them, venerate them, and claim that Ku'ayb speaks to them and tells them things, some of which they like and others which they dislike. The news of what Abrahah wrote to the Negus reached the people of Mecca. Consequently a man of the Banū Mālik b. Kinānah, who was among those charged with intercalating the calendar,[672] summoned two of their young men [i.e. two men of the Banū Mālik b. Kinānah], ordered them to go to the sanctuary in which al-Qalīs was located,[673] and to defecate in it.[674] They did precisely this, and when Abrahah entered the sanctuary and saw their remains, he said: "Who did this?" He was told: "Two Arab men." [Upon hearing this,] he was furious, and said: "I shall not cease until I demolish the House in Mecca." Then he set out [to Mecca], and "the affair of the elephant"[675] took place.

Ku'ayb and the piece of wood that was with it remained in al-Qalīs until al-'Abbās b. al-Rabī' al-Ḥāriṯī,[676] who was governor over Yemen, destroyed it [al-Qalīs] during Abū Ǧa'far's caliphate.[677] He took Ku'ayb out of al-Qalīs, and one of the people of Iraq bought it, cut it into pieces, and built a house with it. Then he was afflicted with leprosy, and the rabble said: "This [happened] because he bought Ku'ayb."

§ 196 Al-Suhaylī said: This church was named al-Qalīs because of its height and elevation.[678] Abrahah subjugated the people of Yemen during the construction of this church and imposed upon them various tasks without compensation. He brought to it materials such as variegated alabaster[679] and

672 See "Nasī'," in EI[2] (A. Moberg).

673 Earlier in this paragraph it was said that the sanctuary (*bayt*) was in al-Qalīs.

674 The traditions concerning the person (or persons) who desecrated this church are discussed in Kister (1972): 63–64.

675 "The affair of the elephant" refers to the expedition that Abrahah made with "the people of the elephant" in order to destroy Mecca and the Ka'bah. According to Muslim sources, the Prophet was born in the year of the elephant (ca. 570 CE); Nicholson (1966): 66–69; "People of the Elephant," in EQ (I. Shahīd).

676 Al-'Abbās b. al-Rabī' b. 'Ubayd Allāh al-Ḥāriṯī. In another source, al-'Abbās is referred to as 'Abd Allāh: Serjeant/Lewcock (1983): 46.

677 The second 'Abbāsid caliph; he reigned from 136/754 to 158/775.

678 See also Ibn Kaṯīr, *Tafsīr*[1], 8:459: "The Arabs named it al-Qullays due to its height, because when someone looked up at it, his cap (*qalansuwah*) would nearly fall off his head." And see also al-Suhaylī, *al-Rawḍ al-unuf*, 1:244–245, who associates the meaning of al-Qullays with the verb *qalasa*: when the food "goes up" (*irtafa'a*) from the stomach to the mouth. However, the word is of Greek origin: *ecclesia*.

679 See also Serjeant/Lewcock (1983): 45.

مثل الرخام المجزع[a] والحجارة المنقوشة بالذهب من قصر بلقيس صاحبة سليمٰن وكان من موضع هذه الكنيسة على فراسخ وكان فيه بقايا من آثار ملكها فاستعان بذلك على ما أراده في هذه الكنيسة من بهجتها وبهائها ونصب فيها صلبانا من الذهب والفضة ومنابر من العاج والآبُنُس وكان أراد أن يرفع في بنائها حتى يشرف منها على عدن.[b]

وكان حكمه في العامل إذا طلعت عليه الشمس قبل أن يأخذ في عمله أن يقطع يده. فنام رجل منهم ذات يوم حتى طلعت الشمس فجاءت معه أمه وهي عجوز فتضرعت إليه تستشفع لابنها فأبى إلا أن يقطع يده. فقالت: "اضرب بمعولك اليوم. فاليوم لك وغدا لغيرك." فقال: "ويحك! ما قلت؟" فقالت: "نعم. كما صار هذا الملك من غيرك إليك فكذلك يصير منك إلى غيرك." فأخذته موعظتها وأعفى الناس من العمل فيها بعدُ.[c]

---

٩ وأعفى: في الأصل "واعفا".

---

a قارن الصالحي، سبل الهدى، ١: ٢٥٠ ("فبنى لهم كنيسة هائلة بصنعاء رفيعة البناء مزخرفة الأرجاء، فسمتها العرب القُلّيس لارتفاعها لأن الناظر إليها، يكاد تسقط قلنسوته عن رأسه لارتفاع بنائها، ونقل من قصر بلقيس ما تحتاج إليه، واستذَلَّ أهلَ اليمن في بنيان هذه الكنيسة، وبناها بالرخام المجزَّع والأبيض والأحمر والأصفر والأسود").

b راجع الأزرقي، أخبار مكة[1]، ١: ٢١٦ ("وكان أبرهة قد أجمع أن يبني القُلَّيس حتى يظهر على ظهره فيرى منه بحر عَدَن").

c قارن الأزرقي، أخبار مكة[1]، ١: ٢١٦ ("وكان أبرهة عند بناء القُلَّيس قد أخذ العُمال بالعمل أخذًا شديدًا، وكان آلى أن لا تطلع الشمس على عامل لم يضع يده في عمله، فيؤتى به إلا قطع يده. قال: فتخلف رجل ممن كان يعمل فيه حتى طلعت الشمس، وكانت له أم عجوز، فذهب بها ولدها لتستوهبه من أبرهة، فأتته وهو بارز للناس، فذكرت له علّة ابنها، واستوهبته منه. فقال: لا أكذب نفسي ولا أفسد على عمالي. فأمر بقطع يده. فقالت له أمّه: اضْربْ بمعولك، ساعي بهر، اليوم لك، وغدًا لغيرك، ليس كل الدهر لك. فقال: أدنوها، فقال لها: إن هذا الملك [يكون] لغيري؟ قالت: نعم، وكان أبرهة قد أجمع أن يبني القُلَّيس حتى يظهر على ظهره فيرى منه بحر عَدَن، فقال: لا أبني حَجَرًا على حَجَر بعد يومي هذا. وأعفى الناس من العمل").

stones ornamented with gold from the palace of Bilqīs [Queen of Sheba],[680] who was Solomon's companion. It [the palace] was [a few] *farsaḫs* from the location of this church, and inside it were the remains of the relics of her rule. He made use of this to achieve the magnificence and splendor that he desired for this church. He affixed gold and silver crosses in it [the church] and made pulpits of ivory and ebony. He wanted to raise the edifice until he could get a view of ʿAdan from it.

With regard to workers, his rule was to cut off their hand[s] if they began [i.e. came] to work after sunrise [i.e. late].[681] One day, one of the workers slept until sunrise, and his mother, who was an old woman, came with him. She beseeched him [Abrahah], asking forgiveness for her son, but he insisted on cutting off his [her son's] hand. She said: "Strike with your pickaxe today! This day belongs to you, but tomorrow belongs to someone else." He said: "Woe unto you! What did you say?" She said: "Yes! Just as this kingship passed to you from someone else, it will likewise pass from you to someone else." Her admonition influenced him and following this, he exempted the people from working in it [the church].

680 See "Bilqīs," in *EI*³ (A. Havemann).

681 Lit. "If the sun rose before they began their work."

فلما هلك ومُزقت الحبشة كل ممزق وأقفر ما حول هذه الكنيسة فلم يعمرها أحد وكثرت حولها السباع والحيات[a] وكان كل من أراد أن يأخذ شيئا منها أصابته الجن فبقيت من ذلك العهد بما فيها من العُدد والخشب المرصع | بالذهب والآلات المفضضة التي تساوي قناطير من المال لا يستطيع 47b أحد أن يأخذ منها شيئا إلى زمن أبي العباس السفاح. فذكر له أمرها وما يتهيب من جنها وجِنّانِها فلم يَرُعه ذلك وبعث إليها [أبا] العباس بن الربيع عامله على اليمن معه أهل الحزْم والجلاد فخربها وحصلوا منها مالا كبيرا ببيع ما أمكن بيعه من رخامها وآلاتها.[b] فعفا بعد ذلك رسمها وانقطع خبرها ودرست آثارها. وكان الذي يصيبهم من الجن ينسبونه إلى كُعَيْب وامرأته صنمين كانت {الكنيسة} بنيت عليهما فلما كسر كعيب وامرأته أصيب الذي كسرهما بجذام فافتتن بذلك رَعاع الناس وطَغاتُهم وقالوا: "أصابه كعيب."

وذكر أبو الوليد الأزرقي أن كعيبا كان من خشب طوله ستون ذراعا والله أعلم.

§197 قال ابن شبة: واتخذت جهينة بيتا بالنقعين بين جب والأعوص واسمه الهُجم وحموا له واديا كانوا يحجون إليه. وكان الذي بناه منهم {ويسدنه} ويقوم بأمره عبد المدان بن حُرَيث. وسمعت

---

٥ أبا ... الربيع : كذا في الأصل بدلا من "العباس بن الربيع". ٨ الكنيسة : في الأصل "بالكنيسة". || كسرهما : وضع المقريزي ثلاث نقط تحت الكلمة إشارة إلى تلفظها بالسين. ٩ وطَغاتُهم : كذا (التشكيل). ١١ بالنقعين : وضع المقريزي رمز "ع" تحت الكلمة إشارة إلى تلفظها بالعين. ١٢ ويسدنه: في الأصل "وتسدنه".

---

a قارن الحلبي، السيرة الحلبية، ١: ٩٩ ("ولما هلك صاحب الفيل وقومه عزت قريش وهابتهم الناس كلهم، وقالوا: أهل الله لأن الله معهم. وفي لفظ: لأن الله سبحانه وتعالى قاتل عنهم، وكفاهم مؤنة عدوهم الذي لم يكن لسائر العرب بقتاله قدرة، وغنموا أموال أصحاب الفيل: أي ومن حينئذ مزقت الحبشة كل ممزق، وخرب ما حول تلك الكنيسة التي بناها أبرهة؛ فلم يعمرها أحد، وكثرت حولها السباع والحيات ومردة الجن").

b قارن الازرقي، أخبار مكة[١]، ١: ٢١٧ ("فلم يزل القُلَّيس على ما كان عليه، حتى ولّى أبو جعفر المنصور أمير المؤمنين، العباس بن الربيع بن عبيد الله الحارثي اليمن، فذكر العباس ما في القُلَّيس من النقض والذهب والفضة، وعظم ذلك عنده، وقيل له: إنك تصيب فيه مالًا كثيرًا وكنزًا، فتاقت نفسه إلى هدمه وأخذ ما فيه").

When he died and the Ethiopians were destroyed, everything surrounding this church was destitute, no one lived there, and there were many predatory animals and serpents around it. Anyone who wished to take something from it became possessed by the *ǧinn*. From that period it remained with everything that was inside it, including the materials, wood inlaid with gold, and silver-coated tools that were worth a tremendous sum of money. No one could take anything from it until the time of Abū l-ʿAbbās al-Saffāḥ.[682] He was told about its condition and about the [peoples'] fear of its *ǧinn* and serpents, but this did not scare him. He sent al-ʿAbbās b. al-Rabīʿ,[683] who was his governor over Yemen, to it, along with resolute and courageous men. He [al-ʿAbbās b. al-Rabīʿ] destroyed it, and they obtained a great deal of money from it by selling the alabaster and tools that could be sold. Afterwards, its remains were obliterated, information about it no longer circulated, and its relics were wiped out. They associated the *ǧinn* that possessed them with Kuʿayb and his wife, two idols on which the church had been built. When Kuʿayb and his wife were destroyed, the one who destroyed them was afflicted with leprosy, and the rabble and impious people strayed from the right path and said: "Kuʿayb afflicted him [with the disease]."

Abū l-Walīd al-Azraqī[684] reported that Kuʿayb was made of wood, [and that] it was sixty cubits long, but Allāh knows best.

§ 197 Ibn Šabbah said: Ǧuhaynah adopted a sanctuary in al-Naqʿayni, between Ǧubb and al-Aʿwaṣ, called al-Huǧam. They declared the valley to which they used to make pilgrimage[s] its *ḥimá* [protected space]. The Ǧuhaynah member who built it, and who was its custodian and caretaker, was ʿAbd al-Madān b. Ḥurayṯ,[685] but I heard some mention that its caretaker

682 The first ʿAbbāsid caliph (d. 136/754).

683 Not Abū l-ʿAbbās b. al-Rabīʿ as erroneously read by al-Maqrīzī.

684 On Abū l-Walīd al-Azraqī, the compiler of *Aḫbār Makkah*, see "al-Azraḳī," in *EI*² (J.W. Fück).

685 In other sources he is referred to as ʿAbd al-Dār b. Ḥuḍayb or Huḏayl; see "Ḳuḍāʿa," in *EI*² (M.J. Kister).

من يذكر أن الذي كان يقوم بأمره سُوَيد، حوَّط عليه. وأنشدني عمر بن عبد الرحمٰن الجهني لعبد المدان بن حريث: [الكامل]

ولقد أُريتُ بأن تقام بنية ليست بظلم أو {تطيف بمأثم}
فإذا الذين إذا الأمور تقُسِمَت لاذوا بريهة أو جوالب قوزم[a]

§198 خبر ذات أنواط

خرج الترمذي من حديث سفيٰن عن الزهري عن سنان بن أبي سنان عن أبي واقد الليثي أن رسول الله ﷺ لما خرج إلى حنين مر بشجرة للمشركين يقال لها ذات أنواط يعلقون عليها أسلحتهم. فقالوا: "يٰرسول الله اجعل لنا ذات أنواط كما لهم ذات أنواط." فقال النبي ﷺ: "سبحان الله هذا كما قال قوم موسى ﴿ٱجْعَلْ لَنَا إِلَٰهًا كَمَا لَهُمْ آلِهَةٌ﴾. والذي نفسي بيده لتركبن سَنن من كان قبلكم."
قال أبو عيسى: هذا حديث حسن صحيح.[b]

---

٣ تطيف بمأثم: في الأصل: "تقمن ما اثم" (راجع ياقوت، معجم البلدان).

٤ قوزم: أضاف المقريزي الحاشية التالية في الهامش الأيسر بجانب هذه الكلمة: "حـ صنم".

---

a قارن ياقوت، معجم البلدان، ٤: ٤١١ ("كان رجل من جهينة يقال له عبد الدار بن حُدَيب قال يوما لقومه: هَلُمّ نبني بيتاً بأرض من دارهم يقال لها الحَوْراءُ نضاهي به الكعبة ونعظمه حتى نستميل به كثيراً من العرب، فأعظموا ذلك وأبَوْا عليه، فقال في ذلك:

ولقد أرَدْتُ بأنْ تُقامَ بَنِيّةٌ ليست بحَوْبٍ أو تطيف بمأثم
فأبى الذين إذا دُعوا لعظيمة راغوا ولاذوا في جوانب قَوْدم
يَلْحَون إلّا يؤمروا، فإذا دُعوا وَلَّوْا وأعرض بعضهم كالأبكم
صفح منافعه ويغمض كلمة في ذي أفاويه غموض المَنْسِم")

b راجع الترمذي، سنن، ٤: ٤٩–٥٠.

was Suwayd. He built a wall[686] around it. ʿUmar b. ʿAbd al-Raḥmān al-Ǧuhanī recited to me [verses] that were composed by ʿAbd al-Madān b. Ḥurayṯ: [*al-kāmil*]

It was shown to me in a dream that an edifice will be set up,
which is not [associated with] wrongdoing, and does not encompass sin.
But then, those who seek refuge at the time when the intentions [of the different groups] are divided,[687]
[...] or [...] of Qawzam [?].

§198 The account of Ḏāt Anwāṭ[688]

Al-Tirmiḏī[689] quoted Sufyān's *ḥadīṯ* on the authority of al-Zuhrī < Sinān b. Abī Sinān[690] < Abū Wāqid al-Layṯī:[691] When the Messenger of Allāh, may Allāh bless and save him, set out to Ḥunayn,[692] he passed by a tree called Ḏāt Anwāṭ that belonged to the polytheists, on which they suspended their weapons. They [the Muslims] said: "O Messenger of Allāh! Make [another] Ḏāt Anwāṭ for us just as they have a Ḏāt Anwāṭ." The Prophet, may Allāh bless and save him, said: "Allāh be praised! This is exactly what the people of Mūsá said: 'Make for us a god, as they have gods.'[693] I swear by the One in whose hand is my soul, you will surely follow the paths of those who have lived before you." Abū ʿĪsá[694] said: This is a *ḥadīṯ* of good authority.

---

9 Qawzam : [Qawzam is] an idol (marginal gloss in al-Maqrīzī's hand). Yāqūt, *Muʿǧam al-buldān*, 4:411 has Qawdam, which he defines as the name of a mountain. This source also provides a clearer version of the above-mentioned line: "But those who turn away when called upon for an important event refused and found refuge beside Qawdam." For a translation of this variant, see Klinke-Rosenberger (1941): 54.

---

686 Or a fence; perhaps, "He demarcated its boundaries"?

687 *Iḏā l-umūr tuqussimat*; the translation of this part of the verse follows Bravmann (1972): 40.

688 *Nawṭ* (pl. *anwāṭ*) denotes a thing that is suspended.

689 Abū ʿĪsá Muḥammad b. ʿĪsá l-Tirmiḏī (d. 279/892): "al-Tirmidhī," in *EI*² (G.H.A. Juynboll).

690 On whom see Ibn Saʿd, *al-Ṭabaqāt*¹, 7:246.

691 One of the Prophet's Companions; Ibn Ḥaǧar, *al-Iṣābah*¹, 7:370–371.

692 A valley on one of the roads of al-Ṭāʾif; it was the site of a famous battle that took place after the conquest of Mecca; "Ḥunayn," in *EI*² (H. Lammens [Abd al-Hafez Kamal]).

693 Qurʾān (*al-Aʿrāf*), 7:138.

694 I.e. al-Tirmiḏī (see above, n. 689).

§199 ورواه عمر بن شبة من طريق ابن أبي فديك عن كثير بن عبد الله المزني عن أبيه عن جده قال: | غزونا مع النبي ﷺ عام الفتح ونحن ألف ونيف ففتح الله له مكة وحنينا حتى إذا كنا بين 48a حنين والطائف إذا نحن بشجرة دَفواء[a] سدرة كان يناط بها السلاح فسميت ذات أنواط تعبد من دون الله[b] فلما رآها النبي ﷺ صُرف[c] عنها في يوم صائف إلى ظل هو أدنى منها فقال له رجل: "يٰرسول الله اجعل لنا ذات أنواط كما لهم ذات أنواط." فقال النبي ﷺ: "أيها المسلمون قلتم والذي نفس محمد بيده كما قالت بنو إسرائيل ﴿يَا مُوسَى ٱجْعَلْ لَنَا إِلٰهًا كَمَا لَهُمْ آلِهَةٌ﴾." فقال: "﴿أَغَيْرَ ٱللّٰهِ أَبْغِيكُمْ إِلٰهًا وَهُوَ فَضَّلَكُمْ عَلَى ٱلْعَالَمِينَ﴾."

§200 ورواه من طريق ابن المبٰرك قال: أخبرنا معمر عن الزهري قال: حدثني من سمع أبا واقد الليثي قال: خرجنا مع النبي ﷺ قبل حُنين فمررنا بسدرة فقلنا: "يٰرسول الله اجعل لنا ذات أنواط

---

a راجع ابن منظور، لسان العرب، "دفو" ("والدَّفْواءُ: الشجرة العظيمة. وفي الحديث: أَن النبي، صلى الله عليه وسلم، في بعض أَسفاره أَبْصَرَ شجرةً دَفْواء تُسَمَّى ذاتَ أَنْواط لأَنه كان يُناطُ بها السلاحُ وتُعْبَدُ دونَ الله عز وجل. والدَّفْوَاءُ: العظيمة الظَّلِيلةُ الكثيرةُ الفُروع والأَغْصان وتَكُونُ المائلَةَ").

b قارن الآلوسي، روح المعاني، ٩: ٤٢ ("كان يناط بها السلاح فسميت ذات أنواط فكانت تعبد من دون الله").

c قارن الطبراني، المعجم الكبير، ١٧: ٢١ ("فلما رآها رسول الله ﷺ انصرف عنها في يوم صائف الى ظل هو أدنى منها").

§ 199 ʿUmar b. Šabbah narrated it [the *ḥadīṯ* of Ḏāt Anwāṭ] with a chain of transmission going back to[695] Ibn Abī Fudayk[696] on the authority of Kaṯīr b. ʿAbd Allāh al-Muzanī[697] < his father < his [Kaṯīr's] grandfather, who said: We carried out a raid with the Prophet, may Allāh bless and save him, in the year of the conquest of Mecca with a thousand and some of our men [i.e. from Muzaynah], and Allāh granted him victory in Mecca and Ḥunayn. When we were between Ḥunayn and al-Ṭāʾif, we saw a great, shady[698] *sidrah* tree, on which weapons were suspended. It was called Ḏāt Anwāṭ and it was worshipped besides Allāh. When the Prophet, may Allāh bless and save him, saw it, he was diverted from it, despite the fact that it was a hot day, to a place that was less shaded. Then someone said to him: "O Messenger of Allāh! Make [another] Ḏāt Anwāṭ for us just as they have a Ḏāt Anwāṭ." The Prophet, may Allāh bless and save him, said: "O Muslims! I swear by He in whose hand is Muḥammad's soul, you have said exactly what the Banū Isrāʾīl said: 'Moses, make for us a god, as they have gods'."[699] He said: "What, shall I seek a god for you other than Allāh, who has preferred you above all beings?"[700]

§ 200 He [Ibn Šabbah] also narrated it [the *ḥadīṯ* of Ḏāt Anwāṭ] with a chain of transmission going back to[701] Ibn al-Mubārak,[702] who said, Maʿmar[703] informed us on the authority of al-Zuhrī, who said, someone who heard Abū Wāqid al-Layṯī related to me [the *ḥadīṯ* of Ḏāt Anwāṭ as follows]: We [the Muslims] set out with the Prophet, may Allāh bless and save him, in the direction of Ḥunayn, passed by a *sidrah* tree, and said: "O Messenger of Allāh! Make [another] Ḏāt Anwāṭ for us just as they have a Ḏāt Anwāṭ." The infidels

695 *Min ṭarīq*; see note 112.

696 Muḥammad b. Ismāʿīl b. Abī Fudayk (d. ca. 200/816): al-Ḏahabī, *Siyar aʿlām al-nubalāʾ*, 9:486–487.

697 Kaṯīr b. ʿAbd Allāh b. ʿAmr b. ʿAwf al-Muzanī l-Madanī (d. ca. 158/775): al-Mizzī, *Tahḏīb al-kamāl*, 24:136–140.

698 *Dafwāʾ*; see Lane (1863–1893): 895 (providing several meanings for the phrase *shağarah dafwāʾ*).

699 Qurʾān (*al-Aʿrāf*), 7:138.

700 Qurʾān (*al-Aʿrāf*), 7:140.

701 *Min ṭarīq*; see note 112.

702 Ibn al-Mubārak ʿAbd Allāh b. ʿAbd al-Raḥmān al-Ḥanẓalī (d. 118 or 119); "Ibn al-Mubārak," in *EI*² (J. Robson).

703 On Maʿmar b. Rāšid al-Baṣrī (d. ca. 153/770), a *mawlá* of the Azd, see Ibn ʿAsākir, *Dimašq*, 59:390–423.

كما لهم ذات أنواط.“ قال: وكان الكفار ينوطون سلاحهم بسدرة ثم يكونون حولها. فقال النبي ﷺ: ”لتركبن سنن من كان قبلكم. هذا كما قالت بنو إسرائيل لموسى ﴿ٱجْعَل لَّنَآ إِلَٰهًا كَمَا لَهُمْ ءَالِهَةٌ﴾“ انتهى.

§ 201 وكانت للعرب أنصاب واحدها نُصُب. قال الله تعالى ﴿حُرِّمَتْ عَلَيْكُمُ ٱلْمَيْتَةُ وَٱلدَّمُ وَلَحْمُ ٱلْخِنزِيرِ وَمَآ أُهِلَّ لِغَيْرِ ٱللَّهِ بِهِۦ وَٱلْمُنْخَنِقَةُ وَٱلْمَوْقُوذَةُ وَٱلْمُتَرَدِّيَةُ وَٱلنَّطِيحَةُ وَمَآ أَكَلَ ٱلسَّبُعُ إِلَّا مَا ذَكَّيْتُمْ وَمَا ذُبِحَ عَلَى ٱلنُّصُبِ وَأَن تَسْتَقْسِمُوا۟ بِٱلْأَزْلَٰمِ ذَٰلِكُمْ فِسْقٌ﴾. فالنصب حجارة تجمع في موضع من الأرض يقربون لها وليست بأصنام.[a] قال ابن جريج: النصُب ليست بأصنام الصنم يُصَور ويُنقَش وهذه حجارة تنصَب ثلاثمائة وستون حجرا ومنهم من يقول ثلاثمائة منها لخزاعة فكانوا إذا ذكوا نضحوا الدم على ما أقبل من الكعبة وشرحوا اللحم وجعلوه على الحجارة.[b] فقال المسلمون: ”يارسول الله كان أهل الجاهلية يعظمون البيت بالدم فنحن أحق | أن نعظمه.“ فكان النبي ﷺ لم يكره ذلك. 48b
فأنزل الله تعالى ﴿لَن يَنَالَ ٱللَّهَ لُحُومُهَا وَلَا دِمَآؤُهَا﴾ الآية.

٤-٦ حُرِّمَتْ ... فِسْقٌ : شكل المقريزي الآية كما يلي: حُرمت عليكم الميتةُ والدمُ ولحم الخنزير وما أُهِلَّ لغير الله به والمُنْخَنقة والموْقُوذَة والمُتَرَدِّيَة والنَطيْحَةُ وما أكلَ السبُعُ إلا ما ذكيتم وما ذُبِحَ على النُصُب وأن تَسْتَقسِمُوا بالأزْلَام ذلكم فِسْق. ١١ ٱللَّهَ لُحُومُهَا : شكل المقريزي هاتين الكلمتين كما يلي: اللهَ لحومُها.

---

a قارن الطبري، جامع البيان، ٨: ٧٠ (”والنُّصُبُ، الأوثانُ من الحجارةِ، جماعةُ أنصابٍ كانت تُجْمَعُ في الموضع مِن الأرضِ، فكان المشرِكون يُقَرِّبون لها، وليست بأصنامٍ“).

b قارن الجصاص، أحكام القرآن، ٥: ٧٠ (”كان الناس في الجاهلية إذا ذبحوا لطخوا بالدم وجه الكعبة وشرحوا اللحم ووضعوه على الحجارة“).

used to suspend their weapons on a *sidrah* tree, and then they would remain around it. The Prophet, may Allāh bless and save him, said: "You will surely follow the paths of those who have lived before you. This is exactly what the Banū Isrāʾīl said to Mūsá: 'Make for us a god, as they have gods'."[704] Unquote.

§ 201 The Arabs had *anṣāb*. Its singular is *nuṣub*.[705] Allāh, the Exalted, said: "Forbidden to you are carrion, blood, the flesh of swine, what has been hallowed to other than Allāh, the beast strangled; the beast beaten down, the beast who falls to his death, the beast gored, and that devoured by beasts of prey—excepting that which you have sacrificed duly—as also things sacrificed to idols (*nuṣub*), and partition by the divining arrows; that is ungodliness."[706] *Nuṣub* are stones that were gathered at a certain place on the ground, and to which sacrifices were offered. They are not *aṣnām*. Ibn Ǧurayǧ said: *Nuṣub* are not *aṣnām*. A *ṣanam* is formed and engraved, whereas these are stones that are set up. [There were] three hundred sixty stones, and some say that three hundred of them belonged to the Ḫuzāʿah. When they slaughtered [sacrifices], they sprinkled the blood towards the Kaʿbah, cut the meat into slices, and placed it on the stones. The Muslims said: "O Messenger of Allāh! The people of the Ǧāhiliyyah used to venerate the House [i.e. the Kaʿbah] with blood, but we have a better right to venerate it." The Prophet, may Allāh bless and save him, did not disapprove of this, and Allāh, the Exalted, revealed: "The flesh of them shall not reach Allāh, neither their blood" and so on with the verse.[707]

---

704 Qurʾān (*al-Aʿrāf*), 7:138.

705 There are different opinions as to whether *nuṣub* is a singular or plural noun. Later in this paragraph, this word seems to be treated as plural. For the definitions of the word *anṣāb*, see also Lane (1863–1893): 2800; "Nuṣub," in *EI*[2] (F. Fahd); "Idols and Images," in *EQ* (G. Hawting).

706 Qurʾān (*al-Māʾidah*), 5:3.

707 Qurʾān (*al-Ḥaǧǧ*), 22:37.

§ 202 وقال ابن أبي نجيح عن مجاهد في قوله تعالى ﴿وَمَا ذُبِحَ عَلَى ٱلنُّصُبِ﴾ قال: حجارة كانت يذبح عليها أهل الجاهلية. وفي رواية: حجارة حول الكعبة يذبح عليها أهل الجاهلية ويبدلونها إذا {شاؤوا} بحجارة أعجب إليهم منها. وعن قتادة: النصب حجارة كان أهل الجاهلية يعبدونها ويذبحون لها. فنهى الله عن ذلك. وفي رواية: النصُب أنصاب أهل الجاهلية. وعن ابن عباس رضي الله عنه: النصب أنصاب كانوا يذبحون ويهلون عليها. وقال ابن سيدة: والنُصُبُ والنُصْبُ كل ما عُبد من دون الله والجمع أنصاب. وقال الزجاج: النصُب جمع واحدها نِصَاب. قال: وجائز أن يكون واحدا وجمعه أنصاب. والأنصاب حجارة كانت حول الكعبة تُنصَب فَيُهَلّ عليها ويُذبَح لغير الله تعالى.[a]

§ 203 قال ابن إسحاق: وكانت رُضَا بيتا لبني ربيعة بن كعب بن سعد بن زيد مناة بن تميم. وله يقول المُسْتَوغر بن ربيعة بن كعب بن سعد حين هدمها في الإسلام: [الكامل]

ولقد شددت على رضاء شدة فتركتها قفراً بقاع أسحما[b]

---

٢ رواية: كشط المقريزي نهاية هذه الكلمة وكلمة أخرى تليها، ثم أضاف الياء والتاء المربوطة وأطال الياء.
٣ شاؤوا: في الأصل "شاوا". ١٠ أسحما: وضع المقريزي رمز "ح" تحت الكلمة إشارة إلى تلفظها بالحاء.

---

a راجع ابن سيدة، المحكم، ٨: ٣٤٣.

b قارن ابن الكلبي، الأصنام، ٣٠ ("وقال المستوغِر في كسره رُضًى في الإسلام، فقال:
ولقد شَدَدْتُ على رُضَاء شَدّةً فتَرَكْتُها تلًّا تُنازِع أَسْحَمَا")
وقارن أيضا السهيلي، الروض الأنف، ١: ٣٧٩
("ولقد شَدَدْتُ على رُضَاء شَدَّةً فتركتها قفرا بقاع أَسْحَمَا
يريد: تركتُها سَحْمَاءَ من آثار النار").

§ 202 Ibn Abī Naǧīḥ[708] said on the authority of Muǧāhid regarding His saying, the Exalted: "as also things sacrificed to idols (*nuṣub*),"[709] [that the word *nuṣub* denotes] stones on which the people of the Ǧāhiliyyah used to make sacrifices. According to another opinion, [they were] stones around the Kaʿbah, on which the people of the Ǧāhiliyyah used to make sacrifices and which they would replace, if they wished, with stones that were more pleasing to them. On the authority of Qatādah: *Nuṣub* are stones that the people of the Ǧāhiliyyah worshipped and to which they made sacrifices. Allāh forbade this. According to another opinion, *nuṣub* are the *anṣāb* of the people of the Ǧāhiliyyah. On the authority of Ibn ʿAbbās, may Allāh be pleased with him: *Nuṣub* are *anṣāb* on which they used to make sacrifices, and over which they used to invoke the name of their deity before slaughtering an animal. Ibn Sīdah said: *Nuṣub* and *nuṣb* are anything that was worshipped apart from Allāh. The plural [of these two words] is *anṣāb*. Al-Zaǧǧāǧ said: The [word] *nuṣub* is plural; its singular is *niṣāb*. He [also] said: It may be that it is singular, and its plural is *anṣāb*.[710] *Anṣāb* are stones that were set up around the Kaʿbah, over which the name of some deity was invoked before slaughtering an animal, and on which [offerings] were sacrificed for [deities] other than Allāh, the Exalted.

§ 203 Ibn Isḥāq said: Ruḍā was a sanctuary that belonged to the Banū Rabīʿah b. Kaʿb b. Saʿd b. Zayd Manāt b. Tamīm. Al-Mustawġir[711] b. Rabīʿah b. Kaʿb b. Saʿd said [the following verse] about it, when he destroyed it after the advent of Islam: [*al-kāmil*]

I assaulted Ruḍāʾ,
    and left it deserted on a black plain.[712]

---

708 ʿAbd Allāh b. Abī Naǧīḥ, a *mawlá* of Ṯaqīf (d. ca. 132/750): Ibn Saʿd, *al-Ṭabaqāt*¹, 8:44; al-Ḏahabī, *Siyar aʿlām al-nubalāʾ*, 6:125–126.

709 Qurʾān (*al-Māʾidah*), 5:3.

710 See also Lane (1863–1893): 2800.

711 Al-Mustawġir was in fact his epithet. His name was ʿAmr b. Rabīʿah b. Kaʿb b. Saʿd b. Zayd Manāt b. Tamīm; see Ibn al-Kalbī, *al-Aṣnām*, 30. For more on al-Mustawġir, see Al-Jallad (2021): 1–2.

712 This verse is also translated in Wellhausen (1897): 58; Ibn Hišām, *The Life of Muhammad* 39. Presumably, the plan became "black" after the idol was burned.

§204 بس بيت كانت تعبده غطفان. بناه ظالم بن أسعد بن ربيعة بن عامر بن مالك بن مُرة بن عوف بن سعد بن ذبيان بن بغيض بن ريث بن غطفان بن سعد بن قيس بن عيلان بن مضر بن نزار بن معد بن عدنان. قال زهير بن جناب الكلبي: [الوافر]

نخلي بعدها غطفان بسا   وما غطفان والأرض الفضاء

§205 بيت النار وهو بيت في مغارة عظيمة يخرج منها لهيب النيران. كان أهل اليمن في أيام التبابعة يتحاكمون إليها فيما يختلفون فيه والمحق لا يمسه منها سوء والمبطل تتلفه.[a]

§206 السَّعِيْدَة بيت كانت العرب تحجه في الجاهلية.

١–٣ بناه ... عدنان: الزيادة بخط المقريزي في الهامش الأيسر من الأسفل إلى الأعلى، ثم في الهامش الأعلى من الأعلى إلى الأسفل ويشير إليها رمز ¬ بعد "غطفان". ٢ عيلان: وضع المقريزي رمز "ع" تحت الكلمة إشارة إلى تلفظها بالعين. ٤ نخلي: في الأصل "نخلا". ٥–٦ بيت ... تتلفه: كشط المقريزي نصا آخر قبل أن يصححه كما هو الآن.

a راجع الطبري، تاريخ، ٢: ٩٠٥ ("وكانت باليمن فيما يزعم أهل اليمن نار تحكم بينهم فيما يختلفون فيه تأكل الظالم ولا تضرّ المظلوم").

§ 204 Buss was a sanctuary that was worshipped by Ġaṭafān.[713] It was built by Ẓālim b. Asʿad b. Rabīʿah b. ʿĀmir b. Mālik b. Murrah b. ʿAwf b. Saʿd b. Ḏubyān b. Baġīḍ b. Rayṯ b. Ġaṭafān b. Saʿd b. Qays b. ʿAylān b. Muḍar b. Nizār b. Maʿadd b. ʿAdnān. Zuhayr b. Ǧanāb al-Kalbī[714] said: [*al-wāfir*]

Afterwards, the Ġaṭafān left Buss,
and what have the Ġaṭafān to do with a spacious tract of land?[715]

§ 205 A fire temple is a sanctuary in a big cave, from which flames of fire emerge. During the days of the Tabābiʿah [pl. of Tubbaʿ], the people of Yemen used to seek its judgment concerning matters on which they disputed. If one was telling the truth, no harm befell him from it, while the liar was annihilated by it.

§ 206 Al-Saʿīdah was a sanctuary to which the Arabs made pilgrimage in the Ǧāhiliyyah.

713 For reports that discuss Buss, see Kister (1986): 43–52; Lecker (1989): 37–41.
714 A tribal leader and poet of the Kalb; "Zuhayr b. Dj̲anāb," in *EI*² (M. Lecker).
715 This verse is also translated in Kister (1986): 43.

Bibliography

Primary Sources

Abū ʿAlī l-Fārisī, *al-Ḥuǧǧah*

Abū ʿAlī l-Ḥasan b. Aḥmad al-Fārisī (d. 377/987), *al-Ḥuǧǧah li-l-qurrāʾ al-sabʿah*, ed. Badr al-Dīn Qahwaǧī and Bašīr Ǧuwayǧātī (Damascus: Dār al-Maʾmūn li-l-Turāṯ, 1984), 7 vols.

Abū Ḥayyān, *al-Baḥr al-muḥīṭ*

Abū Ḥayyān Muḥammad b. Yūsuf (d. 745/1344), *al-Baḥr al-muḥīṭ fī l-tafsīr*, ed. Ṣidqī Muḥammad Ǧamīl (Beirut: Dār al-Fikr, 2010), 11 vols.

Abū Nuʿaym, *Dalāʾil al-nubuwwah*

Abū Nuʿaym Aḥmad b. ʿAbd Allāh al-Iṣfahānī (d. 430/1038), *Dalāʾil al-nubuwwah*, ed. Muḥammad Rawwās Qalʿaǧī and ʿAbd al-Barr ʿAbbās (Beirut: Dār al-Nafāʾis, 1406/1986), 2 vols. (continuous pagination).

Abū Nuʿaym, *Ḥilyat al-awliyāʾ*

Ḥilyat al-awliyāʾ wa-ṭabaqāt al-aṣfiyāʾ (Cairo: Maktabat al-Ḫānǧī; repr. Beirut: Dār al-Fikr, 1387/1967), 10 vols.

Abū Nuʿaym, *Iṣbahān*

Ḏikr aḫbār Iṣbahān, ed. Sven Dedering (Leiden: Brill, 1934), 2 vols.

Abū Nuʿaym, *Maʿrifat al-ṣaḥābah*

Maʿrifat al-ṣaḥābah, ed. ʿĀdil b. Yūsuf al-ʿAzzāzī (Riyadh: Dār al-Waṭan li-l-Našr, 1998), 7 vols.

Abū Nuʿaym, *Taʾrīḫ Iṣbahān*

Kitāb Taʾrīḫ Iṣbahān, ed. Sayyid Kasrawī Ḥasan (Beirut: Dār al-Kutub al-ʿIlmiyyah, 1990), 2 vols.

Abū Ṭālib, *Dīwān*

Abū Ṭālib, *Dīwān Abī Ṭālib*, ed. Muḥammad al-Tūnǧī (Beirut: Dār al-Kitāb al-ʿArabī, 1994).

Abū ʿUbaydah, *al-Dībāǧ*

Abū ʿUbaydah Maʿmar b. al-Muṯanná (d. ca. 210/825), *Kitāb al-Dībāǧ*, ed. ʿAbd Allāh b. Sulaymān and ʿAbd al-Raḥmān b. Sulaymān (Cairo: Maktabat al-Ḫānǧī, 1991).

Al-Aḫfaš al-Aṣġar, *Kitāb al-Iḫtiyārayn*

Abū l-Ḥasan ʿAlī b. Sulaymān b. al-Mufaḍḍal al-Aḫfaš al-Aṣġar (d. 315/927), *Kitāb al-Iḫtiyārayn al-Mufaḍḍaliyyāt wa-l-Aṣmaʿiyyāt*, ed. Faḫr al-Dīn Qabāwah (Damascus: Dār al-Fikr, 1999).

Al-Aʿlam al-Šantamarī, *Šarḥ dīwān ʿAlqamah*

Yūsuf b. Sulaymān al-Aʿlam al-Šantamarī (d. 476/1083), *Šarḥ dīwān ʿAlqamah b. ʿAbadah al-faḥl*, ed. Ḥannā Naṣr al-Ḥittī (Beirut: Dār al-Kitāb al-ʿArabī, 1993).

Al-Ālūsī, *Rūḥ al-maʿānī*

Maḥmūd b. ʿAbd Allāh al-Ālūsī (d. 1854), *Rūḥ al-maʿānī fī tafsīr al-Qurʾān al-ʿaẓīm wa-l-sabʿ al-maṯānī* (Beirut: Dār Iḥyāʾ al-Turāṯ al-ʿArabī, 198–), 30 vols.

Al-Āmidī, *al-Muʾtalif wa-l-muḫtalif*

al-Ḥasan b. Bišr al-Āmidī (d. 370/981 or 982), *al-Muʾtalif wa-l-muḫtalif*, ed. ʿAbd al-Sattār Aḥmad Farrāǧ (Cairo: Dār Iḥyāʾ al-Kutub al-ʿArabiyyah, 1381/1961).

Anon., *al-Manāsik*

Anon., *Kitāb al-Manāsik wa-amākin ṭuruq al-ḥaǧǧ wa-maʿālim al-ǧazīrah*, ed. Ḥamad al-Ǧāsir (Riyadh: al-Yamāmah, 1401/1981).

Al-Aʿšá, *Dīwān šiʿr al-Aʿšá*

Maymūn b. Qays al-Aʿšá (d. after 4/625), *Dīwān šiʿr al-Aʿšá Maymūn b. Qays b. Ǧandal maʿa šarḥ Abī l-ʿAbbās Ṯaʿlab* (*Kitāb al-Ṣubḥ al-munīr fī šiʿr Abī Baṣīr*), ed. R. Geyer (Vienna: Adolf Holzhausens Nachfolger, 1928).

Al-ʿAskarī, *al-Awāʾil*

Abū Hilāl al-ʿAskarī (d. ca. 400/1010), *al-Awāʾil*, ed. Muḥammad al-Miṣrī and Walīd Qaṣṣāb (Damascus: Wizārat al-Ṯaqāfah wa-l-Iršād al-Qawmī, 1975), 2 vols.

Al-ʿAwtabī, *al-Ansāb*

Salamah b. Muslim al-ʿAwtabī (fl. 5th/11th c.?), *al-Ansāb*, ed. Iḥsān al-Nuṣṣ (Muscat, 1427/2006^{4}), 2 vols.

Al-ʿAynī, *ʿUmdat al-qārī*

Badr al-Dīn Maḥmūd b. Aḥmad al-ʿAynī (d. 855/1451), *ʿUmdat al-qārī šarḥ Ṣaḥīḥ al-Buḫārī* (Beirut: Dār al-Fikr, 1998), 16 vols.

Al-Azraqī, *Aḫbār Makkah*^{1}

Muḥammad b. ʿAbd Allāh al-Azraqī (d. ca. 250/865), *Aḫbār Makkah wa-mā ǧāʾa fīhā mina l-āṯār*, ed. ʿAbd al-Malik b. Duhayš (Mecca: Maktabat al-Asadī, 2003), 2 vols.

Al-Azraqī, *Aḫbār Makkah*^{2}

Aḫbār Makkah wa-mā ǧāʾa fīhā mina l-āṯār, ed. Rušdī Malḥas ([Beirut:] Dār al-Andalus, n.d.), 2 vols.

Al-Baġawī, *Šarḥ al-sunnah*

al-Ḥusayn b. Masʿūd al-Farrāʾ al-Baġawī (d. ca. 516/1122), *Šarḥ al-sunnah*, ed. Šuʿayb al-Arnāʾūṭ (Beirut: al-Maktab al-Islāmī, 1393/1403), 16 vols.

Al-Baġawī, *Tafsīr*

Maʿālim al-tanzīl, on margin of al-Ḫāzin, *Tafsīr al-Ḫāzin*, ʿAlāʾ al-Dīn ʿAlī b. Muḥammad al-Baġdādī. *Lubāb al-taʾwīl fī maʿānī l-tanzīl* (Cairo: al-Istiqāma, 1381; repr. Beirut: Dār al-Fikr, 1399/1979), 4 vols.

Al-Baġdādī, *Ḫizānat al-adab*

ʿAbd al-Qādir b. ʿUmar al-Baġdādī (d. 1093/1682), *Ḫizānat al-adab wa-lubb lubāb lisān al-ʿarab*, ed. ʿAbd al-Salām Muḥammad Hārūn (Cairo: Maktabat al-Ḫānǧī, 1996), 13 vols.

Al-Bakrī, *Muʿǧam mā staʿǧam*

Abū ʿUbayd ʿAbd Allāh b. ʿAbd al-ʿAzīz al-Bakrī (d. 487/1094), *Muʿǧam mā staʿǧam min asmāʾ al-bilād wa-l-mawāḍiʿ*, ed. Muṣṭafá l-Saqqā (Beirut: ʿĀlam al-Kutub), 4 vols.

Al-Balāḏurī, *Ansāb al-ašrāf*

Aḥmad b. Yaḥyá l-Balāḏurī (d. ca. 279/892), *Ansāb al-ašrāf*, vol. 1, ed. Muḥammad Ḥamīdullāh (Cairo: Dār al-Maʿārif, 1959); vol. 4, i, ed. I. ʿAbbās (Wiesbaden: Franz Steiner, 1979); vol. 5, ed. I. ʿAbbās (Weisbaden and Beirut: Bibliotheca Islamica, 1996).

Al-Bayhaqī, *Dalāʾil al-nubuwwah*

Aḥmad b. al-Ḥusayn al-Bayhaqī (d. 458/1066), *Dalāʾil al-nubuwwah wa-maʿrifat aḥwāl ṣāḥib al-sharīʿah*, ed. ʿAbd al-Muʿṭī Qalʿaǧī (Beirut: Dār al-Kutub al-ʿIlmiyyah, 1985), 7 vols.

Al-Bayhaqī, *Šuʿab al-īmān*

Šuʿab al-īmān, ed. Zaġlūl (Beirut: Dār al-Kutub al-ʿIlmiyyah, 1410/1990), 9 vols.

Al-Buḫārī, *Ṣaḥīḥ*

Muḥammad b. Ismāʿīl al-Buḫārī (d. 256/870), *Ṣaḥīḥ al-Buḫārī*, ed. Muṣṭafá Dīb al-Baġā (Damascus: Dār Ibn Kaṯīr, 1987), 7 vols.

Al-Ḏahabī, *Mīzān al-iʿtidāl*

Muḥammad b. Aḥmad al-Ḏahabī (d. 748/1348), *Mīzān al-iʿtidāl fī naqd al-riǧāl*, ed. ʿAlī Muḥammad al-Baǧāwī (Beirut: Dār al-Maʿrifah, 1963), 4 vols.

Al-Ḏahabī, *Siyar aʿlām al-nubalāʾ*

Siyar aʿlām al-nubalāʾ, ed. Šuʿayb al-Arnāʾūṭ et al. (Beirut: Muʾassasat al-Risālah, 1401–1409/1981–1988), 25 vols.

Al-Ḏahabī, *Taḏkirat al-ḥuffāẓ*

Taḏkirat al-ḥuffāẓ (Hyderabad: Dāʾirat al-Maʿārif al-ʿUṯmāniyyah, 1376/1956; repr. Beirut: Dār Iḥyāʾ al-Turāṯ al-ʿArabī, n.d.), 3 vols.

Al-Dāraquṭnī, *al-Muʾtalif wa-l-muḫtalif*

ʿAlī b. ʿUmar al-Dāraquṭnī (d. 385/995), *al-Muʾtalif wa-l-muḫtalif*, ed. Muwaffaq b. ʿAbd Allāh b. ʿAbd al-Qādir (Beirut: Dār al-Ġarb al-Islāmī, 1986), 5 vols.

Al-Dimašqī, *Nuḫbat al-dahr*

Šams al-Dīn Muḥammad al-Dimašqī (d. 727/1327), *Nuḫbat al-dahr fī ʿaǧāʾib al-barr wa-l-baḥr*, ed. A.F. Mehren (Saint-Petersburgh: Académie Impériale des Sciences, 1865).

Al-Dīnawarī, *al-Muǧālasah*

Abū Bakr Aḥmad b. Marwān al-Dīnawarī (d. 333/944), *al-Muǧālasah wa-ǧawāhir al-ʿilm*, ed. Abū ʿUbaydah Mašhūr b. Ḥasan (Beirut: Ǧamʿiyyat al-Tarbiyah al-Islāmiyyah, 1998), 10 vols.

Al-Fākihī, *Aḫbār Makkah*

Muḥammad b. Isḥāq al-Fākihī (d. ca. 272/885), *Aḫbār Makkah fī qadīm al-dahr wa-ḥadīṯihi*, ed. ʿAbd al-Malik b. ʿAbd Allāh b. Duhayš (Beirut: Dār Ḫiḍr, 1994), 6 vols.

Al-Fārābī, *Dīwān al-adab*

Abū Ibrāhīm Isḥāq b. Ibrāhīm al-Fārābī (d. 350/961), *Dīwān al-adab* [*aw awwal muʿǧam ʿarabī murattab bi-ḥasab al-abniyah*], ed. Aḥmad Muḫtār ʿUmar (Cairo: al-Hayʾah al-ʿĀmmah li-Šuʾūn al-Maṭābiʿ al-Amīriyyah, 1974–1987), 4 vols.

Al-Fāsī, *Šifāʾ al-ġarām*

Muḥammad b. Aḥmad al-Fāsī (d. 832/1429), *Šifāʾ al-ġarām bi-aḫbār al-balad al-ḥarām*, ed. ʿUmar ʿAbd al-Salām Tadmurī (Beirut: Dār al-Kitāb al-ʿArabī, 1985), 2 vols.

Firdawsī, *Epic of the Kings*

Firdawsī, *The Shah-nama, the National Epic of Persia*, trans. R. Levy (London: Routledge & K. Paul, 1967).

Al-Ǧāḥiẓ, *al-Buḫalāʾ*

ʿAmr b. Baḥr al-Ǧāḥiẓ (d. 255/868–869), *Kitāb al-Buḫalāʾ*, ed. Aḥmad al-ʿĀmirī and ʿAlī l-Ǧāzim (Beirut: Dār al-Kutub al-ʿIlmiyyah, 1997), 2 vols.

Al-Ǧāḥiẓ, *al-Ḥayawān*

Kitāb al-Ḥayawān, ed. ʿAbd al-Salām Hārūn (Cairo: Maṭbaʿat Muṣṭafá l-Bābī l-Ḥalabī, 1965–1969), 8 vols.

Al-Ġarnāṭī, *Tuḥfat al-albāb*[1]

Abū Ḥamīd al-Ġarnāṭī l-Andalusī (d. 565/1169–1170), *Le Tuḥfat al-albāb de Abū Ḥamīd al-Andalusī al-Ġarnāṭī*, ed. Gabriel Ferrano (Paris: Imprimerie Nationale, 1925).

Al-Ġarnāṭī, *Tuḥfat al-albāb*[2]

Tuḥfat al-albāb wa-nuḫbat al-iʿǧāb, ed. Ismāʿīl al-ʿArabī (Morocco: Dār al-Āfāq al-Ǧadīdah, 1993).

Al-Ǧaṣṣāṣ, *Aḥkām al-Qurʾān*

Aḥmad b. ʿAlī l-Rāzī l-Ǧaṣṣāṣ (d. 370/981), *Aḥkām al-Qurʾān*, ed. Muḥammad Ṣādiq Qamḥāwī (Beirut: Dār Iḥyāʾ al-Kutub al-ʿArabiyyah/Muʾassasat al-Taʾrīḫ al-ʿArabī, 1992), 5 vols.

Al-Ḥalabī, *al-Sīrah al-Ḥalabiyyah*

ʿAlī b. Ibrāhīm al-Ḥalabī (d. 1044/1635), *al-Sīrah al-Ḥalabiyyah fī sīrat al-Amīn al-Maʾmūn* (*Insān al-ʿuyūn*) (Cairo: Dār al-Maʿrifah, n.d.), 3 vols.

Al-Hamdānī, *al-Iklīl*

al-Ḥasan b. Aḥmad al-Hamdānī (d. ca. 334/945), *al-Iklīl min aḫbār al-Yaman wa-ansāb Ḥimyar: Al-Kitāb al-ʿāšir fī maʿārif Hamdān wa-ansābihā wa-ʿuyūn aḫbārihā*, ed. Muḥibb al-Dīn al-Ḫaṭīb (Cairo: al-Maṭbaʿah al-Salafiyyah wa-Maktabatuhā, 1368/1949).

Al-Ḥarbī, *Ġarīb al-ḥadīṯ*

Ibrāhīm b. Isḥāq al-Ḥarbī (d. 285/898), *Ġarīb al-ḥadīṯ*, ed. Sulaymān b. Ibrāhīm b. Muḥammad al-ʿĀyid (Mecca: Ǧāmiʿat Umm al-Qurá, 1985), 3 vols.

Al-Ḫargūšī, *Šaraf al-muṣṭafá*

ʿAbd al-Malik b. Muḥammad al-Ḫargūšī (d. ca. 407/1016), *Šaraf al-muṣṭafá*, ed. Nabīl Āl Bāʿalawī ([Mecca:] Dār al-Bašāʾir al-Islāmiyyah, 1424/2003), 6 vols.

Ḥassān, *Dīwān*

Ḥassān b. Ṯābit (d. ca. 40/659), *Dīwān of Ḥassān Ibn Ṯābit*, ed. W. ʿArafat (London: E.J.W. Gibb Memorial Series, 1971), 2 vols.

Al-Ḫaṭīb al-Baġdādī, *al-Asmāʾ al-mubhamah*

Aḥmad b. ʿAlī l-Ḫaṭīb al-Baġdādī (d. 463/1071), *Kitāb al-Asmāʾ al-mubhamah fī l-anbāʾ al-muḥkamah*, ed. ʿIzz al-Dīn ʿAlī l-Sayyid (Cairo: al-Ḫānǧī, 1992).

Al-Ḫaṭīb al-Baġdādī, *Taʾrīḫ Baġdād*

Taʾrīḫ Baġdād (Cairo: al-Ḫānǧī, 1931), 14 vols.

Al-Hayṯamī, *Maǧmaʿ al-zawāʾid*

ʿAlī b. Abī Bakr al-Hayṯamī (d. 807/1405), *Maǧmaʿ al-zawāʾid wa-manbaʿ al-fawāʾid* (Beirut: Dār al-Kitāb al-ʿArabī, 1967), 10 vols.

Al-Ḥāzimī, *ʿUǧālat al-mubtadī*

Abū Bakr Muḥammad b. Abī ʿUṯmān al-Ḥāzimī (d. 584/1188), *ʿUǧālat al-mubtadī wa-fuḍālat al-muntahī fī l-nasab*, ed. ʿAbd Allāh Kannūn (Cairo: al-Hayʾah al-ʿĀmmah li-Šuʾūn al-Maṭābiʿ al-Amīriyyah, 1965).

Al-Ḫāzin, *Tafsīr*¹

ʿAlāʾ al-Dīn ʿAlī b. Muḥammad al-Ḫāzin al-Baġdādī (d. 741/1341), *Lubāb al-taʾwīl fī maʿānī l-tanzīl* (Beirut: Dār al-Kutub al-ʿIlmiyyah, 1995), 4 vols.

Al-Ḫāzin, *Tafsīr*²

Lubāb al-taʾwīl fī maʿānī l-tanzīl (Cairo: al-Istiqāmah, 1381 AH; repr. Beirut: Dār al-Fikr, n.d.), 4 vols.

Ḫidāš b. Zuhayr, *Šiʿr*

Ḫidāš b. Zuhayr, *Šiʿr Ḫidāš b. Zuhayr al-ʿĀmirī*, ed. Yaḥyá l-Ǧabūrī (Damascus: Majmaʿ al-Luġah al-ʿArabiyyah, 1986).

Al-Ḥimyarī, *al-Rawḍ al-miʿṭār*

Muḥammad b. ʿAbd al-Munʿim al-Ḥimyarī (d. 900/1495), *al-Rawḍ al-miʿṭār fī ḫabar al-aqṭār*, ed. Iḥsān ʿAbbās (Beirut: Maktabat Lubnān, 1975).

Al-Ḥuṭayʾah, *Der Dīwān*

Ǧarwal b. Aws al-Ḥuṭayʾah (d. after 41/661), *Der Dīwān des Ǧarwal b. Aus al-Ḥuṭejʾa*, ed. Ignaz Goldziher (Leipzig: F.A. Brockhaus, 1893).

Al-Ḥuṭayʾah, *Dīwān*

Dīwān al-Ḥuṭayʾah bi-riwāyat wa-šarḥ Ibn Sikkīt, ed. Nuʿmān Muḥammad Amīn Ṭāhā (Cairo: Maktabat al-Ḫānǧī, 1987).

Ibn ʿAbd al-Barr, *al-Istīʿāb*

Abū ʿUmar Yūsuf b. ʿAbd al-Barr (d. 463/1070), *al-Istīʿāb fī maʿrifat al-aṣḥāb*, ed. ʿAlī Muḥammad al-Biǧāwī (Cairo: Maṭbaʿat Nahḍat Miṣr, 1980), 4 vols.

Ibn ʿAbd Rabbihi, *al-ʿIqd al-farīd*

Aḥmad b. Muḥammad b. ʿAbd Rabbihi (d. 328/940), *al-ʿIqd al-farīd*, ed. ʿAbd al-Maǧīd Qamīḥah et al. (Beirut: Dār al-Kutub al-ʿIlmiyyah, 1983), 9 vols.

Ibn Abī Ḥātim, *al-Ǧarḥ wa-l-taʿdīl*
'Abd al-Raḥmān b. Muḥammad b. Abī Ḥātim (d. 327/938), *Kitāb al-Ǧarḥ wa-l-taʿdīl* (Beirut: Dār al-Kutub al-ʿIlmiyyah, 1952), 9 vols.

Ibn ʿAdī, *al-Kāmil*
ʿAbd Allāh b. ʿAdī l-Ǧurǧānī (d. 365/976), *al-Kāmil fī ḍuʿafāʾ al-riǧāl* (Beirut: Dar al-Fikr, 1404/1984), 9 vols.

Ibn ʿAsākir, *Dimašq*
ʿAlī b. al-Ḥasan b. Hibat Allāh b. ʿAsākir (d. 519/1125), *Taʾrīḫ madīnat Dimašq*, ed. ʿUmar b. Ġarāmah al-ʿAmrawī (Beirut: Dār al-Fikr, 1415–1419/1995–1998), 80 vols.

Ibn ʿAsākir, *Muḫtaṣar Taʾrīḫ Dimašq*
Muḫtaṣar Taʾrīḫ Dimašq li-Ibn ʿAsākir, ed. Rūḥiyyah al-Naḥḥās, Riyāḍ ʿAbd al-Ḥamīd Murād, and Muḥammad Muṭīʿ al-Ḥāfiẓ (Damascus: Dār al-Fikr, 1984–1988), 29 vols.

Ibn al-Aṯīr, *al-Kāmil fī l-taʾrīḫ*[1]
ʿIzz al-Dīn Abū l-Ḥasan ʿAlī, known as Ibn al-Aṯīr (d. 630/1233), *al-Kāmil fī l-taʾrīḫ* (Beirut: Dār Ṣādir-Dār Bayrūt, 1965–1966), 13 vols.

Ibn al-Aṯīr, *al-Kāmil fī l-taʾrīḫ*[2]
al-Kāmil fī l-taʾrīḫ, ed. Abū l-Fidāʾ ʿAbd Allāh al-Qāḍī (Beirut: Dār al-Kutub al-ʿIlmiyyah, 1987), 11 vols.

Ibn al-Aṯīr, *Usd al-ġābah*
Usd al-ġābah fī maʿrifat al-ṣaḥābah, ed. ʿAlī Muḥammad Muʿawwaḍ and ʿĀdil Aḥmad ʿAbd al-Mawǧūd (Beirut: Dār al-Kutub al-ʿIlmiyyah, 1994), 7 vols.

Ibn ʿAṭiyyah, *al-Muḥarrar al-waǧīz*
ʿAbd al-Ḥaqq b. Ġālib b. ʿAṭiyyah (d. 546/1152), *al-Muḥarrar al-waǧīz fī tafsīr al-kitāb al-ʿazīz*, ed. ʿAbd Allah b. Ibrāhīm al-Anṣārī (Cairo: Dār al-Fikr al-ʿArabī, 2000?), 15 vols.

Ibn Baškuwāl, *Ġawāmiḍ al-asmāʾ*
Abū l-Qāsim Ḫalaf b. ʿAbd al-Malik b. Baškuwāl (d. 578/1183), *Ġawāmiḍ al-asmāʾ al-mubhamah*, ed. ʿIzz al-Dīn ʿAlī l-Sayyid and Muḥammad Kamāl al-Dīn ʿIzz al-Dīn (Beirut: ʿĀlam al-Kutub, 1987), 2 vols.

Ibn Durayd, *Ǧamharat al-luġah*
Muḥammad b. al-Ḥasan b. Durayd (d. 321/933), *Ǧamharat al-luġah*, ed. Ramzī Baʿlabakkī (Beirut: Dār al-ʿIlm li-l-Malāyīn, 1987–1988), 3 vols.

Ibn Durayd, *al-Ištiqāq*
al-Ištiqāq, ed. ʿAbd al-Salām Muḥammad Hārūn (Cairo: al-Ḫānǧī, 1378/1958).

Ibn Durayd, *Taʿlīq*
Taʿlīq min Amālī Ibn Durayd, ed. Muṣṭafá l-Sanūsī (Kuwait: al-Maǧlis al-Waṭanī li-l-Ṯaqāfah wa-l-Funūn wa-l-Ādāb, 1984).

Ibn al-Faqīh, *Muḫtaṣar Kitāb al-Buldān*
Abū Bakr Aḥmad b. Muḥammad al-Hamaḏānī, known as Ibn al-Faqīh (d. ca. 289/902), *Muḫtaṣar Kitāb al-Buldān* (Leiden: Brill, 1885).

Ibn al-Ǧawzī, *Kašf al-muškil*

'Abd al-Raḥmān b. 'Alī b. al-Ǧawzī (d. 597/1201), *Kašf al-muškil min ḥadīṯ al-Ṣaḥīḥayn*, ed. 'Alī Ḥusayn al-Bawwāb (Riyadh: Dār al-Waṭan li-l-Našr, 1997), 4 vols.

Ibn al-Ǧawzī, *al-Muntaẓam*

al-Muntaẓam fī ta'rīḫ al-mulūk wa-l-umam, ed. Muḥammad 'Abd al-Qādir and Muṣṭafá 'Abd al-Qādir (Beirut: Dār al-Kutub al-'Ilmiyyah, 1992), 15 vols.

Ibn al-Ǧawzī, *Ṣifat al-ṣafwah*

Ṣifat al-ṣafwah, ed. Fāḫūrī and Qal'aǧī (Beirut: Dār al-Ma'rifah, 1399/1979), 4 vols.

Ibn Ḥabīb, *al-Muḥabbar*

Muḥammad b. Ḥabīb (d. 245/860), *Kitāb al-Muḥabbar*, ed. Ilse Lichtenstaedter (Hyderabad: Dā'irat al-Ma'ārif al-'Uṯmāniyyah, 1361/1942; repr. Beirut: al-Maktab al-Tiǧārī, n.d.).

Ibn Ḥabīb, *al-Munammaq*

Kitāb al-Munammaq fī aḫbār Qurayš, ed. Ḫuršīd Aḥmad Fāriq (Beirut: 'Ālam al-Kutub, 1405/1985).

Ibn Ḥaǧar, *Fatḥ al-bārī*

Abū l-Faḍl Aḥmad b. 'Alī b. Ḥaǧar al-'Asqalānī (d. 852/1449), *Fatḥ al-bārī bi-šarḥ Ṣaḥīḥ al-Buḫārī*, ed. 'Abd al-'Azīz b. 'Abd Allāh b. Bāz (Beirut: Dār al-Fikr, 1993), 18 vols.

Ibn Ḥaǧar, *al-Iṣābah*[1]

al-Iṣābah fī tamyīz al-ṣaḥābah, ed. 'Ādil Aḥmad 'Abd al-Mawǧūd and 'Alī Muḥammad Mu'awwaḍ (Beirut: Dār al-Kutub al-'Ilmiyyah, 1995), 8 vols.

Ibn Ḥaǧar, *al-Iṣābah*[2]

al-Iṣābah fī tamyīz al-ṣaḥābah, ed. 'Alī Muḥammad al-Biǧāwī (Cairo: Dār Nahḍat Miṣr, 1392/1972), 8 vols.

Ibn Ḥaǧar, *Tahḏīb al-tahḏīb*

Tahḏīb al-tahḏīb, ed. Muṣṭafá 'Abd al-Qādir (Beirut: Dār al-Kutub al-'Ilmiyyah, 1994), 12 vols.

Ibn Ḫallikān, *Wafayāt al-a'yān*

Aḥmad b. Muḥammad b. Ibrāhīm b. Abī Bakr b. Ḫallikān (d. 681/1282), *Wafayāt al-a'yān wa-anbā' abnā' al-zamān*, ed. Iḥsān 'Abbās (Beirut: Dār Ṣādir, 1972), 8 vols.

Ibn Ḥamdūn, *al-Taḏkirah al-Ḥamdūniyyah*

Muḥammad b. al-Ḥasan, known as Ibn Ḥamdūn (d. 562/1167), *al-Taḏkirah al-Ḥamdūniyyah*, ed. Iḥsān 'Abbās and Bakr 'Abbās (Beirut: Dār Ṣādir, 1996), 10 vols.

Ibn Ḥammād, *al-Fitan*

Nu'aym b. Ḥammād (d. 228/843), *al-Fitan*, ed. Suhayl Zakkār (Beirut: Dār al-Fikr, 1993).

Ibn Ḥanbal, *al-Musnad*

Aḥmad b. Ḥanbal (d. 241/855), *al-Musnad* (Cairo: al-Maṭba'ah al-Maymaniyyah, 1313/1895; repr. Beirut: al-Maktab al-Islāmī/Dār Ṣādir, n.d.), 6 vols.

Ibn Ḥazm, *Ǧamharat ansāb al-ʿarab*
ʿAlī b. Aḥmad b. Saʿīd b. Ḥazm al-Andalusī (d. 456/1064), *Ǧamharat ansāb al-ʿArab*, ed. ʿAbd al-Salām Hārūn (Cairo: Dār al-Maʿārif, 1382/1962).

Ibn Ḥibbān, *Taʾrīḫ al-ṣaḥābah*
Abū Ḥātim Muḥammad b. Aḥmad b. Ḥibbān al-Bustī (d. 354/965), *Taʾrīḫ al-ṣaḥābah allaḏīna ruwiya ʿanhum al-aḫbār*, ed. Ibn al-Ḍinnāwī (Beirut: Dār al-Kutub al-ʿIlmiyyah, 1988).

Ibn Ḥibbān, *al-Ṯiqāt*
al-Ṯiqāt (Hyderabad: Dāʾirat al-Maʿārif al-ʿUṯmāniyyah, 1983; repr. Beirut: Muʾassasat al-Kutub al-Ṯaqāfiyyah, 1995), 10 vols.

Ibn Hišām, *al-Sīrah al-nabawiyyah*
Abū Muḥammad ʿAbd al-Malik b. Hišām (d. ca. 218/833), *al-Sīrah al-nabawiyyah*, ed. Muṣṭafá l-Saqqā, Ibrāhīm al-Ibyārī and ʿAbd al-Ḥafīẓ Šalabī (Cairo: Muṣṭafá l-Bābī l-Ḥalabī, 1936; repr. Beirut: Iḥyāʾ al-Turāṯ al-ʿArabī, 1971), 4 vols.

Ibn Hišām, *The Life of Muhammad*
The Life of Muhammad: A Translation of [*Ibn*] *Isḥāq's Sīrat rasūl Allāh, with Introduction and Notes*, trans. A. Guillaume (London: Oxford University Press, 1955).

Ibn al-Kalbī, *al-Aṣnām*
Hišām b. Muḥammad b. al-Kalbī (d. ca. 204/819), *Kitāb al-Aṣnām*, ed. Aḥmad Zakī Bāšā (Cairo: al-Dār al-Qawmiyyah li-l-Ṭibāʿah wa-l-Našr, 1924).

Ibn al-Kalbī, *Ǧamharat al-nasab*
Ǧamharat al-nasab, ed. Nāǧī asan (Beirut: ʿĀlam al-Kutub-Maktabat al-Nahḍah al-ʿArabiyyah, 1407/1986).

Ibn al-Kalbī, *Nasab Maʿadd*
Nasab Maʿadd wa-l-Yaman al-kabīr, ed. Nāǧī Ḥasan (Beirut: ʿĀlam al-Kutub, 1988).

Ibn Kaṯīr, *al-Bidāyah wa-l-nihāyah*
Abū l-Fidāʾ Ismāʿīl b. ʿUmar b. Kaṯīr (d. 774/1373), *al-Bidāyah wa-l-nihāyah*, ed. ʿAbd al-Ḥamīd Hindāwī (Sidon: al-Maktabah al-ʿAṣriyyah, 2001), 10 vols.

Ibn Kaṯīr, *al-Sīrah al-nabawiyyah*
al-Sīrah al-nabawiyyah, ed. Muṣṭafá ʿAbd al-Wāḥid (Beirut: Dār Iḥyāʾ al-Turāṯ al-ʿArabī, 1964), 4 vols.

Ibn Kaṯīr, *Tafsīr*[1]
Tafsīr al-Qurʾān al-ʿaẓīm (Beirut: Dār al-Kutub al-ʿIlmiyyah, 1998), 9 vols.

Ibn Kaṯīr, *Tafsīr*[2]
Tafsīr al-Qurʾān al-ʿaẓīm, ed. Muṣṭafá l-Sayyid Muḥammad et al. (Cairo: Muʾassasat Qurṭubah, 1421/2000), 15 vols.

Ibn Manẓūr, *Lisān al-ʿarab*
Muḥammad b. Mukarram, known as Ibn Manẓūr (d. 711/1311), *Lisān al-ʿarab* (Beirut: Dār Ṣādir, 1994), 15 vols.

Ibn Qāniʿ, *Muʿǧam al-ṣaḥābah*
ʿAbd al-Bāqī b. Qāniʿ (d. 351/962), *Muʿǧam al-ṣaḥābah*, ed. Ṣalāḥ b. Sālim al-Maṣrātī (Medina: Maktabat al-Ġurabāʾ al-Aṯariyyah, 1997), 3 vols.

Ibn Qayyim al-Ǧawziyyah, *Iġāṯat al-lahfān*
Šams al-Dīn Muḥammad b. Abī Bakr, known as Ibn Qayyim al-Ǧawziyyah (d. 751/1350), *Iġāṯat al-lahfān min maṣāʾid al-šayṭān*, ed. ʿIṣām Fāris al-Ḥarastānī (Beirut: Muʾassasat al-Risālah, 1994), 2 vols.

Ibn Qudāmah, *al-Istibṣār*
Muwaffaq al-Dīn ʿAbd Allāh b. Qudāmah al-Maqdisī (d. 620/1223), *al-Istibṣār fī nasab al-ṣaḥābah min al-anṣār*, ed. ʿAlī Nuwayhiḍ (Beirut: Dār al-Fikr, 1972).

Ibn Qutaybah, *Ġarīb al-ḥadīṯ*
ʿAbd Allāh b. Muslim b. Qutaybah (d. 276/889), *Ġarīb al-ḥadīṯ* (Beirut: Dār al-Kutub al-ʿIlmiyyah, 1988), 2 vols.

Ibn Qutaybah, *al-Maʿānī*
Kitāb al-Maʿānī l-kabīr fī abyāt al-maʿānī (Beirut: Dār al-Nahḍah al-Ḥadīṯah, 198–), 3 vols.

Ibn Quṭlūbuġā, *al-Ṯiqāt*
Zayn al-Dīn Qāsim b. Quṭlūbuġā (d. ca. 879/1474), *al-Ṯiqāt mimman lam yaqaʿ fī l-kutub al-sittah*, ed. Ḥāmid ʿAbd Allāh al-Maḥallāwī (Beirut: Dār al-Kutub al-ʿIlmiyyah, 2019), 7 vols.

Ibn Saʿd, *al-Ṭabaqāt*[1]
Muḥammad b. Saʿd, *al-Ṭabaqāt al-kubrá*, ed. Muḥammad ʿAbd al-Qādir (Beirut: Dār al-Kutub al-ʿIlmiyyah, 1997), 9 vols.

Ibn Saʿd, *al-Ṭabaqāt*[2]
Kitāb al-Ṭabaqāt al-kabīr, ed. ʿAlī Muḥammad ʿUmar (Cairo: Maktabat al-Ḫānǧī, 2001), 11 vols.

Ibn Sayyid al-Nās, *ʿUyūn al-aṯar*
Muḥammad b. ʿAbd Allāh b. Yaḥyá b. Sayyid al-Nās (d. 659/1261), *ʿUyūn al-aṯar fī funūn al-maġāzī wa-l-šamāʾil wa-l-siyar*, ed. al-Ḫaṭrāwī and Mittū (Medina: Maktabat Dār al-Turāṯ, Beirut: Dār Ibn Kaṯīr, 1992), 2 vols.

Ibn Sīdah, *al-Muḫaṣṣaṣ*
ʿAlī b. Ismāʿīl, known as Ibn Sīdah (d. 458/1066), *Kitāb al-Muḫaṣṣaṣ* (Cairo: al-Maṭbaʿah al-Kubrá l-Amīriyyah, 1898), 17 books in 6 vols.

Ibn Sīdah, *al-Muḥkam*
al-Muḥkam wa-l-muḥīṭ al-aʿẓam, ed. ʿAbd al-Ḥamīd Hindāwī (Beirut: Dār al-Kutub al-ʿIlmiyyah, 2001), 11 vols.

Ibn Šabbah, *Taʾrīḫ al-Madīnah*
ʿUmar b. Šabbah (d. 262/878), *Taʾrīḫ al-Madīnah al-munawwarah*, ed. Fahīm Muḥammad Šaltūt (n.p., [1979]; repr. Beirut: Dār al-Turāṯ and al-Dār al-Islāmiyyah, 1990), 4 vols.

Al-Iṣfahānī, *al-Aġānī*
Abū l-Farağ ʿAlī b. Ḥasan al-Iṣfahānī (d. 356/967), *Kitāb al-Aġānī*, ed. ʿAbd al-Amīr ʿAlī Muhannā and Samīr Ğābir (Beirut: Dār al-Fikr, 1997), 27 vols.

Al-Kalāʿī, *al-Iktifāʾ*
Sulaymān b. Mūsá l-Kalāʿī (d. 634/1237), *al-Iktifāʾ bi-mā taḍammanahu min maġāzī rasūli llāh wa-l-ṯalāṯah al-ḫulafāʾ*, ed. Muḥammad Kamāl al-Dīn ʿIzz al-Dīn ʿAlī (Beirut: ʿĀlam al-Kutub, 1417/1997), 4 vols.

Al-Kattānī, *al-Risālah al-mustaṭrafah*
Muḥammad b. Jaʿfar al-Kattānī (d. 1345/1927), *al-Risālah al-mustaṭrafah bayān mašhūr kutub al-sunnah al-mušarrafah* (n.p., n.d.; repr. Cairo: Maktabat al-Kulliyyāt al-Azhariyyah, n.d.).

Kumayt b. Zayd, *Dīwān*
Kumayt b. Zayd (d. 126/744), *Dīwān al-Kumayt b. Zayd al-Asadī*, ed. Muḥammad Nabīl Ṭurayfī (Beirut: Dār Ṣādir, 2000).

Al-Maqdisī, *al-Badʾ wa-l-taʾrīḫ*
Muṭahhar b. Ṭāhir al-Maqdisī (d. ca. 355/966), *al-Badʾ wa-l-taʾrīḫ*, ed. Cl. Huart (Paris, 1899–1919; repr. Baghdad: Maktabat al-Muṯanná, n.d.), 6 vols.

Al-Maqrīzī, *al-Ḫiṭaṭ*
Aḥmad b. ʿAlī l-Maqrīzī (d. 845/1442), *al-Mawāʿiẓ wa-l-iʿtibār bi-ḏikr al-ḫiṭaṭ wa-l-āṯār*, ed. Ayman Fuʾād Sayyid (London: Muʾassasat al-Furqān lil-Turāṯ al-Islāmī, 2013), 7 vols.

Al-Maqrīzī, *Imtāʿ al-asmāʿ*
Imtāʿ al-asmāʿ bi-mā li-l-nabī min al-aḥwāl wa-l-amwāl wa-l-ḥafadah wa-l-matāʿ, ed. Muḥammad ʿAbd al-Ḥamīd al-Numaysī (Beirut: Dār al-Kutub al-ʿIlmiyyah, 1999), 15 vols.

Al-Masʿūdī, *Murūğ al-ḏahab*
ʿAlī b. al-Ḥusayn al-Masʿūdī (d. 345/956), *Murūğ al-ḏahab wa-maʿādin al-ğawhar*, ed. Ch. Pellat (Beirut: Manšūrāt al-Ğāmiʿah al-Lubnāniyyah, 1966–1979), 7 vols.

Al-Māturidī, *Taʾwīlāt*
Muḥammad b. Muḥammad al-Māturidī (d. 333/944), *Taʾwīlāt ahl al-sunnah*, ed. Muḥammad Mustafīḍ al-Raḥmān (Baghdad: Maṭbaʿat al-Iršād, 1983).

Al-Māwardī, *al-Ḥāwī l-kabīr*
ʿAlī b. Muḥammad al-Māwardī (d. 450/1058), *al-Ḥāwī l-kabīr fī fiqh maḏhab al-Imām al-Šāfiʿī*, ed. ʿAlī Muḥammad Muʿawwaḍ and ʿĀdil Aḥmad ʿAbd al-Mawğūd (Beirut: Dār al-Kutub al-ʿIlmiyyah, 1994), 19 vols.

Al-Māwardī, *al-Nukat wa-l-ʿuyūn*
al-Nukat wa-l-ʿuyūn: tafsīr al-Māwardī (Beirut: Dār al-Kutub al-ʿIlmiyyah, 2000), 6 vols.

Al-Maydānī, *Mağmaʿ al-amṯāl*
Aḥmad b. Muḥammad al-Maydānī (d. 518/1124), *Mağmaʿ al-amṯāl*, ed. Muḥammad

Muḥyī l-Dīn ʿAbd al-Ḥamīd (Cairo: Maṭbaʿat al-Sunnah al-Muḥammadiyyah, 1374/1955), 2 vols.

Miskawayh, *Taǧārib al-umam*

Aḥmad b. Muḥammad Miskawayh (d. 421/1030), *Taǧārib al-umam*, ed. A. Emami (Tehran: Soroush Press, 1997–2002), 7 vols.

Al-Mizzī, *Tahḏīb al-kamāl*

Yūsuf b. al-Zakī ʿAbd al-Raḥmān al-Mizzī (d. 742/1341), *Tahḏīb al-kamāl fī asmāʾ al-riǧāl*, ed. Baššār ʿAwwād Maʿrūf (Beirut: Muʾassasat al-Risālah, 1405–1413/1985–1992), 35 vols.

Al-Muʿāfá, *al-Ǧalīs al-ṣāliḥ*

Al-Muʿāfá b. Zakariyyāʾ (d. 390/1000), *al-Ǧalīs al-ṣāliḥ al-kāfī wa-l-anīs al-nāṣiḥ al-šāfī*, ed. Muḥammad Mursī l-Ḫūlī and Iḥsān ʿAbbās (Beirut: ʿĀlam al-Kutub, 1413/1993), 4 vols.

Al-Mubarrad, *al-Kāmil fī l-luġah wal-adab*

Muḥammad b. Yazīd al-Mubarrad (d. 286/900), *al-Kāmil fī l-luġah wa-l-adab*, ed. Muḥammad Abū l-Faḍl Ibrāhīm (Cairo: Dār al-Fikr al-ʿArabī, 1417/1997), 4 vols.

Al-Mufaḍḍal al-Ḍabbī, *al-Mufaḍḍaliyyāt*

Abū l-ʿAbbās al-Mufaḍḍal b. Muḥammad al-Ḍabbī (d. ca. 163/780), *al-Mufaḍḍaliyyāt*, ed. Aḥmad Muḥammad Šākir and ʿAbd al-Salām Muḥammad Hārūn (Cairo: Dār al-Maʿārif, 1994).

Muǧāhid, *Tafsīr*

Abū l-Ḥaǧǧāǧ Muǧāhid b. Ǧabr al-Makkī (d. bet. 100/718 and 104/722), *Tafsīr al-Imām Muǧāhid b. Ǧabr*, ed. ʿAbd al-Salām Abū Nīl (Cairo: Dār al-Fikr al-Islāmī l-Ḥadīṯah, 1989).

Muġulṭāy, *Ikmāl tahḏīb al-kamāl*

Muġulṭāy b. Qilīǧ al-Ḥanafī (d. 762/1361), *Ikmāl tahḏīb al-kamāl fī asmāʾ al-riǧāl*, ed. ʿĀdil b. Muḥammad and Usāmah b. Ibrāhīm (Cairo: al-Fārūq al-Ḥadīṯah, 2001), 12 vols.

Muqātil, *Tafsīr*

Abū l-Ḥasan Muqātil b. Sulaymān (d. 150/767), *Tafsīr Muqātil b. Sulaymān*, ed. Aḥmad Farīd (Beirut: Dār al-Kutub al-ʿIlmiyyah, 2003), 3 vols.

Muslim, *Ṣaḥīḥ*

Abū l-Ḥusayn Muslim b. al-Ḥaǧǧāǧ al-Naysābūrī (d. 261/875), *Ṣaḥīḥ Muslim*, ed. Muḥammad Fuʾād ʿAbd al-Bāqī (Beirut: Dār al-Fikr, 1999), 5 vols.

Al-Muttaqī l-Hindī, *Kanz al-ʿummāl*

Al-Muttaqī l-Hindī, ʿAlī b. ʿAbd al-Malik (d. 976/1567), *Kanz al-ʿummāl fī sunan al-aqwāl wal-afʿāl*, ed. Ṣafwat al-Saqqā and Bakrī l-Ḥayyānī (Beirut: Muʾassasat al-Risālah, 1985), 16 vols.

Naṣr, *al-Amkinah*

Abū l-Fatḥ Naṣr b. ʿAbd al-Raḥmān al-Fazārī l-Iskandarānī (d. ca. 561/1166), *al-Am-*

kinah wa-l-miyāh wa-l-ǧibāl wa-l-āṯār, ed. Ḥamad al-Ǧāsir (Riyadh: Markaz al-Malik Fayṣal, 2004), 2 vols.

Al-Nawawī, *Tahḏīb al-asmāʾ*
Abū Zakariyyāʾ al-Nawawī (d. 676/1277), *Tahḏīb al-asmāʾ wa-l-luġāt* (Cairo, n.d.; repr. Beirut: Dār al-Kutub al-ʿIlmiyyah, n.d.), 2 vols.

Al-Nuwayrī, *Nihāyat al-arab*
Aḥmad b. ʿAbd al-Wahhāb al-Nuwayrī (d. 733/1333), *Nihāyat al-arab fī funūn al-adab* (Cairo: Maṭbaʿat Dār al-Kutub al-Miṣriyyah, 1923–1929), 13 vols.

Al-Qālī, *al-Amālī*
Ismāʿīl b. al-Qāsim al-Qālī (d. 356/967), *Kitāb al-Amālī* (Cairo: al-Hayʾah al-Miṣriyyah al-ʿĀmmah lil-Kitāb, 1975–1976), 2 vols.

Al-Qalqašandī, *Maʾāṯir al-ināfah*
Abū l-ʿAbbās Aḥmad b. ʿAbd Allāh al-Qalqašandī (d. 821/1418), *Maʾāṯir al-ināfah fī maʿālim al-ḫilāfah*, ed. ʿAbd al-Sattār Aḥmad Farrāǧ (Beirut: ʿĀlam al-Kutub, 1964), 3 vols.

Al-Qalqašandī, *Ṣubḥ al-aʿšá*
Ṣubḥ al-aʿšá fī ṣināʿat al-inšāʾ (Cairo: Dār al-Kutub al-Miṣriyyah, 1913–1919), 15 vols.

Al-Qasṭallānī, *Iršād al-sārī*
Aḥmad b. Muḥammad al-Qasṭallānī (d. 923/1517), *Iršād al-sārī li-šarḥ Ṣaḥīḥ al-Buḫārī* (Cairo: Būlāq, 1905), 10 vols.

Al-Qurṭubī, *al-Ǧāmiʿ*
Muḥammad b. Aḥmad al-Qurṭubī (d. 671/1272), *al-Ǧāmiʿ li-aḥkām al-Qurʾān* (Cairo: Dār al-Kutub, 1967; repr.), 20 vols.

Al-Rāġib al-Iṣfahānī, *Tafsīr*
Abū l-Qāsim al-Ḥusayn b. Muḥammad al-Rāġib al-Iṣfahānī (d. early 5th/11th c.), *Tafsīr al-Rāġib al-Iṣfahānī min awwal sūrat Āl ʿImrān wa-ḥattá nihāyat al-āyah 112 min sūrat al-Nisāʾ*, ed. ʿĀdil b. ʿAlī b. Aḥmad al-Šaddī, PhD dissertation (Mecca: Ǧāmiʿat Umm al-Qurá, 2005), 4 vols.

Al-Rāzī, *Mafātīḥ al-ġayb*
Abū ʿAbd Allāh Faḫr al-Dīn al-Rāzī (d. 606/1209), *Mafātīḥ al-ġayb* (*al-tafsīr al-kabīr*) (Beirut: Dār al-Fikr, 1981), 32 vols.

Al-Ṣafadī, *al-Wāfī bi-l-wafayāt*
Ṣalāḥ al-Dīn Ḫalīl b. Aybak al-Ṣafadī (d. 769/1363), al-*Wāfī bi-l-wafayāt*, ed. Aḥmad al-Arnāʾūṭ and Turkī Muṣṭafá (Beirut: Dār Iḥyāʾ al-Turāṯ al-ʿArabī, 1420/2000), 29 vols.

Al-Šahrastānī, *al-Milal wa-l-niḥal*
Muḥammad b. ʿAbd al-Karīm al-Šahrastānī (d. 548/1153), *Kitāb al-Milal wa-l-niḥal* (Leipzig: Otto Harrassowitz, 1923).

Al-Ṣāliḥī, *Subul al-hudá*
Muḥammad b. Yūsuf al-Ṣāliḥī (d. 942/1536), *Subul al-hudá wa-l-rašād fī sīrat ḫayr*

al-ʿibād, ed. Muṣṭafá ʿAbd al-Wāḥid (Cairo: al-Mağlis al-Aʿlá li-l-Šuʾūn al-Islamiyyah, 1972–1990), 8 vols.

Al-Samʿānī, *al-Ansāb*

ʿAbd al-Karīm b. Muḥammad al-Samʿānī (d. 562/1167), *al-Ansāb*, ed. ʿAbd Allāh ʿUmar al-Barūdī (Beirut: Dār al-Ğinān, 1408/1988), 5 vols.

Al-Samhūdī, *Wafāʾ al-wafā*

ʿAlī b. ʿAbd Allāh al-Samhūdī (d. 911/1506), *Wafāʾ al-wafā bi-aḫbār dār al-Muṣṭafá*, ed. Qāsim al-Sāmarrāʾī (London and Jedda: Muʾassasat al-Furqān li-l-Turāṯ al-Islāmī, 1422/2001), 4 vols.

Sībawayhi, *Kitāb Sībawayhi*

Abū Bišr ʿAmr b. ʿUṯmān, known as Sībawayhi (d. ca. 180/796), *Kitāb Sībawayhi*, ed. ʿAbd al-Salām Muḥammad Hārūn (Cairo: Maktabat al-Ḫānğī, 1988), 5 vols.

Al-Singārī, *Manāʾiḥ al-karam*

ʿAlī b. Tāğ al-Dīn al-Sinğārī (d. 1125/1713), *Manāʾiḥ al-karam fī aḫbār Makkah wa-l-bayt wa-wulāt al-ḥaram*, ed. Ğamīl ʿAbd Allāh Muḥammad al-Miṣrī (Mecca: Wizārat al-Taʿlīm al-ʿĀlī, Ğāmiʿat Umm al-Qurá, 1998), 6 vols.

Al-Suhaylī, *al-Rawḍ al-unuf*

ʿAbd al-Raḥmān b. ʿAbd Allāh al-Suhaylī (d. 581/1185), *al-Rawḍ al-unuf fī tafsīr al-Sīrah al-nabawiyyah li-Ibn Hišām*, ed. ʿAbd al-Raḥmān al-Wakīl (Cairo: Dār al-Kutub al-ʿIlmiyyah, 1967), 7 vols.

Al-Suyūṭī, *al-Durr al-manṯūr*

Ğalāl al-Dīn al-Suyūṭī (d. 911/1505), *Tafsīr al-durr al-manṯūr fī l-tafsīr al-maʾṯūr* (Beirut: Dār al-Fikr, 1414/1993).

Al-Suyūṭī, *al-Ḫaṣāʾiṣ*

al-Ḫaṣāʾiṣ al-kubrá, ed. Muḥammad Ḫalīl Harās (Cairo: Dār al-Kutub al-Ḥadīṯah, 1387/1967).

Al-Ṭabarānī, *al-Aḥādīṯ al-ṭiwāl*

Abū l-Qāsim Sulaymān b. Aḥmad al-Ṭabarānī (d. 360/971), *al-Aḥādīṯ al-ṭiwāl*, ed. Muṣṭafá ʿAbd al-Qādir ʿAṭā (Beirut: Dār al-Kutub al-ʿIlmiyyah, 1412/1992).

Al-Ṭabarānī, *al-Muʿğam al-kabīr*

al-Muʿğam al-kabīr, ed. Ḥamdī ʿAbd al-Mağīd al-Salafī (Cairo: Maktabat Ibn Taymiyyah, 1405/1985), 24 vols.

Al-Ṭabarī, *Ğāmiʿ al-bayān*

Abū Ğaʿfar Muḥammad b. Ğarīr al-Ṭabarī (d. 310/923), *Tafsīr al-Ṭabarī: Ğāmiʿ al-bayān ʿan taʾwīl āy al-Qurʾān*, ed. ʿAbd Allāh b. ʿAbd al-Muḥsin al-Turkī (Cairo: Hağar, 2001), 26 vols.

Al-Ṭabarī, *History*

The History of al-Ṭabarī, vol. 1, trans. F. Rosenthal (Albany: State University of New York Press, 1989); vol. 2, trans. W.M. Brinner (Albany: State University of New York Press, 1987); vol. 5, trans. C.E. Bosworth (Albany: State University of New York Press,

1999); vol. 6, trans. W. Montgomery Watt and M.V. McDonald (Albany: State University of New York Press, 1988); vol. 8, trans. M. Fishbein (Albany: State University of New York Press, 1997); vol. 25, trans. Kh.Y. Blankinship (Albany: State University of New York Press, 1989); vol. 39, E. Landau-Tasseron (Albany: State University of New York Press, 1998).

Al-Ṭabarī, *Taʾrīḫ*

Taʾrīḫ al-rusul wa-l-mulūk, ed. M.J. De Goeje et al. (Leiden: Brill, 1964), 14 vols.

Al-Ṯaʿlabī, *al-Kašf wa-l-bayān*

Aḥmad b. Muḥammad al-Ṯaʿlabī (d. 427/1035), *al-Kašf wa-l-bayān*, ed. Abū Muḥammad b. ʿĀšūr (Beirut: Dār Iḥyāʾ al-Turāṯ al-ʿArabī, 2002), 10 vols.

Al-Tibrīzī, *Šarḥ*

Yaḥyá b. ʿAlī l-Tibrīzī (d. 502/1109), *Šarḥ al-qaṣāʾid al-ʿašr*, ed. Muḥammad Muḥyī l-Dīn ʿAbd al-Ḥamīd (Cairo: Maṭbaʿat Muḥammad ʿAlī Ṣubayḥ, 1964).

Al-Tirmiḏī, *Sunan*

Muḥammad b. ʿĪsá l-Tirmiḏī (d. 279/892), *Sunan al-Tirmiḏī*, ed. Baššār ʿAwwād Maʿrūf (Beirut: Dār al-Ġarb al-Islāmī, 1996), 6 vols.

Ṭufayl al-Ġanawī, *Dīwān*

Ṭufayl al-Ġanawī (d. after ca. 608), *The Poems of Ṭufail ibn ʿAuf al-Ghanawī and aṭ-Ṭirimmāḥ ibn Ḥakīm aṭ-Ṭāʾyī* (sic), ed. F. Krenkow (London: Luzac & Co., 1927).

Al-Wāqidī, *al-Maġāzī*

Muḥammad b. ʿUmar al-Wāqidī (d. 207/822), *Kitāb al-Maġāzī*, ed. Marsden Jones (London: Oxford University Press, 1966), 3 vols.

Al-Yaʿqūbī, *Taʾrīḫ*

Aḥmad b. Abī Yaʿqūb al-Yaʿqūbī (d. ca. 292/905), *Taʾrīḫ* (Beirut: Dār Ṣādir and Dār Bayrūt, 1379/1960), 2 vols.

Yāqūt, *Muʿǧam al-buldān*

Abū ʿAbd Allāh Yāqūt b. ʿAbd Allāh al-Ḥamawī (d. 626/1229), *Muʿǧam al-buldān* (Beirut: Dār Ṣādir, 1977), 5 vols.

Al-Zamaḫšarī, *al-Fāʾiq*

Maḥmūd b. ʿUmar al-Zamaḫšarī (d. 538/1144), *al-Fāʾiq fī ġarīb al-ḥadīṯ* (Beirut: Dār al-Kutub al-ʿIlmiyyah, 1996), 4 vols.

Al-Zarqānī, *Šarḥ*

Muḥammad b. ʿAbd al-Bāqī l-Zarqānī (d. 1122/1710), *Šarḥ al-ʿallāmah al-Zarqānī ʿalá l-Mawāhib al-laduniyyah bi-l-minaḥ al-Muḥammadiyyah*, ed. Muḥammad ʿAbd al-ʿAzīz al-Ḫālidī (Beirut: Dār al-Kutub al-ʿIlmiyyah, 1996), 12 vols.

Al-Zaylaʿī, *Taḫrīǧ al-aḥādīṯ*

ʿAbd Allāh b. Yūsuf b. Muḥammad al-Zaylaʿī (d. 762/1361), *Taḫrīǧ al-aḥādīṯ wa-l-āṯār al-wāqiʿah fī Tafsīr al-Kaššāf li-l-Zamaḫšarī*, ed. Sulṭān b. Fahd al-Ṭabīšī (Riyadh: Wizārat al-Awqāf al-Suʿūdiyyah, 2003), 4 vols.

Al-Zubayr b. Bakkār, *Ǧamharat nasab Qurayš*

Abū ʿAbd Allāh al-Zubayr b. Bakkār b. ʿAbd Allāh b. Muṣʿab (d. 256/ 870), *Ǧamharat nasab Qurayš wa-aḫbārihā*, ed. ʿAbbās Hānī l-Jarrāḫ (Beirut: Dār al-Kutub al-ʿIlmiyyah, 2010), 2 vols.

Secondary Sources

Abbās (n.d.)

Abbās, I., "Two Hitherto Unpublished Texts on Pre-Islamic Religion," in *Actes du 8me Congrès de Union Européenne des Arabisants et Islamisants (1976)* (Aix-en-Provence: Edisud, n.d.): 7–16.

al-Andalusī (1991)

al-Andalusī, Ṣāʿid b. Aḥmad, (d. 462/1070), *Science in the Medieval World: "Book of the Categories of Nations,"* translated and edited by Sema'an I. Salem and Alok Kumar (Austin: University of Texas, 1991).

Al-Jallad (2001)

Ahmad Al-Jallad, "On the Origins of the God Ruḍaw and Some Remarks on the Pre-Islamic North Arabian Pantheon," *JRAS* series 3 (2001): 1–13.

Andrae (1960)

Andrae, T., *Mohammed: The Man and His Faith*, trans. Th. Menzel (New York: Harper & Row, 1960). Originally appeared under the title *Mohammed, sein Leben und sein Glaube* (Gottingen: Vandenhoeck and Ruprecht, 1932).

Arberry (1983)

The Koran Interpreted / Translated with an Introduction by Arthur J. Arberry, (Oxford: Oxford University Press, 1983).

Atallah (1969)

Atallah, W., *Les Idoles de Hicham Ibn al-Kalbi* (Paris, 1969).

al-Azmeh (2014)

al-Azmeh, A. *The Emergence of Islam in Late Antiquity* (Cambridge: Cambridge University Press, 2014).

Bauden (2014)

Bauden, F., "Taqī al-Dīn Aḥmad ibn ʿAlī al-Maqrīzī," in A. Mallett (ed.), *Medieval Muslim Historians and the Franks in the Levant* (Leiden and Boston: Brill, 2014): 161–200.

Bauden (forthcoming)

"Maqriziana XIV: Al-Maqrīzī's Last Opus (*al-Ḫabar ʿan al-bašar*) and Its Significance for the Historiography of the Pre-Modern Islamicate World."

Beeston (1981)

Beeston, A.F.L., "Some Notes on Classical Arabic Syntax," *JSS* 26/1 (1981): 21–30.

Behrens-Abouseif (1989)
Behrens-Abouseif, D., *Islamic Architecture in Cairo: An Introduction* (Cairo: American University in Cairo Press, 1989).
Bosworth (1994)
Bosworth, C.E., "Abū Ḥafṣ al-Kirmānī and the Rise of the Barmakids," *BSOAS* 57.2 (1994): 268–282.
Bravmann (1972)
Bravmann, M.M., "Heroic Motives in Early Arabic Literature," in idem (ed.), *The Spiritual Background of Early Islam: Studies in Ancient Arab Concepts* (Leiden: Brill, 1972): 39–122.
Bravmann (1977)
"Some Specific Forms of Hypotaxis in Ancient Arabic," in idem (ed.), *Studies in Semitic Philology* (Leiden: Brill, 1977): 295–321.
Brünnow/Fischer (2008)
Brünnow, R.-E., and A. Fischer, *Chrestomathy of Classical Arabic Prose Literature, 8th Revised Version* (Wiesbaden: Harrassowitz, 2008).
Buhl (1930)
Buhl, F., *Das Leben Muhammeds*, trans. H.H. Schaeder (Leipzig 1930; repr. Heidelberg: Quelle & Meyer, 1955). Originally appeared in Danish, 1903.
Caskel (1966)
Caskel, W., and G. Strenziok, *Ǧamharat an-Nasab: Das genealogische Werk des Hišām ibn Muḥammad al-Kalbī* (Leiden: Brill, 1966), 2 vols.
Chwolson (1856)
Chwolson, D., *Die Ssabier und der Ssabismus* (St. Petersburg: Buchdruckerei der Kaiserlichen Akademie der Wissenschaften, 1856), 2 vols.
Cook (1999)
Cook, M., "Ibn Qutayba and the Monkeys," *SI* 89 (1999): 43–74. Reprinted in idem, *Studies in the Origins of Early Islamic Culture and Tradition* (Aldershot: Ashgate 2004), no. XI.
Cook (2004)
Studies in the Origins of Early Islamic Culture and Tradition (Aldershot: Ashgate, 2004).
Corbin (1986)
Corbin, H., "Sabian Temple and Ismailism," in idem, *Temple and Contemplation*, trans. P. Sherrard (London: Routledge and Kegan Paul, 1986): 132–182.
Crone (1980)
Crone, P., *Slaves on Horses: The Evolution of the Islamic Polity* (Cambridge: Cambridge University Press, 1980).
Crone (2016)
"Tribes without Saints," in H. Siurua (ed.), *The Qur'ānic Pagans and Related Matters* (Leiden: Brill, 2016): 422–475.

Dozy (1881)
Dozy, R.P.A., *Supplément aux dictionnaires arabes* (Leiden: E.J. Brill, 1881), 2 vols.
Fahd (1968)
Fahd, T., *Le Panthéon de l'Arabie centrale à la veille de l'Hégire* (Paris: P. Geuthner, 1968).
Faris (1952)
Faris, N.A. (trans.), *The Book of Idols: Being a Translation from the Arabic of the Kitāb al-Aṣnām by Hishām Ibn al-Kalbī* (Princeton: Princeton University Press, 1952).
Geyer (1928)
Geyer, R., *Gedichte von Abū Baṣīr Maymūn ibn Qays al-Aʿšá* (London: Luzac & Co., 1928).
Goldfeld (1973)
Goldfeld, I., "ʿUmyānis the Idol of Khawlān," *Israel Oriental Studies* 3 (1973): 108–119.
Goldziher (1966)
Goldziher, I., *Muslim Studies*, ed. S.M. Stern, trans. C.R. Barber and S.M. Stern (London: George Allen & Unwin, 1966), 2 vols.
Graf (2010)
Graf, D.F. [with S. Tairan], "Jurash, cite caravanière sur la route de l' encens," *L'Archéo Thema, Revue d'archéologie et d'histoire* 9 (juillet-août): 24–29.
Green (1992)
Green, T., *The City of the Moon God* (Leiden: Brill, 1992).
Grunebaum (1953)
von Grunebaum, G.E., "Review of: *The Book of Idols: Being a Translation from the Arabic of the Kitāb al-Aṣnām by Hishām Ibn al-Kalbī*; N.A. Faris," *JAOS* 73/1 (1953): 44–46.
Guillaume (1960)
Guillaume, A., *New Light on the Life of Muhammad* (Manchester: Manchester University Press, [1960]).
Guillaume (1964)
"Stroking an Idol," *BSOAS* 27/2 (1964): 430.
Hawting (1980)
Hawting, G.R., "The Disappearance and Rediscovery of Zamzam and the 'Well of the Kaʿba,'" *BSOAS* 43/1 (1980): 44–54.
Hawting (1984)
"The Origin of Jedda and the Problem of Shuʿayba," *Arabica* 31 (1984): 318–326.
Hawting (1999)
The Idea of Idolatry and the Emergence of Islam: From Polemic to History (Cambridge: Cambridge University Press, 1999).
Hell (1933)
Hell, J., *Neue Huḏailiten-Diwane* (Leipzig: Harrassowitz, 1933).

Henninger (1981)
Henninger, J., "Pre-Islamic Bedouin Religion," in M.L. Swartz (ed.), *Studies on Islam* (New York and Oxford: Oxford University Press, 1981): 3–22. Originally published under the title "La religion bédouine préislamique," in F. Gabrieli (ed.), *L'antica società beduina* (Rome: Istituto di Studi Orientali, 1959): 115–140. Reprinted in F.E. Peters (ed.), *The Arabs and Arabia on the Eve of Islam* (Aldershot: Ashgate, 1999): 109–128.

Höfner (1970)
Höfner, M., "Die vorislamischen Religionen Arabiens," in H. Gese, M. Höfner, and K. Rudolph (eds.), *Die Reliqionen Altsyriens, Altarabiens und der Mandäer* (Stuttgart: Kohlhammer, 1970): 233–402.

Howell (1889–1911)
Howell, M.S., *A Grammar of the Classical Arabic Language* (Allahabad: North-Western Provinces Government Press, 1880–1911), 4 vols. in 11 books.

Jeffery (1938)
Jeffery, A., *The Foreign Vocabulary of the Qur'ān* (Baroda: Oriental Institute, 1938).

Jones (2011)
Early Arabic Poetry: Select Poems, edition, translation, and commentary by Alan Jones, 2nd ed. (Reading: Ithaca Press, 2011).

King (2002)
King, G.R.D., "The Prophet Muḥammad and the Breaking of the *Jāhiliyyah* Idols," in J.F. Healey and V. Porter (eds.), *Studies on Arabia in Honour of Professor G. Rex Smith* (Oxford: Oxford University Press, 2002): 91–122.

King (2004)
"The Paintings of the Pre-Islamic Kaʿba," *Muqarnas* 21 (Essays in Honor of J. M. Rogers) (2004): 219–229.

Kister (1965)
Kister, M.J., "Mecca and Tamīm (Aspects of Their Tribal Relations)," JESHO 8 (1965): 113–163. Reprinted, with additional notes, in idem, *Studies in Jāhiliyya and Early Islam* (London: Variorum Reprints, 1980), no. I.

Kister (1970)
"'Bag of Meat': A Study of an Early Ḥadīth," BSOAS 33 (1970): 267–275.

Kister (1972)
"Some Reports Concerning Mecca from Jāhiliyya to Islam," JESHO 15 (1972): 61–93. Reprinted, with additional notes, in idem, *Studies in Jāhiliyya and Early Islam* (London: Variorum Reprints, 1980), no. II.

Kister (1979)
"Some Reports Concerning al-Ṭā'if," JSAI 1 (1979): 1–18. Reprinted in idem, *Studies in Jāhiliyya and Early Islam* (London: Variorum Reprints, 1980), no. XI.

Kister (1980)
Studies in Jāhiliyya and Early Islam (London: Variorum Reprints, 1980).

Kister (1980a)

"'Labbayka, Allāhumma, Labbayka ...' On a Monotheistic Aspect of a Jāhiliyya Practice," *JSAI* 2 (1980): 33–57. Reprinted in idem, *Society and Religion from Djahiliyya to Islam* (Aldershot: Ashgate, 1990), no. I.

Kister (1986)

"Mecca and the Tribes of Arabia: Some Notes on Their Relations," in M. Sharon (ed.), *Studies in Islamic History and Civilization in Honour of Professor David Ayalon* (Jerusalem: Cana, and Leiden: E.J. Brill, 1986): 33–57.

Kister (1990)

Society and Religion from Djahiliyya to Islam (Aldershot: Ashgate, 1990).

Kister (1991)

"Land Property and *Jihād*: A Discussion of Some Early Traditions," *JESHO* 34/3 (1991): 270–311.

Kister (1994)

"'And He Was Born Circumcised': Some Notes on Circumcision in Ḥadīth," *Oriens* 34 (1994): 10–30. Reprinted in idem, *Concepts and Ideas at the Dawn of Islam* (Aldershot: Ashgate, 1997), no. VII.

Kister (1997)

Concepts and Ideas at the Dawn of Islam (Aldershot: Ashgate, 1997).

Klinke-Rosenberger (1941)

Klinke-Rosenberger, R., *Das Götzenbuch: Kitab al-asnam* (Leipzig: Otto Harrassowitz, 1941).

Kohlberg (2003)

Kohlberg, E., "Vision and the Imams," in E. Chaumont (ed.), *Autour du regard: Mélanges Gimaret* (Leuven: Peeters, 2003): 125–157.

Kowalski (1934)

Kowalski, T., "Zu dem Eid bei den alten Arabern," *AO* 6 (1934): 68–81.

Krone (1992)

Krone, S., *Die altarabische Gottheit al-Lāt* (Frankfurt a.M.: Peter Lang, 1992).

Lammens (1928)

Lammens, H., *L'Arabie occidentale avant l'Hégire* (Beirut: Imprimerie Catholique, 1928).

Lane (1863–1893)

Lane, E.W., *Madd al-qāmūs. An Arabic-English Lexicon* (London and Edinburgh: Williams and Norgate, 1863–1893), 8 vols.

Lecker (1989)

Lecker, M., *The Banū Sulaym: A Contribution to the Study of Early Islam* (Jerusalem: Institute of Asian and African Studies, The Hebrew University, 1989).

Lecker (1993)

"Idol Worship in Pre-Islamic Medina (Yathrib)," *Le Muséon* 106 (1993): 331–346.

Reprinted in idem, *Jews and Arabs in Pre- and Early Islamic Arabia* (Aldershot: Ashgate, 1998), no. I.

Lecker (1994)
"Kinda on the Eve of Islam and during the *Ridda*," JRAS (1994): 333–356. Reprinted in idem, *Jews and Arabs in Pre- and Early Islamic Arabia* (Aldershot: Ashgate, 1998), no. XV.

Lecker (1995)
Muslims, Jews and Pagans: Studies on Early Islamic Medina (Leiden: Brill, 1995).

Lecker (1995a)
"The Conversion of Ḥimyar to Judaism and the Jewish Banū Hadl of Medina," *WO* 26 (1995): 129–136.

Lecker (1997)
"Zayd b. Thābit, 'a Jew with Two Sidelocks': Judaism and Literacy in pre-Islamic Medina (Yathrib)," in *JNES* 56 (1997): 259–273. Reprinted in idem, *Jews and Arabs in Pre- and Early Islamic Arabia* (Aldershot: Ashgate, 1998), no. III.

Lecker (1998)
Jews and Arabs in Pre- and Early Islamic Arabia (Aldershot: Ashgate, 1998).

Lecker (2001)
"Were Customs Dues Levied at the Time of the Prophet Muḥammad," in *al-Qanṭara* 22 (2001), 19–43. Reprinted in idem, *People, Tribes and Society in Arabia around the Time of Muḥammad* (Aldershot: Ashgate, 2005), no. VII.

Lecker (2002)
"The Levying of Taxes for the Sassanians in Pre-Islamic Medina (Yathrib)," in *JSAI* 27 (2002), 109–126.

Lecker (2005)
People, Tribes and Society in Arabia around the Time of Muḥammad (Aldershot: Ashgate, 2005).

Lecker (2005a)
"Was Arabian Idol Worship Declining on the Eve of Islam?," in idem, *People, Tribes and Society in Arabia around the Time of Muḥammad* (Aldershot: Ashgate, 2005): 1–43 (no. III).

Lecker (2012)
"Wadd, the Weaponed Idol of Dūmat al-Jandal and the *Quṣṣāṣ*," in I. Sachet and Ch. Robin (eds.), *Dieux et déesses d'Arabie, images et représentations* (Paris: De Boccard, 2012): 131–138.

Lecker (2014)
"Notes about Censorship and Self-Censorship in the Biography of the Prophet Muḥammad," *al-Qanṭara* 35 (2014): 233–254.

Lecker (2015)
"Wāqidī (d. 822) vs. Zuhrī (d. 742): The Fate of the Jewish Banū Abī 'l-Ḥuqayq," in

Ch.J. Robin (ed.), *Le Judaïsme de l'Arabie antique: Actes du Colloque de Jérusalem (février 2006)* (Paris: Brepols, 2015): 495–509.

Lecker (forthcoming)
"Idol Worship in Pre-Islamic Yamāma," forthcoming in *Festschrift Ch. Robin*. Online at https://huji.academia.edu/MichaelLecker.

Levi Della Vida (1938)
Levi Della Vida, G., *Les Sémites et leur rôle dans l'histoire religieuse* (Paris: Paul Geuthner, 1938).

Lichtenstaedter (1975)
Lichtenstaedter, I., "A Note on the Gharānīq and Related Qur'anic Problems," *Israel Oriental Studies* 5 (1975): 54–61.

Little (1974)
Litte, D.P., "The Recovery of a Lost Source for Bāḥrī Mamlūk History: Al-Yūsufī's *Nuzhat al-Nāẓir fī Sīrat al-Malik al-Nāṣir*," JAOS 94/1 (1974): 42–54.

Lyall (1913)
Lyall, C.J., *The Diwans of ʿAbīd ibn al-Abraṣ, of Asad, and of ʿĀmir ibn aṭ-Ṭufail* (Leiden: Brill, and London: Luzac, 1913).

Lyall (1918)
The Mufaḍḍaliyyāt: An Anthology of Ancient Arabian Odes, Volume Two: Translation and Notes (Oxford: Clarendon Press, 1918).

Margoliouth (1905)
Margoliouth, D.S., *Mohammed and the Rise of Islam* (London: G.P. Putnam's Sons, 1905).

Melamede (1934)
Melamede, G., "The Meetings at al-ʿAḳaba," *Le Monde Oriental* 28 (1934): 17–58.

Müller (1994)
Müller, W., "Adler und Geier als altarabische Gottheiten," in I. Kottsieper et al. (eds.), *'Wer ist wie du, Herr, unter den Göttern?' Studien zur Theologie und Religionsgeschichte Israels für Otto Kaiser zum 70. Geburtstag* (Göttingen: Vandenhoeck und Ruprecht, 1994): 91–107.

Munt (2012)
Munt, H., "Writing the History of an Arabian Holy City: Ibn Zabāla and the First Local History of Medina," *Arabica* 59 (2012): 1–34.

Munt (2014)
The Holy City of Medina: Sacred Space in Early Islamic Arabia (New York: Cambridge University Press, 2014).

Nicholson (1966)
Nicholson, R., *A Literary History of the Arabs* (London: Cambridge University Press, 1966; 1st ed. London, 1907).

Nöldeke (1887)
Nöldeke, Th., "Review of Wellhausen, *Reste arabischen Heidenthumes*," ZDMG 41 (1887): 707–726.
Paret (1957)
Paret, R., *Mohammed und der Koran. Geschichte und Verkündigung des arabischen Propheten* (Stuttgart: W. Kohlhammer Verlag, 1957).
Peters (1999)
Peters, F.E. (ed.), *The Arabs and Arabia on the Eve of Islam* (Aldershot: Ashgate, 1999).
Pellat (1969)
Pellat, Ch., *The Life and Works of Jāḥiẓ* (Berkeley: University of California Press, 1969).
Reitemeyer (1903)
Reitemeyer, E., *Beschreibung Ägyptens im Mittelalter aus den geographischen Werken der Araber* (Leipzig: Seele, 1903).
Rice (1952)
Rice, D.S., "Medieval Ḥarrān: Studies on Its Topography and Monuments, I," *Anatolian Studies* 2 (1952): 36–84.
Robertson Smith (1907)
Robertson Smith, W., *Kinship and Marriage in Early Arabia* (London: Adam and Charles Black, 1907).
Robertson Smith (1972)
The Religion of the Semites (New York: Shocken Books, 1972).
Robin (2009)
Robin, Ch.J., "ʿAmmīʾanas, dieu de Khawlān (Yémen)," in M.A. Amir-Moezzi, J.D. Dubois, C. Jullien, and F. Jullien (eds.), *Pensée grecque et sagesse d'Orient. Hommage à Michel Tardieu* (Turnhout: Brepols, 2009), 537–560.
Robin (2015)
"La Grande Église d'Abraha à Ṣanʿāʾ Quelques remarques sur son emplacement, ses dimensions et sa date," in C. Vassilios (ed.), *Interrelations between the Peoples of the Near East and Byzantium in Pre-Islamic Times, Semitica Antiqva* 3 (2015): 105–129.
Robinson (2000)
Robinson, C.F., *Empire and Elites after the Muslim Conquest: The Transformation of Northern Mesopotamia* (Cambridge: Cambridge University Press, 2000).
Rubin (1986)
Rubin, U., "The Kaʿba: Aspects of Its Ritual Functions and Position in Pre-Islamic and Early Islamic Times," JSAI 8 (1986): 97–131.
Rubin (1990)
"Ḥanīfiyya and Kaʿba: An Inquiry into the Arabian Pre-Islamic Background of Dīn Ibrāhīm," JSAI 13 (1990): 85–112. Reprinted in idem, *Muḥammad the Prophet and Arabia* (Surrey: Ashgate, 2011), no. x.

Rubin (1995)
The Eye of the Beholder: The Life of Muhammad as Viewed by the Early Muslims (A Textual Analysis) (Princeton, NJ: Darwin Press, 1995).

Rubin (2007)
"The Hands of Abū Lahab and the Gazelle of the Kaʿba," *JSAI* 33 (2007): 93–98. Reprinted in idem, *Muḥammad the Prophet and Arabia* (Surrey: Ashgate, 2011), no. XII.

Rubin (2011)
Muḥammad the Prophet and Arabia (Surrey: Ashgate, 2011).

Rubin (2011a)
"Quraysh and Their Winter and Summer Journey: On the Interpretation of Sura 106," in idem, *Muḥammad the Prophet and Arabia* (Surrey: Ashgate, 2011), no. XIII

Seidensticker (2010)
Seidensticker, Tilman, "Sources for the History of Pre-Islamic Religion," in *The Qurʾān in Context*, ed. Angelika Neuwirth, Nicolai Sinai, Michael Marx (Leiden: Brill, 2010): 293–322.

Serjeant (1989)
Serjeant, R.B., "Dawlah, Tribal Shaykhs, the Manṣab of the Waliyyah Saʿīdah, *qasāmah*, in the Faḍlī Sultanate, South Arabian Federation," in M.M. Ibrahim (ed.), *Arabian Studies in Honour of Mahmoud Ghul: Symposium at Yarmouk University December 8–11, 1984* (Wiesbaden: Harrassowitz, 1989): 134–160. Reprinted in idem, *Customary and Sharīʿah Law in Arabian Society* (Aldershot: Ashgate, 1991), no. V.

Serjeant (1991)
Customary and Sharīʿah Law in Arabian Society (Aldershot: Ashgate, 1991).

Serjeant/Lewcock (1983)
Serjeant, R.B., and R. Lewcock, "The Church (al-Qalīs) of Ṣanʿāʾ and Ghumdān Castle," in idem (eds.), *Ṣanʿāʾ: An Arabic Islamic City* (London: World of Islam Festival Trust, 1983): 44–48.

Shahid (1979)
Shahid, I., "Byzantium in South Arabia," *Dumbarton Oaks Papers* 33 (1979): 23–94.

Stummer (1944)
Stummer, F., "Bemerkungen zum Götzenbuch des Ibn al-Kalbî," *ZDMG* 98 (1944): 377–394.

Tannous (forthcoming)
Tannous, J., "What is Syriac? Explorations in the History of a Name," in K. Akalin and Z. Duyu (eds.), *The Syriac Identity: Receptions and Interpretations/Süryani Kimliği: Kabul ve Yorumlama* (provisional title).

Tritton (1959)
Tritton, A.S., "Notes on Religion in Early Arabia," *Le Muséon* 72 (1959): 191–195.

Ullmann (1970–2004)

Ullmann, M. (ed.), *Wörterbuch der klassischen arabischen Sprache, unter Mitwirkung der Akademien der Wissenschaften in Göttingen, Heidelberg und München und der Akademie der Wissenschaften und der Literatur in Mainz* (Wiesbaden: Harrassowitz, 1970–2004), 2 vols in several parts.

van Bladel (2010)

van Bladel, K., "The Bactrian Background of the Barmakids," in A. Akasoy, Ch. Burnett, and R. Yoeli-Tlalim (eds.), *Islam and Tibet: Interactions along the Musk Routes* (Burlington, VT: Ashgate, 2010): 45–87.

van Ess (2001)

van Ess, J., "Die Pest von Emmaus: Theologie und Geschichte in der Fruhzeit des Islams," *Oriens* 36 (2001): 248–267.

Watt (1953)

Watt, W.M., *Muhammad at Mecca* (Oxford: Clarendon Press, 1953).

Wiet (1953)

Wiet, G., *L'Égypte de Murtadi* (Paris: Imprimerie Nationale, 1953).

Wellhausen (1882)

Wellhausen, J., *Muhammed in Medina. Das ist Vakidi's Kitab alMaghazi in verkürzter deutscher Wiedergabe* (Berlin: G. Reimer, 1882).

Wellhausen (1884–1899)

Skizzen und Vorarbeiten (Berlin: G. Reimer, 1884–1899), 6 vols.

Wellhausen (1897)

Reste arabischen Heidentums (Berlin: Verlag von Walter de Gruyter, 1897).

Wensinck (1975)

Wensinck, A.J., *Muhammad and the Jews of Medina*, trans. and ed. W. Behn (Freiburg im Breisgau: K. Schwarz, 1975). Originally appeared under the title *Mohammed en de Joden te Medina* (Leiden: Brill, 1908).

Wright (1896–1898)

Wright, W., *A Grammar of the Arabic Language* (Third Edition), trans. and ed. W. Wright, rev. W.R. Smith and M.J. de Goeje (Cambridge: Cambridge University Press, 1896–1898), 2 vols.

Yarshater (2008)

Yarshater, Ehsan, "Iranian National History," in *The Cambridge History of Iran*, vol. 3: *The Seleucid, Parthian and Sasanid Periods*, part 1, ed. Ehsan Yarshater (Cambridge: Cambridge University Press, 2008): 359–478.

Yazigi (2008)

Yazigi, M., "ʿAlī, Muḥammad, and the *Anṣār*: The Issue of Succession," *JSS* 53 (2008): 279–303.

List of Quoted Manuscripts

Cairo, Dār al-Kutub al-Miṣriyyah, 5251
Cairo, Institut français d'archéologie orientale, 30/2
Cairo, Maktabat al-Azhar, Abāẓah 6733

Istanbul, Süleymaniye Kütüphanesi, Aya Sofya 3364
Istanbul, Süleymaniye Kütüphanesi, Aya Sofya 3365
Istanbul, Süleymaniye Kütüphanesi, Fatih 4339
Istanbul, Topkapı Sarayı Müzesi Kütüphanesi, 2926/4

Strasbourg, Bibliothèque nationale et universitaire, 4244

Index of Qurʾānic Verses

Page and line numbers between parentheses refer to the translation.

البقرة [2] *al-Baqarah*

إِنَّ ٱلصَّفَا وَٱلْمَرْوَةَ مِنْ شَعَائِرِ ٱللَّهِ فَمَنْ حَجَّ ٱلْبَيْتَ أَوِ ٱعْتَمَرَ فَلَا جُنَاحَ عَلَيْهِ أَنْ يَطَّوَّفَ بِهِمَا وَمَنْ تَطَوَّعَ خَيْرًا فَإِنَّ ٱللَّهَ شَاكِرٌ عَلِيمٌ [158] 148:7–8 (149:17–20); 150:1–3 (151:3–6)

النساء [4] *al-Nisāʾ*

أَلَمْ تَرَ إِلَى ٱلَّذِينَ أُوتُوا نَصِيبًا مِنَ ٱلْكِتَابِ يُؤْمِنُونَ بِٱلْجِبْتِ وَٱلطَّاغُوتِ وَيَقُولُونَ لِلَّذِينَ كَفَرُوا هٰؤُلَاءِ أَهْدَىٰ مِنَ ٱلَّذِينَ آمَنُوا سَبِيلًا [51] 220:1–2 (221:1–4)

إِنْ يَدْعُونَ مِنْ دُونِهِ إِلَّا إِنَاثًا [117] 132:12–13 (133:24–25)

إِنْ يَدْعُونَ مِنْ دُونِهِ إِلَّا إِنَاثًا وَإِنْ يَدْعُونَ إِلَّا شَيْطَانًا مَرِيدًا [117] 132:11 (133:21–22)

المائدة [5] *al-Māʾidah*

وَمَا ذُبِحَ عَلَى ٱلنُّصُبِ [3] 172:5 (173:7–8); 282:1 (283:2)

حُرِّمَتْ عَلَيْكُمُ ٱلْمَيْتَةُ وَٱلدَّمُ وَلَحْمُ ٱلْخِنْزِيرِ وَمَا أُهِلَّ لِغَيْرِ ٱللَّهِ بِهِ وَٱلْمُنْخَنِقَةُ وَٱلْمَوْقُوذَةُ وَٱلْمُتَرَدِّيَةُ وَٱلنَّطِيحَةُ وَمَا أَكَلَ ٱلسَّبُعُ إِلَّا مَا ذَكَّيْتُمْ وَمَا ذُبِحَ عَلَى ٱلنُّصُبِ وَأَنْ تَسْتَقْسِمُوا بِٱلْأَزْلَامِ ذٰلِكُمْ فِسْقٌ [3] 280:4–6 (281:6–11)

الأنعام [6] *al-Anʿām*

وَجَعَلُوا لِلَّهِ مِمَّا ذَرَأَ مِنَ ٱلْحَرْثِ وَٱلْأَنْعَامِ نَصِيبًا فَقَالُوا هٰذَا لِلَّهِ بِزَعْمِهِمْ وَهٰذَا لِشُرَكَائِنَا فَمَا كَانَ لِشُرَكَائِهِمْ فَلَا يَصِلُ إِلَى ٱللَّهِ وَمَا كَانَ لِلَّهِ فَهُوَ يَصِلُ إِلَىٰ شُرَكَائِهِمْ سَاءَ مَا يَحْكُمُونَ [136] 192:8–10 (193:18–21)

الأعراف [7] *al-Aʿrāf*

ٱجْعَلْ لَنَا إِلٰهًا كَمَا لَهُمْ آلِهَةٌ [138] 276:9 (277:18); 280:2 (281:4)

يَا مُوسَى ٱجْعَلْ لَنَا إِلٰهًا كَمَا لَهُمْ آلِهَةٌ [138] 278:6 (279:14–15)

أَغَيْرَ ٱللَّهِ أَبْغِيكُمْ إِلٰهًا وَهُوَ فَضَّلَكُمْ عَلَى ٱلْعَالَمِينَ [140] 278:6–7 (279:15–16)

إِنَّ ٱلَّذِينَ تَدْعُونَ مِنْ دُونِ ٱللَّهِ عِبَادٌ أَمْثَالُكُمْ [194] 206:6 (207:12–13)

يوسف [12] *Yūsuf*

وَمَا يُؤْمِنُ أَكْثَرُهُمْ بِٱللَّهِ إِلَّا وَهُمْ مُشْرِكُونَ [106] 106:5 (107:11–12)

الحج [22] *al-Ḥağğ*

وَجَدْتُهَا وَقَوْمَهَا يَسْجُدُونَ لِلشَّمْسِ مِنْ دُونِ ٱللَّهِ [18] 210:2 (211:2–5)

لَنْ يَنَالَ ٱللَّهَ لُحُومُهَا وَلَا دِمَاؤُهَا [37] 280:11 (281:21)

al-Furqān [25] الفرقان

وَٱلَّذِينَ لَا يَشْهَدُونَ ٱلزُّورَ [72] 62:1 (63:2)

al-Naml [27] النمل

وَجَدْتُهَا وَقَوْمَهَا يَسْجُدُونَ لِلشَّمْسِ مِنْ دُونِ ٱللَّهِ [24] 208:10 (209:23–24)

Fāṭir [36] فاطر

مَنْ كَانَ يُرِيدُ ٱلْعِزَّةَ [10] 206:5 (207:8–9)

al-Zuḫruf [43] الزخرف

وَمَنْ يَعْشُ عَنْ ذِكْرِ ٱلرَّحْمَٰنِ نُقَيِّضْ لَهُ شَيْطَانًا فَهُوَ لَهُ قَرِينٌ [36] 236:1–2 (237:2–3)

al-Ǧāṯiyah [45] الجاثية

أَفَرَأَيْتَ مَنِ ٱتَّخَذَ إِلَٰهَهُ هَوَاهُ [23] 204:3–4 (205:6–7); 234:5 (235:10–11); 238:4–5 (239:11–12)

al-Naǧm [53] النجم

ٱللَّاتَ وَٱلْعُزَّى [19] 236:10 (237:19–239:1)

أَفَرَأَيْتُمُ ٱللَّاتَ وَٱلْعُزَّى [19] 236:6 (237:10–11); 238:1 (239:3–4)

أَفَرَأَيْتُمُ ٱللَّاتَ وَٱلْعُزَّى وَمَنَاةَ ٱلثَّالِثَةَ ٱلْأُخْرَى [19–20] 246:10 (247:18–249:1)

أَفَرَأَيْتُمُ ٱللَّاتَ وَٱلْعُزَّى وَمَنَاةَ ٱلثَّالِثَةَ ٱلْأُخْرَى أَلَكُمُ ٱلذَّكَرُ وَلَهُ ٱلْأُنْثَى تِلْكَ إِذًا قِسْمَةٌ ضِيزَى إِنْ هِيَ إِلَّا أَسْمَاءٌ سَمَّيْتُمُوهَا أَنْتُمْ وَآبَاؤُكُمْ مَا أَنْزَلَ ٱللَّهُ بِهَا مِنْ سُلْطَانٍ [19–23] 232:1–2 (233:2–5)

وَأَنَّهُ هُوَ رَبُّ ٱلشِّعْرَى [49] 210:4 (211:7)

Nūḥ [71] نوح

لَا تَذَرُنَّ آلِهَتَكُمْ وَلَا تَذَرُنَّ وَدًّا وَلَا سُوَاعًا [23] 84:3–4 (84:7–8); 132:2 (133:4–5)

وَقَالُوا لَا تَذَرُنَّ آلِهَتَكُمْ وَلَا تَذَرُنَّ وَدًّا وَلَا سُوَاعًا وَلَا يَغُوثَ وَيَعُوقَ وَنَسْرًا وَقَدْ أَضَلُّوا كَثِيرًا وَلَا تَزِدِ ٱلظَّالِمِينَ إِلَّا ضَلَالًا [23–24] 130:6–7 (131:11–13)

al-Muddaṯṯir [75] المدثر

وَٱلرُّجْزَ فَٱهْجُرْ [5] 146:5 (147:12)

Index of Prophetic Traditions

Page and line numbers between parentheses refer to the translation.

أريت أبا بني كعب هؤلاء عمرو بن لحي بن قمعة بن خندف يجر قصبه في النار قد آذي أهل النار بريحه 100:4–5 (101:8–10)

أريت الجنة وأريت النار فإذا فيها عمرو بن لحي يتأذى أهل النار بريحه 98:8–100:1 (99:16–101:1)

أول من سيب السوائب أبو خزاعة عمرو بن عامر وإني رأيته في النار يجر أمعاءه فيها 96:6–7 (97:12–13)

رأيت عمرو بن لحي بن قمعة بن خندف أبا بني كعب هؤلاء يجر قصبه في النار 96:9 (97:17–18)

رأيت عمرو بن لحي بن قمعة بن خندف في النار يجر قصبه على رأسه فروة فقلت له من معك في النار فقال من بيني وبينك من الأمم 98:2–4 (99:5–8)

رأيت عمرو بن عامر الخزاعي يجر قصبه في النار وكان أول من سيَّب السوائب 92:1–2 (93:2–4)

رأيت عمرو بن لحي يجر قُصْبَه في النار فسألته عمن بيني وبينه من الناس فقال هلكوا 86:2–3 (87:4–6)

رأيت عمرو بن عامر يجر قصبه في النار كان سيب السائبة وبحر البحيرة 96:4–5 (97:8–9)

رأيت عمرو بن لحي يجر قصبه في النار وأشبه من رأيت به معبد بن أكثم الكعبي 86:5–6 (87:11–12); 88:5–6 (89:11–12), 94:5–6 (95:12–14)

قد علمت أول من نصب النصب وسيب السوائب وغير دين إبرٰهيم عمرو بن لحي وقد رأيته يجر قصبه 96:1–2 (97:3–5)

يا أكثم رأيت عمرو بن لحي بن قمعة بن خندف يجر قصبه في النار فما رأيت رجلا أشبه برجل منك به ولا بك منه 88:4–6 (89:9–10)

Index of Verses of Poetry

p. / ص	meter / البحر	rhyme / القافية	beginning of first hemistich / أول البيت
284	*al-wāfir* / الوافر	الفضاء	نخلى بعدها
124	*al-ṭawīl* / الطويل	الثعالب	أرب يبول
190	*al-munsariḥ* / المنسرح	شَرْب	إني وما مار
158	*al-ṭawīl* / الطويل	فاذهبوا	وقالوا وألقوا
240	*al-kāmil* / الكامل	فالغبغب	يا عام
180	*al-ṭawīl* / الطويل	ورَسُوْبُ	يُظاهِر
240	*al-ṭawīl* / الطويل	بغبغب	يميني
246	*al-kāmil* / الكامل	الخزرج	إني حلفت
126	*al-wāfir* / الوافر	الصباح	وسار بنا
134	*al-raǧaz* / الرجز	{السراحا}	إنا اختلفنا
214	*al-sarīʿ* / السريع	الجلْسَدِ	(…)
154	*al-ṭawīl* / الطويل	سعد	أتينا إلى سعد
248, 250	*al-kāmil* / الكامل	سِنْداد	أهل الخورنق
158	*al-kāmil* / الكامل	محمد	أَوْدَى ضَمار
200	*al-ṭawīl* / الطويل	جَمْد	بنى لي
118	*al-ṭawīl* / الطويل	هُجَّدِ	لخياك {ود}
116	*al-basīṭ* / البسيط	تلد	يا جامعًا
170	*al-wāfir* / الوافر	دوارُ	ألا ⟨يا⟩ ليت
138	*al-ḫafīf* / الخفيف	عصر	أنا مأوى
228	*al-wāfir* / الوافر	الصبور	تركت اللات
216	*al-wāfir* / الوافر	السُعَيْر	حَلَفتُ بمائرَاتٍ
260	*al-raǧaz* / الرجز	الموتورا	لو كنت
258	*al-ṭawīl* / الطويل	تذكرا	وذكرته
174	*al-mutaqārib* / المتقارب	دَوّروا	ويوم {بخربَةَ}
200	*al-sarīʿ* / السريع	والخميس	أبلغ بني النجار
128	*al-wāfir* / الوافر	يَريش	يَريش الله

(*cont.*)

p. / ص	meter / البحر	rhyme / القافية	beginning of first hemistich / أول البيت
140	*al-wāfir* / الوافر	إساف	عليه الطير
128	*al-rağaz* / الرجز	الطريق	قُولا لِنَهْم
132	*al-munsariḥ* / المنسرح	ورق	حلفت بالنَسْر
192	*al-ṭawīl* / الطويل	نتفرق	رضِيعي
124	*al-wāfir* / الوافر	سُواع	ألم يَرْهَبك
124	*al-wāfir* / الوافر	سُوَاع	تراهم حول
188	*al-ṭawīl* / الطويل	المجامع	وإني أخو جرم
196, 198	*al-rağaz* / الرجز	عبادك	يا ذا الكفين
230	*al-rağaz* / الرجز	سبحانك	يا عُز
166	*al-ṭawīl* / الطويل	باطل	تبرأ من
190	*al-ṭawīl* / الطويل	والقَمَل	حلفت يمينا
182	*al-ṭawīl* / الطويل	أفعل	ذَهَبْتُ
216	*al-basīṭ* / البسيط	واحتمِلوا	لا أعرفنَّك
200	*al-ṭawīl* / الطويل	وفضول	لنا الجبل
192	*al-wāfir* / الوافر	والحَلال	مَنَحْناهُن
152	*al-ṭawīl* / الطويل	ونائل	وحيث يُنيخ
204	*al-wāfir* / الوافر	قال	وما قُرس
142	*al-ṭawīl* / الطويل	ونائل	وملقى
156	*al-ṭawīl* / الطويل	عرمرم	إذًا لحللنا
182	*al-rağaz* / الرجز	غنم	إذا لقيت
116	*al-wāfir* / الوافر	النعيمُ	ألا تلك المسرة
188	*al-ṭawīl* / الطويل	المواسم	ألم ينهكم
156	*al-ṭawīl* / الطويل	وعائم	تخبر من لاقيت
120	*al-basīṭ* / البسيط	عَزَما	حياك {وُد}
178	*al-rağaz* / الرجز	كلثوم	رب أريك
190	*al-kāmil* / الكامل	المُتَيَقِن	فالقريتين
226	*al-ṭawīl* / الطويل	غَنْم	لقد أُنكِحَت

(cont.)

أول البيت beginning of first hemistich /	القافية / rhyme	البحر / meter	ص / p.
نَفَرَت	يَقْدُم	*al-kāmil* / الكامل	184
وعند الشارق	عُظْم	*al-wāfir* / الوافر	198
ولقد شددت	أسحما	*al-kāmil* / الكامل	282
تبعت	هوان	*al-ṭawīl* / الطويل	212
الحمد لله	{الدرن}	*al-rağaz* / الرجز	170
وقد آلَتْ	متحرفينا	*al-wāfir* / الوافر	246
فقلنا إذا	تَمُورها	*al-ṭawīl* / الطويل	202
وإني وتركي	يدينها	*al-ṭawīl* / الطويل	236
⟨و⟩ كعبة نجران	بأبوابها	*al-mutaqārib* / المتقارب	266
فيا عزُ	وشمِري	*al-ṭawīl* / الطويل	230
نام الخلي	وِسَادي	*al-kāmil* / الكامل	250, 252

Index of Names

People

ʿAbbās b. ʿAbd al-Muṭṭalib 143
ʿAbbās b. Mirdās 159, 161
al-ʿAbbās b. al-Rabīʿ al-Ḥāriṯī 271, 275
ʿAbd Allāh b. Abī Bakr b. Muḥammad b. ʿAmr b. Ḥazm 87
ʿAbd Allāh b. ʿĀmir 257
ʿAbd Allāh b. Ǧubayr 27
ʿAbd Allāh b. Masʿūd 7n, 91n, 97
ʿAbd Allāh b. Muḥammad b. ʿAqīl 87, 95
ʿAbd Allāh b. Rawāḥah 28, 165, 167
ʿAbd Allāh al-ʿUmānī 15
ʿAbd Allāh b. Unays al-Ǧuhanī 31
ʿAbd Allāh b. Uzayhir 19
ʿAbd Allāh b. Yazīd (b. Qanṭas) al-Huḏalī 6, 7, 22
ʿAbd al-ʿAzīz b. ʿImrān al-Zuhrī 239
ʿAbd al-ʿAzīz b. Wadīʿah al-Muzanī 247
ʿAbd al-Ḥakīm b. Abī Namir 99, 101
ʿAbd al-Ḥamīd b. Ǧaʿfar 17
ʿAbd Ḥarīš b. Murrah b. ʿAmr b. Ḥanẓalah b. Yarbūʿ 163
ʿAbd Kulāl 201
ʿAbd al-Madān b. Ḥurayṯ 275, 277
ʿAbd al-Maǧīd b. Suhayl 21
ʿAbd al-Malik b. ʿAbd al-ʿAzīz b. Saʿīd b. Saʿd b. ʿUbādah 34
ʿAbd al-Muṭṭalib b. Hāšim 32, 143, 153n, 201
ʿAbd Qays b. Ḫufāf b. ʿAbd Ǧarīš 163n
ʿAbd Qays b. Ḫufāf b. ʿAbd Ḥarīš 163
ʿAbd al-Raḥmān b. Abī Sabrah al-Ǧuʿfī 13
ʿAbd Wadd (b. ʿAwf b. Kinānah; *see also*: tribes) 115
ʿAbd al-Wahhāb b. ʿAbd al-Maǧīd 143
ʿAbd Yālīl 38, 39
Abrahah al-Ašram 19n, 269, 271, 273
Abraham 21n, 36, 67, 97, 99, 101, 105, 107, 225
Abū l-ʿAbbās al-Saffāḥ 71n, 275
Abū ʿAbs b. Ǧabr 27, 28
Abū l-Aḥwaṣ ʿAwf b. Mālik 97
Abū ʿAlī l-Qālī 61, 261
Abū ʿĀṣim al-Ḍaḥḥāk b. Maḫlad 147
Abū Bakr (caliph) 7, 18, 37, 91n, 235
Abū Bakr b. Abī Šaybah 209
Abū Bakr b. Muḥammad b. ʿAmr b. Ḥazm 87
Abū Bāsil al-Ṭāʾī 4
Abū Burdah b. Niyār 27
Abū l-Dardāʾ 28, 30n, 167
Abū Duǧānah 26
Abū l-Faraǧ al-Iṣfahānī 259
Abū Ǧaʿfar al-Manṣūr 71n, 147n, 271
Abū Ǧamad 201
Abū Ġassān 229, 239
Abū l-Ǧawzāʾ 237
Abū Ḥarb b. Ḫuwaylid 9
Abū l-Ḥāriṯ Muḥammad b. al-Ḥāriṯ 12, 13
Abū Ḥātim (= Muḥammad b. Ḥātim) 149
Abū Ḥātim al-Siǧistānī 253
Abū l-Ḫaṭṭāb al-Kinānī 243
Abū l-Hayṯam b. al-Tayyihān 26
Abū Ḫirāš al-Huḏalī 125, 227
Abū Hurayrah 19, 89, 93, 95, 97
Abū Isḥāq al-Muʿtaṣim 77
Abū Karib Asʿad 131n, 269n
Abū Kaṯīr Ṣāliḥ (or Yasār/Našīṭ/ Dīnār) b. al-Mutawakkil 17
Abū Kubrān al-Murādī 13, 14
Abū Lahab 37, 229
Abū Maryam al-Ṯaqafī 209
Abū Muḥammad al-Warrāq 8
Abū Musāfiʿ al-Ašʿarī 37
Abū l-Muṭahhar 121
Abū Nuʿaym 7, 8, 11n, 22n
Abū Raǧāʾ al-ʿUṭāridī 207
Abū Ruhm b. Muṭʿim al-Arḥabī 129n
Abū Salamah b. ʿAbd al-Raḥmān 143
Abū Ṣāliḥ al-Hāšimī Bāḏām (or Bāḏān) 4, 209
Abū Ṣāliḥ al-Sammān 89, 97
Abū Ṣirmah (= Abū Qays Ṣirmah b. Abī Anas?) 27
Abū Sufyān b. Ḥarb 21, 40, 137, 247
Abū Ṭalḥah (of the Banū l-Naǧǧār) 25
Abū Ṭālib 143n, 153, 225
Abū Tiǧrāt 20, 21, 22
Abū l-Ṭufayl ʿĀmir b. Wāṯilah 233
Abū ʿUbayd al-Qāsim b. Sallām 11, 127n

Abū ʿUbaydah (Maʿmar b. al-Muṯanná) 10, 253, 261
Abū ʿUbaydah b. ʿAbd Allāh 99
Abū Uḥayḥah Saʿīd b. al-ʿĀṣ 229
Abū ʿUṯmān al-Nahdī 19n, 205
Abū Wāqid al-Layṯī 277, 279
Abū l-Yamān al-Ḥakam b. Nāfiʿ 95
Abū l-Zubayr al-Makkī 29
Abū Zufar al-Kalbī 12
Adam 63, 83, 85, 109, 111, 113
ʿAdī b. Ḥātim 179
ʿĀḏīmūn (Agathadaimon) 63
Aḥmad b. Muʿāwiyah 243
Aḥmad b. Yūnus 151
Aḫnūḫ 109, 113
Akṯam b. al-Ǧawn/Akṯam b. Abī l-Ǧawn 87n, 89, 91, 101
Aʿlá and Anʿam (*see also*: tribes) 113, 127
ʿAlī b. Abī Ṭālib 4, 26, 37, 40, 87n, 179, 181, 209, 247, 249
ʿAlī b. Ḥarb al-Mawṣilī 15, 16, 17
ʿAlqamah b. ʿAbadah al-Tamīmī 179
ʿĀmir al-Ǧādir (*see also*: tribes, and ʿĀmir al-Aǧdār) 115
ʿĀmir b. al-Ṭufayl 171, 241n
ʿAmr b. ʿAdī l-Laḫmī 251n
ʿAmr b. al-ʿĀṣ 35
ʿAmr b. Ǧabalah b. Wāʾilah al-Kalbī 10, 11
ʿAmr b. al-Ǧamūḥ 29, 30, 31, 165, 169
ʿAmr b. Ḥabīb b. ʿAmr b. Šaybān b. Muḥārib 219
ʿAmr b. Hind 251n
ʿAmr al-Huḏalī (the father of Sāʿid b. ʿAmr) 7, 23
ʿAmr b. Luḥayy/ʿAmr b. ʿĀmir 85, 87, 89, 91, 93, 95, 97, 99, 101, 103, 105, 113, 115, 123, 127, 129, 131, 137, 153, 225
ʿAmr b. Maymūn al-Awdī l-Maḏḥiǧī 5
ʿAmr b. Murrah 12
ʿAmr b. Qusṭ 87
ʿAmr b. Ṭayyiʾ 113
Anas b. Mālik 25
ʿAntarah b. al-Aḫras 4
al-Aʿšá, Maymūn b. Qays b. Ǧandal 193, 217, 265
Asad b. ʿAbd Allāh al-Baǧalī 73
Asʿad Abū Karib (*see* Abū Karib Asʿad)
Asʿad b. Zurārah 26, 30
Ašʿaṯ b. Isḥāq 151
ʿĀṣim b. Bahdalah 243
ʿĀṣim b. ʿUmar b. Qatādah 30–31, 35n
al-ʿAskarī, al-Ḥasan b. ʿAbd Allāh 13n, 91
Asmāʾ 227
Ašras b. ʿAbd Allāh al-Sulamī 73n
al-Aswad b. ʿAmr 239
al-Aswad b. Masʿūd 40
al-Aswad b. Yaʿfur 249
ʿAṭāʾ b. Abī Rabāḥ 81
ʿAṭāʾ al-Ḫurāsānī 81n, 243
ʿAṯʿaṯ b. Waḥšī l-Ḫaṯʿamī 259
ʿAwf b. ʿAfrāʾ 26
ʿAwf b. Kinānah b. ʿAwf b. ʿUḏrah b. Zayd 115
al-ʿAwwām b. Ǧuhayl 13
al-Azdahāq (*see* al-Ḍaḥḥāk)
al-Azraqī 275

al-Bakrī 123n, 257
al-Balāḏurī 127n
al-Bāqir, Muḥammad b. ʿAlī 121
al-Barāʾ b. Maʿrūr 29, 165
Barmak 71, 73, 75
Bašīr b. Saʿd 165
Bawlān (*see also*: tribes) 177
Bayān b. Bišr al-Baǧalī 17, 18
al-Bayhaqī 14, 16
Bilāl b. Rabāḥ 22
Bilqīs (Queen of Sheba) 273
Bišr b. Abī Ḫāzim al-Asadī 141
al-Buḫārī 4n, 81, 91, 93, 263

Cleopatra 75

al-Ḍaḥḥāk (al-Azdahāq) 75
al-Ḍaḥḥāk b. Muzāḥim 221
al-Dāraquṭnī 185n
Dāwūd b. Abī Hind 149, 235
Ḍimām b. Ṯaʿlabah 10
Ḍirār b. al-Ḫaṭṭāb 219n
Ḏū l-Aʿwād 251
Ḏubāb (a man of Saʿd al-ʿAšīrah) 13, 14, 211, 213
Ḏū Nuwās 131, 269n
Durayd b. al-Ṣimmah 175
Duyayk 37n

al-Faḍl b. Yaḥyá b. Ḫālid b. Barmak 75
al-Fārābī 257

Farwah b. ʿAmr 26
Farwah b. Musayk al-Murādī 14n
Fuhayrah bt. al-Ḥāriṯ b. Muḍāḍ al-Ǧurhumī 103

Ǧābir b. ʿAbd Allāh 29, 87, 95
Ǧābir b. al-Ṣaqʿab al-Nahdī 191
al-Ǧadd b. Qays 29, 165
Ǧaḏīmah al-Abraš 251n
Ǧaʿfar b. Abī Ḫallās al-Kalbī 185
Ǧaʿfar b. Abī l-Muġīrah al-Qummī 151, 239
al-Ǧāḥiẓ 257
Ǧarīr b. ʿAbd Allāh 17, 18, 131, 261, 263
Ǧarīr b. ʿAbd al-Ḥamīd 97, 151
al-Ǧawālīqī 253
Ǧayrūn b. Saʿd b. ʿĀd 77
Ǧubayr b. Muṭʿim 20, 23
Ǧunayd b. ʿAbd al-Raḥmān al-Murrī 73

Ḥākim b. ʿAṭāʾ al-Sulamī 8
Ḫālid b. ʿAbd Allāh al-Qasrī 13n, 73n
Ḫālid b. Barmak 71n, 73
Ḫālid b. Saʿīd 12
Ḫālid b. al-Walīd 40, 117, 229, 231, 233
Ḥammād b. Salamah 38n, 205, 235
Ḥarb b. Muḥammad 15
al-Ḫargūšī 7, 10n
al-Ḥāriṯ b. Abī Šamir 179
al-Ḥāriṯ b. ʿAmr (Ibn al-Kalbī's informant) 11
al-Ḥāriṯ b. ʿAmr b. ʿAdī 251n
al-Ḥāriṯ b. Kaʿb 225
al-Ḥāriṯ b. Tamīm b. Saʿd b. Huḏayl 123
al-Ḥāriṯ b. ʿUbayd Allāh b. ʿĀmir al-Ġiṭrīf 33–34
al-Ḥasan al-Baṣrī 133
al-Ḥasan b. Kaṯīr b. Yaḥyá b. Abī Kaṯīr 17
Hāšim b. ʿAbd Manāf 143n
Ḥassān b. Maṣād 117
Ḥassān b. Ṯābit 22
al-Ḫaṭṭāb 243
Ḥawwāʾ bt. Yazīd 169
al-Ḥāzimī (*see* Muḥammad b. Mūsá l-Ḥāzimī)
Hermes the First 63
Ḫidāš b. Zuhayr 259
Hilāl b. Umayyah 28
Hind bt. ʿUtbah 21
Hišām b. ʿAbd al-Malik 11, 73
Hišām b. Sulaymān al-Maḫzūmī 99
Hišām b. Yūsuf al-Ṣanʿānī 81
Ḥumayd al-Ṭawīl 205
Hūšang 77
Hušaym b. Bašīr 149
al-Ḥuṣayn b. Yazīd al-Ḥāriṯī 127
al-Ḥuṭayʾah al-ʿAbsī 119
Ḥuyayy b. Aḫṭab 221
Ḫuzāʿī l-Muzanī 5, 181, 183
Ḫuzaymah b. Mudrikah b. Ilyās b. Muḍar 135
Ḫuzaymah b. Ṯābit 28

Ibn ʿAbbās 4, 63, 81, 85, 205, 209, 221, 237, 243, 283
Ibn Abī Fudayk 279
Ibn Abī Naǧīḥ 283
Ibn Abī l-Zinād 101
Ibn ʿAǧlān al-Nahdī 205
Ibn Buraydah 155
Ibn Durayd 13n, 15n, 33n, 61, 253
Ibn Ǧurayǧ 81, 99, 281
Ibn Ḥabīb 255
Ibn Ḥaǧar 6n, 7, 8, 9n, 10, 13n
Ibn Ḥibbān 8, 16n, 89
Ibn Hišām 10, 27n, 30, 61n, 103, 127n, 225, 227, 247
Ibn al-Ḥudādiyyah al-Ḫuzāʿī 239
Ibn Isḥāq 4n, 27n, 29n, 30, 31, 34, 35, 87, 89, 103n, 105, 127, 155, 193, 225, 227, 247, 283
Ibn al-Kalbī 3, 4, 9, 10, 11, 12, 13, 14, 15, 16, 22, 31, 41n, 89, 125n, 129n, 181, 185
Ibn Mākūlā 185n
Ibn Mandah 11n, 14, 17
Ibn Mazrūʿ 99
Ibn al-Mubārak 279
Ibn Qutaybah 153
Ibn Šabbah (*see* ʿUmar b. Šabbah)
Ibn Saʿd 6, 7, 8, 9, 10, 11n, 12, 17, 18, 22n, 28
Ibn Šāhīn 14
Ibn Sīdah 61, 223, 283
Ibn Šihāb al-Zuhrī 29n, 38, 39, 91, 93n, 95, 97, 277, 279
Ibn Umm Duʾād 251
Ibn ʿUqbah 38
Ibn Waqšah 14, 211
Ibn Zabālah 8
Ibn Zayd 211
Ibn al-Zibaʿrá 137

Ibn al-Zubayr 36
Ibrāhīm al-Hağarī 97
Ibrāhīm b. al-Mundir 99
Idrīs (*see also*: Aḫnūḫ) 63, 77, 113
ʿIkrimah b. Abī Ğahl 20, 21, 22
ʿImlāq or ʿImlīq b. Lāwad [Lud] b. Sām [Shem] b. Nūḥ [Noah] 103
Imruʾ al-Qays b. Ḥuğr al-Kindī 9n, 175n, 259, 261
ʿIṣām al-Kalbī 10
Ishmael 89, 101, 105, 107, 139
Ismāʿīl (b. ʿAbd Kulāl) 201
Ismāʿīl b. Abī Ḫālid 17
Ismāʿīl b. Ibrāhīm 149

Kaʿb b. al-Ašraf 221
Kaʿb b. Māmah 251
Kaʿb b. ʿUğrah 25n, 167
Kābul Šāh 71
al-Kalbī 4, 15, 38n, 127n, 209, 253, 255
Kardam b. Sufyān al-Ṯaqafī 23
Katīr b. ʿAbd Allāh al-Muzanī 279
Kay Kāʾūs 77n
al-Kumayt b. Zayd 247

Layṯ b. Saʿd 97

Maʿbad b. Akṯam al-Kaʿbī 87, 89, 95
Maʿdī Karib 131
Mahlāʾīl b. Qaynān 63, 109, 111, 113
Mālik b. Anas 97
Mālik b. Ḥāriṯah al-Ğadarī 117, 119
Mālik b. Kulṯūm 177, 179, 181
Mālik b. Marṯad b. Ğušam 129
Mālik b. Namaṭ al-Hamdānī 129
Maʿmar b. Rāšid 279
al-Manṣūr (*see* Abū Ğaʿfar al-Manṣūr)
Manūčihr 69
al-Maqrīzī 1, 29, 67n, 73n, 79n, 85n, 89n, 93n, 109n, 123n, 125n, 127n, 131n, 139n, 157n, 159n, 163n, 175n, 177n, 179n, 185n, 187n, 191n, 199n, 203n, 227n, 229n, 249, 251n, 253n, 259n, 261n, 267n, 275n, 277n
Marwān b. al-Ḥakam 21
Maṭar al-Warrāq 149
al-Māturīdī 223
Matūšalaḫ [Methuselah] b. Aḫnūḫ 109
Māzin b. al-Ġaḍūbah 15–17
al-Miqdād b. al-Aswad 99
Mirdās b. Abī ʿĀmir 159
Muʿāḏ b. ʿAmr b. al-Ğamūḥ 28, 30, 31n, 165, 169
Muʿāḏ b. Ğabal 28, 31, 165
al-Muʿāfá b. Zakariyyāʾ 14
Muʿāwiyah b. ʿAbd al-ʿUzzá b. Zarrāʿ (read: Ḍirāʿ?) al-Ğarmī 187
Muʿāwiyah b. Abī Sufyān 12, 13, 21, 36n, 37, 75, 137n
Muʿāwiyah b. al-Muġīrah b. Abī l-ʿĀṣ 21
al-Mubarrad 63, 173, 225, 261
Mudliğ b. al-Miqdād b. Ziml b. ʿAmr 12, 13
Muğāhid b. Ğabr al-Makkī 133, 139, 173, 193, 207, 211, 221, 243, 283
al-Muġīrah b. Šuʿbah 38, 39, 40, 239
Muḥammad b. ʿAbbād al-Maḫzūmī 63n, 235
Muḥammad b. ʿAbd al-Raḥīm al-Qaysī 139
Muḥammad b. ʿAmr 143
Muḥammad b. Ğaʿfar b. al-Zubayr b. al-ʿAwwām 27n
Muḥammad b. Ḥātim (*see also*: Abū Ḥātim) 121, 147
Muḥammad b. al-Ḥusayn al-Qaṭṭān 16
Muḥammad b. Ibrāhīm b. al-Ḥāriṯ al-Taymī 89
Muḥammad b. Kaʿb al-Quraẓī 83
Muḥammad b. Maslamah 27
Muḥammad b. al-Munkadir 147
Muḥammad b. Mūsá l-Ḥāzimī 255
Munabbih b. Šubayl 39
al-Mundir al-Akbar (al-Mundir III) 251n, 253, 255
al-Mundir b. ʿAmr 26, 28
Mūsá (Moses) 277, 279, 281
Mūsá b. al-Ğumhūr al-Tinnīsī l-Simsār 16
Mūsá b. ʿUbaydah 147
Muṣʿab b. ʿUmayr 30
Muslim b. al-Ḥağğāğ 91, 263
al-Mustawġir b. Rabīʿah b. Kaʿb b. Saʿd 283
al-Muʿtaṣim (*see* Abū Isḥāq al-Muʿtaṣim)
Muṭʿim al-Arḥabī 129

al-Nābiġah 241
al-Nābiġah al-Ḏubyānī 121
Negus 269, 271
Nīzak Ṭarḫān 73
Noah 67, 79, 81, 83, 85, 103, 111, 113, 133

Nuʿaym b. Ḥakīm 209
al-Nuʿmān b. al-Mundir 249, 259
Numayr b. Muḥammad b. ʿUqayl al-Ẓafarī 9

Pharaoh 79

Qābīl (Cain) b. Ādam 111
al-Qālī (*see* Abū ʿAlī l-Qālī)
al-Qaʿnabī 97
Qārib b. al-Aswad 39
Qatādah b. Diʿāmah 133, 147, 205, 233, 239, 283
Qaṭan b. Šurayḥ 117
Qays b. Abī Ḥāzim al-Baǧalī 17, 263
Qays b. ʿĀṣim 157n
Qays b. al-Ḫaṭīm 169
Qays b. al-Hayṯam al-Sulamī 75
Quṣayy b. Kilāb 20, 36, 153
Quṭrub 223

Rabīʿah b. Ḥāriṯah b. ʿAmr b. ʿĀmir 103
al-Rāġib al-Iṣfahānī 223
al-Raḥḥāl 111
Rāšid b. ʿAbd Rabbihi al-Sulamī 5, 7–9, 125
al-Rāzī 223
Ribʿī b. Raddād 199
Rustam 199

Šabābah b. Sawwār 209
al-Šaʿbī 149
Saʿd b. Muʿād 27, 30
Saʿd b. Sayal al-Azdī 36
Saʿd b. ʿUbādah 26, 28, 34, 28
Saʿd b. Zayd 34n, 40, 247n
al-Saffāḥ (*see* Abū l-ʿAbbās al-Saffāḥ)
Sahl b. Ḥunayf 27
Ṣaḫr b. al-Ǧaʿd al-Ḫuḍrī 237
Saʿīd b. ʿAbd al-Raḥmān b. Abzá 151
Saʿīd b. ʿAmr al-Huḏalī 20, 22
Saʿīd b. Ǧubayr 149, 205, 207, 221, 235, 239
Saʿīd b. al-Musayyab 91, 93, 95, 97
Saʿīd b. al-Walīd b. ʿAmr al-Abraš al-Kalbī 11
Sāʿidah al-Huḏalī 6–7
Ṣāliḥ b. Ḥayyān 155
Ṣāliḥ b. Kaysān 91, 93n, 95n
Salīṭ b. Qays 27
Salmá bt. ʿAmr 143n
al-Samhūdī 8
al-Šarqī b. al-Quṭāmī 12, 13, 225

Šaybah b. ʿUṯmān 36, 37
Šaybān b. ʿAbd al-Raḥmān 147, 233
Sayf b. ʿUmar 14n
Ṣayfī (of the Banū Bawlān) 177
Šayḫū l-ʿUmarī 79
Seth b. Adam 63, 85, 109, 111
Sinān b. Abī Ḥāriṯah al-Murrī 191
Sinān b. Abī Sinān 277
Solomon 273
Šuʿayb b. Abī Ḥamzah 95
Sufyān b. Arḥab 129n
Sufyān b. ʿUyaynah 237, 277
Suhayl b. Abī Ṣāliḥ 97
al-Suhaylī 61, 271
Surāqah b. Mālik b. Ǧuʿšum al-Mudliǧī 189
Suwayd 277

al-Ṭabarānī 15, 16, 17
al-Ṭabarī, Muḥammad b. Ǧarīr 83
Ṯaʿlabah b. ʿAnamah al-Salamī 31
Ṭalḥah b. ʿUbayd Allāh 235
Tammām b. Muḥammad 13
Ṭāriq b. ʿAbd al-Raḥmān 17, 18
al-Tirmiḏī 277
al-Ṭufayl b. ʿAmr al-Dawsī 195, 197
Ṭufayl al-Ḫayl 159
al-Ṭufayl b. Ubayy 87, 95

ʿUbādah b. al-Ṣāmit 167
ʿUbayd Allāh b. ʿAmr 87, 95
Ubayy b. Kaʿb 87, 95
Ukaydir b. ʿAbd al-Malik al-Kindī 117
ʿUmar b. ʿAbd al-ʿAzīz 21, 37n, 235
ʿUmar b. ʿAbd al-Raḥmān al-Ǧuhanī 277
ʿUmar b. Abī Bakr al-Muʾammalī 99, 101
ʿUmar b. al-Ḫaṭṭāb 37, 125n, 243
ʿUmar b. Šabbah 1, 29, 38, 87, 95, 97, 107, 113, 121, 123, 127, 129n, 131, 133, 135, 139, 155, 163, 169, 171n, 175, 181, 187, 203n, 227, 237, 239, 243, 247, 249, 257, 263, 275, 279
ʿUmārah b. Ḥazm 25
ʿUmayr b. ʿAdī b. Ḫarašah 28
Umayyah b. al-Askar al-Layṯī 183
Umm Hāniʾ bt. Abī Ṭālib 4, 209n
Umm Maʿbad 89, 91n
Umm Sulaym bt. Milḥān 25
ʿUrwah b. Masʿūd al-Ṯaqafī 38n, 40
ʿUrwah b. al-Zubayr 30, 83, 133

Usāmah b. Zayd b. Ḥāriṯah 143
Usayd b. al-Ḥuḍayr 27, 28
ʿUṯmān b. Abī l-ʿĀṣ 39n
ʿUṯmān b. Abī Sulaymān 99
ʿUṯmān b. ʿAffān 17, 39n, 71, 75

Waḍḍāḥ al-Yaman 201
al-Walīd b. Ǧumayʿ 233
Wāqid b. ʿAmr 30n
al-Wāqidī 6, 7, 10, 17, 20, 21, 22, 25n, 30n

Yaḥyá b. ʿAbd al-Malik b. Ismāʿīl al-Sulamī 9
Yaḥyá b. ʿAbd al-Raḥmān b. Ḥāṭib 143
Yaḥyá b. Hāniʾ b. ʿUrwah 13, 14
Yaʿqūb al-Qummī 121, 151
Yaʿqūb b. Zayd 147
Yaʿqūbī 37
Yard (Jared) b. Mahlāʾīl 109, 111, 113
Yazīd, ʿAbd al-Masīḥ and Qays 267
Yazīd b. al-Aswad al-Ǧarašī 5
Yazīd b. al-Hād 95, 97
Yazīd b. Muʿāwiyah 13n
Yazīd b. al-Muhallab 121
Yazīd b. Saʿīd al-ʿAbsī 13
Yūnus b. Muḥammad 121, 147, 233

al-Zaǧǧāǧ 221, 283
Ẓālim b. Asʿad b. Rabīʿah 285
Zayd b. ʿAmr b. Nufayl 22, 145, 227
Zayd b. Ḥāriṯah 143
Zayd al-Ḫayl 157
Ziml b. ʿAmr 12
Ziyād b. Labīd 26
al-Zubayr b. Bakkār 99, 137, 153
Zuhayr b. Abī Sulmá l-Muzanī 191
Zuhayr b. Ǧanāb al-Kalbī 285
Zuhayr b. Ḥarb 97, 151
al-Zuhrī (*see* Ibn Šihāb al-Zuhrī)

Places

al-ʿAblāʾ/al-ʿAbalāt 257, 261
ʿAdan 273
Aǧaʾ (a mountain) 175
ʿAmq 183
al-Andalus 75
al-ʿAqīq (a watering-place) 189
al-ʿAqīq (of Medina) 203
ʿArafah 107
al-Aʿwaṣ 275
ʿAyn/Māʾ al-Rasūl 8, 9
ʿAyn Šams 77

Baghdad 16, 97n, 147n, 223n
Bāǧir 15
Baḥrayn 191n
Balḫ 69, 75
Balḫaʿ 131, 133
Balqāʾ 103
Barḏaʿah 17
Bāriq 249
Baṣra 191n
Bayt al-Maqdis 243
Buss 1
(*see also*: idols and sanctuaries)
Buṯhān 32, 169
Buwānah 22, 23, 203
(*see also*: idols and sanctuaries)
Damascus 12, 77
Dār al-Nadwah 37n
Ḏāt Ǧabalayni 181
Ḏāt ʿIrq 1
Ḏū l-Ǧalīl and [Ḏū] l-Salam 183
Ḏū Ġawānah 119
Dūmat al-Ǧandal 81, 113, 115, 117n, 133

Egypt 77, 97n
Euphrates 33n, 255

Farġānah 77

Ǧammāʾ al-ʿĀqir 203
al-Ǧawf 81, 133
al-Ǧazīrah 137
Ǧubb 275
Ǧuraš 127
Ǧurǧān 73

Ḥaǧr 199
Ḫānkāh of Šayḫū 79
Ḥarbah 175
Ḥarrān 77
al-Ḫawarnaq 249, 251

al-Ḥawrāʾ 203
Ḫaybar 19, 221n
Ḫaywān 129
al-Ḥazz 34
Ḥiǧāz 8n, 15, 123, 203, 269
al-Ḥīrah 249n, 251n, 253, 255
Hīt 137
al-Ḥudaybiyyah 123n
Ḥunayn 39, 277, 279
Ḥurāḍ 227, 231
Ḫurāsān 71, 73, 75n

India 85, 109, 255
Iraq 77, 271

Jedda 111, 113, 115, 155

Kashmir 73
Kufa 32, 257

Maʾāb (Moab) 103
Maḏḥiǧ (a hill in Yemen) 127
Manbiǧ 77
Manf 79
Marsūġ 199
al-Marwah 149, 151
Mecca 1, 2, 5, 6, 7, 14, 18, 19, 20–22, 23, 24, 25, 33, 34n, 35, 37, 40, 71, 87, 99n, 103, 105, 107, 111n, 123n, 129, 139, 143, 149, 151, 161, 165n, 171, 189n, 191n, 207n, 209n, 213, 221, 225, 229n, 233, 239n, 245, 247, 249, 257, 263n, 271, 277n, 279
Medina 1, 2, 8, 10, 12, 13, 23–33, 34, 35, 38, 73, 83n, 87n, 91n, 95n, 143n, 147n, 161, 165n, 167n, 197n, 203n, 221n, 239n, 247
Miná 241
Mūhiq 203
al-Mušallal 33, 34n, 247
al-Muzdalifah 107

al-Naǧafah 191
Naǧrān 6, 131n, 265, 267, 269
Naḫlah 225, 227, 239
Naʿmān 6, 7
Namirah 161
al-Naqʿayni 275
Nūd (a mountain in India) 109

al-Qāhirah al-Muʿizziyyah 77, 79
al-Qaryatayni 191
Qudayd 1, 33, 239, 247

Raḍwá 189
Ruhāṭ 7, 8, 9, 33n, 36, 123, 133

Sabaʾ 81, 131, 133
al-Sadīr 249, 251, 253, 255
al-Ṣafā 149, 151
al-Šām (greater Syria) 77, 103, 187, 237, 263n
Samāʾil 15
Šamanṣīr (a mountain) 123n
Ṣanʿāʾ 75, 129, 269
Sarāt mountains 19n, 34, 157
Ṣaydā (Sidon) 77
al-Sind 71, 121n
Sindād 33n, 249, 251, 255, 257
Sirḥān 81n
al-Ṣ.l.b (a watering-place) 191
Suqām 231, 233, 239
Ṣūr (Tyre) 77

Tabālah 9n, 17, 257, 259, 263
Ṭāʾif 38, 39, 225, 237, 239, 243, 247, 257, 277n, 279
Tihāmah 113, 115, 225

Udad (a well) 137
Uḥud 32, 34
ʿUmān 16, 17, 61n
Umm al-Ḥarratayn 201

Yalamlam 22, 23
al-Yamāmah 1, 199
Yanbuʿ 33n
Yaṯrib 23, 24n, 247
Yemen 35n, 127, 129, 201n, 257, 265, 271, 275, 285

Zamzam 141, 153, 155

Tribes

ʿAbd al-Ašhal (of al-Aws) 26, 27, 28, 30, 31, 40, 163, 169n
ʿAbd al-Dār (of Qurayš) 30, 36, 153, 155
ʿAbd al-Madān (of al-Ḥāriṯ b. Kaʿb) 265
ʿAbd Wadd (*see also*: personal names) 117
ʿAdī b. al-Naǧǧār 25n, 26, 27, 32, 163
al-Adīm (of Ḫawlān) 193
al-ʿAǧlān (clients of ʿAmr b. ʿAwf) 33
al-ʿAǧlān b. ʿAttāb b. Mālik b. Kaʿb (of Ṯaqīf) 39, 227n
al-Aḥlāf and Mālik (of Ṯaqīf) 39
Aḥmas (of Baǧīlah) 17, 18, 263
Aʿlá (*see also*: personal names) 127
ʿAmr b. Qays ʿAylan 7
ʿĀmir al-Aǧdār (*see also*: ʿĀmir al-Ǧādir) 115n
ʿĀmir b. ʿAwf (of Kalb) 10, 11
ʿĀmir al-Ǧādir (*see also*: personal names) 115, 117
ʿĀmir b. Rabīʿah 203
ʿĀmir b. Ṣaʿṣaʿah 171n, 187n, 203n, 259n
ʿAmr b. ʿAwf (of al-Aws) 26, 28, 33, 163
Anas Allāh b. Saʿd al-ʿAšīrah 13, 14, 211
ʿAnazah 185, 215
al-ʿAnqāʾ 161
Asad 87n, 141n, 143n, 149n, 209, 243n, 259, 261
Ašǧaʿ 199
ʿAttāb b. Mālik (of Ṯaqīf) 39, 227n, 237
Awd b. Ṣaʿb b. Saʿd al-ʿAšīrah 131
al-Aws 5n, 26, 27, 28, 31, 32, 33, 34, 40, 161n, 163, 169n, 201n, 221n, 247
al-Azd 15n, 19, 32, 33, 34, 61n, 103, 115n, 157, 259, 279n
Azd Šanūʾah 33
Azd al-Sarāt 19, 157n, 259
Azd ʿUmān 61n

Baǧīlah 17, 18, 73n, 131n, 259, 263n, 265
Bakr b. Wāʾil 34n, 193n, 215, 219, 249, 265
Balī 26, 27, 171, 203
Bawlān (*see also*: personal names) 177
Bayāḍah (of al-Ḫazraǧ) 26

Ḍabbah 171
Daws 19, 157, 195, 257, 263, 265
Dīnār b. al-Naǧǧār 32, 163
Duhmān (of Ǧuhaynah) 12
Ḏū l-Kalāʿ (of Ḥimyar) 81, 133
Ḏū Ruʿayn 131

Fazārah 191, 193

Ǧaʿdah 187
Ġanī b. Aʿṣur 171
Ġanm 227
Ǧarm 187, 189
Ġassān 33, 179
Ġaṭafān 121n, 187, 191n, 199, 285
al-Ġaṭārīf (of al-Azd) 33, 34, 157
Ǧuḏām 187, 189, 209
Ǧuʿfī (of Saʿd al-ʿAšīrah) 14
Ǧuhaynah 12, 171, 199, 203, 275
Ǧurhum 37n, 101, 103, 105, 139
Ǧušam (of Hawāzin) 175
Ġuṭayf (of Murād) 14, 81, 133

Hamdān 13, 81, 113, 129, 133
Ḥanīfah 199, 213
al-Ḥāriṯ b. ʿAbd Allāh b. Yaškur b. Mubaššir 34, 157
al-Ḥāriṯ b. al-Ḫazraǧ 32, 165n, 167n, 169
al-Ḥāriṯ b. Kaʿb (of Maḏḥiǧ) 265
Ḥāriṯah (of al-Aws) 26, 27, 31, 163
Hāšim (of Qurayš) 225
Ḫaṯʿam 18, 19, 249, 257, 259, 261, 265
Ḫaṭmah (of al-Aws) 26, 28, 163
Hawāzin 97n, 187, 189, 259
Ḫawlān 5, 6n, 193
al-Ḫazraǧ 5n, 25, 26, 28, 32, 33, 34, 87n, 143n, 161n, 163, 165n, 167n, 169, 201, 247
Ḥimyar 75, 81, 113, 131, 133, 201, 209, 269
Hind b. Ḥarām b. Ḍinnah b. ʿAbd b. Kabīr b. ʿUḏrah 12, 215
Ḥiṭāmah (of Ṭayyiʾ) 15, 16
Huḏayl 6, 7, 8, 22, 23, 33, 81, 113, 123, 125, 133
Ḫuzāʿah 20, 33, 37n, 87n, 89n, 97, 99, 103, 221n, 247, 281

Iyād 251

Kaʿb (of Ḫuzāʿah) 87n, 97, 101
Kaʿb b. al-Ḥāriṯ b. Buhṯah b. Sulaym 9

Kahlān 113
Kalb 10–11, 81, 113, 115n, 133, 177, 185, 285n
Kinānah 7, 34n, 107, 123, 155, 189, 209, 219, 225, 239n, 271
Kindah 32, 259n

Laḫm 187, 189, 209
Lihb 155

Maʿadd b. ʿAdnān 113
al-Maʿāfir 203
Maḏḥiǧ 127
Maḫzūm (of Qurayš) 20, 37
Mālik b. al-Naǧǧār 25, 26, 30, 32, 163
Milkān and Mālik (of Kinānah) 155
Muʿattib (of Ṯaqīf) 39, 239n, 247
Muʿāwiyah (of al-Aws) 163
Muḥārib 175
Murād 14, 81, 127, 133
Murrah (of Ġaṭafān) 121n, 171, 191, 193
Muzaynah 5, 7, 181, 183, 199, 279

al-Nabīt (of al-Aws) 31
al-Naḍīr 37n, 221n
al-Naǧǧār (of al-Ḫazraǧ) 25, 26, 27, 30, 32, 87n, 163, 201
Nāǧiyah (of Murād) 127
Nahd 6n, 191, 205
Nahšal b. Dārim (of Tamīm) 249
Nihm (of Hamdān) 129
Numayr 171

Qasr (of Baǧīlah) 18, 263n
Qawāqilah (of al-Ḫazraǧ) 163, 167n
Qaynuqāʿ 167n
Qays ʿAylan 7, 33n, 34n, 123, 171n, 209
Quḍāʿah 15n, 18, 19n, 32, 33, 99n, 113, 185, 187, 205n
Qurayš 20, 22, 23, 33, 41, 83n, 91n, 99, 107, 119n, 135, 137, 143n, 145n, 147n, 153n, 155, 159, 209, 221, 225, 231, 233n, 235, 239, 245n, 249
Qurayẓah 24, 221n, 269n

Rabīʿah 159, 191, 211
Rabīʿah (of Qays ʿAylān) 33n
Rabīʿah b. Kaʿb b. Saʿd b. Zayd Manāt b. Tamīm 283

Saʿd al-ʿAšīrah 13, 14, 131, 211, 213
Saʿd b. Bakr 10, 123
Saʿd Huḏaym 32, 33
Ṣāhilah (of Huḏayl) 7
Sāʿidah (of al-Ḫazraǧ) 26, 28
Salimah (of al-Ḫazraǧ) 26, 28, 29, 30, 31, 87n, 163, 165n, 169
Šaybān (of Sulaym) 225, 227
Šubayl b. al-ʿAǧlān 39, 227n
Sulaym 7, 8, 9, 32, 123, 149, 159, 161n, 171, 201, 225, 227n, 229n

Tamīm 147n, 151n, 157n, 209, 283
Ṯaqīf 23, 38, 39, 105, 227n, 237, 239, 247, 283n
Ṭasm 229
Ṭayyiʾ 4, 15, 16, 18, 19, 113, 127, 157n, 159, 175, 177n, 181, 191, 203, 209, 221n

Ubāmah (var. Umāmah) of Bāhilah b. Aʿṣur 257
ʿUḏrah 12, 171, 215
ʿUlaym (of Kalb) 177
Umayyah (of al-Aws) 163
ʿUqayl b. Kaʿb 9

Wāqif (of al-Aws) 26, 28

Yaqdum and Yaḏkur (of ʿAnazah) 185

Ẓafar (of al-Aws) 31, 163, 169n
Ẓafar (of Sulaym) 8, 9
Zaʿūrāʾ 26, 169n
Zayd b. Ṣayfī (of Ṭayyiʾ) 181
Zurayq (of al-Ḫazraǧ) 163

Idols and sanctuaries

al-ʿAbd 203
Aḥmas 193
ʿĀʾim 157
Allāt 5, 10, 19n, 22, 38–40, 41n, 105, 225, 227n, 229, 231, 233, 235, 237, 239, 243, 245, 247
ʿAmm Anas (or ʿUmyānis) 6n, 193
ʿAmrah (or ʿAmr) 10, 11
ʿAwḍ 215, 217

Barkulān 203
al-Bayḍāʾ 199
al-Bihām 163
Buss 285
(*see also*: places)
Buwānah 22, 23
(*see also*: places)

Ḍamār 159
Ḏāt Anwāṭ 255n, 277, 279
al-Dawār (*see also*: technical terms) 175
al-Dībāǧ 29, 165
Ḏū l-Ḫalaṣah 9n, 17–19, 131n, 257, 259, 261, 263, 265
Ḏū l-Kaʿabāt 249, 251n
Ḏū l-Kaffayn 22, 195, 197
Ḏū l-Šará 157

al-Fals 4, 40n, 175, 177, 179, 181
Farrāḍ (or Farrāṣ) 13, 14, 211, 213
fire temple 285

Ǧalsad 213, 215
Ġanm (an idol of Daws) 195
Ġanm (an idol of Qurayš) 229
Ġayyān 163
green house 79
Ġumdān 75
al-Ǧuṯā 205

al-Ḥalāl 191, 193
al-Ḫamīs 32, 33, 201
al-Ḥarīš 163
al-Ḥibs 163
Hubal 3, 21, 22, 34n, 36, 103, 135, 137
al-Huǧam 275
Ḥumām 12, 215

Ḥusā 163
Huzzam 32, 169

Isāf 21, 22, 101, 105, 139, 141, 143, 145, 147, 149, 153, 155
Isāf/Sāf (an idol of the Banū Salimah) 163, 165

Kaʿbah 1, 3, 18, 19, 22n, 32n, 34, 36–37, 38, 40, 69, 71, 77, 99, 103, 105, 107, 115n, 135, 137, 139, 141, 145, 147, 149, 153, 155, 171, 173, 209, 221, 225, 227, 231, 233n, 239, 263n, 265, 269, 271n, 281, 283
Kaʿbah of Naǧrān 265, 267
al-Kaʿbah al-Yamāniyyah and al-Kaʿbah al-Šāmiyyah 18, 263
Kāwusān 77
Kuʿayb and Kuʿayb's wife 269, 271, 275
Kulāl 201

Manāf 29, 30, 31n, 165n, 169, 171
Manāt 1, 5n, 22, 29n, 30n, 31n, 33–35, 40, 41n, 169n, 179n, 231, 233, 239, 243, 247, 249
al-Mudawwar 77
al-Mukaymin 203

Nāʾilah 22, 101, 105, 139, 141, 143, 145, 147, 149, 151, 153, 155
Nasr 81, 83, 85, 111, 113, 131, 133
Nawbahār 69, 71, 73, 75
Nuhm 5, 181, 183

al-Qalīs 269, 271, 273, 275
Qawzam 277
al-Qayn 163
Qurs 203

al-Rabbah 38, 39n, 40, 239
Riyām 269
Ruḍā (an idol of Ṭayyiʾ and Rabīʿah) 159
Ruḍā (an idol of the Banū Rabīʿah b. Kaʿb b. Saʿd b. Zayd Manāt b. Tamīm) 283

Saʿd 155
Šafr 163

Ṣaḫr 163
al-Saʿīdah 32, 33, 34, 285
al-Samḥ 163
Šams 163
Samūl 163
al-Šāriq 199
al-Suʿayr 185, 217
al-Šurayr 195
Suwāʿ (a name of two idols) 5, 6–9, 22, 36, 81, 83, 85, 111, 113, 123, 125, 131, 133, 231

al-Ṭimm 163

al-Uqayṣir 187, 189, 191
al-ʿUrayf 191
al-ʿUzzá 1, 5, 10, 19n, 22, 33n, 38, 41, 117n, 225, 227, 229, 231, 233, 235, 237, 239, 243, 245, 247

Wadd 81, 83, 85, 111, 113, 115, 117, 119, 121, 123, 131, 133
Wudd 119n

Yālīl 203
Yaġūṯ 13, 19n, 81, 83, 85, 111, 113, 127, 131, 133
Yaʿūq 81, 83, 85, 111, 113, 129, 131, 133

Zaʿbal 213
Zabr 29, 165

Index of Quoted Titles in *al-Ḫabar ʿan al-bašar*

Dīwān al-adab (al-Fārābī) 257

Kitāb al-Aġānī (Abū l-Farağ al-Iṣfahānī) 259
Kitāb Aḫbār Makkah (Ibn Šabbah) 87, 95
Kitāb al-Amṣār (al-Ğāḥiẓ) 257
Kitāb al-Buldān (al-Kalbī) 253
Kitāb al-Ištiqāq (al-Mubarrad) 255
Kitāb al-Muḥkam (Ibn Sīdah) 61
Kitāb Nasab Qurayš (al-Zubayr b. Bakkār) 99
Kitāb Tuḥfat al-albāb (al-Zubayr b. Bakkār) 139

Maʾdubat al-udabāʾ (al-Nīsābūrī) 257

Index of Sources in *al-Ḫabar ʿan al-bašar*

(Abū ʿAlī l-Qālī) 261
see also al-Amālī
(Abū Bakr b. Abī Šaybah) 209
(Abū Ġassān) 229, 239
(Abū Ḥātim al-Siǧistānī) 253
(Abū ʿUbayd al-Qāsim b. Sallām) 127n
[*Aḫbār Makkah*] (al-Azraqī) 275
[*al-Amākin*] (Muḥammad b. Mūsá l-Ḥāzimī) 255
[*al-Amālī*] (Abū ʿAlī l-Qālī) 61
(al-ʿAskarī) 91

(al-Balāḏurī) 127n

Dīwān al-adab (al-Fārābī) 257

[*Ǧamharat al-luġah*] (Ibn Durayd) 61, 253
[*Ġarīb al-ḥadīṯ*] (Ibn Qutaybah) 153

(Ibn Ḥabīb) 255
(Ibn Ḥibbān) 89
(Ibn Isḥāq) 155
see also al-Sīrah
(Ibn al-Kalbī) 89, 181, 185

(al-Kalbī) 127n, 209, 255
see also Kitāb al-Buldān
[*al-Kāmil fī l-luġah wal-adab*] (al-Mubarrad) 63, 173, 261
Kitāb al-Aġānī (Abū l-Faraǧ al-Iṣfahānī) 259
Kitāb Aḫbār Makkah (ʿUmar b. Šabbah) 87, 95, 97
Kitāb al-Amṣār (al-Ǧāḥiẓ) 257
Kitāb al-Buldān (al-Kalbī) 253
Kitāb al-Ištiqāq (al-Mubarrad) 255
Kitāb al-Muḥkam (Ibn Sīdah) 61
[*Kitāb al-Muḥkam*] (Ibn Sīdah) 223, 283
Kitāb Nasab Qurayš (al-Zubayr b. Bakkār) 99
Kitāb Tuḥfat al-albāb (Muḥammad b. ʿAbd al-Raḥīm al-Qaysī) 139

Maʾdubat al-udabāʾ (al-Nīsābūrī) 257
[*Mafātīḥ al-ġayb*] (al-Rāzī) 223
[*al-Muʿarrab*] (al-Ǧawālīqī) 253
[*Muʿǧam mā staʿǧam*] (al-Bakrī) 123n, 257

[*al-Rawḍ al-unuf*] (al-Suhaylī) 61, 271

[*Ṣaḥīḥ al-Buḫārī*] (al-Buḫārī) 81, 91, 93, 263
[*Ṣaḥīḥ Muslim*] (Muslim) 91, 263
[*al-Sīrah*] (Ibn Hišām) 103, 127n, 225, 227, 247
[*al-Sīrah*] (Ibn Isḥāq) 87, 89, 105, 127, 193, 225, 227, 247, 283
[*Sunan al-Tirmiḏī*] (al-Tirmiḏī) 277

[*Tafsīr al-Ṭabarī*] (Abū Ǧaʿfar Muḥammad b. Ǧarīr al-Ṭabarī) 83
[*Taʾwīlāt ahl a-sunnah*] (al-Māturīdī) 223
[*Tafsīr al-Rāġib al-Iṣfahānī*] (al-Rāġib) 223

(ʿUmar b. Šabbah) 107, 113, 121, 123, 127, 129, 131, 133, 135, 139, 155, 163, 169, 171, 175, 181, 187, 227, 237, 239, 243, 247, 249, 257, 263, 275, 279
see also Kitāb Aḫbār Makkah

(al-Zubayr b. Bakkār) 147, 153
see also Kitāb Nasab Qurayš

Index of Glosses

Anʿam 127

Bāriq 251

Ḍamār 159
Ḏū l-Aʿwād 251

The family of Muḥarriq (*āl Muḥarriq*) 251

ġanū 253

Ḫallās 185

Isāf 139

Mālik b. Kulṯūm 177

Qawzam 277

Ruhāṭ 123

al-Sadīr 251
Šaybān 227
Sindād 249, 251

ṯābit al-awtād 253

wa-l-bayt (and the sanctuary) 249

Yaʿfur 249
Yaqdum and Yaḏkur 185

zūrā 261

Index of Technical Terms

aḥzāb 10n, 147n
anṣāb, nuṣub 81, 97, 145, 173, 217, 241, 281, 283
aṣḥāb al-uḫdūd 269
ʿaṯan 6n
ʿatīrah 15, 183n

badanah, pl. *budn* 103n, 107
al-baḥīrah 89, 91, 95, 97, 99, 101, 105
baṭn 31, 32, 34
bayt (sanctuary) 13, 18, 31, 32, 36, 38, 41, 61, 147, 249n, 251n, 271n
bayt al-aṣnām 18n, 61
Bayt al-Midrās 24, 28

dawār (*see also*: idols and sanctuaries) 171, 173, 207

ġabġab 39, 40, 227, 239, 241
Ǧāhiliyyah 5, 18, 20, 22, 23, 25, 26, 27, 29, 91, 149, 151, 173, 175, 205, 229, 257, 263, 281, 283, 285
al-ġarānīq al-ʿulá 231, 233
al-ǧibt 221, 223
ǧinn, ǧinnī 6, 7, 12, 14, 85, 103, 113, 161, 211, 213, 275

ḥadīṯ 3, 4, 9n, 13, 15, 17, 19, 81, 87, 89n, 91, 93n, 95, 97, 99, 143n, 145n, 149, 209n, 237, 263, 277, 279
ḥafr 187n
ḥaǧǧ 1n, 105, 107
ḥāǧib (chamberlain) 11
ḥāǧib, pl. *ḥuǧǧāb* (custodian/guardian of an idol) 227, 233
al-ḥāmī 89, 93, 99
ḥanīf 2, 22, 27n, 99n, 145n
ḥanīfiyyah 99
ḥaram 18, 105
ḫātam 13n
hātif 8, 13
al-ḥaṭīm 137, 139, 141, 153
ḥiǧr 139n
hiǧrah 1, 22, 24, 30, 35, 91n, 129n, 161
ḥillah tribes 33n, 34n
ḥilm 229
ḥimá 157n, 231, 275
ḫizānah 36, 40

ihlāl 107n
iḥrām 1, 23, 107n
isnād 4, 6n, 8, 10, 12, 14n, 15, 17n, 22, 29, 38n
istiqsām 9n

Kisrá 71
kunyah 8n, 103, 249

liwāʾ 5

maʿbūd 265
maǧlis 32, 34
maḥill 247n
al-masʿá 143
masḥ 20n
mawlá 4, 17, 37n, 87n, 95n, 147n, 149n, 209n, 243n, 253n, 279n, 283n
mīqāt 1, 23
muḫaḍram 4, 119n, 125n, 259n
munāfiq, pl. *munāfiqūn* 25
mušrik, pl. *mušrikūn* 25

nisbah 4, 11n, 15, 113n

qaryah ǧāmiʿah 123n
qayl 125n, 259n
qurrah 189n

raʾī 14, 103, 113n
ruǧz/riǧz 147

al-sāʾibah 89, 91, 93, 97, 99, 101, 105
sādin, pl. *sadanah* (custodian/guardian of an idol) 227, 233
ṣanam, pl. *aṣnām* 5, 6n, 8n, 10, 13, 16n, 18n, 19n, 20, 22, 23, 25n, 29, 31n, 38n, 41n, 61, 157n, 175n, 243n, 281
saqb 1219
Satanic verses 11n, 233n
sawīq 105, 237, 239, 243
šurṭah 12

ṭāġiyah 23, 38, 40
ṭāġūt, pl. *ṭawāġīt* 18, 39n, 91, 93, 221, 223, 225, 265
talbiyah 33, 34n, 107
Tubbaʿ, pl. Tabābiʿah 131, 269, 285

ʿumrah 1n, 105, 107

wafd, pl. *wufūd* 6, 7, 9, 10, 11n, 12, 13, 17, 18
al-waṣīlah 89, 93, 99
waṯan, pl. *awṯān* 6n, 7n, 23, 26, 27n, 32n, 35n, 61, 235n
wuqūf (of pilgrims) 105

al-zūn, al-zūnah 18n, 31n, 61
al-zūr 61, 63

Facsimile of MS *Fatih 4339*
(Istanbul, Süleymaniye Kütüphanesi),
Fols. 30a–48b

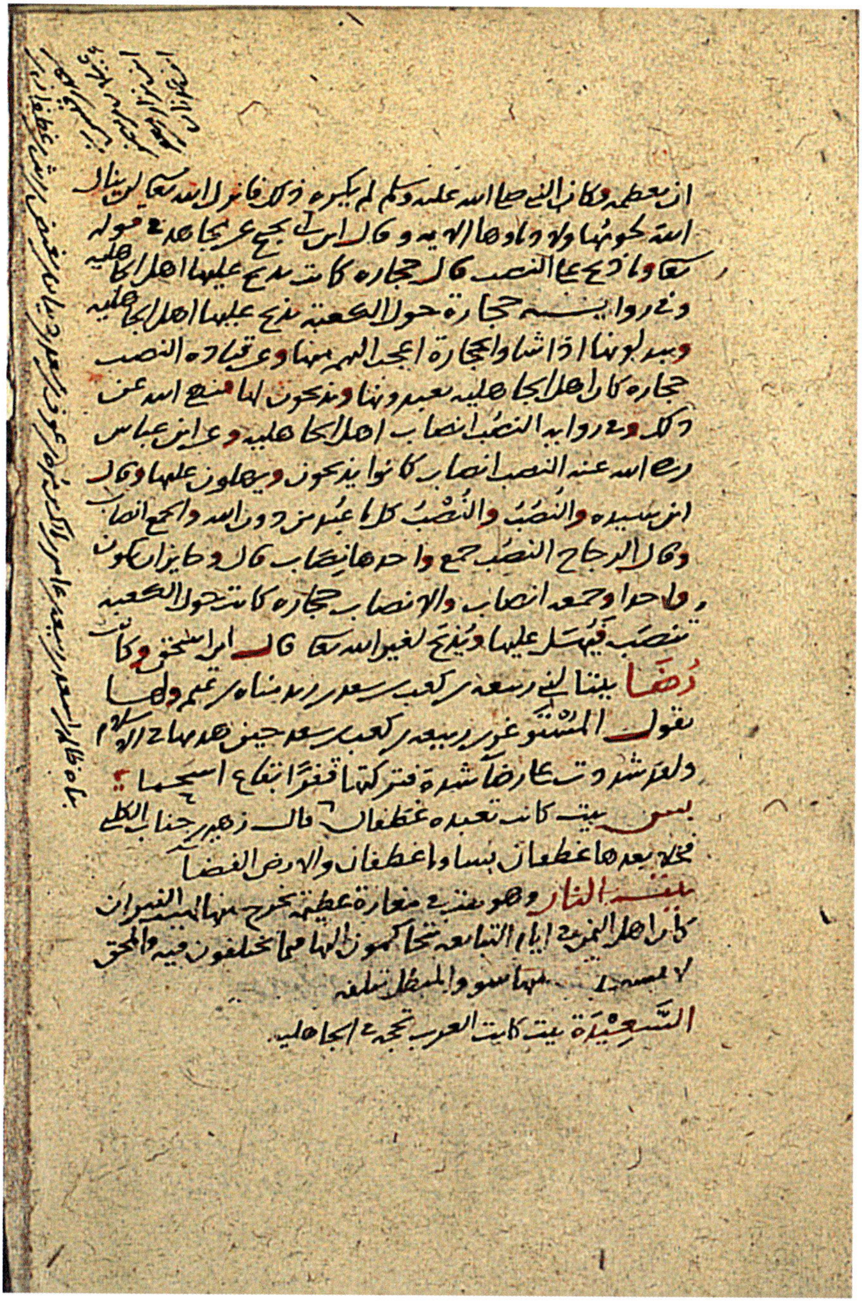
ان معظمه وكان النبي صلى الله عليه وسلم لم يكره ذلك فانزل الله تعالى لن ينال
الله لحومها ولا دماؤها الآية وقال ابن ابي نجيح عن مجاهد في قوله
تعالى وما ذبح على النصب قال حجارة كانت يذبح عليها اهل الجاهلية
وفي رواية حجارة حول الكعبة يذبح عليها اهل الجاهلية
ويبدلونها اذا شاوا بحجارة اعجب اليهم منها وعن قتادة النصب
حجارة كان اهل الجاهلية يعبدونها ويذبحون لها فنهى الله عن
ذلك وفي رواية النصب انصاب اهل الجاهلية وعن ابن عباس
رضي الله عنه النصب انصاب كانوا يذبحون ويهلون عليها وقال
ابن سيده والنصُب والنُّصْب كل ما عُبد من دون الله والجمع انصاب
وقال الزجاج النصُب جمع واحدها نِصاب قال وجايز ان يكون
واحدا وجمعه انصاب والانصاب حجارة كانت حول الكعبة
تنصب فيُهلّ عليها ويُذبح لغير الله تعالى قال ابن اسحق وكانت
رُضا بيتا لبني ربيعة بن كعب بن سعد بن زيد مناة بن تميم ولها
يقول المستوغر بن ربيعة بن كعب بن سعد حين هدمها في الاسلام
ولقد شددت على رضا شدة فتركتها قفرا بقاع اسحما
بس بيت كانت تعبده غطفان قال زهير بن جناب الكلبي
فخلا بعدها غطفان بسا وغطفان والارض الفضا
بيت النار وهو في مغارة عظيمة يخرج منها النيران
كان اهل اليمن في ايام التبابعة يتحاكمون اليها فيما يختلفون فيه والمحق
لا [illegible] منها سوء والمبطل تلفحه
الشَّعيرة بيت كانت العرب تحج في الجاهلية.

48b

 | DOI:10.1163/9789004499867_010

48

غزونا مع النبي صلى الله عليه وسلم عام الفتح ونحن الف ونيف ففتح الله له
مكة وحنينا حتى اذا كنا بين حنين والطايف اذا نحن بشجرة
دفوا بسدره كان يناط بها السلاح فسميت ذات انواط تعبد
من دون الله فلما راها النبي صلى الله عليه وسلم صرف عنها في يوم
صايف الى ظل هو ادنى منها فقال له رجل يا رسول الله اجعل
لنا ذات انواط كما لهم ذات انواط فقال النبي صلى الله عليه وسلم
انها السنن قلتم والذي نفس محمد بيده كما قالت بنو اسرايل
يا موسى اجعل لنا الاها كما لهم الهة قال اغير الله ابغيكم الاها
وهو فضلكم على العالمين ورواه من طريق ابن المبرك قال اخبرنا
معمر عن الزهري قال حدثني من سمع ابا واقد الليثي قال خرجنا
مع النبي صلى الله عليه وسلم قبل حنين فمررنا بسدرة فقلنا يا رسول
الله اجعل لنا ذات انواط كما لهم ذات انواط قال وكان الكفار
ينوطون سلاحهم بسدرة ثم يعكفون حولها فقال النبي صلى الله
عليه وسلم لتركبن سنن من كان قبلكم هذا كما قالت بنو اسرايل
لموسى اجعل لنا الاها كما لهم الهة انتهى وكانت للعرب
انصاب واحدها نصب قال الله تعالى حرمت عليكم الميتة
والدم ولحم الخنزير وما اهل لغير الله به والمنخنقة والموقوذة
والمتردية والنطيحة وما اكل السبع الا ما ذكيتم وما ذبح
على النصب وان تستقسموا بالازلام ذلكم فسق قال النصب
حجارة تجمع في موضع من الارض يغرسون لها وليست باصنام
قال ابن جريج النصب ليست باصنام الصنم يصور وينقش
وهذه حجارة تنصب ثلثماية وستون حجرا فمنهم من يقول
ثلثماية منها لخزاعة فكانوا اذا ذبحوا نضحوا الدم على ما اقبل من
الكعبة وشرحوا اللحم وجعلوه على الحجارة فقال المسلمون
يا رسول الله كان اهل الجاهلية يعظمون البيت بالدم فنحن احق

بالذهب والآلات المفضضة التي تساوي قناطير من المال لا يستطيع
أحد أن يأخذ منها شيئاً إلى زمن أبي العباس السفاح فذكر له أمرها
وما يتهيب من جنها وحياتها فلم يرعه ذلك وبعث إليها أبا العباس
ابن الربيع عامله على اليمن معه أهل الحزم والجلد فخربوها وحصلوا
منها مالاً كثيراً ببيع ما أمكن بيعه من رخامها وآلاتها فعفا بعد ذلك
رسمها وانقطع خبرها ودرست آثارها وكان الذي يصيبهم من
الجن ينسبونه إلى كُعَيْب وامرأته صنمين كانت الكنيسة بنيت
عليهما فلما كسر كعيب وامرأته أصيب الذي كسرها بجذام فافتتن
بذلك رعاع الناس وطغامهم وقالوا أصابه كعيب وذكر أبو الوليد
الأزرقي أن كعيباً كان من خشب طوله ستون ذراعاً والله أعلم
قال ابن شبة واتخذت جهينة بيتاً بالقنعيين بين حبة والأعوص
واسمه الهجم وهو الذي وادياً كانوا يحجون إليه وكان الذي سباه منهم
وتسدنه ويقوم بأمره عبد الدار بن حُرَيْث وسمعت من يذكر أن
الذي كان يقوم بأمره سُوَيد حوَّط عليه وأنشدني عمر عبد الرحمن
الجهني لعبد الدار بن حريث

ولقد أردت بأن تقام بنية ليست بظلم أو تقى مآثم
فإذا الذين إذا الأمور تعيّمت لا ذو دابر بجة أو جوالب قوزم صح

خبر ذات أنواط خرج الترمذي من حديث سفيان عن الزهري
عن سنان بن أبي سنان عن أبي واقد الليثي أن رسول الله صلى الله عليه وسلم
لما خرج إلى حنين مر بشجرة للمشركين يقال لها ذات أنواط يعلقون
عليها أسلحتهم فقالوا يا رسول الله اجعل لنا ذات أنواط كما لهم ذات
أنواط فقال النبي صلى الله عليه وسلم سبحان الله هذا كما قال قوم
موسى اجعل لنا إلهاً كما لهم آلهة والذي نفسي بيده لتركبن سنن
من كان قبلكم قال أبو عيسى هذا حديث حسن صحيح ورواه عمر بن شبة
من طريق ابن أبي فديك عن كثير بن عبد الله المزني عن أبيه عن جده قال

غزونا

47b

47

فعدا رجلان من النساة من بني مالك بن كنانة فقيمين منهم فامرهما ان يذهبا الى
البيت الذي فيه القليس فيحدثا فيه ففعلا ذلك فدخل ابرهة البيت
فرأى اثارهما فقال من فعل هذا فقيل له رجلان من العرب فغضب
وقال لا انتهي حتى اهدم البيت الذي بمكة فسار وكان من امر الفيل ما
كان فلم يزل كعيب والخشبة التي معه في القليس حتى هدمه
العباس بن الربيع الحارثي في خلافة ابي جعفر وهو عامل على اليمن
واخرج كعيبا من القليس فابتاعه رجل من اهل العراق فقطعه وبنا
به دارا فجذم فقال رعاع من الناس هذا من شراه كعيبا وقال
السهيلي وسميت هذه الكنيسة القَلِيْس لارتفاع بنائها وعلوها
قال وكان ابرهة قد استذل اهل اليمن في بنيان هذه الكنيسة وجشمهم
فيها انواعا من السُخرَة وكان ينقل اليها العُدد من الرخام المجزع والحجارة
المنقوشة بالذهب من قصر بلقيس صاحبة سليمن وكان من موضع
هذه الكنيسة على فراسخ وكان فيه بقايا من اثار ملكها فاستعان
بذلك على ما اراده في هذه الكنيسة من بهجتها وبهائها ونصب فيها
صلبانا من الذهب والفضة ومنابر من العاج والآبنوس وكان اراد
ان يرفع في بنائها حتى يشرف منها على عدن وكان حكمه في العامل
اذا طلعت عليه الشمس قبل ان ياخذ في عمله ان تقطع يده فنام رجل
منهم ذات يوم حتى طلعت الشمس فجاءت معه امه وهي عجوز فتضرعت
اليه تستشفع لابنها فابى الا ان تقطع يده فقالت اضرب بمعولك
اليوم فاليوم لك وغدا لغيرك فقال ويحك ما قلت فقالت نعم كما صار
هذا الملك من غيرك اليك فكذلك يصير منك الى غيرك فاخذته موعظتها
واعفى الناس من العمل فيها بعدُ فلما هلك ومزقت الحبشة كل
ممزق واقفر ما حول هذه الكنيسة فلم يعمرها احد وكثرت حولها
السباع والحيات وكان كل من اراد ان ياخذ شيئا منها اصابته
الجن فبقيت من ذلك العهد بما فيها من العُدد والخشب المرصع

47a

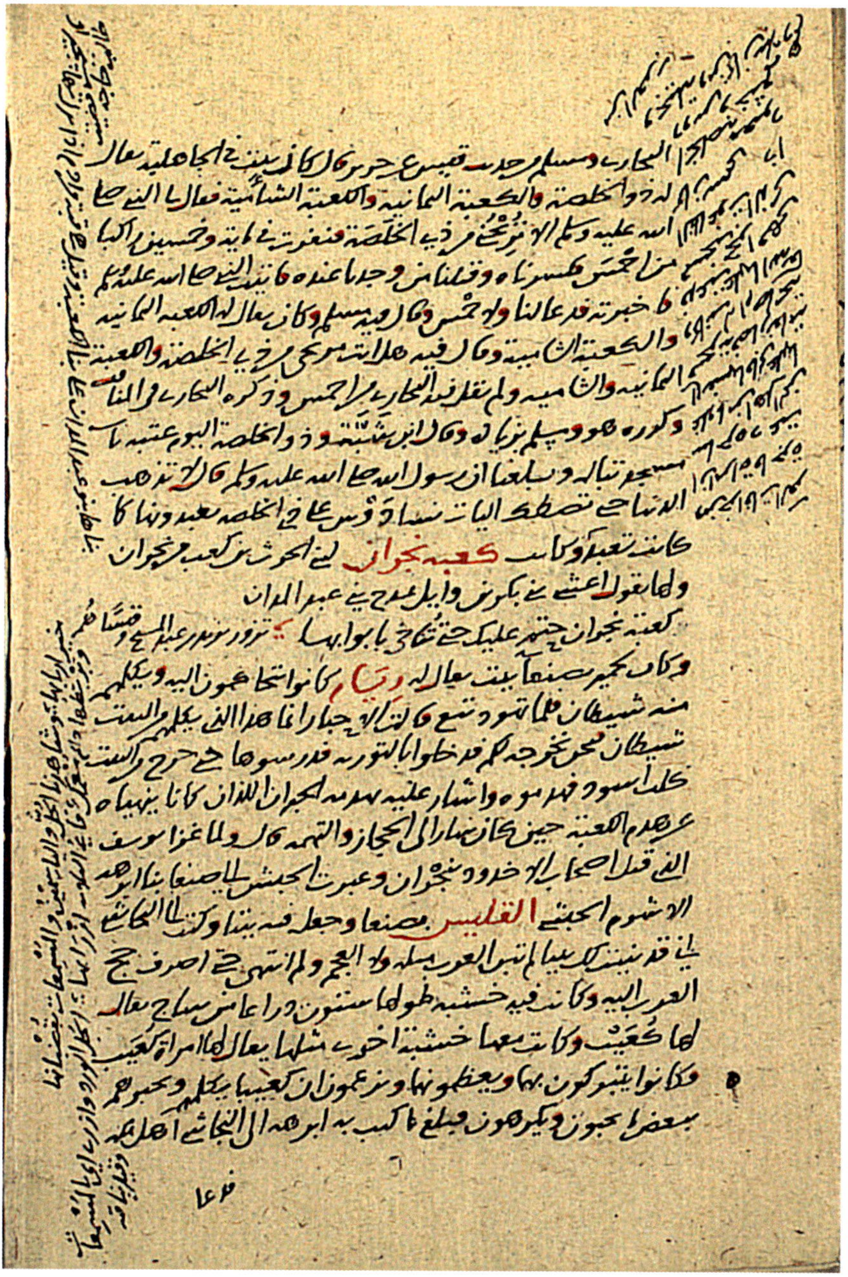
البخاري ومسلم من حديث قيس عن جرير قال كان بيت في الجاهلية يقال
له ذو الخلصة والكعبة اليمانية والكعبة الشامية فقال لي النبي صلى
الله عليه وسلم الا تريحني من ذي الخلصة فنفرت في مائة وخمسين راكبا
من احمس فكسرناه وقتلنا من وجدنا عنده فاتيت النبي صلى الله عليه وسلم
فاخبرته فدعا لنا ولاحمس وقال فيه مسلم وكان يقال له الكعبة اليمانية
والكعبة الشامية وقال فيه هل انت مريحي من ذي الخلصة والكعبة
اليمانية والشامية ولم يقل فيه البخاري من احمس وذكره البخاري في المناقب
وذكره هو ومسلم بزيادة وقال ابن هشام وذو الخلصة اليوم عتبة باب
مسجد تبالة وبلغنا ان رسول الله صلى الله عليه وسلم قال لا تذهب
الدنيا حتى تصطك اليات نساء دوس على ذي الخلصة يعبدونها كما
كانت تعبد وكانت كعبة نجران لبني الحرث بن كعب من نجران
ولها يقول الاعشى في بكر بن وائل يمدح بني عبد المدان
كعبة نجران حتم عليك حتى تناخي بابوابها تزور يزيد وعبد المسيح وقيسا هم
وكان لحمير صنما بيت يقال له رئام كانوا يتحاكمون اليه ويكلمهم
منه شيطان فلما تهود تبع قالت له الاحبار انما هذا الذي يكلمهم الشيطان
شيطان فخل نخرجه لكم فدخلوا بالتورية فدرسوها حتى خرج
كلب اسود فهدموه واشار عليه بهدمه الحبران اللذان كانا نهياه
عن هدم الكعبة حين كان سار الى الحجاز والتهمة قال ولما غزا يوسف
الذي قتل اصحاب الاخدود بنجران وعبرت الحبشة بنى بصنعا ابرهة
الاشرم الحبشي القليس بصنعا وجعله فيه بيتا وكتب الى النجاشي
اني قد بنيت لك بيتا لم تبن العرب مثله ولا العجم ولم انته حتى اصرف حج
العرب اليه وكانت فيه خشبة طولها ستون ذراعا من ساج يقال
لها كعيب وكانت معها خشبة اخرى مثلها يقال لها امراة كعيب
فكانوا يتبركون بهما ويعظمونهما ويزعمون ان كعيبا يكلمهم ويخبرهم
ببعض ما يحبون ويكرهون فبلغ ما كتب به ابرهة الى النجاشي اهل مكة
١٤٢

46b

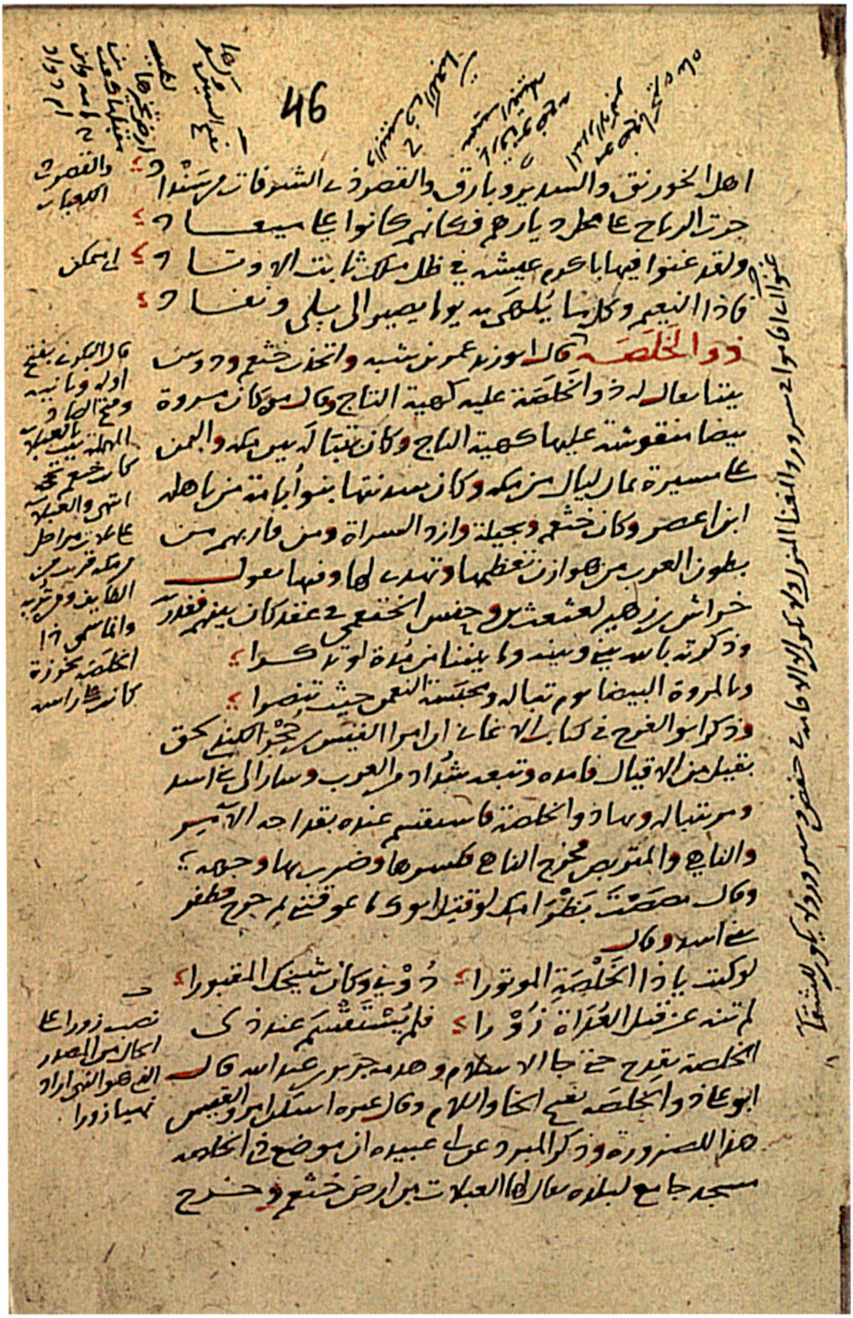

46

اهل الخورنق والسدير وبارق والقصر ذي الشرفات من سنداد
جرت الرياح على محل ديارهم فكانهم كانوا على ميعاد
ولقد غنوا فيها بانعم عيشة في ظل ملك ثابت الاوتاد
فاذا النعيم وكل ما يلهى به يوما يصير الى بلى ونفاد

ذو الخلصة قال ابو زيد عمر بن شبة واتخذت خثعم ودوس
بيتا يقال له ذو الخلصة عليه كهيئة التاج وقال غيره كانت مروة
بيضا منقوشة عليها كهيئة التاج وكانت بتبالة بين مكة واليمن
على مسيرة سبع ليال من مكة وكان سدنتها بنو امامة من باهلة
ابن اعصر وكانت خثعم وبجيلة وازد السراة ومن قاربهم من
بطون العرب من هوازن تعظمها وتهدي لها وفيها يقول
خداش بن زهير لعثعث بن وحشي الخثعمي في عقد كان بينهم فغدر

وذكرته بالله بيني وبينه وما بيننا من مدة لو تذكرا
وبالمروة البيضا يوم تبالة ومحبسة النعم حيث تنصرا

وذكر ابو الفرج في كتاب الاغاني ان امرا القيس بن حجر الكندي لحق
بقيل من الاقيال فامده وتبعه شذاذ من العرب وسار الى بني اسد
ومر بتبالة وبها ذو الخلصة فاستقسم عنده بقداحه الامر
والناهي والمتربص فخرج الناهي فكسرها وضرب بها وجهه
وقال مصصت بظر امك لو قتل ابوك ما عوقتني ثم خرج فظفر
ببني اسد وقال

لو كنت يا ذا الخلص الموتورا مثلي وكان شيخك المقبورا
لم تنه عن قتل العداة زورا

فلم يستقسم عند ذي
الخلصة بقدح حتى جاء الاسلام وهدمه جرير بن عبد الله قال
ابو عبيد ذو الخلصة بفتح الخا واللام وقال غيره اسكن ابن العبيس
هذا للضرورة وذكر المبرد عن ابي عبيدة ان موضع ذي الخلصة
مسجد جامع لبلدة يقال لها العبلات من ارض خثعم وخرج

[margin:] قال البكري بفتح اوله وثانيه وفتح الصاد المهملة بيت بالعبلات كانت خثعم تحجه انتهى والعبلات على مراحل من مكة قرب من الطائف ومن تربة وانما سمي ذا الخلصة لخرزة كانت في راسه

[margin:] نصب زورا على الانكار من المصدر الذي هو النهي اراد نهيا زورا

46a

هو الذي كانت تحجه الاعراب في الجاهلية الجهلا
وفي ديوان الادب للفارابي سنداد اسم
نهر والشرفات الشماريخ واحدها
شرفه

45*b

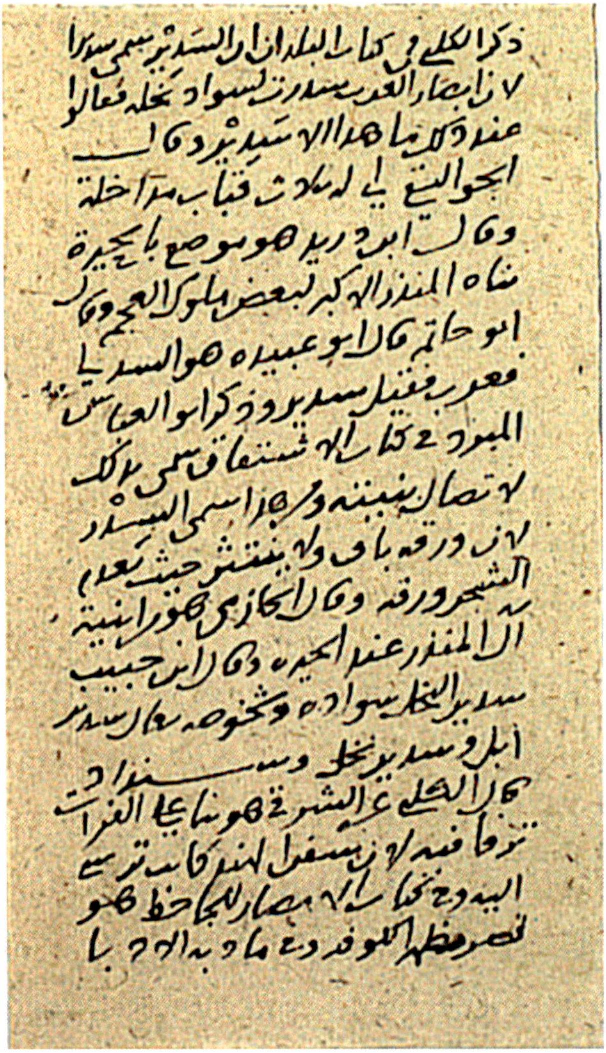
ذكر الكلبي في كتاب البلدان ان السدير يسمى سديرا
لان ابصار العرب تسدر لسواد نخله فقالوا
عند ذلك ما هذا الا سدير وقال
الجوالنبع لي له ثلاث قباب متداخلة
وقال ابو زيد هو موضع بالحيرة
بناه المنذر الاكبر لبعض ملوك العجم وقال
ابو حاتم قال ابو عبيدة هو السدلي
معرب فقيل سدير وذكر ابو العباس
المبرد في كتاب الاشتقاق يسمى بذلك
لاتصال بنيته ومجاز اسمي السدر
لان ورقه باق ولا ينتثر حيث يعدل
الشجر ورقه وقال الحازمي هو بناء بنته
آل المنذر عند الحيرة وقال ابن حبيب
سدير النخل سواده وشخوصه يقال سدير
ابل وسدير نخل وسواد
قال الكلبي في الشرقي هو نهر على الفرات
ترعا فيه لانه يشتغل لانه كانت ترسي
اليه وفي كتاب الامصار للجاحظ هو
قصر عظيم الكوفة دون ما دونه الى با

45*a

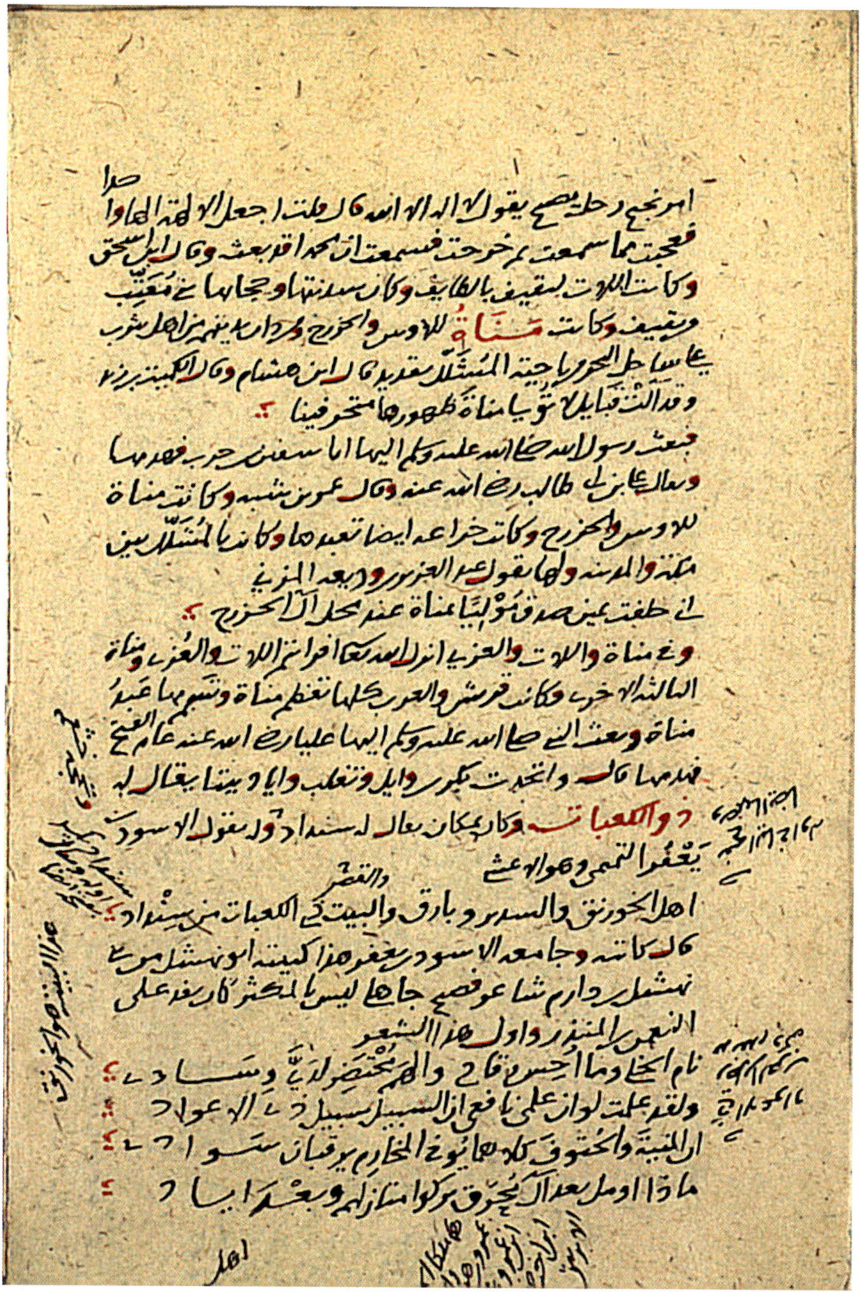
ابن نجيح رجلا يصيح يقول لا اله الا الله قال قلت اجعل الآلهة الها واحدا
فعجبت مما سمعت ثم خرجت فسمعت ان محمدا قد بعث وقال ابن اسحق
وكانت اللات لثقيف بالطايف وكان سدنتها وحجابها بني معتب
من ثقيف وكانت مناة للاوس والخزرج ومن دان بدينهم من اهل يثرب
على ساحل البحر من ناحية المشلل بقديد قال ابن هشام وقال الكميت بن زيد
وقد آلت قبائل لا تولي … مناة ظهورها متحرفينا
فبعث رسول الله صلى الله عليه وسلم اليها ابا سفيان بن حرب فهدمها
ويقال علي بن ابي طالب رضي الله عنه وقال عمر بن شبه وكانت مناة
للاوس والخزرج وكانت خزاعة ايضا تعبدها وكانت بالمشلل بين
مكة والمدينة ولها يقول عبد العزى بن وديعة المزني
اني حلفت يمين صدق برة … بمناة عند محل آل الخزرج
وفي مناة واللات والعزى انزل الله تعالى افرايتم اللات والعزى ومناة
الثالثة الاخرى وكانت قريش والعرب كلها تعظم مناة وتسمي بها عبد
مناة وبعث النبي صلى الله عليه وسلم اليها عليا رضي الله عنه عام الفتح
فهدمها قال واتخذت بكر بن وائل وتغلب واياد بيتا يقال له
ذو الكعبات وكان بمكان يقال له سنداد وله يقول الاسود بن
يعفر التميمي وهو الاعشى
اهل الخورنق والسدير وبارق … والبيت ذي الكعبات من سنداد
قال كاتبه وجامعه الاسود بن يعفر هذا كنيته ابو نهشل من بني
نهشل بن دارم شاعر فصيح جاهلي ليس بالمكثر كان يفد على
النعمان بن المنذر واول هذا الشعر
نام الخلي وما احس رقادي … والهم محتضر لدي وسادي
ولقد علمت لو ان علمي نافعي … ان السبيل سبيل ذي الاعواد
ان المنية والحتوف كلاهما … يوفي المخارم يرقبان سوادي
ماذا اؤمل بعد آل محرق … تركوا منازلهم وبعد اياد

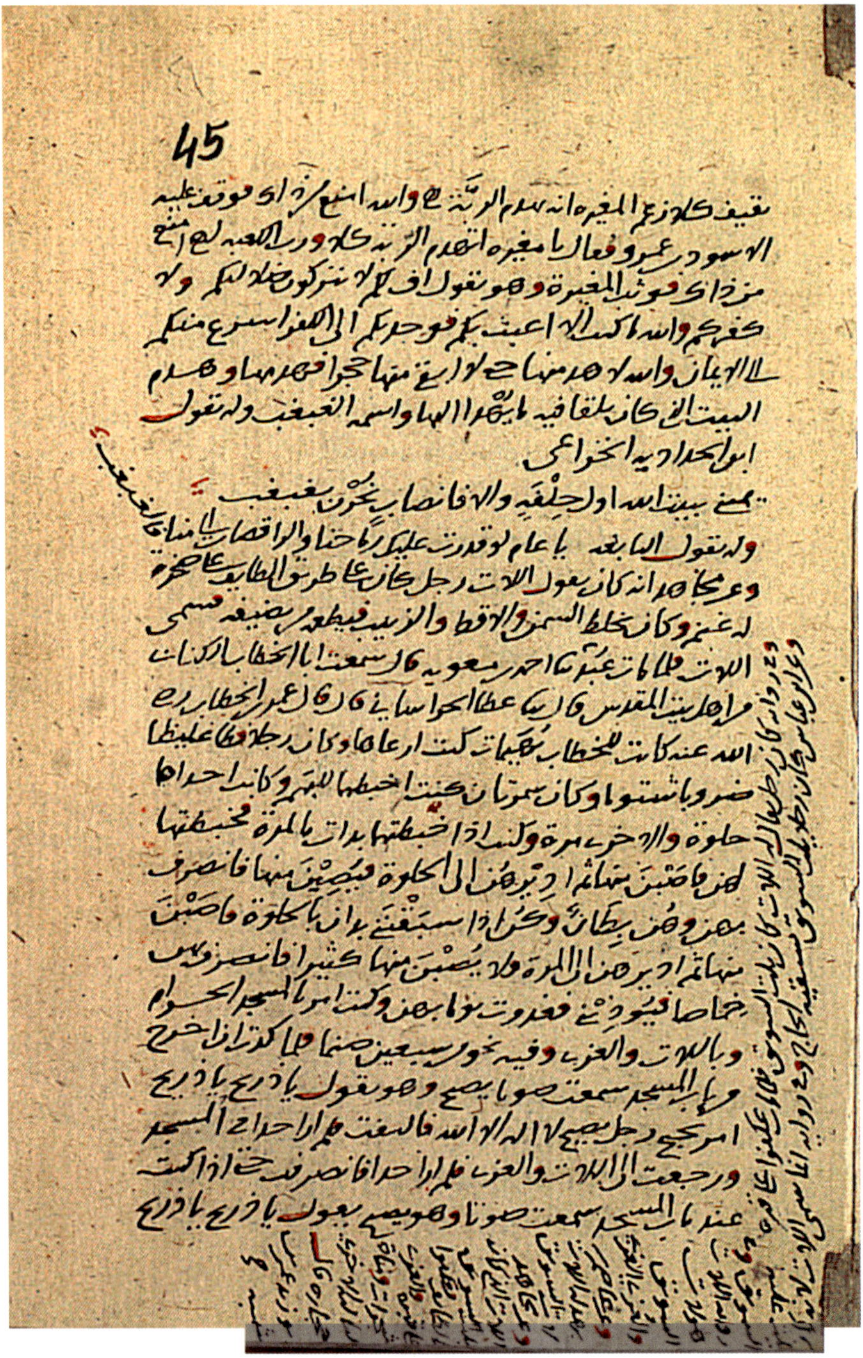
45

ثقيف كلا زعم المغيرة انه يهدم الربة قال والله اشبع من ذا اي فوقف عليه
الاسود بن عمرو فقال يا مغيرة اتهدم الربة كلا ورب الكعبة لم اشبع
من ذا اي فوثب المغيرة وهو يقول اف لكم لا تتركون ضلالكم ولا
كفركم والله ما كنت الا اعبث بكم فوجدتكم الى الكفر اسرع منكم
الى الايمان والله لاهدمنها حتى لا ابقي منها حجرا فهدمها وهدم
البيت الذي كان يلقا فيه ما يتقرب الى الربة واسمه الغبغب وله يقول
ابو الحداديه الخزاعي

يمنى بيتا لله اول حلفة والا فانصاب يخرن بغبغب

وله يقول النابغة يا عام لو قدرت عليك رماحنا والراقصات الى منا فالغبغب
وعن مجاهد انه كان يقول اللات رجل كان على طريق الطايف على صخرة
له غنم وكان يخلط السمن والاقط والزبيب فيطعم من يضيفه فسمي
اللات فلما مات عبدوه ثنا احمد بن معوية قال سمعت ابا الخطاب الكناني
من اهل بيت المقدس قال ثنا عطا الخراساني قال قال عمر ابن الخطاب رضي
الله عنه كانت للخطاب حكيمات كنت ارعاها وكان رجلا فظا غليظا
ضروبا شتوما وكان يامرني ان اخبط لها للبهم وكانت احداها
حلوة والاخرى مرة وكنت اذا خبطتها بدات بالمرة فخبطتها
لهن فاصبن منها ثم ادبرهن الى الحلوة فيصبن منها فانصرف
بهن وهن بطان وكن اذا سبقنني بدات بالحلوة فاصبن
منها ثم ادبرهن الى المرة فلا يصبن منها كثيرا فانصرف بهن
خماصا فيوجعني فغدوت يوما بهن وكنت امر بالمسجد الحرام
وباللات والعزى وفيه نحو سبعين صنما فلما كدت اخرج
من المسجد سمعت صوتا يصيح وهو يقول يا ذريح يا ذريح
امر نجيح رجل يصيح لا اله الا الله فالتفت فلم ار احدا خارج المسجد
ورجعت الى اللات والعزى فلم ار احدا فانصرفت حتى اذا كنت
عند باب المسجد سمعت صوتا وهو يصيح يقول يا ذريح يا ذريح

الحجارة فيعبدون الآخر ويطرحون الأول فأنزل الله تعالى أفرأيتم من اتخذ
إلهه هواه ثلاث آيات وقال حماد بن سلمة عن داود بن أبي هند عن
محمد بن عباد المخزومي أن قريشا قالت قيضوا لأصحاب محمد فقيضوا
لكل رجل منهم وليه يأخذه فقيضوا لأبي بكر الصديق رضي الله عنه طلحة
ابن عبيد الله فأتاه فقال يا أبا بكر قم إلي قال إلام تدعوني قال إلى
اللات والعزى قال وما اللات قال ربنا قال وما العزى قال
بناته قال فمن أمهم إذا قال فسكت وأقبل على القوم فقال أجيبوه
عني فسكتوا فقال يا أبا بكر قم إلي أشهد أن لا إله إلا الله وأن محمدا
عبده ورسوله قال فأنزل الله تعالى ومن يعش عن ذكر الرحمن
نقيض له شيطانا فهو له قرين قال ابن شبة **واللات**
كانت لثقيف بالطائف وموضعها الذي كانت به تحت منارة مسجد
الطائف اليسرى وكانت اللات صخرة مربعة وكان سدنتها
من ثقيف إلى بني عتاب بن مالك الثقفيين وكان سفيان بن عيينة يقول
هي شجرة ولها يقول صخر الجعد الخضري

وإني وتركي وصل كأس لكالذي تبرأ من لات وكان يدينها

وقال أبو الجوزاء عن ابن عباس رضي الله عنه في قوله تعالى اللات
والعزى قال كان رجل يلت السويق وعن قتادة في قوله أفرأيتم
اللات والعزى قال أما اللات فكانت بالطائف وأما العزى
فكانت بسقام شعب ببطن نخلة وأما مناة فكانت بقديد آلهة
يعبدونها وقال جعفر عن سعيد كانت قريش يعبدون اللات وهو
حجر أبيض حينا من الدهر فإذا وجدوا ما هو أحسن منه طرحوا الأول
وعبدوا الآخر فأنزل الله تعالى فيهم أفرأيت من اتخذ إلهه هواه الآية
قال عمر بن شبة حدثني أبو غسان حدثني عبد العزيز بن عمران الزهري
قال إن النبي صلى الله عليه وسلم بعث إلى اللات المغيرة بن شعبة يهدمها
فأقدم قال والله لأعجبن ثقيفا فلما صعد عليها تحانق ثم صرع فقالت

ثقيف

44

وبا عزان لم تقتلي المرء خالدا فبوئي باثم عاجلا او تنصّري
فاقبل اليها خالد بالسيف وهو يقول يا عزّ كفرانك لا سبحانك
اني رايت الله قد اهانك فضربها خالد بالسيف ثم انصرف وسال
النبي صلى الله عليه وسلم فاخبره الخبر فقال تلك العزى ولن تعبد
العزى بعد اليوم ابدا قال وبلغني انهم حموا لها واديا يقال له
سقام وهو من ناحية حراض يشبهونه بحرم الكعبة وانه لم يحم
لسواع وبلغني انهم كانوا يقولون اللات والعزى ومناة الثالثة
الاخرى بنات الله ويقولون اذا طافوا بالكعبة اللات والعزى
ومناة الثالثة الاخرى فانهن لغرانيق العلى وان شفاعتهن
لترتجى قال الله تعالى افرايتم اللات والعزى ومناة الثالثة الاخرى
الكم الذكر وله الانثى تلك اذا قسمة ضيزى ان هي الا اسماء سميتموها
انتم واباوكم ما انزل الله بها من سلطان وقال يونس بن بكير عن
شيبان عن قتادة قال بعث النبي صلى الله عليه وسلم خالد بن الوليد رضي
الله عنه الى شعب سقام ليكسر العزى فقال سادنها يا خالد بن
الوليد احذركها ان لها شدة لا يقوم لها شيء فمشى اليها خالد بن
الوليد بالفاس فهشم انفها وقال الوليد بن جميع عن ابي الطفيل
قال لما افتتح النبي صلى الله عليه وسلم مكة بعث خالد بن الوليد الى
العزى فاتاها وهي على ثلاث سمرات فهدم البيت وقطع السمرات
ثم اتى النبي صلى الله عليه وسلم فاخبره فقال ارجع فانك لم تصنع
شيئا فرجع فلما راته السدنة وهم حجابها امعنوا وامعنوا في
الجبل وقالوا يا عزى خبليه يا عزى اعوريه فاتاها فاذا امراة
عريانة ناشرة شعرها تحثوا التراب على راسها فعممها
بالسيف حتى قتلها ثم رجع الى النبي صلى الله عليه وسلم فاخبره فقال
تلك العزى وعن عمر بن عبد العزيز قال ان المشركين كانوا يعبدون العزى
وهو حجر ابيض الحين من الدهر ثم يجدون ما هو احسن منه من

[illegible]

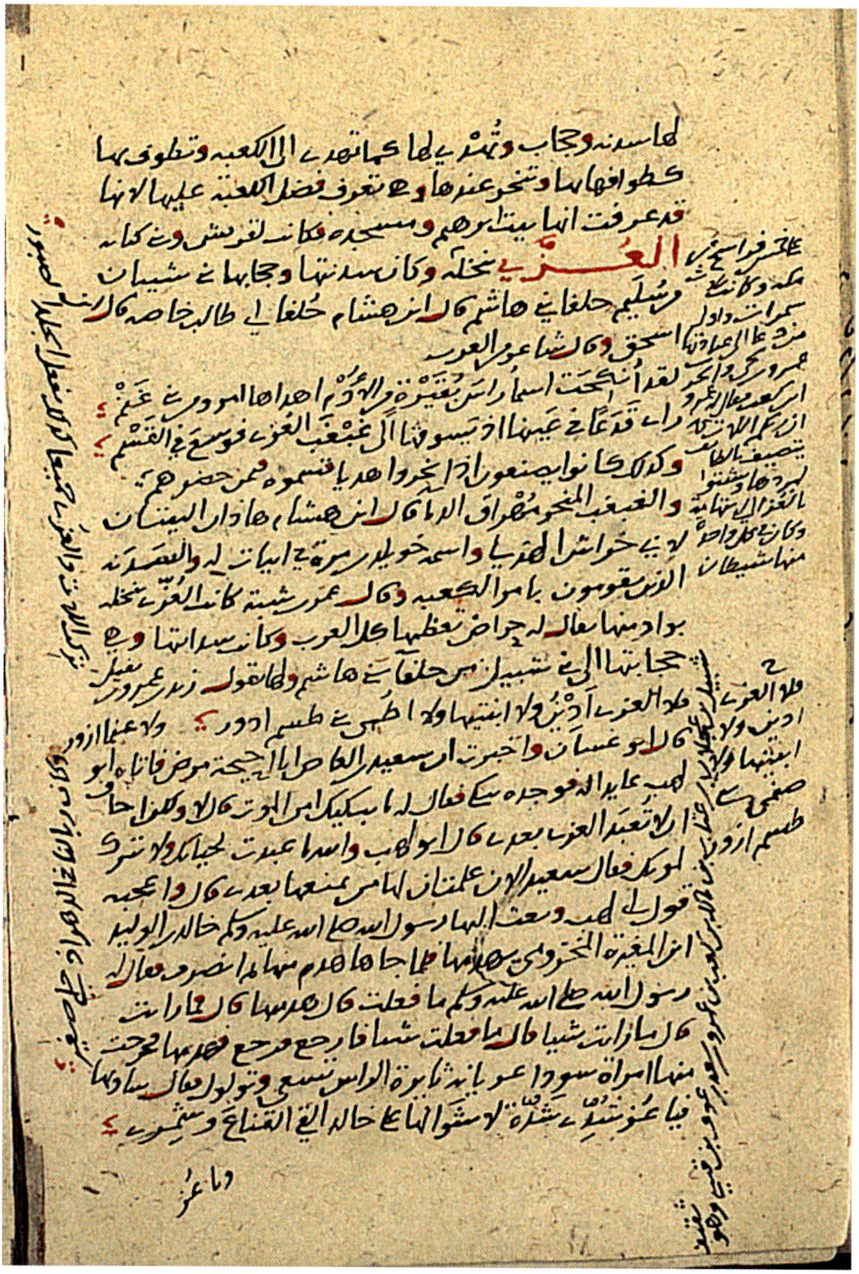
لها سدنة وحجاب وتهدي لها كما تهدي إلى الكعبة وتطوف بها
كطوافها بها وتنحر عندها وهي تعرف فضل الكعبة عليها لأنها
قد عرفت أنها بيت إبرهيم ومسجده فكانت لقريش وبني كنانة
العزى بنخلة وكان سدنتها وحجابها بني شيبان
من سليم حلفاء بني هاشم قال ابن هشام حلفاء أبي طالب خاصة قال ابن
إسحق وقال شاعر من العرب
لقد أنكحت أسماء رأس بقيرة ... من الأدم أهداها امرؤ من بني غنم
رأى قدعا في عينها إذ يسوقها ... إلى غبغب العزى فوسع في القسم
وكذلك كانوا يصنعون إذا نحروا هديا قسموه فيمن حضرهم
والغبغب المنحر ومهراق الدماء قال ابن هشام هذان البيتان
لأبي خراش الهذلي واسمه خويلد بن مرة في أبيات له والسدنة
الذين يقومون بأمر الكعبة وقال عمر بن شبة كانت العزى بنخلة
بواد منها يقال له حراض يعظمها كل العرب وكانت سدانتها و
حجابتها إلى بني شيبان من حلفاء بني هاشم ولها يقول زيد بن عمرو بن نفيل
فلا العزى أدين ولا ابنتيها ولا صنمي بني طسم أدور ... ولا غنما أزور
قال أبو غسان وأخبرت أن سعيد بن العاص أبا أحيحة مرض فأتاه أبو
لهب عائدا له فوجده يبكي فقال له ما يبكيك أمن الموت قال لا ولكني أخاف
أن لا تعبد العزى بعدي قال أبو لهب والله ما عبدت لحياتك ولا تترك
لموتك فقال سعيد الآن علمت أن لها من يمنعها بعدي قال وأعجبه
قول أبي لهب وبعث إليها رسول الله صلى الله عليه وسلم خالد بن الوليد
ابن المغيرة المخزومي يهدمها فجاءها فهدم منها ثم انصرف فقال له
رسول الله صلى الله عليه وسلم ما فعلت قال هدمتها قال هل رأيت
قال ما رأيت شيئا قال ما فعلت شيئا فارجع فرجع فهدمها فخرجت
منها امرأة سوداء عريانة ثائرة الرأس تسعى وتولول فقال سادنها
فيا عز شدي شدة لا شوى لها ... على خالد ألقي القناع وشمري
وما عز

43b

43

فصل في ذكر الجبت والطاغوت

قال الله تبارك وتعالى ألم تر إلى الذين أوتوا نصيبا من الكتاب يؤمنون
بالجبت والطاغوت ويقولون للذين كفروا هؤلاء أهدى من
الذين آمنوا سبيلا يعني تعالى بذلك اليهود ونزلت هذه الآية في
كعب بن الأشرف وحيي بن أخطب لما لقيا قريشا فقال لهما المشركون
انحن أهدى أم محمد وأصحابه فانا أهل السدانة والسقاية وأهل
الحرم فقالا بل أنتم أهدى من محمد وهما يعلمان أنهما كاذبان وإنما
حملهما على ذلك الحسد فأنزل الله تعالى هذه الآية فعن ابن عباس رضي
الله عنه أنه قال الجبت الأصنام والطاغوت تراجمة الأصنام وعن
مجاهد وابن زيد الجبت السحر والطاغوت الشيطان وعن سعيد بن
جبير الجبت الساحر والطاغوت الكاهن وعن الضحاك الجبت
حيي بن أخطب والطاغوت كعب بن الأشرف وقال الزجاج كل ما
عبد من دون الله فهو جبت وطاغوت وقال قطرب الجبت
الجبس وهو الذي لا خير عنده قلبت السين تاء وقال الراغب
الجبت والطاغوت في الأصل اسمان لصنمين ثم صارا يستعملان
في كل باطل ولذلك قيل ما عبد من دون الله فهو طاغوت ولذلك
فسر مرة بالصنم ومرة بالشيطان ومرة بالسحر ومرة بكل ما
يعبد من دون الله وقال الرازي وهما كلمتان وضعتا لمن
كان في غاية الشر والفساد وقال الماتريدي والطاغوت
مشتق من الطغيان سمي بذلك كل من انتهى في الطغيان غايته حتى
استجاز أن يعبد دون الله وقال ابن سيدة والطاغوت ما
عبد من دون الله عز وجل يقع على الواحد والجمع والمذكر والمؤنث
وزنه فعلوت إنما هو طيغوت قدمت الياء قبل الغين وهي
مفتوحة وقبلها فتحة فقلبت ألفا وقال ابن اسحق وكانت العرب
قد اتخذت مع الكعبة طواغيت وهي بيوت تعظمها كتعظيم الكعبة

قال لما كان فلم يكن الا قليل حتى سمعنا بظهور النبي صلى الله عليه وسلم فعلت
تبعت رسول الله اذ جا بالهدى وخلفت فراضا بدار هوان
شددت عليه شدة فتركته كان لم يكن والدهر ذو حدثان
فلما رايت الله اظهر دينه اجبت رسول الله حين دعاني
فاصبحت للاسلام ما عشت ناصرا والقيت فيه كلكلي وجراني
فمن مبلغ سعد العشيرة اني شريت الذي يبقى باخر فاني

زعبل صنم لبني حنيفة

الجلسند صنم قال كما يعثر من يمشي الى الجلسند يعني
يقول يتعثر لانه يمشي منكسا راسه

جمام صنم كان لبني عنزة وكانوا يعظمونه وكان في هذيل
حرام بن ضنة بن عبد بن كبير عذره وكانوا يعترون عنده

عوض صنم لبكر كلها قال رجل من عنزة قديم
حلفت بمائرات حول عوض وانصاب تركن لدى السعير
اجوب الدهر ارضا شطر عمرو ولو يلقى بساحتها بعيرا
وقال الاعشى لا اعرفنك ان جدت عداوتنا والتمس النصر منكم عوض تحتمل
عوض بالضم فسر واحتمل الرجل غضب

السقب من ولد الناقة الذكر ولا يقال للانثى سقبة وكان
لبني بكر بن وائل بن قاسط رافق سقب يعبدونه فاغار عليهم عمرو بن
حبيب بن عمرو بن شيبان بن محارب بن فهر بن مالك بن النضر بن كنانة فاخذ
السقب الذي يعبدونه فاكله فقيل له آكل السقب لذلك

42

دون الله يعني الأوثان يقول لا جعل الا شكلا وقال أبو بكر بن أبي شيبة نا
شبابة نا نعيم بن حكيم عن أبي مريم عن علي رضي الله عنه قال انطلق بي
رسول الله صلى الله عليه وسلم حتى أتى الكعبة فقال اجلس فجلست
إلى جنب الكعبة وصعد على منكبي ثم قال انهض فنهضت به فلما
رأى ضعفي تحته قال اجلس فجلست فنزل عني وجلس لي وقال
لي يا علي اصعد على منكبي فصعدت على منكبيه ثم نهض بي فخيل إلي
أني لو شئت نلت أفق السماء فصعدت على الكعبة وتنحى رسول
الله فقال لي ألق صنمهم الأكبر صنم قريش وكان من نحاس وكان
موتدا بأوتاد من حديد إلى الأرض فقال لي رسول الله عالجه فجعلت
أعالجه والنبي صلى الله عليه وسلم يقول إيه إيه فلم أزل أعالجه حتى
استمكنت منه فقال لي اقذفه فقذفته فنزوت أو نزلت وقال
الكلبي عن أبي صالح عن ابن عباس قال كانت العرب تعبد النجوم وكانت
حمير تعبد الشمس وذلك قول الله تعالى وجدتها وقومها يسجدون
للشمس من دون الله وكانت كنانة تعبد القمر وكانت تميم تعبد
الدبران وكانت لخم وجذام تعبد المشتري وكانت طي تعبد الثريا
وكانت قيس تعبد الشعرى وكانت بنو أسد تعبد عطارد وكانت
ربيعة تعبد المرزم وذلك قول الله تعالى ألم تر أن الله يسجد له من في
السموات ومن في الأرض والشمس والقمر والنجوم إلى أن هووا كله
مسخر له وعن مجاهد في قوله تعالى وأنه هو رب الشعرى قال له
كوكب خلف الجوزا كانوا يعبد وكان لسعد العشيرة صنم يقال
له فراض وكان يقال لسادنه ابن وقشة وهو من بني
أنس الله بن سعد العشيرة وكان له رئي من الجن يخبره بما يكون فأتاه
يوما وعنده رجل من بني أنس الله يقال له ذباب فنظر إليه فقال يا
ياذباب م
ذباب فقال يا ذباب اسمع العجب العجاب بعث الله أحمد بالكتاب
يدعو بمكة فلا يجاب فقال له ذباب ما تقول فقال لا أدري هكذا

وكانوا يعظمونه

من كان يعبده وبالبلد كان صنما لجهينة بالحوراء من ارض الحجاز
على ساحل البحر وكان للعافر صنم يقال له تَسْرُعلان وكان
لبني عامر بن ربيعة صنم يقال له قرس وكان شنية بوانه وله يقول السلمي
وما قرس وان عظمتموه بزيد دفع يعم وله قباله
والعَسد كان لطي وكان بموهق والجثا كان صنما لبني نهد
وله يقول ابن عجلان النهدي
فقلنا اذا لا ينكل القوم عنكم لعمرو والجثا اللات الدهر تمورها
وعن سعيد بن جبير عن ابن عباس رضي الله عنه في قوله تعالى افرايت من
اتخذ الهه هواه قال كان احدهم يعبد الحجر فاذا راى ما هو احسن
منه رمى به وعبد الاخر وقال حماد بن سلمة عن حميد عن ابي عثمن قال
كنا في الجاهلية اذا احملنا حجرا على بعير نعبده فراينا حجرا احسن
منه القيناه واخذنا الذي هو احسن وكنا اذا سقط الحجر عن
البعير قلنا قد سقط الاهكم فالتمسوا حجرا اخر وعن قتادة
قال حدثني عن ابي عثمن قال كان اهل الجاهلية اذا حجوا عمدوا
الى حجرهم الذي كانوا يعبدونه فشدوه على بعير ابلهم فاذا سار
ذلك البعير نادي مناديهم ان ربكم قد سار فسيروا فان سار يومه
اجمع ساروا معه وان هو برك من ساعته نادي مناديهم ان
ربكم قد نزل فانزلوا وان وجدوا حجرا احسن من حجرهم الاول
اخذوه ورموا بالاخر فاذا كان من الغد دارهم وصبوا عليه
البانهم واطعمتهم وذبحوا له فيظل اولادهم جياعا وتظل كلابهم
شبعا عليها يضحك بهما الشيطان ويتلعب بهم وعن ابي رجا قال
كنا نضع الحجر الابيض ونرى احسن منه الحجر الاسود فيتصل
ونجمع الرمل فنحلب فيه ونصلي له وعن مجاهد في قوله من كان
مريد العزة قال لعبادة الاوثان وعن سعيد بن جبير في قوله تعالى
ان الذين تدعون من دون الله عباد امثالكم يقول الذين تدعون من
دون

41b

41

الى
الله صلى الله عليه وسلم اما حلوق واسكت فانك تستشهد واما الطير
خرجت منك فهو زوج حتى يصعد به الى السما واما المراة التي ادخلتك
في بطنها فهي الارض فقال الطفيل يا رسول الله اني قد قلت شعرا فانشدك
فقال رسول الله صلى الله عليه وسلم انشد ما قلت قال قلت
يا ذا الكفين لست من عبادكا فقال رسول الله صلى الله عليه وسلم
صدقت قال قلت ميلادنا اقدم من ميلادكا فقال
رسول الله صلى الله عليه وسلم صدقت قال قلت
انا حشوت النار في فوادكا فقال رسول الله صلى الله عليه وسلم
انا اعلم وكان الشارق صنما لحنيفة وكان بحجر اليمامة
وكان في موضع سوق الخلق وله يقول ربعي بن دواد
وعند الشارق المرح المراح بكل كتيبة وبكل عظيم
قضينا حجنا وبرين منا كما حلت معاقد كل شطيم
وكان باليمامة اخمية يقال لها مرشوخ وهي اليوم الاكمة التي
يقال لها اكمة المصلي يصلب عليها عبيد فارس يقال له رستم
وكانوا يحجون اليها وكان الذي يحج يجلس على راسها ثم ياخذ انسان
برجله فيجره حتى يهبطه الى الارض اربع مرات وزعم رجل من
اشجع قال كانت البيضا نحرمها اشجع وبطون من غطفان
وجهينة ولها يقول المزني
لنا الجبل العالي الحرام الذي ترى على الارض اماذبه وفضول
فكيف تعاف الضيم ترفع راسه باقدام ام الحوتين حلول
وكان لحمير صنم يقال له كلال وكانوا يعبدونه قال وضاح اليمن
بنا اسمعيل بحا مو ثلا وعبد كلال قبله وابو حمد
والخميس كان لبني سليم والخزرج والانصار وله يقول
عبد المطلب بن هاشم البلغ في النجار ان جيتهم اني منهم وابنهم والخميس
وكان بحمى المعافر بالعقيق العينه صنم يقال له الكيمن ١٧١٧

والجلال كان صنما لبني مرة وكان بكاما يقال له الصلب وله يقول

متجنّا هن مرة يوم أضحى غداة حجيج أحمس والجلال

وأحمس كان صنما لبني فزارة وله يقول الأعشى

رضيعي لبانٍ ثدي أم تعاسما بأحمس عوض الدهر لا نتفرق

وعم أنس كان لخولان بأرضها وكان يقسم له من قسم الله تعالى

قال مجاهد كانت خولان إذا ذبحت ذبيحة يسمون عليها باسم الله واسم

صنمهم ويقسمون له من زرعهم فإذا هبت الريح فأمالت ما جعلوا للصنم

إلى ما جعلوا لله لم يجعلوا لله فيه شيئا وإذا هبت الريح فأمالت ما جعلوا

لله إلى ما جعلوه لصنمهم جعلوه للصنم فأنزل الله عز وجل في ذلك وجعلوا

لله مما ذرأ من الحرث والأنعام نصيبا فقالوا هذا لله بزعمهم وهذا لشركائنا

فما كان لشركائهم فلا يصل إلى الله وما كان لله فهو يصل إلى شركائهم

ساء ما يحكمون واتخذت دوس أصناما منها صنم يقال له الشريو

وآخر يقال له غنم وآخر يقال له ذو الكفين وكان الطفيل بن

عمرو الدوسي يقول كنت سادنا لذي الكفين فإن كنت لأغبقه

اللبن حتى تلغ فيه الكلاب وإن صبيانا ليتضاغون ما يمنعني أن

أسقيهم ذلك اللبن إلا فرقا من الصنم ثم إني فكرت في أمره فوجدته حجرا

لا يضر ولا ينفع فعمدت إليه فحرقته بالنار ثم أقبلت إلى رسول الله صلى

الله عليه وسلم حتى إذا كنت ببعض الطريق رأيت رؤيا ظننت أنها لما

صنعت بالصنم فجئت رسول الله صلى الله عليه وسلم فقلت إني كنت سادنا

لصنم لنا والله إن كنت لأغبقه اللبن حتى يلغ فيه الكلاب ما يمنعني منه

إلا فرقا منه وإني فكرت فيه فوجدته حجرا لا يضر ولا ينفع فحرقته

بالنار ثم أقبلت إليك حتى إذا كنت ببعض الطريق رأيت رؤيا فظننتها

لما صنعت بالصنم فقال رسول الله صلى الله عليه وسلم خيرا رأيت اقصص

رؤياك فقلت رأيت بطني انشق فخرجت منه طير خضر صعدت بي إلى

السماء ورأيت رأسي حلق ورأيت امرأة أدخلتني فرجها فقال رسول

الله

40b

الخامس ٢٦

40

للصنم فاراد هدمه فقيل له انه الاه فتركه وقال في ذكر البيتين [illegible]
شبه وكان لقضاعه ولخم وجذام واهل الشام ومن والاهم من غطفان
صنم يقال له الاقيصر وكانوا يحجونه فيحلقون روسهم عنده فكان
كلما حلق رجل منهم راسه القى مع شعره قبضة من دقيق فكانت
هوازن تنتابهم في ذلك الوقت فان ادركه قبل ان يلقي الدقيق مع ذلك
الشعر قال بعضهم اعطنيه فاني من هوازن ضارع وان فاته اخذ ذلك
الشعير بما فيه مع القمل والدقيق فخبزه واكله فاختصمت جرم
وبنو جعدة الى النبي صلى الله عليه وسلم في ماء يقال له العقيق فقضى به
الله عليه وسلم لجرم فقال معوية بن عبد العزى بن زراع الجرمي

واني اخو جرم كما قد علمتم ؛ اذا اجتمعت عند النبي المجامع
فان انتم لم تقنعوا بقضايه ؛ فاني بما قال النبي لقانع
الم تر جرما انجدت وابوكم ؛ مع القمل حفر الاقيصر شارع
اذا قرة جاءت يقول اصب بها ؛ سوى القمل اني من هوازن ضارع
فما انتم من هوة الناس كلهم ؛ بلى ذنب ما انتم واكارع
وانتم كالخنصرين اخستما ؛ فانتما من طولها الاصابع

وقال سراقة بن مالك بن جعشم المدلجي من بني كنانه

الم ينهكم عن شتمنا لا اباكم ؛ جذام ولخم اعرضت في المواسم
وكل قضاعي كان جفانه ؛ حياض برضوى والانوف رواغم
عما تنهكوا من قبضة الذل منكم ؛ فلا المرو يستحيي ولا المرو طاعم

والاقيصر يقول زهير بن ابي سلمى المزني

حلفت يمينا بالاقيصر جاهدا ؛ وما سحقت فيه المقادم والقمل

وكان صنم يقال له الغريف لبني نهم ايضا وله يقول جابر بن
الصعب النهدي اني وامارنا الغريف واقرقوا بالجلهتين بن شرب
والاه ربيعة كان في النخعة وكان لطي ورسعه وله يقول سيار بن
حارثة المزني فالغريقين الاه ربيعة اثارها حملوا عن المستبقين

40a

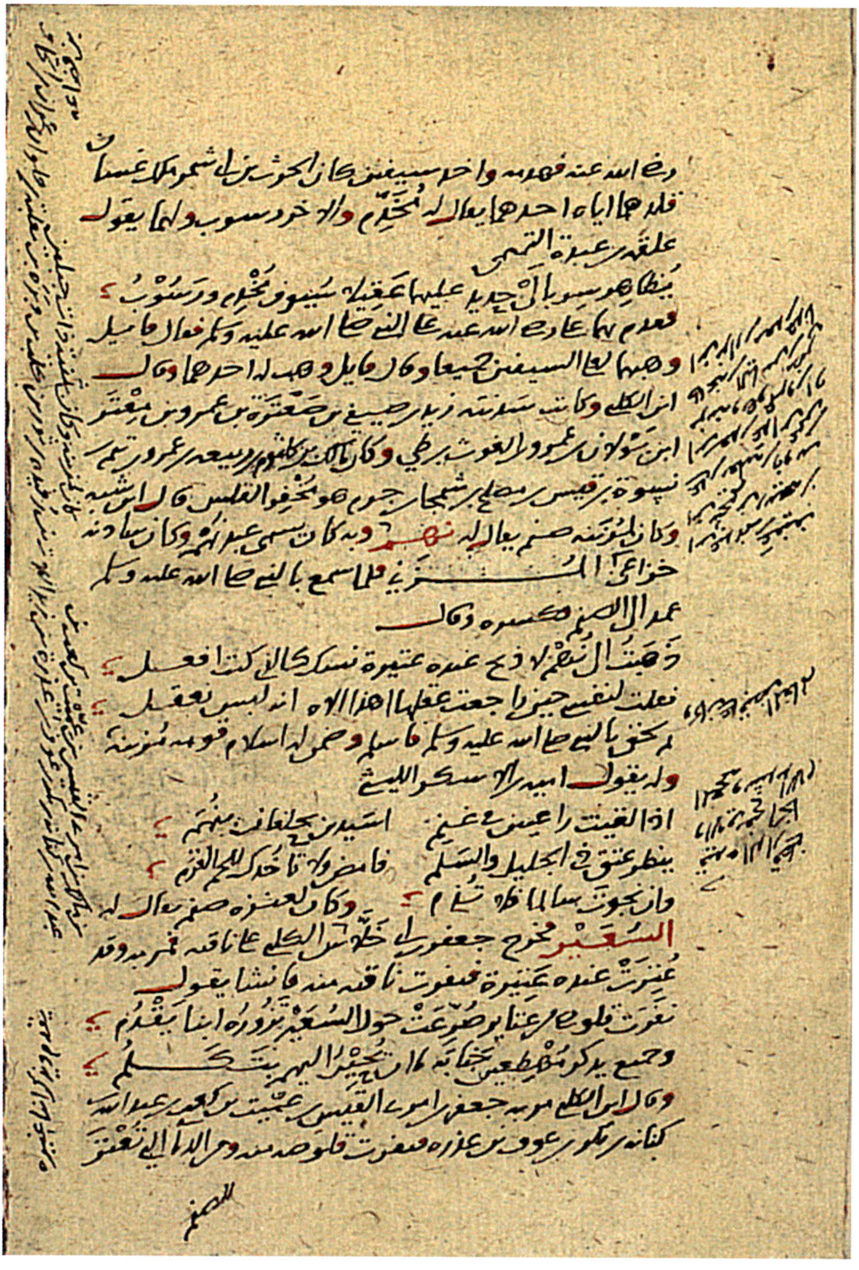
رضى الله عنه فهدمه واخذ سيفين كان الحرث بن ابي شمر ملك غسان
قلدهما اياه احدهما يقال له مخذم والاخر رسوب ولهما يقول
علقمة بن عبدة التميمي
مظاهر سربالي حديد عليهما عقيلا سيوف مخذم ورسوب
فقدم بهما على رضى الله عنه على النبي صلى الله عليه وسلم فقال قايل
وهبهما له السيفين جميعا وقال قايل ووهب له احدهما وقال
ابن الكلبي وكانت سدنته زياد بن صيفي بن صعترة بن عمرو بن معتر
ابن سلوان بن عمرو الغوث بن طي وكان بالكلب بن كلثوم بن ربيعة بن عمرو بن تيم
نسيوه بن قيس بن مصلح بن شمجار جرم هو بحفو الفلس قال ابن شبه
وكان لمزينة صنم يقال له نهم وبه كان يسمى عبد نهم وكان سادنه
خزاعي المزني فلما سمع بالنبي صلى الله عليه وسلم
عمد الى الصنم فكسره وقال
ذهبت الى نهم لاذبح عنده عتيرة نسك كالذي كنت افعل
فقلت لنفسي حين راجعت عقلها اهذا اله ابكم ليس يعقل
ثم لحق بالنبي صلى الله عليه وسلم فاسلم وضمن له اسلام قومه مزينة
وله يقول امية بن الاسكر الليثي
اذا لقيت راعيين في غنيمة   اسيدين يحتلفان بينهم
ينظر عتق في الجليل والسلم   فامضوا تاخذكم اللحم الغرم
وان يجوب سالما فلا تسلم   وكان لعنزة صنم يقال له
السعير فخرج جعفر بن ابي خلاس الكلبي على ناقته فمر به وقد
عترت عنده عنزة عتيرة فنفرت ناقته منه فانشا يقول
نفرت قلوصي من عتاير صرعت حول السعير تزوره ابنا يقدم
وجموع يذكر مهطعين جنابه ما ان يحير اليهم بتكلم
وقال ابن الكلبي مرة جعفر امرؤ القيس عتيبة بن كعب بن عبد الله
كنانه بن بكر بن عوف بن عذره فنفرت قلوصه منه ومر الدال التي تعتر
الصنم

39b

39

منصوبة وكانوا يذبحون عندها عتايرهم وعن مجاهد في قوله
وما ذبح على النصب قال كان حول الكعبة حجر يذبح عليه اهل
الجاهلية ويبدلونه اذا شاوا بالحجر احب اليهم منه كان اشبه
وكان لطي صنم يقال له الفُلُس وكان احمر طويلا في وسط
جبلهم الذي يقال له اجا اسود كانه تمثال انسان فكانوا يعبدونه
ويهدون له ويذبحون عنده ولا ياتيه خايف الا امن عنده ولا يطرد
احد طريدة فيلجا بها اليه الا تركت فلم تُخفَر وكان اخر من
سدنته بنو بولان وبولان هو الذي بدا بعبادته فكان اخر من
سدنه منهم رجل يقال له صيفي فانطلق صيفي يوما فاطرد ناقة
خلية لامراة من كلب من بني عليم كانت جارة لمالك بن كلثوم
الشمجي وكان شريفا فارسا فانطلق بها حتى وقفها بفنا
الفلس وخرجت جارة مالك فاخبرته بذهابه بناقتها فركب
فرسه عريانا واخذ رمحه ثم خرج في اثره فادركه وهو عند
الفلس والناقة موقوفة عند الفلس فقال له خل عن ناقة جارتي
فقال انها لربك قال خل سبيلها فقال اتخفر الهك فبوا له
الرمح فحل عقالها فانصرف بها مالك واقبل السادن على الفلس
ونظر الى مالك ثم رفع يده فقال رب ان مالك بن كلثوم ؎
اخفرك اليوم بناب علكوم ؎ وكنت قبل اليوم غير مغشوم ؎
يحرضه عليه والفا ذلك اليوم عدي بن حاتم قد ذبح عنده وجلس
هو ونفر معه يتحدثون بما صنع مالك وفزع لذلك عدي بن حاتم
وقال انظروا ما يصيبه في يومه او غده فلما مضت له ايام ولم
يصبه شي رفض عدي عبادته وعبادة الاصنام وتنصر فلم
يزل نصرانيا حتى جا الله بالاسلام فكان مالك اول من اخفره
وكان بعد ذلك اذا طرد السادن طريدة اخذت منه فلم يزل
الفلس يعبد حتى ظهر النبي صلى الله عليه وسلم فبعث اليه علي بن ابي طالب

بن ربيعة بن عمرو بن تيم
بن شمشون بن قيس
بن منظر الشمجي بن ثعلبة
ابن عمرو بن الغوث
ابن طي

[illegible]

فقالت امراته اهلكتني يا ابن رواحة وخرج وجا ابو الدردا وامراته
تبكي فقال ما لك قالت اخوك ابن رواحة دخل فصنع ما ترى فغضب
ثم فكر فقال لو كان عند هذا خير لدفع عن نفسه فاتى النبي صلى الله
عليه وسلم فاسلم وكان لكعب بن عجرة تاخر اسلامه وله صنم في بيته
وكان عبادة بن الصامت له صديقا فدخل منزله يوما وكعب غايب بسيرله
فكسر صنمه فلما جا كعب فراى ما صنع به قال ما عند هذا طايل واتى
منزل عبادة فظن عبادة انه يريد ان يقع به فقال قد رايت انه لو كان
عنده طايل ما تركك تفعل به ما رايت قال وكانت حوا بنت يزيد
امراة قيس بن الحطيم فقالت كان قيس لا يرام فعدوت يوما على صنمه
فكسرته فلما دخل نظر اليه وقال ما هذا الا انت فعلت هذا قلت لا ولكن
الشاة نطحته فقام الى الشاة فذبحها قال واتخذت بلحرث بن
الخزرج صنما يقال له هزم وكان موضعه في مجلسهم الذي يقال له الهزم
ببطحان وكان لبني سلمة صنم يقال له مناف فعدا عليه رهط
منهم يقال له الجموح فربطه بكلب ثم طرحه في بير فوجده فيها فقال
الحمد لله الجليل ذي المنن   فتبح بالفعل ميناما ذا الـ ور
اقسم لو كنت الها لم تكن   انت وكلب وسط بير في قرن
قال وكان الدوار ان العرب تاخذ من الحرم بسبعة احجار
بقدر عرض الكعبة وطولها الا انه مدور ثم يدورون حوله فيدور
الرجال اربعة اطواف والنسا ثلثة وكانت دوار في سبع قبايل
من العرب ليس في غيرهم في خثعم ونمير وسوة وجهينة
وباهلة وعنزة وسليم وفي ذلك يقول عامر بن الطفيل ورا بني
قينات لغني بن اعصر يطفن وفيهن جمال
الا ليت اخواني غنيا عليهم كما امسوا خر دوار
ويقال ان عامرا كان عاهرا فاجرا وكانت هذه الحجارة التي كانوا
يدورون حولها تسمى الدوار ويقال لها ايضا النصف وكانت عند

منصوبة

38b

38

مبطلا لما غلب عليه فخرج حتى اتى مكة فوجد النبي صلى الله عليه وسلم قد
هاجر الى المدينة فطلبه حتى جا المدينة فاسلم قال وكان لكل بطن
والاوس والخزرج وهم الانصار صنم في بيت لجماعة البطن يكرمونه
ويعظمونه ويذبحون له وكان في بني عبد الاشهل صنم يدعا الحريش
وصنم في بني حارثة يقال له صخر وصنم في بني ظفر يقال له
شمس وصنم في بني معوية يقال له البهام وصنم في بني عمرو بن عوف
يقال له الغين وصنم في بني خطمة يقال له شفر وصنم للعواقلة
يقال له الحيس وصنم في بني امية يقال له غيان وصنم في
بني سلمة يقال له اساف وصنم في بني عدي النجار يقال له عمول
وصنم في بني دينار النجار يقال له حسا وصنم في بني مالك بن النجار
يقال له الطم وصنم في بني زريق يقال له السيح ولكل رجل شريف
صنم من هذه الاصنام وكان في بيت عمرو بن الجموح صنم يقال له
مناف كسره معاذ بن جبل رضي الله عنه ومعاذ بن عمرو بن الجموح
والبرا بن معرور وصنم يقال له الدباج وصنم لجدير بن قيس
يقال له الزنبور فلما قدم السبعون الذين شهدوا العقبة جعلوا
يكسرون الاصنام فدخل عبد الله بن رواحة رضي الله عنه على شيخ
منهم قديم فربط مع صنمه ميتة ثم وضعه على بابه فاصبح الشيخ
فراه فقال من صنع هذا بالاهنا فقيل له هذا عمل ابن رواحة فاتاه
ابن رواحة فقال له اما تستحي وانت من كبرا انا تعبد خشبة انت
عملتها بيدك فقال الشيخ اني غير متعرض له اخاف على صبيتي
فضحك بشير سعد وقال وهل عنده ضر او نفع فكسره عبد الله بن
رواحة واسلم الشيخ وكان ابو الدردا اخر داره اسلاما وكان
عبد الله بن رواحة يدعوه الى الاسلام فيابا وكان له صديقا فتحينه
فلما خرج ابو الدردا دخل عبد الله منزله فكسر صنمه وهو يقول
تبرا من اسما الشياطين كلها الا كل ما يدعا مع الله باطل

والیه نسب عبد حريش
ابن مرة بن عمرو بن
حنظلة بن يربوع
جد عبد قيس
خفاف بن عمير
[illegible]

38a

تخبو منه قيت ان قد هزمتهم ولو بدرا سيما جم له وعايم
وكان بالسراة صنم يقال له ذو الشرى كان لبني الحرث بن يشكر
ولدوس وله يقول رجل من الغطارف
اذا لحللنا دون ما حول ذي الشرى وشج العدى منا خميس عرمرم
ورضا كان لربيعة وطي وله يقول طفيل الخيل
وقالوا الفوا الاحبوا في رحالهم ورضا قد تخافون فاذهبوا
وكان ضمار صنما لبني سليم كان منهم لمرداس بن ابي عامر ابي عباس
ابن مرداس وكان قد جعل عليه سيفين من ذهب وجعله في بيت
فكان يتعاهده في الايام فيسائله عن الشي فيكلمه الشيطان من جوفه
فلما هلك مرداس اوصى به ابنه عباسا فكان عباس يتعاهده مثل
ما كان ابوه يتعاهد منه فسمع عباس ليلة من البيت الذي فيه الصنم صوتا
فخرج يسحب ثوبيه اباه فسمع صوتا من جوف الصنم يقول
اودى ضمار وكان يعبد مرة قبل الكتاب الى النبي محمد
قل للقبائل من سليم كلها هلك الانيس وعاش اهل المسجد
ان الذي ورث النبوة والهدى بعد ابن مريم من قريش مهتد
فكتم ذلك عباس ولم يذكره لاحد وخرج الى ابل له بعقيق تمرة فبينما هو
مستلق في روضة من رياض العقيق اذ سمع صوتا وهو يقول
بشر الجن وابلاسها ان قد وضعت المطي احلاسها
ومنعت السما احراسها فرفع راسه فاذا هو بطير فطلبه من
في بعض تلك الجبال فلم يقدر عليه فرجع الى مكانه فبينا هو هناك اذ سمع
صوتا يقول ان النور الذي وقع من السما يوم الاثنين وليلة الثلاثا
في وادي العنقا فرفع راسه فاذا هو بحيات على نشز فطلبه فانحمل حيث
لم يره فرجع الى اهله فقال هل اتاكم خبر من قبل مكة قالوا نعم بلغنا ان
نبيا خرج بمكة فوقع في قلبه الاسلام فخرج متوجها الى مكة وقال
لاهله اني منطلق الى مكة فان كان محمد حقا لم اسبق اليه وان كان

مبطلا

الصفا وثن يقال له اساف وعلى المروة وثن يقال له نايلة فكان المشركون
يطوفون بينهما فلما كان الاسلام قال ناس لرسول الله صلى الله عليه
وسلم ان اهل الجاهلية كانوا يطوفون بين الصفا والمروة للوثنين
اللذين كانا عليهما وليسا من شعاير الله فنزلت هذه الاية ان الصفا
والمروة من شعاير الله فمن حج البيت او اعتمر فلا جناح عليه ان يطوف
بهما وفي رواية محمد بن داود عن عامر قال كان على الصفا وثن يقال له اساف
وعلى المروة وثن يقال له نايلة فكان اهل الجاهلية اذا طافوا بينهما
مسحوها فلما جاء الاسلام قال المسلمون ان اهل الجاهلية انما كانوا
يسعون بينهما من اجل هذين الصنمين قال فنزلت ان الصفا والمروة من
شعاير الله فمن حج البيت او اعتمر فلا جناح عليه ان يطوف بهما ومن
تطوع خيرا فان الله شاكر عليم قال فجعله تطوع خير ثنا زهير بن
جرير عن اشعث عن جعفر عن سعيد قال لما كان يوم فتح مكة جاءت
عجوز شمطا حبشية تخمش وجهها وتدعو بالويل قال فذكر
ذلك للنبي صلى الله عليه وسلم فقال تلك نايلة قد ايست ان تعبد في بلدكم
هذا ابدا ثنا احمد بن يونس نا يعقوب عن جعفر عن ابن ابزى قال لما
كسرت نايلة جاءت عجوز حبشية شمطا تخمش وجهها وتدعو
بالويل فقيل للنبي صلى الله عليه وسلم فقال تلك نايلة ايست ان تعبد
ببلدكم هذه ابدا قال ابن شبة وكان سَعْد صنما
لبني ملكان وقال الكلبي كانت صخرة بساحل جدة وكانت صخرة
طويلة ويقال كان لبني لهب فاقبل رجل منهم بابل له يطيفها بسعد
يرجو بركته فلما رات الابل ما عليه من الدما والذبايح نفرت وتفرقت
فلم تكد تجمع فرماه الكناني بحجر وقال

اتينا الى سعد ليجمع شملنا فشتتنا سعد فلا نحن من سعد
وهل سعد الا صخرة بتنوفة من الارض لا تدعو لغي ولا رشد

وكان للازد بالسراة صنم يقال له عايم وله يقول زيد الخيل

37

اراسافا وابن نايله * قد نعيا للسايله * كل الذي ينطق فيه القايله

ولا ساف يعول يشوب حازم الاسد

عليه الطير ما يدنون منه مقامات العوارك من اساف *

ولهما يقول عبد المطلب بن هاشم

ويلتقي رجال الاشعرين ركابهم بمفضى السيول من اساف ونايل *

وهما اليوم حجران بمكة قد نبتا في دار عباس بن عبد المطلب التي في
المسعا حدثنا عبد الوهاب بن عبد المجيد نا محمد بن عمرو عن ابي سلمة ويحيى
بن عبد الرحمن بن حاطب عن اسامة بن زيد بن حارثة عن ابيه قال خرج النبي صلى الله
عليه وسلم وهو مردفي الى نصب من الانصاب فذبحنا له شاة وجعلناها
في التور فلقينا زيد بن عمرو بن نفيل فابى ان ياكل منها وكان صنمان من نحاس
يقال لهما اساف ونايلة مستقبل الكعبة يتمسح بهما الناس اذا طافوا
مسنها
فقال النبي صلى الله عليه وسلم لا تمسهما ولا تمسح بهما فقلت في نفسي لا
حتى انظر ما يقول فمسستها فقال الم تنه عن هذا قال والذي اكرمه
ما مسستها حتى انزل عليه الكتاب وثنا ابو عاصم عن ابي يحيى عن عبيدة
موسى ثنا يعقوب بن زيد قال ومر النبي صلى الله عليه وسلم بقضيب يشير به
اليهما حتى اتى على اساف ونايلة فامر بهما فجعلا او طرحا ثم قال
قولوا قالوا يا رسول الله ما نقول قال قولوا صدق الله وعده ونصر
عبده وهزم الاحزاب وحده ثنا محمد بن حاتم ثنا يونس بن محمد ثنا
شيبان عن قتادة والرجز فاهجر قال هما صنمان كانا عند اساف
ونايلة يمسح وجوههما من اتى عليهما من المشركين فامر الله تعالى نبيه صلى
الله عليه وسلم ان يهجرهما ويجانبهما وثني عن سعيد بن جبير كان
اساف ونايلة رجلا وامراة فجرا في الكعبة فمسخا حجرين فاتخذا
صنمين يعبدان من دون الله فلما افتتح النبي صلى الله عليه وسلم مكة
امر بهما فكسرا وعن مطر قال عبد اساف ونايلة اربعين سنة
ثنا ابو حاتم انا هشيم انا داود بن ابي هند عن الشعبي قال كان على

الصفا

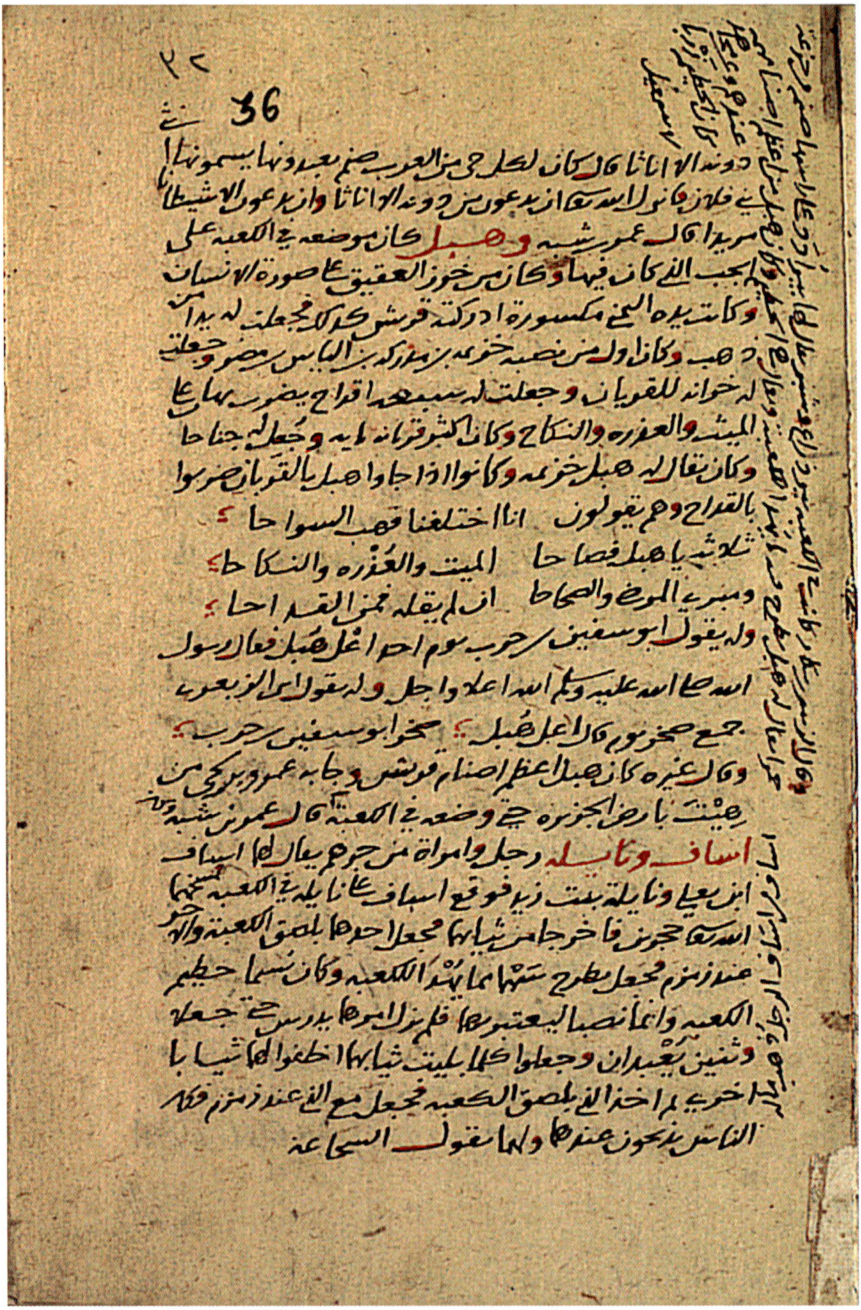

٢٢

36

دونه الا اناثا قال كان لكل حي من العرب صنم يعبدونها يسمونها انثى
بني فلان فانزل الله تعالى ان يدعون من دونه الا اناثا وان يدعون الا شيطانا
مريدا قال عمر بن شبه وهبل كان موضعه في الكعبة على
الجب الذي كان فيها وكان من خرز العقيق على صورة الانسان
وكانت يده اليمنى مكسورة ادركته قريش كذلك فجعلت له يدا من
ذهب وكان اول من نصبه خزيمة بن مدركة بن الياس بن مضر وجعلت
له خزانة للقربان وجعلت له سبعة اقداح يضربون بها على
الميت والعذرة والنكاح وكان اكثر قربانه ابله وجعل له جناحا
وكان يقال له هبل خزيمة وكانوا اذا جاؤا هبل بالقربان ضربوا
بالقداح وهم يقولون انا اختلفنا فهب السراحا
ثلاثة يا هبل فصاحا الميت والعذرة والنكاحا
والبرء في المرضى والصحاحا ان لم تقله فمر القداحا
وله يقول ابو سفين بن حرب يوم احد اعل هبل فقال رسول
الله صلى الله عليه وسلم الله اعلى واجل وله يقول ابن الزبعرى
جمع صخر من قال اعل هبل فخر ابو سفين بن حرب
وقال غيره كان هبل اعظم اصنام قريش وجاء به عمرو بن لحي من
هيت بارض الجزيرة حتى وضعه في الكعبة قال عمر بن شبة وكان
اساف ونايلة رجل وامراة من جرهم يقال له اساف
ابن يعلى ونايلة بنت زيد فوقع اساف على نايلة في الكعبة فمسخهما
الله تعالى حجرين فاخرجا من ثيابهما فجعل احدهما بلصق الكعبة والاخر
عند زمزم فجعل يطرح بينهما ما يهدى للكعبة وكان يسمى حطيم
الكعبة وانما نصبا ليعتبر بهما فلم يزل امرهما يدرس حتى جعلا
وثنين يعبدان وجعلوا كلما بليت ثيابهما اخلفوا لهما ثيابا
اخرى ثم اخذ الذي بلصق الكعبة فجعل مع الاخر عند زمزم فكان
الناس يذبحون عندهما ولهما يقول السجاعة

36a

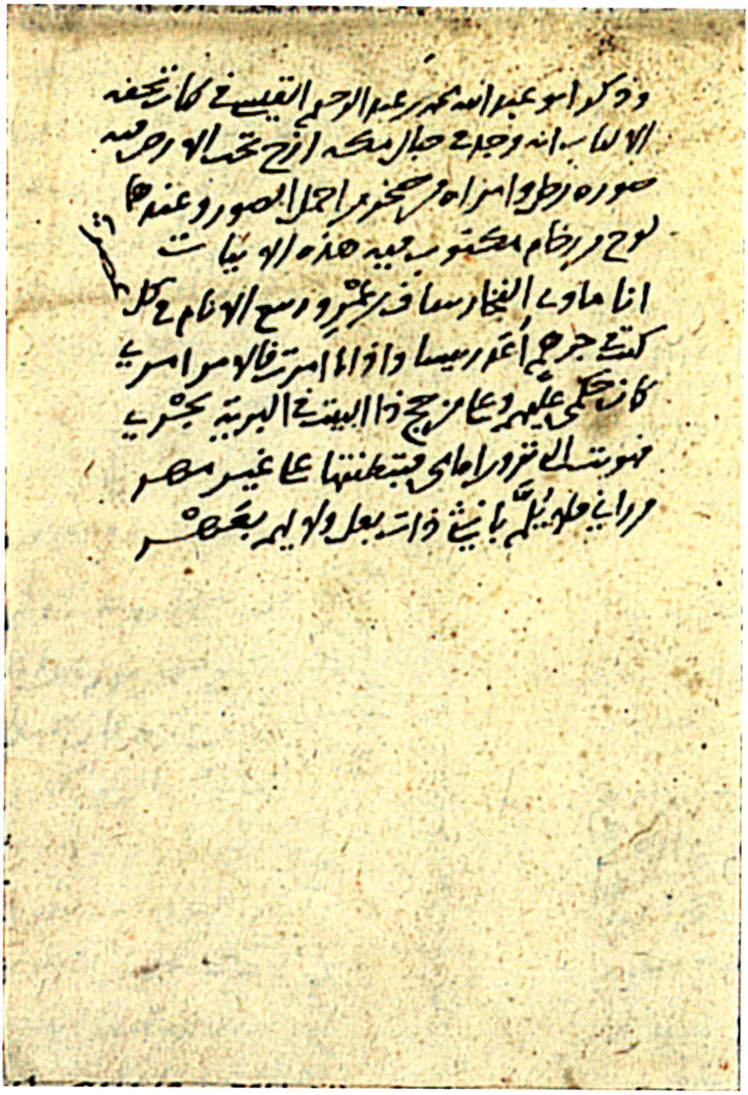
وذكر ابو عبد الله محمد بن عبد الرحيم القيسي في كتاب تحفة
الالباب انه وجد في جبال مكة ازج تحت الارض فيه
صورة رجل وامراة من حجر من اجمل الصور وعندها
لوح من رخام مكتوب عليه هذه الابيات
انا ماوي النجار سافرت عمرو وسع الانام في كل
كيتي جرجم اعمر ريسا واذا ما امرت فالامر امري
كان حكمي عليهم وعنا من حج ذا البيت في البرية يجري
فهو بين السرور واماي فيسطعنها عنا غير مصر
ورايت علو يلم بانيت ذات بعل ولو لم بعصر

35*a

يريش الله في الدنيا ويبري ولا يبري يعوق ولا يريش

قال عمر بن شبة وأجابت حمير عمرو بن لحي فدفع إلى الرجل من
ذي رعين يقال له معدي كرب نسرا فكان بموضع من أرض
سبا يقال له بلخع تعبده حمير ومن والاها فلم يزالوا يعبدونه
حتى هودهم ذو نواس ولم تزل هذه الأصنام تعبد حتى بعث الله تبارك
وتعالى محمدا صلى الله عليه وسلم وأمر بهدمها وبعث جرير بن عبد الله
البجلي إلى نسر فهدمه وفي هذه الخمسة الأصنام أنزل الله تعالى وقالوا
لا تذرن آلهتكم ولا تذرن ودا ولا سواعا ولا يغوث ويعوق ونسرا
وقد أضلوا كثيرا ولا تزد الظالمين إلا ضلالا وقال غيره لم تزل حمير
تعبد نسرا إلى أن انتقلت أيام تبع عن عبادة الأصنام إلى اليهودية
وفي نسر يقول رجل من آل ذي رعين في قتيل قتله رجل من بني
أود بن صعب سعد العشيرة

حلفت بالنسر لا أصالحكم ما اهتز في رأس أثلة ورق

وذكر ابن شبة عن قتادة في قوله تعالى ولا تذرن آلهتكم ولا تذرن ودا
ولا سواعا الآية قال كان ود لهذا الحي من كلب بدومة الجندل
وكان سواع لهذيل برهاط وكان يغوث لبني غطيف من مراد
بالجوف من سبا وكان يعوق لهمدان ببلخع وكان نسر لذي
الكلاع من حمير وكانت هذه الآلهة التي يعبدها هؤلاء في العجم قبل
قوم نوح والله أعلم أتشعرون عودا أو طينة أو حجرا عبدها
العرب بعد ذلك وعن عروة بن الزبير وذكر قوم نوح عليه
وقول بعضهم لبعض لا تذرن آلهتكم ولا تذرن ودا ولا سواعا
ولا يغوث ويعوق ونسرا قال كانت هذه في قوم نوح ثم
صارت في العرب وقال مجاهد كانت هذه الأصنام أسماء قوم
صالحين فماتوا فعبدهم قوم نوح واتخذوهم آلهة فدعاهم إلى تركها
فقالوا لا تذرن آلهتكم هذه الأسماء وعن الحسن في قوله تعالى إن يدعون

من دونه

وكان برهاط من ارض الحجاز فقال رجل من العرب يذكره

تراهم حول قبلتهم عكوفا كما عكفت هذيل على سواع

تظل جنابه صرعى لديه عتائر من ذخائر كل راع

وقال ابو خراش الهذلي يذكر سواعا

الم بن تبكر من عتر وخوف جنوح الآثمين على سواع

وله يقول راشد بن عبد ربه السلمي ونظر الى ثعلبين وهما يبولان عليه

ارب يبول الثعلبان براسه لقد ذل من بالت عليه الثعالب

قال واجابت مذحج عمرو بن لحي فدفع الى انعم بن عمرو المرادي

يغوث فكان باكمة باليمن يقال لها مذحج تعبده مذحج ومن

والاها وقال غيره ان عمرو بن لحي دفع يغوث الى الاعلم وهو انعم

بن عمرو والى اعلى بن عمرو وكانت مذحج ومن والاها تعبده فارادت

ناجية من مراد اخذه منهم فهربوا به الى الحصين بن ... الحارث

فوجبت بهم واكرمهم وزوج صاحبه ابنته بغير مهر وساقها

اليه وهو رجل من اهله وفيه قيل

وسار بنا يغوث الى مراد فناجزناهم قبل الصباح

وقال ابن اسحق وانعم من طي واهل جرش من مذحج اتخذوا يغوث

بجرش قال ابو زيد واجابت همدان فدفع عمرو بن لحي الى مالك

ابن مرثد بن جشم بن حاشد بن جشم بن خيوان بن نوف بن همدان

يعوق فكان بقرية يقال لها خيوان تعبده همدان

ومن والاها من اهل اليمن وقال غيره خيوان من صنعا على

ليلتين مما يلي مكة وفي يعوق يقول مالك الارحبي لنعم

في شان قتيل كان منهم

فوكد لنهم اقصى بانهم جار بكل الطريق

يا قومنا لا تعتدوا بيننا وبينكم يعوق

وقال مالك بن نمط الهمداني

ثم قالت يا جامعا جامع الاحشاء والكبد يا ليت امك لم تولد ولم تلد ∴
ثم اكبت عليه فشهقت شهقة فماتت وقال ايضا يومئذ حسان بن
مصاد ابن عم الاكيدر وكان كلاب بن حارثة نصف ودا يقول كان
على صورة رجل كاعظم ما يكون من الرجال متزر بحلة متردّ
باخرى عليه سيف متقلده وقد تنكب قوسا وبين يديه حربة
فيها لواء وكنانة فيها سهام وفي ود يقول الحطيئة العبسي
فحياك ودّ اما هداك لفتية وركب باعلى ذي غوانة مجمر ∴
وله يقول النابغة الذبياني
حياك ودّ فانا لا يحل لنا لهو النساء وان الدين قد عزما ∴ قال
حدثنا محمد بن حاتم ثنا يونس بن محمد ثنا يعقوب القمي ثنا ابو المطهر عن ابي
جعفر محمد بن علي انهم ذكروا عنده وهو قائم يصلي يزيد بن المهلب
فلما انفتل من صلاته قال ذكرتم يزيد بن المهلب اما انه قتل في اول
ارض عبد فيها غير الله ثم ذكر ودا فقال كان ود رجلا مسلما
كان محببا في قومه فلما مات عسكروا حول قبره وجزعوا عليه فلما
راى ابليس جزعهم عليه تشبه في صورة انسان فقال اري
جزعكم على هذا فهل لكم ان اصور لكم مثله فيكون في ناديكم فتذكرونه
به قالوا نعم قال فصور لهم مثله فوضعوه في ناديهم وجعلوا يذكرونه
فلما راى ما بهم من ذكره قال هل لكم ان اجعل في منزل كل رجل
منكم تمثالا مثله فيكون في بيته فتذكرونه قالوا نعم قال فمثل لكل
اهل بيت تمثالا مثله فجعلوا يذكرونه وادرك ابناؤهم فجعلوا
يرون ما يصنعون وتناسلوا ودرس امر ذكرهم اياه حتى اتخذوه
الها من دون الله اولاد اولادهم فكان اول ما عبد غير الله في
الارض ود قال ابو زيد واجابت عمرو بن لحي هذيل بن مدركة
فدفع الى رجل منهم يقال له الحرث بن تميم بن سعد بن هذيل سواعا
فكانت هذيل وكنانة وشكير وسعد بكر وسافلة قيس يعبدونه

وكان

34b

34

فاحتمل الماء الاصنام حتى القاها الى جدة فنضب الماء عنها وانكشفت فلم تزل
مدفونة حتى استخرجها ابليس لمشركي العرب فدعاهم اليها فاجابوه
فاخذت قضاعة ودا فعبدوه في دومة الجندل ثم توارثوه حتى
صار الى كلب فعبدوه حتى جاء الاسلام واخذت اعلى وانعم
ابنا عمرو من طي يغوث وكان لكهلان يعوق ثم توارثه بنوها
حتى صار الى همدان وكان لبني معد بن عدنان سواع حتى صار
لهذيل وكان لحمير نسر وذكر ابو زيد عمر بن شبة ان عمرو بن لحي
قال له رئيه يوما اجب ابا ثمامة فقال له لبيك من تهامة
فقال له ارحل بلا ملامة قال جير ولا اقامة قال ائت ضف
جدة تجد فيها اصناما معدة فاوردها ارض تهامة ولا تهب
ثم ادع العرب الى عبادتها تجب فاتى شط جدة فاستثارها
ثم حملها حتى وردها تهامة وحضر الحج فدعا العرب
الى عبادتها فاجابه عوف بن كنانة بن عوف بن عذرة بن زيد
فدفع اليه ودا فحمله فكان بدومة الجندل وسمى ابنه عبد
ود فهو اول عربي سمي عبد ود ثم سميت العرب بعده وجعل
عوف ابنه عامرا الذي يقال له عامر الاجدار سادنا له فلم تزل
بنوه يسدنونه حتى جاء الله بالاسلام فكان مالك بن حارثة
الاجداري يذكر انه راه وقال كان ابي يبعثني اليه باللبن فيقول اسقه
الهك فاشربه قال ثم رايت خالد بن الوليد بعد كسره اجذاذا
وكان النبي صلى الله عليه وسلم وجهه لهدمه من غزوة تبوك فحالت بينه وبين
هدمه بنو عبد ود وبنو عامر الاجدار فقاتلهم فقتلهم فكسره فقتل
يومئذ رجل من بني عبد ود يقال له قطن بن شريح فاقبلت امه وهو
مقتول فقالت

الا تلك المودة لا تدوم ولا يبقى على الدهر النعيم
ولا يبقى على الحدثان غفر بشاهقة له ام رؤوم

34a

ان هولا يفخرون عليكم ويزعمون انهم بنو ادم دونكم فهل يسركم ان
اجعل لكم شبه ادم فتاتونه كل وقت فتطوفون به فقالوا
وددنا ذلك فنحت لهم خمسة اصنام وهي ود وسواع ويغوث
ويعوق ونسر فعبدوها وما زالوا على عبادتها حتى بعث الله تعالى
نوحا فنهاهم عن عبادتها فابوا عليه تركها فلما كان الطوفان
جعل الموج يدفعها بشدة جريته الماء حتى قذفها الى البحر جدة فلما
نضب ما الطوفان انكشفت ويقال ان ودا وسواعا ويغوث
ويعوق ونسرا كانوا قوما صالحين ماتوا جميعا في شهر فجزع
عليهم ذوو اقربائهم فاتاهم رجل من بني قابيل بن ادم يقال له الرجال
فقال لهم وقد اشتد حزنهم يا قوم قد علمتم اني اتقن الناس صنعة
فهل لكم ان اعمل مثل صورهم لا تنكرون منهم قليلا ولا كثيرا غير
ان لا اقدر ان انفخ فيهم الروح فقالوا نعم فنحت لهم الاصنام الخمسة على
صورهم وذلك على عهد يرد بن مهلائيل بن قينان بن انوش بن
شيث بن ادم فكان الرجل منهم يجي فاذا نظر الى الاصنام ذكر
عمه وابن عمه كانهم هم فيستغفر لصاحبه ويترحم عليه حتى
هلك ذلك القرن ثم جا قرن بعدهم فعظموا تلك الاصنام اشد
تعظيما من القرن الاول ثم جا القرن الثالث فقالوا ما عظم اولينا
هولا الا وهم يرجون شفاعتهم عند الله فعبدوهم وبالغوا في
تعظيمهم وصار الامر يزداد عظما حتى اعتقدوا انها تشفع وتضر
فلما بعث الله اليهم اخنوخ وهو ادريس بن يرد بن مهلائيل نبيا دعاهم
الى عبادة الله ورفض الاصنام فابوا ذلك فرفعه الله اليه ولم
يزد ذلك الامر الا عظما حتى ادرك نوح وبينه وبين ادم عشرة
اجيال فبعثه الله اليهم رسولا وهو ابن اربع مائة وثمانين سنة
فدعاهم في نبوته مائة وعشرين سنة ثم امره الله ان يصنع الفلك
وحمل فيها من امره فركب معه ثمانون نفسا وارسل الله الطوفان

فاحتمل

33

تعظيم البيت والطواف به والحج والعمرة والوقوف على عرفة والمزدلفة
وهدي البدن والإهلال بالحج والعمرة مع إدخالهم فيه ما ليس منه
فكانت كنانة وقريش إذا أهلوا قالوا لبيك اللهم لبيك لبيك لا شريك
لك إلا شريك هو لك تملكه وما ملك فيوحدونه بالتلبية ثم
يدخلون معه أصنامهم ويجعلون ملكها بيده يقول الله تبارك
وتعالى لمحمد صلى الله عليه وسلم وما يؤمن أكثرهم بالله إلا وهم مشركون
أي ما يوحدونني بمعرفة حقي إلا جعلوا معي شريكا من خلقي
وذكر ابن هشام أن إسمعيل عليه السلام لما سكن مكة وولد له بها أولاد وكثروا
بها حتى ملؤوها وأجلوا من كان بها من العماليق ضاقت عليهم مكة
فانتشروا في البلاد وكان سبب عبادتهم الأوثان والحجارة أنه كان لا
يظعن من مكة ظاعن إلا احتمل معه حجرا من حجارة الحرم معظما له
ويقال إن آدم عليه السلام لما مات افترق أولاده فرقتين فرقة
تمسكت بالدين والصلاح وفرقة مالت إلى المعاصي والفساد
فاعتزل أهل الصلاح وصعدوا الجبل [illegible] مغارة هناك وأقام
أهل الفساد في الأرض فكانوا يستغوون من نزل إليهم من
أهل الجبل هذا وقد اشتغلوا على تابوت آدم فصور لهم الشيطان
صورة آدم ليتخذوها بدلا من تابوته فعظموها دهرا طويلا
حتى جاء بعدهم من غلا في تعظيمها حتى رأى عبادتها دينا فعبدها
وصارت صنما وعمل مثلها عدة أصنام ويقال إن آدم لما
بالهند على الجبل الذي أهبط عليه فكانوا يطوفون بقبره تبركا به
ثم افترقوا في الديانة فأوحى الله تعالى إلى [illegible] خنوخ بن يرد
بن مهلاييل بن قينان بن أنوش بن شيث بن آدم أن لا يطوف بقبر
آدم كافر وأن يحول بينهم وبينه فلا يصلون إليه وأن يخلي
بين المؤمنين وبين قبره فكان المؤمنون من ولد آدم يطوفون
بقبره كلما أرادوا ومنعوا أهل الكفران من ذلك واشتد
ذلك عليهم وحزنوا لمفارقته فلما رأى إبليس ذلك منهم قال لهم

33a

حدثني بعض اهل العلم ان عمرو بن لحي خرج من مكة الى الشام في
بعض اموره فلما قدم مآب من ارض البلقاء وبها يوميذ العماليق وهم
ولد عملاق ويقال عمليق بن لاوذ بن سام بن نوح راهم يعبدون
الاصنام فقال لهم ما هذه الاصنام التي اراكم تعبدون قالوا له
هذه اصنام نعبدها فنستمطرها فتمطرنا ونستنصرها
فتنصرنا فقال لهم افلا تعطوني منها صنما فاسير به الى ارض
العرب فيعبدونه فاعطوه صنما يقال له هبل فقدم به مكة
فنصبه وامر الناس بعبادته وتعظيمه انتهى وكان عمرو بن لحي
حين غلبت خزاعة على البيت ونفت جرهم عن مكة قد جعلته العرب
ربا لا يبتدع بدعة الا اتخذوها شرعة لانه كان يطعم الناس
ويكسو في الموسم فربما نحر في الموسم عشرة الاف بدنة وكسا عشرة
الاف حلة وبلغ من وكان يلت السويق للحاج على صخرة معروفة
تسمى صخرة اللات وكان الذي يلت من ثقيف فلما مات قال لهم
عمرو بن لحي انه لم يمت ولكن دخل في الصخرة ثم امرهم بعبادتها
وان يبنوا عليها بيتا يسمى اللات فدام امره وامر بنيه على هذا
بمكة ثلاثماية سنة فلما هلك عمرو سميت تلك الصخرة اللات
مخففة التا واتخذت صنما وقال ابن اسحق وزعموا ان اول ما
كانت عبادة الحجارة في بني اسمعيل انه كان لا يظعن من مكة
ظاعن منهم حين ضاقت عليهم والتمسوا الفسيح في البلاد الا حمل
معه حجرا من حجارة الحرم تعظيما للحرم فحيثما نزلوا وضعوه
فطافوا به كطوافهم بالكعبة حتى سلخ ذلك بهم الى ان كانوا
يعبدون ما استحسنوا من الحجارة واعجبهم حتى خلف الخلوف
ونسوا ما كانوا عليه واستبدلوا بدين ابرهيم واسمعيل غيره
فعبدوا الاوثان وصاروا الى ما كانت عليه الامم قبلهم من الضلالات
وفيهم على ذلك بقايا من عهد ابرهيم عليه السلام يتمسكون بها من

فهو اول من غير دين ابرهيم واسمعيل واول من بحر البحيرة وسيب السائبة واول من نصب وثنا بعد جرهم ويقال انه الذي استخرج اساف ونايلة ونصبها

تعظيم

32b

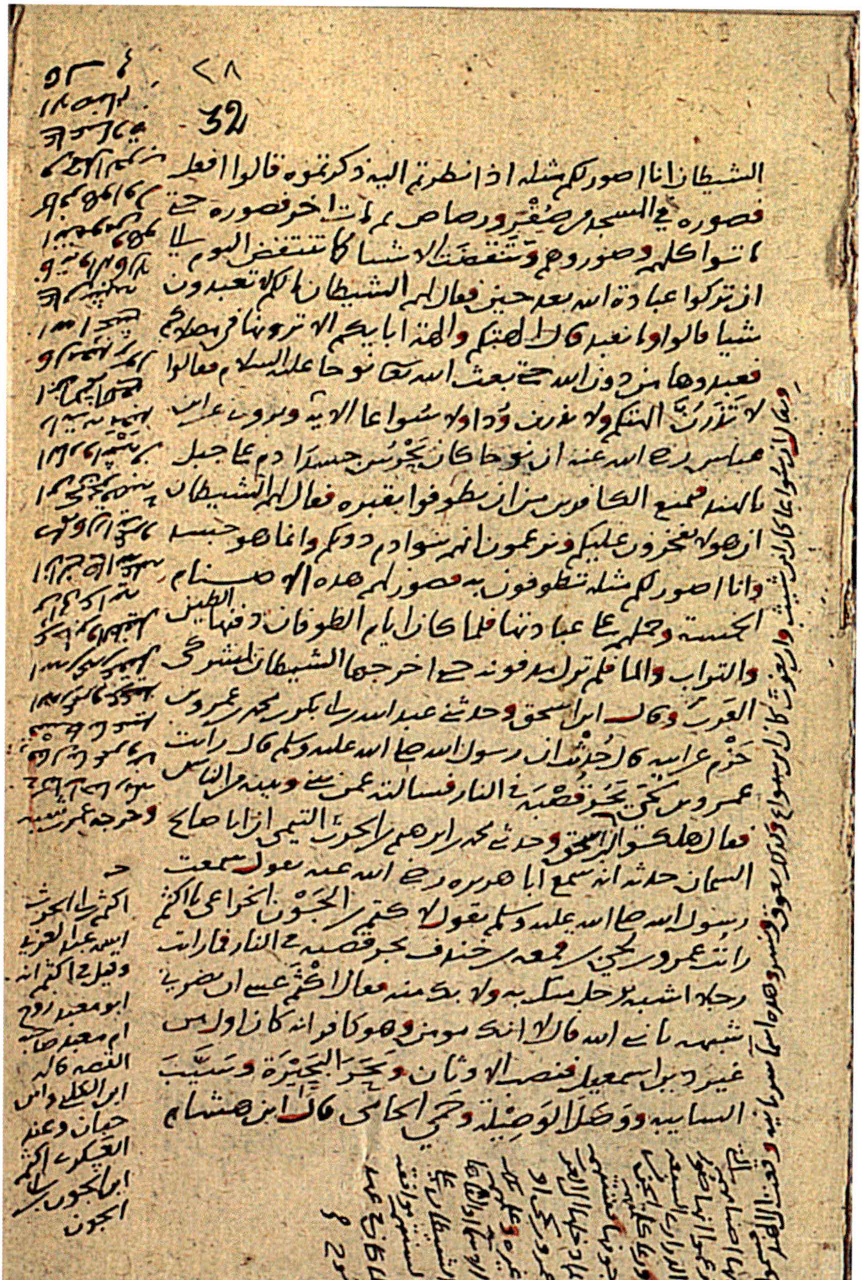
٢٨
32

الشيطان انا اصور لكم مثله اذا نظرتم اليه ذكرتموه قالوا افعل
فصوره في المسجد من صفر ورصاص ثم جاء اخر فصوره حتى
اتوا كلهم فصوروهم وتنقصت الاشيا كما تنتقص اليوم الى
ان تركوا عبادة الله بعد حين فقال لهم الشيطان ما لكم لا تعبدون
شيا قالوا وما نعبد قال الهتكم والهة ابايكم الا ترونها في مصلاكم
فعبدوها من دون الله حتى بعث الله تعالى نوحا عليه السلام فقالوا
لا تذرن الهتكم ولا تذرن ودا ولا سواعا الاية وروي عن ابن
عباس رضي الله عنه ان نوحا كان يحرس جسد ادم على جبل
بالهند فيمنع الكافرين من ان يطوفوا بقبره فقال لهم الشيطان
ان هولا يفخرون عليكم ويزعمون انهم بنو ادم دونكم وانما هو جسد
وانا اصور لكم مثله تطوفون به فصور لهم هذه الاصنام
الخمسة وحملهم على عبادتها فلما كان ايام الطوفان دفنها الطين
والتراب والما فلم تزل مدفونة حتى اخرجها الشيطان لمشركي
العرب وقال ابن اسحق وحدثني عبد الله بن ابي بكر بن محمد بن عمرو بن
حزم عن ابيه قال حدثت ان رسول الله صلى الله عليه وسلم قال رايت
عمرو بن لحي يجر قصبه في النار فسالته عمن بيني وبينه من الناس
فقال هلكوا قال ابن اسحق وحدثني محمد بن ابرهيم بن الحرث التيمي ان ابا صالح
السمان حدثه انه سمع ابا هريرة رضي الله عنه يقول سمعت
رسول الله صلى الله عليه وسلم يقول لاكثم بن الجون الخزاعي يا اكثم
رايت عمرو بن لحي بن قمعة بن خندف يجر قصبه في النار فما رايت
رجلا اشبه برجل منك به ولا بك منه فقال اكثم عسى ان يضرني
شبهه يا نبي الله قال لا انك مومن وهو كافر انه كان اول من
غير دين اسمعيل فنصب الاوثان وبحر البحيرة وسيب
السايبة ووصل الوصيلة وحمى الحامي قال ابن هشام

حـ
اكثم بن الجون
ابيه عبد العزى
وقيل في اكثم انه
ابو معبد زوج
ام معبد صاحب
القصة قاله
ابن الكلبي وابن
حبان وعند
العسكري اكثم
ابن الجون بن ابي
الجون

32a

حديث رايت عمرو بن لحي يجر قصبه في النار خرجه
البخاري ومسلم من طريق صالح بن كيسان عن ابن شهاب
قال سمعت سعيد بن المسيب يقول البحيرة التي يمنع درها
للطواغيت فلا يحلبها احد من الناس والسايبة التي
كانوا يسيبونها لالهتهم فلا يحمل عليها شيء قال ابن المسيب
وقال ابو هريرة قال رسول الله صلى الله عليه وسلم رايت
عمرو بن عامر الخزاعي يجر قصبه في النار وكان اول من
سيب السوايب زاد البخاري بعد هذا والوصيلة
الناقة البكر تبكر في اول نتاج الابل ثم تثني بعد بانثى
وكانوا يسيبونها لطواغيتهم ان وصلت احداهما
بالاخرى ليس بينهما ذكر والحام فحل الابل يضرب الضراب
المعدود فاذا قضى ضرابه ودعوه للطواغيت واعفوه
من الحمل فلم يحمل عليه شيء وسموه الحامي رواه ابن الهاد عن
ابن شهاب عن سعيد عن ابي هريرة سمعت النبي صلى الله عليه
وسلم وقال لنا ابو اليمان انا شعيب عن الزهري سمعت
سعيدا قال البحيرة بهذا قال وقال ابو هريرة سمعت
النبي صلى الله عليه وسلم نحوه وخرج ابو زيد عمر بن
شبة في كتاب اخبار مكة حدثنا عبيد الله بن عمرو عن

31**b

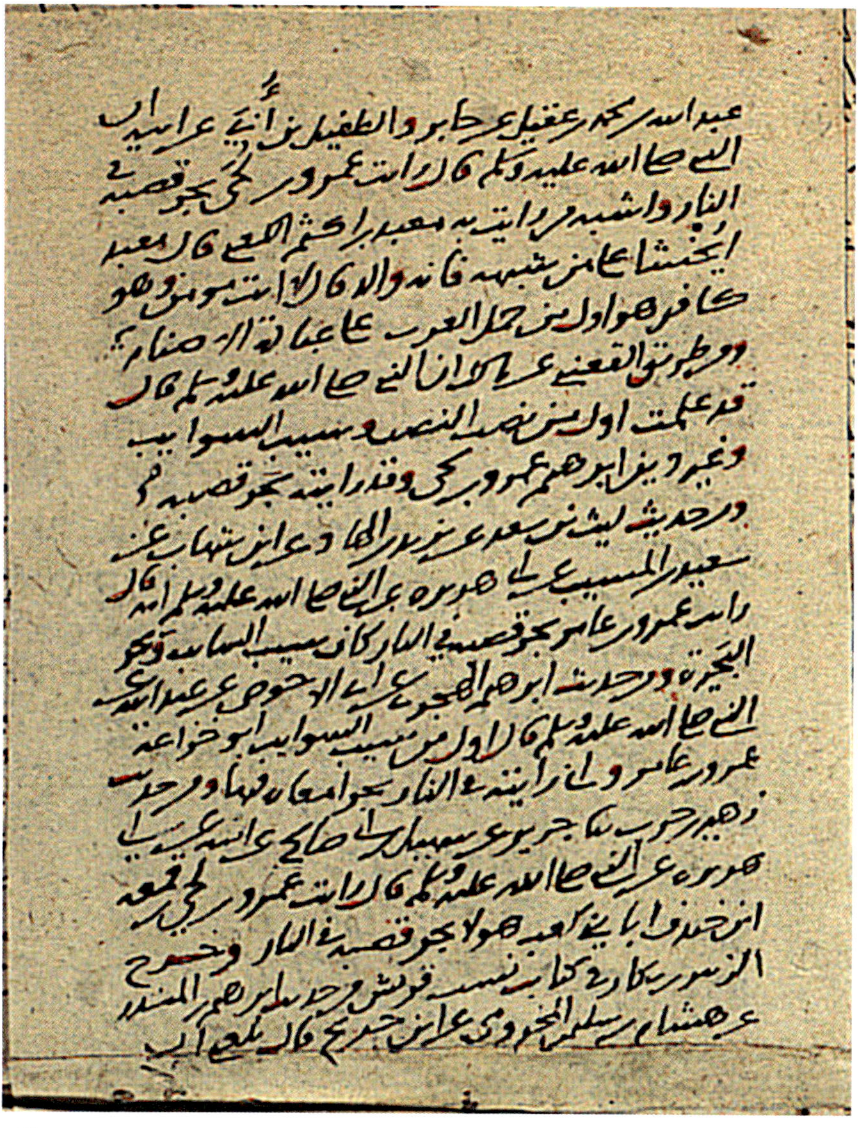

عبد الله بن محمد بن عقيل عن جابر و الطفيل بن أبي عن ابيه ان
النبي صلى الله عليه وسلم قال رايت عمرو بن لحي يجر قصبه في
النار واشبه من رايت به معبد بن اكثم الكعبي قال معبد
ايخشى علي من شبهه فانه والد قال لا انت مومن وهو
كافر هو اول من حمل العرب على عبادة الاصنام
ومن طريق القعنبي عن ... ان النبي صلى الله عليه وسلم قال
قد علمت اول من نصب النصب وسيب السوايب
وغير دين ابرهيم عمرو بن لحي وقد رايته يجر قصبه في
ومن حديث ليث بن سعد عن يزيد بن الهاد عن ابن شهاب عن
سعيد بن المسيب عن ابي هريره عن النبي صلى الله عليه وسلم انه قال
رايت عمرو بن عامر يجر قصبه في النار كان سيب السايبه وبحر
البحيره ومن حديث ابرهيم الهجري عن ابي الاحوص عن عبد الله عن
النبي صلى الله عليه وسلم قال اول من سيب السوايب ابو خزاعة
عمرو بن عامر واني رايته في النار يجر امعاه فيها ومن حديث
زهير بن حرب نا جرير عن سهيل بن ابي صالح عن ابيه عن ابي
هريره عن النبي صلى الله عليه وسلم قال رايت عمرو بن لحي بن قمعه
ابن خندف ابا بني كعب هولا يجر قصبه في النار وخرج
الزبير بن بكار في كتاب نسب قريش من حديث ابرهيم بن المنذر
عن هشام بن سليمان المخزومي عن ابن جريج قال بلغني ان

31**a

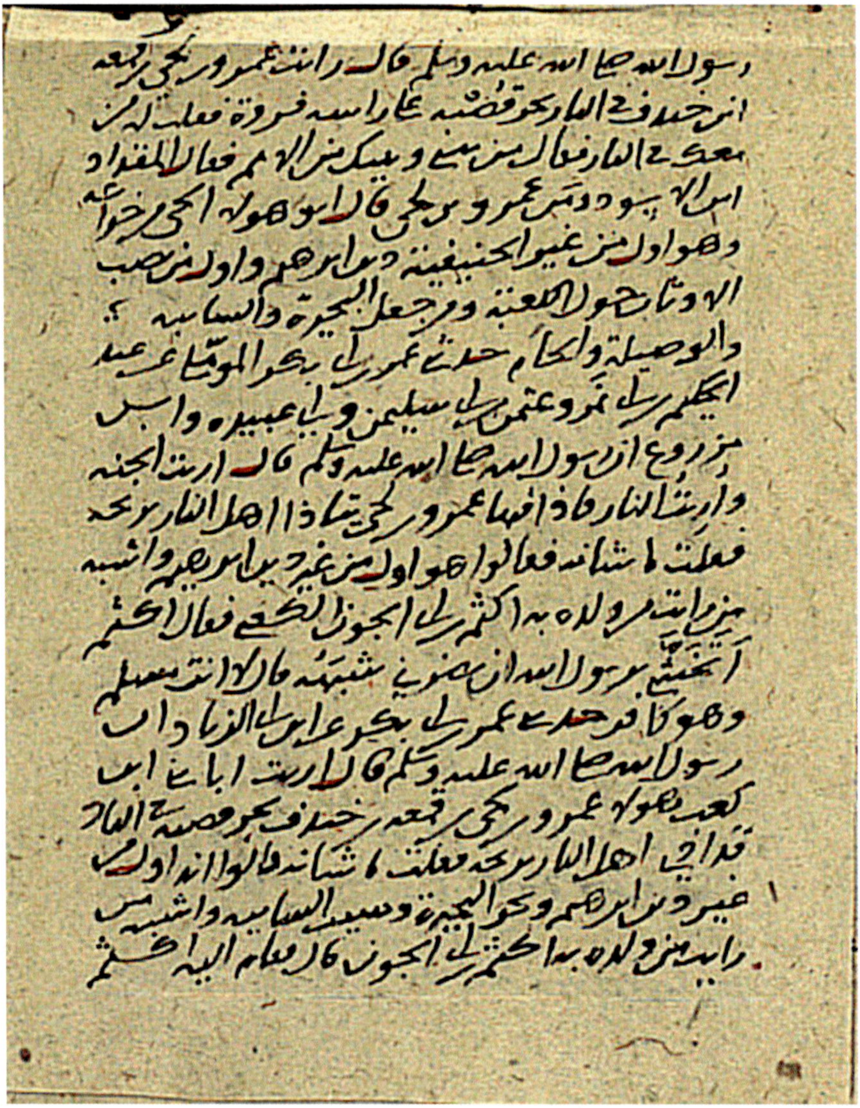

رسول الله صلى الله عليه وسلم قال رايت عمرو بن لحي بن قمعة
ابن خندف في النار يجر قصبه على راسه فروة فقلت له من
معك في النار فقال من بيني وبينك من الامم فقال المقداد
ابن الاسود ومن عمرو بن لحي قال ابو هو ليه الحي خزاعة
وهو اول من غير الحنيفية دين ابرهيم واول من نصب
الاوثان حول الكعبة ومن جعل البحيرة والسايبة
والوصيلة والحام حدثنا عمرو بن بحر المومل عن عبد
الحكم بن عمرو عثمن بن سليمن وابا عبيدة وابن
هرمز رووا ان رسول الله صلى الله عليه وسلم قال اريت الجنة
واريت النار فاذا فيها عمرو بن لحي بينا ذا اهل النار ريحه
فقلت ما شانه فقالوا هو اول من غير دين ابرهيم واشبه
من رايت من ولده به اكثم بن الجون الكعبي فقال اكثم
أتخشى يا رسول الله ان يضرني شبهه قال لا انت مسلم
وهو كافر حدثنا عمرو بن بحر عن ابن الزناد ان
رسول الله صلى الله عليه وسلم قال رايت ابا بني
كعب هؤلا عمرو بن لحي بن قمعة بن خندف يجر قصبه في النار
قد اذى اهل النار ريحه فقلت ما شانه قالوا انه اول من
غير دين ابرهيم وبحر البحيرة وسيب السايبة واشبه من
رايته منهم لده به اكثم بن الجون قال فقام اليه اكثم

31*b

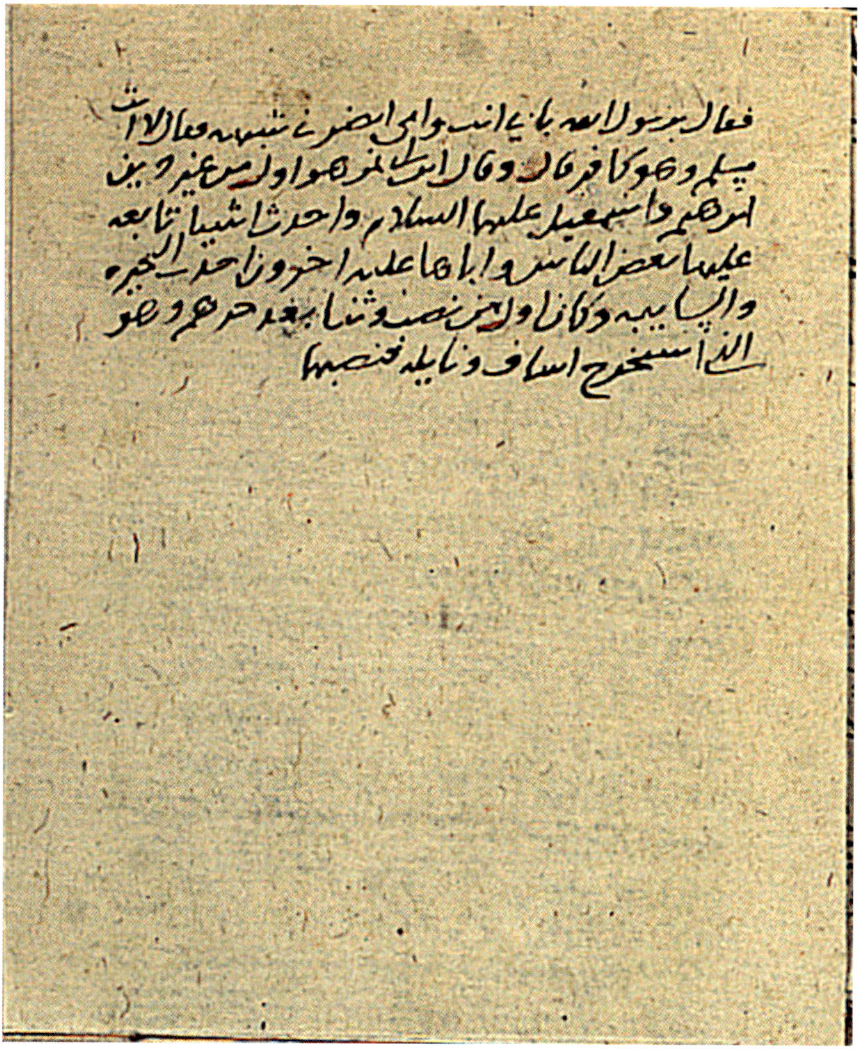

فقال يا رسول الله بابي انت وامي ايضرني شبهه فقال لا انت
مسلم وهو كافر قال وقال ابن الكلبي هو اول من غير دين
ابرهيم واسمعيل عليهما السلام واحدث اشيا تابعه
عليها بعض الناس واباها عليه اخرون احدث البحيرة
والسايبة وكان اول من نصب وثنا بعد جرهم وهو
الذي استخرج اساف ونايلة فنصبها

31*a

كانت بمنف على أسماء السبعة السيارة ولم يزل هذا البيت إلى حين منف
حتى قطعه الأمير شيخو العمري في أعوام بضع وخمسين وسبعمائة ومنه
استكمل باب خانكاه شيخو بخط صليبة جامع ابن طولون ظاهر
القاهرة المعزية وقد زعم قوم أن أول من عبد الأصنام قوم
نوح عليه السلام وفيه نظر لأن الأصنام كانت قبل زمن نوح بدهر
وخرج البخاري من حديث هشام عن ابن جريج وقال عطاء عن ابن
عباس رضي الله عنه صارت الأوثان التي كانت في قوم نوح في العرب
أما ود كانت لكلب بدومة الجندل وأما سواع فكانت لهذيل
وأما يغوث فكانت لمراد ثم لبني غطيف بالجوف عند سبا وأما يعوق
فكانت لهمدان وأما نسر فكانت لحمير لآل ذي الكلاع أسماء رجال
صالحين من قوم نوح فلما هلكوا أوحى الشيطان إلى قومهم أن انصبوا
إلى مجالسهم التي كانوا يجلسون أنصابا وسموها بأسمائهم ففعلوا فلم
تعبد فلما هلك أولئك ونسخ العلم عبدت وحكى أبو جعفر محمد بن جرير
الطبري أن ودا وسواع ويغوث ويعوق ونسرا نفرا من بني آدم
غير أنه قوم نوح التي كانوا يعبدونها وأنهم كانوا قوما صالحين فيما
بين آدم ونوح وكان لهم أتباع يقتدون بهم فلما ماتوا قال أصحابهم الذين
كانوا يقتدون بهم لو صورناهم كان أشوق لنا إلى العبادة إذا ذكرناهم
فصوروهم فلما ماتوا وجاء آخرون دب إليهم إبليس فقال إنما كانوا
يعبدونهم وبهم يستسقون المطر فعبدوهم فابتدأ عبادة الأوثان من
ذلك الوقت وحكى أن هذه الخمسة هي أسماء أصنام قوم نوح وعن
الثعلبي أن جماعة وروي عن عروة بن الزبير وغيره قال
اشتكى آدم عليه السلام وعنده بنوه ود وسواع ويغوث
ويعوق ونسر وكان ود أكبرهم وأبرهم به
وعن محمد بن كعب كان لآدم خمس بنين ود وسواع ويغوث
ويعوق ونسر وكانوا عبادا فمات رجل منهم فحزنوا عليه فقال

الشيطان

31b

ولده فاستولى على يد هشام بن عبد الملك بن مروان فسماه عبد العزيز واليه
ينسب البرامكة وخرب هذا الهيكل قتيبة بن الهيثم السلمي سنة
احدى واربعين في اول خلافة معوية بن ابي سفين وكان بناء عظيما 31
حوله اروقة وبلا غاية وستون مقصورة بن سبع سكني سدنته
وقومته ويقال ان غمدان بصنعا بناه الضحاك المعروف
بالازدهاق على اسم الزهرة ثم سكنه الملوك من حمير الى ان خربته
الحبشة ثم خرب ما بقي منه امير المومنين عثمن بن عفان رضي الله عنه
وكان في الجبل الفاصل بين جزيرة الاندلس وبين الارض الكبيرة
هيكل الزهرة يقال له كلا وبطره وكان بفرغانة بيت
يقال له كاوسان بناه احد ملوك الطبقة الاولى من الفرس على
اسم الشمس خربه امير المومنين ابو اسحق المعتصم وزعموا ان الكعبة
بيت زحل وان ادريس عليه السلام نص عليه ووصى ان يحج اليه
ويقال ان موضع جامع بني امية بدمشق هو بيت المشتري
بناه جيرون بن سعد بن عاد وان بيت المريخ بمدينة صور من الساحل
الشامي وان عين شمس خارج القاهرة المعزية من ارض مصر كان
هيكل الشمس بناه اوشهنج اول ملوك الطبقة الاولى من الفرس
على اسم الشمس وقيل بناه غيره وان بيت الزهرة بمدينة منبج
وبيت عطارد بمدينة صيدا من الساحل الشامي وبيت القمر
هو قلعة مدينة حران يقال له المدور وما زال عامرا الى ان خربه
الططر في اعوام بضع وستين وسبع مائة عند تغلبهم على العراق
والشام وكان بمدينة منف التي يقال لها مدينة فرعون من ارض
مصر البيت الاخضر وهو حجر مانع لا يعمل فيه الحديد الا بجهد
كان قطعة واحدة قد نقش فيه صور وكتابة وعلى وجه بابه
صور حيات قد نشرت صدورها لو اجتمع الالوف من الناس لما قدروا
ان يحركوه لعظمه وثقله يقال انه بيت القمر وانه احد بيوت سبعة

ويقال ان خربه الفضل
ابن يحيى بن خالد
بن برمك لما دخل
بلخ وبناه مسجدا

31a

ابرهيم عليه السلام واثبت ان فوق الشمس قوة قاهرة للكل وكان
وشيانه وشابهم ما تقدم ذكره وكان القوم يتقربون الى الهياكل
تقربا الى الروحانيين لتقربهم الى البارى تعالى لاعتقادهم ان
الهياكل ابدان الروحانيين كانوا ومن يتقرب الى شخص فقد
تقرب الى روحه فلما اصلوا هذا الاعتقاد بنوا اثنى عشر
هيكلا وهي هيكل العلة الاولى وهيكل العقل
وهيكل السياسة وهيكل الصورة وهيكل النفس
وكانت هذه الهياكل الخمسة كلها مستديرة وهيكل
زحل وهو مسدس وهيكل المشترى وهو مثلث
وهيكل المريخ وهو مربع وهيكل الشمس وهو مربع ايضا
وهيكل الزهرة وهو مثلث مستطيل في جوف مربع
وهيكل عطارد وهو مثلث في جوف مربع مستطيل
وهيكل القمر وهو مثمن وكانت اصنامهم في هذه الهياكل
ولها صلوات يصلونها لكل كوكب من السبعة يوم مخصوص
يزعمون انه رب في ذلك اليوم وتكون صلاتهم في ذلك اليوم ثلث مرات
عند طلوع الشمس وعند زوالها وعند غروبها فيصلون لزحل
يوم السبت ويصلون للمشترى يوم الاحد ويصلون للمريخ يوم
الاثنين ويصلون للشمس يوم الثلثا ويصلون للزهرة يوم
الاربعا ويصلون لعطارد يوم الخميس ويصلون للقمر يوم الجمعة
وزعموا ان الكعبة البيت الحرام هيكل زحل وهذا الكلام
تقادم عليه الدهور وكثر القصود له من شان زحل الثبات
وكان ببلخ نوبهار بناه منوشجهر احد ملوك الطبقة
الاولى من الفرس على اسم القمر ليضاهي به الكعبة وجعل حوله الاصنام
والبسوه الحرير الى ان دانت الفرس بالمجوسية فعملوه بيت نار
وقيل ... وكانت ملوك الفرس من الاكاسرة والاشكانية وملوك ...

في اخبار ابرهيم عليه السلام

وعظموه وحجوا اليه من الافاق ... العرب ... الكعبة

خالد

30b

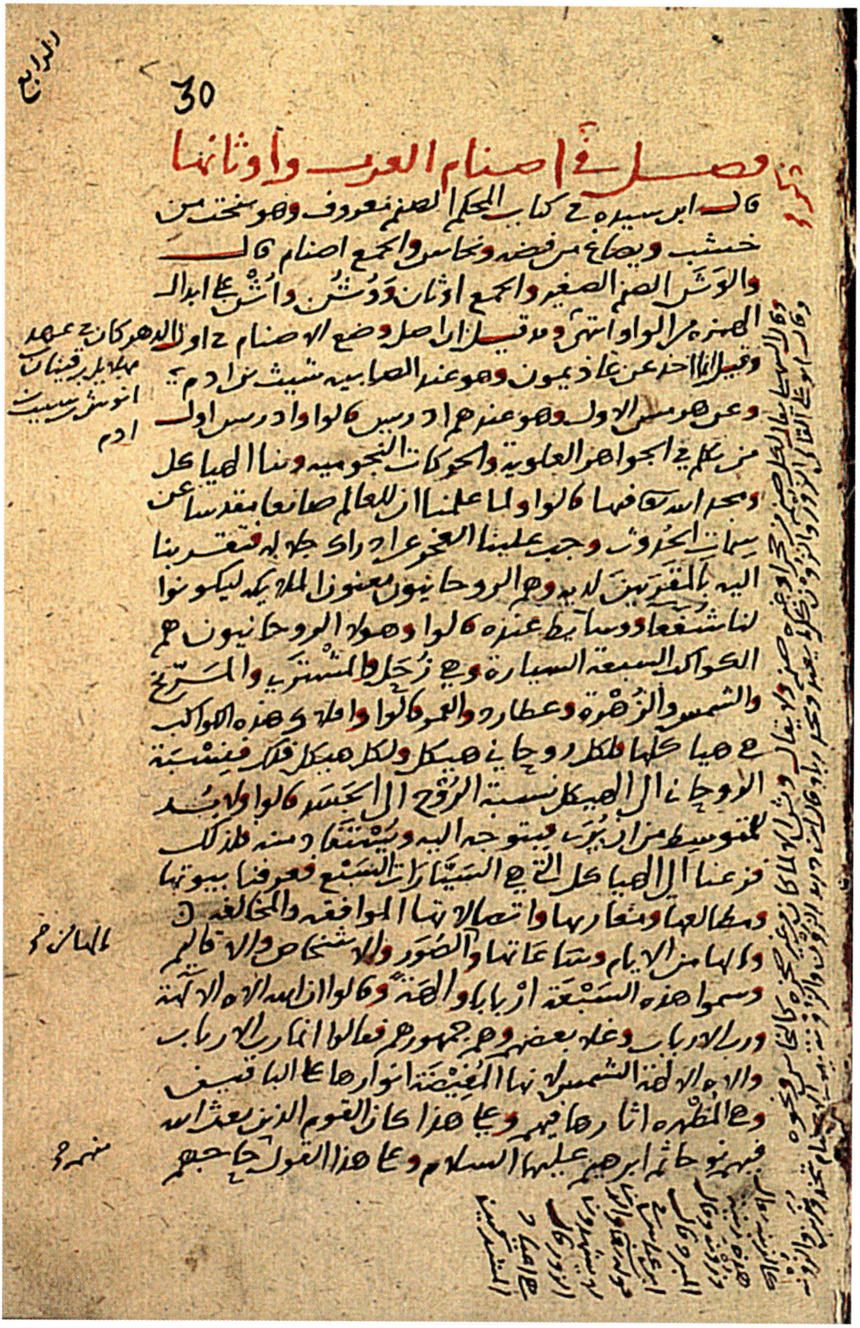

30

فصل في اصنام العرب واوثانها

قال ابن سيده في كتاب المحكم الصنم معروف وهو ينحت من
خشب ويصاغ من فضة ونحاس والجمع اصنام قال
والوثن الصنم الصغير والجمع اوثان ووُثْن واُثْن على ابدال
الهمزة من الواو انتهى ومن قال ان اصل وضع الاصنام في اول الدهر
وقيل انما اخذ عن عاذيمون وهو عند الصابية شيث بن ادم
وعن هرمس الاول وهو عندهم ادريس قالوا وادريس اول
من تكلم في الجواهر العلوية والحركات النجومية وبنا الهياكل
ومجد الله تعالى فيها قالوا ولما علمنا ان للعالم صانعا مقدسا عن
سمات الحدوث وجب علينا العجز عن ادراك جلاله فتقربنا
اليه بالمقربين لديه وهم الروحانيون يعنون الملائكة ليكونوا
لنا شفعاء ووسايط عنده قالوا وهولاء الروحانيون هم
الكواكب السبعة السيارة وهي زحل والمشتري والمريخ
والشمس والزهرة وعطارد والقمر قالوا وافلاك هذه الكواكب
هي هياكلها فلكل روحاني هيكل ولكل هيكل فلك فنسبة
الروحاني الى الهيكل نسبة الروح الى الجسد قالوا ولا بد
للمتوسط من ان يرى فيتوجه اليه ويستشفع به فلذلك
فزعنا الى الهياكل التي هي السيارات السبع فعرفنا بيوتها
ومطالعها ومغاربها واتصالاتها الموافقة والمخالفة
وكلها من الايام وساعاتها والصور والاشخاص والاقاليم
وسموا هذه السبعة اربابا والهة وقالوا ان الله اله الالهة
ورب الارباب وغلا بعضهم وهم جمهورهم فقالوا انما رب الارباب
واله الالهة الشمس لانها المفيضة انوارها على الباقيين
وهي المظهرة اثارها فيهم وعلى هذا كان القوم الذين بعث الله
فيهم نوحا ثم ابرهيم عليهما السلام وعلى هذا القول حاجهم

30a

Printed in the United States
by Baker & Taylor Publisher Services